CW00350669

Emptiness in the Mind-Only School of Buddhism

A

Philip E. Lilienthal

BOOK

The Philip E. Lilienthal imprint honors special books
in commemoration of a man whose work
at the University of California Press from 1954 to 1979
was marked by dedication to young authors
and to high standards in the field of Asian Studies.
Friends, family, authors, and foundations
have together endowed the Lilienthal Fund,
which enables the Press to publish under this imprint
selected books in a way that reflects the taste and judgment
of a great and beloved editor.

Emptiness in the Mind-Only School of Buddhism

Jeffrey Hopkins

Dynamic Responses to Ḏzong-ka-ḇa's
The Essence of Eloquence: I

UNIVERSITY OF CALIFORNIA PRESS

Berkeley   Los Angeles   London

University of California Press
Berkeley and Los Angeles, California

University of California Press, Ltd.
London, England

First paperback printing 2003

© 1999 by
The Regents of the University of California

Library of Congress Cataloging-in-Publication Data

Hopkins, Jeffrey.
Emptiness in the mind-only school of Buddhism / Jeffrey Hopkins.
p. cm.
"A Philip E. Lilienthal book."
Includes bibliographical references and index.
ISBN 0-520-23908-3 (pbk : alk. paper)
1. Tsoṅ-kha-pa Blo-bzaṅ-grags-pa, 1357-1419. Legs bśad sñiṅ po.
2. Sunyata. 3. Vijñaptimātratā. I. Tsoṅ-kha-pa Blo-bzaṅ-grags-pa,
1357-1419. Legs bśad sñiṅ po.
BQ7950.T754L4335 1999
294.3'420423—dc21 98-46315
CIP

Printed in the United States of America

11 10 09 08 07 06 05 04 03
10 9 8 7 6 5 4 3 2 1

The paper used in this publication meets the minimum
requirements of ANSI/NISO Z39.48-1992 (R 1997)
(*Permanence of Paper*). ♾

Contents

PART THREE: *Synopsis*

PART FOUR: *Critical Edition in Tibetan Script*

Preface

This book is the first of a three-volume series of related but stand-alone works on the first two sections of Ḏzong-ka-ḇa's[a] *The Essence of Eloquence.*[b] The focus of all three volumes is the exposition of emptiness in the Mind-Only School according to numerous Tibetan and Mongolian scholars over the last six centuries who have tried both to find and to create consistency in his often terse and cryptic tract.

This first volume is in four parts:

- A historical and doctrinal introduction
- A translation of the General Explanation and the Section on the Mind-Only School in *The Essence of Eloquence* with frequent annotations in brackets, footnotes, and backnotes
- A detailed synopsis of the translation
- A critical edition in Tibetan script of these sections in *The Essence of Eloquence.*

The second volume, *Reflections on Reality,* will:

- place reactions to Ḏzong-ka-ḇa's text in historical and social context by examining the tension between allegiance and rational inquiry in monastic colleges,
- expand on the religious significance of the three natures of phenomena
- present Jo-nang-ḇa[c] views on the thoroughly established nature and Ge-luk-ḇa[d] criticisms,
- explain the reasonings establishing mind-only as means to overcome basic dread of reality, and
- consider how Ḏzong-ka-ḇa and his commentators present the provocative issue of the relationship between two types of emptiness in the Mind-Only School and compare how the topic of two emptinesses is debated today in America, Europe, and Japan, thereby demonstrating how the two forms of scholarship refine and enhance each other.

---

[a] *tsong kha pa blo bzang grags pa;* 1357-1419.

[b] *drang ba dang nges pa'i don rnam par phye ba'i bstan bcos legs bshad snying po;* Peking 6142, vol. 153. For a translation of the complete text, see Robert A. F. Thurman, *Tsong Khapa's Speech of Gold in the Essence of True Eloquence* (Princeton, N.J.: Princeton University Press, 1984). A Chinese translation was completed in Hla-s̄a on the day commemorating Buddha's enlightenment in 1916 by Venerable Fa Zun, "Bian Liao Yi Bu Liao Yi Shuo Cang Lun," in *Xi Zang Fo Jiao Jiao Yi Lun Ji* (Taipei: Da Sheng Wen Hua Chu Ban She, 1979), vol. 2, 159-276.

[c] *jo nang pa.*

[d] *dge lugs pa.*

The third volume, *Absorption in No External World,* will examine a plethora of fascinating points on the three natures raised in six centuries of commentary through:

- identifying the teachings in the first wheel of doctrine,
- probing the meaning of "own-character" and "established by way of its own character,"
- untangling the implications of D̄zong-ka-b̄a's criticisms of Wonch'uk, and
- treating many engaging points on the three natures and the three non-natures, including (1) how to apply these two grids to uncompounded space; (2) whether the selflessness of persons is a thoroughly established nature; (3) how to consider the emptiness of emptiness; and (4) the ways the Great Vehicle schools delineate the three natures and the three non-natures.

I became involved with D̄zong-ka-b̄a's *The Essence of Eloquence* in 1982, while under a Fulbright Senior Fellowship in India. I was visiting at the S̄har-d̄zay[a] College of Gan-den[b] Monastic University, resettled in south India after the Tibetan diaspora beginning in 1959. I was checking with the abbot, La-d̄i Rin-b̄o-chay—who is a reincarnate lama (most abbots in the Ge-luk-b̄a[c] sect are not recognized reincarnate lamas) from the southeastern province of Tibet called Kam[d]—my translations of D̄zong-ka-b̄a's presentation of Yoga Tantra in his *Great Exposition of Secret Mantra*[1] and his exposition of the view of emptiness in his *Medium Exposition of the Stages of the Path.*[2] I checked the translations by orally retranslating the texts into Tibetan. Before our meetings, I would not look at the Tibetan text, so that my retranslation would be from the English as much as possible. The Tibetan of stock phrases was obvious, and thus, since he knew no English, he could not confirm my choice of translation-equivalents; however, he was skilled at rapidly criticizing or confirming my reading of the syntax of a sentence and thus its basic structure and meaning. We sometimes would pause to discuss an issue troubling to me or one on which he wanted to explore my understanding.

One day fairly early in my two-month stay at S̄har-d̄zay College, he informed me that the Dalai Lama would probably come to Gan-den University to teach D̄zong-ka-b̄a's *The Essence of Eloquence.* Since the text is renowned for its difficulty, I knew that I must prepare for the event; so I obtained a copy and started reading it. However, I found that little of the content was staying with me, and, since translation is, for me, an effective mode of focusing concentra-

---

[a] *shar rtse;* literally, East Point.

[b] *dga' ldan* (*tuṣita*).

[c] This is one of four major orders of Tibetan Buddhism. It came to be the dominant form, in terms of numbers, and is the order from which the Dalai Lamas come.

[d] *khams.*

tion and of retaining material, I decided to use it as an exercise to immerse myself in the text, despite the fact that my long-time friend, Professor Robert Thurman, then of Amherst College and now of Columbia University, had translated the entire text and would be publishing it. Translation would promote my own understanding, even if nothing significantly different from Thurman's work emerged.[a] It turned out that I found it useful to add into the translation in brackets and in footnotes a great deal of material from six centuries of commentary to place *The Essence of Eloquence* in its subsequent context in Ge-luk-b̄a scholarship and to indicate the historical context of the composition.

* * *

I want to express my profound gratitude to fifteen Tibetan and three Mongolian scholars with whom I have worked on comparative systems of tenets (both Buddhist and non-Buddhist), on *The Essence of Eloquence* and/or its commentaries, and on related topics. I list these in order to show how what we learn depends on others' help—an illustration of Buddha's focal teaching, dependent-arising.

In the order of the first teachings received from these scholars (for full references to the texts see the bibliography):

The late Ge-s̄hay Nga-w̄ang-w̄ang-gyel of the Go-mang College of Dre-b̄ung Monastic University: portions of Jam-ȳang-shay-b̄a's *Great Exposition of Tenets*

Professor Ge-s̄hay Hlün-drup-sö-b̄a of the Jay College of S̄e-ra Monastic University and the University of Wisconsin: Ḡön-chok-jik-may-w̄ang-b̄o's *Precious Garland of Tenets* (see Sopa and Hopkins, *Cutting through Appearances: The Theory and Practice of Tibetan Buddhism*)

The late Ge-s̄hay Ḡel-den of the Go-mang College of Dre-b̄ung Monastic University: D̄zong-ka-b̄a's *Extensive Commentary on the Difficult Points of "The Afflicted Intellect and the Mind Basis-of-All": Ocean of Eloquence*

The late Ken-sur Nga-w̄ang-lek-den, abbot emeritus of the Tantric College of Lower Hla-s̄a and ge-s̄hay in the Go-mang College of Dre-b̄ung Monastic University (in Tibet): except for the chapter on the Autonomy School, all of Jam-ȳang-shay-b̄a's *Great Exposition of Tenets* and Nga-w̄ang-b̄el-den's *Annotations* (the chapter on the Consequence School twice); D̄zong-ka-b̄a's *Extensive Explanation of (Chandrakīrti's) "Supplement to (Nāgārjuna's) 'Treatise on the Middle'": Illumination of the Thought;* all but twenty-five folios of Jam-ȳang-shay-b̄a's *Great Exposition of the Middle;* lectures on the Consequence School at the University of Wisconsin (which I translated)

The late Professor Ge-s̄hay Gen-dün-l̄o-drö of the Go-mang College of Dre-

[a] I did my own translation without reference to Thurman's and, several years into my work on the text, checked my translation against his.

b̄ung Monastic University and the University of Hamburg: many aspects of Jam-ȳang-shay-b̄a's *Great Exposition of Tenets;* a portion of Gyel-tsap's *Explanation of (Dharmakīrti's) Commentary on (Dignāga's) "Compilation of Prime Cognition": Unerring Illumination of the Path to Liberation;* recorded teachings to Professor Joe Wilson on Jam-ȳang-shay-b̄a's *Great Exposition of Tenets* on the Mind-Only School; and lectures on calm abiding (which I translated; see Lodrö and Hopkins, *Walking through Walls,* republished in restructured form as *Calm Abiding and Special Insight*)

Ke-d̄zün-sang-b̄o Rin-b̄o-chay of the N̄ying-ma order, founder of a monastery in Boda, Nepal, and a retreat center in the hills: tenet systems as presented in L̄ong-chen-rap-jam's *Precious Treasury of the Supreme Vehicle* and *Precious Treasury of Tenets: Illuminating the Meaning of All Vehicles*

The late Ge-s̄hay D̄a-drin-rap-d̄en of the Jay College of S̄e-ra Monastic University: the Fifth Dalai Lama's *Instructions on the Stages of the Path to Enlightenment: Sacred Word of Mañjushrī* and many discussions on epistemology

La-d̄i Rin-b̄o-chay, abbot emeritus of and ge-s̄hay in the S̄har-d̄zay College of Gan-den Monastic University: Pur-bu-j̄ok's small and middling Collected Topics; Ge-s̄hay Jam-b̄el-sam-pel's *Presentation of Awareness and Knowledge;* Pur-bu-j̄ok's *Explanation of the Presentation of Objects and Object Possessors as well as Awareness and Knowledge* and *The Topics of Signs and Reasonings in the "Great Path of Reasoning";* Jam-ȳang-shay-b̄a's *Great Exposition of the Concentrations and Formless Absorptions;* and lectures on the Mind-Only School and other systems of tenets (which I translated)

Den-ma L̄o-chö Rin-b̄o-chay, abbot emeritus of the N̄am-gyel College and ge-s̄hay in the L̄o-s̄el-l̄ing College of Dre-b̄ung Monastic University: Jam-ȳang-shay-b̄a's *Seventy Topics;* the sections on the two truths, the concentrations, and the formless absorptions in Paṇ-chen S̄ö-nam-drak-b̄a's *General-Meaning Commentary on the Perfections;* Ḡön-chok-jik-may-w̄ang-b̄o's *Presentation of the Grounds and Paths: Beautiful Ornament of the Three Vehicles* and *Thorough Expression of the Natures of the One Hundred Seventy-Three Aspects of the Three Exalted Knowers*

The late Ken-sur Ye-s̄hay-tup-d̄en, abbot emeritus of and ge-s̄hay in the L̄o-s̄el-l̄ing College of Dre-b̄ung Monastic University: D̄zong-ka-b̄a's *The Essence of Eloquence;* Paṇ-chen S̄ö-nam-drak-b̄a's *Garland of Blue Lotuses;* the section on Mind-Only in B̄el-jor-hlün-drup's *Lamp for the Teaching* and in A-ku L̄o-drö-gya-tso's *Precious Lamp;* a large portion of the first Dalai Lama's *Great Treatise on Prime Cognition: Adornment of Reasoning;* and lectures on the two truths in the Great Exposition School and the Sūtra School (which I translated)

The late Ge-s̄hay L̄o-sang-gya-tso of the L̄o-s̄el-l̄ing College of Dre-b̄ung Monastic University, principal of the School of Dialectics in Dharmsala, India: presentation of the two truths in the Middle Way Consequence School as found in D̄zong-ka-b̄a's *Illumination of the Thought*

Ge-s̄hay Tup-d̄en-gya-tso of the Go-mang College of Dre-b̄ung Monastic University: large parts of Jam-ȳang-shay-b̄a's *Great Exposition of the Interpretable and the Definitive* and Gung-tang's *Difficult Points;* parts of Gung-tang's *Annotations* and A-ku L̄o-drö-gya-tso's *Precious Lamp*

Ge-s̄hay B̄el-den-drak-b̄a of the L̄o-s̄el-l̄ing College of Dre-b̄ung Monastic University: S̄er-s̄hül's *Notes* in its entirety and the introduction and the section on Mind-Only in Ke-drup's *Opening the Eyes of the Fortunate*

Gen L̄o-sang-d̄en-dzin of the Go-mang College of Dre-b̄ung Monastic University (in Hla-s̄a): the three wheels of doctrine in Gung-tang's *Difficult Points* and the beginning of the Mind-Only section in D̄zong-ka-b̄a's *The Essence of Eloquence*

Ge-s̄hay Ye-s̄hay-tap-kay of the L̄o-s̄el-l̄ing College of Dre-b̄ung Monastic University: Jay-d̄zun Chö-ḡyi-gyel-tsen's *General Meaning of (D̄zong-ka-b̄a's) "Differentiating the Interpretable and the Definitive": Eradicating Bad Disputation* and Paṇ-chen S̄ö-nam-drak-b̄a's *Garland of Blue Lotuses* in their entirety

Ge-s̄hay Ḡön-chok Tse-ring of the S̄har-d̄zay College of Gan-den Monastic University: Gung-ru Chö-jung's *Garland of White Lotuses* in its entirety and part of Jik-may-dam-chö-gya-tso's *Port of Entry*

I want to express my heartfelt appreciation to His Holiness the Dalai Lama, whom I first met in 1972 in Dharmsala. When he asked me to translate his *Key to the Middle Way,* I said that I would do so if he would answer whatever questions I had, and he responded affirmatively. This opened the way to working on seven books with him, often based on having become his interpreter on lecture tours in the United States in 1979, 1981, 1984, 1987, 1989, and 1996; in Canada in 1980; in Malaysia, Singapore, and Australia in 1982; in Great Britain in 1984; and in Switzerland in 1985. These experiences opened me to many topics that I otherwise would not have encountered. I also attended his lectures on Nāgārjuna's Six Collections of Reasoning, D̄zong-ka-b̄a's *Medium Exposition of the Stages of the Path,* and Maitreya's *Sublime Continuum of the Great Vehicle,* the last being from the viewpoints of many Tibetan commentators. He truly sees the forest from the trees.

Extended explanations by the above Tibetan and Mongolian scholars made it possible for me to present this and the two other volumes on the Mind-Only School.

It was most fortunate that John C. Powers, then a graduate student in the University of Virginia Buddhist Studies program, wanted to translate *Sūtra Unraveling the Thought,* a foundational text of the Mind-Only School, which we read word by word in tutorial over several years. Also, Cyrus Stearns's completion of his fascinating thesis on S̄hay-rap-gyel-tsen, D̄zong-ka-b̄a's chief opponent in *The Essence of Eloquence,* was most timely and illuminating.

Many thanks to William Magee, who read through the entire text of this volume and made many editorial suggestions; to Paul Hackett, who provided copious bibliographical assistance; and to Craig Preston, who created a new diacritics font and modified a Tibetan font. Many thanks also to the four seminar classes at the University of Virginia that tackled earlier versions of the three-volume series and helped me to see how to shape my work.

Jeffrey Hopkins
University of Virginia

Technical Notes

It is important to recognize that:

- footnotes are marked "a, b, c..."; backnotes are marked "1, 2, 3...." References to texts are mostly given in the backnotes, whereas other information, more pertinent to the reading of the material at hand, is given in the footnotes. Footnote references in italics indicate that the note includes a linkage to a chapter in *Reflections on Reality* or an issue treated in *Absorption in No External World;*
- I have translated the term *drang don* (*neyārtha*) sometimes as "interpretable meaning" and other times as "requiring interpretation," or a variant thereof. There is no significance to the multiple translation other than variety and clarity, the latter being to emphasize that the scripture requires interpretation;
- full bibliographical references are given in the footnotes and backnotes at the first citation in each chapter;
- citations of the *Sūtra Unraveling the Thought* include references to the edited Tibetan text and French translation of it in consultation with the Chinese by Étienne Lamotte in *Saṃdhinirmocanasūtra: L'Explication des mystères* (Louvain: Université de Louvain, 1935) and to the English translation from the *stog* Palace edition of the Tibetan by John C. Powers, *Wisdom of Buddha: Saṁdhinirmocana Sūtra* (Berkeley, Calif.: Dharma, 1995). There is also a translation from the Chinese by Thomas Cleary in *Buddhist Yoga: A Comprehensive Course* (Boston: Shambhala, 1995), in which the references are easily found, as long as chapter 7 of Lamotte and Powers is equated with chapter 5 of Cleary as per the Chinese edition that he used (see appendix 2, p. 457ff.). Passages not cited in D̄zong-ka-b̄a's text are usually adaptations of Powers's translation as submitted for his doctoral dissertation;
- in this volume, references are made to *Reflections on Reality* by chapter since it is not yet finished. The issues in *Absorption in No External World* are arranged in numbered sequence, and thus references to it are by issue number;
- cross-references to the Translation, Synopsis, and Text are given throughout the book. Those to the Translation are indicated by page numbers in square brackets; those to the Synopsis, by page numbers in parentheses; and those to the Text, by page numbers in curly brackets (braces);
- in part 2, the translation of the first two sections of D̄zong-ka-b̄a's *The*

Essence of Eloquence, the two section titles and the twelve chapter titles have been constructed closely following Ḏzong-ka-ḇa's own outline;

- the Sanskrit for quotations in part 2 is found in the footnotes to the Tibetan Text, with references in the footnotes or backnotes to the Translation to the corresponding page number and footnote in the Tibetan Text;
- in part 3, a synopsis of Ḏzong-ka-ḇa's text, almost all references are omitted since they are easily found in the corresponding section of the Translation;
- the names of Indian Buddhist schools of thought are translated into English in an effort to increase accessibility for non-specialists;
- for the names of Indian scholars and systems used in the body of the text, *ch, sh,* and *ṣh* are used instead of the more usual *c, ś,* and *ṣ* for the sake of easy pronunciation by non-specialists; however, *chchh* is not used for *cch.* In the notes the usual transliteration system for Sanskrit is used;
- transliteration of Tibetan is done in accordance with a system devised by Turrell Wylie; see "A Standard System of Tibetan Transcription," *Harvard Journal of Asiatic Studies* 22 (1959): 261-267;
- the names of Tibetan authors and orders are given in "essay phonetics" for the sake of easy pronunciation; for a discussion of the system used, see the technical note at the beginning of my *Meditation on Emptiness* (London: Wisdom, 1983; rev. ed., Boston: Wisdom, 1996), 19-22. The system is used consistently, with the result that a few well-known names are rendered in a different way: for example, "Lhasa" is rendered as "Hla-s̄a" since the letter "h" is pronounced before the letter "l"; and
- an English-Tibetan-Sanskrit glossary will be given at the end of the third volume, *Absorption in No External World.*

PART ONE:
INTRODUCTION

1. The Voice

In an earlier work, *Meditation on Emptiness*,[3] I attempted to present a multifaceted view of a Tibetan tradition of Buddhism by adopting the literary convention of assuming the voice of the tradition. My intention was to re-create for the reader facets of my encounter with the tradition by letting the tradition present itself, thereby drawing the reader into its culture, much as I had over the period of a decade. I hardly need mention that there is no way merely "to let the tradition present itself"; this is a literary convention that, given the writer's creativity and background in the culture, can yield a narrative voice through which certain aspects of that culture can come to life for the reader. My primary intention was to present a philosophical tradition, but without editing out what did not fit into my view of what philosophy is. I was fascinated with what seemed to be a cacophony of perspectives within the tradition and wanted the reader to experience my sense of the clash of perspectives.

Again and again, I had been faced with an analysis of phenomena, presented carefully and logically, that appealed to my most rational (or just plain sensible) side, but then this was juxtaposed with an utterly fabulous view of history that has, for instance, Padmasambhava living for 1,773 years and Shāntarakṣhita living for 999. Again and again, what for me was philosophical precision was seamlessly combined with "religion through story," accounts of fabulous events that were, at once, childishly amusing and mythically moving. Painstaking investigation of objects that could originate only from the data of actual experience was set side by side with a cosmogony, told not as if it were other beings' distant accounts but almost as if the tellers had been present there and were giving an eye-witness report.

I wanted the reader to be drawn into a position of being attracted and repelled, clarified and confused, without an overarching voice that claimed to have made sense out of what, for me, was incongruous. By "assuming the voice of the tradition," especially of a particular lama whose storytelling capacities were so great that he could seemingly *encompass* the tradition, I could easily avoid the arrogance of pretending to have a privileged position and could convey the majesty of horizon of a tradition of spiritual development—that culminates in omniscience—as well as its non-analytical acceptance of fables and its psychologically evocative stories. Thus, I intended not to shrink from the fabulous aspects of the tradition that, by their very improbability, undercut the claim—made in much of its philosophy—to an utterly rational perspective.

I wanted to show, within the raucousness of these facets of the tradition, the fascinatingly intricate nature of its philosophical and psychological analysis, which is built around a conflict between appearance and reality. By putting the reader in the context of the tradition "as it is," rather than as what I had hoped it would be (witness the European accounts of Theravāda Buddhism earlier in this century as if a purely rational religion had finally been found), I intended to convey some of the richness of its context as well as the impossibility of a simpleminded perspective on the tradition.

Thus, my primary aims were (1) to evince a respect for the directions, goals, and horizons of the culture itself without falling prey to the arrogance either of swallowing an Asian tradition as if it had all the answers or of pretending to have a privileged position and (2) to re-create for the reader my varied reactions to this diverse culture, without attempting to resolve the tensions between these conflicting aspects. The risk I took in adopting the "voice of the tradition" was that, for those who could not stand the tension of my not having a one-sided perspective, I could appear to be at a level that Wilfred Cantwell Smith[4] describes as adulation, the third of five attitudes toward other cultures—attitudes of superiority, relativism, adulation, benefiting from learning *about* other cultures, and benefiting from learning *from* other cultures about ourselves. I viewed my position as more like the fifth stage, about which Smith says:[5]

> In the prospect of learning not only *about* other cultures and other ages but also *from* them, including especially learning from them about ourselves, we profit most, as well as being intellectually most correct, as we discover that their very otherness is a stage that we are today in process of leaving behind.

By dwelling on its own perspectives and not forcing a fabricated synthesis, I was maintaining a respect for the tradition as a part of *our* world culture. However, the danger was that I could be viewed, by those uncomfortable with the multiplicity of perspectives, as having swallowed the tradition uncritically, whole hog, 1,773-year lifespans and all. The risk, I determined, was worth taking since, at minimum, the tradition would be allowed to speak, rather than being stultified in what I perceive to be the all-too-frequent nihilistic relativism that, upon uncovering the historical strata of traditions, assumes that such investigation is sufficient. Historical analysis is not only beneficial but also necessary to this field, but to be satisfied with it is to miss a great deal of the dynamics of a culture. Though such scholarship has the grand goal of exposing traditional claims of extrahistorical revelations of the truth by pointing out that revelations cannot occur except within a context, it too often succumbs to the view that what arises in dependence upon conditions—because it does not have the self-existence it seems to have—is as good as nonexistent, non-functional, dead. Worldviews, in the hands of scholarship that does not realize the dynamic contextuality of even its own perspective, lose their very life. I was trying to give the other side of the coin.

The literary device of, for the most part, assuming the voice of the tradition afforded me a framework for presenting a Tibetan tradition as a living phenomenon with its own horizons. My own historical imbeddedness was clear from a list (in the introduction to *Meditation on Emptiness*) of thirty-two common views of the philosophy of the Middle Way School that evidence showed are not shared with this particular Tibetan tradition. The conflict between how the Middle Way School is presented in works of contemporary American, European, Indian, and Japanese scholarship and how a Tibetan tradition presents itself formed the underlying theme of the book.

Now that I am thirty-seven years into an encounter with Tibetan Buddhism, my current endeavor, while sharing many of the same goals, is different. Here, although I also seek to convey the experience of a participant-observer (what observer is not a participant to some extent?), the voice is that of the participant-observer myself. Again, I seek to convey some of the multifaceted richness of Tibetan Buddhist traditions but more through the medium of what at least seems to be my own voice. As before, I call my approach "multifaceted," not "holistic," since I assume that no presentation can convey the whole picture. What most who describe their work as holistic mean is just that it communicates aspects that others, or more likely they themselves, had not previously thought to include. If they really meant that in however many hundred pages they could convey a whole tradition, their wings of feathers and wax of Icarian arrogance would certainly melt and plunge them down to drown in the ocean of inanity.

What I risk here—now that my voice is more my own and now that I have emerged from the facilitative garment of the guise of merely "reporting" a tradition—is inadvertently to communicate that I have found a privileged position from which my observations somehow *encompass* Tibetan culture. Rather, my hope is that, as before, the style may help to open horizons. My aim is to contribute to what Smith so aptly describes as "we all" talking with each other about "us human beings," "as heirs of many cultures."[6]

2. The Text

The Ge-luk-b̄a order of Tibetan Buddhism was founded by the yogi-scholar D̄zong-ka-b̄a L̄o-sang-drak-b̄a[a] (1357-1419), the fourth in a family of six sons in the D̄zong-ka region of the northeastern province of Tibet called Am-do.[b] He took layperson's vows at the age of three from the Fourth Karma-b̄a Röl-b̄ay-dor-jay[c] and novice monastic vows at seven. He studied and practiced in Am-do until age sixteen, when he left for central Tibet, never to return to Am-do. There, Chö-jay Don-drup-rin-chen[d] advised him to study the Five Great Books of Indian Buddhism (described below, p. 9ff.), which became the basic curriculum of sūtra study in the monasteries that D̄zong-ka-b̄a and his followers established. From childhood, his study and practice was interlaced with tantra, and thus it is only a misimpression outside of Tibetan, Mongolian, and Chinese circles that he was not deeply involved with tantrism.

He studied a great deal with masters of the Ḡa-gyu[e] and S̄a-ḡya[f] orders. As Stephen Batchelor says in *The Tibet Guide:*[g]

> Tsongkhapa was born in 1357 in Amdo, the northeastern province of Tibet. During the time of the Third Dalai Lama his birthplace was marked by the erection of the Kumbum Jampa Ling Monastery near Xining. While still very young he was recognized as possessing unusual spiritual qualities and as a young man was sent to Central Tibet to further his understanding of Buddhism in the more cultured region of the country. The first monastery he visited was that of Drigung, where he studied medicine and the doctrines of the Kagyu lineage. From here he proceeded to Netang, Samye, Zhalu, and Sakya monasteries. He met his main teacher Rendawa at Tsechen Monastery just outside Gyantse. For many years he studied the full range of Buddhist philosophy, including the more esoteric tantric systems. He then retreated to Olka, north of the Brahmaputra downstream from Tsetang, and

---

a *tsong kha pa blo bzang grags pa.*

b *a mdo.*

c *karma pa rol pa'i rdo rje* (1340-1383).

d *chos rje rin chen don grub.*

e *bka' brgyud.*

f *sa skya.*

g Stephen Batchelor, *The Tibet Guide: Central and Western Tibet* (Boston: Wisdom, 1998), 129-131. For a short biography, see Geshe Ngawang Dhargey, "A Short Biography," in *Life and Teachings of Tsong Khapa,* ed. Robert A. F. Thurman, trans. mainly by Khamlung Tulku (Dharmsala, India: Library of Tibetan Works and Archives, 1982), 4-39. For an inspired and inspiring account, see Robert A. F. Thurman, *Tsong Khapa's Speech of Gold in the Essence of True Eloquence* (Princeton, N.J.: Princeton University Press, 1984), 65-89.

spent the next four years in intense retreat. Upon returning to society he found himself much in demand as a teacher. One place where he taught was the hill in Lhasa on which the Potala was eventually built. Together with Rendawa he stayed for some time at Reting, where he composed his most famous work, *The Great Exposition of the Stages on the Path to Enlightenment.* After another meditation and writing retreat at Chöding Hermitage (above where Sera monastery now is), he founded, in 1409, the famous annual Mönlam (prayer) festival in Lhasa, which, after a twenty-five year hiatus, was reinaugurated in 1986. (In the political unrest that followed the demonstrations of 1987 and 1988, it was canceled in 1989 and by 1994 had not been resumed.)

After the prayer festival Tsongkhapa decided to found his own monastery. He selected Mt. Drokri, a mountain upstream from Lhasa, and called the monastery "Ganden," Tibetan for "Tushita," the pure land where the future Buddha Maitreya resides. Within a year seventy buildings had been completed, but it was not until 1417 that the main hall of the monastery was consecrated.

Tsongkhapa died at Ganden two years later, in 1419, and shortly before his death passed the mantle of succession to Gyeltsab Je, one of his two chief disciples. Gyeltsab Je held the position of Ganden Tripa (Throne Holder of Ganden) until his own death twelve years later, when it passed to Tsongkhapa's other chief disciple Khedrup Je. The post of Ganden Tripa was later given to the senior Dharma Master of one of the two main Ganden Colleges, Jangtse and Shartse. It was a five-year post for which to qualify one must first have obtained a geshe degree with highest honors (*lharampa*), proceeded to the abbotship of one of the two Lhasa tantric colleges, and from there been appointed Dharma Master of either Jangtse or Shartse college. The tradition has been continued in India. It is the Ganden Tripa, *not* the Dalai Lama, who heads the Gelukpa order.

During his lifetime Tsongkhapa was regarded as a remarkable spiritual figure whose genius and saintliness held him above the sectarian differences of his times. Although greatly inspired by the example of Atisha, to the point of attributing authorship of his own major written work to him, and by the spirit of the Kadampa tradition, Tsongkhapa nonetheless studied widely with representatives of all the major orders in Tibet and assimilated their lineages. It is uncertain whether he intended to form his own order, though he must have realized it was liable to happen. He could not have foreseen, though, the dimensions this order (the Gelukpa) would eventually assume and the political power it would wield.

Over the following centuries Ganden Monastery grew to the size

> of a small township, delicately perched along the high sheltered slopes of the mountain. By 1959 this calm, secluded center of learning and contemplation housed more than five thousand monks, but with the Chinese occupation the monks were forced to scatter, and by the mid-sixties the monastery was nearly deserted. The final blow came with the cultural revolution. Coerced by the Chinese and caught up in the frenzy and terror of the times, the local Tibetans demolished the buildings. For many years only jagged ruins remained. The greater religious freedom permitted after the death of Mao allowed the laborious and gradual reconstruction of the monastery to begin. One by one the buildings emerged from out of the rubble and monks trickled back to their former home. Yet, perhaps because of its symbolic power as the stronghold of the previous spiritual rule as well as its distance from the capital, Ganden has been rebuilt largely through private funds and has received scant support from the government. Four hundred monks are officially allowed to live here now, although there are around six hundred actually in residence.

It strikes me that the construction of seventy buildings in one year and Ḏzong-ka-ḇa's later instruction to two students to build other monastic universities in the Hla-s̄a[a] Valley—Dre-ḇung[b] coming to have 2,000 monastic residents one year after commencement of construction[7]—suggest that he did indeed intend to form a new order. In any case, the writings of his immediate followers, such as Gyel-tsap,[c] Ke-drup,[d] and the latter's brother Ba-s̄o-chö-ḡyi-gyel-tsen,[e] clearly indicate the raising of Ḏzong-ka-ḇa to the status of saint and founder of a new religious order.

His followers eventually came to have great influence throughout a vast region stretching from Kalmuck Mongolian areas, where the Volga empties into the Caspian Sea (in Europe), to Outer and Inner Mongolia, and the Buriat Republic of Siberia, as well as to most parts of Tibet and Ladakh. Ḏzong-ka-ḇa established a system of education centered in large monastic universities—eventually in three areas of Tibet which became some of the prime centers of religious education.

The form Buddhism took in Tibet was greatly influenced by the highly developed form of the religion present in India through the twelfth century and

---

a *lha sa.*

b *'bras spungs.*

c *rgyal tshab dar ma rin chen,* 1364-1432.

d *mkhas grub dge legs dpal bzang,* 1385-1438, born in the western province of Tibet, *gtsang,* in *ldog gzhung.* See José Ignacio Cabezón, *A Dose of Emptiness: An Annotated Translation of the* stong thun chen mo *of mKhas grub dGe legs dpal bzang* (Albany, N.Y.: State University of New York Press, 1992), 14.

e *ba so chos kyi rgyal mtshan,* born 1402.

even later; the geographic proximity and perhaps relatively undeveloped culture of the region provided conditions for extensive, systematic transfer of highly developed scholastic commentaries and systems of practice. Unlike many of its East Asian counterparts, Tibetan Buddhism is centered not on Buddha's word as found in sūtras and tantras but on Indian commentaries, many of which never made their way to East Asia. Scholasticism, therefore, often (but not always) occupies a more central place in aspects of Tibetan culture than it does farther east.

These Ge-luk-b̄a colleges came to share a curriculum that is based on Five Great Books of Buddhist India[a]—a program of study that begins around age eighteen and lasts for about twenty-five years—but they use different textbooks that are commentaries on those Great Books. To prepare students for study of these texts, the curriculum begins with a class on introductory debate that serves to establish the procedure of outwardly combative but inwardly probing analysis used throughout the course of study. The debate format is at once individualistic, in the aim to win one-on-one debates, and group-stimulated, in the sense that information and positions are acquired from fellow debaters in an ongoing network of communication and shared appreciation of insight. As further preliminaries, the classes study Awareness and Knowledge,[b] which is basic psychology, and Signs and Reasonings,[c] which is basic reasoning. Then begins the first of the Five Great Books: the coming Buddha Maitreya's *Ornament for Clear Realization,*[d] a rendering of the hidden teaching on the path structure in the Perfection of Wisdom Sūtras, which, according to the tradition, were spoken by the Buddha of this age, Shākyamuni. In the standard Ge-luk-b̄a educational curriculum, six years are spent studying Maitreya's *Ornament for Clear Realization*—a highly elaborate compendium on the paths that is not practiced in Tibet in its own form. Rather, the long period of study is used to enrich understanding of a complex structure of spiritual development that pro-

---

[a] In his condensation of D̄zong-ka-b̄a's biography, Geshe Ngawang Dhargey ("A Short Biography," 9, 11) speaks of the Five Great Books as if such a category predates D̄zong-ka-b̄a; this is possible, although it necessary to pursue whether Geshe Ngawang Dhargey is overlaying a system of education that developed based on D̄zong-ka-b̄a's advice or a system that his successors founded. For a list of the seventeen texts that D̄zong-ka-b̄a taught in a three-month teaching, see Geshe Ngawang Dhargey, "A Short Biography," 13-14.

[b] Translation of a typical text with commentary can be found in Lati Rinbochay and Elizabeth Napper, *Mind in Tibetan Buddhism* (London: Rider, 1980; Ithaca, N.Y.: Snow Lion, 1980; reprint, Ithaca, N.Y.: Snow Lion, 1986).

[c] Translation of a typical text with commentary can be found in Katherine Rogers, *A Tibetan Manual of Logic: An Introduction to Reasoning in the Ge-luk-b̄a Monastic Educational System,* (Ann Arbor, Mich.: University Microfilms, 1993).

[d] *mngon rtogs rgyan, abhisamayālaṃkāra;* Peking 5184, vol. 88. A notable exception is the curriculum at the monastery of the Paṇ-chen Lama, D̄ra-s̄hi-hlün-b̄o Monastic University (*bkra shis lhun po*), where Dharmakīrti's *Pramāṇavārttika* is the topic of this initial long period of study.

vides an all-encompassing worldview daunting in its intricacy. Though the structure of the path, as it is presented in this text, does not provide the rubric of actual practice, much of its import is brought over to "stages of the path" literature, the practical implementation of which is certified by the great number of short texts in this genre aimed at daily meditation. The more complex system is dauntingly elaborate, such that it provides a perimeter within which the more practical teachings can be implemented.

Classes on Maitreya's text (and the others) meet with a teacher for about two hours daily and then for two sessions of debates, each about two hours. Every year throughout the twenty-five-year program, time is taken out for pursuit of the second of the Great Books, Dharmakīrti's *Commentary on (Dignāga's) "Compilation of Prime Cognition"*[8]—largely epistemological and logical studies.

Having settled the path structure through the study of Maitreya's *Ornament for Clear Realization,* the class passes on to the third Great Book, Chandrakīrti's *Supplement to (Nāgārjuna's) "Treatise on the Middle,"* [a] to ex-

[a] *dbu ma la 'jug pa, madhyamakāvatāra;* Peking 5261, Peking 5262, vol. 98. Since Chandrakīrti often refers to Nāgārjuna's *Treatise on the Middle* (*dbu ma'i bstan bcos, madhyamakaśāstra*) merely by the appellation *madhyamaka,* the *madhyamaka* of "*madhyamakāvatāra*" is held to refer to a text propounding the middle, specifically Nāgārjuna's *Treatise on the Middle.* My translation of *avatāra* (*'jug pa*) as "supplement" is controversial; others use "introduction" or "entrance," both of which are attested common translations in such a context. My translation is based on the explanation by Dzong-ka-ba that Chandrakīrti was filling in holes in Nāgārjuna's *Treatise on the Middle; ;* see Tsong-ka-pa, Kensur Lekden, and Jeffrey Hopkins, *Compassion in Tibetan Buddhism* (London: Rider, 1980; reprint, Ithaca, N.Y.: Snow Lion, 1980), 96-99. Among the many meanings of the Tibetan term for *avatāra, 'jug pa* can mean "to affix" or "to add on." To summarize the oral teachings of the late Kensur Nga-wang-lek-den:

> *Avatāra* means "addition" in the sense that Chandrakīrti's text is a supplement historically necessary so as to clarify the meaning of Nāgārjuna's *Treatise on the Middle.* He wanted to make clear that the *Treatise* should not be interpreted according to the Mind-Only system or according to the Middle Way Autonomy School (*dbu ma rang rgyud pa, svatantrikamādhyamika*), the founding of which is attributed to Bhāvaviveka. During Nāgārjuna's lifetime, Bhāvaviveka had not written his commentary on the *Treatise,* nor had he founded his system; therefore, it was necessary later to supplement Nāgārjuna's text to show why it should not be interpreted in such a way. Moreover, it is said that Chandrakīrti sought to show that a follower of Nāgārjuna should ascend the ten grounds by practicing the vast paths necessary to do so. This is because some interpret the Middle Way perspective as nihilistic. They see it as a means of refuting the general existence of phenomena rather than just their inherent existence and conclude that it is not necessary to engage in practices such as the cultivation of compassion. Therefore, in order to show that it is important to engage in three central practices—compassion, non-dual understanding, and the altruistic mind of enlightenment—and to ascend the ten Bodhisattva grounds, Chandrakīrti—in reliance on Nāgārjuna's *Precious*

plore for two years the emptiness of inherent existence. Emptiness is the primary content of path consciousnesses and is the explicit teaching of the Perfection of Wisdom Sūtras.

The next Great Book is Vasubandhu's *Treasury of Manifest Knowledge*,[9] a compendium of the types and natures of afflicted phenomena and their causes as well as the pure phenomena that act as antidotes to them and the states of cessation brought about by these antidotes; this takes two years. The last Great Book is Guṇaprabha's *Aphorisms on Discipline*,[10] again studied for two years. At the end, there are several years for review and preliminary rounds of debate in preparation for the yearly debate competition.

D̄zong-ka-b̄a wrote commentaries on Maitreya's *Ornament for Clear Realization* and Chandrakīrti's *Supplement to (Nāgārjuna's) "Treatise on the Middle,"* and his two main students, Gyel-tsap and Ke-drup, wrote commentaries on Dharmakīrti's *Commentary on (Dignāga's) "Compilation of Prime Cognition."* Gyel-tsap also wrote a commentary on Maitreya's text, which is said to reflect D̄zong-ka-b̄a's more mature thinking later in his life.

These commentaries by D̄zong-ka-b̄a and his two chief disciples are used by the colleges, along with Tibetan commentaries by Chim Jam-b̄ay-ȳang[a] and the First Dalai Lama, Gen-dün-drup,[b] on Vasubandhu's *Treasury of Manifest Knowledge* and Tso-na-wa's[c] and the First Dalai Lama's commentaries on Guṇaprabha's *Aphorisms on Discipline*, but D̄zong-ka-b̄a's works are not the chief textbooks in the monastic colleges. Given that the basic structure of the monastic university is to divide into camps that stimulate intellectual exchange, the main textbooks are sub-sub-commentaries written by prominent scholars, which present the aforementioned commentaries in a clearer format and attempt to resolve issues unclear (or confused) in those texts. These commentaries, called the college's "textbook literature,"[d] are the main focus, elevated even

Garland—wrote this supplementary text.

See Jeffrey Hopkins, *Buddhist Advice for Living and Liberation: Nāgārjuna's Precious Garland* (Ithaca, New York: Snow Lion, 1998).

This Tibetanized reading of *'jug pa* as "supplement" accords with the Tibetan term *rtags 'jug* (*liṅgāvaṃtāra* [Sarat Chandra Das, *A Tibetan-English Dictionary* (Calcutta: 1902; reprint, Delhi: Motilal Banarsidass, 1969, 1970; compact reprint, Kyoto, Japan: Rinsen Book Company, 1981), 535) "the affixing of gender," referring to the usage of letters—identified by gender in Tibetan grammar—in various positions in a syllable. It also perhaps accords with the fifth meaning given in Vaman Shivaram Apte, *Sanskrit-English Dictionary* (Poona, India: Prasad Prakashan, 1957), 163, "Any new appearance, growth, rise," though it seems that not much of a case can be made from the Sanskrit. Of course, such a supplement also serves as an introduction, or means of entry, to Nāgārjuna's *Treatise*.

a *mchims 'jam pa'i dbyangs.*

b *dge 'dun grub;* 1391-1475, retrospectively called the First Dalai Lama when S̄ö-nam-gya-tso, the reincarnation of his reincarnation, received the title of Dalai.

c *mtsho na wa rin chen bzang po.*

d *yig cha.*

to a status of primary concern and adherence. Despite my dubbing them "sub-sub-commentaries," their significance in the community is focal. (Perhaps due to Protestant emphasis on early Christianity, we often unwarrantedly assume that the focus of religious systems is on their founder and early history, whereas the focus in this system is on the thought of the author of the textbook literature, perhaps as a door to the thought of the founder of their sect but more likely as the embodiment of his thought appropriate to one's own time. I do not deny that the "door analogy" leads back eventually to Shākyamuni Buddha; rather, it seems that the *focus* is on the more current.)

Students identify with the college units to the point where, as a friend put it, one wonders what significance the general monastic university has. Their members' adherence to these units is so strong that the Chinese communists, upon their recent minor relaxation of religious suppression in Tibet, have not allowed the colleges to reopen. Out of fear of the loyalty so successfully inculcated in these units, they have, by refusing to let them reopen, stifled the basic structure that promotes vigorous intellectual interchange. The lack of easy communication in Tibet and the consequent highly factional and parochial nature of the society are reflected in the monks' intense adherence to these colleges, but the other, perhaps more powerful, factor is the esthetic appreciation of intellectual confrontation that is a result of the almost endless number of scholastic disputes between the colleges.

Composition Of *The Essence of Eloquence*

This work is the most famous of the five texts that D̄zong-ka-b̄a wrote on the view of emptiness.[11] In 1402, at the age of forty-five, he wrote the *Great Exposition of the Stages of the Path,*[12] which has a long and complicated section on special insight[a] into emptiness. Five years later, when he was fifty, he began writing a commentary on Nāgārjuna's *Treatise on the Middle,*[13] called *Ocean of Reasoning,*[14] at Chö-ding[b] Hermitage above what became S̄e-ra Monastic University on the northern outskirts of Hla-s̄a, but in the midst of explicating the first chapter, he foresaw that there would be interruptions if he stayed there. Thus, he left Chö-ding Hermitage for another hermitage at S̄e-ra, Ra-ka Precipice.[c] Indeed, the Yung-lo Emperor of the Ming Dynasty sent a representative to Chö-ding Hermitage who, not finding him there, proceeded to Hla-s̄a. D̄zong-ka-b̄a then came to Hla-s̄a, where he was asked to come to China to teach. Referring to his advancing age and wish to be in retreat, he sent images of the Buddha in his stead, thereby avoiding embroilment in politics.

Returning to Ra-ka Precipice, he began writing the *Treatise Differentiating*

---

a *lhag mthong, vipaśyanā.*

b *chos sdings.*

c *rva kha brag;* perhaps the meaning of the name is Goat-Face Crag.

Interpretable and Definitive Meanings: The Essence of Eloquence. I imagine that he felt the need to compose his own independent work on the view of emptiness in the Great Vehicle schools as background for his commentary on Nāgārjuna's treatise, before returning to the complications of these schools' stances. If this is so, he wrote *The Essence* as an overarching structure in which that commentary could be understood.

After completing *The Essence* in 1408,[a] he returned to commenting on Nāgārjuna's text. Then, at age fifty-eight in 1415, he went on to write the *Medium Exposition of the Stages of the Path,*[15] and finally, at age sixty-one, one year before his death, he wrote a commentary on Chandrakīrti's *Supplement to (Nāgārjuna's) "Treatise on the Middle."*

Request For The Teaching

The person or persons who request the teaching that leads to the writing of a text are usually listed in the colophon, but Ḏzong-ka-ḇa's *The Essence of Eloquence* does not list anyone.[16] Nevertheless, Jay-ḏzün Chö-ḡyi-gyel-tsen[b] reports in his biography of Ke-drup,[c] one of Ḏzong-ka-ḇa's two main disciples, that Ḏzong-ka-ḇa composed the text in response to questions concerning the interpretable and the definitive from the S̄a-ḡya scholar Ȳak-truk S̄ang-gyay-ḇel-wa,[d] also known as Ȳak Mi-pam-chö-ḡyi-l̄a-ma.[e] Called Ȳak-truk (Ȳak-Child) since he was the student of Abbot/Professor[f] Ȳak-yu,[g] he was of sufficient stature that the Omniscient Rong-bo[h] took him as a lama. Ḡön-chok-jik-may-w̄ang-ḇo reports that Ȳak-truk S̄ang-gyay-ḇel-wa was a great scholar and that Ḏzong-ka-ḇa's teacher, the S̄a-ḡya scholar Ren-da-wa Shön-nu-l̄o-drö,[i] and he were re-

---

[a] For the date, see Leonard W. J. van der Kuijp, "Apropos of a Recent Contribution to the History of Central Way Philosophy in Tibet: *Tsong Khapa's Speech of Gold*" in *Berliner Indologische Studien* 1 (Reinbek, Germany: Verlag für Orientalistische Fachpublikationen, 1985), 68, n. 2.

[b] *rje btsun chos kyi rgyal mtshan;* 1469-1546.

[c] The material on the person requesting the teaching is drawn from W̄el-mang Ḡön-chok-gyel-tsen's *Notes on (Ḡön-chok-jik-may-w̄ang-ḇo's) Lectures* (381.5-382.3) and Jik-may-dam-chö-gya-tso's *Port of Entry* (15.4-15.6).

[d] *g.yag phrug sangs rgyas dpal ba / g.yag ston sangs rgyas dpal ba;* 1348-1414.

[e] *g.yag mi pham chos kyi bla ma.*

[f] *mkhan po.* Nowadays in Ge-luk-ḇa circles, this term tends to mean "abbot," but in other contexts it also was and is used to refer to a rank of scholarly authority.

[g] *g.yag yu.*

[h] *kun mkhyen rong bo / rong ston shes bya kun gzigs;* 1367-1449. He is called *śākya rgyal mtshan* in W̄el-mang Ḡön-chok-gyel-tsen's *Notes on (Ḡön-chok-jik-may-w̄ang-ḇo's) Lectures* (382.5).

[i] *red mda' ba gzhon nu blo gros;* 1349-1412. A S̄a-ḡya lama, he was Ḏzong-ka-ḇa's main teacher. It is reported in W̄el-mang Ḡön-chok-gyel-tsen's *Notes on (Ḡön-chok-jik-may-w̄ang-ḇo's) Lectures* (382.4) that "except for being included in Ḏzong-ka-ḇa's lineage of lama-

nowned in the S̄a-ḡya sect as the "Ȳak-Shön duo."[a]

Ḡön-chok-jik-may-w̄ang-b̄o[17] reports that Ȳak-truk S̄ang-gyay-b̄el-wa, having received D̄zong-ka-b̄a's *The Essence of Eloquence* in answer to his questions, read it and thereupon developed great ascertainment, such that he wanted to go to listen to his teachings. However, his students intervened, telling him that, since he himself was an aged, eminent, scholar, it would damage his reputation, and thus they did not let him. Given the tendency of Tibetan (and every other) culture to create exalted reputations through fabrication and hyperbole, it is difficult to determine whether this account reports Ȳak-truk S̄ang-gyay-b̄el-wa's actual response to D̄zong-ka-b̄a's text or just a creative apologetic for why a respected scholar did not become D̄zong-ka-b̄a's student after reading this most central and most profound of his works on the view of emptiness. In this century, for instance, a Tibetan scholar from the Go-mang[b] College, Gen-dün-chö-pel,[c] whose powers of intellect are unquestioned, wrote a text, *Ornament for the Thought of Nāgārjuna,*[d] criticizing D̄zong-ka-b̄a's presentation of emptiness in the Consequence School, but some contemporary Ge-luk-b̄a scholars, operating no doubt on the principle that no one of any intelligence who was versed in D̄zong-ka-b̄a's thought could criticize him, have made claims that Ge-dün-chö-pel did not author the text. They say that one of his students wrote it (at least from a certain point to the end) but credited himself with only being the scribe.[e]

The working principle that anyone of caliber who studied D̄zong-ka-b̄a's works could not possibly criticize them in preference to another interpretation has caused me to wonder whether it may have been operating in the account of why Ȳak-truk S̄ang-gyay-b̄el-wa did not become D̄zong-ka-b̄a's student. In a

teachers because he gained difficult points with respect to Mādhyamika as well as Logic-Epistemology (*tshad ma, pramāṇa*) from him, there is no one prior to the Foremost Great personage [D̄zong-ka-b̄a] in terms of the transmission of the exposition of *The Essence.*" Since it is clear that Ḡön-chok-jik-may-w̄ang-b̄o recognizes his founder's life-story of relying on many teachers, I take the meaning to be that the main points made in this text cannot be found in others' works.

a *g.yag gzhon gnyis;* Jik-may-dam-chö-gya-tso's *Port of Entry,* 15.5.

b *sgo mang.*

c *dge 'dun chos 'phel;* 1905-1951.

d *klu sgrub dgongs rgyan.* Donald S. Lopez Jr. is translating this work.

e Indeed, the text stylistically is in two parts, one clearly being Ge-dün-chö-pel's own prose, as is attested by his biographer, the other being constructed from notes on his teachings. Ge-dün-chö-pel was ultimately accused of being a communist and was arrested and imprisoned for two years; his case is cited by many forward-thinking Tibetans as a prime example of the conservative excesses of the old government. See my condensation of his biography in Gedün Chöpel and Jeffrey Hopkins, *Tibetan Arts of Love* trans. and intro. by Jeffrey Hopkins (Ithaca, N.Y.: Snow Lion, 1992), 11-32. For a thorough account of his life, see Heather Stoddard, *Le mendiant de L'Amdo,* Recherches sur la Haute Asie, 9 (Paris: Société d'Ethnographie, 1985).

similar fashion, I doubt the story, widely renowned among Ge-luk-b̄a scholars, that the great fifteenth-century S̄a-ḡya scholar D̄ak-tsang S̄hay-rap-rin-chen,[a] who detailed contradictions in D̄zong-ka-b̄a's works,[18] eventually accepted the correctness of D̄zong-ka-b̄a's position and "wrote a stanza of praise." It strikes me as highly implausible that this prolific scholar would have confined himself to a single stanza had his view changed so dramatically.

In the Tibetan culture of reincarnation, creative reformulation of history is not limited even to a single lifetime; the lists of previous incarnations of a great figure sometimes become not even thinly disguised attempts to subsume other sects under one's own banner. For instance, the eighteenth-century Mongolian scholar of the Ge-luk-b̄a order, J̄ang-ḡya Röl-b̄ay-dor-jay,[b] friend and lama of the Ch'ien-lung Emperor, is said to be the reincarnation of Mar-b̄a Chö-ḡyi-l̄o-drö,[c] the great translator and teacher of Mi-la-re-b̄a,[d] both of whom are central to the Ḡa-gyu sect of Tibetan Buddhism! One of my Ge-luk-b̄a teachers, in a rather matter-of-fact way, reported that Ke-drup, one of D̄zong-ka-b̄a's two most important disciples, was an incarnation of L̄ong-chen-rap-jam,[e] who represents the crowning development of the N̄ying-ma-b̄a sect in the fourteenth century and in many respects is to the N̄ying-ma-b̄a sect what D̄zong-ka-b̄a is to the Ge-luk-b̄a sect. I was speechless. The sectarian rewriting of history is endless. Still, it is not that all Tibetans gullibly swallow these manipulations, for most Tibetan scholars are critical of such constructive hyperbole; cynicism is not limited to persons from other cultures, just as disbelief in American political and commercial advertising is not limited to non-Americans.

Whether or not Ȳak-truk S̄ang-gyay-b̄el-wa was satisfied with D̄zong-ka-b̄a's answers to his questions as presented in *The Essence of Eloquence,* the text became **the** central source of philosophical fascination for a long tradition of Ge-luk-b̄a scholarship divided among competing colleges.

The Steel Bow And Arrow

The Essence of Eloquence is considered to be so challenging that it is called his steel bow and steel arrow.[f] As the eighteenth- and nineteenth-century commentator W̄el-mang Ḡön-chok-gyel-tsen,[g] from the Am-do Province[h] of Tibet,

---

a *stag tshang lo tsā ba shes rab rin chen,* born 1405.

b *lcang skya rol pa'i rdo rje,* 1717-1786. For a short biography, see *Reflections on Reality,* chap. 3.

c *mar pa chos kyi blo gros,* 1012-1097.

d *mi la ras pa,* 1040-1123.

e *klong chen rab 'byams / klong chen dri med 'od zer,* 1308-1363.

f *lcags mda' lcags gzhu.*

g (*dbal mang dkon mchog rgyal mtshan;* 1764-1853), *Notes on (Ḡön-chok-jik-may-w̄ang-b̄o's) Lectures,* 381.4-381.5.

h Born in *bsang khog tshar tsha.* For dates and birthplaces of Am-do scholars, see Tenzin

says, just as it is hard to pull a steel bow to its full extent but if one can, the arrow will course over a great area, so even the words—not to consider the meaning—of this text are difficult to understand but, when understood, yield great insight. The metaphor states a martial challenge to the reader, calling for heroic strength of intellectual will; the work is viewed as one of genius, difficult to control because of its often cryptic brevity but yielding profound insight if pursued with analytical fortitude. (The metaphor also may be a polite way of communicating that the book is so abstruse and sometimes apparently self-contradictory that it takes tremendous effort to attempt to construct a consistent account of Ḏzong-ka-ḇa's thought.) Thus, among his five great works on the view of emptiness the steel bow and arrow is just *The Essence of Eloquence.*

This daunting challenge to take up the steel bow and arrow, repeated from generation to generation, has been accepted by so many brilliant Tibetan and Mongolian scholars, testing their strength on the steel bow and arrow, that we have a veritable treasure-trove of expositions. The emphasis on reasoning in the Ge-luk-ḇa sect—combined with the impetus gained from the culture's parochialism such that small units came to be emphasized to the point of overwhelming the whole—spawned a dynamic tradition of commentarial exposition. Each educational unit sought to have its own distinctive literature on a topic in order both to promote analytical inquiry and to establish the claims of the greatness of the local leader. Disagreement even with Ḏzong-ka-ḇa, the founder of the sect, is promoted within the bounds of not openly criticizing his works but doing so under various polite facades. Through such techniques, an atmosphere of considerable intellectual freedom is fostered, prompting the writing of many commentaries on a fundamental text like his *The Essence of Eloquence.*

The first is found in a work by Ḏzong-ka-ḇa's student Ke-drup (1385-1438), called *Opening the Eyes of the Fortunate: Treatise Brilliantly Clarifying the Profound Emptiness.*[19] Ke-drup views his work as bringing considerable clarity to Ḏzong-ka-ḇa's explanation:[20]

> Even though our Omniscient Foremost One [Ḏzong-ka-ḇa] has already extended the kindness of completely clarifying the systems of the great chariots [great leaders] in his *Differentiating the Interpretable and the Definitive: The Essence of Eloquence,* the power of intelligence of present-day beings is very weak, and, therefore, all of these beings, subsumed in a state like intellectually undeveloped childhood, cannot open even a portion of [Ḏzong-ka-ḇa's presentations that are] like words [used in] the Vajra [Vehicle whose meaning is hard to understand]. Having understood that they are just not penetrating [his words], I will show to listeners with very few words just those meanings—like a treasure beneath the ground—such that they are like

Palbar, *The Tragedy of My Homeland* (*nga'i pha yul gyi ya nga ba'i lo rgyus*) (Dharmsala, India: Narthang, 1994).

olives[a] resting in the palm of their hands. Stay with your ears inclined!

Ke-drup puts the blame for not understanding Ḏzong-ka-ḇa's profound intent on the low intellectual level of "present-day beings," but, given that Ke-drup was Ḏzong-ka-ḇa's own student and was writing his exposition approximately twenty years after the master's work[b] and thus not after centuries of possible decay of intelligence, his decrying the intellectual level of his compatriots hints at Ḏzong-ka-ḇa's lack of clear exposition relative to his audience. Ke-drup obviously takes delight in providing such clarity on several major issues.

His exposition is synthetic, in that he draws from the entire scope of Ḏzong-ka-ḇa's works on the view of emptiness, and thus this work is not strictly a commentary on *The Essence of Eloquence.* However, in the section on the Mind-Only view of emptiness, his exegesis is largely limited to *The Essence of Eloquence.* Still, since his presentation is oriented to several key issues and follows his own order, he does not provide either a section-by-section summation or exploration of a great number of issues in *The Essence of Eloquence.*

Such a summation subsequently was provided by N̄yel-ḏön B̄el-jor-hlün-drup[c] (1427-1514) of the Jay College of S̄e-ra Monastic University,[d] who wrote an exposition of Ḏzong-ka-ḇa's text in a genre called a "difficult points commentary,"[e] most likely around the end of the fifteenth century or the beginning of the sixteenth. His text, entitled *Commentary on the Difficult Points of (Ḏzong-ka-ḇa's) "The Essence of Eloquence": Lamp for the Teaching,*[21] cites all of Ḏzong-ka-ḇa's text (with a few unintended omissions) and summarizes its meaning except when the original seemed adequately clear. Since B̄el-jor-hlün-drup only occasionally expands on issues, the strength of his commentary is its restatement, usually in brief but clear form, of the entire text, making it a good introduction. He does not touch on scores of difficult issues, and thus its use is preliminary.

Later, Gen-dün-gya-tso[f] (1476-1542), retrospectively called the Second

---

a *skyu ru ra* (*āmalakī*). The term also is used for a sour medicinal fruit, *Emblica officinalis Linn.*, said to cure diseases of phlegm, bile, and blood; see Sarat Chandra Das, *A Tibetan-English Dictionary* (Calcutta: 1902; reprint, Delhi: Motilal Banarsidass, 1969, 1970; compact reprint, Kyoto, Japan: Rinsen Book Company, 1981), 103. The usage here is to indicate something that is perfectly clear in front of the eyes.

b Ḏzong-ka-ḇa wrote *The Essence* in 1407-1408 (Thurman, *Tsong Khapa's Speech of Gold,* 88), and Ke-drup wrote *Opening the Eyes of the Fortunate* sometime between 1424-1428 (Cabezón, *Dose of Emptiness,* 17).

c *gnyal* [also spelled *gnyan*] *ston dpal 'byor lhun grub.* A student of L̄o-drö-rin-chen-seng-ḡe (*blo phros rin chen seng ge*), he was taught *The Essence of Eloquence* by Nyen-ḇo Shākya Gyel-tsen (*nyan po śākya rgyal mtshan*), who was taught the text by both of Ḏzong-ka-ḇa's main students, Gyel-tsap and Ke-drup.

d *se ra byes.*

e *dka' 'grel.*

f *dge 'dun rgya mtsho.*

Dalai Lama when his reincarnation Sö-nam-gya-tso received the title of Dalai[a] from the Mongolian chieftain Altan Khan, wrote a section by section exposition on the entire text in the same genre as Bel-jor-hlün-drup, called *Commentary on the Difficult Points of "Differentiating the Interpretable and the Definitive" from the Collected Works of the Foremost Holy Omniscient [Dzong-ka-ba].*[22] Like Bel-jor-hlün-drup's work, it assumed considerable importance since it covers Dzong-ka-ba's complete text. When Ge-luk-ba scholars criticize it, the format is largely one of pretending to reframe his actual intent. The attention that it receives today is testimony to its stature in the tradition, since a text even from a Dalai Lama easily can be ignored.

Difficult issues are faced in print in a genre of literature used in monastic colleges called "general meaning,"[b] which are often supplemented with "decisive analyses."[c] In their more advanced forms, these textbooks on seminal Indian texts actively stimulate the intellect through juxtaposing assertions that are, or appear to be, contradictory and through making often highly elaborate and esthetically attractive reformulations of assertions in order to create coherence. In this genre, the intellectual fervor behind the topics and the format of philosophical confrontation—which is not accompanied by concluding practical summations—suggest that the aim is not what usually would be considered practice, that is, meditation cultivating what has been studied, but endless intellectual reflection. This perspective has resulted in the flowering of intellectual pursuits in Tibet but calls into question the injunctions to practical implementation. It appears that internal practice has given way to external debate on major and minor issues, but the emphasis on intellectual development also stems from stark recognition that these matters are not easily penetrated, requiring much intellectual exploration, and that immersion in topics—even to the point of entering into a maze of conceptuality—can bear fruit over lifetimes. At least, this is the system's self-justification for the pursuit of ever more refined conceptualization.

Also around the beginning of the fifteenth century, two scholars—who during the long and varied course of their education studied with the same teacher[d]—wrote general-meaning commentaries on Dzong-ka-ba's *The Essence of Eloquence.* Paṇ-chen Sö-nam-drak-ba[e] (1478-1554) wrote his *Distinguishing through Objections and Answers (Dzong-ka-ba's) "Differentiating the Interpretable and Definitive Meanings of All the Scriptures, The Essence of Eloquence": Garland of Blue Lotuses,*[f] and Jay-dzün Chö-gyi-gyel-tsen (1469-1544/46) wrote his *Gen-*

a *tā le.* This is a translation of the last two syllables of his Tibetan name, "gya-tso" (*rgya mtsho*).

b *spyi don.*

c *mtha' dpyod.*

d Jam-yang-dön-yö-bel-den (*'jam dbyangs don yod dpal ldan;* 1445-1524).

e *paṇ chen bsod nams grags pa.*

f The late Ken-sur Ye-shay-tup-den reported that Paṇ-chen Sö-nam-drak-ba also wrote a *eral Meaning of (Ḏzong-ka-ḇa's) "Differentiating the Interpretable and the Definitive": Eradicating Bad Disputation: A Precious Garland,*[23] in which he often refutes views held by Paṇ-chen S̄ö-nam-drak-ḇa.[a] Both of these texts are mostly limited to commenting on the introductory and Mind-Only sections of Ḏzong-ka-ḇa's work. Among the monastic colleges near Hla-s̄a, the former came to be used by the S̄har-ḏzay College of Gan-den Monastic University and the L̄o-s̄el-l̄ing[b] College of Dre-ḇung Monastic University; the latter came to be used by the Jang-ḏzay[c] College of Gan-den Monastic University and the Jay College of S̄e-ra Monastic University.

Gung-ru Chö-jung[d] wrote a much more extensive work, often highly critical of other commentaries and containing particularly good "word commentaries" on Ḏzong-ka-ḇa's text, called *Decisive Analysis of (Ḏzong-ka-ḇa's) "Differentiating the Interpretable and the Definitive, The Essence of Eloquence": Garland of White Lotuses.*[24] This came to be used by the Go-mang Dre-ḇung Monastic University. Two texts[25] similar to those by Jay-ḏzün Chö-ḡyi-gyel-tsen and Paṇ-chen S̄ö-nam-drak-ḇa, but structured around the three wheels of doctrine, were written by Ḏen-ḇa-dar-gyay[e] (1493-1568); these came to be used by the M̄ay College of S̄e-ra Monastic University.[f] Afterward, followers of these scholars wrote other commentaries (listed below), usually to support their colleges' textbooks as issues of controversy and need for greater clarity came to the fore.

The last major development in college literature—in the sense of changing the basic curriculum—came more than a century later, with the production of a revised set of monastic textbooks by Jam-ȳang-shay-ḇa[g] (1648-1721). A long, involved treatment of the introductory and Mind-Only sections of Ḏzong-ka-

"decisive analysis" entitled *Eliminating Qualms about Difficult Topics in (Ḏzong-ka-ḇa's) "The Essence of Eloquence"* (*legs bshad snying po'i dka' gnad dogs gcod*) but that, despite an extensive search, it has not been found.

[a] Jay-ḏzün Chö-ḡyi-gyel-tsen refutes several of Paṇ-chen S̄ö-nam-drak-ḇa's positions, and thus it seems likely that Paṇ-chen S̄ö-nam-drak-ḇa's text was written first even though he was nine years younger than Jay-ḏzün Chö-ḡyi-gyel-tsen. However, there are many ambiguities involved in trying to determine the historical order of texts written by contemporaries since positions finally put to print could have been part of an earlier, oral tradition.

[b] *blo gsal gling.*

[c] *byang rtse.*

[d] Whether he preceded or followed Paṇ-chen S̄ö-nam-drak-ḇa and Jay-ḏzün Chö-ḡyi-gyel-tsen is unclear; nevertheless, he refutes positions that they held. I obtained a copy of his seemingly unobtainable *Garland of White Lotuses* from the Inner Mongolian scholar L̄o-sang-ḏen-dzin (*blo bzang bstan 'dzin*) while studying at Go-mang College in the fall of 1988. He had received it from Ḡum-bum Monastic University in eastern Tibet just outside Si-ling, the capital of Am-do Province (Ch'ing-hai), where I later purchased copies. Gung-ru Chö-jung's text on the twenty types of *saṅgha* is still used by the Go-mang tradition.

[e] *bstan pa dar rgyas.*

[f] *se ra smad.*

[g] *'jam dbyangs bzhad pa ngag dbang brtson grus.*

ḇa's text, his text presents a sometimes lengthened but more often condensed and refined version of Gung-ru Chö-jung's *Decisive Analysis.* Jam-ȳang-shay-ḇa often merely copies his predecessor but sometimes corrects what he found to be errors; he also sharpens criticisms of Jay-d̄zün Chö-ḡyi-gyel-tsen's and Paṇ-chen S̄ö-nam-drak-ḇa's texts (D̄en-ḇa-dar-gyay seemingly being ignored). Jam-ȳang-shay-ḇa's text, entitled *Decisive Analysis of (D̄zong-ka-ḇa's) "Differentiating the Interpretable and the Definitive": Storehouse of White Lapis-Lazuli of Scripture and Reasoning Free from Error: Fulfilling the Hopes of the Fortunate,*[26] replaced that by Gung-ru Chö-jung as the textbook on this topic for the Go-mang College of Dre-ḇung Monastic University near Hla-s̄a, and he installed it as the textbook for this topic at the D̄ra-s̄hi-kyil[a] Monastic University in Am-do Province, which he founded.

After Jam-ȳang-shay-ḇa, a series of Am-do scholars rose to the challenge of D̄zong-ka-ḇa's text. Jam-ȳang-shay-ḇa's reincarnation, Ḡön-chok-jik-may-w̄ang-ḇo[b] (1728-1791), who was born in Am-do N̄ang-ra,[c] northwest of D̄ra-s̄hi-kyil, gave lectures on the text in 1782,[27] which were written down by his student W̄el-mang Ḡön-chok-gyel-tsen (1764-1853),[d] born in Am-do S̄ang-kok-tsar-tsa.[e] The length and complexity of Gung-ru Chö-jung's and Jam-ȳang-shay-ḇa's works, as well as their intricate probing of D̄zong-ka-ḇa's sources (and thus reopening of issues), led to brilliant analyses by a gifted scholar of possibly Mongolian descent, Gung-tang Ḡön-chok-d̄en-ḇay-drön-may[f] (1762-1823), who was born in Am-do Dzö-ge,[g] south of D̄ra-s̄hi-kyil; he became the chief student of Ḡön-chok-jik-may-w̄ang-ḇo. Gung-tang Ḡön-chok-d̄en-ḇay-drön-may began but did not finish two commentaries in the genres of "annotations" and "difficult points" on the Mind-Only section of D̄zong-ka-ḇa's text, usually from Jam-ȳang-shay-ḇa's viewpoint but with considerable adjustment of the latter's views, largely within the facade of explaining Jam-ȳang-shay-ḇa's text. Occasionally he prefers Gung-ru Chö-jung's interpretations to Jam-ȳang-shay-ḇa's, and, conversely, at other times he explains away deficiencies in the latter's presentation as due to merely cribbing Gung-ru Chö-jung's.

To get a handle on the plethora of commentaries, one of Gung-tang's students, Dön-drup-gyel-tsen[h] (not from Am-do but in this tradition), wrote a text

[a] *bkra shis 'khyil.*

[b] *dkon mchog 'jigs med dbang po.*

[c] *snang ra.*

[d] W̄el-mang Ḡön-chok-gyel-tsen also was a student of Gung-tang Ḡön-chok-d̄en-ḇay-drön-may.

[e] *bsang khog tshar tsha.*

[f] *gung thang dkon mchog bstan pa'i sgron me.* For a brief biography, see E. Gene Smith, *University of Washington Tibetan Catalogue* (Seattle, Washington: University of Washington Press, 1969), 1: 81-82.

[g] *mdzod dge.*

[h] *don grub rgyal mtshan.*

entitled *Extensive Explanation of (D̄zong-ka-b̄a's) "Treatise Differentiating the Interpretable and the Definitive, The Essence of Eloquence," Unique to Ge-luk-b̄a: Four Intertwined Commentaries.*[28] It refers to four sets of works (and other minor texts) on D̄zong-ka-b̄a's *The Essence of Eloquence* found in the four major scholastic colleges around Hla-s̄a, as well as to the Second Dalai Lama's *Lamp Illuminating the Meaning.* The four sets are:

L̄o-s̄el-l̄ing College of Dre-b̄ung Monastic University
- Paṇ-chen S̄ö-nam-drak-b̄a's *Garland of Blue Lotuses* (also used as main textbook by S̄har-d̄zay College of Gan-den Monastic University)
- Tsül-kang Lek-b̄a-dön-drup's[a] *Commentary on the Difficult Points*

Go-mang College of Dre-b̄ung Monastic University
- Gung-ru Chö-jung's *Garland of White Lotuses*
- Jam-ȳang-shay-b̄a's *Great Exposition of the Interpretable and the Definitive*
- Gung-tang's *Annotations*
- Gung-tang's *Difficult Points*

Jay College of S̄e-ra Monastic University
- B̄el-jor-hlün-drup's *Lamp for the Teaching*
- Jay-d̄zün Chö-ḡyi-gyel-tsen's General-Meaning Commentary (also used as main textbook by Jang-d̄zay College of Gan-den Monastic University)
- S̄hay-rap-w̄ang-b̄o's[b] *Differentiating the Interpretable and the Definitive*
- D̄ra-d̄i Ge-s̄hay Rin-chen-dön-drup's[c] *Ornament for the Thought*

M̄ay College of S̄e-ra Monastic University
- D̄en-b̄a-dar-gyay's *General Meaning*
- D̄en-b̄a-dar-gyay's *Decisive Analysis*[d]

(I have used all of these texts except for two that I could not locate, Tsül-kang Lek-b̄a-dön-drup's *Commentary on the Difficult Points* and S̄hay-rap-w̄ang-b̄o's *Differentiating the Interpretable and the Definitive.*) Rather than a grand synthesis of these many commentaries, Dön-drup-gyel-tsen's text provides very short compilations of stances on many issues, and thus its usefulness is limited. It is likely that he was seeking to place Gung-tang's brilliant analyses in a wider framework of scholastic interaction by identifying in brief terms the positions of other scholars.

That Gung-tang did not finish his two commentaries drew another of Jam-

---

[a] *tshul khang legs pa don grub.*

[b] *shes rab dbang po.*

[c] *pra sti dge bshes rin chen don grub.* He flourished in the mid-seventeenth century and was born in Am-do *dpa' ris pra sti.*

[d] Dön-drup-gyel-tsen indicates that, in addition to these four sets, he consulted other texts, such as the *zur rgol* by Kyung-truk-b̄a (*'khyung 'phrug pa*), a text from the Jang-d̄zay College of Gan-den Monastic University, which is used in addition to Jay-d̄zün Chö-ḡyi-gyel-tsen's *General-Meaning Commentary.*

ȳang-shay-b̄a's followers, A-ku L̄o-drö-gya-tso,[a] who was born in Am-do D̄za-yü,[b] southeast of D̄ra-s̄hi-kyil, and flourished in the early twentieth century (1851-1930), to write a "difficult points commentary" that also includes very short sections on the Autonomy and Consequence Schools. At times he abbreviates Gung-tang's opinions and at others explains issues that Gung-tang only indicates require more thought.[c]

Another early-twentieth-century follower but frequent critic of Jam-ȳang-shay-b̄a, Jik-may-dam-chö-gya-tso[d] (1898-1946), born in Am-do A-wa,[e] north of D̄ra-s̄hi-kyil, wrote a comprehensive commentary on D̄zong-ka-b̄a's entire text. Entitled *Treatise Distinguishing All the Meaning of (D̄zong-ka-b̄a's) "The Essence of Eloquence": Illuminating the Differentiation of the Interpretable and the Definitive: Port of Entry to "The Essence of Eloquence,"*[29] it lists and examines the positions of many of the above authors. A synthetic, lengthy tome in two volumes on D̄zong-ka-b̄a's entire text, it provides extensive detail on the entire scope of commentaries.

Among these, the works by Gung-ru Chö-jung, Jam-ȳang-shay-b̄a, Gung-tang, A-ku L̄o-drö-gya-tso, and Jik-may-dam-chö-gya-tso are most effective when read in series. Since Gung-ru Chö-jung's text was the basis for this tradition and since Jam-ȳang-shay-b̄a often condenses his predecessor's more free-flowing presentation, Gung-ru Chö-jung's work provides both a clear introduction and increased access to the twists and turns of the later texts. Many difficulties in Jam-ȳang-shay-b̄a's textbook that can hinder continued reading are handled by Gung-tang's brilliant and incisive analyses, whose work, therefore, can be understood only within its context as a supplement to Jam-ȳang-shay-b̄a's. A-ku L̄o-drö-gya-tso's text is indispensable because it explains many points that Gung-tang leaves hanging; still, it cannot stand alone since its flow

---

a *a khu blo gros rgya mtsho;* also known as Gung-tang L̄o-drö-gya-tso.

b *tsa yus.*

c Mention also should be made of J̄o-ne Paṇḍita L̄o-sang-gya-tso (*co ne paṇḍita blo bzang rgya mtsho*), who was born in Am-do *chos dpal zhing* in *co ne* and flourished in the early twentieth century. He gave lectures on D̄zong-ka-b̄a's *The Essence of Eloquence* in 1927, from which notes were taken by Pa-bong-ka-b̄a Jam-b̄a-d̄en-dzin-trin-lay-gya-tso (1878-1941), entitled *Presentation of the Interpretable and the Definitive, Brief Notes on the Occasion of Receiving Profound [Instruction from J̄o-ne Paṇḍita L̄o-sang-gya-tso] on (D̄zong-ka-b̄a's) "The Essence of Eloquence."* The text is brief and somewhat haphazard, since it was intended merely as personal notes.

d *'jigs med dam chos rgya mtsho;* 1898-1946. He was recognized as the reincarnation of *'jigs med bsam gdan;* his poetic name is Mi-pam-ȳang-j̄en-gay-b̄ay-dor-jay (*mi pham dbyangs can dges* [or *dgyes*] *pa'i rdo rje*). He wrote sixteen volumes of works. This work is dependent on teachings received from Gi-d̄eng L̄o-sang-b̄el-d̄en (*sgi steng blo bzang dpal ldan*) over more than eight months beginning in October/November of 1928 plus earlier teachings received from the same teacher over three years on the Naturelessness School. In the colophon he humbly says that he was setting down what this master taught.

e *a ba,* or *'gar tse nyin,* in *reb gong gser mo ljongs.*

is so bound to Jam-ȳang-shay-b̄a's and Gung-tang's expositions. Jik-may-dam-chö-gya-tso's text, on the other hand, is a massive synthesis.

In July 1996, when the Fourteenth Dalai Lama,[a] born in Am-do D̄ak-tser[b] in 1935, came to Gethsemani in Kentucky for a Buddhist-Christian dialogue, I reported to him that I had twenty commentaries[c] on D̄zong-ka-b̄a's text and was using eighteen. The next day, when he asked me what commentary I thought was best, I answered, "Gung-tang's analyses are very good, but Jik-may-dam-chö-gya-tso's text is superb." He quickly got up, went to his suitcase, and took out the green Kalimpong edition of *The Essence* that he always has with him. He opened it to reveal that the margins were filled with notes in his own hand which he explained were mostly from Jik-may-dam-chö-gya-tso's commentary. He said he cut out blank pages for notes when the margins were not sufficient.

Jik-may-dam-chö-gya-tso's contributions are such that he could be called the "scholar of scholars" of D̄zong-ka-b̄a's *The Essence of Eloquence*.

1. He covers all four sections of D̄zong-ka-b̄a's text in detail in two volumes—the Prologue and the Mind-Only School (356 folios), and the Autonomy School and Consequence School (299 folios)

> Unlike almost all of the other commentators from across the full breadth of the Tibetan cultural region, he did not desist from commenting on the sections on the Autonomy School and Consequence School, the omission usually being excused on the grounds that these schools are covered respectively in textbooks on Maitreya's *Ornament for Clear Realization* and Chandrakīrti's *Supplement to (Nāgārjuna's) "Treatise on the Middle."* Although there are three texts from the Se-ra Jay College that treat the entire text, they are not nearly as expansive. That by N̄yel-d̄ön B̄el-jor-hlün-drup does not even consider a great many issues. That by S̄er-s̄hül L̄o-sang-pün-tsok[d] gives an intriguingly unbiased treatment of difficult points in the Mind-Only section but offers only a "word commentary"[e] on the rest. That by D̄a-drin-rap-d̄en[f] is simply a word commentary. (The latter two are discussed below.) It is reported[g] that Gung-tang Ḡön-chok-d̄en-

a *bstan 'dzin rgya mtsho.*

b *stag mtsher;* southeast of *sku 'bum,* where D̄zong-ka-b̄a was born.

c The total now is twenty-six.

d *ser shul dge bshes blo bzang phun tshogs.*

e *tshig 'grel.*

f *tre hor dge bshes rta mgrin rab brtan,* 1920-1986. In Europe and America his published name is usually written Geshe Rabten. For a biography, see B. Alan Wallace, trans. and ed., *The Life and Teachings of Geshé Rabten* (London: George Allen and Unwin, 1980).

g By Geshe Thupten Gyatso.

b̄ay-drön-may's seventh incarnation was supposed to finish his commentary, but he is now seemingly too old to do so.

2. He does not use the facade of defending the textbook literature he originally studied

   All of the other post-sixteenth-century commentaries (except S̄er-s̄hül in places) play the game of pretending to re-explain the subtleties of their own textbook literature, but Jik-may-dam-chö-gya-tso does not shy away from frequently and openly criticizing Jam-ȳang-shay-b̄a and even Gung-tang Ḡön-chok-d̄en-b̄ay-drön-may. It is reported[a] that twenty ge-s̄hays from D̄ra-s̄hi-kyil sought to proceed to Rep-gong to debate with Jik-may-dam-chö-gya-tso after publication of his text in order to defend Jam-ȳang-shay-b̄a but the debate never took place.

3. He lists and analyzes the opinions of more Ge-luk authors

   His biographer, Tsay-d̄en-shap-drung Jik-may-rik-b̄ay-l̄o-drö,[b] says without exaggeration that he studied around forty such texts.

4. He pays close attention to the commentary by the seventh-century Korean scholar, Wonch'uk, on the *Sūtra Unraveling the Thought*[c]

   In the Mind-Only section, he cites Wonch'uk's commentary at least twenty-two times. He uses it for explanation of terms, for revealing the sources of several of D̄zong-ka-b̄a's and Gung-tang Ḡön-chok-d̄en-b̄ay-drön-may's points, for including the opinions of Paramārtha, and as a vehicle for developing topics.

5. He gives more definitions and etymologies than other authors do

For these reasons Jik-may-dam-chö-gya-tso's massive commentary is most helpful in organizing and penetrating the plethora of opinions on topics within Ge-luk circles. By giving his own independent opinions he keeps from falling into the deadness of a mere list of others' positions.

His weakness is that he does not consider in detail the works of the scholar-yogi that D̄zong-ka-b̄a marked out as his chief opponent, Döl-b̄o-b̄a S̄hay-rap-gyel-tsen[d] (see p. 47ff.) Detailed analysis of S̄hay-rap-gyel-tsen's *Ocean of Definitive Meaning, Fourth Council,* and so forth, would have fleshed out the context of *The Essence of Eloquence.* This failing is particularly intriguing since

[a] By Geshe Thupten Gyatso.

[b] *tshe tan zhab drung 'jigs med rigs pa'i blo gros* in *mkhas dbang 'jigs med rigs pa'i blo gros kyi gsung rtsom pod dang po* (mtsho sngon: mi rigs dpe skrun khang, 1987), 228.13.

[c] For discussion of Wonch'uk's commentary, see p. 39ff.

[d] *dol po pa shes rab rgyal mtshan;* 1292-1361.

Gung-tang Ḡön-chok-d̄en-b̄ay-drön-may does do this to some extent. Also, Jik-may-dam-chö-gya-tso does not consider the opinions of non-Ge-luk scholars subsequent to D̄zong-ka-b̄a, such as the intriguing S̄a-ḡya scholar, Shākya-chok-den.[a] Thus, his range is limited even if he is indeed a scholar of scholars.

Two twentieth-century commentaries from the Jay College of S̄e-ra Monastic University also are particularly helpful. The first is a remarkably unbiased synthetic commentary by S̄er-s̄hül L̄o-sang-pün-tsok, called *Notes on (D̄zong-ka-b̄a's) "Differentiating the Interpretable and the Definitive": Lamp Illuminating the Profound Meaning.*[30] In a genre called "separate annotations,"[b] S̄er-s̄hül Ge-s̄hay makes reasoned choices among many of the above-mentioned commentaries on a plethora of key issues about the prologue and Mind-Only sections—allegiance to his college not dictating his preferences. The text's lack of bias is a tribute to the author's towering intellect and dedication to content. Still, being a series of disconnected annotations, it has to be read along with *The Essence* and, preferably, with the major commentaries since his annotations are historically rooted. For the sections on the Autonomy and Consequence Schools S̄er-s̄hül Ge-s̄hay gives a fleshed out "word commentary" embedded within *The Essence,* thereby serving as a helpful entry to those parts of *The Essence.*

Another twentieth-century work on D̄zong-ka-b̄a's entire text, a "difficult points" commentary by D̄a-drin-rap-d̄en, does not evince S̄er-s̄hül Ge-s̄hay's lack of bias, but I found it very helpful in reading the text and preparing a translation—much of the bracketed material in my translation being from this work. It provides helpful rephrasings, inserted into D̄zong-ka-b̄a's text, drawn from B̄el-jor-hlün-drup's and the Second Dalai Lama's commentaries and also including the extensive outline found in Ge-s̄hay L̄o-sang-ge-lek's[c] *Mirror Illuminating the Meaning of the Thought of (D̄zong-ka-b̄a's) "Treatise Differentiating the Interpretable and the Definitive: The Essence of Eloquence."*[31] S̄er-s̄hül Ge-s̄hay's and D̄a-drin-rap-d̄en's works are synthetic representatives of different genres aimed at providing easier access—the former to central issues and the latter to the organization, syntax, flow of ideas, and so forth.

Much like the famed twenty-one Indian commentaries on Maitreya's *Ornament for Clear Realization,* the number of commentaries on D̄zong-ka-b̄a's *The Essence of Eloquence* written over the last six centuries[d] signifies both the seminal importance of the text in the Tibetan cultural region and the vibrancy of the scholarly tradition. To make D̄zong-ka-b̄a's often cryptic text more accessible, I have used eighteen of the twenty-six commentaries I have located, citing seventeen in the Translation as sources for annotation in brackets and in notes.[e]

---

a *gser mdog paṇ chen śākya mchog ldan,* 1428-1509.

b *zur mchan.*

c *dge bshes blo bzang dge legs.*

d Ge-s̄hay Ye-s̄hay-tap-kay has assembled a list of fifty-six commentaries.

e See p. 59ff. for an alphabetical list with college identifications where appropriate.

3. The Worldview

Ḍzong-ka-ḅa's text is often so brief with abrupt, unannounced shifts of topic, unspecified references, omissions, and seeming contradictions that it has been subjected to continuing, briskly argued analysis over the last six centuries by persons committed both to ferreting out its meaning and to maintaining diversity of opinion. It is virtually impossible to plunge right into it without becoming lost. The seemingly endless investigation of his system—performed by his followers through juxtaposing various facets of it and through probing enigmatic remarks hinting at penetration of profound issues—takes place within a worldview that is the floor for inquiry. Thus, in preparation for approaching the steel bow and arrow, it is necessary first to gain an overview of the issues involved, the theater for grand and petty dramas.

Three Natures

In Buddhism in general, suffering is viewed as being induced by actions[a] motivated by afflictive emotions,[b] which, in turn, are grounded in misperception of the nature of phenomena. More specifically, the *Sūtra Unraveling the Thought,* on which the Asaṅga based his system to a great degree, frames this process as stemming from the superimposition of a false status—called an imputational nature[c]—on impermanent phenomena. These phenomena are called "other-powered natures"[d] because they are objects under the influence of something other than themselves—that is, under the influence of causes and conditions. Other-powered natures do not have the power to stay for a second moment. No matter what they are—bodies, minds, tables, chairs, houses—most beings see them falsely, as if they were solid and could remain, as if they were under their own power, whereas actually they cannot remain even for a second moment since they are under the influence of the force of causes and conditions outside themselves. More specifically, those causes and conditions are predispositions, internal seeds, etchings on the mind by former perceptions that, when activated, produce an appearance of an object and a consciousness that pays attention to it. The same seed causes the appearance of the object and the appearance of the subject, much as in a dream.

---

a *las, karma.*

b *nyon mongs, kleśa.*

c *kun btags pa'i rang bzhin, parikalpitasvabhāva.*

d *gzhan dbang gi rang bzhin, paratantrasvabhāva.* For a thorough analysis of the three natures in the Yogic Practice (that is, Mind-Only) School in India, see Ake Boquist, *Trisvabhāva: A Study of the Development of the Three-Nature-Theory in Yogācāra Buddhism,* ed. Tord Olsson, Lund Studies in African and Asian Religions, 8 (Lund, Sweden: University of Lund, 1993). See also *Reflections on Reality,* chaps. 3 and 11-15.

The imputational nature that is falsely imputed to them is often described as the superimposition that subject and object are different entities—distant and cut off—whereas actually they are not. It is not being said that a table, for instance, appears to be a table but is not a table; rather, a table falsely appears to be distant and cut off from, for instance, the eye consciousness that is perceiving it. The table exists, but not in the manner in which it appears to exist. For example, during a magical display created by putting a salve on a small object such as a pebble and using a mantra that affects the eye consciousness of all present, a pebble appears to be a horse but is not; similarly, a table appears to be distant and cut off from an eye consciousness perceiving it but is not. Nonetheless, it seems external through the power of unreal ideation.[a] This is not necessarily current conceptuality thinking, "This is a different entity from my eye consciousness." Rather, through past repeated misperception of objects, predispositions were established for the false appearance of objects. By the power of these predispositions, phenomena presently appear to be distant and cut off from the perceiver even in raw sensation.

Another important mode of the imputational nature is the establishment of phenomena by way of their own character as the referent of a conceptual consciousness or of a word.[b] Imputation is done in terms of entities and attributes. The entity is, for example, a table; its attributes are, for instance, that it is large and scratched, old but serviceable. A nonexistent imputational nature of the table is that it is established **by way of its own character** as an object expressed by words for entities and attributes and as the referent of thoughts about entities and attributes.

Those are the most crucial imputational natures, belief in which produces all the ills of cyclic existence[c] and failure to know all that can be known. Contrary to such superimpositions, the final mode of being of other-powered natures, their emptiness of these imputational natures, is called the "thoroughly established nature."[d] The distinguishing feature of a thoroughly established nature is that it is a final object of observation by a path of purification. It must be something cognizance of which will remove obstructions built on unfounded misperceptions; thus, it is thoroughly established. Through reflecting on the thoroughly established nature, one overcomes misconceptions with respect to phenomena. Also, the thoroughly established nature is permanent, in the sense that it does not change moment by moment. In addition, although a thoroughly established nature—an emptiness—itself is not a virtue, the consciousness that pays attention to it is the supreme of all virtuous phenomena; the quality of the consciousness is extended to the object of the consciousness,

---

a For discussion of this term, see p. 307ff.

b *rang 'dzin rtog pa'i zhen gzhir rang gi mtshan nyid kyis grub pa;* also, *gzugs gzugs zhes rjod pa'i sgra 'jug pa'i 'jug gzhir rang gi mtshan nyid kyis grub pa.*

c *'khor ba, saṃsāra.*

d *yongs su grub pa'i rang bzhin, pariniṣpannasvabhāva.*

and thus in this sense the thoroughly established nature is the supreme virtue.

In this way, the three natures are three aspects, so to speak, of each and every phenomenon. The object itself is an other-powered nature which is the basis of the falsely imaged imputational nature and is the basis of thoroughly established nature, which is the other-powered nature's emptiness of that imputational nature. The thrust of the theory when applied in this way is liberative, first identifying a false status (the imputational nature) of objects (other-powered natures) belief in which induces suffering and finitude, and then, in order to gain liberation, realizing the emptiness (the thoroughly established nature) of that status (the imputational nature) falsely imputed to objects (other-powered natures). In this way the three natures can be applied to each and every phenomenon.

Hence, it can be seen that the question of the status of subjects and objects is central to the view of emptiness in the Mind-Only School and that realization of emptiness, in turn, is central to the process of overcoming the afflictive emotions that bind persons in cyclic existence and obstruct them from full altruistic expression. The issue is not merely a matter of how subject and object are **conceptualized** in treatises but whether the apprehended-object is innately **experienced** as an entity external to the apprehending-subject. Not merely speculative, the topic is at the heart of the process of release from suffering, for pain is viewed as being induced by actions motivated by afflictive emotions which, in turn, are grounded in this misconception of the nature of phenomena.

In the seventh chapter of the *Sūtra Unraveling the Thought,* Buddha is depicted as saying:[32]

> Superimposing the imputational nature onto other-powered natures and thoroughly established natures, sentient beings designate the convention that other-powered natures and thoroughly established natures are of the character of the imputational nature. In just the way that they designate such conventions, their minds are thoroughly infused with such designations of conventions, and due to relation with the designation of conventions or due to the dormancies of designations, they manifestly conceive other-powered natures and thoroughly established natures to be of the character of the imputational nature. In just the way that they manifestly conceive this, in that same way—due to the causes and conditions of manifestly conceiving other-powered natures as being of the imputational nature—in the future other-powered natures are thoroughly generated.
>
> On that basis, they become thoroughly afflicted by the afflictions that are the afflictive emotions. Also, they are thoroughly afflicted by the afflictions that are actions and by the afflictions that are the production of a lifetime. For a long time, they transmigrate as hell-beings,

> animals, gods, demi-gods, or humans and travel about within these transmigrations, not passing beyond cyclic existence.

Misconception of the nature of phenomena leads to an afflictive process that binds beings within a round of suffering.

Dzong-ka-ba, in *The Essence of Eloquence* (220), succinctly summarizes the import of the sūtra:

> The *Sūtra Unraveling the Thought* says that through manifestly conceiving the imputational nature in other-powered natures, [all] afflictive emotions are produced and, due to that, karmas are accumulated whereby one revolves in cyclic existence. Also, it says that if one sees other-powered natures as without the nature of the character of the imputational character, those are overcome in that order.

Release from suffering is viewed as a process of perceiving the actual nature of phenomena such that the superimposition that serves as the basis of the round of suffering is eradicated. In the seventh chapter of the *Sūtra Unraveling the Thought,* Buddha is depicted as saying to the Bodhisattva Paramārthasamudgata:[33]

> Because, hearing these doctrines, they do not conceive other-powered natures in the manner of the imputational character, they believe, thoroughly differentiate, and realize properly that [other-powered natures] are [self-]production-non-natures,[a] character-non-natures, and ultimate-non-natures....Moreover, on this basis, they thoroughly develop aversion toward all compositional phenomena, become completely free from desire, become completely released, and become thoroughly released from the afflictions that are the afflictive emotions, the afflictions that are actions, and the afflictions that are births.
>
> With respect to that, Paramārthasamudgata, through just this path and through just this procedure, even sentient beings who have the lineage of the Hearer Vehicle attain the unsurpassed accomplishment and blissful nirvana. Through just this path and through just this procedure, sentient beings who have the lineage of the Solitary Realizer Vehicle and those who have the lineage of the Vehicle of a One Gone Thus attain the unsurpassed accomplishment and blissful nirvana. The path of thorough purification of Hearers, Solitary Realizers, and Bo-

---

[a] It seems that this phrase has to be explained as meaning that they realize that other-powered natures are not established—in the manner of the imputational nature—by way of their own character. Otherwise, it would be indicating that other-powered natures themselves are not established by way of their own character, a position that would contradict the sūtra itself in the same chapter, as will be cited later (pp. 97 and 292, and *Reflections on Reality,* chap. 7), where Buddha says that whatever does not exist by way of its own character is not produced.

dhisattvas is only this one, and their purification is also one—there is no second.

The sūtra clearly calls for overcoming suffering by removing a false superimposition that induces the afflictive emotions driving the process of cyclic existence.

Asaṅga describes this afflictive psychological process in the "Chapter on Suchness" in his *Grounds of Bodhisattvas,*[34] and Dzong-ka-ba (221) summarizes Asaṅga in order to make the material more accessible:

> Conceptualization [that factors imputed] in the manner of entity and attribute [are established by way of their own character] and conceptualization apprehending amorphous wholes generate the foundations of [fictional] proliferations—the things that are the objects observed by conceptuality. In dependence upon that, the view of the transitory [as substantially established I and mine] is generated, and through this the other afflictive emotions are produced, whereby one travels in cyclic existence. However, if through the four examinations and the four thorough knowledges one understands the objects apprehended by conceptuality as nonexistent, those [afflictive emotions and so forth] are overcome.

The process is as follows:

- First, phenomena are misconceived in a false way to be established by way of their own character as the referents of designations for entities ("body") and attributes ("beautiful")
- That leads to improper thought mis-imagining qualities of cleanliness, happiness, permanence, and self
- That, in turn, engenders the perception that the self is substantially established and that mind, body, and so forth belong to a substantially established self
- That leads to the afflictive emotions of desire, hatred, and so forth; these produce actions which establish potencies in the mind—perpetuating the process of suffering in a round of painful existence

Since the afflictive emotions that bind beings in the beginningless round of birth, aging, sickness, and death are based on a false conceptualization of entities and their attributes, to understand the path of purification in the Yogic Practice School it is imperative to investigate what this false conceptualization is. It is also crucial to explore whether, as Ge-luk-ba scholars claim, it involves a misconception of a difference of entity between subject and object.

Such false conceptualization has come to be understood in Ge-luk-ba interpretations as follows:

> Although objects are not established by way of their own character as the referents of terms or of conceptual consciousnesses and although

> subject and object are not different entities, they appear even in raw sensation to be so established. Due to assenting to this seeming status, beings are drawn into afflictive emotions—misconceiving themselves and others to be substantially established in the sense of being self-sufficient and then, as a consequence of this, generating desire, hatred, confusion, enmity, jealousy, and so forth. These afflictive emotions, in turn, result in actions, which establish potencies in the mind that keep beings bound in cyclic existence.

Seen in the perspective of this worldview, the central issue of this inquiry is not merely theoretical. Rather, in this interpretation, it is undeniable that objects appear to be established by way of their own character as the referents of terms or of conceptual consciousnesses and appear to be different entities from the consciousnesses that perceive them. Thus this is an investigation into whether these appearances are true or false and hence whether the emotions founded upon assumptions of the status of phenomena based on these appearances are false. The aim of the system is for practitioners to engage in reasoned analysis, such that a decision that phenomena appear falsely is reached, whereupon, in combination with profound concentration, they can overcome the pull of this false appearance and thereby undo the psychological processes that give rise to the afflictive emotions and consequent contaminated actions. Hence, the basic issue is the unhealthy psychology of cyclic existence and the process of liberation from such unhealthy states.

The perspective is of a worldview of bondage due to misconception and liberation by way of knowledge. Developing over time, beginning most likely with early strata of the *Grounds of Bodhisattvas*[a] and culminating in Asaṅga's *Summary of the Great Vehicle,*[35] there came to be a view that the sufferings of sentient beings are founded on a misperception of the nature of phenomena in such a dualistic way.[b] Specifically, phenomena falsely appear to be established by way of their own character as the referents of the imputations of entities and attributes in such a manner that namer and named—subject and object—seem to be different entities, whereas they are not. By assenting to this false appearance, beings are drawn into a series of detrimental mental states, exaggerating the status of phenomena, such that counterproductive emotions are generated. These lead to actions that, in turn, deposit predisposing potencies in the mind in latent form, which, when activated, perpetuate further the round of powerless suffering.

Because the process of becoming afflicted with suffering is built on ignorance—both a lack of knowledge of the true status of phenomena and an active assent to false appearance of phenomena—the situation of beings is fraught with potential, both for more pain in the future and for release from bondage

---

a See *Reflections on Reality,* chap. 21.

b I do not mean to suggest that there were not other such views prior to this period.

through the acquisition of wisdom. That wisdom is the earth-shattering knowledge that phenomena are not established by way of their own character as the referents of the imputations of entities and attributes and hence that namer and named, subject and object, are not different entities. The overcoming of innate tendencies, ingrained over countless lifetimes, to assent to false appearance requires that wisdom be teamed with powerful, one-pointed concentration to the point where the true nature of objects can be perceived in non-conceptual, totally non-dual cognition, which must be reentered again and again. The psychology of limited, counterproductive states is thus transformed through philosophical penetration of the true status of things, thereby undoing an afflictive process built on the failure to analyze appearances. In this way, the philosophical enterprise has powerful ramifications for psychological improvement—theoretical study leading to transformation of character.

Artificial And Innate Superimpositions

According to Ḏzong-ka-ḇa and his followers, the conception that other-powered natures such as mind, body, and house are established by way of their own character as the referents of conceptual consciousnesses apprehending them in the manner entities and attributes is the chief superimposition explicitly treated in the seventh chapter of the *Sūtra Unraveling the Thought*, the "Questions of Paramārthasamudgata." Other-powered natures' emptiness of such a superimposed nature is their thoroughly established nature. The superimposed factor itself is an imputational nature.

Consciousnesses engaged in such superimposition are of two types, artificial[a] (that is, intellectually acquired) and innate.[b] The former are delusive consciousnesses that have as their basis the reasonings and/or the scriptures of a mistaken system. No matter how ingrained or habitual these become and no matter how much one becomes unaware or unconscious of them, as long as the initial impetus comes from reasonings and/or scriptures, the mistakenly conceiving consciousness is called "artificial." The innate, on the other hand, is not dependent on reasoning and scripture or on training in a mistaken system or even on learning language and thus exists even among babies, animals, insects, and so forth.

About the artificial, Ḏzong-ka-ḇa (194) identifies the systems that assert such a status as being true:

> With respect to superimposition, there are two, artificial and innate, and within the artificial there are the systems of Others' Schools and of

a *kun btags, parikalpita.*

b *lhan skyes, sahaja.*

> the two Proponents of [Truly Existent External] Objects among our own schools [the Great Exposition[a] and the Sūtra Schools[b]].

He identifies (1) non-Buddhist schools that, as the late Ḏa-drin-rap-ḏen says,[36] have many modes of assertion that terms and conceptual consciousnesses operate through the power of the things which are their referents and (2) what are, in this tradition, held to be the two Lesser Vehicle[c] schools. These are systems that assert the tenet that objects are established by way of their own character as the referents of conceptual consciousnesses. Later, in the context of stating the Mind-Only position that objects are not established by way of their own character as the referents of conceptual consciousnesses, Ḏzong-ka-ḇa (201) adds:

> For this reason, even the Hearer schools have assertions of tenets that are superimpositions opposite to this—that is, holding that forms and so forth are established by way of their own character as imputed by names as entities and attributes.
>
> It is as follows: In refuting this, Asaṅga's *Grounds of Bodhisattvas* refutes it also with [Buddhist] scripture, and since it is not suitable to refute Other Schools [Non-Buddhists] with the scriptures of one's own teacher, our own schools also must exist among those who are being refuted, and since the Proponents of Non-Nature[d] or a specific type of Yogic Practitioner are not being refuted, [these have to be Buddhist] Hearer schools. Hence, [on the occasion of refuting this, Asaṅga] does not quote passages from the *Sūtra Unraveling the Thought* but refutes them with three passages[e] established for them.

---

a *bye brag smra ba, vaibhāṣika.*

b *mdo sde pa, sautrāntika.*

c *theg dman, hīnayāna.* The term "Lesser Vehicle" (*theg dman, hīnayāna*) has its origin in the writings of Great Vehicle (*theg chen, mahāyāna*) authors and was, of course, not used by those to whom it was ascribed. Substitutes such as "non-Mahāyāna," "Nikāya Buddhism," and "Theravādayāna" have been suggested in order to avoid the pejorative sense of "Lesser." However, "Lesser Vehicle" is a convenient term in this particular context for a type of tenet system or practice that is seen in Tibetan scholarship to be surpassed but not negated by a "higher" system. The "Lesser Vehicle" is not despised, most of it being incorporated into the "Great Vehicle." The monks' and nuns' vows are Lesser Vehicle, as is much of the course of study in Ge-luk-ḇa monastic universities—years of study are put into the topics of Epistemology (*tshad ma, pramāṇa*), Manifest Knowledge (*chos mngon pa, abhidharma*), and Discipline (*'dul ba, vinaya*), all of which are mostly Lesser Vehicle in perspective.

d *ngo bo nyid med par smra ba, niḥsvabhāvavādin.* These are the so-called Proponents of the Middle (*dbu ma pa, mādhyamika*), but the Proponents of Mind-Only consider themselves to be the Proponents of the Middle since they propound a middle free from the two extremes, and thus Ḏzong-ka-ḇa often refers to this school by a name acceptable to all schools.

e For the three passages see p. 202, footnote a.

That Buddhist schools are being refuted by Asaṅga is known, not because he cited them by name but because he used Buddhist scriptures to refute this notion, it being the custom not to make use of scriptural citation from other than the opponent's own tradition.

At the point where we left the preceding quote, D̄zong-ka-b̄a (194) says about innate superimpositions:

> With respect to the innate [type of superimposition], since the superimposition of a self of persons will be shown later [in the section on the Consequence School, I] will explain [here the innate] superimposition of a self of phenomena. This is because the imputation of a self of phenomena by [other schools of] tenets is for the sake of confirming the self of phenomena that is conceived innately and because the main of the objects of reasoned negation is also that [innately conceived self of phenomena].

The innate superimposition being refuted is one that beings engage in without stimulus from formal systems of any sort but, nevertheless, is supported by certain systems, in this case both non-Buddhist and Low Vehicle Buddhist schools. This inborn error cannot be one that requires education for its inception or one that would be either obviously silly or refutable by reasoning in the Low Vehicle schools of tenets; Great Vehicle reasoning is required to refute it.

The innate erroneous conception being identified here is not that the name of the object is the object or that the object is its name, since even the Low Vehicle schools realize that such is not the case, and it is obvious that anyone endowed with common sense can understand that saying, "gold," does not produce gold. Rather, it is the conception that objects are established by way of their own character as the referents of conceptual consciousnesses or of words. A **consequence** of such would be that a person who had not learned the name of an object would know its name merely from seeing the object; however, the conception that the name of the object is the object or that the object is its name is not innate, no matter how great the impact of understanding this can be. Rather, the **absurd** consequences are **reasons** refuting that objects are established by way of their own character as the referents of conceptual consciousnesses or of words; thus, the reasons should not be confused with the status of objects that the reasons refute.

Also, what is being refuted is not merely that objects are the referents of a conceptual consciousness or that objects are the referents of terms. For objects are indeed the referents of a conceptual consciousness and of terms. Put more simply, we can think about objects, and our terms can indeed refer to objects (how else could we ever ask for noodle soup and get it?). Hence, what is being refuted is that objects are **established by way of their own character** as the referents of conceptual consciousnesses and of terms. D̄zong-ka-b̄a (195) makes this point clearly:

> Those imputational factors—which are such that a consciousness conceiving imputational factors to be established by way of their own character is asserted to be a consciousness conceiving a self of phenomena—are the nominally and terminologically imputed factors [in the imputation of] the aggregates and so forth as entities, "This is form," and as attributes, "This is the production of form," and so forth. Since the aggregates and so forth do exist as just those [entities of such nominal and terminological imputation], the [mere] conception that they exist as those [entities of nominal and terminological imputation] is not a superimposition; rather, the conception that the aggregates and so forth **exist by way of their own character** as those entities [of nominal and terminological imputation] is a superimposition.

His point is that objects are indeed referents of our conceptions and terminology but are not established as such by way of their own mode of being. Assent that such referentiality inheres in objects themselves is what must be stopped.

Three Non-Natures

In chapter 7 of the *Sūtra Unraveling the Thought* the Bodhisattva Paramārthasamudgata questions Buddha about his saying in the Perfection of Wisdom Sūtras that "All phenomena are natureless." On the surface, Buddha's statement appears to be nihilistic—denying that any phenomenon has "nature."

In response, Buddha explains that when he said that all phenomena are natureless, he was not making a blanket statement with respect to each and every phenomenon but was referring to the **three** types of phenomena and their respective **three** types of non-nature. Exhibiting the typical Indian delight in esthetically stimulating word-play complications, he identifies the three types of phenomena that are **nature**less as the three **natures**—imputational natures, other-powered natures, and thoroughly established natures. Again cryptically, the three different types of non-nature that the three natures have are identified as character-non-nature,[a] production-non-nature,[b] and ultimate-non-nature.[c]

---

[a] *mtshan nyid ngo bo nyid med pa nyid, lakṣaṇaniḥsvabhāvatā* (Étienne Lamotte, *Saṃdhinirmocanasūtra: L'Explication des mystères* [Louvain: Université de Louvain, 1935], 67 [3], n. 3).

[b] *skye ba ngo bo nyid med pa nyid, utpattiniḥsvabhāvatā* (ibid., 67, n. 4).

[c] *don dam pa ngo bo nyid med pa nyid, paramārthaniḥsvabhāvatā* (ibid., 67, n. 5). This term has two meanings. My general translation is "ultimate-non-nature" since this mirrors the Sanskrit and the Tibetan and is sufficiently ambiguous to allow its two meanings. The first meaning is the actual ultimate-non-nature, the thoroughly established nature, which is both (1) the **ultimate** as the object of observation by a path of purification and (2) the very **non-nature**, that is, the **absence** of the opposite of emptiness, in phenomena. The second meaning refers to fact that other-powered natures are not the ultimate; just as other-powered natures are natureless in terms of production, so they are **natureless** in terms of the **ultimate**—that is to say, they lack being that nature which is the ultimate. (The *Sūtra Unravel-*

And to make the puzzle more complicated, both other-powered natures and thoroughly established natures are said to be ultimate-non-natures.

To start to solve the puzzle (even without knowing the meaning), one first has to line up the three natures with three non-natures—the last of the three non-natures having two types:

Three Natures	*Three Non-Natures*
Imputational natures	Character-non-natures
Other-powered natures	1) Production-non-natures 2) Ultimate-non-natures
Thoroughly established natures	Ultimate-non-natures

Then, based on statements in the *Sūtra Unraveling the Thought,* it is possible to identify the meaning of the three non-natures:

Three Natures	*Three Non-Natures*
Imputational natures	Character-non-natures, in the sense that they are posited by names and terminology and do not exist by way of their own character
Other-powered natures	1) Production-non-natures, in the sense that they arise through the force of other conditions and are not self-produced 2) Ultimate-non-natures, in the sense that they are not objects of observation of paths of purification, that is, are not objects of the ultimate, purifying consciousness
Thoroughly established natures	Ultimate-non-natures, in the sense that they are the ultimate and the very absence of a difference of entity of subject and object and the very absence of establishment by way of a phenomenon's own character as the referent of terms and conceptual consciousnesses

In this way, in the *Sūtra Unraveling the Thought* Buddha interprets the statement in the Perfection of Wisdom Sūtras that "All phenomena are natureless," so that it is not nihilistic.

The *Sūtra Unraveling the Thought* itself says that sharpest Bodhisattvas can, without relying on other sūtras, understand these (superficially nihilistic) statements as referring to the three natures and the three non-natures. As the *Sūtra* says:[37]

> With respect to this, thinking of just these three types of non-nature, the One Gone Thus, by way of the aspect of setting forth sūtras of interpretable meaning, taught the doctrine in this way, "All phenomena are natureless; all phenomena are unproduced, unceasing, quiescent from the start, and naturally thoroughly passed beyond sorrow." Regarding that, when sentient beings who have generated great roots of virtue, have purified the obstructions, have ripened their continuums, who have great faith and have accumulated great collections of merit

ing the Thought is clear on this point; see p. 88ff.). Thus, thoroughly established natures are "ultimate-non-natures," and other-powered natures are also "ultimate-non-natures," but for different reasons.

and wisdom—hear this doctrine, they understand—**just as it is**—this which I explained with a thought behind it, and they develop belief in that doctrine. They also realize, by means of their exalted wisdom, **the meaning just as it is.**

Thus, Ge-luk-ba̅ scholars hold that even for the Proponents of Mind-Only the Perfection of Wisdom Sūtras are the supreme of sūtras, even though their literal reading must be interpreted.

Compatibility Of Emptiness And Idealism

There are many fascinating topics to be considered with respect to the various interpretations of idealism in Europe, and so forth:

- Locke (1632-1704), who leaves an external object as "substance" devoid of secondary qualities such as color, taste, and smell
- Berkeley (1685-1753), who does away with external objects altogether, even as substance, using the mind of God as the mechanism for positing a continuously perceiving consciousness and thus continuity of objects
- Hume (1711-1776), who does away with such a God, to be replaced by the association of ideas, and so forth.

In Buddhism, as expounded by Ge-luk-ba̅ scholars, there are other idealist tendencies including:

- the common tenet of all Buddhist schools (as presented in Ge-luk-ba̅ scholarship) that the definition of an existent as **that which is observed by valid cognition,**[a]
- the common tenet that the mind is predominantly important among all phenomena, and
- denial that external objects generate perceptions but affirmation that other beings are different entities from oneself.

Here I use the term "idealism" in the last sense, only to mean the "absence of external objects"—specifically that an object such as blue does not exist as a separate entity from a consciousness apprehending blue and that a consciousness apprehending blue does not exist as a separate entity from that blue. This is commonly called subjective idealism. It is important to note that subjective idealism in this Buddhist system does not entail that all objects are the same entity as *one particular* subject and thus does not entail solipsism—there are other consciousnesses and their percepts. (Ge-luk-ba̅ scholars "handle" the solipsistic tendencies through reference to Dharmakīrti's proof of the existence of

[a] *tshad mas dmigs pa.*

other beings in his *Proof of Other Continuums,*[38] the very title of which recognizes the idealist nature of his philosophy and its possible mis-interpretation as solipsism.)

Such idealism also does not necessitate the positing of a permanent, pure consciousness that is the ultimate truth, or absolute reality.[a] This would be to overload idealism with notions that it necessarily entails the assertion of a permanent pure consciousness as the ultimate truth and then to propose that Asaṅga in these texts does not propound idealism since it is clear that for him emptiness is the ultimate truth. Asaṅga does indeed propound that emptiness is the ultimate truth, for when he speaks about the path of seeing, for instance, he says not that a meditator sees just mind but that a meditator sees emptiness. Hence, it is unwarranted to take this type of Buddhist idealism to be absolute idealism, which would indeed entail that on the path of seeing a yogi would have to realize just mind; such is not the case.

Although the object of non-conceptual wisdom is not a consciousness but emptiness, this does not entail that mind-only is not a final doctrine. In most[b] Ge-luk-b̄a delineations of the Mind-Only School's view of emptiness, the **emptiness** of a difference of entity between subject and object is the ultimate truth, the object of direct perception on the path of seeing and the path of meditation. According to their standard presentations of the path structure in the Mind-Only School, the emptiness that is directly seen on the paths of seeing and meditation is the absence of a difference of entity between subject and object or the absence of objects' being established by way of their own character as the referents of terms or conceptual consciousnesses. Thus, emptiness so defined not only does not cancel out mind-only but confirms mind-only, the very absence of a difference of entity between subject and object upon which such idealism depends. Understood this way, idealism and emptiness are compatible in one system.

---

[a] Thus it is unfounded to claim that, since Asaṅga teaches that the mind-basis-of-all (*kun gzhi rnam par shes pa, ālayavijñāna*) is impermanent, he could not have taught it in any way other than provisionally, that is to say, merely to lead trainees. Janice D. Willis presents this notion in her *On Knowing Reality: The Tattvārtha Chapter of Asaṅga's Bodhisattvabhūmi* (New York: Columbia University Press, 1979; reprint, Delhi: Motilal Banarsidass, 1982), 21-24. See *Reflections on Reality,* chap. 21 and appendix 3.

[b] For others, see *Reflections on Reality,* chap. 14.

4. The Context

In the section on Mind-Only, Ḏzong-ka-ḇa presents how the *Sūtra Unraveling the Thought* differentiates which of Buddha's scriptures require interpretation and which are definitive. He does this within the fourfold context of:

- Refining the Korean scholar Wonch'uk's seventh-century presentation
- Criticizing the eclectic syncretism of the fourteenth-century Tibetan scholar-adept Jo-nang-ḇa Shay-rap-gyel-tsen (1292-1361), who died four years after Ḏzong-ka-ḇa's birth
- Presenting Indian Mind-Only scholarship in such a way that the architecture of the system can be engaged
- Distinguishing the Mind-Only School from the Consequence School and thus setting the stage for his later exposition of Chandrakīrti's criticism of the Mind-Only School and the Autonomy School

Wonch'uk's Influence In Tibet

Tibetan scholarship on the *Sūtra Unraveling the Thought* is strongly influenced by the *Extensive Commentary on the "Sūtra Unraveling the Thought"*[39] written in Chinese[a] by the seventh-century Korean scholar Wonch'uk[b] and translated into Tibetan. Wonch'uk was born in 612 or 613 in Hsin-lo, a descendant of a prince of the Silla kingdom (the other two kingdoms being Paekje and Koguryo),[c] eighty-two years after the Silla court officially adopted Buddhism.

---

[a] The only extant version of the Chinese is in the supplement to the Kyōto edition of the canon, *Dainihon Zokuzōkyō* (Kyōto, 1905-1912; also Hong Kong Reprint, 1922, 134.d-535.a) and is available in a Chinese version of an ongoing *tripiṭaka* that includes many texts, mostly Chinese works: *Da Zang Jing* (Taipei: Xin Wen Fong Ltd.), 1977, vol. 34, 581-952, and vol. 35, 1-100. It is missing the first portion of the eighth fascicle and all of the tenth fascicle of the original text. These have been reconstructed from the Tibetan by Inaba Shōju: *Enjiki Gejinmikkyōsho Sanitsububan no kanbunyaku* (Kyōto: Hōzōkan, 1949). See Shōtarō Iida, "The Three Stūpas of Ch'ang An," in *Papers of the First International Symposium Commemorating the 30th Anniversary of Korean Liberation* (Seoul, Academy of Korean Studies: 1975), 489, and John C. Powers, *Hermeneutics and Tradition in the Saṃdhinirmocana-sūtra* (Leiden, Netherlands: Brill, 1993), 17, n. 34. For discussion of the number of chapters in Wonch'uk's commentary, see appendix 2 (p. 457).

[b] Tib. *rdzogs gsal / wen tshig / wen tshegs / wanydzeg*, Ch. *Yüan-ts'e*, 613-696. See also Iida, "Three Stūpas of Ch'ang An," 484-497.

[c] The three ancient kingdoms were united as Unified Silla, or Korea, in 668 C.E. The biographical sketch of Wonch'uk is drawn from Iida, "Three Stūpas of Ch'ang An," 484-497, and Shōtarō Iida, "A Mukung-hwa in Ch'ang-an—A Study of the Life and Works of Wonch'uk (613-696), With Special Interest in the Korean Contributions to the Development of Chinese and Tibetan Buddhism," in *Proceedings, International Symposium, Commemorating the 30th Anniversary of Korean Liberation* (Seoul: National Academy of Sciences,

Wonch'uk was ordained as a novice at the age of three, and at fifteen, in 627/628 he traveled to Ch'ang-an,[a] China, capital of the T'ang Dynasty (618-908), where he remained for the rest of his life. He became a master of Mind-Only Buddhism, which was introduced into China in three phases:

- The initial phase began in the first year of the reign of Emperor Hsüan-wu of the Northern Wei dynasty (508) with the arrival of three masters from India—Ratnamati, Bodhiruci, and Buddhashānta. The system that developed was called the Dashabhūmika School (Ch. *Ti-lun*), based on Buddhashānta's translation of Vasubandhu's *Treatise on the "Sūtra on the Ten Grounds"* (*daśabhūmimkasūtraśāstra*)

- During the second phase, a Mahāyānasaṃgraha School (Ch. *She-lun*) formed, based on the translation of Asaṅga's *Summary of the Great Vehicle* (*mahāyānasaṃgraha*)[40] by the Indian monk and sage Paramārtha,[41] who was born in Ujjain, India, in 499, arrived in Guanjou in 546, and remained in China until his death in 569. His translations had a profound effect on forms of Buddhism in China.[42] Wonch'uk, studying under Seng-pien (568-642) and Fa-ch'ang (567/569-645/646) at Yüan-fa Monastery, became conversant with the Mind-Only School as transmitted by Paramārtha during the latter's twenty years of teaching in China. His studies emphasized Vasubandhu's *Treatise on the "Sūtra on the Ten Grounds"* (the primary first-phase text) and Asaṅga's *Summary of the Great Vehicle* (the primary second-phase text). Wonch'uk was strongly influenced by the expositions of Mind-Only doctrines by Sthiramati

- In 645, at age thirty-three, prompted by dreaming that "a *brahmana* gave him fruit until he was completely satisfied,"[43] Wonch'uk went to meet Hsüan-tsang upon the latter's return from India. Hsüan-tsang's return marked the beginning of the third phase of the dissemination of Mind-Only Buddhism into China, the school being called Fa-hsiang (*dharmalakṣaṇa,* Character of Phenomena) or Wei-shih (*vijñaptimātra,* Cognition-Only), this name being based on Hsüan-tsang's influential composition of a text based primarily on Dharmapāla's commentary on Vasubandhu's *Thirty Stanzas on the Establishment of Cognition-Only* (*vi-*

Republic of Korea, 1975), 225-251; Oh Hyung-keun, "The Yogācāra-Vijñaptimātratā Studies of Silla Monks," in *Assimilation of Buddhism in Korea: Religious Maturity and Innovation in the Silla Dynasty,* ed. Lewis R. Lancaster and C. S. Yu (Berkeley, Calif.: Asian Humanities Press, 1991), 105-120; Ahn Kye-hyon, "Buddhism in the Unified Silla Period," in *Assimilation of Buddhism in Korea: Religious Maturity and Innovation in the Silla Dynasty,* ed. Lewis R. Lancaster and C. S. Yu, 1-46; Peter H. Lee, ed., *Sourcebook of Korean Civilization* (New York: Columbia University Press, 1993), vol. 1, 166-171; and Robert E. Buswell, trans., "Wonch'uk (613-696): Memorial Inscription," unpublished manuscript. Buswell related to me that there is nothing in Korean about Wonch'uk's life.

[a] Presently called Xian.

> *jñaptimātratāsiddhi*)[44] called the *Ch'eng wei-shih lun.* In his own text, Hsüan-tsang makes use of ten Indian commentaries on Vasubandhu's *Thirty Stanzas on the Establishment of Cognition-Only* (Dharmapāla, Sthiramati, Chittrabhānu, Nanda, Guṇamati, Hiṇamitra, Jñānachandra, Bandhushrī, Shuddhachandra, and Jinapura). Later the school came to be called the "New Yogācāra," in contradistinction to Paramārtha's "Old Yogācāra"

Hsüan-tsang[45] (600-664) is renowned for his arduous trip to India in 629[46] through Central Asia (begun close to the time that Wonch'uk left Korea for China), during which he:

- survived an attempt on his life by his guide,
- became lost in the desert,
- threatened a hunger strike after the King of Turfan would not let him leave and thereby was granted safe travel to India through the king's letters,
- was captured on the Ganges by bandits who wanted him as a human sacrifice,
- was tutored at Nālandā in Mind-Only doctrines by the 106-year-old scholar-abbot Shīlabhadra, who had been a disciple of Dharmapāla, himself a disciple of Dignāga, who was a disciple of Vasubandhu, half-brother of Asaṅga,
- traveled to Shrī Laṅka, and
- returned to Nālandā where he mainly studied Indian philosophy.

He became so famous in India that when he called on Harṣha, emperor of India, the Emperor bowed to the ground and kissed his feet. Harṣha convened a grand debate for eighteen days so that Hsüan-tsang could "dissipate the blindness of the Hīnayāna and...shatter the pride of the Brahmans."[47] In 645, after an absence of sixteen (or seventeen) years, the triumphant Hsüan-tsang returned to Ch'ang-an, for a tumultuous welcome and an audience with Emperor T'ai-tsung.

Resisting the Emperor T'ai-tsung's request that he renounce his vows so that he could serve as an adviser to him, Hsüan-tsang put his energies into translating some of the 657 texts he brought back with him from India. In time, he translated 74 of them, including the *Sūtra Unraveling the Thought.* As mentioned above, he composed the influential *Ch'eng wei-shih lun,* based mainly on Dharmapāla's *Commentary on (Vasubandhu's) "Thirty Stanzas on the Establishment of Cognition-Only"* but also incorporating, where he found them useful, the views of the nine other Indian commentators given above. At the emperor's request, he also wrote a record of his journey,[48] a storehouse of information on Central Asia and India.

After Emperor T'ai-tsung again requested that Hsüan-tsang give up his vows and he again resisted, the emperor took a deep interest in Buddhism and had nine copies of Hsüan-tsang's newly translated texts distributed to each of the nine divisions of the empire and allowed the ordination of five monks in each of the 3,716 monasteries. In addition, in 648, a year before Emperor T'ai-tsung's death, 300 monks were ordained at the spectacular ceremony dedicating the magnificent Ta-tz'u-en Monastery built by the Crown Prince, Li Chih (soon to become Emperor Kao-tsung). A library and an Institute for the Translation of Scriptures were established within the monastery.

During the reign of Emperor Kao-tsung other monasteries were established, and thus, through his service to two emperors, Hsüan-tsang had great influence on the course of Buddhism in China, it being said that he had 3,000 disciples. When Hsüan-tsang died in 664, the Emperor Kao-tsung canceled his audiences for three days out of respect for the "Jewel of the Empire." However, immediately thereafter, the emperor ordered the cessation of all translation activities, showing that, as Stanley Weinstein says:[49]

> his primary concern was for Hsüan-tsang as an individual—a monk of unusual talent who served the T'ang ruling family loyally—rather than for the Buddhist teachings to which Hsüan-tsang had dedicated his life....This simple, unadorned edict brought to an abrupt close the activities of the most remarkable and productive group of Buddhist translators and scholars ever assembled on Chinese soil.

Hsüan-tsang's two most famous disciples were K'uei-chi (632-682)[a] and Wonch'uk. Hsüan-tsang selected K'uei-chi, born in a noble family in Ch'ang-an, as the chief transmitter of the Mind-Only Buddhism that he brought back from India. Thus, K'uei-chi served as Hsüan-tsang's assistant during the translation of the *Establishment of Cognition-Only* late in his master's life, and he himself wrote four commentaries on the text. K'uei-chi came to be revered as the first patriarch and founder of the sect. As Weinstein says:[50]

> The Yogācāra Buddhist movement of Hsüan-tsang and Ts'u-en [K'uei-chi] dominated the Buddhist world of their day, completely overshadowing the other schools of Buddhism, and when in the latter half of the T'ang Dynasty it finally began to decline, it had already been firmly planted in Japan, where it has continued to the present day as the Hossō Sect, always giving a strong impetus to the Buddhist world.

K'uei-chi's noble lineage and importance in the sect set the stage for conflict with Wonch'uk, whose previous training in Paramārtha's "Old Yogācāra" both

---

[a] More properly called Chi or Tz'u-en, the latter being based on his monastery's name; see Stanley Weinstein, "A Biographical Study of Tz'u-en," in *Monumenta Nipponica* 15, nos. 1-2 (1959): 119-149. For a detailed study of his life and works, see Alan Sponberg, "The Vijñaptimātratā Buddhism of the Chinese Monk K'uei-chi (A.D. 632-682)" (Ph.D. diss., University of British Columbia, 1980).

gave him background for easy access to the new doctrines of Hsüan-tsang and distanced him from the orthodoxy of the new school. It is renowned that his quick wit was such that when Hsüan-tsang showed him his new translations of Asaṅga's *Grounds of Yogic Practice* and Dharmapāla's *Establishment of Cognition-Only,* Wonch'uk understood them immediately and clearly. Undoubtedly, his quick penetration was aided by his previous study, which gave him so much confidence that "he was not overwhelmed by Hsüan-tsang's enormous prestige" and even pointed out a mistranslation by the master.[51] Wonch'uk's vast scholarship enabled him to formulate a synthesis of Old and New Yogācāra, and thus he came to be branded as non-orthodox by Hsüan-tsang's and K'uei-chi's followers.

Based on the *Lotus Sūtra* (*saddharmapuṇḍarīka*), the *Flower Garland Sūtra* (*avataṃsaka*), and so forth, Wonch'uk drew the conclusion that all beings would eventually become fully enlightened and hence there are not three final vehicles (Hearer, Solitary Realizer, and Bodhisattva vehicles) but just one. The notion of one final vehicle was popular in Korean Buddhism at that time and "was used as a symbolic philosophical and religious basis for the unification of the three kingdoms"[52] when Silla, allied with the T'ang Dynasty, defeated the other two Kingdoms—Paekche in 660 and Koguryo in 668—unifying Korea. The single-vehicle interpretation put Wonch'uk at odds with the teachings of Hsüan-tsang and K'uei-chi as well as their followers, the Korean being considered to be an outsider.[a] When Wonch'uk's disciples in China and Silla established their own school, the Korean school debated against the Chinese school of Hsüan-tsang, K'uei-chi, and Hui-chao (650-714).

The intense rivalry between K'uei-chi and Wonch'uk—at least on the level of their chief disciples—led to accounts, discredited by Hatani Ryotai,[53] Stanley Weinstein,[54] and Shōtarō Iida,[55] that Wonch'uk bribed a guard at the gate of the temple where Hsüan-tsang was teaching Dharmapāla's *Establishment of Cognition-Only* to K'uei-chi so that he himself could write a synopsis and, preempting K'uei-chi, give a lecture on the work. Given the extremely high level of erudition that Wonch'uk evinces in his commentary on the *Sūtra Unraveling the Thought,* this account (as well as another similar to it) seems fabricated to discredit him.

Still, it is said that to calm his ambition Wonch'uk took pleasure in mountains and streams and lived in retreat for eight years. Later, as the principal teacher of Hsi-ming Monastery, he wrote a commentary on the *Establishment of Cognition-Only,* but it, along with all but three[b] of twenty-three works

---

[a] It also puts him at odds with Ge-luk-b̄a scholars' interpretations of the Mind-Only School following Asaṅga, though it accords with their interpretations of the Mind-Only School following Dharmakīrti as well as the Middle Way Autonomy School and their own final view as represented in the Middle Way Consequence School.

[b] The three works are his commentary on the *Sūtra Unraveling the Thought,* a *Commentary on the Benevolent King Sūtra,* and an *Essay on the Heart Sūtra;* see Kye-hyon, "Buddhism

fascicles,[a] has apparently not survived. The Emperor Kao-tsung appointed him the leader of a group translating eighteen titles (in 34 fascicles) of scriptures brought to Ch'ang-an around 680 by the Indian monk Divākara. Later Wonch'uk lectured on and assisted in the translation of the *Flower Garland Scripture,* but before the task was completed, he passed away at Fo-shou-chi Monastery on August 25, 696, at the age of eighty-four. A White Stūpa was erected at Hsiang-shan Monastery, in a valley to the north of Mount Lung-men, to commemorate his life, his relics also being distributed to other monasteries associated with him. Another stūpa was built in 1114 at Hsing-chiao Monastery of Ch'ang-an, to the left of Hsüan-tsang's stūpa, where there was also one commemorating K'uei-chi, which was renovated at that time. Wonch'uk and K'uei-chi are also portrayed together in the Wild Goose Pagoda in Ch'ang-an. These are fitting commemorations of the impact of these two scholars, stemming to a great extent from their being the two main disciples of Hsüan-tsang at Ta-tz'u-en Monastery.

In 735 a pilgrim named T'an-kuang (died c. 788)[56] from Ho-hsi, near Tun-huang, traveled to Ch'ang-an, where he stayed at Hsi-ming Monastery—which had been Wonch'uk's monastery a half-century earlier. When T'an-kuang returned to the Tun-huang area in 774, he carried with him Wonch'uk's ten-fascicle commentary on the *Sūtra Unraveling the Thought.* T'an-kuang became a famous teacher, and not long thereafter a renowned scholar in T'an-kuang's lineage, Fa-ch'eng[b] (c. 755-c. 849) became the chief translator under the Tibetan king, Rel-b̄a-j̄en[c] (who reigned 815-841) during the eighty-six-year-period when Tibet controlled the area of Tun-huang. The eventual result was that Wonch'uk's text was translated into Tibetan, probably sometime between 815 and 824.[57] Through this set of circumstances, Wonch'uk's commentary on the *Sūtra Unraveling the Thought* became part of the Tibetan cultural milieu when, early in the fifteenth century, D̄zong-ka-b̄a composed *The Essence of Eloquence.*

D̄zong-ka-b̄a explicitly refers to Wonch'uk's text nine times—three by his name,[d] five by "Chinese *Great Commentary,*"[e] and once within "the commen-

in the Unified Silla Period," 14.

[a] Or 99 or 93, according to Iida, "Mukung-hwa in Ch'ang-an," 233; for a partial listing of Wonch'uk's works, see the same, 233-237. A copy of Wonch'uk's commentary and notes on Hsüan-tsang's *Chen Wei Shi Lun* entitled *Chen Wei Shi Lun Ce Shu,* published early in this century from wood blocks, was found in a Taipei used bookstore and republished by Ci Ji Gong De Hui in 1989 with notes by Chen Hui Jian; my thanks to Chen Shu-chen for the reference.

[b] *chos grub.*

[c] *ral pa can.*

[d] Twice as *wen tsheg* (Translation, 119/ Text, 387; 125/389) and once as *sde snod gsum pa wen tsheg* (Tripiṭaka Wonch'uk, 123/388).

[e] It is apparent that D̄zong-ka-b̄a was unaware that Wonch'uk was born in Korea; it is

taries."[a] There are also two times when, without attribution, he uses Wonch'uk's text as a source for outlines of passages from the *Sūtra Unraveling the Thought*.[b] The number of references and the fact that he does so by name or title of his text eight times are particularly significant, since Ḏzong-ka-ḇa only obliquely refers to one other text written in Chinese—a commentary on the sūtra by Paramārtha that, most likely, he knew only through Wonch'uk's commentary. Also, he does not even mention the name of any Tibetan scholar, including the one whom he is principally refuting, Shay-rap-gyel-tsen (1292-1361), whose opinions he frequently rebukes.[c] Ḏzong-ka-ḇa's open references to Wonch'uk most likely derive from deference to his wide-ranging scholarship and from a wish to correct the opinions of an influential, if temporally distant, scholar.

Among the eleven references, Ḏzong-ka-ḇa disagrees with Wonch'uk four times, refines his opinion five times, and agrees two times. In the course of the section on the Mind-Only School, he:

1. disagrees with Wonch'uk's assertion that "own-character"[d] means the unique character of an object, saying that it means establishment by way of its own character: "the Chinese *Great Commentary*," p. 78;
2. disagrees about the meaning of "the various[e] and manifold[f] constituents": included in "the commentaries," p. 80;
3. implicitly agrees with Wonch'uk's division of the description of the character-non-nature into a (rhetorical) question, answer, questioning of the reason, and answer to that question:[g] p. 86;
4. agrees about the meaning of "permanent, permanent time[h] and everlasting, everlasting time"[i] as former time and later time, respectively: "the Chinese *Great Commentary*," p. 98;
5. refines Wonch'uk's resolution of an apparent conflict between the *Sūtra*

likely that by using the nomenclature of "the Chinese *Great Commentary*" (*rgya nag gi 'grel chen;* 78/370, 98/381, 101/382, 123/388, 126/389), he intends to distinguish Wonch'uk's commentary from another long commentary extant in Tibetan (for discussion of its authorship see appendix 1, p. 453ff.). Ḏzong-ka-ḇa cites this commentary only once, in order to refute it (see p. 156). Ḏzong-ka-ḇa does not cite Jñānagarbha's commentary (Peking 5535, vol. 109), which is only on the eighth chapter, nor does he mention a short one attributed to Asaṅga (Peking 5481, vol. 104). His attention is clearly on Wonch'uk's text.

a *'grel pa rnams;* 80/370.

b 86/373 and 118/387.

c See below, p. 54ff.

d *rang gi mtshan nyid, svalakṣaṇa.*

e *tha dad pa, nānātva.*

f *du ma, anekatva.*

g Ḏzong-ka-ḇa copies Wonch'uk's structuring (Peking 5517, vol. 116, 130.5.4ff).

h *rtag pa rtag pa'i dus.*

i *ther zug ther zug gi dus.*

Unraveling the Thought and Asaṅga's *Summary of Manifest Knowledge:* "the Chinese *Great Commentary,*" p. 101;

6. implicitly refines (that is, abbreviates) Wonch'uk's outline of a sūtra passage: p. 118;
7. refines Wonch'uk's presentation of the four qualities of the first wheel of doctrine: "Wonch'uk," p. 119;
8. praises Wonch'uk's **translation** of a term in the *Sūtra Unraveling the Thought* (this being "in a non-manifest manner" in place of "through the aspect of speaking on emptiness") but refines the **meaning**: "the Chinese *Great Commentary,*" p. 123;
9. disagrees with Wonch'uk for merely saying the four qualities of the middle wheel are so "in relation to the third wheel" and suggests that Wonch'uk should have criticized Paramārtha's explanation: "Tripiṭaka Wonch'uk," p. 123;
10. laconically faults the first part of Wonch'uk's twofold interpretation of the second of the four qualities of the third wheel of doctrine: "Wonch'uk," p. 125; and
11. refines Wonch'uk's nomenclature for the three wheels of doctrine, agreeing that the first wheel is to be called "the wheel of doctrine of the four truths" and that the second is to be called "the wheel of doctrine of no character," but not agreeing that the third is to be called "the wheel of the ultimate, the definitive"; Ḏzong-ka-ḇa insists on "the wheel of good differentiation": "the Chinese *Great Commentary,*" p. 126.

Also, it is highly likely that through Wonch'uk's text Ḏzong-ka-ḇa became aware of the scholarship of Bodhiruci, Dharampāla, Paramārtha, and Hsüan-tsang, all of whom the Tibetan scholar mentions in his separate presentation of the mind-basis-of-all and afflicted intellect,[a] written in his twenties.[58]

Ernst Steinkellner[59] cogently speculates that the Tibetan technique of employing elaborate sectioning and subsectioning of texts may stem from similarly elaborate sectioning in Wonch'uk's commentary. If this is so, Wonch'uk also gave rise to a predominant style of scholarly organization in Tibetan texts that was employed to greater and lesser degrees by scholars in all of the major sects. In any case, through his extensive and erudite commentary on the *Sūtra Unraveling the Thought* Wonch'uk served to stimulate Ḏzong-ka-ḇa (and perhaps others who preceded him)[b] and thereby the various Ge-luk-ḇa traditions that de-

a *Extensive Commentary on the Difficult Points of the Mind-Basis-of-All and Afflicted Intellect: Ocean of Eloquence* (*yid dang kun gzhi'i dka' ba'i gnas rgya cher 'grel pa legs par bshad pa'i rgya mtsho*). See the excellent translation by Gareth Sparham in collaboration with Shōtarō Iida, *Ocean of Eloquence: Tsong kha pa's Commentary on the Yogācāra Doctrine of Mind* (Albany, N.Y.: State University of New York Press, 1993). In that text, Ḏzong-ka-ḇa cites Wonch'uk with regard to the history of Great Vehicle masters (pp. 48-49) and the number of consciousnesses asserted by Mind-Only masters (pp. 153-156).

b Research is needed to determine this.

veloped in the vast Tibetan cultural region. It is clear from the tone of these scholars' comments that they admired Wonch'uk's intelligence and erudition.

S̄hay-rap-gyel-tsen's Innovative Syncretism

The situation is far more complicated with D̄zong-ka-b̄a's near contemporary Döl-b̄o-b̄a S̄hay-rap-gyel-tsen, one of the most influential figures of fourteenth-century Tibet—so influential that much of the Mind-Only section of *The Essence of Eloquence* is framed as a rebuttal to his views.[a] As Cyrus Stearns says:[b]

> Without question, the teachings and writing of Dol po pa, who was also known as "The Buddha from Dol po" (*Dol po sangs rgyas*), and "The Omniscient One from Dol po who Embodies the Buddhas of the Three Times" (*Dus gsum sangs rgyas kun mkhyen dol po pa*), contain the most controversial and stunning ideas ever presented by a great Tibetan Buddhist master. The controversies which stemmed from his teachings are still very much alive today among Tibetan Buddhists, more than 600 years after Dol po pa's death.

S̄hay-rap-gyel-tsen was born in 1292 in a family that practiced tantric rites of the N̄ying-ma order.[60] After receiving tantric initiation at the age of five, he had a vision of Red Mañjushrī, and subsequently his intelligence burgeoned. At twelve he was ordained and at seventeen fled, against his parents' will, to study with Ḡyi-d̄ön Jam-ȳang-drak-b̄a-gyel-tsen[c] in Mustang, where, in a month, he learned the doctrinal language[d] of the (1) path-structure studies associated with the Perfection of Wisdom teachings, (2) epistemology and logic,[e] and (3) phenomenology.[f] His new teacher was called to S̄a-ḡya, then the greatest learning

---

a Wel-mang Ḡön-chok-gyel-tsen's *Notes on (Ḡön-chok-jik-may-w̄ang-b̄o's) Lectures* (399.3) states that S̄hay-rap-gyel-tsen is D̄zong-ka-b̄a's main opponent in *The Essence of Eloquence.*

b Cyrus R. Stearns, *The Buddha from Dol po and His Fourth Council of the Buddhist Doctrine* (Ann Arbor, Mich.: University Microfilms, 1996), 2. Stearns's excellent work is the source for much of what follows, except for the parts drawn from the *Ocean of Definitive Meaning.* See also Cyrus R. Stearns, "Dol-po-pa Shes-rab-rgyal-mtshan and the Genesis of the *gzhan-stong* Position in Tibet," *Asiatische Studien / Études Asiatiques* 59, no. 4 (1995): 829-852; David Seyfort Ruegg, "The Jo Naṅ Pas: A School of Buddhist Ontologists according to the *Grub mtha' sel gyi me loṅ,*" *Journal of the American Oriental Society* 83, no. 1 (1963): 73-91; Matthew Kapstein, *The 'Dzam-thang Edition of the Collected Works of Kun-mkhyen Dol-po-pa Shes-rab-rgyal-mtshan: Introduction and Catalogue* (Delhi: Shedrup Books, 1992); and S. K. Hookham, *The Buddha Within: Tathāgatagarbha Doctrine according to the Shentong Interpretation of the Ratnagotravibhāga* (Albany, N.Y.: State University of New York Press, 1991).

c *skyi ston 'jam dbyangs grags pa rgyal mtshan.*

d *chos skad.*

e *tshad ma, pramāṇa.*

f *chos mngon pa, abhidharma.*

center in Tibet, and two years later Shay-rap-gyel-tsen joined him, where he continued studies on the three above-mentioned topics, as well as Shāntideva's *Engaging in the Bodhisattva Deeds*[61]—simultaneously mastering them in a year and half.

From his master Gyi-dön he also received teachings on the *Kālachakra Tantra* and related sūtras and commentaries that shaped his practice and teachings. After receiving many other teachings, when he was twenty-one his parents, "who had now forgiven him for running away,"[62] made an offering for his own first teaching—this being on the Perfection of Wisdom, epistemology and logic, phenomenology, and discipline. "His teachings were received with unprecedented acclaim, although some criticized him for teaching too many texts at once."[63] At the age of twenty-two, while making a tour of western and central Tibet to learn at other institutions, he first came to be called "Omniscient,"[a] an epithet that even his opponents still use. As Stearns says about the his extremely broad learning and about the importance of Gyi-dön Jam-yang-drak-ba-gyel-tsen to him:[64]

> Up until the age of twenty-nine (1321) he had studied with more than thirty teachers, the most important of whom, Skyi ston 'Jam dbyangs Grags pa rgyal mtshan, had bestowed upon him some seventy initiations and teachings.

At twenty-nine in 1321, however, he was completely humbled when he visited the monastery of Jo-nang and saw "that every man and woman who was seriously practicing meditation had realized the nature of reality through meditation."[65]

In 1322 he returned to Jo-nang, where he received in-depth instruction on the *Kālachakra Tantra* and entered into retreat. During a second retreat for one year (or two or three, depending on the account), he realized the first four branches of the six-branched yoga of the Kālachakra system—individual withdrawal, concentration, stopping-vitality, retention, subsequent mindfulness, and meditative stabilization. Stearns says (brackets mine):[66]

> On the basis of both *pratyāhara* [withdrawal] and *dhyāna* [concentration], he beheld immeasurable figures of the Buddhas and pure lands. On the basis of *prāṇāyāma* [stopping-vitality] and *dhāraṇā* [retention], exceptional experience and realization was born due to the blazing of blissful warmth.

During this retreat Shay-rap-gyel-tsen realized the view of "other-emptiness" (which Dzong-ka-ba seeks so strongly to refute in *The Essence of Eloquence*) but did not speak about it for several years.

In 1326 he was installed as the head of the Jo-nang Monastery and in 1327 began work on a gigantic monument—the Glorious Stūpa of the Constella-

[a] *kun mkhyen.*

tions[a]—which was completed in 1333, restored by Tāranātha in 1621, and recently refurbished in 1990. Either during or after the building of the stūpa, for the first time he taught that conventional phenomena are self-empty, in the sense that they lack any self-nature, whereas the ultimate is other-empty, in the sense that it is empty of the relative but has its own self-nature. This latter realization Shay-rap-gyel-tsen himself stated to be previously unknown in Tibet and spoke of it this way:[67]

> I bow in homage to the gurus, buddhas and kalkīs by whose kindness the essential points which are difficult for even the exalted ones to realize are precisely realized, and to their great *stūpa.*[b]

During this period Shay-rap-gyel-tsen wrote and taught a great deal, while also working on the monument. Even "his *magnum opus* [*The Mountain Doctrine: Ocean of Definitive Meaning*][c] was completed well before the final consecration of the *stūpa* on October 30, 1333."[68]

His view of "other-emptiness," based largely on his profound understanding of the *Kālachakra Tantra* and commentary by Kalkī Puṇḍarīka and bolstered by the *Lion's Roar of Shrīmālādevī Sūtra,*[d] and so forth, was received (soon thereafter or after a passage of time, according to different accounts) with amazement and shock. However, he also was highly lauded and received great offerings from exalted figures of the day, among whom he indeed was one of the greatest. He gave teachings sometimes to thousands of persons and at other times to the luminaries of his period. He was invited, along with Bu-dön Rin-chen-drup[e]—another great master of Kālachakra—to China by the Yüan dynasty (Mongolian) Emperor Toghon Temür. Neither of them went, and to

---

a *dpal ldan rgyu skar gyi mchod rten.*

b In his promise to compose *The Essence of Eloquence* Dzong-ka-ba (p. 68) similarly says that his realization of the view is special:

> Many who had much hearing of the great texts,
> Who worked with much weariness also at the path of reasoning,
> And who were not low in accumulation of the good qualities of clear realization
> Worked hard at but did not realize this topic which,
>
> Having perceived it well through the kindness of the smooth protector and guru [Mañjushrī],
> I will explain with an attitude of great mercy.

The similarities may not be coincidental.

c *ri chos nges don rgya mtsho* (Gangtok, Sikkim: Dodrup Sangyey Lama, 1976).

d *lha mo dpal 'phreng gi seng ge'i sgra zhes bya ba (theg pa chen po'i) mdo, śrīmālādevīsiṃhanāda(mahāyāna)sūtra,* part 48 of *Mahāratnakūṭasūtra,* Peking 760, vol. 24. See the translation by A. Wayman and H. Wayman, *The Lion's Roar of Queen Śrīmālā* (New York: Columbia University Press, 1974); cited at length in Shay-rap-gyel-tsen's *Ocean of Definitive Meaning,* 114.6ff, 181.6ff., and so forth.

e *bu ston rin chen grub,* 1290-1364.

avoid the emperor's displeasure Shay-rap-gyel-tsen "stayed in different isolated areas for four years."[69]

Concerned about the damage to religious centers and so forth that ensued from a protracted power struggle, Shay-rap-gyel-tsen decided "to travel to Lha sa and make prayers to the Jo bo image there, which he felt to be the same as the Buddha himself."[70]

> Dol po pa had become increasingly disturbed by the extensive damage to the Buddhist communities, temples, and shrines in Tibet due to the great political turmoil that had swept through the land during the protracted power struggle between the Sa skya pa in Gtsang [the western province of Tibet] and the newly arisen Phag mo gru in Dbus [Central Tibet].[71]

Thus, in 1358, at the age of sixty-six, he departed from Jo-nang. Along the way, he gave teachings to the Fifteenth Patriarch of Sa-gya, Sö-nam-gyel-tsen,[a] who requested that he compose *The Great Calculation of the Doctrine, Which Has the Significance of a Fourth Council,*[b] along with his own commentary. Shay-rap-gyel-tsen audaciously[72] entitled his work this way because he considered this doctrine to be a presentation suitable to be likened to an addition to the famous three councils in India.

He also gave lectures "that were often so large that people at the edges could not hear the teaching, so it had to be relayed through an interpreter."[73] In the Hla-sa area he was thronged with teachers and others requesting teachings, to the point where "There were so many people listening to the teachings that doors were broken and stairways collapsed."[74]

After six months, when leaving Hla-sa to return to Jo-nang, he was thronged by believers and, again, along the way he taught huge crowds and received the praise of monastic leaders. When he stopped in Sha-lu[c] to debate with Bu-dön, the latter sought to avoid the confrontation, but when Shay-rap-gyel-tsen nevertheless made "the opening exclamation for debate (*thal skad*), the force...produced a crack in the wall of Bu-ston's residence."[75]

In the eleventh month of mouse year (the end of 1360), Shay-rap-gyel-tsen gave a teaching on his *Ocean of Definitive Meaning* and the next day passed away in deep meditation.

> When the corpse was offered into the fire, the smoke rose up only about the length of a spear, then went to the *stūpa* like a streaking arrow, circled it many times, and finally disappeared to the west.[76]

After the crematorium was opened, many clear, crystal-like formations appeared among the ashes, and "ashes from the cremation were gathered and put

a *bsod nams rgyal mtshan.*

b *bka' bsdu bzhi pa'i don bstan rtsis chen po.*

c *zha lu.*

along with other relics into an image of Dol po pa that was in the great *stūpa* he had built."[77]

Less than fifteen years after Shay-rap-gyel-tsen's death, the influential Sa-gya scholar Ren-da-wa Shön-nu-lo-drö (1348-1413), who became Dzong-ka-ba's chief teacher, raised strong objections to Shay-rap-gyel-tsen's teachings, even refuting "the validity of the *Kālachakra Tantra*."[78] Dzong-ka-ba similarly disagreed strongly with Shay-rap-gyel-tsen's doctrine of "other-emptiness" but, along with a vast number of opinions that differed from those of Ren-da-wa, did accept the *Kālachakra Tantra,* as is evidenced by the fact that both of his foremost students wrote texts on the Kālachakra system and several of his students wrote short essays of notes on his teachings on this system.[a]

Shay-rap-gyel-tsen developed a new doctrinal language through an amalgamation of the classical texts of the Mind-Only and Middle Way systems into a Great Middle Way,[b] and he also intertwined the particular vocabulary of the Kālachakra system. As he says:[79]

> *Tantras* should be understood by means of other *tantras.*
> *Sūtras* should be understood by means of other *sūtras.*
> *Sūtras* should also be understood by means of the *tantras.*
> *Tantras* should also be understood by means of the *sūtras.*
> Both should be understood by means of both.

In what are usually considered the classical texts of separate systems, he saw presentations of multiple systems crowned by the Great Middle Way. For instance, he considered separate passages of the *Sūtra Unraveling the Thought,* usually considered to be Mind-Only, to present the views of Mind-Only and the Great Middle Way,[c] the latter being concordant with Ultimate Mind-Only,[d] or Supramundane Mind-Only,[e] which is beyond consciousness.[f] In his *Ocean of Definitive Meaning,*[80] he takes the following passage from chapter 9 of the *Sūtra Unraveling the Thought* to evince the view of the Great Middle Way:[81]

> That which brings about definite emergence [from obstructions] by means of the middle path upon having abandoned the extreme of superimposition and the extreme of deprecation is their wisdom. Moreover, by way of that wisdom they thoroughly and correctly know also, just as it is, the meaning of the doors of liberation with respect to the

[a] Among these are three texts on the six-branched yoga, and so forth: one very short (Peking 6058), another fairly short (6206), and one a bit longer (6168).

[b] *dbu ma chen po.*

[c] He attacks the notion that *Sūtra Unraveling the Thought* has merely a Mind-Only perspective (*Ocean of Definitive Meaning,* 205.2ff.)

[d] *don dam pa'i sems tsam:* ibid., 213.1. Also, "Final Mind-Only" (*mthar thug gi sems tsam:* ibid., 213.4).

[e] *'jig rten las 'das pa'i sems tsam:* ibid., 213.6.

[f] *rnam shes las 'das pa:* ibid., 213.2.

> three doors of liberation—emptiness, wishlessness, and signlessness. They also thoroughly and correctly know, just as it is, the meaning of the natures with respect to the three natures—imputational, other-powered, and thoroughly established.

Not just in sūtras and tantra but also in Indian treatises—usually taken to be strictly Mind-Only—he found passages teaching Mind-Only but others teaching the Great Middle Way.

Thus Shay-rap-gyel-tsen's synthesis was by no means a collage drawing a little from here and a little from there and disregarding the rest. Rather, he had a comprehensive, thorough, and overarching perspective born from careful analysis. For him, others had just not seen what the texts themselves were saying and, instead of that, read into the classical texts the views of single systems. For instance, he says that the mere fact that the three natures and the eight collections of consciousness are taught in Maitreya's *Differentiation of the Middle and the Extremes* does not make it a Mind-Only text, since these are also taught in sūtras and tantras of the Great Middle Way. He adds:[82]

> Moreover, the meaning of the statement in Maitreya's *Differentiation of the Middle and the Extremes,* "All are just name-only," contradicts the view of the Proponents of Mind-Only.

He quotes many sūtras to the same end:[83]

> The *Descent into Laṅkā Sūtra* says that, for the time being, one is taught mind-only, but finally having thoroughly passed beyond that, one is taught the middle without appearance, and that having also passed beyond this, one is taught the middle with appearance and that if one does not arrive at that, one has not seen the profound meaning of the Great Vehicle. It says:
>
> Relying on mind-only,
> One does not imagine external objects.
> Relying on non-appearance,
> One passes beyond mind-only.
>
> Relying on observing reality,
> One passes beyond non-appearance.
> If yogis dwell in non-appearance,
> They do not perceive the Great Vehicle.

In this way, Shay-rap-gyel-tsen's perspective was syncretic, in that he drew from a great variety of sūtras, tantras, and treatises. It was synthetic perhaps only in the sense that he found within these an exposition of a view beyond the traditional schools. It was not a mere putting together of pieces from here and there.

He also criticized the then (and still) popular notion that recognition of conceptions themselves as the Truth Body[a] of a Buddha "would alone bring about enlightenment,"[b] without requiring abandonment of any misconceptions.[c] He complains:[84]

> These days the majority maintains that this very mind itself [*sems nyid*] is *dharmakāya,* self-arisen pristine awareness, and *mahāmudrā,* and many maintain that the concepts are *dharmakāya,* the afflicting emotions are pristine awareness, *saṃsāra* and *nirvāṇa* are indivisible.

Indeed, the works of Shay-rap-gyel-tsen's contemporary, the Nying-ma master Long-chen-rap-jam,[d] are replete with such statements. For instance, in his *Precious Treasury of Tenets: Illuminating the Meaning of All Vehicles,* Long-chen-rap-jam says:

> On the path of the Definition Vehicle one finally becomes tired and exhausted by the asceticism of abandoning [non-virtues] and adopting [virtues]. However, in Mantra everything shines as a help-mate, and thus entities to be abandoned and entities to be adopted are naturally pure.[85]
>
> In Mantra the secrecy of mind is that memories and thought dawn as the sport of reality, whereby the mind shines as self-illuminating self-arisen pristine wisdom.[86]
>
> Since afflictive emotions are naturally purified without abandoning them, the two collections are amassed quickly and completed; thereby, liberation is achieved in one lifetime.[87]

Shay-rap-gyel-tsen considered such teachings to be the secret work of devils.[88] Thus he was bucking two popular trends—(1) separation of the classical texts of the Great Vehicle into isolated systems and of sūtra and tantra into isolated camps and (2) reduction of the final path to self-recognition of basic mind.

Dzong-ka-ba reacted to Shay-rap-gyel-tsen's dynamic synthesis with his own analysis of the classical texts that yielded evidence opposing such an amalgamation. To make this point, he emphasized philosophical controversies between schools that are evident in these texts, thereby evolving his own synthesis. Based on this, he considered Shay-rap-gyel-tsen's positing of Mind-Only, Middle Way, and Great Middle Way to be unfounded. This appears to be the chief impetus behind his writing a text under the rubric not of intertwining texts but

---

a *chos sku, dharmakāya.*

b For a clear and concise exposition of this position, see Stearns, *The Buddha from Dol po,* 151-156; also 171-174.

c For an excellent study of doctrines of enlightenment through seeing basic mind, see David Jackson, *Enlightenment by a Single Means* (Vienna: Verlag der Österreichischen Akademie der Wissenschaften, 1994).

d *klong chen rab 'byams,* 1308-1363.

of distinguishing them and entitling it *Treatise Differentiating Interpretable and Definitive Meanings: The Essence of Eloquence*—even the name of which I see as being in response to Shay-rap-gyel-tsen's magnum opus, entitled *The Mountain Doctrine: Ocean of Definitive Meaning*. Dzong-ka-ba's sense that the separateness of many texts[a] needed to be emphasized is understood only in the context of his reaction to Shay-rap-gyel-tsen's synthesis. Still, the vast amount of distinctions that he had to make in order to "find" his own grand overview of these systems indicates that his perspective is, in its own way, just as creative, synthetic, and syncretic.

The overall structure of the Mind-Only section of *The Essence of Eloquence* and the relationship of each part to Shay-rap-gyel-tsen's views is:

- to show how the *Sūtra Unraveling the Thought* presents the ultimate as a mere absence and thus to undermine Shay-rap-gyel-tsen's view that the ultimate is positive;
- to demonstrate how the founder of the Mind-Only system, the fourth-century north Indian sage Asaṅga, relied primarily on the *Sūtra Unraveling the Thought* and thus to undercut Shay-rap-gyel-tsen's notions that Asaṅga's texts could differ from the presentations in this sūtra;
- to detail the objections—found in chief works by Asaṅga—to doctrines of the Middle Way School and thereby to refute Shay-rap-gyel-tsen's attempt to amalgamate parts of the classical texts by Asaṅga—that are usually recognized as of the Mind-Only School—with classical texts of the Middle Way School to form a Great Middle Way;
- to show how texts by Maitreya and Indian scholars, which are prevalently recognized as Mind-Only, accord with presentations in the *Sūtra Unraveling the Thought* and in those works by Asaṅga and thereby further to undercut Shay-rap-gyel-tsen's finding multiple systems in their texts; and
- to present how the truth behind false superimpositions contrary to the nature of phenomena is realized through opposing misconceptions about the status of phenomena and thereby to counter Shay-rap-gyel-tsen's depiction of manifesting a positive ultimate.[b]

There are ten major refutations that fall into three categories:

1. Pointing out the contradiction that Shay-rap-gyel-tsen asserts that the *Sūtra Unraveling the Thought* is definitive but does not follow its teaching

[a] He did not do this for all texts. For instance, he considered Maitreya's *Ornament for Clear Realization* to contain passages that represent the opinions of the Consequence School subdivision of the Middle Way School and others that represent the views of the Autonomy School subdivision. See Tsong-ka-pa, Kensur Lekden, and Jeffrey Hopkins, *Compassion in Tibetan Buddhism* (London: Rider, 1980; reprint, Ithaca, N.Y.: Snow Lion, 1980), 178-181.

[b] These "refutations" are discussed in the corresponding footnotes, the Synopsis, and *Reflections on Reality*, chap. 17.

that the thoroughly established nature is a mere absence, a mere negative, and, instead of that, asserts that the final reality is positive: p. 92

2. Pointing out the contradiction that the *Sūtra Unraveling the Thought* speaks of the thoroughly established nature as other-powered natures' emptiness of the imputational nature, but Shay-rap-gyel-tsen turns this around and, instead of that, holds that the thoroughly established nature is empty of other-powered natures and imputational natures. This involves the assertion that other-powered natures and imputational natures are self-empty but that the thoroughly established nature is other-empty as well as the correlate assertion that all conventional phenomena are only fancied by a mistaken mind and are not established in the slightest whereas the final reality is truly established: pp. 108, 109, 129, 186, 188, 188, 226
3. Pointing out Shay-rap-gyel-tsen's mistake of concluding that when the *Sūtra Unraveling the Thought* says that the third wheel of doctrine is definitive, it means that all sūtras taught during the third period of Buddha's teaching are definitive, including those propounding that a Buddha is already present in the continuums of each being: pp. 129, 130

In sum, throughout the section on Mind-Only in *The Essence of Eloquence* Dzong-ka-ba, without mentioning Shay-rap-gyel-tsen's name, seeks to refute his positions on the nature of reality and thus his differentiation of which scriptures require interpretation and which are definitive. In the process, Dzong-ka-ba's own views on the Mind-Only School's description of emptiness and the stages of affliction and release become clear.

PART TWO:
ANNOTATED TRANSLATION

Dzong-ka-ba Lo-sang-drak-ba's
Treatise Differentiating Interpretable and Definitive Meanings: The Essence of Eloquence

Prologue and Section on the Mind-Only School

Remarks

The reader may find it helpful to read the corresponding section in the Synopsis before reading the Translation; thus throughout the Translation there are cross-references to the Synopsis that are indicated by pages numbers in parentheses. There are also cross-references to the Text that are indicated by page numbers in curly brackets (braces).

The two section titles and the twelve chapter titles have been added, closely following Ḏzong-ka-ḇa's own outline. Many subsections are given in square brackets, drawn from the commentaries; the purpose of these is merely to announce shifts of topic. Thus I have not tried to keep strict rules of subdividing, since a complete rendering would be overbearing.

References to texts are given in the backnotes, whereas other information, more pertinent to the reading of the translation, is given in the footnotes. Footnote references in italics indicate that the note includes a linkage to a chapter in *Reflections on Reality* or an issue treated in *Absorption in No External World.*

Seventeen Tibetan commentaries on Ḏzong-ka-ḇa's *The Essence of Eloquence* are cited in the notes. These are listed below alphabetically by author's name with the shorter title used in the notes, the author's dates, the largest Tibetan colleges using the text (if applicable), and the full translated title of the text (for the Tibetan title, and other information, see the bibliography).

- A-ku Ḻo-drö-gya-tso's *Precious Lamp* (Gung-tang Ḻo-drö-gya-tso; 1851-1930): Dre-ḇung Go-mang and Ḏra-s̄hi-kyil
  Commentary on the Difficult Points of (Ḏzong-ka-ḇa's) "Treatise Differentiating Interpretable and the Definitive Meanings, The Essence of Eloquence": A Precious Lamp

- Ḇel-jor-hlün-drup's *Lamp for the Teaching* (1427-1514): S̄e-ra Jay
  Commentary on the Difficult Points of (Ḏzong-ka-ḇa's) "The Essence of Eloquence": Lamp for the Teaching

- Ḏa-drin-rap-ḏen's *Annotations* (1920-1986): S̄e-ra Jay
  Annotations for the Difficult Points of (Ḏzong-ka-ḇa's) "The Essence of Eloquence": Festival for the Unbiased Endowed with Clear Intelligence

- Dön-drup-gyel-tsen's *Four Intertwined Commentaries* (fl. late eighteenth and early nineteenth century): Dre-ḇung Go-mang and Ḏra-s̄hi-kyil
  Extensive Explanation of (Ḏzong-ka-ḇa's) "Treatise Differentiating the Interpretable and the Definitive, The Essence of Eloquence," Unique to Ge-luk-ḇa: Four Intertwined Commentaries

- D̄ra-d̄i Ge-s̄hay Rin-chen-dön-drup's *Ornament for the Thought* (fl. mid-seventeenth century): S̄e-ra Jay
  Ornament for the Thought of (D̄zong-ka-b̄a's) "Interpretable and Definitive: The Essence of Eloquence"

- Gung-ru Chö-jung's *Garland of White Lotuses* (fl. most likely in the sixteenth century since he refutes positions like those of Paṇ-chen S̄ö-nam-drak-b̄a and Jay-d̄zün Chö-ḡyi-gyel-tsen): Dre-b̄ung Go-mang and D̄ra-s̄hi-kyil
  Decisive Analysis of (D̄zong-ka-b̄a's) "Differentiating the Interpretable and the Definitive, The Essence of Eloquence": Garland of White Lotuses

- Gung-tang's *Annotations* (Gung-tang Ḡön-chok-d̄en-b̄ay-drön-may, 1762-1823): Dre-b̄ung Go-mang and D̄ra-s̄hi-kyil
  Beginnings of Annotations on (D̄zong-ka-b̄a's) "The Essence of Eloquence" on the Topic of Mind-Only: Illumination of a Hundred Mind-Only Texts

- Gung-tang's *Difficult Points* (Gung-tang Ḡön-chok-d̄en-b̄ay-drön-may, 1762-1823): Dre-b̄ung Go-mang and D̄ra-s̄hi-kyil
  Beginnings of a Commentary on the Difficult Points of (D̄zong-ka-b̄a's) "Differentiating the Interpretable and the Definitive": Quintessence of "The Essence of Eloquence"

- Jam-ȳang-shay-b̄a's *Great Exposition of the Interpretable and the Definitive* (Jam-ȳang-shay-b̄a Nga-w̄ang-d̄zön-drü, 1648-1722): Dre-b̄ung Go-mang and D̄ra-s̄hi-kyil
  Decisive Analysis of (D̄zong-ka-b̄a's) "Differentiating the Interpretable and the Definitive": Storehouse of White Lapis-Lazuli of Scripture and Reasoning Free from Error: Fulfilling the Hopes of the Fortunate

- Jay-d̄zün Chö-ḡyi-gyel-tsen's *General-Meaning Commentary* (1469-1546): S̄e-ra Jay and Gan-den Jang-d̄zay
  General Meaning of (D̄zong-ka-b̄a's) "Differentiating the Interpretable and the Definitive": Eradicating Bad Disputation: A Precious Garland

- Jik-may-dam-chö-gya-tso's *Port of Entry* (1898-1946)
  Treatise Distinguishing All the Meanings of (D̄zong-ka-b̄a's) "The Essence of Eloquence," Illuminating the Differentiation of the Interpretable and the Definitive: Port of Entry to "The Essence of Eloquence"

- Ke-drup's *Opening the Eyes of the Fortunate* (Ke-drup-ge-lek-b̄el-sang, 1385-1438): used by all colleges
  Opening the Eyes of the Fortunate: Treatise Brilliantly Clarifying the Profound Emptiness

- L̄o-sang-w̄ang-chuk's *Notes* (1901-1979): S̄e-ra Jay
  Notes on (D̄zong-ka-b̄a's) "Interpretable and Definitive, The Essence of Eloquence": Lamp for the Intelligent

- Paṇ-chen S̄ö-nam-drak-b̄a's *Garland of Blue Lotuses* (1478-1554): Dre-b̄ung L̄o-s̄el-l̄ing and Gan-den S̄har-d̄zay
  Distinguishing through Objections and Answers (D̄zong-ka-b̄a's) "Differentiating the Interpretable and Definitive Meanings of All the Scriptures, The Essence of Eloquence": Garland of Blue Lotuses

- Second Dalai Lama's *Lamp Illuminating the Meaning* (Gen-dün-gya-tso, 1476-1542): used by all colleges
  Commentary on the Difficult Points of "Differentiating the Interpretable and the Definitive" from the Collected Works of the Foremost Holy Omniscient [D̄zong-ka-b̄a]: Lamp Thoroughly Illuminating the Meaning of his Thought

- S̄er-s̄hül's *Notes* (S̄er-s̄hül Ge-s̄hay L̄o-sang-pün-tsok, fl. in early twentieth century): S̄e-ra Jay
  Notes on (D̄zong-ka-b̄a's) "Differentiating the Interpretable and the Definitive": Lamp Illuminating the Profound Meaning

- W̄el-mang Ḡön-chok-gyel-tsen's *Notes on (Ḡön-chok-jik-may-w̄ang-b̄o's) Lectures* (1764-1853): Go-mang tradition
  Notes on (Ḡön-chok-jik-may-w̄ang-b̄o's) Lectures on (D̄zong-ka-b̄a's) "The Essence of Eloquence": Stream of the Speech of the Omniscient: Offering for Purification

It would be gullible to hold that the commentaries present all of D̄zong-ka-b̄a's meaning, just as it would be arrogant to hold that they present none of it. In this translation, my intention is to provide a plethora of clearly marked annotations to show how various Tibetan and Mongolian scholars attempted to pry open D̄zong-ka-b̄a's often cryptic but much-lauded text on the final nature of phenomena.

TREATISE DIFFERENTIATING INTERPRETABLE AND DEFINITIVE MEANINGS: THE ESSENCE OF ELOQUENCE[a]

[a] See *Absorption,* #1-3.

Prologue

Namo gurumañjughoṣāya (Homage to guru Mañjughosha).[a]

[Expression of Worship to the Teacher, Shākyamuni Buddha][b]

(251) {363}

Homage to the Lord of Subduers,[c] god of gods,
As soon as whose body was seen by those
High-and-mighty with presumptions proclaiming
In the mundane world a great roar of arrogance[d] —

[The gods known as] Bliss-Arising, Cloud Mount, Golden Womb,
Bodiless Lord, Garlanded Belly,[e] and so on—

---

[a] See *Reflections on Reality,* chap. 5. Mañjughoṣha, or Mañjushrī, is the physical manifestation of the compassion of all Buddhas.

[b] Bel-jor-hlün-drup's *Lamp for the Teaching,* 4.6. See *Reflections on Reality,* chap. 5.

[c] *thub dbang, munīndra.* Buddhaguhya (*sangs rgyas gsang ba*) explains that the term *muni* (*thub pa*) means that the person has **restrained** body, speech, and mind (*lus la sogs pa sdams pa ni thub pa zhes bya'o*); see his *Commentary on the "Concentration Continuation Tantra"* (*bsam gtan phyi ma rim par phye ba rgya cher bshad pa, dhyānottarapaṭalaṭīkā*), Peking 3495, vol. 78, 70.1.5. Tibetan oral traditions also take *thub pa* as referring to one who has **overcome** the enemy that is the afflictive emotions. Many translators render *muni* as "sage," but I choose "subduer" because it conveys the sense of conquest that the term has in Tibetan, for *thub pa* means "able," with a sense of being able to overcome someone else. (*Śākya,* the name of this Buddha's clan, also means "able" or "potent," this probably being the reason why the name *śākyamuni* was translated into Tibetan as *śākya thub pa,* with the first part of the compound in transliterated Sanskrit and the second in Tibetan.) The term *dbang po* (*indra*) means "supreme one," "powerful one," "lord," and more loosely "king"; Shākyamuni is depicted as the supreme among Subduers.

[d] Lo-sang-wang-chuk (*Notes,* 84.9) finds possible references to the triad of body, speech, and mind; he takes:

- "high-and-mighty" (*'gying*) as referring to a physical quality (probably since the term can refer to a lion's manner of sitting),
- "roar" (*nga ro*) as referring to a quality of speech, and
- "presumptions" (*rlom pa*) and "arrogance" (*dregs pa*) as referring to a quality of mind.

[e] "Bliss-Arising" (*bde 'byung, śambhu*) is also known as *maheśvara* or *śiva.* Gung-tang (*Difficult Points,* 3.14, 4.11) reports that Maheshvara (Great Lord) is called "Bliss-Arising" not because he himself becomes blissful in dependence upon the goddess Uma but because his body is so supremely satisfying that when others see it, all virtues, including liberation, as well as temporary happiness arise. This is why Maheshvara is called a source of joy.

Gung-tang is refuting the first part of a dual explanation by Bel-jor-hlün-drup (*Lamp for the Teaching,* 5.1) who says:

> Īshvara is called Bliss-Arising because bliss arose in him in dependence upon the goddess Uma. Or, in another way, it is also suitable to take this in accordance with the explanation that he is so called because he has a supremely satisfying body.

Even they became like fireflies [overwhelmed] by the sun and thereupon
Paid respect with their beautiful crowns to his lotus feet.

[Expression of Worship to the Upholders of the Teaching][89]
Respectful homage to Mañjughoṣha and the Regent [Maitreya], great like oceans—
The depth of whose wisdom and mercy is very hard to fathom,[a]
Whose great waves of Bodhisattva deeds ripple widely,[b]

Gung-tang prefers the latter explanation and adds more detail.

"Cloud Mount" (*sprin la zhon, meghavāhana*) is also known as *indra* or *śakra.* Gung-tang (*Difficult Points,* 5.5) reports that Shakra is called "Cloud Mount" because of being mounted on an elephant that, like a cloud, is very large and moves about gently, with magnificent bearing.

"Golden Womb" (*gser gyi mngal, hiraṇyagarbha*) is also known as *brahmā.* Gung-tang (*Difficult Points,* 5.10) reports that Brahmā was born from a golden lotus in the shape of an egg in the midst of a sphere of fire; the egg arose from water, the two halves of which, when they split, became the sky and the earth. See *Absorption,* #6 and 7.

"Bodiless Lord" (*lus med bdag po, anaṅgapati*) is the God of Desire (*'dod lha, kāmadeva*), the demonic Lord of Love (*dga' rab dbang phyug*). According to Gung-tang (*Difficult Points,* 6.5), he shot his five arrows—which cause arrogance, dullness, thorough obscuration, fainting, and mindlessness (Gung-tang gives various renditions of these five, 6.9-7.3)—while Maheshvara was dwelling in asceticism in union with the goddess Uma, thereby causing Maheshvara to fall from his practice. Understanding that this was done by a demon, Maheshvara angered and emitted fire from his third eye of fire—the other two being sun and moon—burning away the body of the Sinful Demon (*bdud sdig can,* an epithet of the God of Desire), who thereby came to be called the "Bodiless Lord."

"Garlanded Belly" (*tha gu'i lto, dāmodara*) is also known as *viṣṇu.* Gung-tang (*Difficult Points,* 3.17) reports that during his youth Viṣhṇu wore a garland of flowers around his waist and that according to one story his wife wanted to put a garland of flowers around his head, but the garland reached only his waist, this being why he is called "Garlanded Belly."

[a] Gung-tang (ibid., 14.1-15.1) says that the words translated here as "depth" (*gting mtha'*) can be taken in two ways—one as indicating the limit of the depth, meaning that the depth of both the wisdom and the mercy of Mañjughoṣha and Maitreya is difficult to fathom. However, in the other interpretation the two syllables are separated:

- Since Mañjughoṣha's wisdom is of one taste with the profound suchness, its depth (*gting*) is difficult to fathom
- Since Maitreya's mercy extends into the limitless (*mtha' yas pa*) techniques of altruism (*gzhan phan gyi thabs*), its extent is difficult to comprehend

Gung-tang's exegesis, at first blush appearing to be overdone, reflects a long tradition of esthetic appreciation for creatively expounding on even single words in ways consonant with the topics of the text.

[b] Gung-tang (ibid., 14.6-14.14) takes "Bodhisattva deeds" as referring to Bodhisattvas' taking on the task of presently displaying—while still Bodhisattvas—the twelve deeds of a Buddha in order to help others. He cites Maitreya's *Ornament for the Great Vehicle Sūtras,* "Knowing the aspects of teaching the circle of a Buddha," and the sūtra passages (in the Per-

Those jewel treasures of eloquence.[a]

I bow down with the top of my head to the feet
Of the honorable Nāgārjuna and Asaṅga who, like the sun, illumined
The supreme teaching of the Conqueror[b] for beings below, on, and above the earth
Through opening well chariot-ways for the two modes[c] of the scriptures[d] of the One Gone to Bliss.[e]

Respectful obeisance to the kings among scholars—

---

fection of Wisdom Sūtras) on the twenty members of the spiritual community (*dge 'dun nyi shu'i mdo*) that speak of Bodhisattvas' emanating as Buddhas and of their turning the wheel of doctrine.

[a] According to Gung-tang (*Difficult Points,* 14.14-15.1), just as oceans are treasures of jewels (pearls and so forth), so Mañjughoṣha and Maitreya are treasures of all the eloquence of the Buddha, and, implicitly, this indicates that Dzong-ka-ba's own eloquence has come in stages transmitted from its source, the Buddha. Gung-tang says that through this illustration, it is indicated that any true preceptual instruction must come through an unbroken transmission of holy persons, like a river having its source in snow.

[b] Gung-tang (*Difficult Points,* 16.8) takes "supreme teaching of the Conqueror" (*rgyal ba'i bstan pa mchog*) as referring to Buddha's teaching in general but even more so to the Great Vehicle of inseparable wisdom and method, since the profound emptiness and the vast Bodhisattva deeds are, respectively, the transmissions (*bka' bab*) of Nāgārjuna and Asaṅga.

[c] Gung-tang (ibid., 15.17-16.8) takes "two modes" (*tshul gnyis*) as referring to two different great ways of positing what requires interpretation and what is definitive—as found in the two systems of the Middle Way School and the Mind-Only School for commenting on the final thought of the Perfection of Wisdom Sūtras. Jay-dzün Chö-gyi-gyel-tsen's *General-Meaning Commentary* (3a.7) has a similar explanation.

[d] *gsung rab, pravacana;* more literally, "high sayings." Rather than the written word, the main field of reference of this term is the spoken word.

Gung-tang (*Difficult Points,* 15.1-15.17) explains that in this context of paying homage to Nāgārjuna and Asaṅga for differentiating the interpretable and the definitive among Buddha's scriptures, this term refers to Buddha's scriptures in general and mainly refers to the Perfection of Wisdom Sūtras since not only the Proponents of the Middle but also the Proponents of Mind-Only hold the Perfection of Wisdom Sūtras to be the chief of all sūtras. For the Proponents of Mind-Only hold that the intended trainees of the Perfection of Wisdom Sūtras are sharper than the intended trainees of the *Sūtra Unraveling the Thought,* since they can understand the three natures and three non-natures just from hearing the Perfection of Wisdom Sūtras, without having to rely on an explanation such as that given in the *Sūtra Unraveling the Thought.*

The Perfection of Wisdom Sūtras are the treasury that is the basis for the differentiation into what requires interpretation and what is definitive, whereas the *Sūtra Unraveling the Thought* and the *Sūtra of the Teachings of Akṣhayamati* are the keys to that treasury, in that they show how to make the differentiation. Gung-tang therefore concludes that here "scriptures" refers not to those two sūtras but to Buddha's scriptures in general and mainly the Perfection of Wisdom Sūtras.

[e] *bde gshegs, sugata;* an epithet of Buddha.

Āryadeva, Shūra,[a] Buddhapālita,
Bhāvaviveka, the honorable Chandrakīrti,
The honorable Vasubandhu, Sthiramati, Dignāga,

The honorable Dharmakīrti,[b] and so forth—
Supreme of those holding the banner of the non-disappearance of the Subduer's teaching,
Those ornaments of Jambudvīpa[c] who through assuming well the two systems of the great openers of the chariot-ways
Opened the eyes of hundreds of hundred thousands[d] of the world's clear-minded.

[Promise of Composition][e] (251) {364}
Many who had much hearing of the great texts,
Who worked with much weariness also at the path of reasoning,
And who were not low in accumulation of the good qualities of clear realization
Worked hard at but did not realize this topic[f] which,

Having perceived it well through the kindness of the smooth[g] protector and guru [Mañjushrī],
I will explain with an attitude of great mercy.

[Exhortation to Listen][h]
Listen intently, O you who wish to be unmatched proponents [of doctrine][i]
With discriminating analysis realizing the suchness of the teaching.

---

a Tibetan scholars with whom I have worked identify Shūra (*dpa' bo*) as Ashvaghoṣha; for references to controversy about such an identification, see David Seyfort Ruegg, *The Literature of the Madhyamaka School of Philosophy in India* (Wiesbaden, Germany: Otto Harrasowitz, 1981), 119-121.

b Of these eight scholars, the first five are the main upholders of the Middle Way School, and the last five, of the Mind-Only School; see Gung-tang, *Difficult Points,* 16.14. They are in chronological order within their respective groups.

c *'dzam gling, jambudvīpa.* Jambudvīpa is the southern continent from among the four continents of this world system but now is taken as referring to this world.

d *bye ba,* "ten millions"; the word has the sense of "countless."

e Bel-jor-hlün-drup's *Lamp for the Teaching,* 7.2. See *Reflections on Reality,* chap. 5.

f See *Absorption,* #4.

g According to Ser-shül (*Notes,* 3a.6-3b.1), "smooth" (*'jam, mañju*) indicates that Mañjushrī is devoid of the roughness of the obstructions to liberation from cyclic existence and the roughness of the obstructions to omniscience. This is not the Bodhisattva Mañjushrī but the one that is the physical manifestation of the wisdom of all Buddhas.

h Bel-jor-hlün-drup's *Lamp for the Teaching,* 4.5, 7.4. See *Absorption,* #5.

i That is, Buddhas.

[Indicating The Great Importance Of Differentiating Which Scriptures Require Interpretation And Which Are Definitive] (251) {365}

The *Superior Sūtra of the Questions of Rāṣhṭapāla* [contained in the *Pile of Jewels Sūtra*] says:[a]

> Due to being endowed with compassion,
> Through hundreds of skillful means and reasonings
> You cause transmigrating beings who wander due to not knowing
> The modes of emptiness, quiescence, and no production
> To enter [into understanding these three doors of liberation].[90]

Thus, it is said that the Compassionate Teacher—perceiving that the thusness[b] of phenomena is very difficult to realize and that, if it is not realized, one [can][91] not be released from cyclic existence—brings about the thorough understanding of that [suchness][92] through many modes of skillful means and many approaches of reasoning.[c] Therefore, those having discrimination[d] must work at a

---

[a] *'phags pa yul 'khor skyong gis zhus pa zhes bya ba theg pa chen po'i mdo, āryarāṣṭrapālaparipṛcchānāmamahāyānasūtra;* Peking 760, vol. 23, chap. 17. For Gung-tang's identification of the sūtra and for the Sanskrit, see p. 365, footnote a.

[b] I translate *de bzhin nyid* (*tathatā*) as "thusness" and *de nyid* (*tattva*) or *de kho na nyid* (*tattva*) as "suchness." That these are equivalent is clear from Jay-d̄zün Chö-ḡyi-gyel-tsen's interchangeable usage of them in his *General-Meaning Commentary* (4b.1):

> Those discriminating persons who seek release [from suffering] should strive at techniques for understanding just what the **suchness** (*de kho na nyid*) of phenomena is because it is said that our Teacher, endowed with compassion, upon perceiving that the **thusness** (*de bzhin nyid*) of phenomena is very difficult to realize and that if it is not realized, one is not released—that is to say, cannot be released—from cyclic existence, causes trainees to understand **suchness** (*de kho na nyid*) thoroughly through many modes of skillful means, such as giving and so forth, and many approaches of reasoning, such as dependent-arising and the lack of being one or many.

(For Gung-tang's different interpretation of "many modes of skillful means," see the next footnote.) I translate another equivalent term, *chos nyid* (*dharmatā*), as "real nature," and another, *yang dag* (*samyak*), in a similar context as "reality."

[c] Gung-tang (*Annotations,* 9.5-9.6) identifies the "many modes of skillful means" as Buddha's temporarily teaching merely a coarse form of selflessness and identifies the "approaches of reasoning" as the reasonings of dependent-arising and so forth used to establish the emptiness of inherent existence. In his *Difficult Points* (35.11), Gung-tang makes an important distinction between *thabs* (*upāya*) as compassion and *thabs* (*upāya*) as skillful means used to lead trainees by way of various techniques; he speaks from a tradition that distinguishes these two. It appears that in many Great Vehicle traditions, especially in East Asia, the two are conflated. See *Reflections on Reality,* chap. 9.

[d] They are discriminative **because** they want liberation (Jay-d̄zün Chö-ḡyi-gyel-tsen's *General-Meaning Commentary,* 4b.1; also, D̄a-drin-rap-d̄en's *Annotations,* 4.5).

technique for thoroughly understanding how suchness is.

Moreover, this depends upon differentiating those meanings that require interpretation and those that are definitive within the scriptures of the Conqueror.[a] Furthermore, the differentiation of those two cannot be done merely through scriptures that state, "This is a meaning to be interpreted; that is a meaning that is definitive." For, [Buddha spoke variously in relation to the thoughts of trainees and][93] (1) otherwise the composition of commentaries on [Buddha's] thought differentiating the interpretable and definitive by the great openers of the chariot-ways [Nāgārjuna and Asaṅga] would have been senseless; (2) also, scriptures [such as the *Sūtra Unraveling the Thought* and the *Teachings of Akṣhayamati Sūtra*][94] set forth many conflicting modes of positing the interpretable and the definitive; and (3) through scriptural passages merely saying [about a topic], "This is so," such cannot be posited, and if, then, **in general** it is not necessarily [suitable to accept whatever is indicated on the literal level in sūtras],[95] mere statements [in sūtra] of, "This is [interpretable, and that is definitive],"[96] also cannot establish **about specifics**, the interpretable and the definitive, [that such is necessarily so].[97]

Therefore, one must seek [Buddha's] thought, following the [two][98] great openers of the chariot-ways [Nāgārjuna and Asaṅga], who were prophesied as differentiating the interpretable and the definitive in [Buddha's] scriptures and who commented on the thought of the interpretable and the definitive and, moreover, settled it well through reasoning that damages[b] the interpretation of the meaning of definitive scriptures as anything else and establishes that, within their being unfit to be interpreted otherwise, [the final mode of subsistence[c]

---

[a] *rgyal ba'i gsung rab **kyi** drang ba dang nges pa'i don.* Gung-tang makes a critical difference between *gsung rab **kyi** drang nges 'byed pa* and *gsung rab **la** drang nges 'byed pa;* I translate the former as "differentiating the interpretable and definitive **within** the scriptures" and the latter as "differentiating the interpretable and definitive **with respect to** the scriptures"; admittedly, the English is no clearer than the Tibetan. According to him (*Difficult Points,* 38.4), the former, "differentiating the interpretable and definitive **within** the scriptures," means to identify what are interpretable and what are definitive scriptures from among the scriptures (*gsung rab **kyi nang nas** drang don gyi gsung rab dang nges don gyi gsung rab gang yin so sor ngos bzung ba la byed*) whereas the latter "differentiating the interpretable and the definitive **with respect to** the scriptures," means to differentiate the interpretable and the definitive with respect to the *meaning* of the scriptures, this requiring extensive delineation of the presentation of the two truths, which itself requires realization of emptiness. Therefore, the latter cannot be required for realization of emptiness, whereas the former can. The latter is called (37.7) "differentiating the interpretable and the definitive on the level of the meaning that is expressed within the scriptures" (*brjod bya don gyi drang nges 'byed pa*) whereas the former is called (38.5) "differentiating the interpretable and the definitive on the level of the words that are the means of expression" (*rjod byed tshig gi drang nges 'byed pa*). See *Reflections on Reality,* chap. 9.

[b] That is, contradicts or invalidates.

[c] *gnas lugs mthar thug.* Among the many meanings of "subsistence," here it means "exis-

explained in them] is definite as [just] that meaning. Therefore, in the end, the differentiation [between the interpretable and the definitive] must be made just by stainless reasoning, because if a proponent asserts a tenet contradicting reason, [that person] is not suitable to be a valid being [with respect to that topic][99] and because the suchness of things also has reasoned proofs which are establishments by way of [logical] correctness.

It is from perceiving the import of this meaning [that differentiation of the interpretable and the definitive cannot be made by scripture alone and that reasoning is required,[100] that Buddha] says:[a]

> Like gold [that is acquired] upon being scorched, cut, and rubbed,
> My word is to be adopted by monastics and scholars
> Upon analyzing it well,
> Not out of respect [for me].[b]

Thus, with respect to differentiating the interpretable and the definitive, there are two parts: the position relying on the *Sūtra Unraveling the Thought* and the position relying on the *Teachings of Akṣhayamati Sūtra.* The presentation of the position relying on the *Sūtra Unraveling the Thought* has two parts: stating what is said in the sūtra and exegesis of its meaning.

---

tence" and not "barely existing" as in "subsistence farming."

[a] For the Sanskrit, see p. 367, footnote a. A goldsmith performs three operations on gold before acquiring it or taking it to be true gold. It is first scorched to test for telltale discolorations (*bsregs, tāpa*). Then it is cut; and finally it is rubbed to determine whether it leaves a gold-identifying streak.

The first step could not be, as some claim, that the gold is melted, since melting would reveal all internal impurities and thus the next step, cutting it, would not be needed. As a last step, it is rubbed most likely on a touchstone, since *nikaṣa* (*brdar*) also means "touchstone" and "a streak or line of gold made on a touchstone" (Vaman Shivaram Apte, *Sanskrit-English Dictionary* [Poona, India: Prasad Prakashan, 1957]).

[b] See *Reflections on Reality,* chap. 6.

THE SŪTRA UNRAVELING THE THOUGHT ON DIFFERENTIATING THE INTERPRETABLE AND THE DEFINITIVE

With regard to stating what is said in the *Sūtra Unraveling the Thought* (255) {368} about differentiating the interpretable and the definitive, there are four parts: a question about dispelling contradiction in the sūtras, the answer dispelling that contradiction, identifying the entities of the three natures, and [Paramārthasamudgata's] offering [to Buddha] the meaning established by these.

1. Questioning Apparent Contradiction

Question About Dispelling Contradiction In The Sūtras (257) {368}

[In the "Questions of Paramārthasamudgata Chapter" of] the *Sūtra Unraveling the Thought,* [Paramārthasamudgata] says:[a]

[a] The Bodhisattva Paramārthasamudgata is questioning Buddha, the Supramundane Victor, about apparent contradictions in his teaching. Ḏzong-ka-ḇa paraphrases and condenses the sūtra; the actual passage (Étienne Lamotte, *Saṃdhinirmocanasūtra: L'Explication des mystères* [Louvain: Université de Louvain, 1935], 65-66 [1], and 192-193; Dön-drup-gyel-tsen's *Four Intertwined Commentaries,* 4.2-6.2; and John C. Powers, *Wisdom of Buddha: Saṃdhinirmocana Sūtra* [Berkeley, Calif.: Dharma, 1995], 95) [the material in bold type has been condensed or omitted in Ḏzong-ka-ḇa's citation]:

Then, the Bodhisattva Paramārthasamudgata asked the Supramundane Victor:

> **Supramundane Victor, when I was here alone in a solitary place, my mind generated the following qualm.** The Supramundane Victor spoke, in many ways, of the own-character of the aggregates. He also spoke of [their] character of production, character of disintegration, abandonment, and thorough knowledge. Just as he did with respect to the aggregates, so he also spoke with respect to the sense spheres, dependent-arising, and the foods. **The Supramundane Victor** also spoke, **in many ways**, of the own-character of the truths as well as **speaking** of thorough knowledge, abandonment, actualization, and meditation. **The Supramundane Victor also spoke, in many ways,** of the own-character of the constituents, as well as **speaking** of the various constituents, manifold constituents, [their] abandonment, and thorough knowledge. **The Supramundane Victor also spoke, in many ways,** of the own-character of the **four mindful establishments,** as well as **speaking** of [their] **classes of** discordances, antidotes, **meditation,** production of that which has not been produced, the abiding of that which has been produced, non-loss, [their] arising again, and increasing and extending. **Just as he did with respect to the mindful establishments, so he spoke with respect to the thorough abandonings, the legs of magical manifestation, the faculties, the powers, and the branches of enlightenment. The Supramundane Victor also spoke, in many ways, of the own-character of the eightfold path of Superiors, as well as speaking of [their] discordances, antidotes, production of that which has not been produced, the abiding of that which has been produced, recollection, [their] arising again, and increasing and extending.**
>
> Also, the Supramundane Victor said [in the middle wheel of the teaching], "All phenomena are natureless; all phenomena are unproduced, unceasing, quiescent from the start, and naturally thoroughly passed beyond sorrow."

The Supramundane Victor[a] [initially] spoke, in many ways, of the own-character[b] of the aggregates [of forms, feelings, discriminations, compositional factors, and consciousnesses, these being that in which one travels in cyclic existence].[101] He also spoke of their character of production [through the force of contaminated actions and afflictive emotions,[102] their] character of disintegration, abandonment[c] [of the contaminated actions and afflictive emotions that are the causes of the

---

> Therefore, I am wondering of what the Supramundane Victor was thinking when he said, "All phenomena are natureless; all phenomena are unproduced, unceasing, quiescent from the start, and naturally thoroughly passed beyond sorrow." I ask the Supramundane Victor about the meaning of his saying, "All phenomena are natureless; all phenomena are unproduced, unceasing, quiescent from the start, and naturally thoroughly passed beyond sorrow."

Lamotte, in his translation into French (p. 192), divides these teachings into five groups in accordance with whether their features are explicitly mentioned—(1) the aggregates, the sense-spheres, the dependent-arising, and the foods; (2) the truths; (3) the constituents; (4) all of the thirty-seven harmonies with enlightenment, except the eightfold path of Superiors; and (5) the eightfold path of Superiors. It should be noted that this division is merely semantic, that is, based on whether their features are explicitly mentioned. A more meaningful division is into the seven categories themselves—(1) the aggregates, (2) the sense-spheres, (3) the dependent-arising, (4) the foods, (5) the truths, (6) the constituents, and (7) the harmonies with enlightenment.

Lamotte identifies the first mention of "constituents" as referring to the eighteen constituents; this accords with Wonch'uk's reading but not with D̄zong-ka-b̄a's. See *Absorption,* #16.

[a] *bcom ldan 'das, bhagavan.* This term is translated in accordance with the etymology favored in Tibet, where it is recognized that *bhagavan* also can be etymologized as "one who possesses the six goodnesses" (*legs pa drug dang ldan pa*), which seems to fit the more widely used translation as "Blessed One." For Sanskrit sources, see the excellent note in Donald S. Lopez, *The Heart Sūtra Explained* (Albany, N.Y.: State University of New York Press, 1988), 196, no. 46.

[b] *rang gi mtshan nyid, svalakṣaṇa* (Lamotte, *Saṃdhinirmocana,* 67 [1], n. 7). Ge-luk-b̄a scholars identify "own-character" as referring either to objects' establishment by way of their own character (*rang gi mtshan nyid kyis grub pa*) or to establishment by way of their own character as the referents of conceptual consciousnesses (*rang 'dzin rtog pa'i zhen gzhir rang gi mtshan nyid kyis grub pa*) or both.

D̄zong-ka-b̄a identifies this "own-character" with the "character" that in Buddha's answer is denied with respect to imputational natures and that unquestionably refers to their being established by way of their own character, since Buddha says in his answer:

> Those [imputational characters] are characters posited by names and terminology and **do not subsist by way of their own character**. Therefore, they are said to be "character-non-natures."

See *Absorption,* #27-51 and the following conclusion on the topic.

[c] See ibid., #13.

contaminated aggregates],[103] and thorough knowledge [that the entities of the aggregates are like a disease[104] or are not established as a substantially existent self].[105] Just as he did with respect to the aggregates, so he also spoke with respect to [the mode of suffering of][106] the sense-spheres[a] [the six objects—visible forms, sounds, odors, tastes, tangible objects, and other phenomena—and the six senses—eye, ear, nose, tongue, body, and mental sense powers], dependent-arising, and the [four] foods[b] [that is, morsels of food, contact, intention, and consciousness]. In a similar fashion, he also spoke of the own-character of the [four] truths,[c] thorough knowledge [of true sufferings as impermanent and miserable],[107] abandonment [of the sources of suffering, contaminated actions and afflictive emotions],[108] actualization [of true cessations],[109] and meditation [cultivating true paths, which are the means for attaining true cessation of suffering][110] as well as the own-character of the constituents, the various[d] [eighteen][111] constituents, and manifold [six][e] constituents,[f] their abandonment, and thorough knowledge as well as the own-character of the thirty-seven harmonies with enlightenment [which are the antidotes to those objects of abandonment,[112] their] discordances [that is, what is to be abandoned],[113] the antidotes [to those objects of abandonment],[114] production of [virtues[115] or antidotes[116]] that have not been produced, the abiding of those that have been produced, non-loss [of antidotes that have been produced,[117] their] arising again[g] [when one has familiarized with them again and again],[118] and increasing [those antidotes through the power of familiarity][119] and extending[h] [them limitlessly].[120]

Also, the Supramundane Victor said [in the middle wheel of the teaching],[121] "All phenomena are natureless; all phenomena are unproduced, unceasing, quiescent from the start, and naturally thoroughly passed beyond sorrow."[i]

Therefore, I am wondering of what the Supramundane Victor was

---

a *skye mched, āyatana.* I have, in other works, translated this term as "sources" since the six types of objects and the six sense powers are *sources* of consciousness. However, "sources" by itself is not evocative, and thus I have opted for "spheres," which strikes me as better than "fields" (often used by translators), because the term refers not just to the six objects but also to the six senses.

b See *Absorption,* #14.

c See ibid., #25.

d See ibid., #16.

e A-ku Lo-drö-gya-tso (*Precious Lamp,* 53.4) explicitly identifies the "manifold" as the six.

f See *Absorption,* #17.

g See ibid., #18.

h See ibid., #10-12, 22.

i For the Sanskrit, see p. 369, footnote c. See ibid., #26.

> thinking when he said [in the middle wheel of the teaching], "All phenomena are natureless; all phenomena are unproduced, unceasing, quiescent from the start, and naturally thoroughly passed beyond sorrow." I [explicitly][122] ask the Supramundane Victor about the meaning of his saying [in the middle wheel of the teaching], "All phenomena are natureless; all phenomena are unproduced, unceasing, quiescent from the start, and naturally thoroughly passed beyond sorrow."

This asks the following question:

> If the statements in some sūtras [that is, in the middle wheel of the teaching][123] that all phenomena are natureless, and so forth, and the statements in some sūtras [in the first wheel of the teaching][124] that the aggregates and so forth have an own-character, and so forth, were left as they are verbally, they would be contradictory. However, since [the Supramundane Victor][125] must be without contradiction, of what were you [Buddha] thinking when [in the middle wheel of the teaching][126] you spoke of non-nature, and so forth?

Through that, [Paramārthasamudgata] implicitly[a] asks of what [Buddha] was thinking when [in the first wheel of the teaching][127] he spoke of the existence of own-character and so forth.[b]

In the Chinese *Great Commentary*[c] [on the *Sūtra Unraveling the Thought* by the Korean scholar Wonch'uk],[d] and so forth,[e] (259) {370} "own-character"[f]

[a] See ibid., #56.

[b] See ibid., #21-24.

[c] See ibid., #8.

[d] Wonch'uk (Peking 5517, vol. 106, chap. 5, 128.5.7) cites scripture, "'Own-character' is the specific character as in, for instance, the explanation, 'Form is obstructive....Consciousness is the knower.'" The uncommon character (*thun mong ma yin pa'i mtshan nyid*), or specific character (*bye brag gi mtshan nyid*), is the defining characteristic of an object that belongs to it alone.

A-ku Lo-drö-gya-tso (*Precious Lamp,* 54.6) reports that a text entitled *zur bkol bzhi'i zin bris* holds that the *Great Commentary* and Wonch'uk's text are not the same since the former has seventy chapters and the latter has sixty-three, but he explains that even though the current edition of Wonch'uk's text has only sixty-three chapters, Gung-tang takes the "Chinese *Great Commentary*" and Wonch'uk's text to be the same.

[e] Jik-may-dam-chö-gya-tso (*Port of Entry,* 140.2) speculates that "and so forth" includes the *Explanation of the Sūtra Unraveling the Thought* (*dgongs 'grel rnam bshad / 'phags pa nges par dgongs pa 'grel pa'i mdo'i rnam par bshad pa, āryasaṃdhinirmocanasūtrasya vyākhyāna*), listed in the table of contents of the Translation of the Treatises (*bstan 'gyur*) of the *sde dge* edition and so forth. He says that this text—which is (also) called *Great Commentary* and is (mistakenly) reputed to be by Asaṅga—refers to the fourth chapter of the sūtra and clearly speaks of the specific character of an object. For discussion of the authorship of this commentary, see appendix 1, p. 453ff.

[f] See *Absorption,* #27-55, 94.

here [in this passage in the *Sūtra Unraveling the Thought*] is explained as the unique character [of the aggregates and so forth], but this is not right.[a] For the sūtra itself at the point of [speaking about] imputational factors[b] clearly speaks of establishment by way of [the object's] own character[c] [and does not speak of the unique character], and since even imputational factors have a unique characterization, there would be the fallacy that the character-non-nature could not be explained with respect to imputational factors.[d]

---

[a] See ibid., #48, 39.

[b] See ibid., #50.

[c] As will be cited in the Translation (p. 86), the *Sūtra Unraveling the Thought* says:

> Those [imputational characters] are characters posited by names and terminology and **do not subsist by way of their own character**. Therefore, they are said to be "character-non-natures."

Ḍzong-ka-ḅa's well-taken point is that the sūtra, when describing how imputational natures are character-non-natures, says that they "do not subsist by way of their own character" (*rang gi mtshan nyid kyis rnam par gnas pa ni ma yin pa, svalakṣaṇena avyavasthitaṃ:* Lamotte, *Saṃdhinirmocana,* 68 [4], n. 1), that is to say, they are not established by way of their own character; the sūtra does not speak about the defining character of an object.

This clear identification in the sūtra itself is the pivot of Ḍzong-ka-ḅa's argument (in his chapter on the Autonomy School) that when Bhāvaviveka says, in the context of criticizing the Mind-Only interpretation of this earlier passage, that to deny "character" of imputational natures is a deprecation, he indicates that he holds that existent imputational natures, such as uncompounded space, are established by way of their own character. Once Bhāvaviveka holds that even imputational natures are established by way of their own character, he must hold that all phenomena are established this way. It then becomes crucial to determine what Bhāvaviveka means by "establishment by way of its own character," Ḍzong-ka-ḅa's answer being that it means that an object is established from its own side, with the consequence that when it is sought among its bases of designation, it is found.

[d] Imputational natures have the unique characteristic or definition of being **just imputed by conceptuality** (*rtog pas btags tsam;* Gung-ru Chö-jung's *Garland of White Lotuses,* 20a.4). Therefore, if the absence of "character" mentioned in Buddha's answer to Paramārthasamudgata's question when discussing imputational natures merely referred to the non-existence of a unique characterization, such an absence could not be posited with respect to imputational natures, since they do indeed have a unique characterization. However, as is obvious in the next chapter, one of the main points of the *Sūtra Unraveling the Thought* is that imputational natures are non-natures in terms of "character," and thus "character" in that context cannot refer to a unique or uncommon character.

Ḍzong-ka-ḅa's point is well taken, but he makes the extension that, therefore, here in this passage when Paramārthasamudgata questions Buddha, "own-character" also cannot refer to the unique characteristic of an object; he sees a necessary equivalence between the "own-character" mentioned here in the question and the "character" mentioned in the answer. However, it seems to me that the "own-character" mentioned in the question could indeed refer to the entity, the unique character, of an object, since such a meaning appears frequently in Buddhist literature and since the format of an **entity** (such as a form) and its **attributes** (such as production and disintegration) is so important in this sūtra. See *Absorption,* #48.

The commentaries [by Wonch'uk and so forth][a] explain "the various and manifold constituents"[b] [mentioned in passage from the *Sūtra Unraveling the Thought* cited above] otherwise, but when these are put together with a later[c]

---

[a] Gung-tang's *Annotations,* 15.4; and Dön-drup-gyel-tsen's *Four Intertwined Commentaries,* 41.2. Wonch'uk (*Great Commentary,* Peking 5517, vol. 106, chap. 5, 129.3.2) says:

> The eighteen constituents in the character of the one being different from the others are called the "various constituents." Just those eighteen constituents as specifics of limitless sentient beings are called the "manifold constituents."

In chapter 4 of the *Explanation of the Sūtra Unraveling the Thought,* vol. 205, 110.2, when these topics are first introduced, the term is defined in a way better translated as "constitution":

> "Various constitutions" refers to the whole range from variously abiding in the lineages of Hearers, Solitary Realizers, and Ones Gone Thus through to the 84,000 behaviors of sentient beings by way of divisions of desire and so forth...."Manifold constitutions" refers in brief to four forms of constitutions with respect to those various constitutions: naturally abiding constitutions, constitutions from previous conditioning, constitutions suitable for purification, and constitutions not suitable for purification, and furthermore to there being limitless forms of each of these.

See also Jik-may-dam-chö-gya-tso, *Port of Entry,* 141.4.

[b] See *Absorption,* #16.

[c] Later in this chapter, Paramārthasamudgata, following the order of the seven topics, speaks about the three natures in terms of the aggregates, sense spheres, dependent-arising, constituents, and foods and then mentions the six and eighteen constituents. He says: (Lamotte, *Saṃdhinirmocana,* 81 [25], and 204; and John C. Powers, *Wisdom of Buddha: Saṁdhinirmocana Sūtra* [Berkeley, Calif.: Dharma, 1995], 131)

> Just as this is applied to the form aggregate, so this also should be applied similarly to the remaining aggregates. Just as this is applied to the aggregates, so this also should be applied similarly to each of the sense-spheres that are the twelve sense-spheres. This also should be applied similarly to each of the limbs of existence that are the twelve limbs of existence. This also should be applied similarly to each of the foods that are the four foods. This also should be applied similarly to each of the constituents that are the six constituents and the eighteen constituents.

That in the very same chapter of the *Sūtra Unraveling the Thought* the constituents are listed as the six and the eighteen constituents provides good evidence that "the various constituents and manifold constituents" must be these. Still, the order must be reversed to accommodate D̄zong-ka-b̄a's statement that these refer to "the eighteen constituents and the six constituents." Indeed, when Gung-tang (*Difficult Points,* 87.7-87.11/37b.3) makes this point, he (or his scribe) unintentionally edits D̄zong-ka-b̄a's text so that it reads "the six constituents and the eighteen constituents" (*khams drug dang khams bco brgyad*). However, since the Delhi NG dkra shis lhun po (484.3), Guru Deva old zhöl (448.6), Zi ling sku 'bum (342.17), and Sarnath gtsang (6.4) editions all read *khams bco brgyad dang khams drug,* this is clearly not a variant reading, but I doubt that Gung-tang intended to edit D̄zong-ka-b̄a's text (even though it conveniently makes the sūtra and D̄zong-ka-b̄a agree) since Gung-tang goes to some length to indicate why only the *six* constituents (that is, the manifold) are mentioned

occurrence in the *Sūtra* [*Unraveling the Thought*], they are to be taken as the eighteen constituents and the six constituents.

"Non-loss"[a] (260) {370} [in the passage from the *Sūtra Unraveling the Thought* cited above] is non-forgetfulness.[b]

after the eighteen (that is, the various). Despite this minor flaw of the ordering of six and eighteen, the internal evidence—that this reference to the "the various constituents and manifold constituents" must be to the eighteen and the six—is good. See *Absorption*, #17.

[a] *mi bskyud pa, asaṃpramoṣatā* (Lamotte, *Saṃdhinirmocana*, 67 [1], n. 26). "Non-forgetfulness" is *mi brjed pa*.

[b] See *Absorption*, #18.

2. Buddha's Answer

The presentation of [Buddha's] answer dispelling that contradiction has two parts: explaining the modes of non-nature in consideration of which [Buddha] spoke of [all phenomena as] natureless [in the Perfection of Wisdom Sūtras] and explaining that in consideration of which he spoke of [all phenomena as] unproduced and so forth [in the Perfection of Wisdom Sūtras]. (261) {371}

Explaining The Modes Of Non-Nature In Consideration Of Which [Buddha] Spoke Of [All Phenomena As] Natureless [In The Perfection Of Wisdom Sūtras] (261) {371}

This section has three parts: a brief indication, an extensive explanation, and showing examples for these.

Brief Indication Of The Modes Of Non-Nature In Consideration Of Which [Buddha] Spoke Of [All Phenomena As] Natureless [In The Perfection Of Wisdom Sūtras] (261) {371}

The *Sūtra Unraveling the Thought* [when Buddha identifies what was behind his saying in the Perfection of Wisdom Sūtras that all phenomena are natureless][128] says:[a]

> Paramārthasamudgata, thinking of three non-natures of phenomena—character-non-nature,[b] production-non-nature,[c] and ultimate-non-

[a] In the last chapter Dzong-ka-ba quoted Paramārthasamudgata's question, and here he quotes Buddha's answer. He has skipped Buddha's introduction to the answer (Étienne Lamotte, *Saṃdhinirmocanasūtra: L'Explication des mystères* (Louvain: Université de Louvain, 1935), 67 [2], and 193; Dön-drup-gyel-tsen's *Four Intertwined Commentaries,* 6.2-6.5; and John C. Powers, *Wisdom of Buddha: Saṁdhinirmocana Sūtra* (Berkeley, Calif.: Dharma, 1995), 97):

> Having been asked that, the Supramundane Victor said to the Bodhisattva Paramārthasamudgata, "Paramārthasamudgata, the thought in your mind, properly generated virtue, is good, good. Paramārthasamudgata, you are involved in [asking] this in order to help many beings, to [bring] happiness to many beings, out of compassionate kindness toward the world, and for the sake of the aims, help, and happiness of all beings, including gods and humans. You are good to think to ask the One Gone Thus about this meaning. Therefore, Paramārthasamudgata, listen, and I will explain that in consideration of which I said, 'All phenomena are natureless; all phenomena are unproduced, unceasing, quiescent from the start, and naturally thoroughly passed beyond sorrow.'"

[b] *mtshan nyid ngo bo nyid med pa nyid, lakṣaṇaniḥsvabhāvatā* (Lamotte, *Saṃdhinirmocana,* 67 [3], n. 3).

[c] *skye ba ngo bo nyid med pa nyid, utpattiniḥsvabhāvatā* (ibid., 67 [3], n. 4).

nature[a]—I taught [in the middle wheel of the teaching],[129] "All phenomena are natureless."[130]

In consideration of all three non-natures, [Buddha] spoke of non-nature [in the middle wheel of the teaching].[b]

Moreover, Asaṅga's *Compendium of Ascertainments* says:[131]

> *Question:* Thinking of what did the Supramundane Victor say [in the middle wheel][132] that all phenomena are natureless?
>
> *Answer:* Here and there[c] he said such through the force of taming[d] [trainees],[133] thinking of three types of non-nature.

Also, Vasubandhu's *The Thirty*[e] (stanza 23) says:[134]

> Thinking of three types of non-nature
> Of the three types of natures [respectively],[135]
> He taught [in the Perfection of Wisdom Sūtras][136]
> That all phenomena are natureless.

Hence (262) {372} [it is contradictory for some, namely, Döl-b̄o-b̄a and others][f] to explain that the statements in the Perfection of Wisdom Sūtras, and so forth, that all phenomena are natureless are in consideration [only][137] of all conventional phenomena [which, according to them, are self-empty in the sense of being empty of their own true establishment][138] but do not refer to the ultimate [which, they say, is itself truly established and empty of being any conventional phenomenon].[139] They thereby contradict the *Sūtra Unraveling the Thought* as well as the texts of Asaṅga and his brother [Vasubandhu] and are also outside the system of the Superior father [Nāgārjuna],[140] his spiritual sons, and so forth.

---

[a] *don dam pa ngo bo nyid med pa nyid, paramārthaniḥsvabhāvatā* (ibid., 67 [3], n. 5). See p. 35, n. c.

[b] See *Absorption,* #57, 58, 61, 61.

[c] Jik-may-dam-chö-gya-tso (*Port of Entry,* 160.4) cogently suggests that "here and there" (*de dang der*) may mean either "in this and that sūtra" (*mdo de dang der*) or "to this and that trainee" (*gdul bya de dang der*).

[d] Jik-may-dam-chö-gya-tso (ibid., 164.2) reports that D̄ra-d̄i Ge-s̄hay Rin-chen-dön-drup (*pra sti dge bshes rin chen don grub, Ornament for the Thought,* 18.16) interprets "through the force of taming" (*'dul ba'i dbang gis*) as "through the force of taming trainees having the lineage of the Middle Way School by means of the literal reading" (*gdul bya dbu ma pa'i rigs can sgras zin des 'dul ba'i dbang gis*). However, Jik-may-dam-chö-gya-tso points out that D̄zong-ka-b̄a himself in the section on the Consequence School glosses "through the force of taming" (*'dul ba'i dbang gis*) with "through the force of trainees' thought" (*gdul bya'i bsam pa'i dbang gis;* Sarnath gtsang edition, 207). It seems to me that both interpretations are suitable.

[e] See *Absorption,* #61.

[f] D̄a-drin-rap-d̄en's *Annotations,* 12.5. W̄el-mang Ḡön-chok-gyel-tsen's *Notes on (Ḡön-chok-jik-may-w̄ang-b̄o's) Lectures* (399.3) reports that S̄hay-rap-gyel-tsen is called "Döl-b̄o-b̄a" (*dol po pa*) because his family lineage is Döl-b̄o (*rus dol po yin pas*).

It is thus: [When Paramārthasamudgata] asks about that in consideration of which [Buddha] spoke of non-nature, he is asking (1) about what [Buddha] was thinking[a] when he taught non-nature and (2) about the modes of non-nature.[b] Also, the answer indicates those two respectively. From between those two, let us explain the first[c] [that is, what Buddha had as the basis in his thought when in the Perfection of Wisdom Sūtras he taught that all phenomena[d] are natureless. There, Buddha] said that the limitless divisions of instances of phenomena ranging from forms through to exalted knowers-of-all-aspects have no nature[e] or inherent nature.[f] These phenomena are included in the three non-natures [that is, three natures[g]—imputational, other-powered, and thoroughly established natures].[h] Thinking that when it is explained how those are

---

[a] D̄zong-ka-b̄a glosses *ci la* ***dgongs*** *nas* with *ci la* ***bsams*** *nas.* This evidence shows that he considers *dgongs* to be a synonym of *bsams* and justifies the translation of *dgongs* as "thinking" or "having thought" or "in consideration of." Hence, here *dgongs* should not be translated as "intention," since this is too close to *dgos pa* ("purpose" or "intention") in the interpretive triad of *dgongs gzhi, dgos pa, dngos la gnod byed* ("the basis in [Buddha's] thought, the purpose, and damage to the explicit [teaching on the literal level]"); see p. 234ff.

[b] According to Ye-s̄hay-tup-d̄en (oral teachings), the latter refers to the reasons for the respective non-natures.

[c] The second topic, the modes of naturelessness, is set forth in the "extensive explanation" that follows after two paragraphs. That section is entitled "extensive explanation of **the modes of non-nature** in consideration of which [Buddha] spoke of [all phenomena as] natureless [in the Perfection of Wisdom Sūtras]." It might seem that D̄zong-ka-b̄a has begun a subsection that has two parts and has failed to announce either the second topic or the detailed explanation, but he has not; the second topic is covered in the detailed explanation that follows. In

> Also, the answer indicates those two respectively. From between those two, let us explain the first (*lan gyis kyang de gnyis rim pa bzhin ston pa las dang po 'chad pa ni;* Text, p. 372; Delhi NG dkra shis lhun po, 485.4),

the agent of "indicates" (*ston*) is "the answer" (*lan gyis*), not D̄zong-ka-b̄a. He is stating that while the answer lays out these two points, he is here explaining only the first.

[d] The Tibetan word I translate as "phenomena" is *chos* (*dharma*) which, from among its ten meanings, is said in Ge-luk scholasticism to mean "that which holds its own entity" (*rang gi ngo bo 'dzin pa*) in this type of context. Even the ultimate is listed as a phenomenon (*chos*), and thus even the final nature of things, or perhaps noumenon, is a phenomenon.

[e] *ngo bo nyid.*

[f] *rang bzhin.*

[g] It is noteworthy that D̄zong-ka-b̄a uses the term "three non-natures" (*ngo bo nyid med pa gsum*) when the term "three natures" (*ngo bo nyid gsum*) would have been more appropriate; indeed this is how D̄a-drin-rap-d̄en (*Annotations,* 13.4) glosses the term. D̄zong-ka-b̄a's usage of "non-natures" suggests that for him the individual three non-natures and the three natures are equivalent (see *Absorption,* #101), as long as the **actual** ultimate-non-nature is restricted to thoroughly established natures (see ibid., #147, 148). To me, it indeed is the case.

[h] See *Absorption,* #73, 72, 101.

naturelessness, it is easy to understand [the individual modes of thought that were behind his statement in the Perfection of Wisdom Sūtras],[141] he included [all phenomena] into the three non-natures [that is, three natures. For] all ultimate and conventional phenomena are included within those three.[a] Also, with respect to the need for [Buddha's] doing thus,[b] in the Mother Sūtras [that is, the Perfection of Wisdom Sūtras] and so forth, all phenomena—the five aggregates, the eighteen constituents, and the twelve sense-spheres—are described as without thingness,[c] without an inherent nature,[d] and natureless.[e] In particular, mentioning all the terminological variants of the ultimate—emptiness,[f] the element of [a Superior's] qualities,[g] thusness,[h] and so forth—he said that these are natureless. Therefore, who with a mind would propound that the ultimate is not among the phenomena about which it is said that phenomena are natureless![i]

Extensive Explanation[j] *Of The Modes Of Non-Nature In Consideration Of Which [Buddha] Spoke Of [All Phenomena As] Natureless [In The Perfection Of Wisdom Sūtras]* (263) {373}

[Character-Non-Nature] (263) {373}

Question: If the phenomena that are said to be natureless are included

---

a Sthiramati's *Commentary on (Vasubandhu's) "The Thirty"* (Peking 5565, vol. 113 311.3.8), similarly says in commentary on stanza 24, "All phenomena are of the nature of the imputational, the other-powered, and the thoroughly established."

b Ḏzong-ka-ḇa is referring to Buddha's explanation—in the *Sūtra Unraveling the Thought*—of the three types of naturelessness in relation to the three natures. According to S̄er-s̄hül L̄o-sang-pün-tsok (*Notes,* 14b.6-15a.3), Ḏzong-ka-ḇa's point is that since the Perfection of Wisdom Sūtras speak of all phenomena as being natureless, it was necessary for Buddha to explain the basis in his thought for all of those phenomena, and thus he grouped them into the three natures and their respective non-natures.

c *dngos po med pa.*

d *rang bzhin med pa.*

e *ngo bo nyid med pa.*

f *stong pa nyid, śūnyatā.*

g *chos kyi dbyings, dharmadhātu.* The translation as "element of [a Superior's] qualities" is based on a note by Nga-w̄ang-ḇel-den (*Annotations, dbu* 8b.8): *khyod la dmigs nas sgom pas 'phags chos kyi rgyu byed pas chos dbyings zhes bya la,* "It is called the element of [a Superior's] qualities (*dharmadhātu, chos dbyings*) because meditation within observing it acts as a cause of the qualities (*dharma, chos*) of Superiors (*ārya, 'phags pa*)." Emptiness, being uncaused, is not itself a cause (element), but meditation on it causes the development of marvelous qualities; thus, emptiness comes to be **called** a cause, an element producing those qualities.

h *de bzhin nyid, tathatā.*

i See *Absorption,* #63-65.

j See ibid., #59.

within the three non-natures, what are those three and what are their modes of non-nature?

Answer: To explain the first non-nature [that is, the character-non-nature, which is posited with respect to imputational natures], the *Sūtra Unraveling the Thought* says:[142]

> Concerning that, what are character-non-natures of phenomena?[a] Those which are imputational characters.[b]
>
> Why? It is thus: Those [imputational characters] are characters posited by names and terminology[c] and do not subsist by way of their own character.[d] Therefore, they are said to be "character-non-natures."

The question and answer in the first two sentences explain that imputational factors are character-non-natures. Then, "Why?" questions the reason for that. In answer to that question, a reason from the negative side—their not being posited by way of their own character—and a reason from the positive side—their being posited by names and terminology—are stated. Through this clear delineation,[e] the latter two [descriptions of non-nature in the sūtra with respect to other-powered natures and thoroughly established natures][143] also should be understood.

The nature of character that imputational factors[f] do not have is to be taken as establishment, or subsisting, by way of their own character.[g] Here, the measure indicated[h] with respect to existing or not existing by way of [an object's] own character is: not to be posited or to be posited in dependence upon names and terminology.[i]

Furthermore, that which is posited [in dependence upon names and terminology] is not necessarily existent [since, for instance, the horns of a rabbit or a difference of entity between subject and object are posited in dependence upon names and terminology but do not exist]. Moreover, the mode of positing [something in dependence upon names and terminology in this Mind-Only

---

a Roughly, this means, "What are without the nature of being established by way of their own character?

b "Imputational character" (*kun btags kyi mtshan nyid, parikalpitalakṣaṇa*) and "imputational nature" (*kun btags kyi rang bzhin / kun btags kyi ngo bo nyid, parikalpitasvabhāva*) are synonymous.

c See *Absorption,* #104.

d As was mentioned earlier (p. 79, footnote c), this line is crucial for identifying that the "character" that imputational natures lack is subsistence, or establishment, by way of their own character.

e See *Absorption,* #59, 60.

f See ibid., #83.

g See ibid., #29, 94.

h *bstan tshod;* see ibid., #96.

i See ibid., #105-109.

system] is very different from the Consequence School's positing existents through the force of nominal conventions [even if the terminology is similar].[144] Therefore, the meaning of existing and not existing by way of [the object's] own character[a] [here in the Mind-Only School] also does not agree [with the interpretation of the Consequence School].[b] However, if one has the conception of [an object as] existing by way of its own character [as described] in this Mind-Only system, one also has the conception of its being established by way of its own character [as described] in the Consequence School. Nevertheless, there are cases in which, though [Proponents of Mind-Only][145] did not conceive certain bases [that is, imputational natures][146] in accordance with the former [description], they would be conceiving such in accordance with the latter [description by the Consequence School, since the Mind-Only School, for instance, holds that anything existent is findable when the object imputed is sought[147] and this is the meaning of "establishment of an object by way of its own character" for the Consequence School].[c]

[Production-Non-Nature][148] (264) {374}

With respect to the second non-nature, the *Sūtra Unraveling the Thought* says:[149]

> What are production-non-natures of phenomena?[d] Those which are the other-powered characters of phenomena.
>
> Why? It is thus: Those [other-powered characters] arise through the force of other conditions and not by themselves.[e] Therefore, they are said to be "production-non-natures."

The nature of production, or intrinsic production,[f] that other-powered natures do not have is production by themselves, since it says, "not by themselves."

---

[a] See ibid., #113-116.

[b] In the Consequence School, objects that are posited through names and terminology do not exist from their own side; also, establishment from an object's own side, for the Consequentialists, requires establishment of the object by way of its own character. The Mind-Only School, however, holds that objects can be posited through names and terminology and still exist from their own side.

[c] See *Absorption,* #110-112.

[d] Roughly, this means, "What phenomena are without the nature of self-production?" See ibid., #76, 77. About "phenomena," see ibid., #71.

[e] Text, p. 87. The Sanskrit (Lamotte, *Saṃdhinirmocana,* 68 [5], n. 1) is: *idaṃ pratyayabalād utpannaṃ na* ***svatas.*** Gung-tang (*Difficult Points,* 125.4) finds great significance in the Tibetan rendering in the agentive (*bdag nyid* ***kyis***) instead of the ablative (*bdag nyid* ***las***). It would seem that the Sanskrit could have been translated into Tibetan either way. See *Absorption,* #67.

[f] *ngo bo nyid kyis skye ba.*

That is production under their own power;[a] it is as Asaṅga's *Compendium of Ascertainments* says:[150]

> Because compositional phenomena are dependent-arisings, they are produced through the power of conditions and not by themselves. This is called "production-non-nature."

This [Mind-Only School] is a system that says that other-powered natures are natureless since they are without the nature of such inherent[b] production;[c] it does not say that other-powered natures are natureless because of not being established by way of their own character [as the Consequence School holds].[d]

[Ultimate-Non-Nature][151] (264) {375}

From between the two modes of positing[e] the third non-nature, [the first to be discussed is] the positing of other-powered natures as without the nature of the ultimate. About this, the *Sūtra Unraveling the Thought* says:[152]

> What are ultimate-non-natures?[f] Those dependently arisen phenomena—which are natureless due to being natureless in terms of production—are also natureless due to being natureless in terms of the ultimate.
>
> Why? Paramārthasamudgata, that which is an object of observation of purification[g] in phenomena I teach to be the ultimate, and other-powered characters are not the object of observation of purification. Therefore, they are said to be "ultimate-non-natures."

Because other-powered natures do not exist as the ultimate nature, they are said

---

a See *Absorption,* #66-70.

b See ibid., #75.

c *rang bzhin gyis skye ba.*

d See *Absorption,* #74.

e See ibid., #128.

f Jik-may-dam-chö-gya-tso's *Port of Entry* (182.6) points out that this question is not limited to the first mode of positing the ultimate-non-nature but is concerned with both modes, since there is no rhetorical question at that point (see p. 90).

g *rnam par dag pa'i dmigs pa, viśuddhālambana* (Lamotte, *Saṃdhinirmocana,* 69 [6], n. 1). Jik-may-dam-chö-gya-tso (*Port of Entry,* 183.4) takes this term to mean "object of observation that is purified [that is, devoid] of contamination" (*zag bcas kyis rnam par dag pa'i lam gyi dmigs pa*). However, other scholars more cogently take the term as referring to an object that is such that meditation upon it purifies obstructions. For instance, Jam-ȳang-shay-b̄a (*Notes,* 506.5), in speaking about the ultimate that is explicitly indicated at this point, qualifies the term "object of observation of purification" (*rnam dag gi dmigs pa*) with the phrase, "that which is such that, when it is observed and then is meditated upon, the obstructions to omniscience become purified" (*gang la dmigs nas bsgom na shes sgrib dag par 'gyur ba*).

to be "ultimate-non-natures."[a] For the ultimate is that through observation of which and familiarization with which obstructions[b] are removed, but obstructions cannot be removed through observing and familiarizing with other-powered natures.

Question: Why are imputational factors not also posited [at this point in the *Sūtra Unraveling the Thought*][153] as ultimate-non-natures?

Answer: If [something] were posited as [an ultimate-non-nature][154] merely through not being an object of observation of purification, that would be true [that is, imputational natures also would have to be posited as ultimate-non-natures]. However, in the context of refuting a misconception, other-powered natures are posited as ultimate-non-natures due to not being objects of observation of purification, whereas imputational factors are not posited [as ultimate-non-natures].[155]

Question: How is that?

Answer: When one understands that obstructions are purified through meditation observing other-powered natures' emptiness of the imputational factor [—for example, through meditating on other-powered natures' emptiness of being established by way of their own character as the referents of words and of conceptual consciousnesses—], there arises the qualm that since, in that case, [the pure exalted wisdom][156] must also observe the other-powered natures that are the substrata [of the quality of emptiness, those other-powered natures] also would be objects of observation of purification, due to which they would be ultimates. [Thus, such a qualm needs to be alleviated with respect to other-powered natures.][157] However, such a qualm does not occur with respect to imputational factors.[c]

The fault of that qualm does not exist.[d] It is like the fact that just as al-

---

[a] See *Absorption,* #127-152, 169.

[b] Notice that D̄zong-ka-b̄a speaks merely of "obstructions," without specifying these to be the obstructions to omniscience. This leaves open the possibility that both the selflessness of persons and the selflessness of phenomena are actual thoroughly established natures. However, as will be seen below (p. 90), when speaking about the second mode of positing the ultimate naturelessness, he limits the discussion to the selflessness of phenomena. See *Absorption,* #153-167.

[c] See ibid., #129-138, 140, 141.

[d] According to Jam-ȳang-shay-b̄a (81.1), when D̄zong-ka-b̄a says, "The fault of that qualm does not exist," his meaning is that it is not the case that whatever is an object of observation by a path of purification is necessarily its **final** object of observation, that is, a thoroughly established nature. According to Jam-ȳang-shay-b̄a's follower Gung-tang (*Difficult Points,* 130.11) however, Autonomists and Consequentialists would have the qualm that since, in the Mind-Only School, other-powered natures are truly established, other-powered natures' status of being established as objects of observation of a path of purification would have to become their final mode of subsistence, in which case they would not be anything other than the final object of observation (that is, that which is comprehended) by a path of purification. A-ku L̄o-drö-gya-tso (94.3), also a follower of Jam-ȳang-shay-b̄a, says the same

though the conception[a] that sound is permanent is overcome by ascertaining sound as impermanent, it is not contradictory that the conception of permanence is not overcome through [merely] observing sound.[b]

Although other-powered natures are not established as the ultimate when [the term] ultimate is taken as [referring to] the object of observation of purification, it will be explained later whether or not they are established as another [type of] ultimate.[c]

[(Actual) Ultimate-Non-Nature][158] (265) {376}

Furthermore, with respect to the second mode of positing the ultimate-non-nature, the *Sūtra Unraveling the Thought* says:[159]

> Moreover, that which is the thoroughly established character of phenomena is also called "the ultimate-non-nature."[d] Why? Paramārthasamudgata, that which in phenomena is the selflessness of phenomena is called their "non-nature." It is the ultimate, and the ultimate is distinguished by just the naturelessness of all phenomena; therefore, it is called the "ultimate-non-nature."

Since the thoroughly established nature of phenomena—the selflessness of phenomena[e]—is the object of observation of purification, it is the ultimate. Also,

---

as Gung-tang. Both Gung-tang and A-ku Lo-drö-gya-tso cite the Omniscient Chö-jung (*chos 'byung*), the author of the old (that is, prior to Jam-ȳang-shay-b̄a) textbook literature of Go-mang College, as their source (Gung-ru Chö-jung's *Garland of White Lotuses,* 33b.5-34a.6), thereby showing that they feel free to adopt interpretations other than those of their leader. Jam-ȳang-shay-b̄a's interpretation seems closer to D̄zong-ka-b̄a's meaning, whereas the other is more inventive. See *Absorption,* #131.

[a] In this context, "conception" (*'dzin*) means "consciousness conceiving."

[b] Given D̄zong-ka-b̄a's wording in this sentence, it strikes me that when he says, "The fault of that qualm does not exist," his meaning may be that it is not the case that taking cognizance of other-powered natures would eliminate obstructions. Jam-ȳang-shay-b̄a's rendition, given two footnotes above, comes down to the same point.

[c] See p. 144 but mainly p. 158 through the end of the chapter. Other-powered natures are ultimate in the broader sense of being ultimately established.

[d] D̄a-drin-rap-d̄en (21.4) takes "ultimate" as the self of phenomena, as did Ge-s̄hay Ge-dün L̄o-drö in an oral discussion, in which case this phrase should be rendered, "Moreover, that which is the thoroughly established character of phenomena is also called 'the non-nature of the ultimate.'" However, I think that the following discussion of "ultimate" here in the sūtra and in D̄zong-ka-b̄a's commentary, as well as the preceding discussion about why other-powered natures are not the ultimate, makes their interpretation problematic, as is confirmed by Gung-tang's *Difficult Points* (135.12). For "ultimate" here refers not to the object of negation, the self of phenomena, but to the ultimacy of the thoroughly established nature.

[e] Here, D̄zong-ka-b̄a specifies the thoroughly established nature as being the selflessness of **phenomena**, seeming to exclude the selflessness of persons; however, in other places he

since it is distinguished by, that is to say, is posited[a] by way of the mere naturelessness of a self in phenomena,[b] it is also called "the non-nature of phenomena," whereby it is called "the ultimate-non-nature."[c]

Also,[d] (266) {377} the *Sūtra Unraveling the Thought* says:[160]

> If the character [that is, entity] of compositional things[e] and the character of the ultimate were different [entities],[161] then just the **mere** selflessness and the **mere** naturelessness [of the self of phenomena] of compositional things would not be [their] ultimate character.

Also, when giving examples [of the three non-natures, the *Sūtra Unraveling the Thought*] says[f] that just as space is posited as the **mere** absence of form [that is,

---

seems to include both. See *Absorption,* #153-167.

a Ḏzong-ka-ḇa glosses the frequently used technical term *rab tu phye ba* with *bzhag pa,* which merely has the sense of "posit"; his reading, therefore, runs contrary to Lamotte's translation (194.6) as "***est manifesté*** par l'irréalité de toutes les choses."

b Notice that Ḏzong-ka-ḇa uses the phrase *chos rnams kyi bdag* rather than *chos kyi bdag;* taken by itself, this phrase seems to leave open the possibility that the self of persons could also be included; however, the previous sentence seems to militate against its inclusion.

c See *Absorption,* #169.

d As background to this point, Ḏa-drin-rap-ḏen (22.3) inserts:

> Someone might wrongly think that an other-powered nature and its thoroughly established nature are different entities just because those two are mutually exclusive, as indeed they are. However, even though they are mutually exclusive, this does not entail that they are different entities.

However, I doubt that Ḏzong-ka-ḇa's main concern is with establishing that an other-powered nature and its thoroughly established nature are not different entities. Rather, his concern here is to offer more evidence that a thoroughly established nature is a "**mere** selflessness" and a "**mere** naturelessness," that is to say, only an elimination of an object of negation, and not something positive, as the Jo-nang-ḇas (and some contemporary American, European, and Japanese scholars) claim. This is confirmed by Ḇel-jor-hlün-drup (19.2), who divides this section into two parts—showing that the thoroughly established nature is a non-affirming negative and refuting, through this, the assertion that it is a positive entity.

e *'du byed, saṃskāra.* In this context, the term may have a wide meaning that also includes permanent phenomena such as uncompounded space; in that case, it would mean "all phenomena," rather than just compositional things, which are necessarily impermanent. However, W̄el-mang Ḡön-chok-gyel-tsen's *Notes on (Ḡön-chok-jik-may-w̄ang-ḇo's) Lectures* (402.1) glosses "compositional things" (*'du byed*) with "compounded things" (*'dus byas*).

f The passage from chapter 7 of the *Sūtra Unraveling the Thought,* cited later in this chapter (p. 94), is:

> Paramārthasamudgata, it is thus: just as, for example, space is distinguished by the mere naturelessness of form [that is, as a mere absence of forms] and pervades everywhere, so from between those [two] ultimate-non-natures, one [that is, the thoroughly established nature] is to be viewed as distinguished by the selflessness of phenomena and as pervading everything.

Lamotte, *Saṃdhinirmocana,* 69 [7], and 194-195; Dön-drup-gyel-tsen's *Four Intertwined*

a mere absence of obstructive contact],[162] so [the thoroughly established nature] is posited as selflessness. Therefore, it is very clear that the thoroughly established nature, which is the selflessness of phenomena,[a] is posited as the non-affirming negation[b] of [dualistic] proliferations that is a mere elimination of a self of phenomena, with compounded phenomena[c] as that which possesses the quality [of emptiness].[d] It is contradictory [for the Jo-nang-b̄as],[e] while asserting the teaching of the meaning of suchness in this sūtra to be definitive, not to posit the immutable thoroughly established nature by way of an elimination-isolate[f]—which is the mere elimination of an object of negation—but rather to assert it as a positive, self-powered [uncontaminated wisdom],[g] whose appear-

---

Commentaries, 8.3-8.4; and Powers, *Wisdom of Buddha,* 101.

[a] Again, D̄zong-ka-b̄a qualifies "thoroughly established nature" with "selflessness of phenomena." Does his specification limit the thoroughly established nature to the selflessness of phenomena, or does it merely give an example of a thoroughly established nature and thus *suggest* that the selflessness of persons is also a thoroughly established nature? See *Absorption,* #153-167.

[b] *med dgag, prasajyapratiṣedha.*

[c] Since each and every phenomenon is a basis or substratum of emptiness, D̄zong-ka-b̄a's specification of compounded phenomena (which does not include such phenomena as uncompounded space) as the substrata has given rise to creative attempts to explain it. Dön-drup-gyel-tsen (*Four Intertwined Commentaries,* 64.6) explains that since the Jo-nang-b̄as assert that compounded phenomena are the **objects** of negation, D̄zong-ka-b̄a deliberately turns this around by asserting that compounded phenomena actually are the **bases** of negation and that the object of negation is an imputational nature. At minimum, the commentary elegantly fits with D̄zong-ka-b̄a's system and with the tenor of the next sentence.

[d] D̄a-drin-rap-d̄en (23.2) adds:

> Hence, it is clear that the final reality and [its] substratum [that is, an other-powered nature and its thoroughly established nature, or a phenomenon and its ultimate truth] are one entity.

However, as mentioned above, the point of the section is not so much that the two truths are one entity but that the thoroughly established nature is a mere elimination of the self that is the object of negation. D̄zong-ka-b̄a, in the next sentence, refers to this mere elimination as an "elimination-isolate" (*bcad ldog*), that is to say, a conceptually isolatable factor that is a mere elimination. This is in opposition to the Jo-nang-b̄as' consideration of the thoroughly established nature to be a positive entity. A-ku L̄o-drö-gya-tso (107.6) correctly sees these two points as connected.

[e] W̄el-mang Ḡön-chok-gyel-tsen's *Notes on (Ḡön-chok-jik-may-w̄ang-b̄o's) Lectures,* 402.1; Dön-drup-gyel-tsen's *Four Intertwined Commentaries,* 65.2; and D̄a-drin-rap-d̄en's *Annotations,* 23.2. S̄hay-rap-gyel-tsen considers the issue of the interpretable and the definitive in his *Ocean of Definitive Meaning,* 173.4ff.

[f] For a discussion of isolates (or conceptually isolatable phenomena), see Daniel E. Perdue, *Debate in Tibetan Buddhism* (Ithaca, N.Y.: Snow Lion, 1992), 695-771; and Georges B. J. Dreyfus, *Recognizing Reality: Dharmakīrti's Philosophy and its Tibetan Interpretations* (Albany, N.Y.: State University of New York Press, 1997), see his index under "distinguisher."

[g] Gung-tang's *Annotations,* 32.3. About the ultimate, S̄hay-rap-gyel-tsen's *Fourth Council*

assert it as a positive, self-powered [uncontaminated wisdom],[a] whose appearance as an object of awareness does not depend on the elimination of an object of negation.[b]

Since this thoroughly established nature is the mere elimination of the nature of self in phenomena,[c] it is called "the ultimate-non-nature of phenomena."[d] However, this is a system that does not assert that the thoroughly established nature is natureless due to the entity of the negation itself not being established by way of its own character[e] [for in the Mind-Only School emptiness, the thoroughly established nature, *is* ultimately established by way of its own character. The Autonomists and Consequentialists, however, assert that emptiness is not ultimately established by way of its own character.][f]

Showing Examples For These (266) {377}

With respect to examples with which those three non-natures are similar, the *Sūtra Unraveling the Thought* says:[163]

> It is thus: for example, character-non-natures [that is, imputational natures] are to be viewed as like a flower in the sky. Paramārthasamudgata, it is thus: for example, production-non-natures [that is, other-powered natures] are to be viewed as like magical creations. From between the [two][164] ultimate-non-natures, one [that is, other-powered natures] is also to be viewed that way.[g] Paramārthasamudgata, it is

---

a Gung-tang's *Annotations,* 32.3. About the ultimate, Shay-rap-gyel-tsen's *Fourth Council* says:

> It is gnosis, never consciousness.
> It is pure, never impure....
> It is immaculate, never stained.

See Cyrus R. Stearns, *The Buddha from Dol po and His Fourth Council of the Buddhist Doctrine* (Ann Arbor, Mich.: University Microfilms, 1996), 203-204.

b See *Reflections on Reality,* chaps. 14 and 15; also *Absorption,* #62-65.

c *chos rnams kyi bdag gi ngo bo.* Notice that here Dzong-ka-ba does not confine the thoroughly established nature to the absence of a self of *phenomena* (which would be *chos bdag gi ngo bo* or *chos kyi bdag gi ngo bo* and not *chos* ***rnams*** *kyi bdag gi ngo bo*) but speaks of it as an absence of self in /of phenomena, and hence it is open to the interpretation that for him not just the absence of a self phenomena but also an absence of a self of persons could be the thoroughly established nature. See *Absorption,* #153-167.

d Given the points Dzong-ka-ba has made above, this sentence cannot, in my opinion, be used to show that the term "ultimate" in "the ultimate non-nature of phenomena" refers to the object of negation, as some contemporary Tibetan scholars hold.

e See *Absorption,* #168.

f Jam-yang-shay-ba's *Great Exposition of the Interpretable and the Definitive,* 84.3-84.4.

g The example of a magician's illusions is to be applied not only to production-non-natures—these being other-powered natures—but **also** to the first of the two ultimate-non-natures—these again being other-powered natures, which are posited as ultimate-non-

> thus: just as, for example, space is distinguished by the mere naturelessness of form [that is, as a mere absence of forms] and pervades everywhere, so from between those [two][165] ultimate-non-natures, one [that is, the thoroughly established nature] is to be viewed as distinguished by the selflessness of phenomena and as pervading everything.

The similarity of imputational factors with a flower in the sky[a] is an example of their merely being imputed by conceptuality and is not an example of their not occurring among objects of knowledge [that is, existents; hence, the exemplification does not indicate that all imputational factors do not exist.][b]

> The *stog* Palace edition (48.6) has a markedly different (and perhaps skewed) reading:
>
> *de dag las gcig kyang don dam pa ngo bo nyid med pa nyid du blta'o/*

In literal translation, this is: "Something other than those is to be viewed as the ultimate-non-nature" and might be rendered more loosely as, "The ultimate-non-nature is, moreover, to be viewed as other than those." The separation of *de dag las* from *ngo bo nyid med pa nyid* suggests that *de dag las* refers to the other two natures or other two examples. However, the other reading, with Jik-may-dam-chö-gya-tso's interpretation of it, is preferable.

Ḏa-drin-rap-ḏen (*Annotations,* 24.5), with strained inventiveness, gives an entirely different interpretation:

> The non-nature of the ultimate [when "ultimate" is taken as] the object of negation is equivalent to the thoroughly established nature. Not only that, but also the two natures other than the thoroughly established nature must be viewed as empty of a self of phenomena; they are to be viewed also [in that way].

In Tibetan, with the sūtra (as Ḏzong-ka-ḇa cites it) in bold print his commentary reads:

> *dgag bya'i* ***don dam pa ngo nyid med pa nyid*** *de ni yongs grub dang don gcig yin la de tsam ma zad yongs grub* ***de las*** *gzhan ngo bo nyid gzhan gnyis* ***kyang*** *chos kyi bdag gis stong par blta dgos pa ni* ***gcig kyang blta bar bya'o***

Taken this way, the sentence in the sūtra would read, "[The two natures other] than that ultimate-non-nature are also to be viewed in another way." This interpretation strikes me as unnecessarily identifying the ultimate as the object of negation and thus is not elegant. (The lack of a nominative case ending in Tibetan allows for ambiguity in situations such as this.)

Lamotte's critical edition (*Saṃdhinirmocana,* 69 [7]) reads *don dam pa ngo bo nyid med pa nyid de las gcig kyang blta bar bya'o,* eliminating one *kyang.*

[a] As Jik-may-dam-chö-gya-tso (*Port of Entry,* 198.4) says, due to an eye disease (*rab rib*) the figure of a flower appears in the sky in the perspective of such a perception, but in fact there is no flower in the sky; just so, imputational natures are established as merely imputed by conceptuality. He identifies this explanation as from Wonch'uk's commentary (Golden Reprint, vol. 128, 820.1).

[b] For instance, uncompounded space is an existent imputational nature, as is an object's being the referent of a term and of a conceptual consciousness (with the qualification that it is not established so **by way of its own character**). As Jik-may-dam-chö-gya-tso (*Port of Entry,* 198.5) says, if there were no imputedly existent phenomena, then all objects of knowledge would absurdly have to be substantially existent. See *Absorption,* #88, 108.

A-ku L̄o-drö-gya-tso (*Precious Lamp,* 112.4) points out that in the Mind-Only School and Consequence School a flower in the sky is taken as an example of conceptual imputation

It will be explained later how other-powered natures are similar to a magician's illusions (see 176ff.). The meaning of the example for thoroughly established phenomena is clear as it is.

[The Damage To Taking Literally The Statements Of Non-Nature][166] (267) {378}

[According to the Mind-Only School] the modes of the non-nature in the statements [in the middle wheel that all phenomena are] natureless are as explained above [to be in consideration of the three non-natures].[167] If, unlike that, one explained [in accordance with the Consequence School] that [the meaning of] non-nature is that all three natures are not established by way of their own character, one would be adhering literally to the [Perfection of Wisdom][168] Sūtras' statements of non-nature. In that case, [according to the Mind-Only School] one would be incurring a view of nihilism, or a view of annihilation. For one would be deprecating all three natures, due to which one would come to have the view that character [that is, establishment of objects by way of their own character] does not exist. For, this [Mind-Only School] is a system in which, if other-powered natures are not established by way of their own character, production and cessation are not feasible[a] due to which [other-powered natures] would be deprecated, and it is a system in which if the thoroughly established nature does not exist by way of its own character, it could not be the basic disposition of things.[b]

Question: Even if it is allowed that the view of no establishment by way of own character deprecates the other two natures, how does it come to deprecate imputational factors?

Answer: If the other two natures do not exist by way of their own character, they become nonexistent, in which case even the bases of imputing imputational factors and the conventions that are the imputers[c] [that is, terms and conceptual consciousnesses][169] would not exist, whereby imputational factors would be utterly nonexistent. This is the reason.

Moreover, in this vein the *Sūtra Unraveling the Thought* says:[170]

> Even though they have interest in that doctrine [of the profound thoroughly established nature], they do not understand, just as it is, the

---

but not as an example of imputational natures not occurring among objects of knowledge, that is, existents, whereas in the Autonomy School it is taken as an example of the fact that the object negated in selflessness does not occur among objects of knowledge.

a The *Sūtra Unraveling the Thought* says (see p. 97):

> That which does not exist by way of its own character is not produced. That which is not produced does not cease.

b *dngos po'i gshis.*

c *'dogs pa po'i tha snyad.*

> profound reality that I have set forth with a thought behind it.[a] With respect to the meaning of these doctrines, they adhere to the terms as only literal: "All these phenomena are only natureless. All these phenomena are only unproduced, only unceasing, only quiescent from the start, only naturally thoroughly passed beyond sorrow." Due to that, they acquire the view that all phenomena do not exist and the view that [establishment of objects by way of their own][171] character does not exist. Moreover, having acquired the view of nihilism and the view of the non-existence of [establishment of objects by way of their own] character, they deprecate all phenomena in terms of all of the characters—deprecating the imputational character of phenomena and also deprecating the other-powered character and thoroughly established character of phenomena.
>
> Why? Paramārthasamudgata, it is thus: If the other-powered character and the thoroughly established character exist [by way of their own character],[172] the imputational character is known [that is, is possible]. However, those who perceive the other-powered character and the thoroughly established character as without character[b] [that is to say, as not being established by way of their own character] also deprecate the imputational character. Therefore, those [persons] are said to deprecate even all three aspects of characters.

In "With respect to the meaning of [these] doctrines, they adhere to the terms as only literal," the terms are the statements in sūtras [such as the Perfection of Wisdom Sūtras][173] teaching non-nature—that all phenomena are ultimately empty of inherent existence, empty of [establishment] by way of their own nature, and empty of [establishment] by way of their own character. This [Mind-Only school] is a system in which holding what is literally indicated in those passages is asserted to be [mistaken] adherence to the literal reading.

[Wrongly] perceiving other-powered and thoroughly established characters to be without character is to view those two as not being established by way of their own character. The passage from "Why?" on through to the end of that citation indicates the reason why all three natures come to be deprecated. It should be known that even if one holds [a position] in accordance with the statement that production and cessation do not exist by way of their own character, one [explicitly][174] deprecates other-powered natures, and thereby one also

---

a Jik-may-dam-chö-gya-tso (*Port of Entry*, 202.2) points out that as the reason why they do not understand it, Wonch'uk says that "they do not have a nature of honesty and just dwell in their own view"; Jik-may-dam-chö-gya-tso takes these to mean that they are not unbiased and are attached to their own view.

He (202.1) glosses "set forth with a thought behind it" (*dgongs te bshad pa*) with "set forth non-literally" (*sgra ji bzhin pa min par bshad pa*).

b This is a source showing that according to the *Sūtra Unraveling the Thought* thoroughly established natures are established by way of their own character.

comes to deprecate the other two [natures—the imputational and the thoroughly established]. For, this [Mind-Only School] is a system in which if production and cessation are not established by way of their own character, production and cessation become nonexistent [since they would not be established in any other way, in which case the bases of imputation of imputational factors and the substrata of the thoroughly established nature would not exist].[175]

Explaining That In Consideration Of Which [Buddha] Spoke Of [Phenomena As] Being Unproduced And So Forth [In The Perfection Of Wisdom Sūtras] (269) {380}

Question: If such is the mode of non-nature, in consideration of what did [Buddha] speak of [phenomena as] unproduced and so forth?

Answer: These were set forth in consideration of the first and last non-natures [that is, character-non-natures and ultimate-non-natures, these being imputational natures and thoroughly established natures respectively].

[Buddha's Speaking Of Phenomena As Being Unproduced And So Forth In Consideration Of Imputational Natures][176] (269) {380}

With regard to the first, the *Sūtra Unraveling the Thought* says:[177]

> Concerning that, thinking of just character-non-natures [that is, thinking of just imputational factors which are not established by way of their own character], I taught that all phenomena are unproduced, unceasing, quiescent from the start, naturally thoroughly passed beyond sorrow.
>
> Why? Paramārthasamudgata, it is thus: That which does not exist by way of its own character is not produced.[a] That which is not produced does not cease. That which is not produced and does not cease is from the start quiescent. That which is quiescent from the start is naturally thoroughly passed beyond sorrow [that is, naturally devoid of the afflictive emotions without depending on an antidote].[178] That which is naturally thoroughly passed beyond sorrow does not have the least thing to pass beyond sorrow.

[Buddha] states as the reason why imputational factors do not have production and cessation the fact that they are not established by way of their own character. Therefore, this also indicates that if production and cessation exist, they [must][179] be established by way of their own character and indicates that other-powered natures have production and cessation that are established by way of their own character.

---

[a] This sentence clearly sets forth the position that all products are established by way of their own character (Jik-may-dam-chö-gya-tso's *Port of Entry,* 208.3).

Since what are devoid of production and cessation are uncompounded, such are unfit to be phenomena of the thorough afflictions, due to which they are indicated as being quiescent from the start and naturally passed beyond sorrow. For sorrow[a] here is the afflictions.[b]

[Buddha's Speaking Of Not Being Produced And So Forth In Consideration Of The Thoroughly Established Nature][180] (269) {381}

Also, with respect to the second, the *Sūtra Unraveling the Thought* says:[181]

> Moreover, thinking of just the ultimate-non-nature, which is distinguished by the selflessness of phenomena, I taught, "All phenomena are unproduced, unceasing, from the start quiescent, and naturally thoroughly passed beyond sorrow."
>
> Why? It is thus: Just the ultimate-non-nature which is distinguished by the selflessness of phenomena only subsists in permanent, permanent time and everlasting, everlasting time.[c] It is the uncompounded final reality[d] of phenomena, devoid of all afflictive emotions. Because that uncompounded [nature] which subsists for permanent, permanent time and everlasting, everlasting time in the aspect of just that reality is uncompounded, it is unproduced and unceasing. Because it is devoid of all afflictive emotions, it is quiescent from the start and naturally thoroughly passed beyond sorrow.

The Chinese *Great Commentary* [by Wonch'uk] explains that "permanent, permanent time" is former, former time and "everlasting, everlasting time" is later, later time.[e]

---

a *mya ngan.*

b The afflictions are identified in the *Sūtra Unraveling the Thought* as threefold—the afflictive emotions, actions (*las, karma*) and the production of a lifetime; see p. 220, footnote a. The afflictive emotions are commonly identified as the six root afflictions (desire, anger, pride, ignorance, doubt, and afflictive view) and the twenty secondary afflictions (belligerence, resentment, concealment of faults, verbal spite, jealousy, miserliness, deceit, dissimulation, haughtiness, harmfulness, non-shame, non-embarrassment, lethargy, excitement, non-faith, laziness, non-conscientiousness, forgetfulness, non-introspection, and distraction). See Jeffrey Hopkins, *Meditation on Emptiness* (London: Wisdom, 1983; rev. ed., Boston, Ma.: Wisdom, 1996) , 255-266.

c *rtag pa rtag pa'i dus* (*nityaṃ nitya-kālaṃ*) and *ther zug ther zug gi dus* (*dhruvaṃ dhruva-kālaṃ*), (Noriaki Hakamaya, "A Consideration on the Byams Shus kyi Le'u," *Indobukkyogaku Kenkyu,* 14, no. 1 [Dec. 1975]: 28). My thanks to John C. Powers for the citation. Lamotte (*Saṃdhinirmocana,* 70 [9], n. 2) has *nityakālaṃ* and *śāśvatakālaṃ*.

d *chos nyid, dharmatā.*

e In his commentary on this section, Wonch'uk (Peking 5517, vol. 106, chap. 5, beginning at 133.2.1; Golden Reprint, vol. 128, 791.2) cites these expressions several times but does not gloss the terms. However, as Jik-may-dam-chö-gya-tso (*Port of Entry,* 210.5) points out, in Wonch'uk's commentary on a passage in the *Sūtra Unraveling the Thought* near the end of the "Subhūti Chapter" (see also Powers, *Wisdom of Buddha,* 63):

> For permanent, permanent time and everlasting, everlasting time, whether Ones Gone Thus appear in the world or do not appear in the world, the abiding of the real nature (*chos nyid, dharmatā*) of phenomena and the element of a [Superior's] qualities (*chos dbyings, dharmadhātu*) just exists.

Wonch'uk (Peking 5517, vol. 106, 100.3.4; Karmapa *sde dge,* vol. 118, 416.5; and Golden Reprint, vol. 128, 610.2) says:

> The thusness (*de bzhin nyid, tathatā*) which is of one taste has not been a oneness **in the past from the very start** and hence [the *Sūtra Unraveling the Thought* speaks of] "permanent, permanent time," and **in the future** also it will not be a oneness, and hence [the sūtra speaks of] "everlasting, everlasting time." During such times the reality of phenomena abides as the element of a [Superior's] qualities (*ro gcig pa'i de bzhin nyid gzod ma nas sngar yang gcig pa nyid ma yin pas rtag pa rtag pa'i dus zhes bya 'o phyis kyang gcig pa nyid ma yin pas ther zug ther zug gi dus zhes bya ste dus 'di lta bu rnams chos rnams kyi chos nyid chos kyi dbyings la rnam par gnas pa'o*).

(What Wonch'uk means by the thoroughly established nature's **not** being a oneness in the past and in the future is unclear to me.)

Another occurrence of these phrases is in the "Guṇākara Chapter" (see also Powers, *Wisdom of Buddha,* 85-86):

> Guṇākara, it is like this: For example, other-powered characters should be viewed as being [under the influence of] the predispositions for conventions that are the imputational nature, like a very clear crystal that is in contact with a color. It is like this: For example, other-powered characters that are apprehended as the imputational character should be viewed as being like the mistaken apprehension of the very clear crystal as a sapphire, a great sapphire, a ruby, an emerald, or gold. Guṇākara, it is like this: For example, the very clear crystal should be viewed as an other-powered character. Guṇākara, it is like this: For example, just as the very clear crystal is not thoroughly established as having the character of a sapphire, a *mahānīla,* a ruby, an emerald, or gold, and is without those natures **in permanent, permanent time and in everlasting, everlasting time**, so other-powered characters are not thoroughly established in permanent, permanent time and in everlasting, everlasting time as having the imputational character, and are without that nature; just that non-establishment or naturelessness is to be viewed as the thoroughly established character.

Jik-may-dam-chö-gya-tso (*Port of Entry,* 210.1), who says that he is drawing from Wonch'uk, points out that **in general** "permanent time" (*rtag pa'i dus*) and "everlasting time" (*ther zug gi dus*) have various meanings according to context. Both terms refer to the past in Asaṅga's *Actuality of the Grounds* when it says, "In permanent time and everlasting time effects are just not fit to exist in causes," whereas in Vasubandhu's *Principles of Explanation* in the context of a discussion of permanent, stable, and everlasting form, permanent means not impermanent; stable (*brtan pa*) means not disintegrating momentarily; and everlasting means the non-disintegration of the continuum, and thus all three refer to the future. Paramārtha (Wonch'uk, Golden Reprint, vol. 128, 609.2) says that everlasting has the sense of naturally existing from before [and] even during future states of the path (*lam gyi mdun rol*

[Indicating That This Explanation And That In Asaṅga's Summary of Manifest Knowledge *Are Not Essentially Contradictory]*[182] (269) {381}

Question: Here [in this[a] passage in the *Sūtra Unraveling the Thought*],[183]

---

gyi gnas bskabs [sic] *na yang/ snga nas rang bzhin gyis yod pa'i phyir ther zug*), and permanent refers to this mode of reality unceasing even during intermediate and final states of the path (*lam gyi bar dang/ tha ma'i gnas skabs na yang/ don gyi tshul 'di 'gag pa med pa'i phyir rtag pa*). However, in the context of the "Subhūti Chapter" of the *Sūtra Unraveling the Thought* Wonch'uk delimits the meaning of "permanent" to the past and "everlasting" to the future, and this same context applies to the "Paramārthasamudgata Chapter."

[a] The qualification "this" is used to accord with Gung-tang (*Difficult Points,* 167.14-168.15) who points out that what Ḏzong-ka-ḇa is about to say is true only with respect to this part of the *Sūtra Unraveling the Thought.* For the sūtra contains another passage that refers to all three non-natures as being the bases in consideration of which Buddha spoke—in the Perfection of Wisdom Sūtras—of phenomena as unproduced and so forth. That passage is exactly opposite to Ḏzong-ka-ḇa's point that although Buddha identifies **all three natures** as being the bases in consideration of which he spoke—in the Perfection of Wisdom Sūtras—of non-nature, he did not identify all three natures as being the basis in consideration of which he spoke—in the Perfection of Wisdom Sūtras—of phenomena as being unproduced, unceasing, quiescent from the start, and naturally being passed beyond sorrow. Instead of this, he identified only imputational natures and thoroughly established natures and their respective non-natures as being behind this teaching. Hence, Gung-tang makes the point that Ḏzong-ka-ḇa's reference should not be to the sūtra in general but just to the present section on the question and answer concerning the thought behind Buddha's teaching that all phenomena are unproduced, and so forth. Indeed, one can understand that this is Ḏzong-ka-ḇa's concern.

The passage that treats **all three** non-natures as the bases in Buddha's thought when he taught in the Perfection of Wisdom Sūtras that all phenomena are unproduced, and so forth, occurs later in the seventh chapter, when Buddha explains how various types of trainees understand his teaching in the Perfection of Wisdom Sūtras (Lamotte, *Saṃdhinirmocana,* 75 [17], and 199; and Powers, *Wisdom of Buddha,* 115):

> Paramārthasamudgata, with respect to this, **thinking of just those three types of non-nature**, the One Gone Thus, by way of the aspect of setting forth sūtras of interpretable meaning, taught doctrine in this way, "All phenomena are natureless; all phenomena are unproduced, unceasing, quiescent from the start, and naturally passed beyond sorrow."

Here, Buddha explicitly explains that he taught that all phenomena are natureless, **unproduced, and so forth**, "thinking of just those three types of naturelessness."

By calling attention to this passage, Gung-tang shows that Ḏzong-ka-ḇa's statement that Buddha does not do this needs to be limited to the present context of his answer to Paramārthasamudgata's question, and he also indicates a possible sūtra source for Asaṅga's explanation in his *Summary of Manifest Knowledge* of the teaching of non-production and so forth in consideration of all three non-natures. Nevertheless, it strikes me that this later passage in the *Sūtra Unraveling the Thought* could be read in the light of Buddha's own earlier explanation, and thus when he says that "thinking of just those three types of naturelessness," he taught that "all phenomena are natureless; all phenomena are unproduced, unceasing, quiescent from the start, and naturally passed beyond sorrow," he does mean that **all** three having treated **all three** [natures][184] as the bases [in consideration of which he spoke][185] of non-nature [in the Perfection of Wisdom Sūtras, Buddha] then did not take the middle non-nature [that is, production-non-natures, or other-powered natures] as the basis [in consideration of which he spoke in the Perfection of Wisdom Sūtras of all phenomena as] being unproduced and so forth [but mentioned only imputational natures and thoroughly established natures]. However, about the basis [in consideration of which Buddha spoke of not being produced and so forth],[186] Asaṅga's *Summary of Manifest Knowledge* also[a] says:[187]

> [In the Perfection of Wisdom Sūtras it is said that all phenomena are natureless] by reason of the fact that imputational factors are natureless in the sense of not having character [that is, establishment by way of their own character], other-powered natures are natureless in the sense of not having [self-]production], and thoroughly established natures are the ultimate-non-nature.
>
> What is the thought giving rise [to the statements that all phenomena are] "unproduced, unceasing, quiescent from the start, and naturally thoroughly passed beyond sorrow"?
>
> In just the ways that they are natureless, so they are not produced. In just the ways that they are not produced, so they do not cease. In just the ways that they are not produced and do not cease, so they are quiescent from the start. In those ways, they are naturally thoroughly passed beyond sorrow.

Thus, what is the meaning of [Asaṅga's] explaining not being produced and so forth in terms of **all three** characters [whereas the *Sūtra Unraveling the Thought* at this point relates these only to imputational and thoroughly established natures]?

Answer: Concerning this, the Chinese *Great Commentary* [by Wonch'uk] explains that:

- the *Sūtra [Unraveling the Thought]*'s not mentioning other-powered natures as the basis in [Buddha's] thought [when he spoke] of not being produced and so forth [in the Perfection of Wisdom Sūtras] is in order to indicate that dependently arisen objects are not nonexistent,[b] whereas

were the bases with respect to which he made **each** of these five teachings but that, as he explained earlier, the bases in consideration of which he made the individual statements are found **within** the three non-natures. For extended discussion, see Jik-may-dam-chö-gya-tso's *Port of Entry,* 214.6-218.1.

[a] Jik-may-dam-chö-gya-tso (*Port of Entry,* 218.1) calls for analysis of what "also" (*kyang*) might mean.

[b] In Wonch'uk's treatment of the thoughts behind Buddha's teaching of no production and so forth in the Perfection of Wisdom Sūtras (Peking 5517, vol. 106, chap. 5, 132.5.1-135.1.5), the reference here (134.2.6) is found in his lengthy and extremely well-

- the explanation in Asaṅga's *Summary of Manifest Knowledge* is in terms of the non-existence of production by itself[a] and of causeless production.[b]

[**Our own system's answer:**][188] Since other-powered natures have production and cessation that exist by way of their own character, the statements concerning no production and no cessation are not in consideration of other-powered natures. Also, since most other-powered natures are included within [the class of] thoroughly afflicted phenomena, [at this point in the *Sūtra Unraveling the Thought*] they are not treated as the basis of the latter two terms [that is, "quiescent from the start" and "naturally thoroughly passed beyond sorrow."][189] That is the thought of this sūtra passage.

---

documented discussion of this specific point (Peking 5517, vol. 106, chap. 5, 133.3.6; and Golden Reprint, vol. 128, 832.6). He says:

> The teaching, in dependence upon imputational natures, in treatises such as the *Very Extensive One Hundred Stanzas* and so forth (*bstan bcos shin tu rgyas pa brgya pa la sogs pa*) that all phenomena are natureless, unproduced, unceasing, and so forth indicates that dependently arisen objects are not nonexistent. Therefore, these sūtras also, thinking of the three natures in general, teach that all phenomena are natureless and, thinking of the first and last natures, teach [that all phenomena] are unproduced, and so forth.

In the next sentence D̄zong-ka-b̄a implicitly criticizes Wonch'uk for referring to the mere existence of dependent-arisings and not their "existence by way of their own character." D̄zong-ka-b̄a's procedure is typical; first, he gives Wonch'uk credit for the general point but then reexplains the issue to improve the presentation. (The remainder of D̄zong-ka-b̄a's explanation—"whereas...causeless production"—accords exactly with Wonch'uk's text.)

[a] D̄a-drin-rap-d̄en's *Annotations* (33.1) glosses "production by itself" (*bdag nyid kyis skye ba*) with "autonomous production" (*rang dbang gis skye ba*).

[b] Wonch'uk (Peking 5517, vol. 106, chap. 5, 134.2.7; and Golden Reprint, vol. 128, 833.2) says:

> Because other-powered entities are produced in dependence upon others but do not have the meaning of being produced by themselves and of being produced causelessly, [Asaṅga's] *Summary of Manifest Knowledge Treatise* and so forth say that stemming from the three aspects of natures, [Buddha] taught that all phenomena are natureless, unproduced, unceasing, quiescent from the start, and naturally thoroughly passed beyond sorrow.

I agree with Gung-tang (*Difficult Points,* 125.4.) that "production by itself" (*bdag nyid kyis skye ba*) means intrinsic production as in the Nihilist School, but it is intriguing to note that D̄zong-ka-b̄a does not criticize Wonch'uk for describing Asaṅga's view of the production that other-powered entities lack as "being produced by themselves **and** being produced causelessly." Wonch'uk indeed seems not to be giving two ways of referring to causeless production but to offer two **different** explanations (autonomous production and causeless production) since, at least in the Tibetan translation, he uses the term "by" (*kyis*) for the first type and connects the two with "and" (*dang*)—*bdag nyid kyis skye ba dang rgyu med las skye ba.* When Jik-may-dam-chö-gya-tso recapitulates Wonch'uk's meaning (*Port of Entry,* 212.40), he gets around the problem by switching "and" to "or" (*'am*), thereby making the second explanation into a gloss of the first. See *Absorption,* #68.

[On the other hand] Asaṅga was thinking that—in terms of the [type of] non-nature that does not exist with respect to each of the three natures—just as they are natureless so they also are unproduced, unceasing, quiescent from the start, and primordially passed beyond sorrow.[a] Thus, he explained it that way in his *Summary of Manifest Knowledge*.[b] [Hence, since the two modes of exposition serve different purposes, they do not conflict in essential meaning.][190]

---

[a] The meaning is clearly stated in B̄el-jor-hlün-drup's *Lamp for the Teaching* (23.7-24.5): There is a basis in [Buddha's] thought for explaining in the Perfection of Wisdom Sūtras that [all] phenomena are unproduced, and so forth, because [Buddha said such] thinking of all three [natures]—imputational, other-powered, and thoroughly established natures.

- Imputational natures are said to be "unproduced" because they are unproduced by way of their own character. They are said to be "unceased" because they do not cease by way of their own character. They are said to be quiescent from the start and naturally passed beyond sorrow because they are not afflicted phenomena [since, as Jik-may-dam-chö-gya-tso (*Port of Entry,* 213.6) adds, they are uncompounded]
- There is a reason for saying that other-powered natures are "unproduced, unceasing," for they are not produced by their own power without depending on conditions and do not cease by their own power. [As Jik-may-dam-chö-gya-tso (*Port of Entry,* 214.2) fleshes out the remaining two, other-powered natures are said to be "quiescent from the start and naturally passed beyond sorrow," because without depending on conditions they do not exist as thoroughly afflicted phenomena.]
- There is a reason for saying that thoroughly established natures are "unproduced, unceasing" because they are not produced and do not cease as the nature that is a self of phenomena. [Or, as Jik-may-dam-chö-gya-tso (*Port of Entry,* 213.2) puts it, thoroughly established natures are "unproduced, unceasing" because they are the suchness that is not produced and does not cease as either a self of persons or a self of phenomena.] They are said to be "quiescent from the start" and "naturally passed beyond sorrow" because they are without afflictions that are the nature of a self of phenomena [that is, that are established by way of their own character as referents of conceptual consciousnesses]. There is entailment because, on this occasion, it is fitting to take "sorrow" as the afflictive emotions [Or, as Jik-may-dam-chö-gya-tso (*Port of Entry,* 214.3) puts it, thoroughly established natures are said to be "quiescent from the start" and "naturally passed beyond sorrow" because of being naturally passed beyond the afflictions in the sense of being established as either of the two selves.]

[b] D̄zong-ka-b̄a is showing that the *Sūtra Unraveling the Thought* itself at this point differs in its presentation from Asaṅga and so forth but that the latter have good reason for treating it the way they do. D̄a-drin-rap-d̄en (*Annotations,* 33.5) indicates that Vasubandhu's *The Thirty* and so forth accord with Asaṅga's presentation.

3. The Three Natures

Identifying The Entities Of The Three Natures (271) {383}

[Imputational Nature Of A Form][191] (271) {383}

Question: If imputational factors are character-non-natures, what are imputational factors themselves?

Answer: About that, in the *Sūtra Unraveling the Thought* [the Bodhisattva Paramārthasamudgata says during his rerendering of the meaning of Buddha's answer]:[192]

> That which is posited by names and terminology[a]—with respect to [other-powered natures which are] (1) the objects of activity of conceptuality,[b] (2) the foundations of imputational characters,[c] and (3) those which have the signs of compositional phenomena[d]—in the character of entities[e] or particulars [such as, "This is][193] a form aggregate,"[f] and that which is posited by names and terminology in the character of entities or the character of particulars[g] [that is, attributes, such as] "the production of the form aggregate," "the cessation of the form aggregate," "the abandonment and thorough knowledge of the form aggregate" are imputational characters.[h]

The three phrases [that is, "the objects of activity of conceptuality," "the foundations of imputational characters," and "those which have the signs of compositional phenomena"][194] indicate the bases of the imputation of imputational factors[—these being other-powered natures].

The rest of it indicates the mode of imputation. The imputation as, "This

---

[a] Jik-may-dam-chö-gya-tso (*Port of Entry,* 228.4) identifies the meaning of "That which is posited by names and terminology" as:

> establishment by way of its own character as an entity for imputation by terms and conceptual consciousnesses (*sgra rtog gis btags pa'i ngo bor rang gi mtshan nyid kyis grub pa*).

[b] *rnam par rtog pa'i spyod yul, vikalpagocara* (Étienne Lamotte, *Saṃdhinirmocanasūtra: L'Explication des mystères* (Louvain: Université de Louvain, 1935), 81 [25], n. 12).

[c] *kun brtags pa'i mtshan nyid kyi gnas, parikalpitalakṣaṇāśraya* (ibid., 81 [25], n. 13).

[d] *'du byed kyi mtshan ma, saṃskāranimitta* (ibid., 81 [25], n. 14).

[e] *ngo bo nyid kyi mtshan nyid, svabhāvalakṣaṇa* (ibid., 81 [25], n. 16).

[f] "This is a form aggregate" is an illustration of the mode of imputation of entities, whereas the rest are illustrations of the mode of imputation of attributes.

[g] *bye brag gi mtshan nyid, viśeṣalakṣaṇa* (Lamotte, *Saṃdhinirmocana,* 81 [25], n. 17).

[h] Ḍa-drin-rap-den (*Annotations,* 34.5.) adds that although these are imputed as form and so forth, they are not actual form and so forth.

is a form aggregate,"[a] is the mode of imputation of an entity, and the imputation as "[This] is the production of a form aggregate,"[b] and so forth is the mode of imputation of particulars, or attributes.[c] These will be explained in detail later (195).[d]

---

a *'di gzugs phung ngo zhes.*

b *gzugs phung skye'o zhes.*

c Wonch'uk (Golden Reprint, vol. 129, 141.5ff) seeks to explain the meaning of the sūtra's speaking of **both** entity and particular on the occasion of **both** entity and particular:

> That which is posited by names and terminology...**in the character of entities or particulars** [such as, "This is] a form aggregate" and that which is posited by names and terminology **in the character of entities or the character of particulars** [that is, attributes, such as] "the production of the form aggregate," "the cessation of the form aggregate," and "the abandonment and thorough knowledge of the form aggregate" are imputational characters.

Following Wonch'uk, Jik-may-dam-chö-gya-tso (*Port of Entry,* 227.6, 236.2) posits two types of imputation each with respect to entity and attribute:

Imputation of just the entity that is an imputation of entity (*ngo bo la kun btags pa'i kun btags su gyur pa'i ngo bo nyid la kun btags pa*)	"This is a form" (*'di ni gzugs so*)
Imputation of a particular that is an imputation of entity (*ngo bo la kun btags pa'i kun btags su gyur pa'i bye brag la kun btags pa*)	"This is a contaminated form" (*'di ni zag bcas kyi gzugs so*)
Imputation of just the entity that is an imputation of attribute (*khyad bar la kun btags pa'i kun btags su gyur pa'i ngo bo nyid la kun btags pa*)	"Form is produced" (*gzugs skye'o*)
Imputation of a particular that is an imputation of attribute (*khyad bar la kun btags pa'i kun btags su gyur pa'i bye brag la kun btags pa*)	"Form is produced momentarily" (*gzugs skad cig la skye'o*)

This is an ingenious way to explain why the sūtra mentions both entity and particular for each type.

d Gung-ru Chö-jung (23b.5) points out that, with regard to the imputation of an entity and an attribute, what is being refuted is not merely the imputation of that which is bulbous, flat based, and capable of holding fluid (which is the defining nature of a pot) as a pot and the imputation of such as the production of a pot. Rather, what is being refuted is that what is bulbous, flat based, and capable of holding fluid is **established by way of its own character** as the object expressed by the term "pot" and that what is bulbous, flat based, and capable of holding fluid is **established by way of its own character** as the object expressed by the term "production of pot." As Ḏzong-ka-ḇa says in chap. 9 (p. 195):

> Those imputational factors—which are such that a consciousness conceiving imputational factors to be established by way of their own character is asserted to be a consciousness conceiving a self of phenomena—are the nominally and terminologically imputed factors [in the imputation of] the aggregates and so forth as entities, "This is form," and as attributes, "This is the production of form," and so forth. Since the aggregates and so forth do exist as just those [entities of such nominal and terminological imputation], the [mere] conception that they exist as

[Other-Powered Nature Of A Form][195] (271) {383}

Question: If other-powered natures are natureless in terms of production, what are other-powered natures?

Answer: About that, in the *Sūtra Unraveling the Thought* [the Bodhisattva Paramārthasamudgata says during his rerendering of the meaning of Buddha's answer]:[196]

> Those which are the objects of activity of conceptuality, the foundations of imputational characters, and have the signs of compositional phenomena are other-powered characters.

The first [that is, "those which are the objects of activity of conceptuality"] indicates of what [type of consciousness other-powered natures] are objects.[a] The

---

> those [entities of such nominal and terminological imputation] is not a superimposition; rather, the conception that the aggregates and so forth **exist by way of their own character** as those entities [of such nominal and terminological imputation] is a superimposition.

Hence, it is not the act of imputation that is being refuted, nor the mere existence of entities and attributes. Rather, it is being refuted that objects are established by way of their own character as the referents of terms for entities and attributes and of conceptual consciousnesses thinking of such.

[a] As Jik-may-dam-chö-gya-tso (*Port of Entry,* 225.6) points out, Wonch'uk (Golden Reprint, vol. 129, 140.6) says that conceptuality refers to both (conceptual) main minds and mental factors. Wonch'uk offers two explanations on how other-powered natures are the objects of activity of conceptual consciousnesses:

- the form aggregate and so forth are the objects of conceptual consciousnesses
- the form aggregate and so forth are observed-object-conditions of conceptual consciousnesses

Wonch'uk himself prefers the first explanation. Jik-may-dam-chö-gya-tso refers to the fact that Gung-tang, in his *Annotations,* indicates that forms and so forth could only be taken as observed-object-conditions in the sense of appearing to conceptual consciousnesses (*snang ba'i dmigs rkyen*) or as **imputed** observed-object-conditions (*dmigs rkyen btags pa ba*)—his meaning being that they could not be **actual** conditions generating consciousnesses, since they would then be external objects. Gung-tang himself, as Jik-may-dam-chö-gya-tso (*Port of Entry,* 265.2) points out, takes object of activity (*spyod yul*) to mean object of observation (*dmigs yul*), with the caveat that whatever is the object of observation of an awareness is not necessarily an object of activity of that awareness:

- since otherwise all conventional phenomena would have to be the objects of activity of an exalted wisdom of a Superior's meditative equipoise directly realizing emptiness (because it is held that the objects of observation of a consciousness directly realizing emptiness are all phenomena, since they are the bases of emptiness even though they are not perceived), and
- since otherwise an omniscient consciousness would have to be an object of activity (that is to say, in the sphere) of a common consciousness of an ordinary being (because an ordinary being can think about an omniscient consciousness).

second [that is, "the foundations of imputational characters"] indicates that they are the bases of imputation of the imputational factor. The third [that is, "those that have the signs of a compositional phenomenon"] indicates their own entities.[a]

[Thoroughly Established Nature Of A Form][197] (272) {383}

Question: If the thoroughly established nature is the ultimate-non-nature, what is it?

Answer: About that, in the *Sūtra Unraveling the Thought* [the Bodhisattva Paramārthasamudgata says during his rerendering of the meaning of Buddha's answer]:[b]

The thoroughly established character is that which is:

- the thorough non-establishment[c]—of just those [other-powered

---

[a] According to D̄a-drin-rap-d̄en (*Annotations,* 35.6), this phrase merely indicates that other-powered natures are "compositional phenomena"—a term which sometimes is equivalent to "compounded phenomena" (*'dus byas, saṃskṛta*) but also may refer to all phenomena (see also p. 91, footnote e).

Jik-may-dam-chö-gya-tso (*Port of Entry,* 226.5) refers to the fact that Wonch'uk (Golden Reprint, vol. 129, 141.3) prefers the second of two interpretations of the phrase "(having) the signs of a compositional phenomenon":

- Having the signs of an object of a consciousness observing a compositional phenomenon
- Having the signs of the aspects of a compounded phenomenon

Jik-may-dam-chö-gya-tso praises the fact that Gung-tang prefers the first in order to include all phenomena. This must be because the looser meaning of "compositional phenomenon" includes permanent phenomena whereas "compounded phenomenon" does not. Still, the term "compositional phenomenon" also could be taken in its stricter sense as compounded phenomenon if we say that the sūtra is referring to the **main** bases of emptiness; see S̄er-s̄hül's *Notes,* 20a.2.

[b] Chap. 7; Lamotte, *Saṃdhinirmocana,* 81 [25], and 204; Dön-drup-gyel-tsen's *Four Intertwined Commentaries,* 21.6; and John C. Powers, *Wisdom of Buddha: Saṁdhinirmocana Sūtra* (Berkeley, Calif.: Dharma, 1995), 131-132. The passage is basically saying that a thoroughly established nature is the non-establishment of the imputational nature in an other-powered nature and that this non-establishment is what must be comprehended in order to bring about purification. The thoroughly established nature is, therefore, not the other-powered nature seen under a different light; it is not the other-powered nature empty of the imputational nature; rather, it is *just* the absence of the imputational nature in the other-powered nature. The thoroughly established nature is a mere absence, a mere negative, of a falsely imagined status; it is not an other-powered nature devoid of that imagined status. This is a central point in D̄zong-ka-b̄a's interpretation, and he has good sources here and elsewhere in the *Sūtra Unraveling the Thought* itself. See *Reflections on Reality,* chap. 15.

[c] It is clear from this usage of "thorough non-establishment" that the term "thoroughly established nature" refers not to something achieved by spiritual practice but to a character of

natures which are][198] the objects of activity of conceptuality, the foundations of imputational characters, and those which have the signs of compositional phenomena—as that imputational character,[a]

- just the naturelessness of only that [imputational] nature,
- the absence of self in phenomena,
- thusness,[b] and
- the object of observation of purification.[c]

"[The absence of self] in phenomena..." identifies as the thoroughly established nature just that selflessness of phenomena called "thusness" through observation of and meditation on which obstructions are purified.[d] What is the selflessness of phenomena? It is "just the naturelessness [of the imputational nature that is the object of negation in the view of selflessness]."[199] "Just" means "only that."[e]

What sort of nature is nonexistent? With "of only that [imputational] nature," it speaks of the imputational nature mentioned before.[f] "Only" eliminates anything else; therefore, it does not refer to the naturelessness [that is, the absence] of the other two natures [that is, other-powered natures and imputational natures as the Jo-nang-b̄as say][g] but means that the non-existence of the

phenomena that is so.

a It is clear that "imputational character" here refers to the object of negation in selflessness, for example, an object's being established by way of its own character as the referent of a conceptual consciousness. Here, the term does not refer to existent imputational characters, such as uncompounded space.

b *de bzhin nyid, tathatā* (Lamotte, *Saṃdhinirmocana,* 82 [25], n. 32).

c *rnam par dag pa'i dmigs pa, viśuddhālambana.*

d See *Absorption,* #153-167.

e *ngo bo nyid ma mchis pa nyid* **de** *nyid ni de kho na zhes pa'i don no;* see the Text, p. 384. The first *de* is a continuative after an implicit *yin* and is not the first syllable of the word *de nyid.* D̄zong-ka-b̄a is saying that *nyid* in *ma mchis pa nyid* means *de kho na.* He emphasizes that the thoroughly established nature is **only** this absence of the imputational nature, that is, of self, which, in terms of the self of phenomena, is identified here mainly as an object's establishment by way of its own character as the referent of a conceptual consciousness. The mere non-establishment or non-existence of this imputational nature in an other-powered nature is a thoroughly established nature. D̄zong-ka-b̄a makes this point in order to set up his refutation of the Jo-nang-b̄a assertion, which will follow soon. (It should be noticed that, for similar reasons, the thoroughly established nature is not the other-powered nature empty of the imputational nature but the other-powered natures' emptiness itself of the imputational nature.) Jik-may-dam-chö-gya-tso (*Port of Entry,* 233.5) refers to chapter 6 of the *Sūtra Unraveling the Thought,* the "Questions of Guṇākara"; see *Absorption,* #97.

f See ibid., #169.

g S̄hay-rap-gyel-tsen's *Ocean of Definitive Meaning* (11.1) says:

Just that final Buddha, the matrix of One Gone Thus, the ultimate clear light, basic element of [superior] qualities, self-arisen exalted wisdom, great bliss, partless nature of only the imputational factor[a] is taken as the thoroughly established nature.

With respect to what is explained by the previous "just those,"[b] the statement "of **just those** [other-powered natures] which are (1) the objects of activity of conceptuality, (2) the foundations of imputational characters, and (3) those which have the signs of compositional phenomena" indicates that other-powered natures are the bases of emptiness.[c] Then, "non-establishment as the imputational character" very clearly [indicates] that the emptiness of the imputational factor in **just those** [other-powered natures][200] is the thoroughly established nature.

[Refuting The Jo-nang-b̄as' Position][201] (272) {384}

Hence, it is contradictory [for the Jo-nang-b̄as][d] to assert that this sūtra's teaching on the mode of emptiness is of definitive meaning and to assert that the last nature's emptiness of the first two natures is the thoroughly established nature[e] [that is to say, that the thoroughly established nature's emptiness of the imputational and other-powered natures is the thoroughly established nature].[202] Also, with respect to the mode of emptiness, it is not [as in the Jo-nang-

> pervader of all is said to be the basis and source of all phenomena and also is said in reality to be the **basis that is empty of all phenomena**, the void basis, and the basis pure of all defilements.

His *Fourth Council* (Cyrus R. Stearns, *The Buddha from Dol po and His Fourth Council of the Buddhist Doctrine* [Ann Arbor, Mich.: University Microfilms, 1996], 203; also 165, n. 24) says, "Therefore, the ultimate [reality] of all profound *sūtra* and *tantra* which finely present thusness, and so forth, is empty of other, never empty of self-nature."

[a] The imputational nature here is the object of negation in the view of selflessness—the establishment of objects by way of their own character as the referents of conceptual consciousnesses and of words.

[b] *de nyid gong mas.* The reason why the phrase "just those" is called "previous" is that it occurs prior to the passage explained in the preceding paragraph.

[c] D̄zong-ka-b̄a stresses that other-powered natures are the **bases** of emptiness in order to counter S̄hay-rap-gyel-tsen's oft-repeated presentation that the thoroughly established nature is the basis of emptiness in that it is empty of imputational natures and other-powered natures. For instance, the *Ocean of Definitive Meaning* (203.3) says:

> It is necessary to become skilled in the thought of the very many references to the other-empty ultimate, **the basis of emptiness**, with the name great-emptiness (***stong gzhi*** *don dam gzhan stong la stong pa chen po'i ming gi gsungs pa shing tu mang ba rnams kyi dgongs pa la mkhas dgos so*).

[d] Jik-may-dam-chö-gya-tso's *Port of Entry,* 232.2. D̄zong-ka-b̄a most likely bases this opinion on S̄hay-rap-gyel-tsen's presentation of what requires interpretation and what is definitive in his *Ocean of Definitive Meaning,* 173.4ff, where he clearly takes the third wheel of doctrine to be definitive.

[e] See *Reflections on Reality,* chaps. 16 and 17.

b̄as' assertion][a] the negation of something that exists somewhere else, like a place's being empty [or devoid] of a pot. Rather, just as a person is without substantial existence, so other-powered natures are empty of being established as the imputational nature. Therefore, the sūtra speaks of "the thorough non-establishment of just those [other-powered natures][203]...as that imputational character."

With respect to the imputational factor of which [other-powered natures][204] are empty, on both occasions of identifying the imputational factor in the sūtra[b] it does not speak of any other imputational factor than just factors imputed in the manner of entities and attributes. I will explain the reason for this later.[c]

---

[a] Jik-may-dam-chö-gya-tso's *Port of Entry,* 232.2. In this vein, S̄hay-rap-gyel-tsen's *Ocean of Definitive Meaning* (188.3) speaks of the ultimate as being other-empty without being self-empty as in the examples of a horse not existing in a bull and a bull not existing in a horse. Also, his *Fourth Council* says (Stearns, *The Buddha from Dol po,* 215), " Not empty of self-nature, but empty of other, was stated by means of similes such as an empty village and an empty vase." The people of an empty village exist somewhere else, as do water and flowers.

[b] According to Paṇ-chen S̄ö-nam-drak-b̄a (*Garland of Blue Lotuses,* 28a.4) and Jik-may-dam-chö-gya-tso (*Port of Entry,* 232.6), the first occasion is constituted by Buddha's answer to Paramārthasamudgata, when he says:

> Concerning that, what are character-non-natures of phenomena? Those which are imputational characters.
>
> Why? It is thus: Those [imputational characters] are characters posited by names and terminology and do not subsist by way of their own character. Therefore, they are said to be "character-non-natures."

This was discussed in the previous chapter (p. 86). The other is that discussed in this chapter (p. 104):

> That which is posited by names and terminology—with respect to [other-powered natures which are] (1) the objects of activity of conceptuality, (2) the foundations of imputational characters, and (3) those which have the signs of compositional phenomena—in the character of entities [such as, "This is] a form aggregate," or the character of particulars [that is, attributes, such as] "the production of the form aggregate," "the cessation of the form aggregate," "the abandonment and thorough knowledge of the form aggregate" are imputational characters.

However, S̄er-s̄hül (*Notes,* 49b.5) identifies the first as the latter of these two and the second as the similar discussion with respect to true sufferings. It is likely that his reason is that in the earlier passage entity and attributes are not mentioned; nevertheless, I prefer Paṇ-chen S̄ö-nam-drak-b̄a's and Jik-may-dam-chö-gya-tso's identification, since those two passages are not repetitious.

[c] Paṇ-chen S̄ö-nam-drak-b̄a (*Garland of Blue Lotuses,* 28b.2) and Jik-may-dam-chö-gya-tso (*Port of Entry,* 233.2) identify the later explanation as (p. 217):

> Although among imputational factors in general there are many, such as all generally characterized phenomena, space, and so forth, the reason why these are not [explicitly] mentioned in the *Sūtra Unraveling the Thought* is that they are not relevant on the occasion of the imputational factor, the emptiness of which is posited as the thoroughly established nature.

[The Three Natures Of Other Phenomena][205] (273) {384}

[Paramārthasamudgata][206] says that in just the way that [the three natures][207] are applied[a] to the form aggregate, three natures each are applied also with respect to each of the remaining four aggregates, the twelve sense-spheres,[b] the twelve [limbs of] dependent-arising, and the four foods, as well as the six and eighteen constituents.[c] With respect to true sufferings, [Paramārthasamudgata] speaks of the bases of imputation[d] as before, [that is, as the objects of activity of concep-

---

The other type of imputational nature of which phenomena are empty is a difference of entity between subject and object. In chapter 12 (p. 194), Ḏzong-ka-ḇa explains the connection between these two types of objects of negation and their emptiness. At the beginning of that discussion he says:

> In many texts of this [system] there is no explanation of a consciousness conceiving a self of phenomena other than that a consciousness conceiving apprehended-object and apprehending-subject as other substantial entities is a consciousness conceiving a self of phenomena. However, the *Sūtra Unraveling the Thought* explains that other-powered natures are not established by way of their own character as factors imputed in the manner of entity and of attribute and that, therefore, the absence of [such] a nature of character is the selflessness of phenomena. Thus, implicitly it teaches that a consciousness conceiving that factors imputed in the manner of entity and attribute are established by way of their own character in other-powered natures is a consciousness conceiving a self of phenomena.

Concluding that section in the same chapter (p. 217), he says:

> Therefore, it is also not that a negation of an otherness of substantial entity between apprehended-object and apprehending-subject is absent in the statements in the *Sūtra Unraveling the Thought* that the emptiness of imputational factors imputed in the manner of entities and attributes is the thoroughly established nature. [Not only that, but also,] in that sūtra on the occasion of [discussing] calm abiding [in the "Questions of Maitreya Chapter"], a refutation of external objects is clearly set forth.

For discussion of the latter point, see *Reflections on Reality,* chap. 20; and *Absorption,* #52, 53 (for another point, see *Absorption,* #87).

a As Gung-tang (*Difficult Points,* 207.11-207.13) says, Buddha is the one who **applies** the three natures to each phenomenon in his answer to Paramārthasamudgata's question, and Paramārthasamudgata is the one who **says** or reports this back to Buddha to demonstrate his understanding. Thus, the agents of "apply" (*sbyar*) and "say" (*gsungs*) are different, Buddha and Paramārthasamudgata respectively.

b See *Absorption,* #139-152.

c It is intriguing that Paramārthasamudgata uses the standard list of phenomena as presented in the Lesser Vehicle in his layout of the three natures, rather than the list of 108 phenomena gleaned from the Perfection of Wisdom Sūtras.

d A-ku Ḻo-drö-gya-tso (*Precious Lamp,* 137.2) points out that the term "basis of imputation" here refers to the basis of imputation of the imputational nature; as in the case of a person, the basis of imputation of the imputational nature is the person itself. The term here does not refer, as it usually does, to the mental and physical aggregates, for instance, that are

tuality, (2) the foundations of imputational characters, and (3) those which have the signs of compositional phenomena, that is to say, as the other-powered natures themselves]. He says that those that are posited by names and terminology as the entity, "true suffering," and as particulars, "thorough knowledge of true sufferings [as objects to be abandoned],"[208] are imputational factors. Also, [Paramārthasamudgata] speaks of other-powered natures, as before, [to be objects of activity of conceptuality, foundations of an imputational factor, and those which have the signs of compositional phenomena]. Also, the thoroughly established nature is as before; he says that it is "the non-nature of just that [imputational] nature." [Paramārthasamudgata says that] such is also likewise to be applied to the remaining truths [that is, true sources, cessations, and paths].

[Three natures each] are also applied to the seven groups of the [thirty-seven] harmonies with enlightenment. [Paramārthasamudgata] speaks of the basis of imputation as before; the imputational factors are factors imputed in the manner of entity [such as] "right meditative stabilization" and of attributes [such as] their respective discordances, antidotes, and so forth mentioned earlier.[a] He speaks of the other two natures [other-powered and thoroughly established natures] in the same way as he did about those of true sufferings.

[Summary]

These [statements] are Paramārthasamudgata's presentation to the Teacher [Buddha] within a style of positing three characters each with respect to each of [the phenomena] ranging from the form aggregate through the branches of the

---

the basis of imputation of a person.

[a] About the thirty-seven harmonies with enlightenment, the *Sūtra Unraveling the Thought* says:

> The Supramundane Victor also spoke, in many ways, of the own-character of the four mindful establishments, as well as speaking of their classes of discordances, antidotes, production of that which has not been produced, the abiding of that which has been produced, non-loss, their arising again, and increasing and extending. Just as he did with respect to the mindful establishments, so he spoke with respect to the thorough abandonings, the legs of magical manifestation, the faculties, the powers, and the branches of enlightenment. The Supramundane Victor also spoke, in many ways, of the own-character of the eightfold path of Superiors, as well as speaking of their discordances, antidotes, production of that which has not been produced, the abiding of that which has been produced, recollection, their arising again, and increasing and extending.

For D̄zong-ka-b̄a's abridgment of this passage, see p. 77.

path, which were mentioned earlier on the occasion of his question about dispelling contradiction. [The context of Paramārthasamudgata's remarks is that he is saying] "I understand[a] the Teacher's explanation of the three non-natures within thinking of such."

---

[a] *bdag gis go'o;* Text, p. 385; Delhi NG *dkra shis lhun po,* 499.4. D̄zong-ka-b̄a is glossing the term *'tshal* in the sūtra (Lamotte, *Saṃdhinirmocana,* 80-81 [25]): *bcom ldan 'das bcom ldan 'das kyis bka' stsal pa'i don bdag gis 'di ltar* ***'tshal*** *te.* In general, *'tshal* has many meanings, among which is "to understand"; Lamotte (*Saṃdhinirmocana,* 81 [25], n. 11) gives the Sanskrit as *pratyeti* and translates it into French (203) as *comprends.*

4. The Overall Meaning

The presentation of [Paramārthasamudgata's] offering [to Buddha] the meaning established by these [passages][a] has two parts: citing the sūtra and explaining its meaning a little.

Citing The Sūtra (274) {386}

Thus, in [Buddha's] scriptures, there are three sets of sūtras:

- [A first wheel][209] teaching that phenomena exist by way of their own character
- [A middle wheel] teaching that phenomena are not established by way of their own character
- [A final wheel] differentiating well whether phenomena are or are not established by way of their own character

Furthermore, these are twofold—(1) that [final set of sūtras] which does and (2) those [first two sets of sūtras] which do not differentiate well the existence and non-existence of nature [with respect to the three natures].[210] That which does is of definitive meaning since it is not to be interpreted otherwise, and those that do not are of interpretable meaning since they must be interpreted otherwise.

Moreover, since the latter are of two types, it is known through the force of the previous explanation [on the occasion of Paramārthasamudgata's question about dispelling contradiction and of Buddha's answer][211] that two sets of sūtras [that is, the first and middle wheels] require interpretation and one [that is, the final wheel][212] is of definitive meaning. Paramārthasamudgata offers to the Teacher the mode in which just the meaning implicitly abiding [in the question and answer and the presentation of the three natures][213] becomes [a differentiation of] the interpretable and the definitive in connection with the three wheels of doctrine by way of a temporal series.[b] In the *Sūtra Unraveling the Thought*

---

[a] As Jik-may-dam-chö-gya-tso (*Port of Entry,* 286.6) says, these are the passages associated with the three previous sections—the question about dispelling contradiction in the sūtras, the answer dispelling that contradiction, and identifying the entities of the three natures.

[b] Gung-tang specifies what is explicitly indicated in a much more developed way (paraphrasing *Difficult Points,* 232.15):

> Buddha has **explicitly** described the mode of pronouncement in the first and middle wheels as:
>
> - not differentiating from within the three natures what are and are not established by way of their own character, and
> - pronouncing in the first wheel that all phenomena equally are established by way of their own character and in the second wheel that all phenomena are

[Paramārthasamudgata does this by saying to Buddha]:[214]

> Initially, in the area of Varaṇāsi in the Deer Park called "Sage's Propounding,"[a] the Supramundane Victor thoroughly turned a wheel of doctrine for those engaged in the Hearer Vehicle,[b] fantastic[c] and mar-

not established by way of their own character.

Buddha has also explicitly indicated the damage to such positions and has explicitly indicated the thought behind the middle wheel (and hence has implicitly indicated the thought behind the first wheel). Through the force of these points, it is **implicitly** indicated that:

- the first two wheels of doctrine require interpretation,* and there is another definitive wheel of doctrine (for example, the *Sūtra Unraveling the Thought*) that differentiates what is and is not established by way of its own character and is definitive
- since these were set forth in a temporal series, a convention of three wheels of doctrine as well as names and meanings of all three wheels are to be associated with the three types of sūtras.

These latter points are what are implicitly indicated here.

*Over Gung-tang's open objection, this clause cogently is added by Jik-may-dam-chö-gya-tso's *Port of Entry* (280.2) with the justification (281.5-282.5) that even if the means of differentiating what requires interpretation and what is definitive are explicitly and extensively set forth in the question and answer, and so forth, it is not **explicitly** indicated that two types of sūtras require interpretation and that one type is definitive, much as when it is proven that a sound is momentary because of being a product, it is not explicitly proven that a sound is impermanent, even though momentariness is the meaning of impermanence.

Jik-may-dam-chö-gya-tso (*Port of Entry,* 280.3ff.) lists various opinions on what is implicitly indicated:

- Jam-ȳang-shay-b̄a's *Decisive Analysis of the Perfections:* the delimitation of the wheels of doctrine to three
- An unidentified text mentioned in Jam-ȳang-shay-b̄a's *Decisive Analysis of the Perfections:* a question about the final wheel
- J̄ang-ḡya's *Presentation of Tenets:* that there are three categories of sūtras to be explained as requiring interpretation or being definitive
- Gung-tang's *Annotations:* associating the conventions (that is, names) of the three wheels with whether they require interpretation or are definitive
- Gung-tang's *Difficult Points:* (see above minus the additional clause)

a *drang song smra ba, ṛṣivadana* (Étienne Lamotte, *Saṃdhinirmocanasūtra: L'Explication des mystères* (Louvain: Université de Louvain, 1935), 85 [30], n. 3). A-ku L̄o-drö-gya-tso (*Precious Lamp,* 141.5) cites an explanation in the *Great Exposition* (*bye brag bshad mdzod chen mo, mahāvibhāṣa*) that it is called Sage's Propounding because it is a place where Buddha, the supreme of sages, propounded doctrine.

b *nyan thos kyi theg pa la yang dag par zhugs pa, śrāvakayānasaṃprasthita* (Lamotte, *Saṃdhinirmocana,* 85 [30], n. 5). Jik-may-dam-chö-gya-tso (*Port of Entry,* 228.4) explains that "vehicle" here means the scriptural collections of the Hearers, these being the Hearer vehicle as verbalizing words (*rjod byed tshig gi theg pa*).

c *ngo mtshar, āścarya* (Lamotte, *Saṃdhinirmocana,* 86 [30], n. 8).

velous[a] which none—god or human—had previously turned in a similar fashion in the world, through teaching the aspects of the four noble truths.[b] Furthermore, that wheel of doctrine thoroughly turned by the Supramundane Victor is surpassable,[c] affords an occasion [for refutation],[d] requires interpretation,[e] and serves as a basis for controversy.[f]

Based[g] on just the naturelessness of all phenomena and based on just the absence of production, the absence of cessation, quiescence from the start, and naturally passed beyond sorrow, the Supramundane Victor turned a second wheel of doctrine, for those engaged in the Great Vehicle,[h] very fantastic and marvelous, through the aspect of speaking on emptiness.[i] Furthermore, that wheel of doctrine turned by the Supramundane Victor is surpassable, affords an occasion [for refutation], requires interpretation, and serves as a basis for controversy.

However,[j] based on just the naturelessness of phenomena and based on just the absence of production, the absence of cessation, quiescence from the start, and naturally passed beyond sorrow, the Supramundane Victor turned a third wheel of doctrine for those engaged in all vehicles,[k] possessed of good differentiation,[l] fantastic and marvelous.[m] This wheel of doctrine turned by the Supramundane Victor is

---

a *rmad du byung ba, adbhūta* (ibid., 86 [30], n. 9).

b See *Absorption,* #19, 20.

c *bla na mchis pa, sa-uttara* (Lamotte, *Saṃdhinirmocana,* 86 [30], n. 14).

d *skabs mchis pa, sa-avakāśa* (ibid., 86 [30], n. 15).

e *drang ba'i don, neyārtha* (ibid., 86 [30], n. 16).

f *rtsod pa'i bzhi'i gnas, vivādādhikaraṇa* (ibid., 86 [30], n. 17).

g *brtsams, ārabhya* (ibid., 86 [30], n. 18). Gung-tang (*Difficult Points,* 236.10) explains that *brtsams* here means "taking such and such as substrata" (*khyad gzhir bzung ba*), although in other places it means that "the thought comes down to such and such" (*dgongs pa der 'bab pa tsam*).

For the Go-mang tradition of Gung-ru Chö-jung, Jam-ȳang-shay-b̄a, Gung-tang, and A-ku L̄o-drö-gya-tso, the second wheel—taking these as its substrata—teaches on the literal level that all phenomena are not established from their own side.

h *theg pa chen po la yang dag par zhugs pa, mahāyānasaṃprasthita* (Lamotte, *Saṃdhinirmocana,* 86 [30], n. 19).

i *stong pa nyid smos pa'i rnam pas, śūnyatāvādākāreṇa* (ibid., 86 [30], n. 20).

j Jik-may-dam-chö-gya-tso (*Port of Entry,* 294.2) points out the disjunctive function of the Tibetan *lags kyi* that follows the description of the middle wheel but not the first, since both require interpretation; it serves to separate out the third wheel.

k *theg pa thams cad la yang dag par zhugs pa, sarvayānasaṃprasthita* (Lamotte, *Saṃdhinirmocana,* 86 [30], n. 21).

l *legs par rnam par phye ba dang ldan pa, suvibhakta* (ibid., 86 [30], n. 22).

m The *stog* Palace edition of the sūtra (70.4) reads "extremely fantastic and extremely unsurpassable, does not afford an occasion [for refutation], is of definitive meaning,[a] and does not serve as a basis for controversy.

Explaining A Little The Meaning Of That [Passage In The *Sūtra Unraveling the Thought*] (274) {387}

There are two parts: explaining a little the meaning of the words of the sūtra

marvelous" (***ha cang yang** ngo mtshar la/ **ha cang yang** rmad du byung ba*). Gung-tang (*Difficult Points,* 247.1-247.5) rejects similar readings (***shin tu** ngo mtshar rmad du byung ba*) in:

- the *rtag brtan* edition (this most likely being an early-seventeenth-century block-print edition prepared at *rtag brtan phun tshogs gling* Monastery built by the great Jo-nang-b̄a master Tāranātha, who was second only in importance to S̄hay-rap-gyel-tsen to the Jo-nang-b̄a School; the monastery was taken over by the Ge-luk-b̄a order in 1650); and
- in Wonch'uk's commentary. (Although Jik-may-dam-chö-gya-tso, 307.5, reports that Wonch'uk's text does not have this reading, the Peking [5517, vol. 106, chap. 5, 170.1.8] does.)

Gung-tang says that he rejects such readings because they contradict many other editions as well as the *Sūtra Unraveling the Thought* as it is cited in Asaṅga's *Compendium of Ascertainments.* I would add that calling the final wheel of doctrine "*extremely* fantastic and *extremely* marvelous" goes against the basic Ge-luk-b̄a position that even for the Proponents of Mind-Only the middle wheel is the supreme teaching for the Bodhisattvas who are sharper than those for whom the third wheel was specifically taught. This is because these sharp Bodhisattvas can understand the doctrine of the three natures and the three non-natures just from hearing the Perfection of Wisdom Sūtras, and so forth (see Gung-tang's *Difficult Points,* 245.10-247.1). For this reason, the version of sūtra accepted in Ge-luk-b̄a circles speaks **only** of the middle wheel as being "*very* fantastic and marvelous."

In the seventh chapter of the *Sūtra Unraveling the Thought,* Buddha speaks about the various types of sentient beings to whom he teaches doctrine, among whom the supreme are these sharp Bodhisattvas (Lamotte, *Saṃdhinirmocana,* 75 [17], and 199; and Powers, *Wisdom of Buddha,* 115):

> Paramārthasamudgata with respect to this, thinking of just these three types of non-nature, the One Gone Thus, by way of the aspect of setting forth sūtras of interpretable meaning, taught the doctrine [of the middle wheel] in this way, "All phenomena are natureless; all phenomena are unproduced, unceasing, quiescent from the start, and naturally thoroughly passed beyond sorrow." Regarding that, [when] sentient beings who have generated roots of virtue, have purified the obstructions, have ripened their continuums, have great faith, and have accumulated great collections of merit and wisdom hear this doctrine, they understand—**just as it is**—this which I explained with a thought behind it, and they develop faith in that doctrine. They also realize, by means of their exalted wisdom, **the meaning just as it is**. Also, through cultivating their realization they very quickly attain the very final state.

It is said that these sharp Bodhisattvas can realize the meaning of the middle wheel of doctrine—that is, the three natures and three non-natures—without relying on an exposition such as that found in the *Sūtra Unraveling the Thought.*

[a] *nges pa'i don, nītārtha* (Lamotte, *Saṃdhinirmocana,* 86 [30], n. 23).

and explaining a little the mode of the interpretable and the definitive.

Explaining A Little The Meaning Of The Words Of The Sūtra (274) {387}

[The First Wheel] (274) {387}

About this, the **place** where the first wheel was turned is indicated by "in the area of Varaṇāsi in the Deer Park [called] 'Sage's Propounding.'"[a] The **trainees** are indicated by "for those engaged in the Hearer vehicle." "Thoroughly turned a wheel of doctrine, fantastic and marvelous which none—god or human—had turned in a similar fashion in the world, through teaching the aspects of the four noble truths" indicates the **entity** of the wheel. The **subjects of expression** from which it stems are indicated by "through teaching the aspects of the four noble truths." A **praise** of that [wheel][215] is indicated by "fantastic and marvelous which none—god or human—had turned in a similar fashion in the world." That it is **not of definitive meaning** is indicated by "Furthermore, that wheel of doctrine thoroughly turned by the Supramundane Victor is surpassable, affords an occasion [for refutation], requires interpretation, and serves as a basis for controversy."[b]

---

[a] The text (24.12) merely refers to "the first phrase" in this sentence, and "the second phrase" in the next sentence; I have supplied the appropriate material.

[b] Unlike Ḏzong-ka-ḇa's sixfold division of the sūtra passage about the first wheel of doctrine—place, trainees, entity, subjects of expression, praise, and its not being of definitive meaning—Wonch'uk divides a slightly longer passage (beginning with an initial statement, "Then, at that time, the Bodhisattva Paramārthasamudgata also offered this to the Supramundane Victor," and then continuing through what Ḏzong-ka-ḇa cited) into two parts with several subdivisions. Wonch'uk's twofold arrangement (*Great Commentary,* Peking 5517, vol. 106, chap. 5, 164.1.5-169.2.2) with these subdivisions and their corresponding passages in the *Sūtra Unraveling the Thought* (using the version cited just above which differs slightly from the Tibetan translation of Wonch'uk's text) is:

1. Indicating that the [first] wheel of doctrine itself is lofty (*yang dag par*)
    a. Indicating the petitioner and the respondent: "Then, at that time, the Bodhisattva Paramārthasamudgata also offered this to the Supramundane Victor"
    b. Indicating the time when it was spoken: "initially"
    c. Indicating the place where it was spoken: "in the area of Varaṇāsi in the Deer Park [called] 'Sage's Propounding'"
    d. Indicating those for whom it was spoken: "for those engaged in the Hearer vehicle"
    e. Indicating the wheel of doctrine: "thoroughly turned a wheel of doctrine through teaching the aspects of the four noble truths"
2. Indicating that the [first] wheel of doctrine is inferior and not of definitive meaning: "fantastic and marvelous which none—god or human—had turned in a similar fashion in the world [but] that wheel of doctrine thoroughly turned by the Supramundane Victor is surpassable, provides an opportunity [for refutation], is of interpretable

With respect to those, Wonch'uk explains:[a]

1. "Surpassable" means that there is a special doctrine higher than this
2. "Affords an occasion" means that there is an occasion of a doctrine more special than this[b]

meaning, and serves as a basis for controversy"

Dzong-ka-ba not only does not use Wonch'uk's twofold division of the sūtra passage but also (1) eliminates the category of indicating the petitioner and respondent as well as that of time and (2) adds the category of praise. He also changes Wonch'uk's category of "indicating the wheel of doctrine" into two categories, entity and subjects of expression. Dzong-ka-ba does all this without mentioning Wonch'uk. It is only at the point of this final section that he cites Wonch'uk's explanation; his disagreement here is, as will be seen, with Wonch'uk's interpretation of one of four qualities.

a Dzong-ka-ba gives two versions of the four qualities mentioned in the *Sūtra Unraveling the Thought* to describe the first turning of the wheel of doctrine. In the first list, he paraphrases Wonch'uk's explanation (Peking 5517, vol. 106, chap. 5, 169.1.6-169.1.8); in the second list, he gives his own interpretation of the four. Wonch'uk himself says:

> Because this wheel of doctrine holds back [or hides] emptiness and teaches [everything] as just existent, it (1) is of interpretable meaning. Because it fully teaches the causes and effects of cyclic existence and nirvana as well as the selflessness of persons and does not teach the reasoning of the emptiness of phenomena, this teaching of [the first wheel of doctrine] (2) is a teaching that has a special [doctrine] higher than it, (3) is a teaching in relation to which there is occasion for [realization of a doctrine]* more special and is susceptible to destruction by others, and (4) is a source of controversy among the twenty sects [of Hearers].

*This addition is Gung-tang's interpretation of Wonch'uk's meaning; see the next footnote.

Wonch'uk puts first what is mentioned in the sūtra as the third quality of this wheel of doctrine—its being of interpretable meaning. As Gung-tang (*Difficult Points,* 228.13) says, this is because Wonch'uk sees the sūtra's first, second, and fourth qualities as being consequences of the first wheel's being of interpretable meaning.

In the first list of four, Dzong-ka-ba essentially paraphrases Wonch'uk, except that he rearranges Wonch'uk's explanation in accordance with the order of the four points in the sūtra. Then, in his own listing of the four points, he objects only to Wonch'uk's rendering of the second; however, he rewords **all** four points. As Gung-tang (*Difficult Points,* 228.18) says, "Since [Dzong-ka-ba] did not make a refutation of the other three, they accord in **meaning** with his own system." Most likely, Gung-tang is suggesting that even if three of Dzong-ka-ba's list agree with Wonch'uk's in meaning, the phraseology is markedly different.

It seems to me that Dzong-ka-ba also does not accept the meaning of Wonch'uk's rendition of the third quality, unless by "exists" Wonch'uk intends not mere existence but **existence by way of its own character**, since Dzong-ka-ba repeatedly says that the issue is not with existence but with **existence by way of its own character**. Also, Dzong-ka-ba cannot accept the first part of the fourth quality as Wonch'uk presents it, since Dzong-ka-ba considers the first wheel's susceptibility to destruction by others through debate to be the meaning of the second quality. He would not, however, have any substantial quarrel with Wonch'uk's description of the first quality.

b In order to avoid redundancy with the first quality, Gung-tang (*Difficult Points,* 240.6) interprets Wonch'uk's presentation of this quality as meaning that there is an occasion **of**

3. Because it does not teach emptiness and teaches [that everything] exists, it requires interpretation
4. That it has controversy means that it is susceptible to destruction by others[a]

realization of a doctrine more special than this.

[a] In Gung-tang's *Difficult Points* (238.5-240.12), a hypothetical opponent points out that Wonch'uk himself makes "destruction by others" as part of his explanation of the sūtra's second quality, that is, "affords an occasion." According to this hypothetical critic, Dzong-ka-ba has misinterpreted "destruction by others" to be part of the sūtra's fourth quality due to the ambiguity of the Tibetan translation of Wonch'uk's rearrangement of these four into his own list. Speaking about the second and fourth qualities of the first wheel (which, in Dzong-ka-ba's re-ordering of Wonch'uk's passage, are the third and fourth qualities), Wonch'uk (cited in Gung-tang's *Difficult Points,* 238.9; see two footnotes previous for a translation of the complete passage) says:

> *skabs khyad par can yod pa'i bstan pa dang/* ***gzhan dag gis gzhig par bya ba dang/*** *sde pa nyis shu po rtsod par smra ba dag gi gnas su gyur pa yin no//*

The ambiguity revolves around whether the second phrase, "is susceptible to destruction by others" (*gzhan dag gis gzhig par bya ba*) goes with the material before it, "is a teaching in relation to which there is occasion for something more special" (*skabs khyad par can yod pa'i bstan pa*) or after it "is a source of controversy among the twenty sects [of Hearers]" (*sde pa nyis shu po rtsod par smra ba dag gi gnas su gyur pa*). Putting it with the material preceding it, the passage reads:

> (3) is a teaching in relation to which there is occasion for something more special and is susceptible to destruction by others, and (4) is a source of controversy among the twenty sects [of Hearers].

Putting it with the material following it, Dzong-ka-ba takes the passage as saying:

> (3) is a teaching in relation to which there is occasion for something more special, and (4) is susceptible to destruction by others and is a source of controversy among the twenty sects [of Hearers].

Dzong-ka-ba puts the second phrase ("is susceptible to destruction by others") with the material following it, but the hypothetical critic objects that it should be put with the material preceding it, citing as evidence Wonch'uk's later explanation of "does not afford an occasion" with regard to the third wheel, where there is no grammatical ambiguity in the Tibetan. The critic's point is extremely well taken, for, about the third wheel, Wonch'uk (Peking 5517, vol. 106, chap. 5, 170.2.2; cited by Dzong-ka-ba, p. 125) does indeed say:

> Because this is supremely fantastic and there is no other exceeding it, it is unsurpassable. **Because it does not afford an occasion for something more superior later and does not afford an occasion for [later] destruction, it does not afford an occasion.** Because it teaches existence and non-existence completely, it is of definitive meaning, and it is not a source of controversy. (*'di mchog tu rmad du byung zhing de las lhag pa gzhan med pas bla na ma mchis pa dang /* ***phyis mchog tu 'gyur ba'i skabs dang gzhig pa'i skabs med pas skabs ma mchis pa dang*** */ yod med rdzogs par bstan pas nges pa'i don dang / rtsod pa smra ba'i gzhi'i gnas min pa'o//*)

In the middle sentence, Wonch'uk clearly puts "occasion for something more superior later" (*phyis mchog tu 'gyur ba'i skabs*) and "occasion for [later] destruction" (*gzhig pa'i skabs*) together in one negative reason clause, from which it can be determined that this is how the

[through debate][216] and serves as a source of controversy among Hearer sectarians

The meaning of the sūtra [concerning these four points] is:

1. There are other [teachings] of definitive meaning higher than this
2. It affords an occasion[a] for [the assessment of] fault by other disputants when its meaning is asserted in accordance with how it is taught. This is even translated as "susceptible to dispute" in [Paramārtha's] Chinese commentary;[b] hence, the meaning is such [and not as Wonch'uk explains it][217]

---

earlier passage about the first wheel should be read (but, of course, without the negative).

Gung-tang gives an elaborate "defense" of Ḏzong-ka-ḇa's apparent slip with regard to the first wheel. In order to maintain the pretense that Ḏzong-ka-ḇa did not make an error (and in order to indicate his own powers of creative interpretation), Gung-tang makes the claim that in Wonch'uk's text "is susceptible to destruction by others" (*gzhan dag gis gzhig par bya ba* or *gzhan gyis gzhig nus pa*) does indeed go with what follows it, "is a source of controversy among the twenty sects" (*sde pa nyis shu po rtsod...*) and not with the preceding, "is a teaching that has a special [doctrine] higher than it" (*skabs khyad par can yod pa'i bstan pa*), despite the fact that *phyis gzhig pa'i skabs med pa* goes with *skabs med pa.* He does this by analyzing Wonch'uk's meaning of "affording an occasion" as being that there is an occasion **of a higher realization** and thus having nothing to do with external debate. He also thereby has to claim that "does not afford an occasion for destruction" (*gzhig pa'i skabs med pa*), which is undeniably tied to "it does not afford an occasion" (*skabs med pa*), refers not to destruction in debate but to the third wheel's not being discarded upon realizing a higher meaning. However, as Gung-tang himself admits, this brings him into conflict with Ḏzong-ka-ḇa's statement that except for the **former** of the two reasons for "not affording an occasion" his own presentation agrees with Wonch'uk's, for Ḏzong-ka-ḇa explains the **latter** of the two reasons "does not afford an occasion for later destruction" (*gzhig pa'i skabs med pa*) as not affording an occasion for destruction in debate and not as "not being discarded upon realizing a higher meaning" as Gung-tang holds. Gung-tang thereby admits the weakness of his otherwise ingenious defense of Ḏzong-ka-ḇa. The admission can be understood only through realizing that he is self-consciously and humorously operating under the dictum that Ḏzong-ka-ḇa somehow has to be made right even when he is not.

[a] As Jik-may-dam-chö-gya-tso (*Port of Entry,* 290.2) explains, "affords an occasion" (*skabs mchis pa*) means "suitable for the assessment of censure" (*klan ka 'jug rung*) and thus allowing for fallacies through reasonings refuting the extreme of superimposition by opponents such as the Proponents of Mind-Only (*sems tsam sogs rgol bas sgro 'dogs kyi mtha' 'gog pa'i rigs pa dag gis rgol ba'i skyon kyi go skabs yod pa*).

[b] This is the text written by Paramārtha (*yang dag bden pa;* 499-569), called *Commentary on the "Sūtra Unraveling the Words"* (*tshig nges par 'grel ba'i mdo'i 'grel pa*); see Wonch'uk (Peking 5517, vol. 106, chap. 5, 170.2.7, and so forth) for citation of the title. The translation into Tibetan of Paramārtha's explanation, as cited by Wonch'uk (170.3.1 and 170.3.4; see also Jik-may-dam-chö-gya-tso's *Port of Entry,* 290.4), uses the term "susceptible to dispute" (*rgol ba dang bcas pa*) in place of "affords an opportunity" (*skabs mchis pa*). Ḏzong-ka-ḇa's own usage of "affords an opportunity" (*skabs mchis pa*) indicates his preference in terms of the **words**; he agrees, however, that Paramārtha's version communicates the **meaning**, and thus he says, "This is even translated as 'susceptible to dispute' in the Chinese commentary

3. Its meaning must be interpreted otherwise
4. Since the Teacher [Buddha] did not clearly differentiate the status [of what from among the three natures exists by way of its own character and what does not],[218] there is controversy disagreeing about the meaning[a]

[by Paramārtha]; hence, the **meaning** is such [and not as Wonch'uk explains it]."

One might think that by "Chinese commentary" Ḏzong-ka-ḇa is referring to Wonch'uk's commentary, but in all five instances of referring to Wonch'uk's text without giving his name (there being three others when he refers to him by name and one when the text is included within "the commentaries"—see p. 44) he refers to it as the "Chinese **Great** Commentary" (*rgya nag gi 'grel **chen***), and furthermore he has just finished listing Wonch'uk's assertions on these four points; thus I have taken "Chinese commentary" as referring to Paramārtha's commentary. Indeed, Ḏzong-ka-ḇa's reference is extremely cryptic, to be deciphered only by searching for "susceptible to dispute" (*rgol ba dang bcas pa*) in Wonch'uk's text and finding that it occurs only in Wonch'uk's citation of Paramārtha's text. (Wonch'uk repeatedly cites Paramārtha's text—sometimes agreeing with it, sometimes disagreeing, and sometimes not expressing an opinion.) In sum, Ḏzong-ka-ḇa is saying that Wonch'uk should have followed Paramārtha on this point.

Paramārtha's commentary on the *Sūtra Unraveling the Thought* seems not to be extant in Chinese, and also a translation into Tibetan is not found in any Tibetan catalogues (thanks to Paul Hackett for the search). Wonch'uk (for example, Peking 5517, vol. 106, chap. 5, 169.4) also refers to a text called "the master Paramārtha's *Purification of Forgetfulness* (*slob dpon yang dag bden pa'i brjed byang*)—an essay written in order to refresh the memory; this latter text seems to me to be in addition to Paramārtha's commentary on the sūtra and not just another name for it, but I could not confirm my hunch, since it was not found either in Tibetan or in Chinese (thanks to Paul Groner for the latter search). Gung-tang (for example, 241.8) refers to Paramārtha's *Purification of Forgetfulness,* but it may be that his sole source for this is Wonch'uk's citations.

A-ku Ḻo-drö-gya-tso (*Precious Lamp,* 172.5) refers to another text by Paramārtha called *Purification of Forgetfulness* which teaches the views of the different sects.

[a] A-ku Ḻo-drö-gya-tso's explanation of these four (*Precious Lamp,* 153.5) in a way that is applicable to the first two wheels of doctrine is particularly clear since it focuses on the literal reading (*sgras zin*):

1. Due to the mode of teaching the literal reading, there are other sūtras of definitive meaning above it.
2. When asserted in accordance with the literal reading, there are opportunities for the assessment of fault by other disputants.
3. Since the literal reading is not literal (*sgra ji bzhin pa*), it requires interpretation.
4. Since whether the three natures are truly existent is not clarified, there are controversies about the literal reading among followers who assert the literal reading.

The third wheel is the opposite:

1. Due to the mode of teaching the literal reading, there are no other sūtras of definitive meaning above it.
2. When asserted in accordance with the literal reading, there is no opportunity for the assessment of fault by other disputants.
3. Since the literal reading is literal, it is definitive.
4. Since whether the three natures are truly existent is clarified, there are no controversies

[The Second Wheel] (275) {388}

With respect to the second wheel, the **subjects of expression** from which it stems [are indicated by] "Based on just the naturelessness of all phenomena and based on just the absence of production, the absence of cessation, quiescence from the start, and naturally passed beyond sorrow." The **trainees** for whom it was turned [are indicated by] "For those engaged in the Great Vehicle." The meaning of "through the aspect of speaking on emptiness" is explained by one commentary[a] as teaching the selflessness of phenomena.[b]

In the Chinese *Great Commentary* [by Wonch'uk], "in a non-manifest manner"[c] also appears [in his citation of the *Sūtra Unraveling the Thought* instead of "through the aspect of speaking on emptiness."[d] Wonch'uk] explains that it means holding back [or hiding][219] the existent.[e] That translation is good. The meaning is that while the latter two wheels are similar in teaching stemming from naturelessness as the subject of expression, the difference in the mode of teaching is that the middle wheel does not differentiate [clearly][220] what has nature and what does not, as explained before, due to which the sūtra says, "in a non-manifest manner," whereas since the latter wheel differentiates these, the sūtra says, "possessed of good differentiation."

Tripiṭaka[f] Wonch'uk mentions no more than that [the middle wheel][g] is

about the literal reading among followers who assert the literal reading.

[a] Jik-may-dam-chö-gya-tso (*Port of Entry,* 292.2) identifies this as the *Explanation of the "Sūtra Unraveling the Thought"* (*dgongs 'grel rnam bshad*); for a discussion of its author, see appendix 1, p. 453ff.

[b] Gung-tang (*Difficult Points,* 244.2) says that this identification is wrong because "emptiness" here just refers to emptiness of establishment by way of its own character.

[c] Wonch'uk (Peking 5517, vol. 106, chap. 5, 169.2.3): *mi mngon pa'i rnam pas.* Gung-ru Chö-jung's *Garland of White Lotuses* (64b.4) and Jam-ȳang-shay-b̄a's *Great Exposition of the Interpretable and the Definitive* (133.6), when citing Wonch'uk, add *stong pa nyid,* making *stong pa nyid mi mngon pa'i rnam pas;* Wonch'uk's text itself reads: *rang bzhin gyis yongs su myang ngan las 'das pa nyid las brtsams nas 'di ltar mi mngon pa'i rnam pas yang dag pa'i chos kyi 'khor lo bskor ba.*

[d] *stong pa nyid smos pa'i rnam pas.* The *stog* Palace edition of the *Sūtra Unraveling the Thought* (70.1) has still another reading: "through the aspect of elaborations" (*spros pa'i rnam pas*). Jik-may-dam-chö-gya-tso (*Port of Entry,* 292.2) points out that the *ska cog* translation of the *Sūtra Unraveling the Thought* reads "having elaborations" (*spros pa dang bcas pa*).

[e] Wonch'uk (Peking 5517, vol. 106, chap. 5, 169.3.2) explains that the first wheel hides emptiness and teaches existence, whereas the second wheel hides existence and teaches emptiness. D̄zong-ka-b̄a considers the rendering of "in a non-manifest manner" preferable to "through the aspect of speaking," but he does not accept the meaning that Wonch'uk assigns to the expression. D̄zong-ka-b̄a gives his own interpretation two sentences below.

[f] Wonch'uk is called this because of his great knowledge of the three scriptural collections—discipline, sets of discourses, and manifest knowledge.

[g] D̄a-drin-rap-d̄en (*Annotations,* 43.5) adds "the first two wheels," but the topic here is only the middle wheel. Wonch'uk (Peking 5517, vol. 106, chap. 5, 169.5.3) says:

surpassable and so forth in relation to the third wheel. Though he states the explanation[a] by the Indian scholar[b] Paramārtha,[c] it does not appear to be good, and thus I will not write it down. Our own system is as before.[d]

[The Third Wheel] (276) {388}

With respect to the third wheel, the **subjects of expression** from which it stems are similar to those of the middle [wheel]. The **trainees** are those engaged in all vehicles; whereas the former two were those of the Small and Great vehicles individually, this is in terms of both.[e] With respect to its good differentia-

> For those reasons, [the Perfection of Wisdom Sūtras] are very profound, fantastic, and marvelous in relation to the wheel of the four truths but in relation to the third are surpassable, providing an occasion, and of interpretable meaning. Because of being of interpretable meaning, they are controversial.

He then cites Paramārtha (see three footnotes below).

[a] Gung-tang (*Difficult Points,* 229.4) cogently takes the reference here as just to the middle wheel, whereas Jik-may-dam-chö-gya-tso (*Port of Entry,* 293.2) interprets Ḏzong-ka-ḇa as referring to Paramārtha's explanations of all three wheels.

[b] *mkhan po;* this word often means "abbot," but it also refers to someone versed in a topic.

[c] With respect to the middle wheel, Wonch'uk (Peking 5517, vol. 106, chap. 5, 169.5.4) cites Paramārtha's *Purification of Forgetfulness* (*brjed byang*), which says:

> Because this middle wheel teaches a Great Vehicle separate from the Small Vehicle, it is not of definitive meaning. Because there is still one vehicle, it is surpassable. Because it is separate from those of the Small Vehicle, there is quarrel and controversy with those of the Small Vehicle. Because it is destroyed by one vehicle, it is susceptible to dispute.

Wonch'uk does not comment on Paramārtha's presentation. For Gung-tang's speculations on why Paramārtha's presentation is not "good," see *Difficult Points,* 229.4-230.7.

[d] Ḏzong-ka-ḇa's reference is to his own list of the four qualities, given above with respect to the first wheel of doctrine (p. 121). His reference is not to Wonch'uk's explanation—just before his own—of the four qualities in terms of the first wheel, as is evident from the fact that he reworded and criticized it.

[e] Jay-ḏzün Chö-ḡyi-gyel-tsen holds that this means that the intended trainees of the *Sūtra Unraveling the Thought* are both the Lesser Vehicle and the Great Vehicle, and thus it is a sūtra common to the Lesser Vehicle and Great Vehicle. Jam-ȳang-shay-ḇa and so forth hold that the intended trainees of the *Sūtra Unraveling the Thought* are Great Vehicle practitioners who explicitly realize that a presentation of the three natures in terms of the selflessness of phenomena is the thought of the middle wheel and implicitly realize that a presentation of the three natures in terms of the selflessness of persons is the thought of the first wheel, and thus it is a Great Vehicle sūtra. According to this interpretation, an intended trainee of the first wheel of doctrine is able to understand mainly a presentation of the three natures in terms of the selflessness of persons in dependence upon the first wheel—this being what the *Sūtra Unraveling the Thought* means by "those engaged in the Hearer Vehicle." An intended trainee of the middle wheel of doctrine is able—without relying on the final wheel of doc-

tion, it, as explained earlier, presents three characters each with respect to each phenomenon—forms and so forth—and differentiates three modes of non-nature with respect to those.[a]

The usage of the proximate term "this" in "**this** wheel of doctrine turned [by the Supramundane Victor]" refers to the wheel of good differentiation just described—the *Sūtra Unraveling the Thought* and those that make such differentiation. It does not refer to sūtras that, although they were spoken in the final period, do not differentiate between the existence and non-existence of nature in this way. The greatness of this wheel is indicated by "unsurpassable, does not afford an occasion [for refutation], is of definitive meaning, and does not serve as a basis for controversy." Wonch'uk explains:[221]

> Because this is supremely marvelous and there is no other exceeding it, it is unsurpassable. Because it does not afford an occasion for some more superior [realization][222] later and does not afford an occasion for [later][b] destruction, it does not afford an occasion. Because it teaches existence and non-existence completely, it is of definitive meaning, and it is not a source of controversy.

Except for [Wonch'uk's unsuitable explanation of] the former [of the two meanings] of no occasion [that is, "it does not afford an occasion for some more superior (realization) later"], his explanations [of the other three qualities][223]

---

trine—to understand mainly a presentation of the three natures in terms of the selflessness of phenomena that is the thought behind the middle wheel—this being what the *Sūtra Unraveling the Thought* means by "those engaged in the Great Vehicle." See A-ku Lo-drö-gya-tso's *Precious Lamp,* 142.4-143.4; also, 145.2. Dzong-ka-ba seems to support this latter view when he says (p. 201):

> In refuting this, Asaṅga's *Grounds of Bodhisattvas* refutes it also with [Buddhist] scripture, and since it is not suitable to refute Other Schools [Non-Buddhists] with the scriptures of one's own teacher, our own schools also must exist among those who are being refuted, and since the Proponents of Non-Nature or a specific type of Yogic Practitioner are not being refuted, [these have to be Buddhist] Hearer schools. Hence, [on the occasion of refuting this, Asaṅga] does not quote passages from the *Sūtra Unraveling the Thought* but refutes them with three passages established for them.

The last sentence suggests that, for Dzong-ka-ba, the *Sūtra Unraveling the Thought* is not common to the Lesser and Great Vehicles.

[a] See *Absorption,* #73, 72.

[b] Wonch'uk (Peking 5517, vol. 106, chap. 5, 170.2.2) has a second "later" (*phyis*), as is confirmed by Gung-tang's *Difficult Points* (240.14), whereas Dzong-ka-ba omits the second, citing only *phyis mchog tu 'gyur ba'i skabs dang gzhig pa'i skabs med pas.*

Gung-tang cogently says that the type of destruction mentioned here does not refer to being overwhelmed in debate, because there would be no sense in using the temporal reference "later," since if the position were so susceptible, it would always be so; rather, destruction refers to developing higher realization that overwhelms one's earlier realization.

appear to be similar in meaning with the opposite of my earlier explanation of the meaning of surpassable and so forth [with respect to the first wheel (see p. 121) and thus are suitable].[a]

The reason why the literal meaning of the two former sets of sūtras affords an occasion of fault but this does not is that the literal meaning [of the former two sets] must be interpreted otherwise whereas this does not need to be. With respect to involving controversy or not, [that the last wheel does not involve controversy] should be taken as that since these sūtras indicate the existence or non-existence of nature [that is, establishment or non-establishment by way of its own character with respect to the three natures], there is no room for controversy when scholars analyze whether the meaning of those sūtras is or is not delineated that way. However, this does not indicate that there are not other controversies [such as the Proponents of the Middle objecting that even though the meaning of the sūtra definitely is what the Proponents of Mind-Only say it is, the sūtra was spoken with a particular intention, and hence does not represent the final system].[224]

Explaining A Little The Mode Of Interpretability And Definitiveness (278) {389}

[Identifying The Conventions For The Three Wheels Of Doctrine And Positing The Three Wheels As Interpretable Or Definitive][225] (278) {389}

The Chinese *Great Commentary* [by Wonch'uk] designates such a first wheel of doctrine as the wheel of doctrine of the four truths;[b] the second, as the wheel of doctrine of no character,[c] and the third as the wheel of the ultimate, the definitive.[d] However, in accordance with the words of this sūtra itself, the third is to

---

[a] Gung-tang admits that his interpretation of Wonch'uk's explanation of the second part of the second quality (see p. 119, footnotes b and a) makes it not accord in meaning with Ḏzong-ka-ḇa's presentation. Thus, he wonders whether Ḏzong-ka-ḇa is referring merely to the fact that both he and Wonch'uk explain that the third wheel is not susceptible to destruction, even if they disagree on what this means. However, since Ḏzong-ka-ḇa clearly says, "his **explanations** [of the other three qualities] appear to be **similar in meaning**," it is likely that Gung-tang is politely saying that Ḏzong-ka-ḇa erred.

[b] Wonch'uk (Peking 5517, vol. 106, chap. 5, 164.1.5) says, "This indicates the first, the wheel of doctrine of the four truths."

[c] Wonch'uk (ibid., 169.2.3) says, "indicates the second, the wheel of doctrine of no character."

[d] *don dam rnam par nges pa'i 'khor lo,* which could also be translated as "the wheel ascertaining the ultimate." I could not find this designation in the Peking edition of Wonch'uk's text at the point in his discussion of the third wheel that corresponds to where he gives the names of the first two wheels (Peking 5517, vol. 106, chap. 5, 169.5.7). Later in the chapter (175.1.1-175.1.4), Wonch'uk quotes Buddha's name for this teaching, this being "the teaching of the ultimate, the definitive meaning" (*don dam nges pa'i don bstan pa*), but I did not find where he speaks of "the third as the wheel ascertaining the ultimate." See the next

be called "the wheel of good differentiation."[a]

Concerning that, this sūtra's positing [scriptures] as interpretable and definitive is by way of the two, non-differentiation or good differentiation. The bases being posited as interpretable or definitive are the three—the statements [in the first wheel] that phenomena equally[b] have nature in the sense of being established by way of their own character, the statements [in the middle wheel] that phenomena equally do not have such, and the good differentiation [in the final wheel] of those [phenomena] that have [such establishment] and those that do not.[c] That this is so is very clear from:

---

footnote for more discussion of Wonch'uk's source for the name.

[a] Gung-tang (*Difficult Points,* 226.4) says:

> The last [wheel] is designated "the wheel of doctrine of the ultimate, the definitive meaning" in the Chinese *Great Commentary,* but the Foremost Lama [Ḏzong-ka-ḇa] calls it "the wheel of good differentiation." (*tha ma la rgya nag 'grel chen las don dam rnam par nges pa'i chos 'khor zhes btags kyang/ rje bla mas legs par rnam par phye ba'i 'khor lo zhes gsungs so*)

When Ḏzong-ka-ḇa says that the name he uses accords with the "words of the sūtra itself," his reference is to the passage in the *Sūtra Unraveling the Thought* when Buddha, speaking of the third wheel, says, "The Supramundane Victor turned a third wheel of doctrine for those engaged in all vehicles, **possessed of good differentiation**, fantastic and marvelous."

However, as Gung-tang (*Difficult Points,* 226.6) points out, the *Sūtra Unraveling the Thought* itself is also the source for Wonch'uk's calling the third wheel "the wheel of the ultimate, the definitive." Near the end of chapter 7, Paramārthasamudgata questions Buddha about the name of the teaching that Buddha has been giving (see also John C. Powers, *Wisdom of Buddha: Saṁdhinirmocana Sūtra* [Berkeley, Calif.: Dharma, 1995], 145):

> Bodhisattva Paramārthasamudgata said to the Supramundane Victor: "Supramundane Victor, what is the name of this teaching in this form of doctrine, which comments on the thought behind your teachings? In what way should we apprehend this?"
>
> The Supramundane Victor said: "Paramārthasamudgata, this is 'the teaching of the ultimate, the definitive meaning.' This is to be apprehended as 'the teaching of the ultimate, the definitive meaning.'"

Gung-tang speculates that, according to Ḏzong-ka-ḇa, Buddha here gives the particular name of **this chapter of the sūtra** and not the name of the third wheel of doctrine, which, as "the wheel of good differentiation," is more parallel to the names of the other two wheels.

[b] See *Absorption,* #44, 55.

[c] Jam-ȳang-shay-ḇa (33.5) offers another interpretation of this sentence:

> The bases being posited as interpretable or definitive are the three—the statements *equally* [present throughout the sūtras of the first wheel] that phenomena have nature in the sense of being established by way of their own character, the statements *equally* [present throughout the sūtras of the middle wheel] that phenomena do not have such, and the good differentiation [in the final wheel] of those [phenomena] that have [such establishment] and those that do not.

See *Absorption,* 108.

- [Paramārthasamudgata's] question concerning dispelling contradictions in the sūtras
- the answer to that
- [Paramārthasamudgata's] presentation of three natures with respect to each phenomenon and thereupon offering how [Buddha] set forth naturelessness in consideration of that, and
- [Paramārthasamudgata's] offering, in dependence upon those, [a presentation of] the interpretable and the definitive from among the three wheels spoken at earlier and later times.

[Identifying The Scriptures Being Posited As Definitive And Requiring Interpretation][226] (278) {390}

Therefore, the first wheel in which—stemming from the four truths—[Buddha] said, during the first period [of his teaching], that [phenomena] exist by way of their own character and so forth is indicated as requiring interpretation. Such is not indicated with respect to all scriptures spoken during the first period; for example, there is no need here [in the *Sūtra Unraveling the Thought*] to eliminate qualms with respect to [Buddha's] setting forth points of training such as in his statement to the five [ascetics] at Varaṇāsi during the first period, "The lower robe should be worn in a circular fashion."[a]

Likewise, [the explanation that] the second [wheel of the teaching requires interpretation] is also in reference to those that set forth naturelessness and so forth. For, sūtras that, although spoken in the second period, do not stem from naturelessness and so forth do not give rise to qualms as in Paramārthasamudgata's question about dispelling contradictions; hence, there is no need here [in the *Sūtra Unraveling the Thought* for Buddha] to indicate that these require interpretation.

Furthermore, the explanation that the third wheel is of definitive meaning is [in reference to] those of good differentiation as explained before, and not all [doctrines spoken during that period]. This is very clear in the *Sūtra [Unraveling the Thought]* itself. For example,[b] when [Buddha] was about to pass beyond sorrow [that is, die], he said that it would be suitable [to use his earlier declarations] concerning similar [ethical] situations [as a basis for deciding new issues that he had not addressed, this teaching] being called the "condensed discipline,"[c] but [even though that instruction occurred during the final period of his teaching] this *Sūtra [Unraveling the Thought]* does not indicate that it is of definitive meaning.

---

[a] "Circular fashion" means not unevenly.

[b] The bracketed material that clarifies the example is from oral commentary by Ye-s̄hay-tup-d̄en.

[c] *'dul ba mdor bsdus.*

[The Purpose Accomplished Through Dividing The Three Types Of Sūtras Into The Interpretable And The Definitive][227] (279) {390}

Question: What was [Buddha] seeking to accomplish through this *Sūtra [Unraveling the Thought]*[228] by differentiating the interpretable and the definitive from among the wheels of doctrine?

Answer: He was seeking for the trainees of this [sūtra] to overcome taking literally the teaching [in the first two wheels of doctrine][229] that phenomena, without differentiation, are established by way of their own character or are not so established and thereupon to teach them (1) that imputational factors are not established by way of their own character, (2) that the other two natures are established by way of their own character, and (3) that the emptiness which is the emptiness of the imputational factor in other-powered natures is the final ultimate that is the object of observation of the path. Hence, the first two wheels are said to require interpretation, and the final is said to be of definitive meaning.

[Indicating That This Refutes Others' Systems][230] (279) {390}

Therefore, some [earlier Tibetan scholars, specifically the Jo-nang-b̄as,[231] wrongly] establish in dependence upon this *Sūtra [Unraveling the Thought]*[232] that all sūtras spoken during the third period are of definitive meaning and then [mistakenly] assert as literal some [sūtras actually] spoken for the sake of leading those having the lineage of Other [Non-Buddhist] Schools who adhere to the propounding of self.[a] Also, they make the differentiation that except for the real nature,[b] all substrata [that is, all conventional phenomena]—aside from being fancied by a mistaken awareness—do not have entities that are established in the slightest, whereas the real nature is truly established. They assert this differentiation of no true establishment and true establishment to be the meaning of the good differentiation [by the final wheel of doctrine][233] mentioned earlier.

Some others [that is, Bu-d̄ön Rin-chen-drup and so forth][c] refute them,

---

[a] See *Reflections on Reality,* chaps. 16 and 17.

[b] *chos nyid, dharmatā.*

[c] A-ku L̄o-drö-gya-tso's *Precious Lamp,* 169.6, 171.5; and Jik-may-dam-chö-gya-tso's *Port of Entry,* 347.1. Bu-d̄ön Rin-chen-drup (1290-1364) and S̄hay-rap-gyel-tsen (1292-1361) are contemporaries. For discussion of Bu-d̄ön's interpretation of the matrix of One Gone Thus, see David S. Ruegg, *Le Traité du Tathāgatagarbha de Bu-ston rin-chen-grub* (Paris: Publications de l'École Française d'Extrême-Orient, 1973).

A-ku L̄o-drö-gya-tso adds that the main opponent, however, is Yar-drok-b̄a Rin-chen-d̄ok (*yar 'brog pa rin chen tog*); see also Gung-tang's *Difficult Points,* 293.17. Yar-drok-b̄a Rin-chen-d̄ok reverses the final two wheels of doctrine, holding that the Perfection of Wisdom Sūtras are the definitive third wheel and the sūtras of the matrix of One Gone Thus are the second wheel, which requires interpretation.

thinking, "If the differentiation of the interpretable and the definitive were in accordance with this *Sūtra [Unraveling the Thought],*[234] it would be as propounded by the opponent [that is, by the Jo-nang-b̄as,[a] and that would be unsuitable]," and thus they say that this mode of [differentiating] the interpretable and the definitive [as presented in the *Sūtra Unraveling the Thought*][235] is not [to be taken] literally.[b]

It appears that, without analyzing in detail:

- the way in which the question about dispelling contradictions in the sūtras arose [this being with regard to the seemingly contradictory teachings in the first wheel that all phenomena are established by way of their own character and in the middle wheel that all phenomena are not established by way of their own character],[236]
- the way the Teacher answered it [this being to indicate the bases in his thought and how it would be extremist to hold that those two wheels of

---

[a] That is to say, all sūtras spoken in the final period would absurdly be definitive. Ge-luk-b̄a scholars, however, hold that there is a difference between the ten sūtras of the matrix of One Gone Thus and the *Sūtra of the Matrix of One Gone Thus* that Buddha himself cites in the *Descent into Laṅkā Sūtra* as requiring interpretation since it speaks of a fully developed Buddha already present in the continuums of sentient beings. As A-ku L̄o-drö-gya-tso (*Precious Lamp,* 169.1, 170.2) puts it, both the Jo-nang-b̄as and Bu-d̄ön have as the source of their confusion the notion that the matrix of One Gone Thus and the fully developed Buddha-essence—called the permanent, stable matrix of One Gone Thus (*rtag brtan snying po*)—are the same. Thus, for Ge-luk-b̄a scholars, the ten sūtras of the matrix of One Gone Thus do not teach this latter type of Buddha-essence which is taught in a different sūtra that is known in Tibet only through the mention of it in the *Descent into Laṅka Sūtra.* They hold that the ten sūtras are actually sūtras concordant with the middle wheel of doctrine because they teach one final vehicle and they teach that all phenomena are without true establishment. They also assert that the thought of the ten sūtras is Consequentialist and that even Asaṅga's commentary on Maitreya's *Great Vehicle Treatise on the Sublime Continuum* (*theg pa chen po rgyud bla ma'i bstan bcos, mahāyānottaratantraśāstra;* Peking 5525, vol. 108) is Consequentialist, not Mind-Only. For S̄hay-rap-gyel-tsen's radically different interpretation of the sūtra passage that Buddha discusses in the *Descent into Laṅka Sūtra,* see *Reflections on Reality,* chaps. 16 and 17.

[b] Gung-tang (*Difficult Points,* 293.12) cites Ke-drup's *General Presentation of the Tantra Sets*:

> Bu-d̄ön Rin-b̄o-chay [wrongly] asserts that those ten sūtras are sūtras of the final wheel, and, [wrongly] assuming that those sūtras teach as the Jo-nang-b̄as say they do, he asserts that they require interpretation. Taking the Nature Body (*ngo bo nyid sku, svabhāvikakāya*) and the matrix of One Gone To Bliss (*bde gshegs snying po, sugatagarbha*) as being equivalent, he asserts that [the matrix of One Gone To Bliss] does not exist in the continuums of sentient beings. He asserts that only the middle [wheel of Buddha's] word is of definitive meaning.

See also the translation by Ferdinand D. Lessing and Alex Wayman, *Mkhas Grub Rje's Fundamentals of the Buddhist Tantras* (The Hague: Mouton, 1968; reprint, Delhi: Motilal Banarsidass, 1978), 51.1.

doctrine are literal, the first being an extreme of permanence and the second being an extreme of annihilation],[237] and

- the way [teachings] are posited as interpretable and definitive in dependence upon this [that is to say, the division not being made by way of time but being made by way of differentiating or not differentiating among the three natures in terms of which are truly established and which is not],[238]

even both of these [that is, the Jo-nang-b̄as and Bu-d̄ön, and so forth][239] appear to be debating merely [about whether all sūtras that were spoken during the third period are definitive or not, in dependence][240] upon the [summary][241] passage [in the *Sūtra Unraveling the Thought*] that makes the division into what requires interpretation and what is definitive.[a]

[a] From D̄zong-ka-b̄a's viewpoint, both the Jo-nang-b̄as and Bu-d̄ön, and so forth, mistakenly consider the matrix of One Gone Thus and a Buddha's Nature Body to be identical. S̄hay-rap-gyel-tsen holds that even a Buddha's Nature Body exists in the continuums of sentient beings, whereas Bu-d̄ön holds the converse, that is, that even the matrix of One Gone Thus does not exist in the continuums of sentient beings (see the previous footnote). Hence, the Jo-nang-b̄as take all sūtras spoken during the third period to be definitive, whereas Bu-d̄ön and so forth hold that the *Sūtra Unraveling the Thought* is not to be taken literally in its differentiation of what is definitive and what requires interpretation with respect to the three wheels of doctrine. (This depiction needs to be researched.)

EXPLICATIONS OF THE *SŪTRA UNRAVELING THE THOUGHT* ON DIFFERENTIATING THE INTERPRETABLE AND THE DEFINITIVE

5. The Importance of the *Sūtra Unraveling the Thought*

The presentation of exegesis of the meaning of the *Sūtra Unraveling the Thought* on differentiating the interpretable and the definitive (284) {392} has two parts: how the master Asaṅga mainly relied upon the *Sūtra Unraveling the Thought* and how suchness is settled in dependence upon that sūtra.

How The Master Asaṅga Mainly Relied Upon The *Sūtra Unraveling the Thought* (284) {392}

In his *Compendium of Ascertainments* Asaṅga quotes the chapters on the ultimate[a] in the *Sūtra Unraveling the Thought:*[242]

> Furthermore, the ultimate possessing five characteristics[b] should be known in accordance with how it occurs in the *Sūtra Unraveling the Thought.*[c]

---

[a] These are the first four chapters of the sūtra. When Ḏzong-ka-ƀa says that Asaṅga "quotes the chapters," he means just what he says, for, except for the introductory chapter, Asaṅga cites the *Sūtra Unraveling the Thought* in its entirety in his *Compendium of Ascertainments* (Peking 5539, vol. 111, 83.2.6-107.5.1).

[b] Jik-may-dam-chö-gya-tso (*Port of Entry,* 356.5) identifies the five:

1. Inexpressible, because it cannot be expressed exactly as it is by terms and conceptual consciousnesses: taught in chapter 1
2. Non-dual, because there are no dualistic phenomena such as the compounded and the uncompounded in the face of meditative equipoise directly perceiving the ultimate: taught in chapter 1
3. Thoroughly transcending the sphere of argumentation, because of not being an object of direct perception by common beings: taught in chapter 2
4. Thoroughly transcending difference and non-difference, because of not being a different entity from the thing that is empty and not being the same conceptual isolate (that is, not being exactly the same) as the thing that is empty: taught in chapter 3
5. Of one taste in everything, because of being the same taste as the mere elimination of the object of negation in selflessness: taught in chapter 4.

Later (p. 159) Ḏzong-ka-ƀa cites a set of five from Maitreya's *Ornament for the Great Vehicle Sūtras* that differ from these. Ƀel-jor-hlün-drup (*Lamp for the Teaching,* 37.4) mistakenly identifies those as the five mentioned here. S̄er-s̄hül (*Notes,* 22a.3-23b.3), based on Gung-tang, cogently argues that Ƀel-jor-hlün-drup is indeed mistaken, since Asaṅga's *Compendium of Ascertainments* itself identifies them as they are here. (S̄er-s̄hül's argument effectively answers a challenge by Jik-may-dam-chö-gya-tso [*Port of Entry,* 363.6] to Gung-tang's claim that Ƀel-jor-hlün-drup is mistaken.)

Ḏa-drin-rap-ḏen (*Annotations,* 49.3-50.2) gives both versions.

[c] Ḏzong-ka-ƀa is paraphrasing Asaṅga, who, after indicating that the ultimate has five

Also, he quotes the chapters[a] on the characters that teach the three characters:[243]

> The characters of phenomena should be viewed in accordance with what occurs in the *Sūtra Unraveling the Thought.*

Also, he quotes the chapters[b] on non-nature that teach about the question and answer concerning dispelling contradictions in the sūtras, the interpretable and the definitive, and so forth:[244]

> The character of naturelessness in phenomena should be viewed in accordance with what occurs in the *Sūtra Unraveling the Thought.*

Similarly, about the eight collections of consciousness[c] and definiteness with

---

characteristics (inexpressible, non-dual, thoroughly transcending the sphere of argumentation, thoroughly transcending difference and non-difference, and of one taste in everything), says that "The characteristics of inexpressibility and non-duality should be viewed in accordance with the *Sūtra Unraveling the Thought,*" whereupon he cites chapter 1 of the sūtra in toto. Prior to citing chapter 2 (84.2.2), Asaṅga says, "The characteristic of thoroughly transcending the sphere of argumentation should be viewed in accordance with the *Sūtra Unraveling the Thought.*" Prior to citing chapter 3 (84.5.2), he says, "The characteristic of thoroughly transcending difference and non-difference should be viewed in accordance with the *Sūtra Unraveling the Thought.*" Prior to citing chapter 4 (86.1.5), he says, "The characteristic of being of one taste in everything should be viewed in accordance with the *Sūtra Unraveling the Thought.*"

a Dzong-ka-ba speaks of plural chapters (*mtshan nyid gsum ston pa'i mtshan nyid kyi le'u* ***rnams***), but the passage he cites precedes only Asaṅga's citation of chapter 6. A-ku Lo-drö-gya-tso (*Precious Lamp,* 175.6), based on Gung-tang's *Annotations,* suggests that the plural is intended also to include chapter 5 which teaches the character of mind. This seems far-fetched, since "that teach the three characters" (*mtshan nyid gsum ston pa'i*) restrictively modifies "the chapters on the characters" (*mtshan nyid kyi le'u rnams*); however, it does serve to draw chapter 5 into Dzong-ka-ba's discussion, which jumped from the first four chapters to the sixth; still, chapter 5 is not absent, since the teaching on the eight collections of consciousness (which is about to be mentioned) is in chapter 5. Jik-may-dam-chö-gya-tso (*Port of Entry,* 366.4) takes the plural marker here as referring to the *entire* chapter.

Da-drin-rap-den's *Annotations* (50.2), in what is likely a scribal error, misidentifies these as chapters 1 through 4.

b Again Dzong-ka-ba speaks of plural chapters (*ngo bo nyid med pa'i le'u* ***rnams***), but the passage he cites precedes only Asaṅga's citation of chapter 7, the "Questions of Paramārthasamudgata." A-ku Lo-drö-gya-tso (*Precious Lamp,* 175.5), based on Gung-tang's *Annotations,* makes the questionable suggestion that the plural marker also includes chapter 8, since it explains that the teaching of external objects requires interpretation. Jik-may-dam-chö-gya-tso (*Port of Entry,* 366.4) takes the plural marker here as referring to the *entire* chapter.

c The eight sets of consciousnesses are the eye, ear, nose, tongue, body, and mental consciousnesses, as well as the afflicted mentality and mind-basis-of-all. With respect to the next item, "definiteness with respect to final lineages," the reference is to the teaching of lineages of practitioners—as Hearers, Solitary Realizers, and Bodhisattvas. According to the Mind-Only School following Asaṅga, since—among these—some Hearers and Solitary Realizers

respect to final lineages, he also quotes the statements in the *Sūtra Unraveling the Thought.*

Moreover, in the "Chapter on Suchness"[a] in the *Grounds of Bodhisattvas,* its *Ascertainment,*[b] and the *Summary of the Great Vehicle,*[c] Asaṅga settles through many various explanations just the statement in the *Sūtra Unraveling the Thought* that other-powered natures' emptiness of factors imputed in the man-

never proceed on to the Great Vehicle, there are three *final* lineages. Others switch from one path to the other, while still others are in a condition beyond hope of escape from cyclic existence. In this way, there are five lineages of persons and three final lineages of practitioners; see *Reflections on Reality,* chap. 4.

Chapter 5 of the *Sūtra Unraveling the Thought* which treats the character of mind (*sems kyi mtshan nyid, cittalakṣaṇa*) and thus the eight collections of consciousness, is cited in Asaṅga's *Compendium of Ascertainments,* Peking 5539, vol. 111, 87.2.1-88.2.1. The material on three final lineages is found in chapter 7, cited in Asaṅga's *Compendium of Ascertainments,* Peking 5539, vol. 111, 89.2.2-93.4.2. Again, D̄zong-ka-b̄a uses a plural marker (*dgongs 'grel nas gsungs pa* ***rnams***), which A-ku L̄o-drö-gya-tso cogently explains refers to the respective passages within those chapters.

[a] *de kho na'i le'u, tattvārthapaṭala.* This is the fourth chapter of the first section (*gzhi'i rnal 'byor gyi gnas, ādhārayogasthāna*) of Asaṅga's *Grounds of Bodhisattvas,* which is the fifteenth section of his *Grounds of Yogic Practice* (*rnal 'byor spyod pa'i sa, yogācārabhūmi*). For a translation of this chapter into English, see Janice D. Willis, *On Knowing Reality: The Tattvārtha Chapter of Asaṅga's Bodhisattvabhūmi* (New York: Columbia University Press, 1979; reprint, Delhi: Motilal Banarsidass, 1982). As Jik-may-dam-chö-gya-tso (*Port of Entry,* 361.5) points out, D̄zong-ka-b̄a's reference is to the whole fourth chapter. He (369.1) also makes the observation that Asaṅga does not quote the *Sūtra Unraveling the Thought* in the *Grounds of Bodhisattvas.*

[b] *de'i rnam par gtan la dbab pa;* in the Peking catalogue the title is given as *rnal 'byor spyod pa'i sa rnam par gtan la dbab pa bsdu ba.* According to Jik-may-dam-chö-gya-tso (*Port of Entry,* 361), the reference is to the entire exposition—in the *Compendium of Ascertainments*—of the chapter on reality in the *Grounds of Bodhisattvas* (*byang sa'i de kho na nyid kyi le'u'i bsdu ba yongs rdzogs*). He identifies this as beginning with *de kho na'i don rnam par shes par 'dod pas mdor bsdud na* and going through *de ni rnam par mi rtog pa zhes bya 'o.* This is the subsection of Asaṅga's *Compendium of Ascertainments* entitled Ascertainment of the Chapter on the Meaning of Suchness (*de kho na'i don gyi le'u'i rnam par gtan la dbab pa;* Peking 5539, vol. 111, 72.1.6-76.1.5), which explains the three natures. It is part of a larger section entitled Ascertainment of the Grounds of Bodhisattvas (*byang chub sems dpa'i sa'i rnam par gtan la dbab pa;* Peking 5539, vol. 111, 60.2.6-118.5.8), which the Peking lists as the tenth section and the Tokyo *sde dge* (*sems tsam,* vols. 8-9) lists as the fifteenth section of Asaṅga's *Compendium of Ascertainments.* (The material cited in D̄zong-ka-b̄a's chapter 8, on the *Compendium of Ascertainments,* is within this larger section but outside the subsection entitled Ascertainment of the Chapter on the Meaning of Suchness that is the reference here.)

[c] Jik-may-dam-chö-gya-tso (*Port of Entry,* 361.6) refers to chapter 2 of the *Summary* (John P. Keenan, *The Summary of the Great Vehicle by Bodhisattva Asaṅga: Translated from the Chinese of Paramārtha* [Berkeley, Calif.: Numata Center for Buddhist Translation and Research, 1992], 39ff).

ner of entities and attributes is the thoroughly established nature. Furthermore, the essential points of the explanation of the meaning of suchness in Maitreya's *Ornament for the Great Vehicle Sūtras,*[a] *Differentiation of the Middle and the Extremes,*[b] and so forth[c] as well as of the teachings in the commentaries on those[d] are in very great agreement with this sūtra.[e] Therefore, in this [Mind-Only][245] system, delineation of the meaning of this sūtra appears to be the root [of its delineation of suchness].[f]

How Suchness Is Settled In Dependence Upon The *Sūtra Unraveling the Thought* (287) {393}

This section has three parts: a general indication of how the two extremes are abandoned, refutation in particular of the extreme of superimposition, and

---

[a] Chapter 7.

[b] Chapter 3.

[c] The Second Dalai Lama identifies "and so forth" as including Maitreya's *Differentiation of Phenomena and the Final Nature of Phenomena* (*chos dang chos nyid rnam par 'byed pa, dharmadharmatāvibhaṅga;* Peking 5524, vol. 108); Jik-may-dam-chö-gya-tso (*Port of Entry,* 362.2) questions this—presumably because it is considered in Ge-luk-b̄a scholarship to be a text of the Naturelessness School—but he does not suggest what "and so forth" does include. Neither Maitreya's *Great Vehicle Treatise on the Sublime Continuum* nor his *Ornament for Clear Realization* (*abhisamayālaṃkāra, mngon par rtogs pa'i rgyan;* Peking 5184, vol. 88) could be D̄zong-ka-b̄a's referent because he considers the former to evince the view of the Consequence School and the latter to evince the views of mainly the Consequence School and, from time to time, the Autonomy School. Thus, what "and so forth" includes remains a question.

[d] Jik-may-dam-chö-gya-tso (*Port of Entry,* 362.3) specifies these as:

- The commentaries on Asaṅga's *Grounds of Bodhisattvas* by Guṇaprabha (Peking 5545, vol. 112) and Sāgaramegha (Peking 5548, vol. 112)
- The commentaries on Asaṅga's *Summary of the Great Vehicle* by Vasubandhu (Peking 5551, vol. 112) and by Asvabhāva (Peking 5552, vol. 113)
- The commentary on Maitreya's *Ornament for the Great Vehicle Sūtras* by Vasubandhu (Peking 5527, vol. 108) and explanation of that commetnary by Sthiramati (Peking 5531, vols. 108-109) and Asvabhāva (Peking 5530, vol. 108)
- The commentary on Maitreya's *Differentiation of the Middle and the Extremes* by Vasubandhu (Peking 5528, vol. 108) and explanation of that commentary by Sthiramati (Peking 5534, vol. 109)

[e] The order of the treatises mentioned in this paragraph mirror the order of those considered in the seventh through tenth chapters of D̄zong-ka-b̄a's *The Essence* (taking into account that the *Summary of the Great Vehicle* does not have a separate chapter).

[f] D̄ra-d̄i Ge-s̄hay Rin-chen-dön-drup's *Ornament for the Thought,* 47.7. A-ku L̄o-drö-gya-tso's *Precious Lamp* (176.3) cogently comments that it is the *Sūtra Unraveling the Thought,* rather than other sūtras such as the *Descent into Laṅkā,* and so forth, that is the root of this system's delineation of suchness.

how, by means of this, [Buddha's] scriptures are differentiated into the interpretable and the definitive.

General Indication Of How The Two Extremes Are Abandoned (287) {393}

The first has three parts: the explanations (1) in Asaṅga's *Grounds of Bodhisattvas,* (2) in Asaṅga's *Compendium of Ascertainments,* and (3) in texts other than those.

6. Asaṅga's *Grounds of Bodhisattvas*

The explanation of how the two extremes are abandoned in Asaṅga's *Grounds of Bodhisattvas* has two parts: the modes of superimpositional and deprecational views and how those two are refuted.

How Views Superimpose Or Deprecate (287) {393}

Question: Asaṅga's *Grounds of Bodhisattvas* says:[246]

> How does [the ultimate nature of phenomena][a] exist?[b] It exists abandoning both the improper estimation that superimposes what does not exist[c] and the improper estimation that deprecates the real.[d]

In his statement that it exists in the manner of abandoning superimposition and deprecation, what are superimposition and deprecation?

Answer: About those two, Asaṅga's *Grounds of Bodhisattvas* says:[247]

> There are those who adhere [to things] upon superimposing a nonexistent own-character, to the nature of imputational words[e] to the phe-

[a] The bracketed material is taken from the sentence (which Dzong-ka-ba does not cite) in Asaṅga's text following the quote, namely, "the ultimate nature of all phenomena" (*chos thams cad kyi don dam pa'i ngo bo nyid*). The subject of the previous sentence is, similarly, "the nature of all phenomena" (*chos thams cad kyi ngo bo nyid*). Šer-šhül (*Notes,* 23b.4) likewise suggests that the subject is "the mode of existence of phenomena, that is, of other-powered natures and so forth" (*gzhan dbang sogs chos rnams yod tshul*), but A-ku Lo-drö-gya-tso (*Precious Lamp,* 177.1) identifies the subject as "the path of the middle way abandoning the two extremes," which appears to follow Sāgaramegha's commentary (Peking 5548, vol. 112). Strangely, Šer-šhül cites Sāgaramegha's commentary in **apparent** confirmation of his own reading even though he does not mirror that commentary; thus, perhaps he is pointing out a different interpretation. Jik-may-dam-chö-gya-tso (*Port of Entry,* 370.6) gives both interpretations and also (377.2) lists many others.

[b] *yod, vidyate.* Since *vidyate* has the sense of "being found by valid cognition," it is often translated into Tibetan as *yod* ("exist"), but in other places it is translated as *rnyed* ("find"). From the translation-choice here, we can see the translators saw the issue as being not the process by which the essential nature of things is found but the manner of its existence.

[c] According to A-ku Lo-drö-gya-tso's *Precious Lamp* (177.2), such an improper estimation is made by the Proponents of the Great Exposition and the Proponents of Sūtra, and so forth, who have gone too far on the positive side.

[d] According to A-ku Lo-drö-gya-tso's *Precious Lamp* (177.3), such an improper estimation is made by the Autonomists and Consequentialists who have gone too far on the negative side.

[e] *'dogs pa'i tshig, prajñaptivāda.* Since words are sounds and thus are other-powered natures that necessarily do have "own-character," this term is glossed as the nature imputed by words (*tshig gis btags pa'i ngo bo*) by Dra-di Ge-shay Rin-chen-dön-drup (*Ornament for the Thought,* 49.10) and Jik-may-dam-chö-gya-tso (*Port of Entry,* 371.3).

nomena of forms and so forth and to the things of forms and so forth,

This sets forth the mode of superimposition. [With respect to deprecation, the same text continues:]

> and there are those who ruin [the doctrine of the Great Vehicle[248] and the correct delineation of suchness by][249] making deprecation—of [other-powered natures, that is to say,] real things ultimately existing with an inexpressible essence,[a] which serve as the bases of the signs of imputed words, the supports of the signs of imputed words—as "not existing in each and every way."[b] These two are to be known as having thoroughly fallen away from this disciplinary doctrine.[c]

The earlier part of that indicates the mode of deprecation, and the rest about ruination indicates that this is a case of having fallen from the profound doctrine of the Great Vehicle.

"The phenomena of forms and so forth and the things of forms and so forth" indicate the bases of imputing imputational factors. "Nature of imputational words" is to be taken as the nature imputed by words [that is, imputational natures][250] and should not be taken as the words that are the means of imputation;[d] this is clearly explained in Asaṅga's *Compendium of Ascertainments* and so forth. Such also should be known with respect to occurrences on other occasions in the *Grounds of Bodhisattvas.* Conceiving that the nature imputed by words is established by way of its own character, whereas [actually] it does not exist by way of its own character, is a superimposition.

"Bases of the signs of imputational words" is explained [in the citation above] by "supports of the signs of imputational words"; this [refers to other-powered natures which are] the bases of imputation of imputational factors. Conceiving that those [other-powered natures] do not exist in all ways, whereas [actually] they ultimately exist in an inexpressible manner, is a deprecation. In that case, that imputational factors ultimately exist is a superimposition and that the other two natures [that is, other-powered and thoroughly established natures] do not ultimately exist is a deprecation, because the first conventionally exists and the other two ultimately exist.

---

[a] S̄er-s̄hül (*Notes,* 24a.5-26a.2), after listing the interpretations of inexpressibility by the Second Dalai Lama, Jam-ȳang-shay-b̄a, Gung-tang, Tsay-d̄en-hla-ram-b̄a (*tshe brtan lha ram pa*), and unnamed others, gives his own interpretation cogently based on the context of the Chapter on Suchness in Asaṅga's *Grounds of Bodhisattvas,* as well as its commentaries. For him, inexpressibility is an object's not being established by way of its own character as the referent of verbalization, that is to say, of terms and conceptual consciousnesses. Jik-may-dam-chö-gya-tso (*Port of Entry,* 380.5-383.3) lists even more interpretations.

[b] For discussion of this phrase see p. 394, footnote d.

[c] That is to say, doctrine, such as the *Sūtra Unraveling the Thought,* that tames afflictive emotions (A-ku L̄o-drö-gya-tso's *Precious Lamp,* 181).

[d] Words themselves, being sounds, are other-powered natures.

When one draws out the counterpart of [Asaṅga's] explanation that viewing that what ultimately exists does not ultimately exist is a deprecation, then viewing that what does not ultimately exist does exist [ultimately] must be explained as a superimposition. On this occasion [in Asaṅga's *Grounds of Bodhisattvas*][251] it is said that conceiving imputational factors to exist **by way of their own character** is a superimposition, but it is not clearly indicated in words that conceiving imputational factors to exist **ultimately** [is a superimposition].[252] However, it is the meaning of the text that if something exists by way of its own character, it ultimately exists; therefore, this is a position that the ultimate existence of imputational factors goes as a superimposition.[a]

The foundations of imputational characters, those which have the signs of a compositional phenomenon, and the bases of imputation in the manner of entities and attributes [explicitly mentioned][253] in the *Sūtra Unraveling the Thought* refer [mainly][254] to other-powered natures. Hence, it is other-powered natures that are explicitly indicated by the statement in this passage [in Asaṅga's *Grounds of Bodhisattvas*[255] that "conceiving] the supports of the signs of imputational words—as 'not existing in all ways'" [is a deprecation].[256] However, if those [other-powered natures] did not ultimately exist, [their real nature,[257] that is, their] thoroughly established nature also would not ultimately exist, whereby there is no fault in explaining [this passage in Asaṅga's *Grounds of Bodhisattvas* as referring] to both [other-powered and thoroughly established natures].[258] For Asaṅga's *Grounds of Bodhisattvas* says:[259]

> When the mere things [or entities][260] that are the phenomena of forms and so forth are deprecated, suchness does not exist, and imputation [that is, imputational natures][b] also do not exist; [thereby][261] both of those [that is, thoroughly established natures and imputational natures][262] also are not feasible.

The mode of deprecating other-powered things is not [constituted by considering them] "not to exist conventionally" or "not to exist in general" [as the extreme of deprecation is described in the Consequence School];[263] rather, it is in accordance with the earlier explanation [by Asaṅga][c] that [conceiving] the

---

[a] Gung-tang (*Annotations,* as cited in Jik-may-dam-chö-gya-tso's *Port of Entry,* 374.3) cogently speculates that Asaṅga uses the vocabulary of ultimate existence with respect to the extreme of deprecation, since Proponents of Non-Nature themselves frequently speak of the extreme of existing ultimately and the extreme of not existing conventionally. Similarly, he speculates that Asaṅga uses the vocabulary of "own-character" with respect to the extreme of superimposition since, as in the *Sūtra Unraveling the Thought,* imputational natures are said to be natureless in terms of **character** (*mtshan nyid ngo bo nyid med pa*).

[b] Ṣer-ṣhül's *Notes,* 271.3, and Ḍa-drin-rap-ḍen's *Annotations,* 56.5. A-ku Lo-drö-gya-tso (*Precious Lamp,* 183.1) glosses this clause (*'dogs pa yang med do*) as "the bases of imputation and [the words that are] the means of imputing also would not exist."

[c] The reference is to Asaṅga's clear statement in the *Grounds of Bodhisattvas* cited above (p. 141):

ultimately existent not to exist [ultimately] is a deprecation.

How To Refute Views That Superimpose Or Deprecate (288) {396}

Question: If those are the modes of superimposition and deprecation, how are those two abandoned?

Answer: Concerning this, the extreme of superimposition is refuted by the teaching that phenomena are ultimately empty of factors imputed in the manner of entity and attribute. This will be explained in detail later [in chapters 10-11].

Deprecation is refuted through the statement in Asaṅga's *Grounds of Bodhisattvas* quoted just above and by a passage just after it:[264]

> It is thus: [to the Autonomists and Consequentialists who say that all phenomena—the aggregates and so forth—exist conventionally and do not exist ultimately, the Proponents of Mind-Only reply:][265]
>
> > For example, if the aggregates of form and so forth exist [by way of their own character], the person is suitable to be imputed [in dependence upon them],[266] whereas if they did not exist [by way of their own character],[267] then, when the things [that are the basis of imputation][268] are nonexistent, a person is not suitable to be imputed [in dependence upon them].[269] Similarly, if the mere things [that is, the other-powered natures][270] that are the phenomena of forms and so forth exist [by way of their own character, the imputational natures[271] that are imputations of entity and attribute by][272] the words imputing the phenomena of forms and so forth are suitable to be imputed [in dependence upon them],[273] whereas if they do not exist [by way of their own character],[274] there is no imputation when the things [that are the basis of imputation][275] are nonexistent. Concerning that, [there is entailment because][276] if the bases of imputation did not exist [by way of their own character], since the bases are nonexistent, the imputing [words][277] also would be nonexistent.[a]

Here there is no way that those who assert the opponent's position in [Asaṅga's] refutation of deprecation could be from other schools [that is to say, non-Buddhist schools]. Also, within our own schools, among the Hearer

---

There are those who ruin [the doctrine of the Great Vehicle and the correct delineation of suchness by] making deprecation—of [other-powered natures, that is to say,] real things **ultimately existing** with an inexpressible essence, which serve as the bases of the signs of imputed words, the supports of the signs of imputed words—as "not existing in each and every way."

[a] Šer-šhül (*Notes,* 2714) takes this clause (*'dogs pa yang med par 'gyur ro*) to mean "imputational natures would be nonexistent."

schools [that is, the Great Exposition School and the Sūtra School] there are none who assert that the things of forms and so forth, which are the bases of the imputation of conventions by way of names and terminology, do not exist by way of their own character. Therefore, in accordance with the explanation in Asaṅga's *Compendium of Ascertainments,*[a] the opponents are proponents of Great Vehicle tenets. Furthermore, they are the Proponents of Non-Nature who propound that phenomena are not established by way of their own character.[b]

Since the Proponents of Non-Nature do not at all assert that in general other-powered natures and so forth do not occur or do not exist conventionally, they propound that these are not **ultimately** established. Therefore, the refutation "if mere things do not exist"[c] is, as explained earlier, a refutation of the non-occurrence of **ultimately** existent real things.

In this [Mind-Only] system, if imputational factors are not established by way of their own character or do not ultimately exist, they do not have to be nonexistent.[d] However, if the other two natures [that is, other-powered and thoroughly established natures] are not established ultimately or by way of their own character, they do not exist.

Since the production of other-powered natures—[such as] minds and

---

a See p. 149ff.

b S̄er-s̄hül (*Notes,* 27a.5-27b.4) cogently points out that in Asaṅga's *Grounds of Bodhisattvas* and *Compendium of Ascertainments* those who hold a view of deprecation and who are being **explicitly** refuted are just the Consequentialists, who propound that phenomena are not established by way of their own character, and do not include the Autonomists, since their system of tenets propounding that phenomena are not ultimately established arose after these texts. To the objection that the Consequence School was not established (by Chandrakīrti) until after these texts, he answers that, nevertheless, prior to these Mind-Only texts there were many followers of Nāgārjuna who propounded that phenomena are not established by way of their own character. He cogently says that this is the reason why D̄zong-ka-b̄a uses the term "Proponents of Non-Nature who propound that phenomena are not established by way of their own character" (and not "Consequentialists").

Jik-may-dam-chö-gya-tso (*Port of Entry,* 399.4) admits that the same can be said for Autonomists, and thus in general the proponents of the extreme of deprecation here include both Consequentialists and Autonomists. Still, striving to have his cake and eat it too, he says that the *Grounds of Bodhisattvas* takes only the Consequentialists to be the opponents and that through refuting them the Autonomists are perforce refuted.

D̄a-drin-rap-d̄en (*Annotations,* 58.6) holds that the reference is specifically to the Consequentialists and adds that, from the viewpoint of the Mind-Only School, since even the Autonomists assert that phenomena do not truly exist, that is, are not established as their own mode of subsistence, they also abide in an extreme of deprecation.

c As Jik-may-dam-chö-gya-tso (*Port of Entry,* 390.5) points out, these exact words (*dngos po tsam med na*) do not appear in the *Grounds of Bodhisattvas;* thus although D̄zong-ka-b̄a puts the material in quotes, he is paraphrasing.

d Uncompounded space, for instance, is not established by way of its own character and does not ultimately exist but conventionally exists.

mental factors—in dependence upon their own causes and conditions is production established by way of its own character, it becomes ultimately existent production. This [Mind-Only][278] system thinks that if it were otherwise [that is, if production were not established by way of its own character or ultimately], it would be reduced to merely the imputation "production" upon the mind's fancying production, and the things that are minds and mental factors would not have [actual] production.

Therefore, it does not hit the mark [for Consequentialists][a] to answer, "Since the production and cessation of other-powered natures is in the perspective of a mistaken awareness's mere conception of production and cessation, production and cessation exist conventionally, whereby there is no deprecation." For, it is like saying, "A rope is a snake in the perspective of a mistaken consciousness that conceives a rope to be a snake, but in general a rope is never established as a snake." One would be asserting that:

- other-powered causes and effects are causes and effects for a mistaken consciousness that conceives causes and effects to be truly established; but
- other-powered natures themselves [actually] are not established as causes and effects.[b]

Though they assert such, it comes to be that there is no way for them to posit [a presentation of actual][279] actions[c] and their effects, which are such that virtues produce pleasures and ill-deeds produce pain, and hence the Consequentialists are not able to avoid deprecation.

If one asserts causes and effects that are not like this, then these are causes and effects established by way of their own character, due to which they are established as ultimately existent objects. Thinking this, [Asaṅga] explains that, if the bases of imputation did not exist [by way of their own character],[280] imputing also would not exist, whereby both [claims by the Consequentialists] (1) that phenomena are merely imputed [by mistaken consciousnesses][281] and (2) that just this is the meaning of suchness are not possible. Hence, such is the chief of annihilatory views. Asaṅga's *Grounds of Bodhisattvas* says:[282]

---

[a] D̄a-drin-rap-d̄en (*Annotations*, 59.6). It is important to note that these are Consequentialists only as the Proponents of Mind-Only see them, not actual ones, since, according to D̄zong-ka-b̄a, Consequentialists would hold not that production is posited merely in the face of a mistaken awareness but that production is validly established, even if it *appears* to be inherently existent to the valid consciousness that certifies its existence.

A-ku L̄o-drö-gya-tso (*Precious Lamp*, 187.3) identifies the respondents as both Autonomists and Consequentialists.

[b] D̄a-drin-rap-d̄en's *Annotations* (60.3) adds: "Since the Consequentialists do not know how to posit cause and effect that are established by way of their own character and thus posit mere cause and effect for a mistaken consciousness, these cannot function as actual cause and effect."

[c] *las, karma.*

Therefore, some persons [that is, only Consequentialists],[283] who have heard sūtras that are difficult to understand, profound, imbued with the Great Vehicle, endowed with the profound emptiness, and taught with a meaning in [Buddha's] thought [that is other than the literal reading][284] do not know, just as it is, the real meaning that is expounded. This being so, they make improper imputations and, with mere conceptions produced from illogicality upon improper analysis, view and propound, "Whoever view that all these [phenomena][285] are exhausted as mere imputations [by conceptuality][286] and that this is suchness are correctly viewing [the nature of phenomena]."

Since, according to them, even the mere things that are the bases of imputation do not exist [by way of their own character],[287] the imputing[a] [persons, conceptual consciousnesses, and terms][b] themselves also come to be nonexistent in all ways, in which case how could a suchness that is a mere imputation exist! Thereby, through this avenue, they deprecate both suchness and imputed [phenomena].[c] Since through that format they deprecate imputation and suchness, it is said that they are to be known as the chief of those having nihilistic views.

Also:[288]

In consideration of that, [the Supramundane Victor] said,[d] "The view of persons [as substantially existent in the sense of being self-sufficient][289] is preferable; the misapprehension of emptiness is not." The former [that is, those viewing the substantial existence of persons][290] are merely obscured with respect to objects of knowledge; they do not deprecate all objects of knowledge and, through that, are not born in a hell. Moreover, they do not ruin others who want the doctrine, and they do not neglect the points of the trainings. However, the latter are the opposite of those. This is the reason [why the former are preferable].

---

a *'dogs pa, prajñaptiḥ.*

b Jik-may-dam-chö-gya-tso's *Port of Entry,* 393.3. Šer-šhül (*Notes,* 28b.6) takes the reference to be to imputational factors (*kun brtags*).

c *btags pa, prajñaptir.* Jik-may-dam-chö-gya-tso (*Port of Entry,* 393.5) takes the term as referring to all phenomena in the assertion by the Proponents of Non-Nature that all phenomena are (just) imputed. This may be the reason why the translators chose here to change the Tibetan term for *prajñapti* from *'dogs pa* to *btags pa.*

d A-ku Ḻo-drö-gya-tso's *Precious Lamp* (187.5) and Dön-drup-gyel-tsen's *Four Intertwined Commentaries* (117.1) identify the scripture as the *Pile of Jewels Sūtra,* which says:

> Kāshyapa, even a huge mountain (*ri rab, meru*) of viewing [the substantial existence] of persons is preferable; the viewing of emptiness by one with the pride of conceit (*mngon pa'i nga rgyal can*) is not.

Thus, the *Grounds of Bodhisattvas* says that:[a] (289) {400}

- the non-existence of something [that is, the imputational nature][291] in whatsoever [other-powered nature][292] is [the thoroughly established nature which is] the emptiness of that [imputational nature],
- the remainder [that is, the other-powered nature][b] exists [ultimately], and
- one who perceives such is non-erroneously oriented to emptiness.[c]

---

[a] Paraphrasing Peking 5538, vol. 110, 144.5.6-144.5.8; see also Willis, *On Knowing Reality: The Tattvārtha Chapter of Asaṅga's Bodhisattvabhūmi* [New York: Columbia University Press, 1979; reprint, Delhi: Motilal Banarsidass, 1982], 18, 44, and 163; for the Sanskrit, see p. 400, footnote a. For a similar discussion in the context of Maitreya's *Differentiation of the Middle and the Extremes,* see p. 183.

[b] The identification of other-powered natures as the remainder that ultimately exists follows Ḏzong-ka-ḇa's commentary below. A-ku Ḻo-drö-gya-tso (*Precious Lamp,* 188.6) identifies the remainder as both the bases of emptiness (other-powered natures) and emptiness (thoroughly established natures). As Jik-may-dam-chö-gya-tso (*Port of Entry,* 400.3-400.6) points out, the latter type of identification accords with that presented in the first two stanzas of chapter 1 of Maitreya's *Differentiation of the Middle and the Extremes* (see p. 182); he draws the cogent conclusion that it must be said that in the explicit teaching at this point in the *Grounds of Bodhisattvas* nothing other than other-powered natures appears, whereas in general this type of passage in Asaṅga's Five Treatises on the Grounds teaches that thoroughly established natures are also among the remainder. A-ku Ḻo-drö-gya-tso adds that meditative equipoise sees emptiness and that the wisdom of subsequent attainment sees the bases of emptiness and emptiness as truly existent.

Janice D. Willis (*On Knowing Reality,* 18, 168) sees this passage of the *Grounds of Bodhisattvas* as indicating that just emptiness remains. For discussion of the remainder according to Maitreya's *Differentiation of the Middle and the Extremes,* see Gadjin M. Nagao, "What Remains in Śūnyatā? A Yogācāra Interpretation of Emptiness," in *Mahāyāna Buddhist Meditation, Theory and Practice,* ed. Minoru Kiyota (Honolulu: University of Hawaii Press, 1978), 66-82; reprinted in *Mādhyamika and Yogācāra: A Study of Mahāyāna Philosophies,* trans. Leslie S. Kawamura (Albany, N.Y.: State University of New York Press, 1991), 51-60. For an excellent study, see Hugh B. Urban and Paul J. Griffiths, "What Else Remains in Śūnyatā?: An Investigation of Terms for Mental Imagery in the Madhyāntavibhāga-Corpus," *Journal of the International Association of Buddhist Studies* 17, no. 1 (1994): 1-25.

[c] Ḏa-drin-rap-ḏen (62.6) explains this as meaning: The non-existence of the entity of the imputational nature that is the object of negation—establishment of objects by way of their own character as the referents of conceptual consciousnesses—in other-powered natures which are the bases of imputation is the thoroughly established nature that is the emptiness of that. The remainder—the mere things that are the bases of imputation and the imputing [words]—exist. Those who perceive such are non-erroneously oriented with regard to emptiness because they understand a composite of appearance and emptiness that clears away the two extremes.

Ṣhay-rap-gyel-tsen (*Ocean of Definitive Meaning,* 203.3-205.2) cites similar passages from the *Sūtra of the Great Emptiness* and explains them as teaching other-emptiness. He also cites a similar passage from Asaṅga's *Summary of Manifest Knowledge* to establish that Asaṅga sets forth the view of the Great Middle Way. It is safe to assume that Ḏzong-ka-ḇa implicitly is seeking to refute his interpretation.

The emptiness—in the things of forms and so forth—of the entities imputed to them by words is the meaning of the earlier phrase ["the non-existence of something, that is, the imputational nature in whatsoever other-powered natures is the thoroughly established nature which is the emptiness of that imputational nature"]. The remaining [ultimate] existence is the [ultimate] existence of the mere things that are the bases of imputation and the mere imputing [words].

That of which [phenomena] are empty is the imputational factor;[a] the bases that are empty are other-powered natures; the emptiness that is the latter's emptiness of the former is the thoroughly established nature. The meaning of the existence and non-existence of those is as explained before [that is, existing **ultimately** and not existing **ultimately**].

In this way, through abandoning the extreme of superimposition, the extreme of [reified] existence is abandoned, and through abandoning deprecation the extreme of non-existence is abandoned, due to which this is distinguished as non-dualistic, and such an emptiness is described as the final ultimate. Asaṅga's *Grounds of Bodhisattvas* says:[293]

> Those things included within the characteristic of being phenomena released from existence and non-existence—these two being the former thingness [that is, the extreme of superimposition][294] and non-thingness [that is, the extreme of deprecation][295]—are non-dualistic. That which is non-dualistic is called the "unsurpassed middle path that has abandoned the two extremes."

---

[a] Ḏa-drin-rap-ḏen (*Annotations,* 63.4) qualifies this as the imputational factor **that is the object of negation** since phenomena are not empty, for instance, of the imputational factor that is their being referents of their respective conceptual consciousness; rather, phenomena are empty of the imputational factor that is their being established **by way of their own character** as the referents of their respective conceptual consciousnesses.

7. Asaṅga's *Compendium of Ascertainments*

The explanation of how the two extremes are abandoned in Asaṅga's *Compendium of Ascertainments*[a] has two parts: (1) stating the opponent's position along with our questions and the opponent's answers about its meaning and (2) refuting the positions of the answers given.

Stating The Opponent's Position Along With Our Questions And The Opponent's Answers About Its Meaning (291) {402}

Asaṅga's *Compendium of Ascertainments* says:[296]

> Some of the Great Vehicle [that is, Proponents of Non-Nature],[b] due to their own misconception [of the Perfection of Wisdom Sūtras as being literally acceptable],[c] say, "Conventionally all exist; ultimately all do not exist."

The Proponents of the Middle speak of a differentiation of the existence and non-existence of phenomena by propounding that "All phenomena do not ultimately exist, but conventionally exist."

Then, the *Compendium of Ascertainments* says:[297]

> Those [Proponents of Non-Nature][298] are to be asked, "Venerable Ones, what is the ultimate (*don dam, paramārtha*) [truth]?[299] What is the concealer (*kun rdzob, saṃvṛti*) [in the face of which conventional phenomena are posited as true,[300] that is to say, as concordant in how they appear and how they exist]?"
>
> When asked this, [the Proponents of Non-Nature][301] answer, "That which is the naturelessness [that is, absence of ultimate existence][302] of all phenomena is the ultimate [truth].[303] That which observes [and apprehends][304] those phenomena—which are without the

---

a Ḏzong-ka-ḇa usually refers to the text as "the *Compendium*" (*bsdu ba, saṃgrahaṇī*).

b A-ku Ḻo-drö-gya-tso's *Precious Lamp,* 191.3. Jik-may-dam-chö-gya-tso (*Port of Entry,* 404.4) identifies the opponents as the Consequentialists and points out that the epithet "some of the Great Vehicle" (*theg pa chen po la la*) indicates that this text, like Asaṅga's *Grounds of Bodhisattvas,* does not deny that Consequentialists are proponents of Great Vehicle tenets but still holds them to be the chief of annihilationists, much as Consequentialists assert that Autonomists have fallen to extremes and yet are Proponents of the Middle.

c A-ku Ḻo-drö-gya-tso (*Precious Lamp,* 191.3) gives this gloss, whereas Ḏa-drin-rap-ḏen (*Annotations,* 64.3) refers to the "explicit teaching" (*dngos bstan*) as not being literally acceptable. The latter does not seem to be sufficient, since, according to many Ge-luk-ḇa interpretations, the Proponents of Mind-Only hold that the **explicit teaching** of the Perfection of Wisdom Sūtras does not require interpretation and that only the **literal reading** (*sgras zin*) does.

nature [of true establishment][305]—as having such a nature is the concealer [that is, the concealing consciousness].[306] Why? Because it conceals [the reality of] what do not [truly][307] exist [through misconceiving them to truly exist], imputes [true existence], verbalizes [or conceives true existence again and again], and makes designations [of true existence in speech]."

The answer that [the Proponents of Non-Nature] give, upon being asked what the two truths[a] are, is treated [in Asaṅga's *Compendium of Ascertainments*] as the opponent's position.

Concerning that, the question here about what the ultimate is concerns an illustration of ultimate truth and not that nonexistent nature[b] due to their nonexistence as which [objects] are said not to exist ultimately. Otherwise, it would not be reasonable [for the Proponents of Non-Nature] to profess [in answer to the above question][308] that the naturelessness of phenomena is the ultimate because the Proponents of the Middle do not posit something as existing ultimately due to existing as the selflessness of phenomena which they assert to be the ultimate.

Also, the question about what the concealer (*kun rdzob, saṃvṛti*) is concerns the concealer [that is, ignorance], in "truths-for-a-concealer" (*kun rdzob bden pa, saṃvṛtisatya*), in the face of which [phenomena other than emptinesses] are posited as truths [in the sense that ignorance mistakenly takes them to exist the way they appear] and is not a question concerning the conventionality [that is, conventional consciousness] in the face of which [phenomena are said] to exist conventionally. Otherwise, it would not be reasonable [for the Proponents of the Middle] to propound [in answer to the above question][309] that [a consciousness] apprehending what are natureless as having nature is the concealer (*kun rdzob, saṃvṛti*). For, since [such a consciousness] is one conceiving true establishment, Proponents of the Middle assert that its conceived object does not exist even conventionally. This is because the nonexistent nature in "naturelessness" must be taken as a truly established entity.

Refuting The Positions Of The Answers Given (292) {403}

This section has two parts: indicating contradictions in others' tenets [namely,

[a] A-ku Lo-drö-gya-tso (*Precious Lamp,* 191.4 and 192.3) treats the first part of the question (the part about the ultimate) as concerning the ultimate truth but takes the second part to be about the concealing consciousness in the face of which objects are (wrongly) posited as being true, that is to say, as having a concordance between how they appear and how they actually exist. Dzong-ka-ba himself gives this interpretation in the next two paragraphs, and thus when he speaks here of the two truths, it seems that he does not mean that the questioner is asking for an illustration of conventional truths but is asking something **concerning** conventional truths.

[b] Da-drin-rap-den (65.5) glosses *med sa* with *med rgyu'i ngo bor.*

in the system of the Proponents of Non-Nature] and dispelling contradictions in our own tenets [that is, in the system of the Proponents of Cognition].

Demonstrating Contradictions In Others' Tenets (292) {403}

[Refuting The Identification Of The Concealer By The Proponents Of Non-Nature][310] (292) {403}

About this, initially, in Asaṅga's *Compendium of Ascertainments,* the refutation of the identification of the concealer (*kun rdzob, saṃvṛti*) [put forth by the Proponents of Non-Nature] is:[311]

> To those [Proponents of Non-Nature] we say this: Do you assert [the concealing consciousness][312] observing [and apprehending][313] the nature [of true establishment whereas there is no such nature][314] to arise from verbal and conventional causes [that is to say, causes which are of its own similar type],[315] or is it asserted to be mere verbalization and convention? If it arises from verbal and conventional causes, then since [that consciousness conceiving true existence][316] arises from verbal and conventional causes, it is not suitable to say that [this consciousness conceiving true existence][317] does not [ultimately][318] exist.
>
> If [this consciousness conceiving true existence][319] is verbal and conventional, [then it must be only imputed by conceptuality, whereby other-powered natures would be only imputed by conceptuality. In that case, other-powered natures would be nonexistent, and therefore][320] being without a basis [of imputation],[321] it is not suitable to call [that conceptual consciousness][322] verbal and conventional [that is, it would not be suitable to say that a consciousness conceiving true existence is only imputedly existent].[323]

The meaning of this is: The concealing [consciousness] (*kun rdzob, saṃvṛti*) apprehending that [phenomena] ultimately have nature, whereas they [actually] do not, is also [itself a factor of] internal verbalization. In that case, is it produced by causes that are of its own earlier, similar type, or is it merely imputed by conventional and verbal conceptuality?[a] If it is produced by causes that are of its own earlier, similar type, then, since it is produced by causes, "it is not suitable to say that it does not exist," that is, that it does not **ultimately** exist. [The reference here is to **ultimate** existence] because this is an occasion of debating about ultimately existing or not ultimately existing and because the opponent [that is, the Proponent of Non-Nature][324] asserts that [other-powered natures][325] do not **ultimately** exist and does not propound that they do not exist in general.

[a] According to A-ku Ḻo-drö-gya-tso (*Precious Lamp,* 192.6), the latter part of the question means, "or is verbalization [that is, a consciousness conceiving true existence] merely imputed by convention and conceptuality?"

If [you say that the concealing consciousness is merely imputed by conceptuality], then [it is answered that] it is not suitable to be just imputed by conceptuality because [its][326] bases of imputation [that is, other-powered natures][327] do not exist, since if conventionalities and verbalizations [like these][328] are only imputed by conceptuality, then others also will only be such [in which case other-powered natures will be nonexistent].[329]

[Refuting The Identification Of The Ultimate By The Proponents Of Non-Nature][330] (292) {404}

With respect to refuting the identification of ultimate [truth by the Proponents of Non-Nature], the same text says:[331]

> We also say [to those Proponents of Non-Nature], "Venerable Ones, why [do you claim that] those [things][332] that are observed [by valid cognition to be established by way of their own character][333] are not existent [by way of their own character]?"[a]
>
> When this is asked, [the Proponents of Non-Nature][334] answer, "[That there is a consciousness conceiving that objects are established by way of their own character does not damage[b] our assertion that objects are not established by way of their own character][335] because [such a consciousness] is an erroneous thing [that is, a wrong consciousness]."[336]
>
> About that, we ask: "Is that erroneous [consciousness][337] asserted to exist [by way of its own character],[338] or is it asserted not to exist [by way of its own character]? If it exists [by way of its own character],[339] then it is not suitable [for you][340] to say that the non-nature [that is, the absence of ultimate existence] of **all** phenomena is the ultimate [since this erroneous consciousness would exist by way of its own character and hence would exist ultimately].[341] If it does not exist [by way of its own character],[342] then [since it would not exist at all][343] it is not suitable [for you] to say that because [this consciousness][344] is an erroneous thing, what is observed [by it][345] is natureless."

The meaning of that is:

---

[a] Ḏa-drin-rap-ḏen's *Annotations,* 68.3-4. A-ku L̄o-drö-gya-tso (*Precious Lamp,* 193.3) renders the meaning as, "While phenomena are observed by valid cognition to be truly established, how could it be right that they do not truly exist?"

[b] The Tibetan word is *gnod pa* (Sanskrit, *bādhā*) which literally means "damage" and "harm." I use this translation-equivalent because, although by extension the term means "refute" or "contradict," I often find Sanskrit and Tibetan philosophical terminology to be far richer in its literal meaning than in its rerendering into what some English-speaking scholars have identified as its philosophical meaning. Much of the psychological punch (pun intended) is lost in such translations.

> [The Proponent of the Mind-Only School says to the Proponent of Non-Nature:][346] While these phenomena are observed to have an own-character, that is to say, establishment by way of their own character, how could it be reasonable to say that [establishment of objects by way of their own character] does not exist? For, this [proposition] is damaged by valid cognition observing such [establishment of objects by way of their own character].
>
> *Objection* [by the Proponent of Non-Nature:[347] Our assertion that phenomena are not established by way of their own character] is not damaged by an awareness observing such because that awareness is a mistaken thing.
>
> *Answer* [by the Proponent of the Mind-Only School]:[348] Then, if that mistaken [awareness] exists by way of its own character, [since it would ultimately have nature,][349] the naturelessness [of **all** phenomena] would not be suitable [to be propounded][350] as the ultimate [truth]. If [this awareness][351] does not exist [by way of its own character],[352] then [since it would be utterly nonexistent] it is not feasible to say that because [this awareness][353] is mistaken, there is no [fault in holding that such establishment does not exist] even though [establishment of objects by way of their own character] is observed [by it].[354]

Here [in Asaṅga's *Compendium of Ascertainments*][a] the analysis also should be done in terms of ultimately existing or not ultimately existing [as it was in the *Grounds of Bodhisattvas,* which is the root text for the *Compendium of Ascertainments*]; however, the import [of (1) analyzing the ultimate and the concealer and (2) analyzing ultimately existing and not ultimately existing] is similar, and the former analysis [in the *Grounds of Bodhisattvas*] is easier to understand. Therefore, it has been explained that way.

[Reason For Not Demonstrating Fallacies With Respect To Imputational Natures And Thoroughly Established Natures Not Ultimately Existing But Demonstrating Fallacies With Respect To Other-Powered Natures Not Ultimately Existing][355] {404}

Thus, here [in the *Compendium of Ascertainments*[356] Asaṅga] does not address the fallacies of [the assertion by the Proponents of Non-Nature that] the two,

---

[a] The bracketed material in this paragraph is drawn from Jik-may-dam-chö-gya-tso's *Port of Entry,* 408.3-408.5. S̄er-s̄hül L̄o-sang-pün-tsok's interpretation (*Notes,* 28b.6-29a.3) is markedly different; according to him, D̄zong-ka-b̄a's concern is with his own switching back and forth between the vocabulary of ultimate existence and existence by way of an object's own character; in his view D̄zong-ka-b̄a wants to make clear that these two are equivalent. Jik-may-dam-chö-gya-tso (*Port of Entry,* 420.5) refutes an assertion similar to L̄o-sang-pün-tsok's by indicating that the referent of "here" in this and in the next paragraph must be to the same text, the *Compendium of Ascertainments.*

imputational natures and thoroughly established natures, do not exist ultimately and exist conventionally; rather, he demonstrates fallacies upon analyzing whether concealing consciousnesses and mistaken consciousnesses ultimately exist or not. This is a refutation of [the position of the Proponents of Non-Nature that] other-powered natures do not ultimately exist but exist conventionally, for since just these [consciousnesses[357] which, being impermanent, are necessarily other-powered natures] are the subjects possessing the quality of the thoroughly established nature and are the imputers, as well as bases of imputation of imputational factors, scholars mainly debate about whether just these ultimately exist or not.

[Indicating That The Explanation Of The Abandonment Of The Two Extremes In The *Compendium Of Ascertainments* Has The Same Essentials As That In The *Grounds Of Bodhisattvas*][358] (293) {405}

Furthermore, Asaṅga's *Compendium of Ascertainments* says:[359]

> It should be known that adherence to other-powered natures and thoroughly established natures as imputational natures is an extreme of superimposition.

Also:[360]

> The extreme of deprecation is deprecation of own-character [by holding] that other-powered natures and thoroughly established natures do not exist [by way of their own character],[361] whereas they [actually] do. One should understand thoroughly the mode of the meaning of suchness in the manner of abandoning those two extremes.

[Asaṅga] speaks of the deprecation of own-character in which [it is held] that the last two natures [that is, other-powered and thoroughly established natures] are not established as existing by way of their own character, whereas they [actually] are. The *Grounds of Bodhisattvas* and this [*Compendium of Ascertainments*][362] have the same way [of positing][363] the extremes of superimposition and deprecation and [the emptiness which is][364] the abandonment of them.

[That Imputational Natures Do Not Exist Is Not This System][365] (293) {405}

Furthermore, the non-existence of imputational factors is so ultimately; it is not that [in general imputational natures][366] do not exist in conventional terms.[a]

[a] *tha snyad du med pa.* Imputational natures such as uncompounded space exist even though the imputational nature that is the object of negation in the view of selflessness does not exist at all. It is a rule of Tibetan interpretations of the Epistemologists (*tshad ma pa*) that since **some** imputational natures exist, the category of imputational natures exists. The category is expressed in Tibetan in the singular—imputational nature—and thus it is said that in general imputational nature exists.

Asaṅga's *Compendium of Ascertainments* says:[367]

> *Question:* Is it to be said that what is posited by way of whatsoever names and whatsoever verbalizations [that is, conceptual consciousnesses[a] to] those [other-powered things such as][368] clear realizations[b] is the entity of those? Or is it to be said that it is not the entity of those?
>
> *Answer:* It is to be said that it is the entity of those conventionally. It is to be said that it is not the entity of those ultimately.

Also, Asaṅga[369] speaks of "that imputational nature which becomes an object of observation by a consciousness [that is produced][370] in dependence upon names

---

[a] As Jik-may-dam-chö-gya-tso (*Port of Entry,* 410.5) says, what is posited by terms and conceptual consciousnesses is that other-powered natures are foundations of reference by terms and conceptual consciousnesses.

According to A-ku Lo-drö-gya-tso (*Precious Lamp,* 194.3), the question is: Are other-powered natures established or not in accordance with how they appear to consciousnesses of terms conceptual consciousnesses? Also, he does not emend "conceptual consciousnesses" (*mngon par* ***rtog*** *pa*) to "clear realizations" (*mngon par* ***rtogs*** *pa*). Thus, to follow him, the translation of the passage should read:

> Is it to be said that those [other-powered things such as] conceptual consciousnesses which are posited by way of whatsoever names and whatsoever verbalizations [that is, conceptual consciousnesses] are entities of those [that is, do they exist the way they appear]? Or is it to be said that they are not entities of those [that is, do they not exist the way they appear]?

Da-drin-rap-den (*Annotations,* 71.4) identifies conceptual consciousnesses as conceptual consciousnesses that associate name and meaning (*ming don 'brel ba'i rtog pa*). His seemingly forced interpretation—adding "to" (*la*)—makes more sense out of the quotation, since Dzong-ka-ba cites the passage to show that imputational natures exist, and thus I have used Da-drin-rap-den's annotation here.

In A-ku Lo-drö-gya-tso's interpretation, the same point is made, in that if forms are conventionally established by way of their own character as the referents of conceptual consciousnesses, then their being such and the appearance of such exists. The meaning of the passage is, in his interpretation, that forms' appearing to be the referents of conceptual consciousnesses is due to predispositions of verbalization and does not subsist in the object by way of its own character.

As Da-drin-rap-den (71.5) says:

> By way of its own nature, without depending on name and conceptuality, form is not established (1) as the form that is the referent of the term "form" or (2) as the basis [of reference] of the term "form" and as the basis of adherence by a conceptual consciousness [apprehending form]. However, it is permissible that it is a basis of those in dependence upon name and conceptuality.

All of these interpretations are basically saying the same thing.

[b] *mngon par rtogs pa.* Jik-may-dam-chö-gya-tso (*Port of Entry,* 410.3) identifies these as the six—contemplation, faith, ethics, true knowledge of clear realization, true knowledge arisen from the finality of clear realization, and final clear realization—and thus as the path, which is an illustration of other-powered natures.

[due to the force of][371] being thoroughly accustomed to verbalization," and then he says,[372] "because it is imputedly existent, not ultimately existent."

Therefore, [since among imputational natures there are some, such as uncompounded space or being a referent of a conceptual consciousness, that exist and others that do not exist],[373] although imputational factors, such as the two selves [of persons and of phenomena],[374] do not occur among objects of knowledge [that is, do not exist], this mere fact does not make **all** imputational factors into not occurring [among existents]. Hence, substantial existence and ultimate existence are refuted [with respect to imputational natures],[375] but [imputational natures in general or, more specifically, existent imputational natures] are posited as imputedly existent and conventionally existent.

For that reason, the explanation in a certain *Great Commentary* on the *Sūtra Unraveling the Thought* (293) {406} is not the thought of that sūtra when this commentary says:[a]

> Imputational factors do not exist as either of the two truths [ultimate or conventional].[376] The dependent-arisings of other-powered natures of apprehended-objects and apprehending-subjects [which are different substantial entities][377] exist conventionally [and do not exist ultimately],[378] like magical creations. The thoroughly established nature is the ultimate, and its existence in the manner of naturelessness also ultimately exists.

[This is not the thought of the *Sūtra Unraveling the Thought,* because] it contradicts the proof of no external objects in Asaṅga's *Summary of the Great Vehicle*[b]—that is made within citing the *Sūtra Unraveling the Thought*—and there-

[a] A-ku Lo-drö-gya-tso cogently holds that Dzong-ka-ba could not be referring to the very short, ten-page commentary on the *Sūtra Unraveling the Thought* falsely attributed to Asaṅga, even though Dzong-ka-ba mentions a commentary by Asaṅga at the end of this paragraph. Indeed, since Dzong-ka-ba is speaking about a **great** commentary on the sūtra, he could not be referring to the very short one entitled *āryasaṃdhinirmocanabhāṣya* (*'phags pa dgongs pa nges par 'grel pa'i rnam par bshad pa;* Peking 5481, vol. 104, 1.1.1-7.5.1), even though the latter is listed by Bu-dön in his history as by Asaṅga. For that attribution see E. Obermiller, *History of Buddhism (Chos-ḥbyung) by Bu-ston* (Heidelberg: Heft, 1932; Tokyo: Suzuki Research Foundation, n.d.), 140. It is likely that Dzong-ka-ba either did not or would not put any stock in the attribution to Asaṅga since, at the end of this paragraph, he draws the conclusion that "there also does not appear to be any need for this master's [that is, Asaṅga's] composing a separate commentary."

For Jik-may-dam-chö-gya-tso's attempt (*Port of Entry,* 413.4) to pin down Dzong-ka-ba's reference, see appendix 1, p. 453ff.

[b] For the specific references from chapters 2 and 3 of Asaṅga's *Summary of the Great Vehicle* (John P. Keenan, *The Summary of the Great Vehicle by Bodhisattva Asaṅga: Translated from the Chinese of Paramārtha* [Berkeley, Calif.: Numata Center for Buddhist Translation and Research, 1992], 39ff), where the "Questions of Maitreya Chapter" of the *Sūtra Unraveling the Thought* is cited, see *Reflections on Reality,* chap. 20.

upon the explanation of external and internal objects and subjects [which are different substantial entities][379] as imputational factors. It also contradicts Asaṅga's *Grounds of Bodhisattvas*[a] and his *Compendium of Ascertainments*.[b] Furthermore, a passage of [Dharmakīrti's] *Ascertainment [of Prime Cognition]*[380] is cited in that [above-mentioned *Great Commentary*].[381] Hence, one [scholar's][c] saying that it was written by Asaṅga is a case of a great absence of analysis.[d] In his *Compendium of Ascertainments* Asaṅga quotes, except for the introductory chapter[e] of the *Sūtra Unraveling the Thought*,[f] most of the remaining chapters and settles well the difficult points; hence, there also does not appear to be any need for this master's [that is, Asaṅga's] composing a separate commentary.

[It Is Not This System That Imputational Natures Do Not Conventionally Exist And Other-Powered Natures Do Not Ultimately Exist][382] (294) {406}

Furthermore, one later [scholar] explains that it is the thought of Asaṅga and his brother [Vasubandhu] that:[g]

---

[a] Jik-may-dam-chö-gya-tso (*Port of Entry*, 412.5) identifies the passage, cited by Dzong-ka-ba (p. 142), as:

> When the mere things [or entities] that are the phenomena of forms and so forth are deprecated, suchness does not exist, and imputation [that is, imputational natures] also do not exist; [thereby] both of those [that is, thoroughly established natures and imputational natures] are also not feasible.

[b] Jik-may-dam-chö-gya-tso (*Port of Entry*, 412.5) identifies the passage, cited by Dzong-ka-ba (p. 151), as:

> If [this consciousness conceiving true existence] is verbal and conventional, [then it must be only imputed by conceptuality, whereby other-powered natures would be only imputed by conceptuality. In that case, other-powered natures would be non-existent, and therefore] being without a basis [of imputation], it is not suitable to call [that conceptual consciousness] verbal and conventional [that is, it would not be suitable to say that a consciousness conceiving true existence is only imputedly existent].

[c] Dzong-ka-ba most likely draws this critique of an unnamed scholar from Bu-dön's *Catalogue of the Translated Doctrine* (*chos bsgyur dkar chag*), which makes this very point to show that the text is not by Asaṅga (see Ernst Steinkellner, "Who Is Byaṅ chub rdzu 'phrul?: Tibetan and non-Tibetan Commentaries on the *Saṃdhinirmocanasūtra*—A Survey of the Literature," *Berliner Indologische Studien* 4, no. 5 [1989]: 239). Bu-dön also does not identify who the scholar is; none of Dzong-ka-ba's commentators does either.

[d] Dharmakīrti, being an indirect student of Dignāga, who was a direct disciple of Asaṅga's half-brother Vasubandhu, is clearly post-Asaṅga, and thus Asaṅga could not have cited him.

[e] See *Absorption*, #9.

[f] Peking 5539, vol. 111, 83.2.6-107.5.1; the *Compendium of Ascertainments* itself runs from vol. 110, 233.1.1-294.5.8 through vol. 111, 121.2.8; thus his citation of almost the entire sūtra is approximately only a seventh of the *Compendium*.

[g] Gung-tang (*Annotations*, *nyu* 94.3) says that the opponent is probably Bu-dön and cites

- the first nature [the imputational nature][383] does not exist even conventionally,
- although the middle one [the other-powered nature][384] exists conventionally, it does not exist ultimately, and
- the latter [the thoroughly established nature][385] ultimately exists.

This also is outside this system [of Mind-Only as commented upon by Asaṅga and Vasubandhu].[386] In particular, the [wrong] assertion—that the meaning of other-powered natures' existing conventionally is just that a **mistaken** consciousness conceives that production, cessation, and so forth exist in them, whereas **in fact** production, cessation, and so forth do not exist—is the final deprecation of other-powered natures, due to which the other two natures are also deprecated. Hence, this is the chief of annihilatory views described earlier in Asaṅga's *Grounds of Bodhisattvas*[a] as a deprecation of all three natures. Know this as an undispellable contradiction in the position of those who assert that the *Sūtra Unraveling the Thought* is of definitive meaning [and assert that other-powered natures are empty of inherent existence].[387]

Dispelling Contradictions In Our Own Tenets [That Is, In The System Of The Proponents Of Cognition] (294) {407}

[Objection By Someone Not Distinguishing Between Ultimately Existing And Ultimate Truth][388] (294) {407}

If, in accordance with statements in Asaṅga's *Grounds of Bodhisattvas* and *Compendium of Ascertainments,* other-powered natures **ultimately exist**, then how does this not contradict [the many statements that other-powered natures are **not ultimates**, such as]:[389]

1. The statement in the *Sūtra Unraveling the Thought*[390] that whatever is a compounded phenomenon is not ultimate:

   If, just as the eight branches of the path of Superiors are of mutually different character, the thusness of those phenomena—the ultimate, the selflessness in phenomena—also was different in character, then thusness, the ultimate, the selflessness in phenomena also would be caused. If it arose from causes, it would be a compounded phenomenon. If it were a compounded phenomenon, it would not be ultimate.

2. The statement in Maitreya's *Differentiation of the Middle and the Ex-*

his history (see Obermiller, *History of Buddhism,* 52); A-ku Lo-drö-gya-tso (*Precious Lamp,* 195.5) similarly reports that this position is clear in Bu-dön's history. However, Bel-jor-hlün-drup (*Lamp for the Teaching,* 44.7), Jik-may-dam-chö-gya-tso (*Port of Entry,* 415.1), and Da-drin-rap-den (*Annotations,* 73.6) identify the scholar as Jo-nang-ba, that is, Shay-rap-gyel-tsen; Ser-shül (*Notes,* 30a.4) similarly thinks it may be Jo-nang-ba Shay-rap-gyel-tsen.

[a] See p. 141ff.

tremes,[391] "The ultimate is single," as well as its commentary [by Vasubandhu],[392] "The ultimate truth is to be known as the single thoroughly established nature"

3. The explanation that an ultimate truth is without production and disintegration which occurs in Maitreya's *Ornament for the Great Vehicle Sūtras* on the occasion of stating that the ultimate truth has five characteristics:[a]

    [The ultimate is] (1) not existent [in the sense of apprehended-object and apprehending-subject being different substantial entities] and not nonexistent [as a mere negative of a difference of entity of subject and object], (2) not the same [that is, not exactly the same as] and not another [entity from the phenomena that are empty], (3) not produced or disintegrating [when thoroughly afflicted phenomena and pure phenomena are produced and cease and hence] not diminished or increasing, (4) also not purified [because of being naturally pure of defilements from the start], and (5) yet becoming purified [of adventitious defilements]. These are characteristics of the ultimate.

And also the statement in Vasubandhu's commentary that:[393]

> [The ultimate][394] does not exist by way of the imputational character or

---

[a] *theg pa chen po'i mdo sde rgyan, mahāyānasūtrālaṃkāra;* VI.1; Peking 5521, vol. 108, 5.1.1; for the Sanskrit, see p. 408, footnote b. For a translation into French, see Sylvain Lévi, *Mahāyānasūtrālaṃkāra: Exposé de la doctrine du grand véhicule selon le système Yogācāra* (Paris: Bibliothèque de l'École des Hautes Études, 1907, 1911; reprint, Shanghai: 1940), 22. The bracketed commentary in this stanza is from A-ku Ḻo-drö-gya-tso's *Precious Lamp,* 197.1-197.4; for another interpretation of the five, see Jik-may-dam-chö-gya-tso's *Port of Entry,* 425.1, and another's (perhaps his own) criticism of A-ku Ḻo-drö-gya-tso's interpretation, 430.3.

Shay-rap-gyel-tsen (*Ocean of Definitive Meaning,* 195.1) cites this passage as showing that the ultimate is other-empty. He takes:

- "not existent" to mean that imputational natures and other-powered natures do not really exist;
- "not nonexistent" to mean that the thoroughly established nature is not not really existent;
- "not the same" to mean that the three natures are not the same entity;
- "not other" to mean that the three natures are not different entities—the reason for this and the previous point being that imputational natures and other-powered natures do not really have entities;
- since the thoroughly established nature that is the basis empty of imputational natures and other-powered natures is uncompounded, it is "not produced or disintegrating, not diminished or increasing";
- since the thoroughly established nature is naturally pure, its entity does not have anything that requires purification; and
- to attain the thoroughly established nature it must "become purified" of adventitious defilements.

other-powered character and does not not exist by way of the thoroughly established character.

4. Also the statement in Asaṅga's *Compendium of Ascertainments:*[395]

 Is it to be said that reasons [that is, mainly the other-powered natures that are the bases of imputation of imputational natures][a] exist conventionally or that they exist ultimately? They are to be said to exist conventionally.

Also:[396]

> Is it to be said that conceptual consciousnesses [that is, contaminated minds and mental factors][397] exist conventionally or that they exist ultimately? It is to be said that they exist conventionally.[398]

[Answers Dispelling Those Contradictions][399] (295) {409}

[Dispelling Contradictions Regarding The First Three Passages][400] *(295) {409}*

I will explain how these statements do not contradict [the ultimate existence of other-powered natures]. There are two ways of positing [phenomena] as existing conventionally and as existing ultimately.

The First Mode Of Positing Existing Conventionally And Existing Ultimately (295) {409}

The first is to posit an existent—that is posited through the force of conventions—as existing conventionally and to posit an existent—that is not posited through the force of conventions but exists by way of its own character—as ultimately existing.[b] For instance, there are the many statements in sūtra that such and such is by the force of worldly conventions[c] and is not so ultimately. This [mode of positing ultimately existing and conventionally existing][401] is the basis of debate about ultimate and conventional existence and non-existence between the Proponents of the Middle and the Proponents of True Existence

---

[a] A-ku Lo-drö-gya-tso (*Precious Lamp,* 197.4) identifies "reasons" (*rgyu mtshan*) this way and also as **all** bases of designation of imputational natures, thus including permanent phenomena; see Jik-may-dam-chö-gya-tso (*Port of Entry,* 432.6) for a source in the *Compendium* itself. Less satisfactorily, Ḍa-drin-rap-ḍen (76.3) identifies "reasons" as the names (or phrases), "This is form," and so forth.

Phenomena are probably called "reasons" (*rgyu mtshan*) because they are reasons, or bases, for verbalizations.

[b] Ḍa-drin-rap-ḍen (77.6) says that this mode of positing conventional and ultimate existence is shared by all Buddhist schools.

[c] Ḍa-drin-rap-ḍen (78.1) identifies "worldly conventions" (*'jig rten gyi tha snyad*) as names (*ming*) and conceptual consciousnesses (*rtog pa*). He points out that the meaning of being posited through the force of names and conceptual consciousnesses differs greatly in the Mind-Only and Consequence Schools.

who are among our own and others' schools.

In terms of this [mode of positing the meaning of ultimate and conventional, according to the Mind-Only School] the first nature explained earlier [that is, existent imputational natures][402] exists conventionally but does not exist ultimately, and the other two natures [that is, other-powered and thoroughly established natures] exist ultimately but do not exist conventionally. Therefore, they are as was [explained earlier] in Asaṅga's *Grounds of Bodhisattvas* and *Compendium of Ascertainments* [where imputational natures are described as not existing ultimately and other-powered natures and thoroughly established natures are described as existing ultimately].[403]

Also, Asaṅga's *Compendium of Ascertainments* says:[404]

> Those[a] which are objects of observation of a consciousness based on names [through the force of][405] being thoroughly conditioned to verbalization—things having the names of the forms and so forth that exist by way of essences of forms and so forth—both do not substantially exist and do not ultimately exist. Hence, it should be known that whereas those phenomena having the names of forms and so forth do not exist as entities of those [that is, as forms and so forth],[406] those imputations[b] by that [conceptuality][407] exist imputedly.
>
> It should be known that objects of observation of [non-conceptual][408] consciousnesses[c]—that have the name of being devoid of thorough conditioning to verbalization—those objects being things having the names of forms and so forth that exist by way of an inexpressible essence, both substantially exist and ultimately exist.

Moreover, with respect to substantial and imputed existence, Asaṅga's *Compendium of Ascertainments* says:[409]

> It should be known that that of which its own character [can][410] be designated without relying on [apprehending phenomena] other than it and [its apprehension][411] does not [need to][412] depend on [apprehension of phenomena] other than it is, in brief, substantially existent. Anything of which its own character [must be][413] designated in reliance on [apprehending][414] other than itself and depending on other than it-

---

[a] A-ku Ḹo-drö-gya-tso (*Precious Lamp*, 198.3) adds the qualification "external objects," but it is difficult to understand how external objects could "exist imputedly" (see the end of the paragraph), since Ḏzong-ka-ḇa takes Asaṅga as holding that imputed existence is not just a figment of the imagination. S̄er-s̄hül (*Notes*, 30b.3) does not add such a qualification.

[b] A-ku Ḹo-drö-gya-tso (*Precious Lamp*, 198.5), again, interprets this as "those imputed external objects exist imputedly;" see the previous footnote.

[c] A-ku Ḹo-drö-gya-tso (ibid., 200.1) takes this as referring to yogic direction perception, whereas S̄er-s̄hül (*Notes*, 32a.6) takes it as referring to directly perceiving consciousnesses such as eye consciousnesses; the latter objects to those who view the passage as referring to self-consciousness.

> self is to be known, in brief, as existing imputedly; it does not substantially exist.

As an example of this, Asaṅga cites the imputation as a self or sentient being in dependence upon the aggregates [since the apprehension of a self or sentient being must depend upon apprehending mental and physical aggregates].[415]

In this [Mind-Only][416] system, the two—(l) imputed existence in which [the object] is not apprehendable without relying on apprehension of other phenomena and [the object] must be apprehended in reliance upon [apprehending other phenomena][417] and (2) establishment by way of its own character without being posited through the force of conventions—are not contradictory. Therefore, although, for instance, the predispositions of the basis-of-all[a] are said to exist imputedly, it is not contradictory that they exist ultimately [or exist by way of their own character][418] in the sense explained earlier. However, [ultimate existence or existence by way of the object's own character][419] is contradictory with imputed existence, in the sense of being imputed by names and conceptuality.

[The Second Mode Of Positing Existing Conventionally And Existing Ultimately [That Is, Existing As A Conventional Truth And As An Ultimate Truth][420] (295) {410}

Maitreya's *Differentiation of the Middle and the Extremes* says:[421]

> The ultimate is asserted as of three aspects—
> Object [that is, thusness], attainment [that is, nirvana], and practice
> [that is, true paths].

Vasubandhu's commentary on this says,[422] "The object-ultimate is thusness [that is, emptiness] because of being the object of the highest exalted wisdom." [In this explanation] the ultimate[b] is taken as the exalted wisdom of uncontaminated meditative equipoise, and since thusness is the object of that exalted wisdom, thusness is called the object of the ultimate[c] or the ultimate object.[d] It is the meaning of selflessness, suchness; it is also the [actual][423] ultimate that is the object of observation of purification. The other two natures [imputational and other-powered natures] do not exist as that [ultimate],[424] whereas the single thoroughly established nature does, due to which Maitreya's *Differentiation of the Middle and the Extremes* clearly says [that the ultimate is single]:[e]

> The objects of activity [of the path][425] of purification are twofold.

---

a *kun gzhi, ālaya.*

b *dam pa, parama.*

c *dam pa'i don, paramasyārtha.*

d *don dam pa, parama-artha.*

e III.12cd; Peking 5522, vol. 108, 20.3.7; for the Sanskrit, see p. 411, footnote a. See *Absorption,* #154.

> [Both][426] are said to be only the **single** [thoroughly established nature].[427]

And Vasubandhu's commentary on that clearly says:[428]

> [They are] said to be the thoroughly established nature. The other natures [imputational and other-powered natures][429] are not objects of the two types of exalted wisdom purifying [obstructions].

The two exalted wisdoms are the exalted wisdoms purifying the two obstructions [to liberation and to omniscience].[430]

[Another's position:] (296) {411} Since this [Mind-Only] system asserts that an exalted wisdom is a self-cognizing consciousness, an exalted wisdom also would be an object [of the exalted wisdom itself, whereby it too would be an object-ultimate and hence an ultimate truth].[a]

Answer: [Maitreya's explanation that the final object observed by the purifying wisdom is the object-ultimate][431] is in consideration of that object in relation to which the meaning of suchness is realized; hence, there is no fault.[b]

---

[a] A-ku L̄o-drö-gya-tso's *Precious Lamp* (207.6) identifies the position as that of the "Jo-nang-b̄as, and so forth," who hold that the uncontaminated primordial wisdom is the ultimate.

[b] This question and answer poses problems to Ge-luk-b̄a commentators because, strictly speaking, they do not call an exalted wisdom, or even an eye consciousness, a self-cognizing consciousness. Rather, a self-cognizing consciousness is a factor accompanying all other-knowing consciousnesses; it is the same entity as those consciousnesses and is itself internally directed. The problem the commentators must unravel is the meaning of the questioner's calling an exalted wisdom a self-cognizing consciousness. There are many interpretations of the question, among which I find S̄er-s̄hül L̄o-sang-pün-tsok's the most cogent. First, let us consider the interpretations of B̄el-jor-hlün-drup, Jam-ȳang-shay-b̄a, and J̄ang-ḡya.

B̄el-jor-hlün-drup (*Lamp,* 48.6) takes the self-cognizing consciousness of the question as an actual one, and thus he has D̄zong-ka-b̄a simply answering that an exalted wisdom is not a self-cognizing consciousness. He re-phrases this passage as:

> *Qualm:* It [absurdly] follows that an exalted wisdom is an object of purification, because this exalted wisdom is a self-knower that experiences itself. If it is accepted [that this exalted wisdom is an object of purification], then since this exalted wisdom would be an ultimate that is an object of observation of purification, it would be a thoroughly established nature.
>
> *Reply:* Proponents of Cognition do not assert an exalted wisdom to be a self-knower that experiences itself, and an exalted wisdom, merely by virtue of its being the object of exalted wisdom, would not become a thoroughly established nature. For, this [passage in Maitreya's *Differentiation of the Middle and the Extremes*]:
>
> > The objects of activity [of the path] of purification are twofold.
> > [Both] are said to be only the single [thoroughly established nature].
>
> is in consideration of the fact that the object in relation to which [a consciousness] is posited as having realized suchness must be a thoroughly established nature.

Therefore, such an ultimate is uncompounded, and in this [Mind-Only system] it is not contradictory that although [an object like an other-powered nature] is not established as such an ultimate, it is ultimately established in the sense of subsisting by way of its own character without being posited through the force of conventions.

It is in reference to the former mode of ultimate existence [that is, existing

---

Jam-ȳang-shay-b̄a (*Great Exposition of the Interpretable and the Definitive,* 166.6-169.1), on the other hand, takes the question as referring to an exalted wisdom of individual self-knowledge (*so sor rang rig pa'i ye shes*), which the questioner fancies as meaning that it knows itself but which Jam-ȳang-shay-b̄a says means that it sees reality directly by itself individually, without any mixture with anything other, such as terminology, conceptuality, and so forth (see A-ku L̄o-drö-gya-tso's *Precious Lamp,* 209.6).

J̄ang-ḡya (225.1-234.5 and especially 226.10; also cited in A-ku L̄o-drö-gya-tso's *Precious Lamp,* 208.4) rejects this interpretation out of hand because no scholar would mistake the meaning of "individual self-knowledge," as Jam-ȳang-shay-b̄a has the questioner doing. J̄ang-ḡya also says that the assertion that an exalted wisdom is a wisdom of individual self-knowledge is not unique to the Mind-Only School and thus there would be no need for D̄zong-ka-b̄a to say "**This** system asserts...." He interprets the question as referring to an actual self-cognizing consciousness that accompanies an exalted wisdom, and thus the questioner's qualm is that since an exalted wisdom of meditative equipoise is an object found by an uncontaminated, unmistaken, self-cognizing consciousness, it would have to be an ultimate truth.

A-ku L̄o-drö-gya-tso (*Precious Lamp,* 208.6) rejects J̄ang-ḡya's interpretation, based on the fact that the sense in which the Mind-Only School asserts that the self-cognizing consciousness that accompanies a consciousness is uncontaminated is that it is not infected with dualistic appearance. Using this fact, he turns J̄ang-ḡya's criticism of Jam-ȳang-shay-b̄a back on him by pointing out that even the self-cognizing consciousness that accompanies a wrong consciousness is uncontaminated—in the sense that it is not infected with dualistic appearance—but **no scholar would wonder** whether a wrong consciousness is an ultimate truth.

Amidst these and other interpretations, I find S̄er-s̄hül's exposition (*Notes,* 35a.6-35b.5) to be the most cogent. He views D̄zong-ka-b̄a as using the vocabulary of "self-cognizing" (*rang rig*) loosely. He says that even though an exalted wisdom itself is not an actual self-cognizing consciousness, the Mind-Only School asserts that with respect to each and every consciousness the self-cognizing consciousness that experiences it, aside from being merely a factor of luminous knowledge, is not another entity from the consciousness that it knows, due to which the conventions that a consciousness experiences and knows itself by itself are used. He cogently says that it is in the context of such coarse conventions that the question and answer are framed. The answer means that even though an exalted wisdom is an object of itself, only that object in relation to which a consciousness is posited as an exalted wisdom realizing suchness—that is to say, emptiness—is posited as a thoroughly established nature; thus, since an object is not posited as a thoroughly established nature merely because of being an object of an exalted wisdom, there is no fault that the exalted wisdom itself would be an ultimate truth.

For a listing of various interpretations of this passage, see Jik-may-dam-chö-gya-tso's *Port of Entry,* 461.5-470.6.

ultimately or by way of its own character] (297) {411} that [Āryadeva][432] says in his *Compilation of the Essence of Wisdom:*[a]

> That a consciousness which is released
> From apprehended-object and apprehending-subject exists **ultimately**[b]
> Is renowned in the texts of the Yogic Practitioners
> Who have passed to the other shore of the ocean of awareness.

In many treatises of the Middle Way School, there is debate with the Yogic Practitioners, at which time debate on the existence and non-existence of other-powered natures also is not done in terms of existing or not existing conventionally but is about existing or not existing ultimately. Therefore, those two ultimates [that is, existing ultimately and existing as the ultimate] must be distinguished well. In the texts of the master [Asaṅga] and his brother [Vasubandhu], there are many presentations of the ultimate based on the latter interpretation [that is to say, as existing as the ultimate truth].

[Dispelling Contradictions Regarding The Fourth Passage][433] (297) {412}

With respect to how the first two natures exist conventionally [that is, as conventionalities], Asaṅga's *Compendium of Ascertainments* gives rationales for why reasons [that is, phenomena that are foundations of verbalizing words][c] and conceptual consciousnesses [that is, minds and mental factors that involve dualistic appearance][d] exist conventionally. That text says:[434]

---

[a] Stanza 26; *ye shes snying po kun las btus pa, jñānasārasamuccaya;* Peking 5251, vol. 95, 144.2.8. Paṇ-chen S̄ö-nam-drak-b̄a (*Utpala Garland,* 43a.5) refers to a commentary on this text by Bodhibhadra (*byang chub bzang po;* Peking 5252). S̄er-s̄hül (*Notes,* 36a.1) points out that a similar passage appears in Jetāri's *Differentiating the Sugata's Texts* (*bde bar gzhegs pa'i gzhung rnam par 'byed pa, sugatamatavibhaṅga;* Peking 5867).

[b] D̄zong-ka-b̄a's point is that this should not be read as:

> That a consciousness which is released
> From apprehended-object and apprehending-subject exists **as the ultimate** (*dam pa'i don du*)
> Is renowned in the texts of the Yogic Practitioners
> Who have passed to the other shore of the ocean of awareness.

Rather, the end of the second line should read "**exists ultimately**," and thus this quote cannot be used to demonstrate that in the Mind-Only School a mind beyond dualism is the ultimate truth.

[c] S̄er-s̄hül's *Notes,* 36b.1.

[d] S̄er-s̄hül (ibid., 36a.4) takes "conceptual consciousnesses" (*rnam rtog*) as referring to all minds and mental factors of the Desire, Form, and Formless Realms that involve dualistic appearance. Thus, this is much wider than the more usual sense of "conceptual consciousness," as in the division of consciousnesses into direct perception and conceptuality. The term also includes the dualistic consciousnesses of both those who are languaged and those

> ...because of thoroughly giving rise to the afflictive emotions and because of being the bases of imputation.[a]

With respect to the first of those two rationales, when one draws out the opposite of the explanation in the *Sūtra Unraveling the Thought* that objects of observation of purification are ultimates, [a phenomenon] is to be posited as existing conventionally [that is, as a conventionality] due to the fact of thoroughly giving rise to afflictive emotions upon its being observed. This accords with Asaṅga's *Summary of Manifest Knowledge.*[b] With respect to the second rationale, [an object] is said to exist conventionally [that is, as a conventionality] due to being an entity imputed through the conventions of names and terminology and due to being a basis of the signs of imputing designations. "Reasons" are described as things that serve as foundations of verbalizing words.

Also, Vasubandhu's *Principles of Explanation* says:[435]

> Thinking of the objects of worldly unmistaken consciousnesses[c] and objects of supramundane consciousnesses, [Buddha] spoke of the two truths, convention-truths and ultimate-truths [respectively].[436] Because verbalizations[d] are conventions,[e] truths that are objects **to be understood by means of** them are convention-truths; [they are those objects][437] to which the verbalizations refer. For example, a ford **to be crossed by means of** the two feet is called a "foot-ford," and a ford **to be crossed by means of** a boat[f] is called a "boat-ford."

[Explaining a different usage of this terminology.] (298) {413} In Asaṅga's *Compendium of Ascertainments,*[g] a Superior's exalted wisdom of meditative

---

who are not.

[a] Ṣer-ṣhül (ibid., 36b.1) praises Gung-tang's *Annotations* for taking the latter explanation as meaning "the main objects found by conventional valid cognitions" (*tha snyad pa'i tshad ma'i rnyed don gtso bo*).

[b] Dön-drup-gyel-tsen's *Four Intertwined Commentaries* (141.2) gives the citation:

> Why is [an object] posited as existing conventionally? Objects of observation that involve thorough affliction exist conventionally.

This is found in the first section, entitled *lakṣaṇasamuccaya;* Walpola Rahula, *La compendium de la super-doctrine (philosophie) (Abhidharmasamuccaya) d'Asaṅga* (Paris: École Française d'Extrême-Orient, 1971), 23.

[c] Or, "mistaken consciousnesses"; see p. 412, footnote a.

[d] Ṣer-ṣhül (*Notes,* 37a.1) takes verbalizations (*brjod pa*) as referring both to terms and to conceptual consciousnesses.

[e] *kun rdzob, saṃvṛti.*

[f] *ko gru,* literally, a leather boat.

[g] The reference is to Peking 5539, vol. 111, 61.5.3 (Tokyo *sde dge, sems tsam,* vol. 8 [*zhi*], 289a.4):

> Is it to be said that consciousnesses of reality exist conventionally, or is it to be said that they exist ultimately? The first [that is, a Superior's exalted wisdom of medi-

equipoise [directly][438] realizing thusness is said to exist ultimately [that is, as an ultimate truth, because the ultimate truth exists as its object of comprehension];[a] this is in consideration that it does not have the two previous grounds for being posited as existing conventionally.[b] It says that the exalted wisdom attained subsequent to such meditative equipoise exists both conventionally and ultimately [that is, as a conventional truth and as an ultimate truth]; from the viewpoint of its observing conventional signs, it is said to exist conventionally [that is, as a conventional truth].[c]

---

tative equipoise] is said to exist ultimately; the second [that is, an exalted wisdom attained subsequent to such meditative equipoise] is said to be both.

See Jik-may-dam-chö-gya-tso's *Port of Entry,* 474.5.

[a] A-ku L̄o-drö-gya-tso's *Precious Lamp,* 217.2. According to D̄a-drin-rap-d̄en's *Annotations* (86.6), it is said to exist ultimately because dualistic appearance has vanished equally for both its appearance and its ascertainment factors.

[b] As explained above, there are two modes of positing something as existing conventionally:

First mode

1. an existent posited through the force of conventions

Second mode

2. an object of observation suitable to give rise to afflictive emotions
3. a basis of the signs of imputing designations

Jik-may-dam-chö-gya-tso (*Port of Entry,* 475.1, 478.2) says that when D̄zong-ka-b̄a speaks of "the two previous grounds for being posited as existing conventionally," these refer to the first two of the three ways of positing something as existing conventionally (items 1 and 2 above, and not the two items in the second mode). He is following Gung-tang's *Annotations* (*tsu* 109.4), which criticizes B̄el-jor-hlün-drup for lack of clarity on this issue.

[c] D̄ra-d̄i Ge-s̄hay Rin-chen-dön-drup's *Ornament for the Thought* (as reported in S̄er-s̄hül's *Notes,* 37a.5) says that it is said to exist ultimately (that is, as an ultimate truth) because emptiness appears to the ascertainment factor (*nges ngor stong nyid shar*) of an exalted wisdom attained subsequent to meditative equipoise. A-ku L̄o-drö-gya-tso (*Precious Lamp,* 217.4) cogently objects to this because emptiness is an **implicit** object of comprehension of such a wisdom (and hence does not appear even though it is realized). He is following Gung-tang (*Annotations, tsu* 110.2), who states that this wisdom is called these two because it realizes both truths—without the qualification "explicitly."

B̄el-jor-hlün-drup (*Lamp for the Teaching,* 50.4) says that such a wisdom exists ultimately because it is established by way of its own character. He thereby weakly skirts the issue of why it is said to exist ultimately in the sense of being an ultimate truth.

D̄a-drin-rap-d̄en (*Annotations,* 87.3) says that from the viewpoint of its being unmistaken in its factor of taking emptiness as the object of its mode of apprehension, it is said to exist ultimately, that is, as an ultimate truth. This exposition is subject to the fault adduced by A-ku L̄o-drö-gya-tso given above.

Jik-may-dam-chö-gya-tso (*Port of Entry,* 480.3-481.4) holds that nothing more need be said than what D̄zong-ka-b̄a says just above, that is, it is said to exist ultimately in consideration that it does not have the two previous grounds for being posited as existing conventionally (see the previous footnote). He says that positing reasons for these two beyond what

[Supporting evidence for the non-contradiction of existing conventionally, that is, as a conventionality, and existing ultimately.] (298) {413} That [an object] exists conventionally [that is, as a conventional truth] due to being a basis of the signs of imputing designations and due to acting as an object of awareness that gives rise to afflictive emotions is not contradictory with its existing ultimately, in the sense of being established by way of its own character. For Vasubandhu's *Principles of Explanation* says:[a]

> *Objection* by a Hearer Sectarian [to a Proponent of the Great Vehicle]:[439] If the statement in the *Ultimate Emptiness,*[b] "Actions[c] and fruitions[d] exist but an agent is not observed," is [in reference to such being so][440] ultimately, how could all phenomena be natureless [as is said in the literal reading of the Perfection of Wisdom Sūtras]?[441] If it is [in

Ḏzong-ka-ḇa himself says goes against Ḏzong-ka-ḇa's own mode of exposition here. It seems to me, however, that Ḏzong-ka-ḇa may have felt that the reasons were obvious and thus did not state them, and thus the reasons need to be expounded in commentary—my own inclination being to agree with Gung-tang and A-ku Ḻo-drö-gya-tso.

[a] This is a paraphrase; according to the Peking edition of Vasubandhu's text (5562, vol. 113, 283.2.7-283.3.3), the passage reads:

> [*Objection* by a Hearer Sectarian:] The *Ultimate Emptiness* says, "Actions exist, and fruitions also exist, but an agent is not observed," Are these so just ultimately or just conventionally? If just ultimately, how could all phenomena be natureless [as is said in the literal reading of the Perfection of Wisdom Sūtras]? If conventionally, then since agents exist conventionally, it could not be said that agents are not observed [since agents do indeed exist conventionally].
>
> [*Answer* by Vasubandhu:] What is this called "conventional"? What is ultimate? Through this, one will understand what exists conventionally and what exists ultimately.
>
> [*Response* by a Hearer Sectarian:] Names, verbalizations, designations, and conventions are conventionalities. The own-character of phenomena [that is to say, establishment by way of own character] is the ultimate.
>
> [*Answer* by Vasubandhu:] Then, in that case, since actions and fruitions exist as names [that is, as conventionalities that are the bases of affixing of names] and also exist as [ultimates established by way of] their own character, let them be considered as both [conventionally existing and existing ultimately], in accordance with how you assert these.

[b] A-ku Ḻo-drö-gya-tso (*Precious Lamp,* 218.1) identifies this as a Perfection of Wisdom Sūtra; Ser-shül (*Notes,* 55b.1-55b.5), as a text asserted by all Hearer schools except those propounding a self, these being the Sammitīyas and so forth; Jik-may-dam-chö-gya-tso (*Port of Entry,* 482.3), as the *Sūtra of the Great Emptiness* (*stong pa nyid chen po'i mdo*); Ḏa-drin-rap-ḏen (*Annotations,* 88.1), as "a Great Vehicle sūtra."

[c] In the Mind-Only School actions (*las, karma*) are the mental factor of intention (*sems pa, cetanā*); see A-ku Ḻo-drö-gya-tso's *Precious Lamp,* 218.6.

[d] According to A-ku Ḻo-drö-gya-tso (*Precious Lamp,* 218.6), the main fruitions (*rnam smin, vipāka*) are the physical life support (*lus rten*), feeling, and so forth.

reference to such being so] conventionally, then, since agents exist in that way, how could it be said that they are not observed?

In answer [Vasubandhu][442] asks, "If one knows what the conventional and the ultimate are, one understands through this [what it means] to exist in those two ways; therefore, what [do you, Hearer Sectarian, take] those two to be?"

[*Response* by a Hearer Sectarian:] Names,[a] verbalizations,[b] designations,[c] and conventions[d] are conventionalities. The own-character [that is to say, the establishment by way of their own character][443] of phenomena is [their] ultimate [existence].[444]

[*Answer* by Vasubandhu:][445] Then, in that case since actions and fruitions exist as names [that is, as conventionalities that are the bases of affixing of names][446] and also exist as [ultimates in the sense of being established by way of][447] their own character, let them be considered as both [conventionally existing, that is, existing as conventionalities, and ultimately existing] in accordance with how you assert these.[448]

The mode of their ultimate existence is the former [that is to say, the first of the two ways of positing the meaning of existing ultimately, this being to exist by way of their own character],[449] and the mode of their existing conventionally is in accordance with the latter [that is, the second of the two ways of positing the meaning of existing conventionally, this being to exist as bases of the imputation of conventions, that is to say, as conventional truths].[e] The meaning is that [actions and fruitions] exist in both ways.

Although [actions and fruitions][450] are asserted as existing as that ultimate [that is, as established by way of their own character], in this [Mind-Only system][451] such is not contradicted by the statement [in sūtra] that ultimately all phenomena are natureless because [that passage in sūtra][452] is not asserted as literally acceptable.

Persons exist conventionally [that is, as conventionalities, in that they exist as a basis of the imputation of a convention][453] but do not substantially exist [because they exist imputedly in dependence on the aggregates].[454] Actions and fruitions exist conventionally [that is, as conventionalities, in that they exist as bases of the imputation of conventions] and also exist substantially [in that they fulfill none of the three meanings of being imputedly existent].[455] Since [those

---

a *ming.*

b *brjod pa.*

c *gdags pa.*

d *tha snyad.*

e Bel-jor-hlün-drup's *Lamp for the Teaching,* 51.6, and Da-drin-rap-den's *Annotations,* 89.2. A-ku Lo-drö-gya-tso (*Precious Lamp,* 218.3) identifies this as existing as an object found by the reasoning consciousness distinguishing a conventionality (*tha snyad dpyod pa'i rigs shes kyi rnyed don du yod pa*).

two,[456] actions and fruitions,] are objects of worldly consciousnesses, they do not exist ultimately in the second sense [that is, as ultimate truths, since they are not final objects of observation of a path of purification],[457] and those two are not objects of a supramundane consciousness because an object of [a supramundane consciousness] is [the emptiness that is][458] the general character [pervading all phenomena in general[459] and is] inexpressible [since its meaning cannot be taken as an object of mind by mere terms].[460]

[That there are two ways of positing conventional and ultimate][a] is very clear also[b] in the explanation in Vasubandhu's *Principles of Explanation*[c] that the earlier objection [raised by the Hearer Sectarian][461] is incurred by certain Proponents of the Great Vehicle [that is, Proponents of the Middle][462] who propound [as literal][463] the statement that all phenomena do not exist in the manner of having their own character but exist conventionally.

[Dispelling another seeming contradiction.] (299) {414} Maitreya's *Differentiation of the Middle and the Extremes* [speaks of three types of conventionalities]:[464]

> Imputational, mental, and likewise
> The verbal are coarse.

It treats conventional truths, the coarse suchness,[d] as the three—imputational conventionalities, mental conventionalities, and verbal conventionalities.[e] Then

---

[a] Šer-šhül (*Notes,* 37b.5) and Jik-may-dam-chö-gya-tso (*Port of Entry,* 490.6), following Gung-tang, interpret this somewhat cryptic sentence this way. However, Ƀel-jor-hlün-drup (*Lamp for the Teaching,* 53.1.-53.4) interprets what is clear not as referring to the two ways of positing conventional and ultimate but as referring to a refutation of Proponents of the Middle; according to his interpretation (in which it is difficult to determine what "also" means) the passage would be translated as follows:

> It is very clear that this exposition—in Vasubandhu's *Principles of Explanation*—of the above debate [raised by the Hearer Sectarian] **also** applies to certain Proponents of the Great Vehicle [that is, Proponents of the Middle] who propound that it is said [in the Perfection of Wisdom Sūtras] that all phenomena do not exist in the manner of having their own character but exist conventionally.

Both interpretations are plausible, but Gung-tang's suits the context better.

[b] That is to say, not just in Asaṅga's *Compendium of Ascertainments* but **also** in Vasubandhu's *Principles of Explanation;* see Šer-šhül's *Notes,* 38a.1.

[c] Peking 5562, vol. 113, 283.3.8.

[d] The thoroughly established nature is the subtle suchness (Jik-may-dam-chö-gya-tso's *Port of Entry,* 485.2) since it is the final mode of being of phenomena.

[e] Jik-may-dam-chö-gya-tso (*Port of Entry,* 485.3) identifies:

- imputational conventionalities (*btags pa'i kun rdzob*) as imputational natures that are imputed by conceptuality to be truly existent whereas they are not truly existent;
- mental conventionalities (*shes pa'i kun rdzob*) as other-powered natures, which are illustrated by unreal ideation (*yang dag pa ma yin pa'i kun rtog*) since it is the principal other-powered nature, and thus come to be called "mental;" and

it relates these three with the three natures [that is, imputational, other-powered, and thoroughly established—treating thoroughly established natures as verbal **conventionalities**, whereas, as explained above, they are ultimate truths. In treating] the latter [that is to say, thoroughly established natures as verbal conventionalities], it should be understood that it is explaining the thought of other sūtras that say that thusness and so forth exist conventionally;[a] [Maitreya is not indicating that thoroughly established natures are **actual** conventionalities].[465]

[Advice That It Is Necessary To Distinguish The Various Modes Of Positing Substantial Existence And Imputed Existence, And So Forth, In The Higher And Lower Tenet Systems] (300) {415}

If, in that way, you distinguish in detail:

- the different ways substantial existence and imputed existence are posited
- the modes of existing conventionally and existing ultimately in the higher and lower tenet systems, and
- the different ways in which these are posited even in one tenet system,

you will be able to delineate well the important tenets. You will also understand the need for the Proponents of the Middle to prove as not ultimately existent many things that the Proponents of True Existence assert to exist imputedly and to exist conventionally. Otherwise, the differentiation of the upper and lower tenet systems would be reduced to mere whimsy.[b]

- verbal conventionalities (*brjod pa'i kun rdzob*) as thoroughly established natures which, although they ultimately cannot be taken as objects by way of terms and conceptual consciousnesses, are suitable to be expressed through many **verbal** forms such as thusness and so forth.

[a] Bel-jor-hlün-drup (*Lamp for the Teaching,* 54.1) cogently explains:

> There is a reason for saying that suchness and the thoroughly established nature exist as verbal conventionalities, because verbalizations are conventionalities and suchness and the thoroughly established nature are referents of verbalizations.

Da-drin-rap-den (*Annotations,* 90.5) says that the meaning is that the **existence** of thusness must be posited by a conventional consciousness.

[b] That is, one's ranking of systems would be based solely on liking one system and not liking another, since their respective assertions and criticisms of each other would not be understood.

8. Maitreya's *Ornament for the Great Vehicle Sūtras*

The description of how the two extremes are abandoned in texts other than those has two parts: the explanations in Maitreya's *Ornament for the Great Vehicle Sūtras* and in his *Differentiation of the Middle and the Extremes.*

Explaining How The Two Extremes Are Abandoned In Maitreya's *Ornament For The Great Vehicle Sūtras* (302) {416}

[The Thought Behind The Teaching That Phenomena Are Natureless][466] (302) {416}

Maitreya's *Ornament for the Great Vehicle Sūtras* says:[467]

> Because [things] are not [produced in the future from] themselves
> And because [having ceased, past objects are] not [produced again] as having their own nature
> And because [present objects] do not abide [for a second moment] in their own entity
> And because [the natures of objects] conceived [by childish beings] do not exist,
> Naturelessness was asserted [in the Perfection of Wisdom Sūtras].

It is explained [in Vasubandhu's commentary][468] that, in consideration of:

- the naturelessness of the three characteristics of compounded things [that is, that things are not produced under their own power, do not abide under their own power, and do not disintegrate under their own power],[469] and
- the non-existence of the natures that are conceived by childish beings [who conceive forms and so forth to be pure, blissful, permanent, and self and to be separate entities from the consciousnesses apprehending them,[470]

Buddha] spoke of [all phenomena as being] natureless [in the Perfection of Wisdom Sūtras].[471] Asaṅga's *Summary of Manifest Knowledge*[472] explains that, in consideration of those two and in consideration of the three non-natures, [Buddha] set forth naturelessness in the Very Extensive [Perfection of Wisdom Sūtras].

Because phenomena depend upon conditions, they do not exist under their own power; therefore, they are natureless. The meaning of this is as explained in Kamalashīla's *Illumination of the Middle*—the non-existence of production by [a thing's] own essence.[a]

---

[a] Jik-may-dam-chö-gya-tso (*Port of Entry,* 502.3) points outs that Jam-ȳang-shay-b̄a identifies this as causeless production but that it is also suitable to identify it, as Gung-tang's *Annotations* and other texts do, as production from self, as is asserted by the Sāṃkhyas, since

Since whatever phenomenon has ceased is not produced again in the entity of that phenomenon, it does not exist [after its cessation] in its own entity; therefore, it is natureless. Since that which has been produced but has not ceased is momentary, it does not abide for a second period in its own entity; therefore, it is natureless. In brief,[a] since (1) a future sprout is not produced through its own power, (2) a past sprout is not produced again as the entity of the sprout, and (3) a present sprout does not abide for a second period of time after its own establishment, the phenomena of the three times are explained as natureless.

Vasubandhu explains that since the natures of cleanliness, happiness, permanence, and self or of an ["]other imputational character["] as these are conceived by childish beings do not exist, [phenomena] are natureless. "Other" [in "other imputational character" in the previous sentence refers to] object and subject conceived as different substantial entities.[b]

[The Thought Behind The Teaching That Phenomena are Unproduced, Unceasing, Quiescent From The Start, And Naturally Passed Beyond Sorrow][473] (303) {417}

Just as [phenomena] are natureless, so they are unproduced; because of not being produced, so they do not cease, and so forth. By using the former ones as reasons, the latter ones are established. Maitreya's *Ornament for the Great Vehicle Sūtras* says:[474]

> Since each serves as the basis of the latter,
> Due to naturelessness are established
> Non-production, non-ceasing, quiescence from the start,
> And naturally passed beyond sorrow.

This has already been explained.[c]

[The Thought Behind The Teaching Of Attaining Forbearance With Respect To The Doctrine Of Non-Production][475] (303) {418}

Also, [Maitreya] explains the [eight] modes of non-production of phenomena

---

Sthiramati and Asvabhāva give both interpretations. Ḏa-drin-rap-ḏen (93.3) identifies this merely as production of things from causes that are the same entity as themselves. In the three non-natures, however, it is more cogent to take causeless production as what is being negated; see *Absorption,* #68.

[a] This sentence is Ḏzong-ka-ḇa's own summation and not a quotation.

[b] This sentence is Ḏzong-ka-ḇa's own comment on Vasubandhu's meaning and not a quotation.

[c] See p. 97ff. A-ku Ḻo-drö-gya-tso (*Precious Lamp,* 221.5) relates this specifically to the explanation in Asaṅga's *Summary of Manifest Knowledge;* see p. 101.

in the statements [in sūtra][476] about attaining forbearance with respect to the doctrine of non-production:[a]

> Forbearance with respect to the doctrine of non-production is set forth
> In terms of a beginning [of cyclic existence],[b] of [phenomena already produced being produced again in that entity] itself, of the other [that is, a sentient being who did not exist earlier in cyclic existence],
> Of the own-character [of imputational natures], of self [that is to say, self-production of other-powered natures], of [thoroughly established natures] becoming other,
> Of the afflictive emotions [in those who have attained knowledge of extinction], and of enhancement [of a Buddha's Truth Body].

[Vasubandhu's] commentary[477] explains that in this [stanza]:

- "Beginning" refers to the non-production of a beginning to cyclic existence
- "Itself" refers to the fact that any phenomenon that was produced earlier is not produced again in the entity of that [phenomenon],[478] "itself" meaning an earlier one
- "Other" refers to non-production in an aspect that did not exist earlier, "other" meaning a later one—the meaning of this is as explained in Kamalashīla's *Illumination of the Middle* that there is no [new][479] production of a sentient being who did not earlier exist in cyclic existence and that

---

[a] XI.52; Peking 5521, vol. 108, 9.1.4; and Lévi, *Mahāyānasūtrālaṃkāra,* vol. 2, 123. For the Sanskrit, see p. 418, footnote c. The bracketed additions in the stanza are drawn from A-ku Lo-drö-gya-tso's *Precious Lamp,* 222.1; Dön-drup-gyel-tsen's *Four Intertwined Commentaries,* 157.5; and Da-drin-rap-den's *Annotations,* 94.4.

A-ku Lo-drö-gya-tso (*Precious Lamp,* 223.2) takes "attaining forbearance with respect to the doctrine of non-production" as referring to attaining forbearance, that is, facility, with respect to the meaning of the selflessness of phenomena. Jik-may-dam-chö-gya-tso (*Port of Entry,* 505.6) adds that through ascertaining the meaning of the non-production of phenomena upon taking the eight non-productions as reasons, one attains forbearance with respect to the doctrine of non-production, that is, selflessness.

Gung-tang (*Annotations, 'u* 114.3) explains that Maitreya's reasons for choosing merely these eight are threefold:

1. To dispel contradictions adduced the Proponents of Truly Existent External Objects who attempt to prove that the Perfection of Wisdom Sūtras are not the word of Buddha, by claiming that the Perfection of Wisdom Sūtras deprecate the presentations of entry into cyclic existence and reversal into nirvana
2. To refute the Proponents of Non-Nature who claim that the Perfection of Wisdom Sūtras are literally acceptable
3. To answer the argument by the Proponents of Non-Nature that the Proponents of Mind-Only deprecate the non-production that is the object with respect to which forbearance is attained

[b] A-ku Lo-drö-gya-tso (*Precious Lamp,* 222.1) glosses "cyclic existence" with compounded phenomena (*'dus byas*).

there is no production of phenomena that did not exist earlier since something of similar type to what ceased earlier is produced[a]

- "Own-character" is in reference to imputational factors; production never exists in them
- "Non-self-production" is in reference to other-powered natures
- "Non-production in the sense of becoming other" is in reference to thoroughly established natures
- "Non-production of afflictive emotions" is in reference to [Foe Destroyers][b] who have attained knowledge of extinction

---

[a] Production is a case of the cause's ceasing and something of a similar type being produced.

[b] A-ku Lo-drö-gya-tso's *Precious Lamp,* 222.2; and Da-drin-rap-den's *Annotations,* 95.5. With respect to the translation of *arhant* (*dgra bcom pa*) as "Foe Destroyer," I do this to accord with the usual Tibetan translation of the term and to assist in capturing the flavor of oral and written traditions that frequently refer to this etymology. Arhants have overcome the foe which is the afflictive emotions (*nyon mongs, kleśa*), the chief of which is ignorance.

The Indian and Tibetan translators of Sanskrit and other texts into Tibetan were also aware of the etymology of *arhant* as "worthy one," as they translated the name of the "founder" of the Jaina system, Arhat, as *mchod 'od* "Worthy of Worship" (see Jam-yang-shay-ba's *Great Exposition of Tenets, ka* 62a.3). Also, they were aware of Chandrakīrti's gloss of the term as "Worthy One" in his *Clear Words: sadevamānuṣāsurāl lokāt pūnārhatvād arhannityuchyate* (*Mūlamadhyamakakārikās de Nāgārjuna avec la Prasannapadā Commentaire de Candrakīrti,* Bibliotheca Buddhica, 4 [Osnabrück, Germany: Biblio Verlag, 1970], 486.5), *lha dang mi dang lha ma yin du bcas pa'i 'jig rten gyis mchod par 'os pas dgra bcom pa zhes brjod la* (409.20, Tibetan Cultural Printing Press ed.; also, Peking 5260, vol. 98, 75.2.2), "Because of being worthy of worship by the world of gods, humans, and demi-gods, they are called Arhants."

Also, they were aware of Haribhadra's twofold etymology in his *Illumination of the Eight Thousand Stanza Perfection of Wisdom Sūtra.* In the context of the list of epithets qualifying the retinue of Buddha at the beginning of the sūtra (see Unrai Wogihara, *Abhisamayālaṃkārālokā Prajñā-pāramitā-vyākhyā, The Work of Haribhadra* [Tokyo: Toyo Bunko, 1932-1935; reprint, Tokyo: Sankibo Buddhist Book Store, 1973], 8.18), Haribhadra says:

> They are called *arhant* [Worthy One, from the root *arh* "to be worthy"] since they are worthy of worship, religious donations, and being assembled together in a group, and so forth. (Wogihara, *Abhisamayālaṃkārālokā,* 9.8-9: *sarva evātra pūjādakṣiṇā-gaṇa-parikarṣādy-ārhatayarhantaḥ;* Peking 5189, vol. 90, 67.5.7: *'dir thams cad kyang mchod pa dang // yon dang tshogs su 'dub la sogs par 'os pas na dgra bcom pa'o*).

Also:

> They are called *arhant* [Foe Destroyer *arihan*] because they have destroyed (*hata*) the foe (*ari*). (Wogihara, *Abhisamayālaṃkārālokā,* 10.18: *hatāritvād* ***arhantaḥ;*** Peking 5189, vol. 90, 69.3.6. *dgra rnams bcom pas na dgra bcom pa'o*).

(My thanks to Gareth Sparham for the references to Haribhadra.) Thus, we are dealing with a considered preference in the face of alternative etymologies—"Foe Destroyer" requiring a not unusual *i* infix to make *ari-han,* with *ari* meaning enemy and *han* meaning to kill, and

- "Non-production of [further][480] enhancement" refers to the Truth Body of a Buddha

The explanation in this way of the mode of non-nature and of the mode of non-production is the system of those [that is, Proponents of the Mind-Only School] who [unlike the Proponents of Non-Nature] do not assert as literal the explanations that all phenomena are ultimately empty of nature and that compounded things are ultimately without production.

Concerning these, the modes of non-nature of:

- the phenomena of the three times, except for that of the present, and
- the former[a] mode of the non-existence of the natures that are conceived by childish beings [that is to say, the conceptions of cleanliness, happiness, permanence, and a substantially existent self][481]

are in common with both Hearer schools [the Great Exposition and Sūtra School Following Scripture. The reason why the present is not included is that] the Proponents of the Great Exposition assert that the activity of abiding takes place after [an object] has been produced and that the activity of disintegration takes place after that.[b]

[Dispelling An Objection By A Proponent Of Non-Nature That It Is Contradictory To Compare Other-Powered Natures To Illusions And Yet Hold That They Truly Exist][482] (304) {419}

Objection: The *Sūtra Unraveling the Thought*[c] says that other-powered na-

thus "Foe Destroyer." Unfortunately, one word in English cannot convey both this meaning and "Worthy of Worship"; thus I have gone with what clearly has become the predominant meaning in Tibet. (For an excellent discussion of the two etymologies of Arhat in Buddhism and Jainism, see L. M. Joshi, *Facets of Jaina Religiousness in Comparative Light,* L.D. Series, 85 [Ahmedabad, India: L.D. Institute of Indology, 1981], 53-58.)

[a] The latter mode of misconception—childish beings' conception that subject and object are different entities—is not described in the Great Exposition and Sūtra Schools, and thus Ḏzong-ka-ḇa specifies "the former mode."

[b] In the Sūtra School, the Mind-Only School, and the Middle Way School, production, abiding, and disintegration take place not serially but simultaneously, since production is the new arising of a compounded phenomenon that was previously nonexistent, abiding is the remaining of the continuum of the phenomena that were the causes, and disintegration is a compounded phenomenon's not remaining a second moment. Thus, the abiding and disintegration of an object do not require any causes other than those that produce the object. See A-ku Ḻo-drö-gya-tso's *Precious Lamp,* 223.6; Ṡer-ṡhül's *Notes,* 38b.6-39a.3; and Geshe Lhundup Sopa and Jeffrey Hopkins, *Cutting through Appearances: The Practice and Theory of Tibetan Buddhism* (Ithaca, New York: Snow Lion, 1989), 194-196.

[c] Ḏzong-ka-ḇa cited the passage in chapter 2 (p. 93):

> Paramārthasamudgata, it is thus: for example, production-non-natures [that is, other-powered natures] are to be viewed as like magical creations.

tures are like illusions and Maitreya's *Ornament for the Great Vehicle Sūtras*[a] also says that all compounded things are like illusions. Therefore, the meaning of those passages could not allow that other-powered natures are truly established.

Answer: There is no certainty that due to describing other-powered natures as like illusions and so forth, these texts do not teach that they are truly established; it depends upon **how** illusions and so forth are used as examples. Concerning this, Maitreya's *Ornament for the Great Vehicle Sūtras* indicates how illusions are used as examples with:[483]

> Unreal ideation[b] is asserted
> To be just like a [basis of a magical] illusion.
> The error of duality is said
> To be just like an illusory aspect.

A basis of [illusory] mistake such as a clod, a stick, and so forth implanted with

---

[a] The reference is to XI.30, which with bracketed material from Vasubandhu's *Explanation of (Maitreya's) "Ornament for the Great Vehicle Sūtras"* (Peking 5527, vol. 108, 75.3.3), is:

> The compounded phenomena spoken of by the fully enlightened, supreme Buddhas in this and that [discourse]
> Are to be known as like magical illusions, dreams, mirages, reflections,
> Shadows, echoes, moons in water, and emanations.
> [Those compounded phenomena] are asserted as the six [internal sense-spheres, like magical illusions], the six [external sense-spheres, like dreams], the two [minds and mental factors, like mirages], two sets of six [the internal sense-spheres, like reflections, and the external sense-spheres, like shadows], and three [the phenomena related with explanation, like echoes; the phenomena related with meditative stabilization, like moons in water; and taking rebirth in mundane existence according to one's own thought, like an emanation].

The Sanskrit in S. Bagchi *Mahāyāna-Sūtrālaṃkāra of Asaṅga* [with Vasubandhu's commentary], Buddhist Sanskrit Texts, 13 (Darbhanga, India: Mithila Institute, 1970), 62, is:

> māyāsvapnamarīcibimbasadṛśāḥ prodbhāsaśrutkopamā
> vijñeyodakacandrabimbasadṛśā nirmāṇatulyāḥ punaḥ/
> ṣaḍ ṣaḍ dvau ca punaśca ṣaḍ dvayamatā ekaikaśaśca trayaḥ
> saṃskārāḥ khalu tatra tatra kathitā buddhairvibuddhottamaiḥ//

See Sylvain Lévi, *Mahāyānasūtrālaṃkāra, exposé de la doctrine du grand véhicule selon le système Yogācāra* (Paris: Bibliothèque de l'École des Hautes Études, 1907), vol. 1, 62; vol. 2, 113.

The Tibetan, given in A-ku Lo-drö-gya-tso (*Precious Lamp,* 224.5):

> *sangs rgyas rnam sangs rgyas mchog rnams kyis de dang de las 'dus byas dag//*
> *gsungs pa sgyu ma rmi lam smig rgyu gzugs brnyan dang 'dra mig yor dang//*
> *brag cha lta bu dang ni chu zla'i gzugs 'dra sprul dang 'drar shes bya//*
> *drug dang drug dang gnyis dang drug tshan gnyis dang gsum por re 'dod//*

[b] For discussion of this term, see p. 307.

the mantra of illusion[a] is similar to ideation, [which by being the main other-powered phenomenon illustrates all] other-powered natures; Vasubandhu[484] explains that this is the meaning of the first two lines. As the meaning of the latter two lines, he explains that appearances in an illusory aspect as the forms of a horse, elephant, and so forth are similar to dualistic appearances of other-powered natures—namely, apprehended-objects and apprehending-subjects—as distant and cut off.[b]

Furthermore, Maitreya's *Ornament for the Great Vehicle Sūtras* says:[c]

> Just like the non-existence of those [elephants and so forth] in this [illusory appearance],
> So the ultimate is asserted [as the non-duality of object and subject in other-powered natures].
> Just like the apprehension of these [illusory appearances as the entities of horses, elephants, and so forth],
> So conventionalities [are asserted as these forms, sounds, and so forth which appear to have a difference of entity between subject and object].

Vasubandhu's commentary explains that:[485]

> Like the non-existence of elephants and so forth in illusory appearances, the absence of duality in apprehended-object and apprehending-subject in other-powered natures is the ultimate, and like the apprehension of illusory appearances as the entities of horses and elephants, so imputations of the unreal [that is, imputations that other-powered

[a] According to Jik-may-dam-chö-gya-tso (*Port of Entry,* 497.4), the clods, sticks, and so forth that are the bases of illusion are similar to other-powered natures, and being implanted with the mantra is similar to being polluted with predispositions for mistaken dualistic appearance.

The mantra, according to a N̄ying-ma text that I read years ago and cannot now locate, is *thi bi thi bi thi bi,* which, amusingly enough, also could be rendered as *thi vi thi vi thi vi,* or TV, TV, TV (as in the American abbreviation for "television").

[b] Vasubandhu himself does not use the phrase "distant and cut off," which is D̄zong-ka-b̄a's psychologically evocative explanatory addition.

[c] XI.16; Peking 5521, vol. 108, 8.3.2; and Lévi, *Mahāyānasūtrālaṃkāra,* vol. 2, 109. For the Sanskrit, see p. 420, footnote a. The bracketed material is drawn from the commentary following it and from S̄er-s̄hül's *Notes,* 39b.2-39b.6. S̄er-s̄hül points out that W̄el-mang Ḡön-chok-gyel-tsen, in his *Notes on (Ḡön-chok-jik-may-w̄ang-b̄o's) Lectures* takes "conventionalities" (*kun rdzob, saṃvṛti*), as referring not to conventionalities but to the concealer of the ultimate, and thus the meaning of the last line is that the appearance of apprehended-object and apprehending-subject as different substantial entities is the concealer (*kun rdzob, saṃvṛti*) of the ultimate. Jik-may-dam-chö-gya-tso (*Port of Entry,* 498.1), following Vasubandhu's commentary, which D̄zong-ka-b̄a cites just below, takes it as referring to conventional truths. Perhaps S̄er-s̄hül and other commentators avoid this interpretation since it seems to suggests that conventional truths do not exist.

natures are established by way of their own character as the referents of conventions or are different substantial entities from the consciousnesses perceiving them][486] are apprehended as conventional truths.

[Not only that, but also the example of a magician's illusion is used in connection with the selflessness of persons, and so forth;][487] Maitreya's *Ornament for the Great Vehicle Sūtras*[a] explains that:

---

[a] The reference is to XI.30, which with bracketed material from Vasubandhu's *Explanation of (Maitreya's) "Ornament for the Great Vehicle Sūtras"* (Peking 5527, vol. 108, 75.3.3), is:

> The compounded phenomena spoken of by the fully enlightened, supreme Buddhas in this and that [discourse]
> Are to be known as like magical illusions, dreams, mirages, reflections,
> Shadows, echoes, moons in water, and emanations.
> [Those compounded phenomena] are asserted as the six [internal sense-spheres, like magical illusions], the six [external sense-spheres, like dreams], the two [minds and mental factors, like mirages], two sets of six [the internal sense-spheres, like reflections, and the external sense-spheres, like shadows], and three [the phenomena related with explanation, like echoes; the phenomena related with meditative stabilization, like moons in water; and taking rebirth in mundane existence according to one's own thought, like an emanation].

For the Sanskrit and Tibetan texts, see p. 177, footnote a.

A-ku Lo-drö-gya-tso (*Precious Lamp,* 225.1-226.3) calls Dzong-ka-ba's exposition of this stanza an unprecedented good explanation in that earlier Indian and Tibetan commentaries do not offer such a clear exposition. He points out that Asvabhāva does not give commentary on the first two examples and that Sthiramati associates them with the nonexistence of external objects—with Tibetan commentators following him. A-ku Lo-drö-gya-tso calls attention to the resultant redundancy with the second set of internal and external sense spheres that occur later in the fourth and fifth example and says that if different meanings are not assigned to them, they would be repetitive. He puts together the eight examples and their eight meanings such that the first two apply to the selflessness of persons and the last six apply to the selflessness of phenomena:

1. Magical illusion—although the six internal sense spheres do not exist as a substantially established person, they seem to be
2. Dream—although the six external sense spheres do not exist as the objects of use by a substantially established person, they seem to be (A-ku Lo-drö-gya-tso points out that there is precedent for this interpretation in Vasubandhu's commentary, but he seems not to have noticed that there is also precedent for Dzong-ka-ba's interpretation of the first, as can be seen in the bracketed translation given above)
3. Mirage—minds and mental factors appearing as external objects having their own substantial entities
4. Reflection—the six internal sense spheres are reflections of karma
5. Shadow—the six external sense spheres arise like a shadow of the six internal sense spheres (see *Port of Entry,* 499.3)
6. Echo—doctrines explained
7. Moon in water—the appearance of explained meanings to meditative stabilization, or

- The six internal sense-spheres [that is to say, the eye, ear, nose, tongue, body, and mental senses] are said in sūtra to be like illusion from the viewpoint of appearing to be [a substantially established] self, living being, and so forth, whereas they are not; and
- The six external sense-spheres [that is to say, visible forms, sounds, odors, tastes, tangible objects, and other phenomena] are said in sūtra to be like dreams from the viewpoint of appearing to be the objects of use of a self of persons [that is, a substantially established person], whereas they are not.

Thus, these were not set forth as examples showing that external and internal compounded phenomena appear to exist inherently, whereas they are empty of inherent existence.

Moreover, when Asaṅga, in his *Summary of the Great Vehicle,*[a] associates

the natural dawning of good qualities related with meditative stabilization in the water-like clarity of meditative stabilization (for the latter, see *Port of Entry,* 499.4 and 508.2-508.4)

8. Emanation—taking rebirth as one wishes in order to help others

Jik-may-dam-chö-gya-tso (*Port of Entry,* 507.4-508.2), feeling uncomfortable with A-ku Ḹo-drö-gya-tso's suggestion that Ḓzong-ka-ḇa has given an explanation with no Indian background, challenges that his explanation is unprecedented since Sthiramati's commentary on the example of dreams mentions **objects of use** and Asvabhāva's commentary mentions that although forms, sounds, and so forth appear as **objects** of consciousness, they are not and hence are like dreams, and thus both could be interpreted as speaking of a dream as an example of the non-existence of external objects or that things are not the objects of use of a substantially existent person.

[a] Peking 5549, vol. 112 224.5.5-225.1.4; Étienne Lamotte, *La somme du grand véhicule d'Asaṅga,* reprint, 2 vols. Publications de l'Institute Orientaliste de Louvain, 8 (Louvain: Université de Louvain, 1973), vol. 1, 38 (II.27), and vol. 2, 122-124; and John P. Keenan, *The Summary of the Great Vehicle by Bodhisattva Asaṅga: Translated from the Chinese of Paramārtha* (Berkeley, Calif.: Numata Center for Buddhist Translation and Research, 1992), 52:

> Why are other-powered entities indicated as like [a magician's] illusions as mentioned before? In order to overcome others' erroneous doubts with respect to other-powered entities.
>
> How do others have erroneous doubts with regard to other-powered entities? It is thus: In order to overcome the doubt of others wondering how a nonexistent could serve as an object of activity [of consciousness], other-powered entities are taught as just like [a magician's] illusions. In order to overcome doubt wondering how minds and mental factors arise without objects, other-powered entities are taught as just like mirages. In order to overcome doubt wondering how, if there are no objects, one gets involved in activities of desire and non-desire, other-powered entities are taught as just like dreams. In order to overcome doubt wondering how, if there are no objects, one could accomplish the wanted effects of virtuous actions and the unwanted effects of non-virtuous actions, other-powered entities are taught as just like reflections. In order to overcome doubt wondering how, if there are no objects, the varieties of consciousness arise, other-powered en-

the examples of illusion and so forth mentioned in the Mother Sūtras [the Perfection of Wisdom Sūtras] with teachings about other-powered natures, he explains that:

- the example of magical illusion is for the sake of overcoming the thought that if external objects do not exist, how could [a consciousness] observe an object;
- the example of a mirage is for the sake of overcoming the thought that if there are no [external] objects, how could mental factors be produced;
- the example of a dream is for the sake of overcoming the thought that if there are no [external] objects, how could one experience the pleasant and unpleasant;
- and so forth.

Also, with respect to using magical illusions and so forth as examples of truthlessness, the individual modes of using them as examples of truthlessness in the Middle Way School and the Mind-Only School should be differentiated without confusion.

---

tities are taught as just like hallucinations. In order to overcome doubt wondering how, if there are no objects, the varieties of expressions arise, other-powered entities are taught as just like echoes. In order to overcome doubt wondering how, if there are no objects, the objects of activities of correctly apprehensive meditative stabilization arise, other-powered entities are taught as just like a moon [reflected in] water. In order to overcome doubt wondering how, if there are no objects, Bodhisattvas whose minds are not distorted are born in accordance with their thought to accomplish the aims of sentient beings, other-powered entities are taught as just like emanations.

See also *Reflections on Reality,* chap. 20.

9. Maitreya's *Differentiation of the Middle and the Extremes* and Other Scholars

How The Two Extremes Are Abandoned In Maitreya's *Differentiation Of The Middle And The Extremes* (305) {422}

This text says:[488]

> Unreal ideation[a] [—ideation being the main other-powered nature—] exists [by way of its own character in that it is produced from causes and conditions].
> Duality [of subject and object in accordance with their appearance as if distant and cut off] does not exist in that [ideation].
> [The thoroughly established nature which is the] emptiness [of being distant and cut off] exists [by way of its own character as the mode of subsistence] in this [ideation].
> Also that [ideation] exists [as an obstructor] to [realization of] that [emptiness].
>
> [Thus, other-powered natures and thoroughly established natures] are not empty [of establishment by way of the object's own character] and are not non-empty [of subject and object being distant and cut off].
> Thereby all [of the mode of thought in the teachings in the Perfection of Wisdom Sūtras, and so forth, of not being empty and of not being non-empty] is explained [thoroughly].
> Due to the existence [of the other-powered nature that is the erroneous ideation apprehending object and subject as distant and cut off, the extreme of non-existence is avoided] and due to the non-existence [of distant and cut off object and subject—in accordance with how they are apprehended by that ideation—as their mode of subsistence, the extreme of existence is avoided, and ideation and emptiness][489] exist.
> Therefore that [thoroughly established nature which is the emptiness of distant and cut off object and subject and which is the voidness of the two extremes in other-powered natures] is the middle path [that is to say, is established as the meaning of the middle].[b]

---

a *yang dag ma yin kun rtog, abhūtaparikalpa.* For discussion of this term, see p. 307.

b Shay-rap-gyel-tsen (*Ocean of Definitive Meaning,* 207.1) cites these stanzas to show that they give a presentation of the three natures in accordance with the "Maitreya Chapter" of the *Twenty-Five Thousand Stanza Perfection of Wisdom Sūtra* and to demonstrate a complete

The first stanza indicates the character of emptiness, and the second indicates that just this is the middle path.

[How The First Stanza Explains Abandonment Of The Two Extremes][490] (307) {422}

Correct knowledge,[a] just as it is, of existence and non-existence is said [in sūtra][b] to be non-erroneous orientation toward emptiness:

consonance of view with the Great Middle Way. For Ḏzong-ka-ḇa's discussion of the "Maitreya Chapter," see 225ff. and 243ff.

[a] In this sentence, Ḏzong-ka-ḇa paraphrases Vasubandhu's commentary (Peking 5528, vol. 108, 121.2.3), which provides this frequently repeated dictum:

> *gang na gang med pa de ni des stong par yang dag pa ji lta ba bzhin du yang dag par rjes su mthong ngo// 'di la lhag ma yod pa gang yin pa de ni 'dir yod par yang dag pa ji lta ba bzhin du rab tu shes te de ltar stong pa nyid kyi mtshan nyid phyin ci ma log par bstan pa yin no//*

The Sanskrit from Gadjin M. Nagao, *Madhyāntavibhāga-bhāṣya* (Tokyo: Suzuki Research Foundation, 1964), 18.4-18.7, is:

> *evaṃ yad yatra nāsti tat tena śūnyam iti yathābhūtaṃ samanupaśyati yat punar atrāvaśiṣtaṃ bhavati tat sad ihāstīti yathābhūtaṃ prajānātīty aviparītaṃ śūnyatā-lakṣaṇam udbhāvitam bhavati/*

See also Ramchandra Pandeya, *Madhyānta-vibhāga-śāstra* (Delhi: Motilal Banarsidass, 1971), 9.15-9.17. Asaṅga's *Grounds of Bodhisattvas* makes a similar statement; see p. 147. As mentioned above (p. 109, footnote c; and p. 147, footnote c), Shay-rap-gyel-tsen (*Ocean of Definitive Meaning,* 203.3-205.2) cites similar passages from the *Sūtra of the Great Emptiness* and explains them as teaching other-emptiness. He also cites a similar passage from Asaṅga's *Summary of Manifest Knowledge* to establish that Asaṅga sets forth the view of the Great Middle Way. It is safe to assume that Ḏzong-ka-ḇa implicitly is seeking to refute his interpretation.

[b] Ke-drup's *Opening the Eyes of the Fortunate* (José Ignacio Cabezón, *A Dose of Emptiness: An Annotated Translation of the* stong thun chen mo *of mKhas grub dGe legs dpal bzang* [Albany, N.Y.: State University of New York Press, 1992], 46), cited also in Dön-drup-gyel-tsen's *Four Intertwined Commentaries* (164.5), seems to identify the reference of "is said" as "in the commentary" (*'grel par*), which refers to Vasubandhu's commentary, and it does indeed say this (Stefan Anacker, *Seven Works of Vasubandhu* [Delhi: Motilal Banarsidass, 1984], 212; David Lasar Friedmann, *Sthiramati, Madhyāntavibhāgaṭīkā: Analysis of the Middle Path and the Extremes* [Utrechtt, Netherlands: Rijksuniversiteit te Leiden, 1937], 14; and F. Th. Stcherbatsky. *Madhyāntavibhāga, Discourse on Discrimination between Middle and Extremes ascribed to Bodhisattva Maitreya and Commented by Vasubandhu and Sthiramati,* Bibliotheca Buddhica, 30 [Osnabrück, Germany: Biblio Verlag, 1970; reprint, Calcutta: Indian Studies Past and Present, 1971], 22). However, A-ku Lo-drö-gya-tso's identification (*Precious Lamp,* 226.5, following Gung-tang's *Annotations, hu* 119.7) of "is said" as referring to a sūtra cited in the commentary is more appropriate to Ḏzong-ka-ḇa's context given the following sentence, which speaks of Maitreya's text as teaching the real emptiness because it teaches this way—A-ku Lo-drö-gya-tso's point being that Maitreya's text would not be teaching in accordance with its commentary. Ser-shül (*Notes,* 40a.1) similarly identifies the

> In something [that is, other-powered natures] the non-existence of something [that is, the imputational nature] is the emptiness of that [imputational nature], and the remainder [that is, the other-powered nature and thoroughly established natures] exist there.

Since[a] this [passage in Maitreya's *Differentiation of the Middle and the Extremes*][491] also[b] indicates this, it teaches the real emptiness.

"In something" [indicates] the bases of emptiness, other-powered natures, [the main of which is] unreal ideation. In the phrase, "the non-existence of something," that which is nonexistent is the imputational factor, the duality of a difference in substantial entity between object and subject. By saying that it does not exist in that, it indicates that the former [other-powered natures][492] are empty of this latter [imputational nature].[493]

If that [imputational nature][494] does not exist, what is there that exists left over after that? [The phrase] "Ideation exists" and the third line indicate that [what are left over after the negation][495] are the two, other-powered natures and thoroughly established natures. The fourth line eliminates another qualm [concerning the reason why common beings do not realize the emptiness of duality that is the mode of subsistence of forms and so forth, this being because they have the mistaken appearance of duality that serves to obstruct it].[496]

Just this explanation by Vasubandhu in this way of the meaning of what is empty and of that of which it is empty is indicated clearly by Sthiramati,[c] whose

---

reference but more vaguely as "sūtra" (*mdo sde*). Friedmann (*Sthiramati, Madhyāntavibhāgaṭīkā,* 96, n. 113) cites Obermiller (*Indian Historical Quarterly,* IX, 1028) as indicating that this dictum is found in Perfection of Wisdom Sūtras.

I take Ke-drup's statement as referring to the general source for the drift of Ḏzong-ka-ḇa's commentary, which Ḏzong-ka-ḇa himself acknowledges below to be Vasubandhu's commentary. As Ke-drup's *Opening the Eyes of the Fortunate* (208.3) says:

> [Vasubandhu's] commentary says that just this is non-erroneous entry into emptiness by way of understanding, "The non-existence of something in something is [its] emptiness of that, and what is left over in that really exists in it."

However, Jik-may-dam-chö-gya-tso (*Port of Entry,* 522.4-523.5) defends the literal reading of Ke-drup's text, in essence pointing out that Ke-drup is saying that Maitreya's text also teaches such and not that Maitreya's text teaches in accordance (*de bzhin*) with its commentary.

[a] In this and the next sentence, Ḏzong-ka-ḇa is putting Vasubandhu's commentary on Maitreya's stanza together with the dictum that Vasubandhu cites just after the commentary.

[b] A-ku L̄o-drö-gya-tso (*Precious Lamp,* 226.5, following Gung-tang's *Annotations, hu* 120.3) indicates that "also" means "not only Maitreya's *Ornament for the Great Vehicle Sūtras* but also...." Otherwise, the reference absurdly would have to be to Vasubandhu's commentary.

However, as was indicated at the end of two footnotes above, Jik-may-dam-chö-gya-tso (*Port of Entry,* 524.5) holds that the reference is to Vasubandhu's commentary.

[c] Sthiramati is renowned as one of four outstanding disciples of Vasubandhu who surpassed their teacher. Sthiramati is said to have surpassed him in Manifest Knowledge (*chos*

Explanation of (Vasubandhu's) Commentary says:[497]

> In order to refute the deprecation of everything by some who think that all phenomena are utterly, utterly without an inherent nature[a] like the horns of a rabbit, [the text] says, "Unreal ideation exists." "Inherently"[b] is an extra word [to be added to "exists"].[c]

The phrase "ideation exists" is not complete just by itself; therefore, a remainder must be added, and it is this: "inherently." Thus, ideation is not just existent but is **inherently** existent or existent in the sense of being **established by way of its own character.**[d] These modes of existence are also similar with respect to thoroughly established natures.

Also, regarding how the second line [of the first stanza—"Duality (of subject and object in accordance with their appearance as if distant and cut off) does not exist in that (ideation),"—]removes a qualm, Sthiramati's *Explanation of (Vasubandhu's) Commentary* says:[498]

> *Question:* Thus, since sūtra explains that "All phenomena are empty [of inherent existence],"[499] does this [inherent existence of ideation, the prime of other-powered natures][500] not contradict sūtra?
>
> *Answer:* It does not contradict sūtra, for [the thought of sūtra is that][501] "the duality [of subject and object in accordance with their appearance as if distant and cut off] does not exist in ideation." Since unreal ideation is devoid of the entities of object and subject [as different substantial entities,[502] all phenomena] are said to be "empty." It is not that [ideation] utterly does not have an inherent nature.[e] Therefore, this does not contradict sūtra.

---

mngon pa, abhidharma); Dignāga, in logic and epistemology; Vimuktasena, in the perfections; and Guṇaprabha, in the discipline. See E. Obermiller, *History of Buddhism (Chos-ḥbyung) by Bu-ston* (Heidelberg: Heft, 1932; Tokyo: Suzuki Research Foundation, n.d.), 2:147ff; and Alaka Chattopadhyaya, *Atīśa and Tibet* (Delhi: Motilal Banarsidass, 1981), 177, n. 3.

a *rang bzhin ye med, sarvathā niḥsvabhāvāḥ.*

b *rang bzhin gyis, svabhāvatas.*

c This qualification of "exists" with "inherently" is a prime source for determining that in the Mind-Only system other-powered natures are established by way of their own character.

Jik-may-dam-chö-gya-tso (*Port of Entry,* 174.6-176.3) points out that since Sthiramati is indicating that other-powered natures such as "unreal ideation" are inherently established, it is implied that (existent) imputational natures are not inherently established, whereas it is widely accepted among Ge-luk-b̄a scholars that in the Mind-Only School **all** phenomena, including existent imputational natures, are inherently established. It seems to me that this potential fault is why Ḏzong-ka-b̄a, in his commentary just following this quotation, glosses "inherently existent" with "established by way of its own character."

d See *Absorption,* #117, 118.

e *rang bzhin ye med pa, sarvathā niḥsvabhāvaḥ;* for the Sanskrit, see p. 423, footnote c.

In answer to [the objection that] if other-powered natures are inherently established, this contradicts the statement that all phenomena are empty of inherent existence, [Sthiramati] says that [Buddha]—thinking that ideation is empty of the nature of existing in accordance with the appearance of apprehended-object and apprehending-subject as distant and cut off in the appearance of external objects and internal subjects—says [that all phenomena] are empty of nature; it is not that they are utterly without an inherent nature,[a] that is, establishment by way of their own character.

The meaning of the brothers' [that is, Asaṅga's and Vasubandhu's] texts accords with just this, and since just this [establishment by way of its own character] also is described as ultimate establishment, the explanation [by the Jo-nang-b̄as and so forth][b] that in this system other-powered natures are empty of themselves[c] is not at all the case.

Furthermore, with respect to how the third line [of Maitreya's first stanza—"(The thoroughly established nature which is the) emptiness (of being distant and cut off) exists in this (ideation)"—] clears away a qualm, Sthiramati's *Explanation of (Vasubandhu's) Commentary* says:[503]

> *Objection:* If in that way the duality [of apprehended-object and apprehending-subject as different entities][504] utterly does not exist like the horns of a rabbit and if unreal ideation ultimately exists inherently, then emptiness would [absurdly] not exist.
>
> *Answer:* That is not the case, for [Maitreya's text says, "The thoroughly established nature which is the] emptiness [of being distant and cut off] exists [by way of its own character] in that [ideation]." Just this which is the non-existence of apprehended-object and apprehend-

---

a *rang bzhin, svabhāva.*

b For a description of S̄hay-rap-gyel-tsen's initial teaching of this doctrine, see Cyrus R. Stearns, *The Buddha from Dol po and His Fourth Council of the Buddhist Doctrine* (Ann Arbor, Mich.: University Microfilms, 1996), 32. A-ku L̄o-drö-gya-tso (*Precious Lamp,* 227.6) explains that this fact also refutes Bu-d̄ön's position that other-powered natures exist only conventionally.

c S̄hay-rap-gyel-tsen holds simply that conventional phenomena are empty of themselves. When he says that other-powered natures and imputational natures are self-empty, this means that he holds that they simply are empty of themselves and do not have the status of existence. This is clear from his statement (Stearns, *The Buddha from Dol po,* 127) that if self-emptiness were the only type of emptiness, then the ultimate would be empty of the ultimate—the thoroughly established nature would be empty of the thoroughly established nature. Rather, he considers the object negated with respect to the thoroughly established nature to be something other than itself—other-powered natures and imputational natures. D̄zong-ka-b̄a, on the other hand, qualifies the object of negation such that it is not the object itself but an exaggerated status of other-powered natures, this being a difference of entity between subject and object, or establishment of objects by way of their own character as the referents of terms and conceptions.

ing-subject [as different entities][505] in unreal ideation is emptiness;[a] therefore, emptiness does not become nonexistent.

Since [Maitreya] says that ideation exists and duality does not exist, the existent is indicated first [that is, in the first line of the stanza], and the nonexistent is indicated next [in the second line]; hence the qualm that emptiness might not [truly] exist arises [since, if emptiness truly exists, it should have been mentioned before the second line and since imputational factors, which do not truly exist, and the thoroughly established nature are similarly uncompounded phenomena].[506] This qualm is cleared away [by the third line of the stanza].

The objection "if ideation **ultimately exists inherently**" is a case of [the objector's] assuming the posture [of the Mind-Only School][507] that if [something] is established by way of its own character, one [also must] assert that it ultimately exists. The answer does not say that such is not asserted; rather, the answer is given in the context of already asserting such.[b]

Furthermore, this master [Sthiramati] says in his *Commentary on (Vasubandhu's) "The Thirty"*:[508]

> Or, in another way, [this][c] work [that is, *The Thirty*][509] was initiated in order to refute two types of proponents: some [that is, Proponents of the Great Exposition and Proponents of Sūtra][510] who single-pointedly think that, like consciousness, objects of knowledge also [exist] just substantially and (2) others [that is, Proponents of Non-Nature][511] who single-pointedly think that, like objects of knowledge, consciousness also exists just conventionally but does not exist ultimately.

Therefore, the statement that other-powered natures are not utterly nonexistent refutes, as in the earlier citation from Asaṅga's *Grounds of Bodhisattvas,*[d] that **ultimately** existent things utterly do not exist or **in each and every way** do not exist. It does not refute an assertion that [other-powered natures] do not occur among objects of knowledge.

The fourth line [in Maitreya's first stanza, "Also that (ideation) exists (as an obstructor) to (realization of) that (emptiness),"] clears away the qualm, "If an emptiness of duality exists forever in ideation, why do not [even short-sighted

[a] Here Sthiramati clearly frames emptiness as a non-affirming negative when he says, "Just this which is the non-existence...."

[b] The ultimate existence of ideation and thus of other-powered natures is opposite to Shay-rap-gyel-tsen's notion that other-powered natures do not exist.

[c] See p. 425, footnote b.

[d] That citation (p. 141) is:

> there are those who ruin [the doctrine of the Great Vehicle and the correct delineation of suchness by] making deprecation—of [other-powered natures, that is to say,] real things **ultimately** existing with an inexpressible essence, which serve as the bases of the signs of imputed words, the supports of the signs of imputed words—as "not existing **in each and every way**."

beings][a] realize it?" It does this by [indicating that] since they have conceptualization of erroneous dualistic appearance, this obstructs [realization of][b] that emptiness.

[How The Second Stanza Indicates The Middle Path] (310) {426}

That phenomena are **uniformly** empty, are **uniformly** non-empty, [ultimately][512] exist, and do not [ultimately] exist are just extremes and are not the middle path; therefore, the second stanza was spoken in order to refute these extremes. All—the compounded phenomena of ideation and the uncompounded phenomenon of emptiness—are not empty [respectively] of ideation and of emptiness and are not non-empty of [a difference of entity between][513] apprehended-object and apprehending-subject. That this explains ["all (of the mode of thought in the teachings in the Perfection of Wisdom Sūtras, and so forth, of not being empty and also of not being non-empty)"] is to be taken in accordance with Vasubandhu's explanation[c] that it agrees with the teaching in the Mother Sūtras and so forth that all these are not uniformly empty and are also not uniformly non-empty. The meaning (311) {426} is not to explain [as the Jo-nang-b̄as do][d] that the non-empty is the thoroughly established nature and the non-non-empty are the other two natures [that is, other-powered natures and imputational natures].[514]

In accordance with the explanations by the master Vasubandhu and his student [Sthiramati],[515] the existent is ideation; the nonexistent is duality [that is, difference of entity between object and subject];[516] and the existent [that is, the remainder] is the mutual existence of the two, ideation and emptiness. This should not be taken in accordance with the [Jo-nang-b̄as'][e] explanation—which is opposite from that of these [masters, Vasubandhu and Sthiramati][517]—that they assert that since, concerning these two [that is, other-powered natures and

---

[a] It seems to me that D̄zong-ka-b̄a's meaning is restricted to the shortsighted (*tshur mthong*), who, by definition, have not realized emptiness even conceptually. However, D̄a-drin-rap-d̄en (*Annotations,* 104.5) takes those who do not realize emptiness as referring to beings up until the path of seeing; this would allow the question to be concerned also with those who have realized emptiness by inference.

[b] D̄a-drin-rap-d̄en (*Annotations,* 104.6) has "direct perception of that emptiness."

[c] S̄er-s̄hül (*Notes,* 40b.1) cites the passage in Vasubandhu's commentary:

> Thus, this agrees with the statements in the Perfection of Wisdom Sūtras and so forth, "All these are not empty and are not non- empty."

[d] A-ku L̄o-drö-gya-tso's *Precious Lamp,* 230.6. In his *Ocean of Definitive Meaning* and elsewhere S̄hay-rap-gyel-tsen repeatedly makes the point that the thoroughly established nature is not self-empty but is only other-empty, whereas other-powered natures and imputational natures are self-empty. See for instance, *Ocean of Definitive Meaning,* 181.5ff.

[e] Jik-may-dam-chö-gya-tso's *Port of Entry,* 515.1. For a clear statement of this by S̄hay-rap-gyel-tsen see, for instance, Stearns, *The Buddha from Dol po,* 124-125.

the thoroughly established nature],[518] the one exists as factually other than the other, they are empty [of each other].

The *Kāshyapa Chapter,* (311) {426} upon setting out each of the two, existence and non-existence, as extremes, says that the middle between these two—which is described as the middle path of individual investigation of phenomena—is the middle path, and Sthiramati[519] explains that [Maitreya's final line, "Therefore that (thoroughly established nature which is the emptiness of distant and cut off object and subject and which is the voidness of the two extremes in other-powered natures) is the middle path,"] is the meaning of this statement [in the *Kāshyapa Chapter*]. Hence, just this mode of cognition-only[a] is described as the meaning of the middle. Therefore, although according to other[b] Proponents of the Middle [that is, the Proponents of Non-Nature],[520] from between those two[c] the latter [that is, the middle path as explained in the *Kāshyapa Chapter*][d] is asserted to be superior to the former [that is, the middle

---

a *rnam pa rig pa tsam, vijñaptimātra.*

b The Proponents of Mind-Only consider themselves to be Proponents of the Middle since they propound the middle; here, "**other** Proponents of the Middle" are the Proponents of Non-Nature.

c Jik-may-dam-chö-gya-tso (526.5-527.3) lists various interpretations of the two:

- Rin-chen-jang-chup (*rin chen byang chub*): phenomena's emptiness of being established by way of their own character as the referents of their respective conceptual consciousnesses and object and subject's emptiness of being other substantial entities
- The lesser Ḏra-ḏi (*pra sti chung ba*): the object, that is, emptiness, and the subject, exalted wisdom
- Gung-tang's *Annotations* (*ce* 125.4): the middle path as explained in Maitreya's *Differentiation of the Middle and the Extremes* and the middle path as explained in the *Kāshyapa Chapter*
- others: the middle path as taught in the Perfection of Wisdom Sūtras and the middle path as taught in the *Kāshyapa Chapter*
- Sha-m̄ar Ge-dün-ḏen-dzin-gya-tso's (*zhwa dmar dge 'dun bstan 'dzin rgya mtsho*) *Notes Concerning Difficult Points in (Ḏzong-ka-ḇa's) "Differentiating the Interpretable and the Definitive: The Essence of Eloquence": Victorious Clearing Away of Mental Darkness* (*drang nges legs bshad snying po'i dka gnas las brtsams pa'i zin bris bcom ldan yid kyi mun sel*): cognition-only taught in Maitreya's *Differentiation of the Middle and the Extremes* and the middle path taught in the second stanza.

Jik-may-dam-chö-gya-tso, himself, follows the last (see the next footnote); I find Gung-tang's explanation to be more cogent.

d A-ku L̄o-drö-gya-tso's *Precious Lamp,* 231.1; S̄er-s̄hül's *Notes,* 40b.3; and Ḏa-drin-rap-ḏen's *Annotations,* 106.6.

Jik-may-dam-chö-gya-tso (*Port of Entry,* 516.1) less cogently takes the latter to be the middle that is taught in the second stanza and takes the former to be the emptiness of subject and object taught in the first stanza; he takes the "other Proponents of the Middle" to be the Yogic Autonomists. According to him, the sentence means that the Yogic Autonomists take the emptiness of true existence to be superior to the emptiness of subject and object as different entities.

path as explained in Maitreya's *Differentiation of the Middle and the Extremes*],[521] this [Mind-Only][522] system treats those two as equivalent.

[How The Two Extremes Are Abandoned By Scholars Following Asaṅga][523] (312) {426}

Thus, [I] have mentioned at various points the modes of exegesis by Vasubandhu and Sthiramati [on how the two extremes are abandoned]. Dignāga also comments on the meanings of the *Eight Thousand Stanza Perfection of Wisdom Sūtra* in his *Summary Meanings of the Eight Thousand Stanza Perfection of Wisdom Sūtra*[a] in agreement with Asaṅga's *Summary of the Great Vehicle* [saying that the explanations in the Perfection of Wisdom Sūtras that phenomena do not inherently exist—that is, do not exist by way of their own character—require interpretation in that they were made in consideration of imputational natures, whereas the final wheel of teaching is of definitive meaning].[524]

Dharmakīrti's *Commentary on (Dignāga's) "Compilation of Prime Cognition"* (314) {426} says that the emptiness of apprehended-object and apprehending-subject as other substantial entities is the suchness of other-powered natures:[b]

> With respect to that [existence of apprehended-object and of apprehending-subject], due to the non-existence [of a difference of substantial entity] of one [of them]
> Both [that is, the difference of substantial entity of both subject to object and object to subject] also deteriorate [that is, are refuted].
> Therefore, that which is the emptiness of duality [of one of them]
> Is the suchness of that [other one] also.

He also comments (315) {427} on the meaning of the statements in sūtras that

---

[a] *brgyad stong don bsdus, prajñāpāramitāpiṇḍārtha.* Ser-shül (*Notes,* 40b.5) identifies where this exposition starts in Dignāga's text, and Jik-may-dam-chö-gya-tso (*Port of Entry,* 536.4) cites the lines; for these as well as for the passage in Asaṅga's *Summary of the Great Vehicle,* see p. 313.

[b] *tshad ma rnam 'grel gyi tshig le'ur byas pa, pramāṇavartikakārikā;* III.213; for the Sanskrit, see p. 427, footnote a. The bracketed material in this stanza is drawn from Ser-shül's *Notes,* 40b.6-41b.1, where he also offers several interpretations. A-ku Lo-drö-gya-tso (*Precious Lamp,* 232.2-232.5) takes the first two lines differently:

> With respect to that [individual exposition of the emptiness of a difference of entity from the viewpoint of apprehended-object and of apprehending-subject], due to the non-existence of one [of them]
> Both also would deteriorate [that is, become nonexistent].

However, A-ku Lo-drö-gya-tso's interpretation does not seem to represent Dzong-ka-ba's stated reason for his citation.

phenomena are without an inherent nature as just this [emptiness of apprehended-object and apprehending-subject]:[525]

> [That the production, abiding, and disintegration that characterize]
> things abide as different [is differentiated in]
> Dependence upon [a consciousness having dualistic appearance to which] those [appear as] different.
> That [appearance of a difference of entity of subject and object] is just polluted [by predispositions of ignorance].
> Hence their difference is also polluted [or false since they are not established in accordance with their appearance as external objects].
>
> Aside from aspects of apprehended-object and apprehending-subject,
> There are no defining characters that have an otherness [of entity].
> Due to the fact that defining characters are empty,
> [The Perfection of Wisdom Sūtras] explain that [phenomena] are without an inherent nature.

The distinction of a thing's production and so forth as being different is not by way of a mere self-cognizing consciousness but is just by a consciousness perceiving dualistically. Since dualistic appearance is also polluted, that is to say, false, what is posited by it is also false. Also, in the aspects of apprehended-object and apprehending-subject there also are no defining characters that are factually other, and furthermore defining characters that appear dualistically do not exist in accordance with how they appear. Due to this, it is explained [in the Perfection of Wisdom Sūtras][526] that [phenomena] are without an inherent nature.

Moreover, (315) {428} Dharmakīrti's *Commentary on (Dignāga's) "Compilation of Prime Cognition"* says:[527]

> The feature of agent [and object involved] in all definitions
> In terms of specifics such as aggregates and so forth
> Are not suchness [that is, not established by way of their own character].
> Due to this also, those [Perfection of Wisdom Sūtras say that][528] these are devoid of character [that is, establishment by way of their own character].

The form aggregate and so forth, that are stated as definiendums and that are suitable [to be referred to] as form[a] and so forth, which are stated as definitions,

[a] That suitable (to be referred to) as form (*gzugs su rung ba, rūpana*) is commonly considered in Ge-luk-b̄a textbooks to be the definition of form. It should be kept in mind that definitions are considered to be the actual things, not verbal descriptions, whereas the **words** describing, or the **words** defining, an object would indeed be a different entity from the thing being defined.

are all qualified by being object and agent.[a] Although their bases [that is, their illustrations] substantially exist, from the viewpoint of their being object and agent [that is, the defined and means of defining] they are not established in suchness. Thus, Dharmakīrti explains that, in consideration of this, [the Perfection of Wisdom Sūtras] say that [all these definitions][529] are empty of character. This is also in common with the Hearer schools.[b]

Dharmakīrti's *Commentary on (Dignāga's) "Compilation of Prime Cognition"* (316) {428} says:[c]

> [A Proponent of Non-Nature says:] All are [ultimately] without the capacity [to perform functions].
> [*Answer* by a Proponent of True Existence:] The capacity [to produce] sprouts and so forth is seen in seeds and so forth.
> [The Proponent of Non-Nature responds:] That is asserted conventionally.

---

[a] They are object and agent in the sense that definitions characterize or cause understanding of their respective definiendums.

[b] The interpretation of this sentence, which is related with the last line of Dharmakīrti's stanza, is controversial. It likely means, as J̄ang-ḡya Röl-b̄ay-dor-jay says in his *Presentation of Tenets* (129.2-130.3), that D̄zong-ka-b̄a means that the Proponents of Sūtra also assert this type of non-duality. Jam-ȳang-shay-b̄a (*Great Exposition of Tenets, nga,* 13b.6), however, takes it as meaning that Hearer sectarians also (*yang*) are included, his meaning being that the latter are included in positing the thought behind the Perfection of Wisdom Sūtras this way. J̄ang-ḡya objects to Jam-ȳang-shay-b̄a's interpretation on the grounds that Devendrabuddhi's and Prajñākaragupta's commentaries as well as those by D̄zong-ka-b̄a's students Ke-drup and Gyel-tsap explain the term also (*kyang*) in Dharmakīrti's text and the term "also" (*yang*) in D̄zong-ka-b̄a's text as referring only to the commonality between the Proponents of Mind-Only and Hearer schools concerning the assertion on the relationship between definition and definiendum, not to a commonality in treating the Perfection of Wisdom Sūtras this way. This is despite the fact that it is agreed that indeed there are later Lesser Vehicle scholars who, after the appearance of Nāgārjuna, accept the Perfection of Wisdom Sūtras as the word of Buddha and thus the frequent statements that there are no Hearer schools who accept the Perfection of Wisdom Sūtras as the word of Buddha refer to "most" Hearer sects. For summaries of the controversy, see Nga-w̄ang-b̄el-den, *Annotations, dngos,* 142.6-143.1; S̄er-s̄hül's *Notes,* 42a.3-42b.2; and Jik-may-dam-chö-gya-tso's *Port of Entry,* 541.2-545.2). S̄er-s̄hül sides with J̄ang-ḡya, as apparently Nga-w̄ang-b̄el-den does.

[c] III.4; for the Sanskrit, see p. 428, footnote g. Translated in accordance with the commentary of Nga-w̄ang-b̄el-den in his *Explanation of the Conventional and the Ultimate in the Four Systems of Tenets* (*grub mtha' bzhi'i lugs kyi kun rdzob dang don dam pa'i don rnam par bshad pa legs bshad dpyid kyi dpal mo'i glu dbyangs*) (New Delhi: Guru Deva, 1972), 39.2-39.6; see the next footnote and p. 316ff.

This makes the same point as what was stated earlier from Asaṅga's *Compendium of Ascertainments*.[a] Fearing that a detailed commentary on these would be too much, I will not write one.

objects of non-mistaken direct perception! Though [you] use the word "conventionality," [you Proponents of Non-Nature] have come to assert ultimate establishment. To indicate this response, [Dharmakīrti] says, "How? Let it be so." (*kun rdzob sgro btags yin pas ji ltar mngon sum ma 'khrul ba'i snang yul du 'gyur te/ ming kun rdzob zhes 'dogs kyang don dam par grub pa'i don khas blangs par song ba'i phyir/ zhes pa'i lan ston par/ ci ste de ltar 'gyur/ zhes so//*)

Nga-w̄ang-b̄el-den renders this line (which in Sanskrit is *astu yathā tathā*) as ***ci ste*** *de ltar 'gyur,* rather than *ji ltar de ltar 'gyur,* yet he uses *ji ltar* and not *ci ste* in his exposition in the first sentence. It strikes me that, rather than seeing correlatives which *yathā tathā* certainly suggest, he takes *ci ste* (or *ji ltar*) as one meaning unit, corresponding to his first sentence, and takes *de ltar 'gyur* as another meaning unit, corresponding to his second sentence. Though odd at first blush, this interpretation of Dharmakīrti's multivalent text is probably not so far-fetched. Nga-w̄ang-b̄el-den at this point is giving the interpretation of Devendrabuddhi, and so forth, who take Dharmakīrti to be a Proponent of Mind-Only; this is not to say that he is representing Devendrabuddhi's line-by-line explanation of this stanza; see Peking 5717, vol. 130, 276.1.7-276.3.3, which offers two interpretations.

[a] See p. 151ff.

10. Superimposition

The refutation in particular of the extreme of superimposition has two parts: identifying the superimposition that is the object of negation and how to refute it.

Identifying The Superimposition—The Object Of Negation (319) {430}

The objects of reasoned negation in this [Mind-Only][530] system are twofold: [deprecational and superimpositional].[531] The deprecation [that other-powered natures and thoroughly established natures do not ultimately exist or do not exist by way of their own character][532] is only posited through tenets [and thus is just artificial,[533] not innate]. Furthermore, deprecation here is in accordance with that explained earlier as the system of the Proponents of Non-Nature among our own [Buddhist] schools.[a]

With respect to superimposition, there are two, artificial and innate, and within the artificial there are the systems of Others' Schools[b] and the systems of the two Proponents of [Truly Existent External] Objects among our own schools [that is, the Great Exposition and the Sūtra Schools].[534]

With respect to the innate [type of superimposition], since the superimposition of a self of persons will be shown later [in the section on the Consequence School,[c] I] will explain [here the innate] superimposition of a self of phenomena. This is because the imputation of a self of phenomena by [other schools of] tenets is for the sake of confirming the self of phenomena that is conceived innately and because the main object of reasoned negation is also that [innately conceived self of phenomena].

In many texts of this system there is no explanation[535] of a consciousness conceiving a self of phenomena aside from saying that a consciousness conceiving apprehended-object and apprehending-subject as other substantial entities is a consciousness conceiving a self of phenomena. However, the *Sūtra Unraveling the Thought*[d] explains that other-powered natures are not established by

---

[a] See the Translation, especially chaps. 6 and 7.

[b] D̄a-drin-rap-d̄en (*Annotations,* 110.3) explains that these are non-Buddhist schools that have many modes of assertion that terms and conceptual consciousnesses operate through the power of the things that are their referents.

[c] A-ku L̄o-drö-gya-tso's *Precious Lamp,* 235.3. The reference is likely to the section on "the uncommon features of realizing selflessness, the coarse and subtle conceptions of self, and so forth." Jik-may-dam-chö-gya-tso (*Port of Entry,* 546.2), however, identifies the reference as being within the section on the Autonomy School.

[d] Jik-may-dam-chö-gya-tso (*Port of Entry,* 548.1) identifies the passage as occurring in chapter 7 during Paramārthasamudgata's offering back to Buddha the meaning of what he

way of their own character as factors imputed in the manner of entity and of attribute and that, therefore, the absence of [such][536] a nature of character is the selflessness of phenomena.[a] Thus, implicitly it teaches that a consciousness conceiving that factors imputed in the manner of entity and attribute are established by way of their own character in other-powered natures is a consciousness conceiving a self of phenomena. Also, Asaṅga's *Grounds of Bodhisattvas, Compendium of Ascertainments,* and *Summary of the Great Vehicle*[b] with much striving establish that the emptiness of what is conceived by such [a consciousness conceiving a self of phenomena] is the final meaning of the middle and is the thoroughly established nature that is the selflessness of phenomena. Therefore, if you do not know what this imputational factor that is a superimposed factor[c] of a self of phenomena on other-powered natures is, you will not know in a decisive way the conception of a self of phenomena and the selflessness of phenomena in this [Mind-Only][537] system.[d]

Those imputational factors—which are such that a consciousness conceiving imputational factors to be established by way of their own character is asserted to be a consciousness conceiving a self of phenomena—are the nominally and terminologically imputed factors [in the imputation of] the aggregates and so forth as entities, "This is form," and as attributes, "This is the production of form," and so forth.[e] Since the aggregates and so forth do exist as just those [entities of such nominal and terminological imputation],[538] the [mere][539] conception that they exist as those [entities of nominal and terminological imputa-

---

has said:

> That which is:
>
> - the thorough non-establishment—of just those [other-powered natures which are] the objects of activity of conceptuality, the foundations of imputational characters, and those which have the signs of compositional phenomena—as that imputational character,
> - just the naturelessness of only that [imputational] nature,
> - the absence of self in phenomena,
> - thusness, and
> - the object of observation of purification
>
> is the thoroughly established character.

For Ḏzong-ka-ḇa's citation, see p. 107.

[a] See *Absorption,* #95, 98, 99, 102, and 103.

[b] These presentations are given below in the section on refuting the superimposition, p. 207ff.

[c] See *Absorption,* #79, 96-98, and 100.

[d] Ḏzong-ka-ḇa here does not delineate *how* one "will not know in a decisive way the conception of a self of phenomena and the selflessness of phenomena of this [Mind-Only] system" if one does not know this type of superimposition of self, but he gives a hint in the last two paragraphs of the chapter (p. 218).

[e] See *Absorption,* #79, 96-98, 100, and 93.

tion] is not a superimposition; rather, the conception that the aggregates and so forth **exist by way of their own character** as those entities [of nominal and terminological imputation] is a superimposition.

[Dispelling Objections To The Presentation That The Establishment Of Forms And So Forth By Way Of Their Own Character As The Foundations Of Name And Conception Is The Self Of Phenomena And That The Negative Of This Is The Subtle Selflessness Of Phenomena][540] (321) {431}

[First Objection: This Contradicts The *Sūtra Unraveling the Thought,* And So Forth][a] (321) {431}

Objection: If the refutation that forms and so forth being objects of names and terminology is established by way of their own character were a refutation of their being explicit objects of [terms[541] that are] means of verbalization, then there would be no need to prove—that other-powered natures are empty of that—to the Proponents of [Truly Existent External] Objects. This is because it is already established for them that the explicit object verbalized and the means of verbalization[b]—meaning-generalities and sound-generalities—are non-[func-

[a] The headings for the four objections and three of the four answers are drawn from A-ku Lo-drö-gya-tso's *Precious Lamp,* 237.5ff. He says (239.4) these are hypothetical qualms (*dogs pa khong bslang*). Jik-may-dam-chö-gya-tso (*Port of Entry* (564.1, 568.1) also calls them hypothetical disputes (*rgol ba khong nas bsus pa*) and hypothetical qualms (*dogs pa khong slong*). With regard to various opinions about the number of qualms, see Jik-may-dam-chö-gya-tso's *Port of Entry,* 568.2-572.5.

[b] The text (p. 431) reads *dngos kyi brjod bya dang rjod byed don spyi dang sgra spyi;* D̄a-drin-rap-d̄en (*Annotations,* 113.1) annotates *rjod byed* such that the text reads *dngos kyi brjod bya dang rjod byed (kyi dngos yul) don spyi dang sgra spyi.* In translation:

> This is because it is already established for them that the explicit object verbalized and (the explicit object of) the means of verbalization, meaning-generalities and sound-generalities, are non-[functioning] things.

In this way he takes both meaning-generalities and sound-generalities as **objects** of verbalization, rather than considering the first as the **object** of verbalization and the second as the **means** of verbalization.

More cogently, however, Jam-ȳang-shay-b̄a (*Great Exposition of the Interpretable and the Definitive,* 186.5) has *rjod byed kyi sgra spyi dang don spyi* (read *rjod* for *brjod,* since the present is used for the verbal agent noun), and thus it is likely that "means of verbalization" modifies only sound-generalities or both sound-generalities and meaning-generalities, though it is more likely that "means of verbalization" modifies only sound-generalities. Also, the parallelism of D̄zong-ka-b̄a's construction suggests that meaning-generalities are the explicit **objects** of verbalization and that sound-generalities are the explicit **means** of verbalization; this is confirmed by a statement in the next chapter (p. 228):

tioning] things. Furthermore, a valid cognition establishing that they are empty of such would not establish the selflessness of phenomena, and through observing and meditating on that [sort of emptiness][542] the obstructions to omniscience would not be purified. Thereby, one would be contradicting (1) the explanation in the *Sūtra Unraveling the Thought* that imputational factors' emptiness of establishment by way of their own character is the thoroughly established nature that is the selflessness of phenomena[a] and (2) the explanation in Asaṅga's *Grounds of Bodhisattvas* that this emptiness is the object of observation for purifying the obstructions to omniscience.[b]

> Concerning the explanation in the *Conquest Over Objections,* it asserts that the appearances to a conceptual consciousness of sound-generalities, **which the means of verbalization**, and meaning-generalities, **which are the objects of verbalization**, are the imputational eye.

In this passage, his meaning is clear since he explicitly ties "means of verbalization" with "sound-generalities" and "objects of verbalization" with "meaning-generalities" (*rjod byed sgra spyi dang brjod bya don spyi:* see the Text, p. 443). The problem is that it is widely held in Ge-luk-b̄a colleges that both meaning-generalities and sound-generalities are explicit **objects** of verbalization, the former being a generic image of an object that appears to one who has a good idea of an object and the latter being a generic image of an object that appears to someone unfamiliar with an object. However, as Nga-w̄ang-b̄el-d̄en says in his *Annotations for (Jam-ȳang-shay-b̄a's) "Great Exposition of Tenets,"* sound-generalities also can be considered to be mental reverberations of mere terms; thus, in this sense, they perhaps could be considered "explicit means of verbalization," a term usually reserved for actual sounds expressing meaning.

a Again, Jik-may-dam-chö-gya-tso (*Port of Entry,* 565.5) identifies the passage as occurring in chapter 7 of the sūtra during Paramārthasamudgata's offering back to Buddha the meaning of what he has said:

> That which is:
>
> - the thorough non-establishment—of just those [other-powered natures which are] the objects of activity of conceptuality, the foundations of imputational characters, and those which have the signs of compositional phenomena—as that imputational character,
> - just the naturelessness of only that [imputational] nature,
> - the absence of self in phenomena,
> - thusness, and
> - the object of observation of purification
>
> is the thoroughly established character.

For D̄zong-ka-b̄a's citation, see p. 107.

b Jik-may-dam-chö-gya-tso (*Port of Entry,* 565.6) identifies the passage as:

> What is the suchness that is the object of activity for purifying the obstructions to objects of knowledge? That which prevents knowledge of objects of knowledge is called an "obstruction." That which is the object of activity of knowledge releasing from those obstructions to objects of knowledge is to be known as the suchness that is the object of activity of knowledge purifying the obstructions to objects of

[Second Objection: It Is Not Reasonable To Consider That The Establishment Of Such Imputational Natures By Way Of Their Own Character Is The Subtle Self And Thereupon To Refute It][543] (321) {431}

[Moreover][544] if it were that, in refuting forms and so forth being the conceived objects of [terms that are][545] means of verbalization[a] [or of conceptual consciousnesses that relate name and meaning],[546] it is refuted that the illustration-isolates[b] of conceived objects exist by way of their own character, one would be refuting that other-powered natures are established by way of their own character [since illustration-isolates, or mere illustrations, of the conceived object of a conceptual consciousness apprehending form, for instance, are forms; however, refuting that these are not established by way of their own character is not feasible because forms, according to the Mind-Only School are, in fact, established by way of its own character].[547]

Also, even if it were being refuted that the self-isolate of the conceived object [of a conceptual consciousness][548] is established by way of its own character, since it is confirmed even for Proponents of Sūtra that the objects of comprehension of an inferential valid cognition[c] are generally characterized phenomena [and][549] do not exist as [functioning] things, this is not feasible.[d]

---

knowledge.

Peking 5538, vol. 110, 142.3.4-142.4.6; for the Sanskrit, Nalinaksha Dutt, *Bodhisattva-bhūmi (Being the XVth Section of Asangapada's Yogacarabhumi),* Tibetan Sanskrit Works Series, 7 (Patna, India: K. P. Jayaswal Research Institute, 1966), book 1, chap. 4, 26.9; and Janice D. Willis, *On Knowing Reality: The Tattvārtha Chapter of Asaṅga's Bodhisattvabhūmi* (New York: Columbia University Press, 1979; reprint, Delhi: Motilal Banarsidass, 1982), 151.

[a] As Jik-may-dam-chö-gya-tso (*Port of Entry,* 572.5-573.3) points out, it is odd to speak of conceived objects of terms, since terms are sounds and thus material and cannot conceive anything. The more usual vocabulary is object expressed by a term (*sgra'i brjod bya*).

[b] Illustration-isolates (*gzhi ldog*) are conceptually isolated illustrations, that is to say, illustrations *simpliciter;* it is a technical term often used to refer to mere illustrations, isolated from the definition and definiendum which they illustrate. A clay pot is an illustration of pot; that which is bulbous, flat bottomed, and capable of holding fluid is the definition, or defining character, of pot; and pot is the definiendum. The term "self-isolate" (*rang ldog*) is a similarly convenient way of referring just to the object itself, pot, and not any of illustrations, such as a copper pot, or its definition.

[c] Gung-ru Chö-jung (*Garland of White Lotuses,* 19b.3) cogently identifies the "objects of comprehension of an inferential valid cognition" as the appearing objects of inferential cognition, these being sound-generalities (*sgra spyi, śabdasāmānya*) and meaning-generalities (*don spyi, arthasāmānya*), which are the appearing objects of conceptual consciousnesses. However, A-ku Lo-drö-gya-tso (*Precious Lamp,* 238.4) identifies this as the factor, for instance, of forms and so forth being objects of name and terminology (*gzugs sogs ming brda'i yul yin pa'i cha lta bu*).

[d] See *Absorption,* #125.

[Third Objection: It Absurdly Follows That Proponents Of Sūtra Realize The Subtle Selflessness Of Phenomena Because The Following Passage Is Established For Both The Proponents Of Sūtra[a] And The Proponents Of Mind-Only And An Emptiness Exceeding It Does Not Appear In The *Sūtra Unraveling the Thought*][550] (321) {431}

Furthermore, there is the passage in the *Transmigration Sūtra:*[b]

[a] The objector mistakenly thinks that because this passage appears in a Low Vehicle sūtra, it must be established for them, that is to say, understood by them. However, the Proponents of Mind-Only would not accept that this passage is established for the Proponents of Sūtra because they do not understand its import.

[b] *srid pa 'pho ba'i mdo, bhavasaṃkrāntisūtra;* Peking 5538, vol. 110, 145.1.6; for the Sanskrit, see p. 431, footnote a. This is cited in Asaṅga's *Grounds of Bodhisattvas;* see Willis, *On Knowing Reality,* 118 and 164. For the edited Tibetan text and an English translation, see N. Ayyaswami, "Bhavasamkrānti Sūtra," *Journal of Oriental Research* [Madras], 5, no. 4 (1931): 246-260, this passage being on p. 259. Robert A. F. Thurman (*Tsong Khapa's Speech of Gold in the Essence of True Eloquence* [Princeton, N.J.: Princeton University Press, 1984], 233, n. 69) refers to a similar passage in Nāgārjuna's *Bhāvasaṃkrānti.*

The bracketed additions in my translation, except where noted, are drawn from Ser-shül's *Notes,* 43a.1-43a.5. Ser-shül says that he is following the *Explanation of (Asaṅga's) "Grounds of Bodhisattvas"* (*rnal 'byor spyod pa'i sa las byang chub sems dpa'i sa'i rnam par bshad pa, yogācāryabhūmau bodhisatttvabhūmivyākhyā;* Peking 5548, vol. 112, 77.4.4-77.5.3) by Sāgaramegha (*rgya mtsho sprin*) but has tried to rearrange it so that it is more straightforward. Specifically, Ser-shül sees the commentary as giving a contorted explanation of *de la de ni* (*sa [saṃvidyate] tatra*), and he asks that his readers analyze whether his rendition is correct. To do this, let us reconstruct Ser-shül's reading of the stanza, which would be:

> The verbalizations [of "This is such and such" with respect to]
> Whatsoever phenomena with whatsoever names
> Do not exist in those [phenomena through the force of their mode of subsistence as they are so imputed].
> This [non-existence of phenomena by way of their own character as referents of names] is the real nature of phenomena.

Ser-shül clearly identifies *de la (tatra)* as referring to names *(ming)* and the other *de (sa)* as referring to phenomena *(chos rnams),* but the Sanskrit does not support his reading since *nāmnā,* being neuter, cannot be the antecedent of *sa,* which is masculine.

Willis (*On Knowing Reality,* 164) translates the passage correctly as:

> Indeed, by whatsoever name whatsoever dharma is mentioned, that dharma is not found therein. For that is the true nature of all dharmas.

She identifies *de la (tatra)* as referring to the names and *de (sa)* as referring to dharma, whereas Ser-shül does the opposite.

Sāgaramegha inventively identifies the two correlatives in *yo yo dharmo 'bhilapyate (chos rnams gang dang gang brjod pa)* differently; he takes one of them as referring to other-powered natures and the other as referring to imputational natures. He then takes *sa* (*de*) as referring to imputational natures and *tatra (de la)* as referring to other-powered natures. In Tibetan:

> *chos rnams gang dang zhes bya ba ni gzhan gyi dbang gi ngo bo nyid do// gang brjod*

Whatsoever phenomena verbalized with whatsoever names
Do not exist in those [names through the force of their mode of subsistence as they are so imputed].
This [non-existence of phenomena by way of their own character as referents of names][551]
Is the real nature of phenomena.

Since this passage is established also for the Hearer Schools, it [absurdly] would not appear that there would be anything exceeding this [emptiness][552] in even the real nature in the *Sūtra Unraveling the Thought* that is the emptiness of imputational factors.

[Fourth Objection: It Is Not Feasible To Explain That This Mode Of Emptiness Is The Object Of Observation That, When Meditated, Purifies The Obstructions To Omniscience][553] (326) {431}

Moreover, this mode of emptiness [that is, other-powered natures' emptiness of the imputational nature as explained in the *Sūtra Unraveling the Thought*][554] does not involve the meaning of cognition-only that is the negation of apprehended-object and apprehending-subject as different substantial entities. Hence, how could it be feasible [for Asaṅga's *Grounds of Bodhisattvas* and so forth][555] to describe it as the selflessness of phenomena that is the object observed by [the path] purifying the obstructions to omniscience?

Therefore, explain the reasons why these contradictions do not exist in this system!

Answer: They will be explained.

[Answer To The First Objection: The Proponents Of Sūtra Have Not Realized That Such Imputational Natures Are Not Established By Way Of Their Own Character][556] (322) {432}

In Asaṅga's *Grounds of Bodhisattvas,* this mode of emptiness [set forth in the *Sūtra Unraveling the Thought*][557] is explained as the object observed by the exalted wisdom purifying the obstructions to omniscience and as the middle path abandoning the two extremes of which there is none higher,[a] and his *Summary*

---

pa zhes bya ba ni kun brtags pa'o// de la zhes bya ba ni gzhan gyi dbang gi ngo bo la yod pa ma yin pa'o//

He thereby manipulates the meaning so that it reiterates the common doctrine that the imputational nature does not exist in the other-powered nature, rather than that the other-powered nature does not exist in the imputational nature, this being what the grammar seems to say.

In Guṇaprabha's commentary (Peking 5545, vol. 112, 5.4), a detailed explanation of the stanza is not given.

[a] Jik-may-dam-chö-gya-tso (*Port of Entry,* 574.5) identifies the passages as:

of the Great Vehicle[a] says that entry by way of this [mode of emptiness][558] is entry into cognition-only. Therefore, this is not already established by the Hearer Schools [that is, the Great Exposition and Sūtra Schools].

[In Combination With The Above Paragraph, The Answer To The Second Objection: Although The Proponents Of Sūtra Say That The Self-Isolate Of The Conceived Object Of A Conceptual Consciousness—For Instance, The Factor Of Being The Referent Of A Conceptual Consciousness Or Of Being Its Conceived Object—Is Not Established By Way Of Its Own Character, They Assert That Objects Are *Established By Way Of Their Own Measure Of Subsistence* As The Referents Of Conceptual Consciousnesses,[b] Whereby They Come To Assert That Objects Are *Established By Way Of Their Own Character* As The Referents Of Conceptual Consciousnesses][559] (322) {432}

For this reason, even the Hearer schools have assertions of tenets that are superimpositions opposite to this—that is, holding that forms and so forth are established by way of their own character as imputed by names as entities and attributes.

[Proof For The Above Two Answers][560] (322) {432}

It is as follows: In refuting this, Asaṅga's *Grounds of Bodhisattvas* refutes it also

---

> What is the suchness that is the object of activity for purifying the obstructions to objects of knowledge? That which prevents knowledge of objects of knowledge is called an "obstruction." That which is the object of activity of knowledge releasing from those obstructions to objects of knowledge is to be known as the suchness that is the object of activity of knowledge purifying the obstructions to objects of knowledge.

Peking 5538, vol. 110, 142.3.4-142.4.6; for the Sanskrit, see Dutt, *Bodhisattvabhūmi*, book 1, chap. 4, 26.9; and Willis, *On Knowing Reality*, 151.

And:

> How is emptiness apprehended well?...is called "apprehending emptiness well" and "thorough realization with correct wisdom."

Peking 5538, vol. 110, 144.5.6-145.1.5; and Willis, *On Knowing Reality*, 163. For Dzong-ka-ba's paraphrase of the beginning of this passage in the present work, see p. 147. By a final "and so forth," Jik-may-dam-chö-gya-tso indicates that there are more passages.

[a] Jik-may-dam-chö-gya-tso (*Port of Entry*, 574.6) identifies this as:

> It is thus: such Bodhisattvas making effort at entering into cognition-only thoroughly understand....Through these, they enter into cognition-only concerning those mental conceptual consciousnesses to which letters and meanings appear.

For the entire quotation, see p. 213ff.

[b] *rtog pa'i zhen gzhir rang gi gnas tshod kyi dbang gis grub pa:* A-ku Lo-drö-gya-tso's *Precious Lamp*, 240.3.

with [Buddhist] scripture,[a] and, since it is not suitable to refute other schools

[a] The reference is to three passages. The first is that from the *Transmigration Sūtra* cited above (p. 200):

> Whatsoever phenomena verbalized with whatsoever names
> Do not exist in those [names through the force of their mode of subsistence as they are so imputed].
> This [non-existence of phenomena by way of their own character as referents of names]
> Is the real nature of phenomena.

The second passage is from the *Collection of Meanings Sūtra* (*don gyi sde tshan dag gi mdo, arthavargīyasūtra*):

> All whatever fraudulences (*kun rdzob, saṃvṛti*) [put forth by consciousnesses concealing suchness] that exist in the world,
> The Subduer does not assert.
> Because he does not make [superimpositional and deprecational] assertions with respect to what is seen and heard,
> He does not assert those. How could he conceive them?

The Sanskrit—as cited in Asaṅga's *Grounds of Bodhisattvas*—from Unrai Wogihara, *Bodhisattvabhūmi: A Statement of the Whole Course of the Bodhisattva (Being the Fifteenth Section of Yogācārabhūmi),* (Tokyo: Seigo Kenkyūkai, 1930-1936), 48.12, is:

> *yāḥ kāścana saṃvṛtayo hi loke*
> *sarvā hi tā munir nopaiti*
> *an-upago hy asau kenopādatīta* [Dutt: *kena upādatīta*]
> *dṛṣta-śrute kāntim a-saṃprakurvan.*

See also Dutt, *Bodhisattvabhūmi,* 33.10. The Tibetan (Peking 5538, vol. 110, 145.2.3) is:

> *'jig rten dag nas kun rdzob gang ci yod//*
> *de kun thub pas zhal gyis mi bzhes te//*
> *gzigs dang gsan la bzhed par mi mdzad pas//*
> *de ni zhal gyis mi bzhes gang gis 'dzin//*

Willis, *On Knowing Reality,* 120 and 164. About this sūtra, Willis (120) says:

> The *Arthavargīya-sūtra* (Tib. *don gyi sde tshan dag mdo*) exists in the Canon under the title *Aṭṭhakavagga.* There it is found as the thirteenth *sutta* of a larger collection entitled the *Mahāviyuhasutta* in the fourth section of the famed *Sutta Nipāta.* The verse cited here is the third of thirteen verses comprising the *Aṭṭhakavagga.*

For the Pāli, and so forth, see the same. Wogihara (*Bodhisattvabhūmi,* 48, n. 6) refers to "Verse No. 897 (Aṭṭhaka-vaggo in Suttanipāta)."

The third passage is from the *Story of Saṃthakatyāyana Sūtra* (*stums byed ka tya'i bu las brtsams te bka' stsal ba'i mdo, saṃthakātyāyanasūtra*):

> The monk Saṃtha does not engage in meditation depending on the earth. He does not engage in meditation depending on any of these: water, fire, and wind, the spheres of [limitless] space, [limitless] consciousness, and nothingness, the spheres of non-discrimination and non-non-discrimination, this world and the next, the two—sun and moon, seeing, hearing, differentiation, knowing, finding, searching, mental investigation, and analysis....

[Non-Buddhists] with the scriptures of one's own teacher, our own schools also must exist among those who are being refuted, and since the Proponents of Non-Nature or a specific type of Yogic Practitioner are not being refuted,[a] [these have to be Buddhist] Hearer schools. Hence, [on the occasion of refuting this,[561] Asaṅga] does not quote passages from the *Sūtra Unraveling the Thought*[b] but refutes them with three passages[c] established for them.

[Indicating That The Absurd Consequence Of The Third Objection, That Is, That Proponents Of Sūtra Would Have To Realize The Subtle Selflessness Of Phenomena, Is Not Reasonable][562] (323) {432}

Concerning that, let us first identify the innate superimposition. Asaṅga's *Compendium of Ascertainments* says:[563]

> About that [superimposition],[564] it should be known by way of five reasons[d] that childish beings [that is, ordinary worldly beings who have

The Sanskrit—as cited in Asaṅga's *Grounds of Bodhisattvas*—from Wogihara (*Bodhisattvabhūmi,* 49.15ff) and Dutt (*Bodhisattvabhūmi,* 33.23) is:

> *iha Saṃtha bhikṣur na pṛthivīṃ niśritya dhyāyati nāpaḥ na tejo* [Dutt: *tejaḥ*] *na vāyuṃ* [Dutt: *vāyum*] *n'ākāśa-vijñān'ākiṃcanya-naivasaṃjñānāsaṃjñāyatanaṃ nemaṃ lokaṃ na paraṃ* [Dutt adds: *lokaṃ*] *nobhau sūryā-candramasau na dṛṣṭa-śruta-mata-vijñātaṃ prāptaṃ paryeṣitaṃ manasānuvitarkitam anuvicāritaṃ* [Dutt: *anuvicāritam*]. *tat sarvaṃ na niśritya dhyāyati....*

Wogihara (*Bodhisattvabhūmi,* 49, n. 4) identifies this sūtra as being Aṅguttara-Nikāya V, 224.28-329.19. The Tibetan (Peking 5538, vol. 110, 145.3.1) is:

> *'di na dge slong sdums byed ni sa la brten cing bsam gtan mi byed do// chu dang/ me dang/ rlung dang/ nam mkha' dang/ ci yang med pa'i skye mched dang/ 'du shes med 'du shes med min skye mched dang/ 'jig rten 'di dang/ 'jig rten pha rol dang/ nyi ma dang/ zla ba 'di gnyis dang/ mthong ba dang/ thos pa dang/ bye brag phyed pa dang/ rnam par shes pa dang/ rnyed pa dang/ btsal ba dang/ yid kyi rjes su btags pa dang/ rjes su dpyad pa de dag thams cad la brten cing bsam gtan mi byed do// ...*

Willis, *On Knowing Reality,* 122-123 and 165-166. Franklin Edgerton (*Buddhist Hybrid Sanskrit Grammar and Dictionary* [New Haven: Yale University Press, 1953; reprint, Delhi: Motilal, 1972]) identifies *saṃtha* as the name of a monk.

a The reason why these schools are not being refuted is that they do not assert that forms and so forth are established by way of their own character as entities of imputation in the manner of entity and attribute; see Jik-may-dam-chö-gya-tso's *Port of Entry,* 576.2.

b It seems to me that Ḏzong-ka-ḇa here indicates that the *Sūtra Unraveling the Thought* is a scripture of the Great Vehicle and not one common to all vehicles; this accords with the Go-mang tradition's presentation but not with Jay-ḏzün Chö-ḡyi-gyel-tsen's, for instance; see p. 124, footnote e.

c See three footnotes above.

d The syntax of the translation follows Ṣer-ṣhül's *Notes* (43a.5-45a.6), who describes the five in detail within citing the *Compendium of Ascertainments.* A-ku Ḻo-drö-gya-tso's *Precious Lamp* (244.1-248.2), citing the same source passages, calls these the five factors or processes

> not realized emptiness][565] adhere to things, which are verbalized objects, as having nature in accordance with names and verbalizations.

As the first reason [from among the five], he explains that when asked what the entity of a thing [such as a form][566] is, one answers, "That entity is form," and does not answer, "Its name is form."

The meaning of this is that when asked what the entity of the meaning of the verbalization "form" is, one says, "Its entity is form," and does not say, "That which is merely nominally imputed with the name 'form' is the entity of the meaning of the verbalization 'form.'" Therefore, when the convention "form" is imputed, if one examines how [for instance][567] blue's being a basis of the imputation of the convention for form appears, it does not appear [to childish beings][568] to be posited by names and terminology but appears as if established through the force of [blue's][569] own mode of subsistence. A consciousness conceiving that blue is established in accordance with how it appears is an [innate][570] superimpositional consciousness conceiving that blue is established by way of its own character as nominally imputed [to be] "form." [This is the conception that imputation in the manner of an entity is established by way of its own character in blue.][571]

That childish beings have this is confirmed by the above explanation [of how one answers the question, "What is the entity of the meaning of the verbalization 'form'?" and so forth],[572] and also the two schools of Proponents of [Truly Existent External] Objects [that is, the Great Exposition School and the Sūtra School] assert that such a mode of apprehension is reasonably founded. Therefore, although [the Sūtra School and Mind-Only School agree that] the **self**-isolate of the object of verbalization by a term [or phrase such as, "Blue is a form,"][573] is imputed by conceptuality, how could this [Mind-Only system] resemble the system [of the Sūtra School][a] in which the **illustration**-isolates of the object of verbalization by a term involve own-character [that is, establishment by way of the object's own character as the referent of terms]![b]

(*rgyu mtshan*): name, reason, conceptuality, thusness, and exalted wisdom (as does Ḏa-drin-rap-ḏen's *Annotations,* 117.2, in a different order); however, Ser-s̄hül (*Notes,* 43a.6) denies that these are to be named this way. Following A-ku Ḻo-drö-gya-tso, the quotation should read:

> About that [superimposition], it should be known that—by way of five factors—childish beings adhere to things, which are verbalized objects, as having nature in accordance with names and verbalizations.

Since it takes convoluted commentary to name these as A-ku Ḻo-drö-gya-tso does, I find Ser-s̄hül's reading preferable. See also Jik-may-dam-chö-gya-tso's *Port of Entry,* 579.2-586.2, 587.5ff.

a Ser-s̄hül (*Notes,* 45b.2) and Jik-may-dam-chö-gya-tso (*Port of Entry,* 578.4) limit the identification to the Sūtra School. Ḏa-drin-rap-ḏen (*Annotations,* 119.4) includes also the Great Exposition School.

b This cryptic passage is interpreted differently by various Ge-luk-ba scholars. Jik-may-dam-chö-gya-tso (*Port of Entry,* 586.4) points out that this passage (without the clarifying brackets) gives the impression that the Mind-Only School disagrees with the Sūtra School on both aspects of its assertion:

- The self-isolate (see p. 198, footnote b; and *Absorption,* #125) of the object of verbalization by a term or phrase such as, "Blue is a form," is imputed by conceptuality (since the meaning-generalities that are the explicit objects of verbalization *simpliciter* abstracted from the phenomena indicated by those terms are imputed by conceptuality)
- The illustration-isolates of the object of verbalization by a term—or the actual phenomena being verbalized abstracted from the other aspects of the process of verbalization—involve own-character, that is to say, establishment by way of their own character as the referent of terms

If it were Ḏzong-ka-b̄a's intention to indicate that the Mind-Only School differs with both aspects of the Sūtra School's position, the passage in question would have to be interpreted as:

> How could this [Mind-Only system] resemble the system [of the Sūtra School] in which although the self-isolate of the object of verbalization by a term [or phrase such as, "Blue is a form,"] is imputed by conceptuality, the illustration-isolates of the object of verbalization by a term involve own-character [that is, establishment by way of the object's own character as the referent of terms]!

As Jik-may-dam-chö-gya-tso says, the passage might seem to be indicating that the Mind-Only School disagrees with both aspects of the Sūtra School's assertion, but the Mind-Only School does not disagree with the first part, that is, that the **self**-isolate of the object of verbalization by a term is imputed by conceptuality; rather, the Mind-Only School disagrees only with the second part of the assertion, namely, that the **illustration**-isolates of the object of verbalization by a term involve own-character, that is, establishment by way of the object's own character as the referent of terms. Thus, I have inserted brackets into the sentence to make clear where the disagreement lies.

Now let us consider what "own-character" in Ḏzong-ka-b̄a's sentence (*de'i gzhi ldog tu* ***rang mtshan*** *'ong ba'i lugs dang ga la mtshungs,* p. 433) means. If "own-character" is taken merely to mean objects that are established by way of its own character, the second part of the passage seems to be saying:

> How could this [assertion of the Mind-Only School] resemble the system [of the Sūtra School] in which there are own-character [that is, objects that are established by way of their own character] among the illustration-isolates of the object of verbalization of a term!

However, since both the Sūtra School and the Mind-Only School accept that there are indeed objects, such as forms, that are established by way of their own character among the illustrations of objects of verbalization, the clause cannot be read this way. Therefore, S̄er-s̄hül (*Notes,* 45a.6ff) accepts Jam-ȳang-shay-b̄a's (*Great Exposition of the Interpretable and the Definitive,* 193.4ff) gloss of the clause, in which "own-character" is taken not as objects that are established by way of their own character but as the object of negation in the selflessness of phenomena—this being the establishment of objects by way of their own character as the referents of terms. As S̄er-s̄hül (*Notes,* 45b.1) says:

> The illustration-isolates of the objects of verbalization of the term "form" are actual forms such as blue, and the Proponents of Sūtra assert that those are **"own-character" [that is, established by way of their own character] as referents of**

Through that, you should also understand the mode of superimposition in the imputation of attributes as well as the mode of superimposition with respect to phenomena other [than forms].[574] Similarly, when object and subject appear dualistically, the conception that both exist as different substantial entities in accordance with their appearance that way is also a superimposition that is a consciousness conceiving a self of phenomena.

The answers to the remainder of the challenge will be explained later.[a]

How To Refute The Superimposition That Is The Object Of Negation (324) {434}

This section has two parts: the actual refutation and dispelling objections with respect to it.

Actual Refutation Of The Superimposition That Is The Object Of Negation (324) {434}

---

the term "form." How could [the Mind-Only system] resemble such a system!

To get around the same problem, A-ku Lo-drö-gya-tso (*Precious Lamp,* 243.4) reverses who is disagreeing with whom but ends up with the same meaning:

> Although Hearer sectarians say that the self-isolate of the object of verbalization by a term is permanent, they assert that [phenomena] are established by way of their own mode of subsistence as the objects of verbalization by terms, and hence they do not resemble the Proponents of Mind-Only, who assert that although the self-isolate of referent of the conventions of terms and conceptual consciousnesses is permanent, there are illustration-isolates, blue and so forth which are specifically characterized phenomena.

Following this interpretation, Dzong-ka-ba's text would read:

> How could this [assertion of the Hearer schools] resemble the system [of the Mind-Only School] in which although the **self**-isolate of the object of verbalization by a term [or phrase such as, "Blue is a form,"] is imputed by conceptuality, there are specifically characterized phenomena among the **illustration**-isolates of the object of verbalization of a term!

See *Absorption,* #125, 126.

[a] A-ku Lo-drö-gya-tso (*Precious Lamp,* 240.6) identifies the remainder as:

1. Showing the contradiction with the *Sūtra Unraveling the Thought* and Asaṅga's *Grounds of Bodhisattvas* if one accepted the absurd consequence of the first objection, namely, that there would be no need to prove to the Proponents of [Truly Existent External] Objects that other-powered natures are empty (however, it appears that this topic was already covered above, p. 200)
2. Responding to the reason cited in the third objection, namely, the claim that the passage in the *Transmigration Sūtra* is established for both the Proponents of Sūtra and the Proponents of Mind-Only; see p. 211.
3. Responding to the fourth objection; see p. 212

[Reasoning Presented In Asaṅga's *Summary Of The Great Vehicle*][575] (324) {434}

So that one might realize reasonings proving that other-powered natures are empty of the imputational factor—such reasonings not being set forth[a] in the *Sūtra Unraveling the Thought*—three reasonings each are set out in Asaṅga's *Grounds of Bodhisattvas*[576] and *Compendium of Ascertainments.*[b] Moreover, Asaṅga's *Summary of the Great Vehicle* states a question:[577]

> What [reasonings][578] make it evident that other-powered entities which appear to be imputational natures are not of such a nature?

In answer to that question, it says[c] [see the footnote for a fleshing out of the stanza]:

---

[a] A-ku Lo-drö-gya-tso (*Precious Lamp,* 254.2) points out that if Dzong-ka-ba were merely saying that such reasonings are not set forth (instead of not **explicitly** set forth) in the *Sūtra Unraveling the Thought,* then he would be subject to the absurd consequence that these reasonings would not be the meaning of the *Sūtra Unraveling the Thought.* The Second Dalai Lama (*Lamp Illuminating the Meaning of (Dzong-ka-ba's) Thought,* 69.5) similarly adds the word "clearly" (*gsal ba*) instead of "explicitly," as does Jik-may-dam-chö-gya-tso (*Port of Entry,* 589.5). However, since the *Sūtra Unraveling the Thought* does not contain even hints of these reasonings and only has pronouncements on the nature of reality, it can be seen that consideration of explicit and implicit teachings can be, according to circumstance, devices for reading into a text a later perspective. Later Indian Buddhism and much of Tibetan Buddhism moved away from mere reliance on Buddha's call to meditative insight and toward reasoned support that both leads to and certifies meditative experience.

[b] Jik-may-dam-chö-gya-tso (*Port of Entry,* 589.6) identifies the passage as beginning with:

> *gal te ngo bo nyid gang gis rgyu mtshan rnam par bzhag pa de la de dang mthun pa nyid kyi ming nye bar 'dogs par byed pa'i phyir....*

[c] Between the question just asked and this stanza there is another sentence, not cited by Dzong-ka-ba, that says the same in prose. With bracketed additions, the meaning of the stanza is clear:

> [If, for instance, a bulbous, flat bottomed thing able to hold fluid were established through the force of its own mode of subsistence as the referent of the verbal convention "pot,"
>
> 1. the imputational nature would exist in] the essence of that [bulbous thing], but this is contradicted by the fact that an awareness [of the name of an object] does not exist prior to [learning its] name,
> 2. [one object that has many names would have to be] many entities, but this is contradicted by the fact that many [names are used for one object], and
> 3. the entities [of many objects that have the same name] would be mixed, but this is contradicted by the fact that [a name is] not restricted [to one object].
>
> Therefore, it is proven [that objects are not established by way of their own character as the referents of terms and conceptual consciousnesses].

The bracketed material is drawn from Nga-wang-bel-den's *Annotations, dngos* 186.6-187.4; and Jam-yang-shay-ba's *Great Exposition of Tenets, nga* 44b.6-45a.3.

Because an awareness does not exist prior to name,
Because manifold, and because unrestricted,
There are the contradictions of being in the essence of that, of many entities,
And of the mixture of entities. Therefore, it is proven.

Establishing [through the first reasoning][579] *that other-powered natures are empty of the imputational nature due to its being contradictory [for the imputational nature] to be in the essence of that phenomenon:* Let us express—in a way easy to understand—how this is. If a bulbous thing's being a referent or foundation of the convention "pot" were established by way of the bulbous thing's own mode of subsistence or its own character, it would not be posited through the force of terminology [that is, language], in which case even an awareness that has the terminology ["pot"] as its object would not depend upon [making the connection of] the terminology [to the object through being taught language]. Hence, an awareness thinking "pot" with respect to a bulbous thing would [absurdly] be generated [just from seeing the bulbous thing][580] prior to imputing the name "pot" [that is to say, prior to learning that it is called "pot"].

Establishing [through the second reasoning[581] *that other-powered natures are empty of the imputational nature] by way of the contradiction that just one object would be many entities of objects:* According to the other party [who holds that an object's being a referent of the convention of its name is established by way of the mode of subsistence of the object], the usage of many names such as Shakra,[a] Indra,[b] Grāmaghātaka,[c] and so forth for one object must be by way of the force of the thing itself [since, according to the other party, this god is established by way of his own character as the referent of those names],[582] and [in that case][583] just as [different meanings dependent upon each of those names][584] appear [individually][585] to conceptual consciousnesses, so [the one object, the sole Shakra, would have to][586] subsist in fact [as individual objects],[587] whereby the [one] object would [absurdly] become many.

Establishing [through the third reasoning[588] *that other-powered natures are empty of the imputational nature] by way of the contradiction that the entities of unmixed objects would be mixed:* According to the other party, when the one name "Upagupta"[d] is used for two beings, there is no difference in [the fact

---

a *brgya byin.*

b *dbang po.*

c *grong 'joms.* Perhaps also *Nagaraghātaka;* see *Mahāvyutpatti* (*Bon-zō-kan-wa yon'yaku taiko Mahabuyuttopatti,* ed. by SAKAKI Ryōzaburō, 2 vols. [Tokyo: Kokusho kankokai, 1981]; reprint, *Quadralingual Mahāvyutpatti,* reproduced by Lokesh Chandra [New Delhi: International Academy of Indian Culture, 1981]), 3847 and 3848; or Puraṃdara; thanks to Christian Lindtner for the latter.

d *nyer sbas.* The life story of Upagupta is told in *The Aśokāvadāna* translated and published in John S. Strong, *The Legend and Cult of Upagupta: Sanskrit Buddhism in North India*

that] an awareness thinking, "This is Upagupta," is generated [with regard to both of them], and [if those two persons of different continuums are established by way of their own character as referents of the one name "Upagupta"][589] the names of those [two][590] and the conceptual consciousnesses [that are aware of such would have to][591] operate with respect to those two [persons][592] through the force of the things themselves. Therefore, those two objects[—the two persons of different continuums—absurdly][593] would be one object [that is, would be one person with one continuum].[594]

Also, even when one conceives that form and so forth being the referents of conceptual consciousnesses is established ultimately or by way of its own character, this is similar to conceiving that form and so forth are established by their own character as the foundations of imputation with a name. Therefore, even those who do not know terminology as in, "The name of this is such and such," have the superimposition of the object of negation, and the reasoning refuting it is also similar.

[Reasoning Presented In Asaṅga's *Grounds Of Bodhisattvas*][595] (325) {435}

In Asaṅga's *Grounds of Bodhisattvas* [the superimposition of other-powered natures being established by way of their own character as the referents of conceptual consciousnesses apprehending them] is refuted thus:[596]

> If a name is later imputed to an object that existed earlier, "This is such and such," then when it has not been so imputed, the entity of that object would be nonexistent. Also, if it is later imputed to an entity that exists even when it is not imputed, then at a time when the name has not been imputed, an awareness thinking, "This is form," would [absurdly] be generated.[a]

[Refuting Attempts By The Proponents Of External Objects To Dispel These Fallacies][597] (325) {435}

The Hearer schools [that is, the Great Exposition and Sūtra Schools] say [in reply]:[598]

> If the explicit object of the imputation of terminology [that is, a term-generality or meaning-generality][b] were established by way of its own character in the entity of that object, then there would be faults such

and Southeast Asia (Princeton, N.J.: Princeton University Press, 1992).

[a] Ḏzong-ka-ḇa briefly presents only the second and third of the three reasonings given in Asaṅga's *Grounds of Bodhisattvas.*

[b] Jam-ȳang-shay-ḇa's *Great Exposition of the Interpretable and the Definitive,* 206.1; and A-ku L̄o-drö-gya-tso's *Precious Lamp,* 258.2. S̄er-s̄hül (*Notes,* 46a.6) refers only to a meaning-generality. Ḏa-drin-rap-ḏen (*Annotations,* 123.5) has "the likeness of form and so forth" (*gzugs sogs kyi 'dra rnam*).

> as that without depending upon making the association of the terminology [with the object through being taught the name of the object], an awareness of the name would be generated, and so forth. However, such fallacies do not accrue to the establishment, by way of its own character, of form and so forth being the foundations of the imputation of terminology and the referents of conceptual consciousnesses.[a]

Though they say this, it is similar.[b]

[Ancillary Points][599] (326) {435}

Thus, form and so forth being the referents of conceptual consciousnesses[c] is an imputational factor posited by name and terminology, but, since it is established by valid cognition, it cannot be refuted.[d] However, that it is established **by way of the thing's own character** is an imputational factor posited only nominally that does not occur among objects of knowledge [that is, does not exist]. Hence, among what are posited by names and terminology there are two [types], those established by valid cognition and those not established by valid cognition.[e] Still, this system asserts that once something is only posited by names and terminology, cause and effect are not suitable to occur in it.[f]

The two Proponents of [Truly Existent External] Objects [that is, the Great Exposition and the Sūtra Schools][g] do not know how to posit forms and so forth as existing if their being established by way of their own character as the referents of conceptual consciousnesses and as the foundations of imputing terminology is negated. This is not the own-character that is renowned to the Epistemologists.[h]

---

a See *Absorption,* #126.

b Jam-ȳang-shay-b̄a (*Great Exposition of the Interpretable and the Definitive,* 206.3) interprets this sentence as meaning:

> The fallacies [that we adduced] cannot be dispelled through this because [your reply] remains with [that is, does not escape] just the fallacies set forth above.

c See *Absorption,* #78-82.

d See ibid., #108.

e See ibid., #88.

f The Consequence School asserts the opposite—that cause and effect are possible and, in fact, only occur in what are merely posited by name and terminology. Thus, as A-ku L̄o-drö-gya-tso (*Precious Lamp,* 258.4) says, the implications of D̄zong-ka-b̄a's saying "this system" (*'di pa,* literally, "those of this system") is that the Consequentialists, in opposition, assert that cause and effect are not suitable to occur in what are established from their own side and in what are not just posited by name and terminology. See *Absorption,* #74.

g These are the two Proponents of Truly Existent External Objects; however, the assertion is perhaps more cogently limited to the Proponents of Sūtra, as S̄er-s̄hül does (*Notes,* 46.1).

h *tshad ma pa, prāmāṇika.* According to A-ku L̄o-drö-gya-tso (*Precious Lamp,* 259.2), D̄zong-ka-b̄a is making the point that this sort of own-character is not limited to those ob-

For example, although the absence of a pot is a non-affirming negative[a] and it and a certain place come together as a common locus [that is, as something that both is a certain place and is without a pot], this does not prevent the fact that the two—a non-affirming negative and a [functioning] thing—are contradictory.[b] Just so, it is also not contradictory that:

- a consciousness's being a referent of conceptual consciousnesses is an imputational factor that is not ultimately established, but
- a consciousness is ultimately established.

[Answer To The Reason Cited In The Third Objection, Namely, The Claim That The Passage In The *Transmigration Sūtra* Is Established For Both The Proponents Of Sūtra And The Proponents Of Mind-Only][600] (322) {436}

Therefore, [the passage from the *Transmigration Sūtra*]:[601]

> Whatsoever phenomena verbalized with whatsoever names
> Do not exist in those [names through the force of their mode of subsistence as they are so imputed].
> This [non-existence of phenomena by way of their own character as referents of names][602]
> Is the real nature of phenomena.

and so forth[c] are sūtra passages confirmed for the Hearer schools, but it is not that the **explanations** [of these passages] by these [schools] do not differ in

jects that perform functions (a category that excludes permanent phenomena) since—according to the Mind-Only School—in the Great Exposition School and the Sūtra School all phenomena, both the permanent (which are **not** able to produce effects) and the impermanent, come to be established by way of their own character as the referents of conceptual consciousnesses and as the foundations of the imputation of terminology. Therefore, in this context "own-character" refers to establishment through the force of objects' own status (*rang gi gnas tshod kyi dbang gis grub pa*) and not to the ability to perform the function of creating an effect, as it does in the system of the "Epistemologists," which here connotes the Proponents of Sūtra, who assert that the definition of own-character is that which is ultimately able to perform a function (*don dam par don byed nus pa*). In other contexts, "Epistemologists" refers also to the Proponents of Mind-Only that follow Dignāga and Dharmakīrti). See *Absorption*, #40, 121-124.

[a] *med dgag, prasajyapratiṣedha*. Unlike an affirming negative, such as the fat Devadatta's not eating during the day (which suggests that he eats at night), a non-affirming negative, such as the absence of a pot on a certain table, does not suggest anything in its place. For a discussion of the various types of negatives and their relationship to the thoroughly established nature, see *Reflections on Reality*, chaps. 14 and 15.

[b] "Contradictory" here obviously does not refer to a dichotomy; rather, the text is saying that these two are mutually exclusive or are contraries.

[c] Ḍzong-ka-ḅa cites only the first line of the above stanza; thus "and so forth" may refer merely to the rest of the stanza or to all three passages; for the other two passages, see p. 202, footnote a.

meaning [from those given by the Mind-Only School, for they do differ].[a] It is like, for example, this [Mind-Only School's][603] explanation of the statement in a Majority School[b] scripture of a "fundamental consciousness" as the basis-of-all [whereas the Majority School takes it as referring to the mental consciousness].[604]

The aforementioned conception that factors imputed in the manner of entity and attribute exist by way of their own character or exist ultimately is the main obstruction to omniscience. Therefore, it is also correct for the non-existence of this as it is conceived by that [consciousness]—this being the meaning that is delineated [when settling the view of selflessness]—to be the object of observation for purifying the obstructions to omniscience.

[Entry Into Cognition-Only Through These Reasonings][605] (326) {436}

[Answer To The Fourth Objection, Namely, That It Is Not Feasible To Explain That This Mode Of Emptiness Is The Object Of Observation That, When Meditated, Purifies The Obstructions To Omniscience Because It Does Not Involve The Meaning Of Cognition-Only That Is The Negation Of Apprehended-Object And Apprehending-Subject As Different Substantial Entities] (326) {436}

Question: How does one enter into cognition-only through these reasonings? [That is, in dependence upon this mode of proof that factors imputed in the manner of entity and attribute are empty of being established by way of their own character, how does one understand cognition-only, that is to say, truly established consciousness without external objects?][606]

Answer: When that phenomena ranging from forms through to exalted knowers of all aspects [that is, omniscient consciousnesses] are the foundations of the imputation of nominal conventions and the referents of conceptual consciousnesses is refuted as ultimately established, one enters into[c] cognition-only which is the non-dualism of apprehended-object and apprehending-subject. In doing this, one thinks:

In dependence upon a verbalizing name [such as "pot"],[d] the verbal-

---

[a] A-ku Lo-drö-gya-tso (*Precious Lamp*, 259.5) says that the Proponents of Truly Existent External Objects treat the stanza in terms of the selflessness of persons, whereas the Proponents of Mind-Only take it as teaching the selflessness of phenomena as the object of observation purifying the obstructions to omniscience.

[b] *phal chen sde pa, mahāsaṃghika.*

[c] That is, understands.

[d] Da-drin-rap-den (127.6) uses "form" as an illustration of a name, and thus he uses "that which is suitable as form" as the verbalized meaning, the latter being the commonly accepted definition, or defining property, of form. Unfortunately, the definition of form is one of the least evocative in Buddhist scholarship, since it merely resorts to common acceptance of what form is, that is, that which is suitable to be called form. Almost any other object defined and

ized meaning [such as that which is bulbous, flat bottomed, and capable of holding fluid], and the relationship between the name and the meaning, [the phenomena ranging from forms through to omniscient consciousnesses] appear to a mental conceptual consciousness [to be established by way of their own subsistence][607] as the entities and the attributes of the objects verbalized. Objects conceived in accordance with such appearance [to be separate entities from their respective conceptual consciousnesses][608] do not exist, and hence unmistaken [consciousnesses] apprehending such also do not exist.[a]

Asaṅga's *Summary of the Great Vehicle* says:[609]

It is thus: such Bodhisattvas making effort at entering into cognition-only thoroughly understand—with respect to the mental verbalization [that is, conceptual consciousnesses][610] to which letters [that is, names][611] and the meanings [to which those names refer][612] appear—that those lettered names are exhausted as only [posited by][613] mental conceptuality [and are not established in accordance with how they appear to refer to the object verbalized. This is the **examination of names**.][614]

They also thoroughly understand that the meaning depending on letters is just exhausted as only a mental verbalization [that is, as only imputed by conceptuality and not established by way of its own character as the referent of the verbalizing name. This is the **examination of meaning**.][615]

Moreover, they thoroughly understand that those names are only exhausted as factors imputed in the manner of entities and in the manner of attributes. [That is, they understand that the two imputational natures in the manner of entities and attributes—which are factors imputed individually by the two types of names imputing entities and attributes—are only exhausted as imputed by conceptuality and are not established by way of their own character. These are the **examinations of factors imputed in the manner of entity and in the manner of attribute**.][616]

---

its definition would be preferable; for instance, pot is a defined object, and its definition, or defining property, is: that which is bulbous, flat bottomed, and capable of holding fluid. Therefore, I have used the latter for the sake of accessibility.

Asaṅga calls the defined object (that is, the definiendum) a "name" and the definition, the "meaning" or actual object, but this does mean that whatever is a defined object is necessarily a name, because a pot, though a defined object, is not just a name, not just a sound. However, it is clear by the fact that definiendums are called names that emphasis is put on considering defined objects to be names in the context of considering definitions and defined objects.

[a] For samples of six centuries of Tibetan commentary on this topic, see *Reflections on Reality*, chaps. 18 and 19.

Therefore, when they apprehend these as just exhausted as only mental verbalization and when they do not apprehend meanings as well as names involving factors imputed in the manner of entities and attributes nor [anything][617] involving [factors imputed] in the manner of entity and attribute [as other than only being imputed by conceptuality, that is to say, when they do not apprehend these][618] as having the factual character [of subsisting as external objects,[619] they attain] the four thorough examinations [which are entities of the path of preparation] and the four thorough knowledges [which are entities of the path of seeing], just as they are in reality. Through these, they enter into cognition-only concerning those mental conceptual consciousnesses to which letters and meanings appear. [By way of establishing that:

- although name, meaning, entity, and attribute *seem* to mental conceptuality to be different entities from the mind,
- the other-powered natures of forms and so forth are the same substantial entity as mind, and
- uncompounded phenomena are the same entity as mind,

they understand that name, meaning, entity, and attribute are of the essence of cognition.][620]

[Objection That The Above Passage Indicates Entry Into Cognition-Only In Terms Of Only Conceptual Consciousnesses And Not Non-Conceptual Sense Consciousnesses][621] (328) {437}

Objection: This refutes apprehended-object and apprehending-subject related with conceptual mental consciousnesses, but it does not refute—through reasoning—apprehended-object and apprehending-subject related with non-conceptual consciousnesses that arise from stable predispositions.[a] Therefore, how could this be feasible for entering into cognition-only?

Answer: [This reasoning can establish that since a sense consciousness is mistaken with respect to its appearing object, apprehended-object and apprehending-subject are not other substantial entities.[622] Hence] there is no fault, for when it is refuted through reasoning that blue's being the referent of a conceptual consciousness—conceiving the apprehended-object as a factuality other

---

[a] *bag chags brtan byung.* According to Lati Rinbochay and Elizabeth Napper (*Mind in Tibetan Buddhism* [London: Rider, 1980; Ithaca, N.Y.: Snow Lion, 1980], 165, n. 36):

> Saying "stable predispositions" distinguishes between consciousnesses which are polluted by a superficial cause of error and those which are not. The predispositions which give rise to direct perceivers are stable in the sense that their continuum will continue as long as does cyclic existence; those that give rise to wrong consciousnesses such as a sense consciousness seeing blue snow mountains or a thought apprehending sound as permanent are unstable in that their continuum can be adventitiously cut off.

[than the consciousness apprehending it]—exists by way of its own character, it will be established that [a consciousness] apprehending blue to which blue's being the referent of a conceptual consciousness appears is mistaken with respect to its appearing object. This is because, when it [that is, blue's being the referent of a conceptual consciousness] appears, it appears as established by way of its own character. When it has been established [that a consciousness apprehending blue to which blue's being the referent of a conceptual consciousness appears is mistaken with respect to its appearing object], it has been established that blue does not exist as another substantial entity from the consciousness perceiving it [but instead is established as cognition-only].[623]

[Objection That A Self-Cognizing Consciousness Would Be Mistaken][624] (328) {437}

Objection: Then, when it is refuted with reasoning that a consciousness's being a referent of a conceptual consciousness is ultimately established, it would be proven that the self-cognizing consciousness—perceiving [the consciousness][625]—is mistaken with respect to its appearing object because when [that consciousness] appears, [its being a referent of a conceptual consciousness][626] appears to be established by way of its own character. Since, when that has been proven, this consciousness would not exist as established by way of its own character as an experiencing entity, a tenet of the Yogic Practitioners would be discarded.

Answer: That fault does not exist because a consciousness's being the referent of a conceptual consciousness does not appear to a self-cognizing consciousness, whereas blue's being a referent of a conceptual consciousness for conception as an external object does appear to [a consciousness] apprehending blue. This is because there is no contradiction in the fact that being the referent [of a conceptual consciousness][627] is not suitable to appear to a self-cognizing consciousness and so forth,[a] for which dualistic appearance has vanished, but appears to [a consciousness] apprehending blue that is endowed with dualistic appearance.

The reason why (328) {438}, when the referent of a conceptual consciousness[b] appears, it must have dualistic appearance is that when its generality appears to a conceptual consciousness, it definitely appears as having an aspect of dualistic appearance. [However] this [fact of necessarily appearing to a conceptual consciousness as having an aspect of dualistic appearance][628] is not the same for consciousness, because even when a generality [of how a self-cognizing consciousness knows a consciousness][c] appears to a conceptual consciousness, it

---

[a] According to A-ku Lo-drö-gya-tso (*Precious Lamp,* 266.3), "and so forth" includes uninterrupted paths directly cognizing emptiness, these being in a totally non-dualistic manner.

[b] Da-drin-rap-den (*Annotations,* 133.4) takes this as "**being** the referent."

[c] Ser-shül's *Notes,* 49b.2: ***shes pa rang rig*** *gis myong tshul gyi spyi.* The Second Dalai

appears as having the aspect of just experience. You cannot say that it **is** the same [that is, that when a self-cognizing consciousness appears to a conceptual consciousness, it must appear as having an aspect of dualistic appearance, citing as your] reason [the well-founded fact] that a conceptual consciousness definitely has dualistic appearance, because the two—a conceptual consciousness's **having** dualistic appearance[a] and an object's appearing **in the aspect** of dualistic appearance[b]—are not equivalent.[c] If that [these are not equivalent][629] were not the case, one would have to assert that a vanishing of dualistic appearance could not appear to conceptuality, but this also is not feasible, because a vanishing of dualistic appearance would not occur [that is, would not exist at all].[d]

Lama's *Lamp Illuminating the Meaning* (86.6) similarly takes Dzong-ka-ba's reference to be to "how the mode of appearance of consciousness to a **self-cognizing consciousness** appears to a conceptual consciousness" (***rnam shes rang rig*** *la snang tshul rtog la snang tshul*). Jam-yang-shay-ba's *Great Exposition of the Interpretable and the Definitive* (235.6) treats it similarly (***rang rig*** *la rnam shes kyi snang ba ji ltar 'char snyam du bsam pa na*). However, Bel-jor-hlün-drup's *Lamp for the Teaching* (86.4) glosses the reference merely as "when a generality of **consciousness** appears to a conceptual consciousness" (***shes pa'i*** *spyi rtog pa la 'char ba na*).

[a] *rtog pa la gnyis snang yod pa:* Text, p. 438.

[b] *yul de gnyis snang gi rnam par 'char ba:* Text, p. 438. Dzong-ka-ba says "in the aspect of dualistic appearance" (*gnyis snang gi rnam par*) whereas just above he says "as having the aspect of dualistic appearance (*gnyis snang gi rnam pa can du*). I do not take the difference to be significant; it is likely that he is seeking to indicate that these two have the same meaning.

[c] A-ku Lo-drö-gya-tso (*Precious Lamp,* 269.2) says that they are not equivalent, in that a conceptual consciousness's having dualistic appearance refers to the fact that a meaning-generality appears in the face of its appearance factor (*rtog pa la gnyis snang yod pa snang ngor don spyi snang ba*), whereas appearance in an aspect of dualistic appearance refers to an appearance to the mode of apprehension (*gnyis snang gi rnam par 'char ba 'dzin stangs la 'char ba*). Roughly speaking, the first refers to the fact that a conceptual consciousness gets at its object through the means of an intervening mental image, whereas the second refers to what the consciousness is understanding; thus, when a conceptual consciousness rightly understands what a self-cognizing consciousness is, it knows it just to be an entity of experience; it does not superimpose a sense of duality on self-consciousness itself even if self-consciousness appears to it through the route of a conceptual meaning-generality.

[d] As Gung-ru Chö-jung (*Garland of White Lotuses,* 112b.2) frames the point:

> It [absurdly} follows that with respect to the subject, the vanishing of dualistic appearance, it would not occur among existents [literally, "among objects of knowledge"] because [according to you] the appearance of its aspect to a conceptual consciousness apprehending it does not occur.

The entailment being used is: if the appearance of something's aspect to a conceptual consciousness apprehending it does not occur, then it would not exist. In other words, everything existent, at least in some vague way, can appear to conceptuality. It would be difficult to say that this refers even to the appearance of an image of a word for something to a conceptual consciousness, but it would also be hard to say that this refers to an inferential consciousness realizing an object such as an omniscient consciousness. It is said that the **exis-**

[Objection That Something Posited Through The Force Of Conceptuality Could Not Appear To A Non-Conceptual Consciousness][630] (329) {438}

Objection: Because blue's being the referent of a conceptual consciousness is just posited through the force of conceptuality, it does not appear to [an eye consciousness, for instance,][631] which is devoid of conceptuality.

Answer: Then, because a magician's illusion is just posited by conceptuality, a magical illusion being a horse or elephant also would [absurdly] not appear to [the sense consciousnesses of an audience whose eyes have been affected[632] by the force of the mantra repeated by the magician, those sense consciousnesses being] devoid of conceptuality.

Therefore, it is also not that a negation of an otherness of substantial entity between apprehended-object and apprehending-subject is absent in the statements in the *Sūtra Unraveling the Thought* that the emptiness of imputational factors imputed in the manner of entities and attributes is the thoroughly established nature. [Not only that, but also,][633] in that sūtra on the occasion of [discussing] calm abiding [in the "Questions of Maitreya Chapter"],[634] a refutation of external objects is clearly set forth.[a]

[Eliminating Qualms About Other Imputational Natures][635] (329) {438}

Although among imputational factors in general there are many, such as all generally characterized phenomena and space,[b] and so forth, the reason why these are not [explicitly][636] mentioned in the *Sūtra Unraveling the Thought*[c] is

---

tence of an omniscient consciousness can be realized prior to realizing an omniscient consciousness, based on realizing with inference the validity of the four noble truths or of emptiness and making the extension that, if someone can be correct about such profound topics, that person must be correct with respect to everything else, even if those other topics, such as the relationship between a particular effect and its particular karmic cause, are even more hidden than the four truths or emptiness, which are only slightly hidden.

Still, since the first four chapters on the ultimate—in the *Sūtra Unraveling the Thought*—emphasize that the ultimate is beyond argumentation and the entire text presents no reasonings to prove that the ultimate is of one taste with phenomena but merely declares it to be so, this dictum that for something to exist it must appear, to some degree, to a conceptual consciousness suggests the influence of the later development of formal epistemology and logic in Indian Buddhist scholarship and its successors in Tibet.

[a] See *Reflections on Reality,* part 4; and *Absorption,* #52, 53.

[b] Jik-may-dam-chö-gya-tso (*Port of Entry,* 631.6) raises the interesting point that, since space is included within "all generally characterized phenomena," it needs to be analyzed why Ḏzong-ka-ḇa mentions it separately. Indeed, why he does is difficult to determine.

[c] Ḏzong-ka-ḇa says that space is "not mentioned in the *Sūtra Unraveling the Thought,*" but Jik-may-dam-chö-gya-tso (*Port of Entry,* 620.6, 625.4-625.6) points out that space is indeed mentioned in the *Sūtra Unraveling the Thought* (see *Absorption,* #139, for six occurrences in the sūtra) as an example for the thoroughly established nature. Thus he cogently interprets Ḏzong-ka-ḇa as meaning that the sūtra at the point of the extensive indication

that they are not relevant on the occasion of the imputational factor, the emptiness of which is posited as the thoroughly established nature.[a] Although many of those are existents that cannot be posited by names and terminology, they are not established by way of their own character because of being only imputed by conceptuality.[b]

[Reasonings (Explicitly) Refuting External Objects][637] (330) {438}

The refutations of apprehended-object and apprehending-subject related with externality are:[c]

1. In Asaṅga's *Summary of the Great Vehicle,* the reasonings of dreams, reflections, and so forth
2. In Vasubandhu's *The Twenty,* the reasoning refuting partless particles
3. By Dharmakīrti [in his *Commentary on (Dignāga's) "Compilation of Prime Cognition"*], the reasoning refuting that the character of an apprehending-subject is produced from the apprehended-object and is similar to the apprehended-object
4. By Dignāga [in his *Examination of Objects of Observation*],[638] the reasoning refuting that an aggregation of particles or an [individual] minute particle is the apprehended-object

[The Need To Know The Mode[639] Of Refuting Imputational Natures As Presented In The *Sūtra Unraveling the Thought*] (331) {438}

When one does not know—with respect to the statements in Asaṅga's *Summary of the Great Vehicle*[d] that all declarations in the Mother Sūtras of

identifying imputational natures does not explicitly say that space, and so forth, are imputational natures since, except for imputational natures in the manner of entity and attribute, space and so forth are not relevant on the occasion of identifying the thoroughly established nature.

[a] See *Absorption,* #85, 89-92.

[b] This seems to contradict an earlier statement that equates being posited by names and terminology with being only imputed by conceptuality (p. 86):

> Here, the measure indicated with respect to existing or not existing by way of [an object's] own character is: not to be posited or to be posited in dependence upon names and terminology.

See *Reflections on Reality,* chap. 13; and *Absorption,* #105-109.

[c] For discussion of these reasonings, see *Reflections on Reality,* chap. 22.

[d] Jik-may-dam-chö-gya-tso (*Port of Entry,* 666.6) identifies the passage as from chapter 2:

> How is one to understand the imputational nature in the teaching of the Very Extensive Great Vehicle [Sūtras] taught by the Buddha? It is to be understood through the teachings in the framework (*rnam grangs*) of non-existence.

Étienne Lamotte, *La somme du grand véhicule d'Asaṅga,* reprint, 2 vols. Publications de l'Institute Orientaliste de Louvain, 8 (Louvain: Université de Louvain, 1973), vol. 1, 37

"does not exist" refute the imputational factor—this mode of refuting the imputation [that objects are established by way of their own character as the referents of conceptual consciousnesses and as the referents of terms][640] in the *Sūtra Unraveling the Thought,* one [wrongly] explains [all the statements of "does not exist" in the Mother Sūtras][641] as only [refuting][642] the imputation of other substantial entities of apprehended-object and apprehending-subject. Thereby, many great unsuitabilities also have to be propounded with respect to the system of the Yogic Practitioners, and it moreover is very difficult for this system to explain the statements that there is no way to hold [objects] as anything—permanent, impermanent, and so forth.[a] For that reason, one also has to propound that statements [in sūtras] about [phenomena as] being unapprehendable as anything are in consideration of the period of meditative equipoise and that statements of apprehendability in which there is a differentiation of "it is this, it is not that" are in consideration of the period subsequent to meditative equipoise, making such a division of time. This is due to being bereft of having anything to say.

The setting out of the four examinations and the four thorough knowledges in Asaṅga's *Grounds of Bodhisattvas,*[643] *Summary of the Great Vehicle,*[644] *Summary of Manifest Knowledge,*[645] and so forth is said to be the excellent door of entry to cognition-only—the means of settling the view of cognition—[and also][646] the antidote to the obstructions to omniscience [which consist of] the conceptuality that serves as the basis of even the afflictive emotions.[b] To understand the meaning of these, it appears to be necessary to understand from the level of subtle detail the reasonings refuting the imputational factor and the superimposition that are objects of negation discussed in the *Sūtra Unraveling the Thought.* In particular, it appears to be necessary to know how through those reasonings an otherness of substantial entity of apprehended-object and apprehending-subject is refuted, whereupon there is entry into cognition-only. Having seen that [many] nevertheless have not even involved themselves in analyzing these, [I] have indicated a mere door of analysis for the intelligent.

(II.26), and vol. 2, 120; and John P. Keenan, *The Summary of the Great Vehicle by Bodhisattva Asaṅga: Translated from the Chinese of Paramārtha* (Berkeley, Calif.: Numata Center for Buddhist Translation and Research, 1992), 51.

a See *Absorption,* #107, 139, 140, and, esp., 145.

b Here Dzong-ka-ba makes the significant point that this false conceptuality not only comprises the obstructions to omniscience but also serves as the basis underlying the afflictive emotions of desire, hatred, and so forth. This does not mean that consciousnesses conceiving subject and object to be different entities (or conceiving that objects are established by way of their own character as the referents of conceptual consciousnesses) are the afflictive obstructions preventing liberation from cyclic existence. Rather, such false conceptuality underlies the afflictive emotions that prevent liberation and itself also prevents the omniscience of Buddhahood.

11. Handling Objections

Dispelling Objections To The Refutation Of The Extreme Of Superimposition (333) {440}

[Dispelling The Objection That This Presentation Contradicts The Sūtra Unraveling the Thought*]*[647] (333) {440}

[Objection:][648] The *Sūtra Unraveling the Thought*[a] says that through manifestly conceiving the imputational nature in other-powered natures, [all][649] afflictive emotions are produced and, due to that, karmas are accumulated whereby one revolves in cyclic existence. Also, it says[b] that if one sees other-

---

[a] The reference is to chapter 7, where Buddha says:

> Superimposing the imputational nature onto other-powered natures and thoroughly established natures, sentient beings designate the convention that other-powered natures and thoroughly established natures are of the character of the imputational nature. In just the way that they designate such conventions, [their] minds are thoroughly infused with such designations of conventions, and due to relation with the designation of conventions or due to the dormancies of designations, they manifestly conceive other-powered natures and thoroughly established natures to be of the character of the imputational nature. In just the way that they manifestly conceive this, in that same way—due to the causes and conditions of manifestly conceiving other-powered natures as being of the imputational nature—in the future other-powered natures are thoroughly generated.
>
> On that basis, they become thoroughly afflicted by the afflictions that are the afflictive emotions. Also, they are thoroughly afflicted by the afflictions that are actions and the afflictions that are the production of a lifetime. For a long time, they transmigrate as hell-beings, animals, gods, demi-gods, or humans, and travel about within these transmigrations, not passing beyond cyclic existence.

Étienne Lamotte, *Saṃdhinirmocanasūtra: L'Explication des mystères* (Louvain: Université de Louvain, 1935), 70 [10], and 196; and John C. Powers, *Wisdom of Buddha: Saṁdhinirmocana Sūtra* (Berkeley, Calif.: Dharma, 1995), 105-107.

[b] The reference is to chapter 7, where Buddha says:

> Because, hearing these doctrines, they do not conceive other-powered natures in the manner of the imputational character, they believe, thoroughly differentiate, and realize properly that [other-powered natures] are [self-]production non-natures, character non-natures, and ultimate non-natures....Moreover, on this basis, they thoroughly develop aversion toward all compositional phenomena, become completely free from desire, become completely released, and become thoroughly released from the afflictions that are the afflictive emotions, the afflictions that are actions, and the afflictions that are births.

Lamotte, *Saṃdhinirmocana,* 72-73 [13], and 197-198; and Powers, *Wisdom of Buddha,* 107-109. I cited the passage in the Introduction (p. 29).

powered natures as without the nature of the character of the imputational character, those are overcome in that order. It then says[a] that the three—Hearers, Solitary Realizers, and Bodhisattvas—through just this path and just this practice attain nirvana, due to which the paths of purification of those [three vehicles][650] and also their purification[b] are one, there being no second.[c] Moreover, [on the level of what is explicitly indicated, the *Sūtra Unraveling the Thought*][651] does not speak of a mode of other-powered natures being empty of an imputational factor other than that [of the selflessness of phenomena][652] explained earlier.

Therefore, do you take the meaning of this sūtra to be that even Hearers and Solitary Realizers [must][653] realize the selflessness of phenomena, or do you not? If you do, this contradicts the earlier explanations of this as uncommon [that is, as comprehended by Bodhisattvas and not by Hearers and Solitary Realizers]. If you do not [take it that Hearers and Solitary Realizers comprehend the selflessness of phenomena],[654] then how do you explain the meaning of the sūtra [that the states of purification are one]?[655]

[*Answer:*][656] About this, (334) {440} Asaṅga's *Grounds of Bodhisattvas* also says that:[657]

> Conceptualization [that factors imputed][658] in the manner of entity and attribute [are established by way of their own character][659] and conceptualization apprehending amorphous wholes[d] generate the

---

a The reference is to chapter 7, where Buddha says:

> Paramārthasamudgata, concerning that, even sentient beings having the lineage of those of the Hearer Vehicle attain a nirvana of unsurpassed achievement and bliss through just this path and just this achievement. Also, sentient beings having the lineage of those of the Solitary Realizer Vehicle and those having the lineage of Ones Gone Thus attain a nirvana of unsurpassed achievement and bliss through just this path and just this achievement. Therefore, this is the sole path of purification of Hearers, Solitary Realizers, and Bodhisattvas, and the purification is also one. Thinking of this, I teach one vehicle, but it is not that there are not varieties of sentient beings—the naturally dull, middling, and sharp—among the types of sentient beings.

Lamotte, *Saṃdhinirmocana,* 73 [14], and 198; Dön-drup-gyel-tsen's *Four Intertwined Commentaries,* 13.2-13.5; and Powers, *Wisdom of Buddha,* 111-112.

b D̄a-drin-rap-d̄en (*Annotations,* 141.3) glosses "purification" as "the emptiness that is the object observed by the path" (*lam gyi dmigs pa'i stong pa nyid*); however, D̄zong-ka-b̄a below (p. 224) describes it as the state of release, that is, nirvana.

c See *Absorption,* #84, 86.

d According to D̄a-drin-rap-d̄en (142.5) this reads, with his interpretive material in brackets:

> ...the conceptualization that apprehends [a self of persons] as an amorphous whole [which arises from the former conception of a self of phenomena] generates....

B̄el-jor-hlün-drup (*Lamp for the Teaching,* 96.6) gives a similar explanation. However, a consciousness conceiving a self of persons, "the view of the transitory," is mentioned just below as arising in dependence upon "conceptualization [that factors imputed] in the manner of entity and attribute [are established by way of their own character] and conceptualization apprehending amorphous wholes." Using just this reasoning, Ser-shül cogently (*Notes,* 51b.4) concludes that "conceptualization apprehending amorphous wholes" is not a conception of a self of persons; rather, he takes it to be the conception that amorphous wholes—such as that a collection of many types of trees is a forest—are established by way of their own character.

The apprehension of amorphous wholes (*ril por 'dzin pa, piṇḍagrāha*), found in a list of eight types of conceptualization in the *Grounds of Bodhisattvas* (Peking 5538, vol. 110, 145.4.5; Unrai Wogihara, *Bodhisattvabhūmi: A Statement of the Whole Course of the Bodhisattva (Being the Fifteenth Section of Yogācārabhūmi),* (Tokyo: Seigo Kenkyūkai, 1930-1936), 50.25; and Nalinaksha Dutt, *Bodhisattvabhūmi (Being the XVth Section of Asangapada's Yogacarabhumi),* Tibetan Sanskrit Works Series, 7 (Patna, India: K. P. Jayaswal Research Institute, 1966), 34.24), is described by Asaṅga as follows:

> What is conceptuality apprehending amorphous wholes? That which, arisen from apprehending a conglomerate of many phenomena as an amorphous whole, acts on just those things imputed with the names of "form" and so forth with the nominal terminology of self, sentient being, living being, and creature and which acts on a home, an army, a forest, and so forth, as well as food, drink, conveyance, clothing, and so forth, with the nominal terminology for those is called "conceptuality apprehending amorphous wholes."

The Sanskrit (Wogihara, *Bodhisattvabhūmi,* 52.4; and Dutt, *Bodhisattvabhūmi,* 35.20) is:

> *piṇḍa-grāha-vikalpaḥ katamaḥ. yas tasminn eva rūp'ādi-saṃjñake vastuni ātma-sattva-jīva-jantu-saṃjñā-saṃketopasaṃhitaḥ piṇḍiteṣu bahuṣu dharmeṣu piṇḍa-grāha-hetukaḥ pravartate gṛha-senā-van'ādiṣu bhojana-pāna-yāna-vastr'ādiṣu ca tat-saṃjñā-saṃketopasaṃhitaḥ. ayam ucayate piṇḍa-grāha-vikalpaḥ.*

The Tibetan (Peking 5538, vol. 110, 146.1.4) is:

> *ril por 'dzin pa'i rnam par rtog pa gang zhe na/ gzugs la sogs par ming btags pa'i dngos po de nyid la bdag dang/ sems can dang/ srog dang/ skye ba po'i ming gi brda dang ldan pa/ khyim dang/ dmag dang/ nags la sogs pa dang/ zas dang/ skom* [text reads: *sgom*] *dang/ bzhon pa dang/ gos la sogs pa de dag la de dag gi ming gi brda dang ldan pa/ chos mang po bsdus pa dag la ril por 'dzin pa'i rgyu las byung ba 'jug pa gang yin pa de ni ril por 'dzin pa'i rnam par rtog pa zhes bya'o//*

See also Christian Lindtner, "A Treatise on Buddhist Idealism: Kambala's Ālokamālā," in *Miscellanea Buddhica,* ed. Christian Lindtner (Copenhagen: Akademisk Forlag, 1985), 167, n. 135.

A-ku Lo-drö-gya-tso (286.6) and Bel-jor-hlün-drup (95.4) give only general commentaries, without identifying whether this is a conception of a self of persons or a conception of a self of phenomena. However, as mentioned above, it is much more likely that this section is describing aspects of the conception of a self of phenomena. In Ge-luk-ba exegesis of the Mind-Only system, the objects of a conception of a self of phenomena are not limited to phenomena other than persons but include persons as well, since the distinctive feature of a conception of a self of phenomena is to conceive that the object in question is established by way of its own character as the referent of a conceptual consciousness, and thus the conception of a self of phenomena can be done with respect to anything, whether a person or an-

> foundations of [fictional] proliferations[a]—the things that are the objects observed by conceptuality. In dependence upon that, the view of the transitory[b] [as substantially established I and mine] is generated, and through this the other afflictive emotions are produced, whereby one travels in cyclic existence. However, if through the four examinations and the four thorough knowledges, one understands the objects apprehended by conceptuality as nonexistent, those [afflictive emotions and so forth][660] are overcome.

In that way, [Asaṅga] asserts that a consciousness conceiving a self of phenomena—which conceives that factors imputed in the manner of entities and attributes are established by way of their own character in phenomena—acts as the root of the view of the transitory [as substantially established I and mine].

That a consciousness conceiving a self of phenomena acts as the basis of a consciousness conceiving a self of persons is also asserted by those Proponents of the Middle [that is, Autonomists] who assert that Hearers and Solitary Realizers do not have realization of the selflessness of phenomena.[c] Concerning that, when the conception of a self of phenomena is extinguished, the conception of a self of persons is overcome, but if the conception of a self of phenomena has not been extinguished, it is not that the conception of a self of persons has not been overcome. Hence, it is not contradictory for one to have been released from cyclic existence although the **final** basis of cyclic existence has not been overcome.

Therefore, even though the statement "just this path" [cited above from the *Sūtra Unraveling the Thought*] refers to the path of realizing other-powered natures as empty of the imputational character, it need not refer to the path of the selflessness of phenomena because Asaṅga's *Summary of Manifest Knowledge*[d] also speaks of other-powered natures' emptiness of the imputational fac-

other phenomenon. The conception of a self of persons, according to most explanations, consists of the apprehension that persons are substantially existent in the sense of being self-sufficient. See *Absorption,* #83, 84, 86.

a Ḏa-drin-rap-ḏen (*Annotations,* 142.6) says that the three above-mentioned conceptions generate "improper mental application conceptualizing cleanliness, happiness, permanence, and self"; however, it is more likely that this phase of the process is limited to the conception of a self of phenomena since the view of the transitory is generated in dependence upon this sequence. In this way, Ser-shül (*Notes,* 52a.1) speculates that the meaning is that the previous three conceptions generate a liking for such superimpositions and, thereby, a proliferation of conceptuality.

b *'jig lta, satkāyadṛṣṭi.*

c Yogic Autonomists assert that Solitary Realizers cognize what is for them merely the **coarse** selflessness of phenomena, this being the non-difference of entity between subject and object; the subtle selflessness is the emptiness of true existence of all phenomena.

d Jik-may-dam-chö-gya-tso (*Port of Entry,* 675.3) cites a passage from *Summary of Manifest Knowledge:*

tor in terms of the selflessness of persons. Since there is no difference between the Great and Small Vehicles with respect to afflictive emotions being purified through realizing the selflessness of persons and with respect to the release [that is, nirvana][661] that is a mere abandonment of afflictive emotions, it is also said [in the *Sūtra Unraveling the Thought*] that the paths of purification and the purification [that is, the state of having been purified] are the same. [Therefore, the above-mentioned contradictions are not incurred.][662]

As the meaning of the Great Vehicle sūtras, the *Sūtra Unraveling the Thought* spells out:

- The positing of the aggregates and so forth as other-powered natures
- The positing of the self of phenomena superimposed on those as the imputational factor
- The positing of their emptiness of that [imputational nature] as the thoroughly established nature that is the selflessness of phenomena

Through the force of this exposition, one can understand that the meaning of the Low Vehicle sūtras is just the presentation of the three natures in which the emptiness of the imputational factor—a self of persons—in other-powered natures—the aggregates—is posited as the thoroughly established nature that is the selflessness of persons.[a] Therefore, it is implicit to the exposition in the *Sūtra Unraveling the Thought* that the trainees for whom the first wheel was spoken are suitable as vessels for realizing the character-non-nature in terms of the selflessness of persons and are not suitable as vessels for realizing the character-non-nature[b] in terms of the selflessness of phenomena. This is the meaning of the statement that the wheel of doctrine of good differentiation is for the sake of those engaged in all vehicles.[c]

> What are the divisions of the character of reality? The selflessness and non-existence of a sentient being, living being, creature, sustainer, person, one born from Manu, and child of Manu in those aggregates, constituents, and sense spheres. Selflessness just exists.

Jik-may-dam-chö-gya-tso then refers to but does not cite the commentary of Jinaputra (*rgyal sras ma*) which states that the emptiness of a self of persons that is imputed to the other-powered natures of the aggregates and so forth is a thoroughly established nature. See *Absorption,* #153-157.

[a] This sentence strongly suggests that the selflessness of persons is a thoroughly established nature, but some hold that it means only that the selflessness of persons is a thoroughly established nature **in terms of the selflessness of persons** but is not an actual thoroughly established nature. See ibid., #153-157.

[b] See ibid., #95.

[c] About the third wheel of doctrine, Paramārthasamudgata, in relating back to Buddha the meaning of what he has said, says (p. 116):

> Based on just the naturelessness of phenomena and based on just the absence of production, the absence of cessation, quiescence from the start, and naturally

[Dispelling The Challenge That This Presentation Contradicts The Conquest Over Objections About The Three Mother Scriptures][a] (335) {441}

passed beyond sorrow, the Supramundane Victor turned a third wheel of doctrine **for those engaged in all vehicles**, possessed of good differentiation, fantastic and marvelous. This wheel of doctrine turned by the Supramundane Victor is unsurpassable, does not afford an occasion [for refutation], is of definitive meaning, and does not serve as a basis for controversy.

According to Jik-may-dam-chö-gya-tso (*Port of Entry*, 298.2):

1. Wonch'uk takes this as meaning that there are cases of all three types of trainees (Hearer, Solitary Realizer, and Bodhisattva) attaining the respective fruits of their paths **in dependence upon** the *Sūtra Unraveling the Thought*
2. Jay-d̄zün Chö-ḡyi-gyel-tsen similarly says that the *Sūtra Unraveling the Thought* has trainees of both the Great and Lesser Vehicles
3. The Second Dalai Lama, Gung-ru Chö-jung, and Jam-ȳang-shay-b̄a as well as the followers of the latter two say that this refers to those **(followers of the Great Vehicle)** who are able to realize—in dependence upon the explanation of the thought of the first two vehicles by the third vehicle—that the thoughts behind the first two vehicles contain the two selflessnesses (that is, the selflessness of persons and the selflessness of phenomena respectively)
4. The *Illumination of the Difficult to Realize* (*rtogs dka'i snang ba*) says that, although the intended trainees of the *Sūtra Unraveling the Thought* are those who have the Great Vehicle lineage, those of duller faculties among them are fit to be led into another (that is, Lesser) vehicle.

Jik-may-dam-chö-gya-tso favors the third opinion, as do I.

[a] *yum gsum gnod 'joms / 'phags pa shes rab kyi pha rol tu phyin pa 'bum pa dang nyi khri lnga stong pa dang khri brgyad stong pa'i rgya cher bshad pa, āryaśatasāhasrikāpañcaviṃsatisāhasrikā-aṣṭadaśasāhasrikāprajñāpāramitābṛhaṭṭīkā;* Peking 5206, vol. 93. The commentary on the "Maitreya Chapter" is 334.2.1-339.3.6. The three mothers are the *One Hundred Thousand Stanza, Twenty-Five Thousand Stanza,* and *Eighteen Thousand Stanza Perfection of Wisdom Sūtras.* Gyurme Dorje and Matthew Kapstein (*The Nyingma School of Tibetan Buddhism: Its Fundamentals and History* [Boston: Wisdom, 1991], vol. 2, 93, n. 1325) mistakenly assert that Ge-luk scholars identify the *Conquest Over Objections about the Three Mother Scriptures* as a commentary solely on the *One Hundred Thousand Stanza Perfection of Wisdom Sūtra* (Peking 5205). Lama Chimpa and Alaka Chattopadhyaya (*Tāranātha's History of Buddhism in India* [Simla, India: 1970; reprint, Delhi: Motilal Banarsidass, 1990], 417) list the latter commentary as by Damṣṭrāsena, and at the end of this section D̄zong-ka-b̄a identifies the *Conquest Over Objections about the Three Mother Scriptures* as by him.

The translation of this section, which goes to the end of the chapter, follows the extensive and cogent explanation by Jik-may-dam-chö-gya-tso's *Port of Entry,* 680.6-698.1; the heading here is from 680.6. Jik-may-dam-chö-gya-tso's interpretation, framed as an interpretation by "others," disagrees with that by Jam-ȳang-shay-b̄a; Jik-may-dam-chö-gya-tso (690.3-693.5) lists and refutes Jam-ȳang-shay-b̄a's many statements that indicate that for him the *Conquest Over Objections* actually is similar in view to the Jo-nang-b̄as and to the Sāṃkhyas.

[*Objection by followers of Döl-bo-ba Shay-rap-gyel-tsen:*[a] According to you, Dzong-ka-ba,] on all occasions of the emptiness of factors imputed in the manner of entity and attribute and factors imputed in the manner of other substantial entities of apprehended-object and apprehending-subject—(1) just other-powered natures must be taken as the bases of emptiness [that is, the things that are empty] and (2) their emptiness in terms of the two above-mentioned [imputational natures] must be taken as the thoroughly established nature. If so, how do you interpret the statement by Vasubandhu in his *Conquest Over Objections about the Three Mother Scriptures* in which he takes the thoroughly established nature as the basis of emptiness and speaks of its emptiness of the other two natures? That text [in a summary statement] says:[b]

> Concerning that [statement in Perfection of Wisdom Sūtras, "The eye is empty of the eye,"][c] "The eye" is the eye of reality [that is, the reality of the eye].[663] "Of the eye" is of (1) the eye that is the imputational factor and (2) the eye that is the imputed. "Empty" means "devoid." Such is likewise to be applied to "The ear is empty of the ear," and so forth.

[Answer:][664] With respect to that, (337) {442} when the thoroughly established nature that is the selflessness of phenomena is delineated in either the Yogic Practice School or the Middle Way School, the bases of emptiness with respect to which [the thoroughly established nature] is delineated are relative to those bases with respect to which a self of phenomena is conceived by a consciousness conceiving a self of phenomena. It is like, for example, the fact that if you wish to remove the suffering of fright from someone upon that person's apprehending a rope as a snake, you must show—upon taking the rope as the

---

[a] *dol po ba rjes 'brang dag:* A-ku Lo-drö-gya-tso's *Precious Lamp,* 287.5; the phrase might mean, "Döl-bo-ba and his followers." About Shay-rap-gyel-tsen's reliance on the *Conquest Over Objections,* Cyrus R. Stearns (*The Buddha from Dol po and His Fourth Council of the Buddhist Doctrine* [Ann Arbor, Mich.: University Microfilms, 1996], 139) says:

> Dol po pa emphasized that the *Bṛhaṭṭīkā* was the work of Vasubandhu, and gave it a place of central importance in his interpretation of *Prajñāpāramitā* thought.

See also David Seyfort Ruegg, *La Théorie du Tathāgathagarbha et du Gotra: Études sur la sotériologie et la gnoséologie du bouddhisme* (Paris: École Française d'Extrême-Orient, 1969), 325-327. For a closely related discussion, see Dzong-ka-ba's refutation of Ratnākarashānti's *Quintessential Instructions on the Perfection of Wisdom* on the issue of what requires and what is definitive (p. 243 ff.) and the accompanying footnotes.

[b] Peking 5206, vol. 93, 230.4.4-230.4.6; chap. 2. Stearns (*The Buddha from Dol po,* 142) cites a similar passage just before this; see the next citation from the *Conquest Over Objections.*

[c] Ser-shül's *Notes,* 52a.5; for a typical passage from the *Twenty-Five Thousand Stanza Perfection of Wisdom Sūtra,* see p. 349. Shay-rap-gyel-tsen (*Ocean of Definitive Meaning,* 196.4) cites a similar explanation in the *One Hundred Thousand Stanza Perfection of Wisdom Sūtra.*

basis of emptiness—that it is empty of a snake. However, it is not suitable to take the rope's **emptiness** of a snake as the basis of emptiness and say that it is empty [of being a rope and a snake] because of existing as factually other [than them].

Furthermore, (338) {442} with respect to the conception of a self of phenomena, such conceptions as that directionally partless minute particles exist and that objects of apprehension composed of them exist or that a moment of consciousness that has no earlier and later temporal parts exists or that a consciousness that is a continuum composed of those exists—these being imputed only by those whose awarenesses have been affected by [mistaken] tenets—occur only among those proponents of tenets and do not exist among other sentient beings. Therefore, though an emptiness that is no more than merely an absence of those [objects of negation][665] is taught, it does not at all harm the innate conception of self that has resided [in the mental continuum] beginninglessly. Therefore, it must be taught that those bases—that the innate conception of self conceives as self—are empty of self in the way that such is conceived. It must be understood that the refutation of imputational factors that are constructed by tenet systems is a branch [of the process] of refuting that [innate conception of self].[666]

This being the case, since ordinary sentient beings conceive just these other-powered internal and external things—eyes, forms, and so forth which are objects seen, heard, and so forth—as self [that is, as objects and subjects that are different entities or as established by way of their own character as the referents of conceptual consciousnesses and of words], emptiness must be delineated within taking just these as the bases of emptiness. The error does not come through holding that the other two natures [that is, other-powered natures and imputational natures] exist as other factualities in the thoroughly established nature. Therefore, how could selflessness be delineated within thinking [as the Jo-nang-b̄as do] that the thoroughly established nature is empty because of existing as factually other than the other two natures!

Furthermore, the conception that a self of phenomena exists is not a conception that some other thing exists, as in the conception that fire exists on a pass. Rather, one conceives that when there is an appearance—[to][667] one's own mind—as external object and internal subject in the manner of being separate, distant, and cut off, these are established in the way that they appear. Hence, as an antidote to this, it is taught that appearances as object and subject are [in fact][668] not established as other substantial entities of apprehended-object and apprehending-subject, but it is not taught that apprehended-object and apprehending-subject do not exist as other factualities with respect to that [thoroughly established nature]. Therefore, Sthiramati's *Explanation of (Vasubandhu's) Commentary on (Maitreya's) "Differentiation of the Middle and the Extremes"*[669] also says that it is not like a temple's being empty of monastics and so forth[a] but like a rope's being empty of a snake. The other mode of emptiness of a self of phenomena [that is, objects' emptiness of establishment by way of their own character as the referents of conceptual consciousnesses] is also that way.

Therefore, without letting it become like the worldly [example] of putting a scapegoat effigy at the western door when a demon is bringing harm at the eastern door, one should meditate on an emptiness that is such that the emptiness of the imputational self as it is conceived in just those other-powered natures—these being the bases apprehended as self—is the thoroughly established nature. If this is done, it will serve as an antidote to the conception of self.[b] If, on the other hand, one meditates on an emptiness the mode of which is other than this style, it will not harm the conception of self at all.

[Showing That The *Conquest Over Objections* Means Something Else And Establishing That It Is Not Contradictory][c] (337) {443}

[Though, from the literal run of the summary statement in the *Conquest Over Objections* quoted above (p. 226), it might seem that the thoroughly established nature's emptiness of imputational natures and other-powered natures is the final reality, this is not the meaning of that text because of what that text says in its extensive explanation.][670] Concerning the explanation in the *Conquest Over Objections,* it asserts that:

- Appearances to a conceptual consciousness of sound-generalities, which are the means of verbalization, and meaning-generalities, which are the objects of verbalization, are the imputational eye
- The appearance as an eye that has the essence of apprehending an object of apprehension, a sense-sphere of form,[d] is the imputed eye
- The thoroughly established nature known by individual self-cognition in meditative equipoise (1) which is inexpressible due to being devoid of the means of verbalization and the objects of verbalization that are sound-generalities and meaning-generalities and (2) which is devoid of individual appearances as the object apprehended [by the eye] and the apprehending-subject which is the eye—is the eye of reality [that is, the reality of the eye][671]

---

[a] In just this way, Ṡhay-rap-gyel-tsen, in his *The Fourth Council* (Stearns, *The Buddha from Dol po,* 215), uses the similes of an empty village and an empty vase.

[b] "Self" here does not mean person but (1) the establishment of objects by way of their own character as the referents of conceptual consciousnesses and of words and (2) the establishment of subject and object as different entities.

[c] Jik-may-dam-chö-gya-tso cogently sees this section as Ḏzong-ka-ḇa's spelling out the meaning of the *Conquest Over Objections* such that it does not contradict Ḏzong-ka-ḇa's own assertions. A-ku Ḻo-drö-gya-tso (*Precious Lamp,* 289.2), however, entitles it "stating the explanation in the *Conquest Over Objections* and indicating that it contradicts the Mother Sūtras."

[d] *gzugs kyi skye mched, rūpāyatana.*

Therefore, about the reality of the eye—which, in the perspective of a Superior's meditative equipoise, is devoid of the dualistic appearances that are (1) the appearance as object of verbalization and means of verbalization and (2) the appearance as apprehended-object and apprehending-subject—[the *Conquest Over Objections*] says that the object of meditative equipoise is empty of the other two natures. This is because the former dualistic appearance [that is, the appearance as object of verbalization and means of verbalization] is the imputational factor[a] and the latter [that is, the appearance as apprehended-object and apprehending-subject] is the imputed.[b]

For, in this way, the *Conquest Over Objections* moreover says [in its extensive explanation]:[672]

> Concerning that, the thing called "the eye" which is apprehended [or appears][c] in the aspect of object of verbalization [that is, meaning-generality][673] and verbalization [that is, term-generality][674] is the imputational eye [this being the first of the two types of dualistic appearance].[675] Its[d] individually appearing in the aspect of an eye abiding in the essence of apprehended-object and apprehending-subject is the imputed eye [which is the latter of the two types of dualistic appearance].[676] The thoroughly established nature that is its voidness of the aspects of object verbalized and verbalization, that cannot be verbalized, that is devoid of having appearance [as apprehended-object and

---

a *kun brtags.*

b *rnam brtags.*

c Jik-may-dam-chö-gya-tso's *Port of Entry,* 684.6.

d Ser-shül (*Notes,* 53b.1) wonders whether *de nyid* in the second and third sentences, which I have translated as "its," have the same sense as *de la* ("concerning that") at the beginning of the citation, which there means "concerning the occasion of identifying the imputational eye" (*kun brtags kyi mig ngos 'dzin skabs de la*). I presume that he means that in this second sentence *de nyid* means "concerning the occasion of identifying the imputed eye" and that in the third sentence it means "concerning the occasion of identifying the eye of reality." Ser-shül seems to be deliberately bending the grammar in order to make sense out of the two *de nyid.* Jik-may-dam-chö-gya-tso (*Port of Entry,* 684.6), however, takes the first as referring to the imputational eye and the second as referring to the imputed, or other-powered, eye.

The Peking edition of the source text (5206, vol. 93, 230.4.3) does not have either *de nyid,* in which case these two sentences read more easily as:

> The individual appearance in the aspect of an eye abiding in the essence of apprehended-object and apprehending-subject is the imputed eye. The thoroughly established nature that is the voidness of the aspects of object verbalized and verbalization, that cannot be verbalized, that is devoid of having appearance [as apprehended-object and apprehending-subject], and that is known by oneself individually is called "the eye of reality."

This version strikes me as being the more likely reading.

> apprehending-subject], and that is known by oneself individually is called "the eye of reality."[a]

Also, [in its extensive explanation] the *Conquest Over Objections* speaks in the context of the absence of dualistic appearance in the face of a Superior's meditative equipoise:[677]

> It is thus: since, when meditating within taking the ultimate to mind, the things that have the signs of compositional phenomena do not appear, know that those do not ultimately exist but exist conventionally.[b]

Therefore, (337) {444} that [mode of explanation aside from describing the mode of appearance in meditative equipoise][678] is not how the thoroughly established nature that is the selflessness of phenomena is delineated as a **view of the basal state.**[c]

The *Conquest Over Objections* (340) {444} explains [in the quotation just above] that what merely exists in the perspective of a Superior's meditative equipoise ultimately exists [in the sense of being what exists in the perspective of an ultimate consciousness]. However [this does not indicate that in the system of the *Conquest Over Objections* an ultimate existent that is able to bear analysis by reasoning analyzing the mode of being is asserted as it is by the Proponents of Mind-Only, since] **all** those [Proponents of Mind-Only and Proponents of Non-Nature] assert that [a consciousness of] meditative equipoise realizes suchness, and thus they only assert that the object [that is, suchness] exists

---

a In brief (Jik-may-dam-chö-gya-tso's *Port of Entry,* 685.2), the meaning is that:

- Conceptual appearances of terms and meanings concerning the eye are the imputational eye, or imputational nature of the eye
- The actual eye is the imputed eye, or other-powered nature of the eye
- The emptiness of those two in the face of meditative equipoise is the eye of reality, or thoroughly established nature of the eye

b Jik-may-dam-chö-gya-tso (*Port of Entry,* 685.3), based on Ḏzong-ka-ḇa's commentary following the quote, reframes the passage:

> When meditating within taking the ultimate to mind, the things that have the signs of compositional phenomena, that is to say, dualistic phenomena, do not appear in the face of a Superior's meditative equipoise [directly realizing emptiness]. Therefore, know that those do not exist as ultimate truths but exist as conventional truths.

c The view of the basal state (*gzhi'i lta ba*) is in contrast to the view in the face of knowledge (*rig ngo lta ba*)—the latter being the state of meditative equipoise directly realizing emptiness. Ḇel-jor-hlün-drup (*Lamp for the Teaching,* 101.5) describes the latter as "the mode of appearance to meditative equipoise, a path state" (*lam mnyam bzhag la snang tshul*) and contrasts it with "delineating the selflessness of phenomena by hearing and thinking in the basal state" (*gzhi chos kyi bdag med thos bsam gyis gtan la 'bebs pa*). In sum, the meaning is that although the *Conquest Over Objections* describes how emptiness appears to a consciousness of direct realization, it does not present how to get at that state through reflecting on phenomena and how they are empty of an imputational nature.

in the perspective of the respective subject. Hence how could this be the ultimate existence about which [the Middle Way School and the Mind-Only School] debate whether [an object] ultimately exists or does not ultimately exist! That [the *Conquest Over Objections*] utterly does not assert an ultimate existent that is able to bear analysis by reasoning analyzing the mode of being [this being the type of ultimate existence about which the Middle Way School and the Mind-Only School debate] is to be known through its expression—on the occasion of the emptiness of emptiness, the emptiness of the ultimate, and the emptiness of the uncompounded—of many refutations specifically aimed at such an assertion [that the ultimate ultimately exists in the sense of being able to bear analysis by reasoning].[a] Fearing it would take too many [words, I] will not write them down.[b]

The Mother Sūtras themselves, having made a presentation of three [natures] each for each [phenomenon][679] ranging from forms through to exalted knowers of all aspects, explain [in agreement with the *Sūtra Unraveling the Thought*][680] that the emptiness of the imputational object of negation [that is, the imputational nature] in the imputed basis of emptiness [that is, an other-powered nature] is the thoroughly established nature, reality. Therefore, the imputed eye's[c] emptiness of the imputational eye[d] must be explained as reality. Consequently, the explanation [in the *Conquest Over Objections*][681] that the meaning of the sūtra [statement that "The eye is empty of the eye,"] is that [reality] is the latter [nature's, that is, the thoroughly established nature's][682] emptiness of the two former [natures, that is, imputational natures and other-powered natures][683] in the face of meditative equipoise also does not appear to be good.

[Proof That Vasubandhu Did Not Author The *Conquest Over Objections*][684] (341) {445}

1. Reference is made in this [*Conquest Over Objections*] to the "*Commentary*"[e] with regard to the eight conceptions[f] of great beings who are Hearers, and

[a] Ḏa-drin-rap-ḏen's *Annotations,* 152.6. Ḏzong-ka-ḇa's implicit point is that Shay-rap-gyel-tsen has mistaken the meaning of the *Conquest Over Objections* in that he has taken it as a source for his assertion that the ultimate is ultimately existent in the sense of its being established by way of its own character. Jik-may-dam-chö-gya-tso (*Port of Entry,* 686.1-687.5) cites passages in the *Conquest Over Objections* to which Ḏzong-ka-ḇa is referring and draws the conclusion that the *Conquest Over Objections* itself specifically refutes other-emptiness.

[b] As Jik-may-dam-chö-gya-tso (*Port of Entry,* 687.5) indicates, Ḏzong-ka-ḇa extensively speaks to this topic in his *Golden Rosary of Eloquence* at the point of discussing the collection of wisdom.

[c] That is, an other-powered nature.

[d] That is, the nonexistent imputational nature falsely imputed to the eye.

[e] *rnam 'grel,* identified two footnotes below.

[f] Ser-shül (*Notes,* 53b.2) lists the eight as: fewer desires, knowing satisfaction, initiating

such is exactly in the *Commentary on the "Twenty-Five Thousand Stanza Perfection of Wisdom Sūtra"*[a] [by Vimuktasena].[b]

2. [The *Conquest Over Objections*] refutes that both other-powered natures and thoroughly established natures are able to bear analysis by the reasoning analyzing the mode of being [and thus refutes that they are truly established].
3. The mode of explanation [in the *Conquest Over Objections*] discords very

---

effort, solitariness, equipoise, establishment in mindfulness, meditative cultivation of wisdom, and liking the dislike of proliferation. He says that in the *Commentary on the "Twenty-Five Thousand Stanza Perfection of Wisdom Sūtra,"* they are mentioned at the point of the third of the twenty-two mind-generations. He explains that not liking proliferation (*spros pa la mi dga' ba*) is described as not liking the proliferations involved in commerce, farming, and so forth.

[a] *nyi khrid nam 'grel / 'phags pa shes rab kyi pha rol tu phyin pa stong phrag nyi shu lnga pa'i man ngag gi bstan bcos mngon par rtogs pa'i rgyan gyi tshig le'ur byas pa'i rnam par 'grel pa, āryapañcaviṃśatisāhasrikāprajñāpāramitopadeśaśāstrābhisamayālaṃkārakārikāvārttika;* Peking 5186, vol. 88, 107.2.2; this is supposedly (see the next footnote) the commentary by **Bhadanta** Vimuktasena, who was the student of Vasubandhu's student. The same eight are also given in another commentary by the same title (Peking 5185, vol. 88, 12.2.7), supposedly by **Ārya**vimuktasena; see Chimpa and Chattopadhyaya, *Tāranātha's History,* 210, n. 8.

[b] According to B̄el-jor-hlün-drup (*Lamp for the Teaching,* 102.3), this is **Bhadanta** Vimuktasena (***btsun pa** grol sde*). (In their translation of *Tāranātha's History* [210, n. 8], Chimpa and Chattopadhyaya cite the Sanskrit of *btsun pa* as *bhaṭṭāraka*). In Tāranātha's *History* (210) he is said to be from Magadha. Based on D̄zong-ka-b̄a's *Golden Rosary of Eloquence,* Jik-may-dam-chö-gya-tso (*Port of Entry,* 690.2) identifies Daṃṣhṭasena as a Kashmiri (*kha che*) and reports (695.2), but with evident reservation, that in the text entitled *ye shes thog tog,* he is said to be from "Siṅgala." In any case, according to B̄el-jor-hlün-drup and Jik-may-dam-chö-gya-tso, he is not to be confused with the earlier **Ārya**vimuktasena who was Vasubandhu's disciple (see Chimpa and Chattopadhyaya, *Tāranātha's History,* 188-189, 210-212). According to B̄el-jor-hlün-drup and Jik-may-dam-chö-gya-tso, D̄zong-ka-b̄a's point is that Vasubandhu would not have cited a text that postdated him. I would add that even if the *Commentary on the "Twenty-Five Thousand Stanza Perfection of Wisdom Sūtra"* is the one by his contemporary **Ārya**vimuktasena, Vasubandhu probably would not have cited it, since it was the custom not to cite works by one's own students.

In his *Golden Rosary* (see E. Obermiller, *Prajñāpāramitā in Tibetan Buddhism* [Delhi: Classics India Publications, 1988], p. 4, n. 7), D̄zong-ka-b̄a adds devastating evidence (cited also by Jik-may-dam-chö-gya-tso, *Port of Entry,* 689.6) for the conclusion that the *Conquest Over Objections* was not composed by Vasubandhu, this being that it also cites (Peking 5206, vol. 93, 300.4.3) "the thought of Shāntirakṣhita" with regard to how long the teaching will remain—making it a complete impossibility for the *Conquest Over Objections* to be by Vasubandhu if the reference is to the eighth-century Indian master by that name.

Stearns (*The Buddha from Dol po,* 140), after citing opinions of scholars from other orders of Tibetan Buddhism that Vasubandhu is indeed the author, says that it seems only D̄zong-ka-b̄a and his followers hold that it is not by Vasubandhu (Stearns recognizes the strength of their evidence). For other opinions, including those found by Ruegg, see Stearns, *The Buddha from Dol po,* 140-141.

> greatly with Vasubandhu's exposition, in his *Principles of Explanation,*[a] that the meaning of the thought of the Mother Sūtras must be taken in accordance with the explanation in the *Sūtra Unraveling the Thought.*

Therefore, Vasubandhu did not compose it. As renowned in earlier ancient essays, it was composed by Daṃṣhṭasena.[b]

---

[a] See the next chapter, pp. 237 and 240.

[b] *mche ba'i sde* (Jik-may-dam-chö-gya-tso's *Port of Entry,* 690.3; and Chimpa and Chattopadhyaya, *Tāranātha's History,* 268, n. 18). The same *History* (417) gives as alternate names *Daṃṣṭrāsena, Diṣṭasena, Daṃṣṭasena, Daṃṣṭrāsena, Daṃṣṭasyana,* and so forth. A-ku L̄o-drö-gya-tso (*Precious Lamp,* 290.1) cites the *'phang thang gi dkar chag* as identifying *Daṃṣṭasena* as the author. In his *La Théorie du Tathāgathagarbha et du Gotra,* 61 and 325, Ruegg identifies the author as Daṃṣṭrāsena.

Bu-d̄ön (E. Obermiller, *History of Buddhism [Chos-ḥbyung] by Bu-ston* [Heidelberg: Heft, 1932; Tokyo: Suzuki Research Foundation, n.d.], 146) identifies the author as Vasubandhu; Obermiller (*History of Buddhism,* 146, n. 1038) refers to D̄zong-ka-b̄a's and Jam-ȳang-shay-b̄a's refutation of this and their identification of the author as "the Kashmirian Daṃṣṭrāsena." For an extensive and thorough-going discussion of the authorship, see Jik-may-dam-chö-gya-tso's *Port of Entry,* 693.5-698.1.

12. Differentiating Scriptures

How, By Means Of This, [Buddha's] Scriptures Are Differentiated Into The Interpretable And The Definitive (342) {446}

[*The Differentiation Of The Three Wheels Of Doctrine As To Requiring Interpretation Or Being Definitive As Per The* Sūtra Unraveling the Thought][685] (342) {446}

[Showing That The First Wheel Of Doctrine Requires Interpretation][686] (342) {446}

When the mode of commentary on the suchness of things by the masters, the brothers [Asaṅga and Vasubandhu], is taken as given above, the description—in the first wheel—of the two, apprehended-object and apprehending-subject, in terms of externality is elucidated as requiring interpretation. The [**factual**] **basis [in Buddha's] thought**[a] is [the appearance of the six types of objects—forms and so forth—to the six types of consciousness as if they were external objects, as is][687] stated in Vasubandhu's *The Twenty:*[b]

> The Subduer spoke about these—
> The seeds from which cognitions respectively arise
> And the appearances [of forms]—
> In a dualistic way as [internal and external] sense-spheres[c] of those
> [cognitions].

---

[a] In the threefold format of basis in Buddha's thought (*dgongs gzhi*), purpose (*dgos pa*), and refutation of the explicit teaching (*dngos la gnod byed*), *dgongs* should not be translated as "intention," since this would too easily be confused with *dgos pa* ("purpose" or "intention"). The triad is also used by Shay-rap-gyel-tsen in his *Ocean of Definitive Meaning,* 337.3ff.

[b] Stanza 9; for the Sanskrit, see p. 446, footnote b. Vasubandhu's own commentary on this stanza is:

> Regarding (1) the seeds—the respective seeds that have undergone a type of transformation [that is, have thoroughly ripened]—from which the cognitions that perceive forms arise and (2) those appearances, the Supramundane Victor respectively spoke of an eye-sense-sphere and a form-sense-sphere of that cognition.

The bracketed material is from Vinītadeva's *Explanation of (Vasubandhu's) [Auto] Commentary on the "Twenty Stanza Treatise"* (*rab tu byed pa nyi shu pa'i 'grel bshad, prakaraṇaviṃśakāṭīkā*), Peking 5566, vol. 113, 318.4.4; Vinītadeva glosses *pariṇāmaviśeṣaprāptād* with what in the extant Tibetan is *yongs su smin pa.* See also Stefan Anacker, *Seven Works of Vasubandhu* (Delhi: Motilal Banarsidass, 1984), 165; and Thomas A. Kochumuttom, *A Buddhist Doctrine of Experience* (Delhi: Motilal Banarsidass, 1982), 265.

[c] *skye mched, āyatana.*

Also, the **purpose** [of his teaching such] is as the same text says:[a]

> That form-sense-spheres and so forth exist [as external objects][688]
> Was said through the force of a thought behind it
> With regard to beings tamed by that,
> Like [the teaching of] spontaneously arisen sentient beings [as substantially established or permanent].

When it is taught that a consciousness viewing forms and so forth arises from external and internal sense-spheres, it is for the sake of realizing that there is no viewer and so forth except for those. The **damage to the literal reading** is the reasonings refuting external objects.

Since an imputational factor imputed to phenomena in the manner of entity and attribute is a phenomenon-constituent[b] and a phenomenon-sense-sphere,[c] statements that those two [that is, phenomenon-constituent and phenomenon-sense-sphere] are established by way of their own character without differentiating [from among phenomena what does and does not exist by way of its own character][d] also require interpretation.

---

[a] Stanza 8; for the Sanskrit, see p. 446, footnote d. See also Anacker, *Seven Works of Vasubandhu,* 165; and Kochumuttom, *Buddhist Doctrine of Experience,* 264-265.

A-ku Lo-drö-gya-tso (*Precious Lamp,* 291.4) explains that the purpose is to cause entry into realizing the selflessness of persons, just as, for example, Nihilists are taught about the existence of spontaneously arisen beings of the intermediate state so that they might understand that there is a basis for the connection of actions in one life and their effects in another life. However, Jik-may-dam-chö-gya-tso (*Port of Entry,* 699.4) speculates that "spontaneously arisen sentient beings" refers merely to a self of persons—that is, the substantial existence of persons—and not to the category of beings by this name among the four types of birth—egg birth, womb birth, birth from heat and moisture, and spontaneous birth. Ser-shül (*Notes,* 54b.2) similarly interprets the example in the fourth line to mean that, for those who like the doctrine of self, Buddha taught a self of persons, having as the fact behind this the existence of beings of the intermediate state.

[b] *chos kyi khams, dharmadhātu.*

[c] *chos kyi skye mched, dharmāyatana.*

[d] Since these two, as categories, contain instances (such as uncompounded space) that are permanent, the categories themselves are considered to be permanent and hence not established by way of their own character. Dzong-ka-ba's more specific reference is to imputational natures that are factors imputed in the manner of entity and attribute, and when it is taught in the first wheel that all phenomena, without differentiation, are established by way of their own character, these imputational natures, being existent, also are included as being established by way of their own character. Since they exist but actually do not exist by way of their own character, such scriptures also (that is, in addition to those teaching external objects) require interpretation.

Jik-may-dam-chö-gya-tso (*Port of Entry,* 699.6) says that, with respect to the teaching that all phenomena are established by way of their own character, the **factual basis in Buddha's thought** is that other-powered natures and thoroughly established natures are established by way of their own character; the **purpose** is to prevent the annihilationist view of

[Showing That The Middle Wheel Of Doctrine Requires Interpretation][689] (343) {447}

[With respect to the **basis in Buddha's thought** behind the middle wheel], Asaṅga's *Summary of Manifest Knowledge*[a] explains that the statements in the Very Extensive [Sūtras][b] that all phenomena are natureless are in consideration of the three non-natures. Also, Asaṅga's *Summary of the Great Vehicle*[c] says that in the Very Extensive [Sūtras]:

1. all statements of "does not exist" indicate [that] imputational factors [are not established by way of their own character][690]
2. the demonstrations of examples of magical illusions and so forth indicate [the naturelessness of self-production in][691] other-powered natures
3. the four purifications[d] indicate thoroughly established natures

holding that imputational natures do not exist at all; and the **damage to the literal reading** is the reasonings proving that imputational natures are not established by way of their own character.

About the following word "also," see *Absorption,* #52, 53.

[a] Peking 5550, vol. 112, 266.1.3-266.1.6, near the end of the section entitled *dharmaviniścayasamuccaya* (*chos rnam par nges pa kun las btus pa*); and Walpola Rahula, *La compendium de la super-doctrine (philosophie) (Abhidharmasamuccaya) d'Asaṅga* (Paris: École Française d'Extrême-Orient, 1971), 142.

Jik-may-dam-chö-gya-tso (*Port of Entry,* 700.3) calls attention to Ḏzong-ka-ḇa's earlier reference to the *Summary of Manifest Knowledge* on the occasion of the way that Maitreya's *Ornament for the Great Vehicle Sūtras* abandons the two extremes; see p. 172.

[b] *shin tu rgyas pa, vaipulya.* Jik-may-dam-chö-gya-tso (*Port of Entry,* 700.3) identifies this as the *One Hundred Thousand Stanza Perfection of Wisdom Sūtra,* but Ḏzong-ka-ḇa's usage of the plural below indicates that he considers other Perfection of Wisdom Sūtras to be included.

[c] Earlier, when Ḏzong-ka-ḇa indicated that Dignāga's *Summary Meanings of the Eight Thousand Stanza Perfection of Wisdom Sūtra* agrees with Asaṅga's *Summary of the Great Vehicle* (p. 190), Jik-may-dam-chö-gya-tso (*Port of Entry,* 537.3) cited the stanza from chapter 2 of the *Summary:*

> Magical illusions and so forth are taught in relation to the dependent.
> Non-existence is taught in relation to the imputational.
> The four purifications are taught
> In relation to the thoroughly established.

Étienne Lamotte, *La somme du grand véhicule d'Asaṅga,* reprint, 2 vols. Publications de l'Institute Orientaliste de Louvain, 8 (Louvain: Université de Louvain, 1973), vol. 1, 38 (II.26); vol. 2, 122; and John P. Keenan, *The Summary of the Great Vehicle by Bodhisattva Asaṅga: Translated from the Chinese of Paramārtha* (Berkeley, Calif.: Numata Center for Buddhist Translation and Research, 1992), 52. For the Tibetan and Sanskrit, see p. 314, footnote b.

[d] A-ku Ḻo-drö-gya-tso (*Precious Lamp,* 231.5-232.2) and Jik-may-dam-chö-gya-tso (*Port of Entry,* 536.6) list these as:

1. the natural purification—emptiness,

Since those [Very Extensive] Sūtras appear to be the Mother Sūtras [that is, the Perfection of Wisdom Sūtras], Asaṅga asserts that the second wheel, which is described as requiring interpretation, consists of just those [sūtras] as well as those [that teach][692] in accordance with it.[a]

Furthermore, Vasubandhu's *Principles of Explanation* refutes the assertion that the explanations—in the Mother Sūtras[b]—of naturelessness and so forth are literal and says:[693]

> It is set out in the *Sūtra Unraveling the Thought* that all such statements that "All phenomena are natureless," and so forth are not of definitive meaning.

Therefore, he asserts the Mother Sūtras as the second wheel.[c]

The way (344) {447} that the second wheel is explained to require interpretation differs very greatly from the way that the statements in the first wheel of apprehended-object and apprehending-subject come to require interpretation. For:

---

2. the stainless purification—true cessations,
3. the path purification—the thirty-seven harmonies with enlightenment,
4. the observational purification—the scriptural collections of the Great Vehicle.

[a] Paṇ-chen Sö-nam-drak-b̄a's *Garland of Blue Lotuses* (6a.7-6b.3) offers two interpretations of this sentence. His concern is that it seems to suggest that the second wheel includes not only the extensive, middling, and brief Perfection of Wisdom Sūtras but also those that teach in accordance with it. He feels that if it does, the meaning of "those that teach in accordance with it" must be restricted, since he does not accept that the *King of Meditative Stabilizations Sūtra* is an actual second wheel sūtra even though it teaches in accordance with the Perfection of Wisdom Sūtras. Therefore, in his first interpretation, he accomplishes his aim by severely restricting the meaning of "those that teach in accordance with it" to the *Condensed Perfection of Wisdom Sūtra* and so forth. In his second interpretation, he takes the sentence structure differently, such that it would read:

> Since those [Very Extensive] Sūtras appear to be the Mother Sūtras [the Perfection of Wisdom Sūtras], Asaṅga (1) asserts that the second wheel, which is described as requiring interpretation, consists of just those [sūtras] and (2) asserts that those [that teach] in accordance with it [can, from the fact that Asaṅga explains that the statements in them on the literal level that other-powered natures and thoroughly established natures are not truly established require interpretation, be understood as also of interpretable meaning].

The second interpretation evinces considerable creative reformulation by an inventive commentator.

[b] D̄a-drin-rap-d̄en's *Annotations* (156.6) identifies Vasubandhu's passage as the one that D̄zong-ka-b̄a cites below (p. 240) in the detailed explanation of how the middle wheel of doctrine is proved to require interpretation (Peking 5562, vol. 113, 278.5.7-279.3.2); however, it may also include everything up to 281.4.2, which D̄zong-ka-b̄a now cites.

[c] Some reverse the last two wheels; they identify the Perfection of Wisdom Sūtras as the definitive, third wheel of doctrine and the *Sūtra Unraveling the Thought,* and so forth, as the second wheel. See p. 129, footnote c.

1. **The [basis in Buddha's] thought** when he spoke of the eye sense-sphere and visible-form sense-sphere as existing is that he said this in consideration of (a) the respective seed called a "predisposition of fruition," from the ripening of which an eye consciousness arises, and (b) the appearance [of form]; but the meaning of [his] thought is not suitable to be **the meaning that is expressed** by those Low Vehicle sūtras. However, the three modes of non-nature which are that in consideration of which he spoke of non-nature [in the middle wheel] are explained as being the meaning of the Mother Sūtras.
2. Also, the existence of sense-spheres that are external objects is explained as the meaning of Low Vehicle sūtras, but the assertion—without differentiating modes of non-nature—that [phenomena] do not ultimately have a nature at all is not explained to be the meaning of the Mother Sūtras[a]

Therefore, these [texts, such as Asaṅga's *Compendium of Ascertainments,* Asaṅga's *Summary of the Great Vehicle,* Vasubandhu's *Principles of Explanation,* and so forth][694] are not making the commentary that:

- although the explanation that all phenomena, without distinction, are ultimately natureless[b] is the meaning of the Mother Sūtras, it requires interpretation.

Rather, they are explaining that:

- [those sūtras] require interpretation from the viewpoint that—since such is not suitable to be taken literally—the meaning [that is expressed by those sūtras][695] is not definitive as just that [which is the literal reading,] and their meaning still needs to be explained.

The mode of explanation is to comment in this way:

---

a Jik-may-dam-chö-gya-tso (*Port of Entry,* 700.6) cogently rephrases these points:

- In the first wheel the basis in Buddha's thought (this being the seed from which a consciousness arises and the appearance of, for instance, form to an eye consciousness **as if** it is an external object) is necessarily not what is expressed (since what is expressed is the existence of external objects and the non-existence of external objects is not suitable to be taught to the intended trainees of the first wheel), but in the middle wheel the basis in Buddha's thought (this being the three non-natures teamed with the three natures) necessarily is what is expressed, since the three non-natures, teamed with the three natures, is suitable to be taught to sharp Proponents of Mind-Only who are the intended trainees of the middle wheel
- In the first wheel the literal reading (this being the existence of external objects) is necessarily what is expressed, but in the middle wheel the literal reading (this being that all phenomena are natureless) necessarily is not what is expressed (since what is expressed is the three non-natures, teamed with the three natures).

b *don dam* ***par*** *ngo bo nyid med pa.*

> Since imputational phenomena[a] are not established by way of their own character, they are non-natures ultimately[b] [that is, are without the nature of existing ultimately or by way of their own character]. Since other-powered phenomena are not established as the ultimate which is the object of purification, they are non-natures ultimately[c] [that is, are without the nature of being the ultimate]. Also, since thoroughly established phenomena are the ultimate [which is the object observed by a path of purification][696] and also are the non-existence of phenomena as entities of self, they are non-natures ultimately[d] [that is, are without the nature of that ultimacy which is the self of phenomena].

Therefore, because they do not assert that those who hold [the Mother Sūtras][697] to be of literal meaning are the [intended][698] trainees for whom the Mother Sūtras were spoken,[e] they assert that the intended trainees of those [Mother Sūtras] realize the meaning of those sūtras as it is commented on by the *Sūtra Unraveling the Thought* [but without relying on the *Sūtra Unraveling the Thought*].[699] Hence, the thought of the latter two wheels is one and the same.

[Showing That The Final Wheel Of Doctrine Is Definitive][700] (345) {448}

The *Sūtra Unraveling the Thought* refutes those [Consequentialists and so forth][701] who, though they are devoted[f] to the Very Extensive Sūtras, hold them

---

a See *Absorption*, #85.

b *don dam* ***par*** *ngo bo nyid med pa.*

c *don dam* ***par*** *ngo bo nyid med pa.*

d *don dam* ***par*** *ngo bo nyid med pa.* Ḏa-drin-rap-ḏen (158.5) cogently takes "ultimate" here as referring to the object of negation. His point is well taken because one should not confuse "non-natures ultimately" (*don dam* ***par*** *ngo bo nyid med pa*) with "ultimate-naturelessness" (*don dam* ***pa*** *ngo bo nyid med pa*), in which "ultimate" *don dam pa* refers to the ultimate, or thoroughly established nature, itself. The latter is the ultimate-non-nature that is the third of the three non-natures constituting Buddha's thought behind the teaching in the Perfection of Wisdom Sūtras that phenomena are natureless. Here Ḏzong-ka-ḇa is using the terminology of the Perfection of Wisdom Sūtras, that is, "ultimately natureless" or "non-natures ultimately" (*don dam* ***par*** *ngo bo nyid med pa*), with respect to each of the three natures with individual meanings; see individual identifications of these in brackets in the translation.

e Those who hold the Mother Sūtras to be of literal meaning are the Proponents of Non-Nature, and, according to the Mind-Only School, they are not the intended trainees of the middle wheel of doctrine; the intended trainees of the middle wheel are sharp Proponents of Mind-Only themselves; see Jik-may-dam-chö-gya-tso's *Port of Entry*, 702.5. The Proponents of Non-Nature, however, are the intended trainees of the **literal reading** of the Perfection of Wisdom Sūtras.

f *mos.*

to be literal and thereupon propound that the meaning of those sūtras is the literal meaning. It then clearly explains that there is a meaning of those sūtras that is not the literal meaning. Therefore, that [*Sūtra Unraveling the Thought*][702] is said to be of definitive meaning, and since the Mother Sūtras do not clearly differentiate this meaning and are unsuitable to be held as literal, they require interpretation.

[Detailed Explanation Of How The Middle Wheel Of Doctrine Is Proved To Require Interpretation][703] (345) {448}

The **damage to the literal reading** [of the Perfection of Wisdom Sūtras] is just the former statements that if taken to be literal, they would involve deprecation, such that all three characters would be conceived as not established by way of their own character.[a] Furthermore, Vasubandhu's *Principles of Explanation* says:[704]

> The Perfection of Wisdom [Sūtras] indicate many times, for instance, that all phenomena are natureless and so forth. However, they say that those who wish to enter into the flawlessness of Bodhisattvas [should train in the Perfection of Wisdom] and...they also teach the individual disclosure of all ill deeds, and so forth.

Having explained that, Vasubandhu shows that if naturelessness and so forth were literal, there would be internal contradictions:[705]

> If the words of naturelessness and so forth [in the Mother Sūtras] were of only literal meaning, they would contradict all of these. As there would be nothing to be adopted [in practice], it would not be suitable to adopt [a practice] within thinking, "From this cause such and such will arise." Or, one would wonder what thing to be adopted exists to be adopted. Therefore, those words [speaking of naturelessness][706] definitely should not be taken as of literal meaning. Then, as what? As having another thought [behind them].[b]

With respect to the mode of contradiction, if [phenomena] were natureless, one would be propounding that objects of adoption [in practice] and the wish to attain [levels of the path,] as in, "Because of wishing to attain such and such, one should train in the Mother [that is, the perfection of wisdom]," would not be suitable, and one would be propounding that the causes and effects involved in great resources [resulting] from giving and so forth would not be feasible.

---

a There is no fault in considering imputational natures not to be established by way of their own character, but it is wrong to hold that *all* three natures are not established by way of their own character.

b *dgongs pa can.*

[The mode of contradiction] is mainly held to be the unfeasibility of other-powered natures.

Even those [that is, the Proponents of Non-Nature][707] who assert the Mother Sūtras as of definitive meaning make an assertion in accordance with the statements again and again [in the literal reading of the Perfection of Wisdom Sūtras]—about adoption [of virtues] and discarding [of non-virtues] as well as cause and effect and so forth—in the following way: "Furthermore, these are in worldly conventions but not ultimately." They do not assert that in general entities of these [phenomena] utterly do not exist or do not exist conventionally.

The meaning is that [the Proponents of Non-Nature] assert that, although ["ultimately"][708] is not affixed to each [negation] in the sūtra, since it is already affixed in general, the absence of **ultimate** existence is literal, and [Vasubandhu adduces the fault that][709] if the absence of ultimate existence is literal, cause and effect and so forth would not be feasible. For, Asaṅga's *Grounds of Bodhisattvas* and *Compendium of Ascertainments* also explain that [the position] that everything is not ultimately established is a deprecation and refute such.

[*Advice to Tibetans who claim to be Proponents of Non-Nature.* (346) {449} In the Mind-Only School], the differentiation between interpretable and definitive scriptures that are set forth stemming from the ultimate derives from whether there is or is not damage by reasoning to the literal reading. Concerning the damage indicated here [to the literality[710] of the Perfection of Wisdom Sūtras], if you [Tibetans as Proponents of Non-Nature] know well how to refute the ultimate existence [of phenomena][711] and know well how to posit cause and effect as well as bondage and release, and so forth, as validly established within the context of these being phenomena with respect to which such [ultimate existence] has been negated, then your answer hits the mark [in the sense that, in accordance with a proper interpretation of the Consequence School, it can refute Vasubandhu's challenge of internal contradiction]. Otherwise, propounding that "If the production of a sprout is established by valid cognition, it becomes ultimate production; [hence] a sprout is produced in the perspective of a mistaken consciousness fancying production, and thereby all those are feasible conventionally," cannot dispel the damage [by reasoning[712] put forward in Vasubandhu's objections]. Therefore, it would be splendid if you relied on this mode of commentary by the Yogic Practitioners [rather than attempting such a misguided version of the doctrine of the Naturelessness School, thereby making many deprecations].[a]

[a] Dzong-ka-ba describes these misguided persons as those who hold that phenomena are not established by valid cognition, and thus his reference cannot be to Autonomists but must be to those who claim to be Proponents of Non-Nature but cannot figure out how an elimination of inherent existence is compatible with the valid certification of phenomena. A-ku Lo-drö-gya-tso (*Precious Lamp,* 293.3) identifies these as earlier Tibetans and other quarters (*bod snga ma dang gzhan phyogs*). For Dzong-ka-ba's extensive presentation on overidentifi-

Although [in the Mind-Only School][713] there are many approaches with respect to commenting [on a scripture] as requiring interpretation [such as the four intentions and the four thoughts],[a] those with intelligence should know that the Yogic Practitioners' way of commenting on the second wheel as requiring interpretation is just in accordance [with what was explained above, that is, their not being literally acceptable].[714]

[*Identifying The Three Wheels Of Doctrine According To The* Sūtra Unraveling the Thought][715] (347) {450}

The three stages of wheels of doctrine mentioned in the *Sūtra Unraveling the Thought* are posited, not by way of the assemblies of [Buddha's] circle[b] or by way of periods in the Teacher's life[c] and so forth but by way of topics of expression. Furthermore, those are in terms of delineating the meaning of selflessness:

- Initially, at Varaṇāsi, he spoke of the selflessness of persons; [thus] there is one cycle [of teaching], in which the true establishment of the phenomena of the aggregates and so forth, except for a few, is not refuted and true existence is mentioned frequently[d]

cation of the object of negation in selflessness, see Elizabeth Napper, *Dependent-Arising and Emptiness* (London: Wisdom, 1989), 101-122, 176-180, 311-321.

[a] A-ku Ḻo-drö-gya-tso's *Precious Lamp,* 293.5. Jam-ȳang-shay-b̄a (*Great Exposition of Tenets, nga,* 9b.7) lists the four:

Four Thoughts (*dgongs pa bzhi, catvāro 'bhiprāyā*)
Thinking of sameness (*mnyam pa nyid la dgongs pa, samatābhiprāya*)
Thinking of another meaning (*don gzhan la dgongs pa, arthāntarābhiprāya*)
Thinking of another time (*dus gzhan la dgongs pa, kālāntarābhiprāya*)
Thinking of a person's attitude (*gang zag gi bsam pa la dgongs pa, pudgalāntarābhiprāya*)

Four Intentions (*ldem dgongs bzhi, catvāro 'bhisaṃdhaya*)
Intending entry (*gzhug pa la ldem por dgongs pa, avatāranābhisaṃdhi*)
Intending the characters (*mtshan nyid la ldem por dgongs pa, lakṣaṇābhisaṃdhi*)
Intending an antidote (*gnyen po la ldem por dgongs pa, pratipakṣābhisaṃdhi*)
Intending translation (*sbyor ba la ldem por dgongs pa/ bsgyur ba la ldem por dgongs pa, pariṇāmābhisaṃdhi*).

For discussion of these, see *Absorption in No External World,* chap. 19.

Jik-may-dam-chö-gya-tso (*Port of Entry,* 705.4), however, takes D̄zong-ka-b̄a's reference not as different modes within the Mind-Only School but as the contrasting way in which the Middle Way School determines what requires interpretation and what is definitive, and thus he glosses this as "such as whether the passage is literal or not, whether the ultimate truth is taken as the main topic taught or not, and so forth."

[b] Jik-may-dam-chö-gya-tso (*Port of Entry,* 705.5) identifies the Jo-nang-b̄as as the proponents of this notion.

[c] Jik-may-dam-chö-gya-tso (ibid., 705.6) identifies Chim, the Translator Tro, and the Translator Chak (*mchims khro chag*) as the proponents of this notion.

[d] According to Jam-ȳang-shay-b̄a (*Great Exposition of the Interpretable and the Definitive,*

- Then, there is one cycle in which, without [clearly][716] making distinctions, true establishment is refuted [on the literal level][717] with respect to all of the phenomena of the aggregates and so forth[a]
- Then, there arose one cycle in which, with respect to those, he individually differentiated the mode of the first nature [that is, the imputational nature] as not established by way of its own character and the other two [that is, other-powered natures and thoroughly established natures] as established by way of their own character

Therefore, [the wheels of doctrine that are the bases for differentiation—in the "Questions of Paramārthasamudgata Chapter" of the *Sūtra Unraveling the Thought* and in the texts commenting on its thought—of what requires interpretation and what is definitive][718] are taken in terms of these [modes of teaching subject matter].[719] Other sūtras that teach in a way other than these modes of teaching are not in any sensible way bases of this analysis of the interpretable and the definitive.

[Presenting Ratnākarashānti's Mistaken Mode Of Differentiating The Interpretable And The Definitive][720] (347) {450}

Ratnākarashānti's *Quintessential Instructions on the Perfection of Wisdom* says:[721]

> The meaning of whatsoever sūtra that is literal is just of definitive meaning. That meaning does not have a second meaning. Since it is said, "The meaning of this is just ascertained," it is a definitive meaning. Through what is the meaning ascertained? Through (1) just that sūtra, (2) a sūtra other than it, and (3) both.

He asserts the first [that is, those whose meaning is ascertained through themselves][722] to be the *Descent into Laṅkā*, the *Sūtra Unraveling the Thought,* and so forth; he does this thinking that these clearly differentiate the existence and non-existence of nature [that is to say, establishment or non-establishment by way of its own character with respect to the three natures].[723] He asserts the second [that is, those whose meaning is ascertained through another sūtra][724] to be the *Eight Thousand Stanza Perfection of Wisdom Sūtra,* and so forth, thinking that these do not possess differentiation of the existence and non-existence of nature as such is done in the *Sūtra Unraveling the Thought.* He asserts the third

27.3), the last sentence should be rendered as:

> Initially, at Varaṇāsi, he spoke of the selflessness of persons; [thus] there is one cycle [of teaching], in which the true establishment of the phenomena of the aggregates and so forth—[these being] *no more than a few* [of the one hundred and eight phenomena]—is not refuted and true existence is mentioned frequently.

See *Absorption,* #21, 32, 36.

[a] See ibid., #37and 38.

[that is, those whose meaning is ascertained through themselves and through another sūtra][725] as being the *Twenty-Five Thousand Stanza Perfection of Wisdom Sūtra,* and so forth,[a] thinking (1) that the "Questions of Maitreya Chapter" [in those sūtras] has an explanation [that those very sūtras] require interpretation, thereby abandoning the error of adhering [to such teachings] as of literal meaning, and (2) that the *Sūtra Unraveling the Thought* also comments that [these sūtras] require interpretation. This is due to the fact that the middling length [Perfection of Wisdom Sūtra, that is, the *Eight Thousand Stanza Perfection of Wisdom Sūtra*] does not have a "Questions of Maitreya Chapter." According to him, the three characters posited by the "Questions of Maitreya Chapter" [in the *Twenty-Five Thousand Stanza Perfection of Wisdom Sūtra* and so forth][b] and the explanation [of the three characters] by the *Sūtra Unraveling the Thought* are asserted as having the same meaning.

[Refuting Ratnākarashānti's Mode Of Differentiating The Interpretable And The Definitive][726] (348) {451}

If those two [that is, the "Questions of Maitreya Chapter" in the *Twenty-Five Thousand Stanza Perfection of Wisdom Sūtra* and the *Sūtra Unraveling the Thought*][727] had the same meaning, such would be correct, but [they do not, for]:[728]

- Vasubandhu establishes that the naturelessness and so forth mentioned in the Mother Sūtras [which include the *Twenty-Five Thousand Stanza Perfection of Wisdom Sūtra*] require interpretation in accordance with [how] other sūtras such as the *Sūtra Unraveling the Thought* and so forth [say that such teachings require interpretation]
- He indicates that, in a literal reading, the Mother Sūtras themselves have contradictions between what is said in them earlier and later [and thereby establishes that they require interpretation];[729] he does not establish this

[a] A-ku Lo-drö-gya-tso (*Precious Lamp,* 296.5) identifies "and so forth" as "the *Hundred Thousand Stanza Perfection of Wisdom Sūtra,* and so forth." However, Cyrus R. Stearns (*The Buddha from Dol po and His Fourth Council of the Buddhist Doctrine* [Ann Arbor, Mich.: University Microfilms, 1996], 137-138) refers to the 72nd chapter of the *Twenty-Five Thousand Stanza Perfection of Wisdom Sūtra* and the 83rd chapter of *Eighteen Thousand Stanza Perfection of Wisdom Sūtra* and states that a "Questions of Maitreya Chapter" "is not found in other versions of the *Prajñāpāramitā.*" For a typical passage, see p. 348.

[b] Through criticizing and correcting Ratnākarashānti on the issue of what is definitive and what requires interpretation, Dzong-ka-ba indirectly seeks to undermine Shay-rap-gyel-tsen's synthesis of the second- and third-wheel teachings; see the Synopsis, p. 348ff. The "Questions of Maitreya Chapter" of the 18,000- and 25,000-"stanza" Perfection of Wisdom Sūtras are counted as one in the list of five sūtras of definitive meaning that Shay-rap-gyel-tsen studied under Gyi-dön Jam-yang-drak-ba-gyel-tsen at Sa-gya (see Stearns, *The Buddha from Dol po,* 19, n. 17).

through the "Questions of Maitreya Chapter" [of the *Twenty-Five Thousand Stanza Perfection of Wisdom Sūtra* and so forth]

Therefore, this [explanation by Ratnākarashānti][730] is not the thought of the brothers [Asaṅga and Vasubandhu].[a]

Since [the presentations of the three natures by][731] these two [sūtras, (1) the "Questions of Maitreya Chapter" in the *Twenty-Five Thousand Stanza Perfection of Wisdom Sūtra* and (2) the *Sūtra Unraveling the Thought*][732] are quite similar, it is difficult to differentiate them. However, if those two had the same meaning, it would not be suitable [for even the Middle Way School][733] to explain that the meaning of the thought of the Mother Sūtras is that all phenomena are natureless ultimately but exist conventionally [since the "Questions of Maitreya Chapter" of the *Twenty-Five Thousand Stanza Perfection of Wisdom Sūtra* would be saying that such teaching is not definitive. The Middle Way School absurdly] would have to accord with the Cognition School [on the topic of the three natures]. As a point to be analyzed this is very important; it will be explained on the occasion of the Middle Way School.[b]

---

[a] B̄el-jor-hlün-drup's *Lamp for the Teaching,* 112.6. The reference could be just to "the brother," that is, Vasubandhu, but it is more likely to both, although D̄zong-ka-b̄a here has not made an explicit case for Asaṅga.

[b] D̄zong-ka-b̄a analyzes this issue in detail in the section on the Consequence School, in a subsection entitled "Showing that the two, the *Sūtra Unraveling the Thought* and the 'Questions of Maitreya Chapter' are not similar"; two-thirds of that explanation is translated and discussed in Shōtarō Iida, *Reason and Emptiness* (Tokyo: Hokuseido Press, 1980), 262-269. For a condensation of its meaning drawn from the works of Jam-ȳang-shay-b̄a, see p. 348ff. The reason why it is "very important" is that it is crucial to his delineation of the difference between the Mind-Only and Middle Way Schools and thus the impossibility of an amalgamation of the thought of the classical so-called Mind-Only and Middle Way Indian scholars, as is done by S̄hay-rap-gyel-tsen.

PART THREE:
SYNOPSIS

Remarks

In his *Treatise Differentiating Interpretable and Definitive Meanings: The Essence of Eloquence* Ḏzong-ka-ḇa, after a prologue, presents an analysis of scriptural interpretation from the viewpoint of the Mind-Only School. He focuses on the Mind-Only School's explication of Buddha's own statements[a] about interpretation in the seventh chapter of the *Sūtra Unraveling the Thought,* called the "Questions of the Bodhisattva Paramārthasamudgata," giving a lengthy treatment of passages in this chapter of the sūtra, during which he presents opinions sometimes following and sometimes refining the Korean scholar Wonch'uk but solely criticizing renditions of doctrine by the Tibetan scholar S̄hay-rap-gyel-tsen of the Jo-nang-ḇa School.

Then Ḏzong-ka-ḇa discusses major Indian commentarial literature on differentiating scriptures in the Mind-Only School—first detailing the importance of the *Sūtra Unraveling the Thought* for Asaṅga's Mind-Only system and then explicating significant portions—that deal with emptiness, the differentiation of what requires interpretation and what is definitive, and related topics—in Asaṅga's *Grounds of Bodhisattvas* and *Compendium of Ascertainments,*[b] and Maitreya's *Ornament for the Great Vehicle Sūtras*[c] and *Differentiation of the Middle and the Extremes*[d] as well as briefly mentioning twelve other Indian treatises.[e] He openly refutes only one Indian scholar, the eleventh-century Ratnākarashānti.

An annotated translation of the prologue and the section on the Mind-Only School is given in part 2, but the text is often so brief and the shifts of topic so abrupt that detailed synopses of these chapters in a more free-flowing style may be helpful. Given the six centuries of scholarship, almost every point has spawned discussion; many of these are addressed in footnotes in the Translation, found in part 2, while other issues are considered in my *Reflections on Reality* and *Absorption in No External World,* as indicated by footnotes to the Translation. (The page numbers in square brackets after the headings refer to the corresponding part of the Translation, and the page numbers in curly brackets refer to the Tibetan text.)

---

[a] Whether Shākyamuni Buddha actually spoke this sūtra or not, the tradition being examined takes the former to be the case; thus, as a literary device, I shall use the assumption of the tradition since the authorship of the text is not the issue here.

[b] *gtan la dbab pa sdu ba, viniścayasaṃgrahaṇī;* Peking 5539, vol. 110-111.

[c] *theg pa chen po'i mdo sde rgyan, mahāyānasūtrālaṃkāra;* Peking 5521, vol. 108.

[d] *dbus mtha' rnam 'byed, madhyāntavibhaṅga;* Peking 5522, vol. 108.

[e] For a list of these, see p. 285.

Prologue

Overview. Ḏzong-ka-ḇa begins *The Essence of Eloquence* [65] {363} with a brief obeisance in Sanskrit to Mañjughoṣha, or Mañjushrī. The prologue that follows the obeisance and precedes the section on the Mind-Only School is in four basic movements—the first three being standard precursors to the actual subject matter of a text:

- Expression of worship
- Promise of composition
- Exhortation to listen
- Call for reasoned analysis in order to determine the reality of phenomena in the midst of divergent scriptures

Expression Of Worship [65] {363}

The first expression of worship is to Shākyamuni Buddha from the viewpoint of his overwhelming—through his teaching of dependent-arising—worldly deities such as Maheshvara, Indra, Brahmā, the demonic Lord of Love, and Viṣhṇu. Ḏzong-ka-ḇa then makes worship to the upholders of the teaching, these being Mañjughoṣha and Maitreya who are the divine sustainers of Shākyamuni Buddha's teaching and who passed it respectively through Nāgārjuna and Asaṅga. Also included are other great masters of the Middle Way School—Āryadeva, Shūra, Buddhapālita, Bhāvaviveka, and Chandrakīrti—and of the Mind-Only School—Vasubandhu, Sthiramati, Dignāga, and Dharmakīrti.

Promise Of Composition [68] {364}

In his promise to compose the text, Ḏzong-ka-ḇa stakes the claim that he has realized a profound topic that others in Tibet failed to penetrate—the meaning of suchness, emptiness. This leads to a call to his listeners (and readers) to pay close attention.

The Necessity For Reasoned Analysis [68] {365}

Ḏzong-ka-ḇa cites a passage from the *Superior Sūtra of the Questions of Rāṣhṭapāla* that speaks of the multiplicity of Buddha's doctrines that arise from his skill in means. This provides the context for a multistaged argument that it is necessary, given the seeming contradictions in Buddha's manifold teachings on reality, to rely on reasoning to determine the final mode of being of phenomena:[734]

1. In order to be released from cyclic existence it is necessary to realize suchness—emptiness, the thoroughly established nature
2. To realize suchness, it is not sufficient to train only in scriptures that require interpretation; rather, one must engage properly in hearing and thinking on definitive scriptures
3. The determination that a sūtra is definitive cannot be made by the mere fact that there is a scripture saying that it is definitive. For, just as in general it is not necessarily suitable to assert what is indicated on the literal level of a sūtra since Buddha spoke variously in accordance with the needs of trainees—for instance, sometimes he said that there are no external objects and sometimes he said that there are—so, more specifically, it is not suitable to accept a scriptural statement that a certain sūtra is definitive and that another requires interpretation. For instance, Buddha said in the *Teachings of Akṣhayamati Sūtra* that the type of teachings classified as the middle wheel of his doctrine is definitive but in the *Sūtra Unraveling the Thought* said that such requires interpretation. Therefore, through scriptural citation alone, one cannot differentiate which sūtras require interpretation and which are definitive
4. Also, persons such as us cannot make the differentiation through our own powers of mind, nor can we make it following just any of the many schools and great adepts. Hence, the differentiation must be made following either Nāgārjuna or Asaṅga, the two great "chariots" (that is, great leaders) prophesied by the Conqueror Buddha himself as differentiating the interpretable and the definitive
5. To follow Nāgārjuna or Asaṅga does not mean just to read texts written by them; rather, it means analytically to delineate what is definitive and what requires interpretation within Buddha's scriptures in dependence upon the stainless reasonings through which Nāgārjuna and Asaṅga opened up their respective traditions—the Middle Way School and Mind-Only School. These are reasonings through the power of the fact (and not through citation of scripture) that refute all ambiguities that might allow interpreting the Conqueror's thought otherwise and that establish just what his thought is
6. Thus, the process meets back just to pure analysis (a) of emptiness—the mode of subsistence of phenomena that is the uttermost meaning to be delineated—and (b) of the paths of reasonings—the uttermost means of delineation—set forth by the two great chariots, Nāgārjuna and Asaṅga

Ḏzong-ka-ḇa concludes with the famous scriptural quote that Buddha's doctrines are to be examined the way a goldsmith analyzes gold before purchasing it—by scorching it, cutting it, and rubbing it with a special cloth.

He immediately indicates that his exposition of how to differentiate what requires interpretation and what is definitive is in two parts—the presentations in the *Sūtra Unraveling the Thought* and in *Teachings of Akṣhayamati Sūtra,* corresponding to the presentations in the Mind-Only School and the Middle Way School. (Within the Middle Way School, the Autonomy School also makes extensive use of the *Sūtra Unraveling the Thought;* hence Paṇ-chen Sö-nam-drak-ba[735] structures his textbook such that the presentation in the *Sūtra Unraveling the Thought* itself has two parts—the Mind-Only School and the Middle Way School. Under the latter category, he treats how the two divisions of the Middle Way School—the Autonomy School[736] and the Consequence School[737] treat the *Sūtra Unraveling the Thought.* After those,[738] he considers how the Autonomy School[739] and the Consequence School[740] present the interpretable and the definitive according to the *Teachings of Akṣhayamati Sūtra.*[a] The Autonomy School takes the *Sūtra Unraveling the Thought* literally but with a reading different from the Mind-Only School, whereas the Consequence School holds that although the thought of the sūtra is as the Proponents of Mind-Only say it is, Buddha's own thought is different, and thus the sūtra is not to be taken literally.)

[a] It is interesting to note that since Paṇ-chen Sö-nam-drak-ba's exposition ends at 101a.1, his presentation of the Middle Way School is only twenty-five folios.

MIND-ONLY SCHOOL: THE *SŪTRA UNRAVELING THE THOUGHT* ON DIFFERENTIATING THE INTERPRETABLE AND THE DEFINITIVE

Overview of Chapters 1 Through 4

Dzong-ka-ba's exposition of how the *Sūtra Unraveling the Thought* presents the differentiation of what requires interpretation and what is definitive [73] {368} begins in chapter 1 with the sūtra's depiction of a question put to Shākyamuni Buddha by the Bodhisattva Paramārthasamudgata about apparent contradictions in his teachings in the first two wheels of doctrine. Chapter 2 centers around Buddha's short and long answers to Paramārthasamudgata's question—explaining what was behind his teaching in the middle wheel of doctrine, in which he said that all phenomena are natureless and are unproduced, unceasing, quiescent from the start, and naturally thoroughly passed beyond sorrow. The principal format is Buddha's exposition that all phenomena are not natureless, and so forth, in the same way, and that it should be understood that all phenomena can be divided into the three categories called the three natures, each of which has its own type of non-nature; thus there are three natures and three non-natures.

Chapter 3 discusses the three natures through considering Paramārthasamudgata's rerendering of Buddha's teaching. Chapter 4 presents the overall meaning established by the above movements in the *Sūtra Unraveling the Thought* through giving the sūtra's presentation of the three wheels of doctrine, again as per Paramārthasamudgata's rerendering of Buddha's teaching.

Throughout these four chapters, Dzong-ka-ba, while relying on Wonch'uk's presentation, seeks to correct many points; also in chapter 1 he excoriates Shay-rap-gyel-tsen for completely missing what for him is a crucial point and again in chapter 4 criticizes opinions of both Shay-rap-gyel-tsen (1292-1361) and Bu-dön Rin-chen-drup (1290-1364). Let us turn to these chapters in more detail.

1. Questioning Apparent Contradiction

Overview. This chapter [75] {368} has three basic movements:

1. Explaining Paramārthasamudgata's question about apparent contradictions in Buddha's teachings
2. Criticizing Wonch'uk's rendering of two points
3. Glossing the meaning of a word in the sūtra

Paramārthasamudgata's Question [75] {368}

Ḏzong-ka-ḇa immediately cites the *Sūtra Unraveling the Thought* without even mentioning who is speaking, this being the Bodhisattva Paramārthasamudgata. In this citation, Paramārthasamudgata contrasts the teachings of the first two wheels of doctrine. In the first wheel of doctrine Buddha spoke of a multiplicity of phenomena which are arranged in seven groups—the five mental and physical aggregates, the twelve sense-spheres, the twelve links of dependent-arising, the four foods, the four noble truths, the eighteen and six constituents, and the thirty-seven harmonies with enlightenment. About the first wheel, Paramārthasamudgata describes the teachings on the aggregates, sense-spheres, dependent-arising, and foods as having five features:

1. own-character
2. production
3. disintegration
4. abandonment
5. thorough knowledge

The teachings on the four truths are described as having two features:

1. own-character
2. thorough knowledge (of true sufferings), abandonment (of true sources of suffering), actualization (of true cessations), and meditation (cultivating true paths)

The teachings on the constituents are described as having three features:

1. own-character
2. abandonment
3. thorough knowledge

The teachings of the thirty-seven harmonies with enlightenment are described as having eight features:

1. own-character
2. discordances

3. antidotes
4. production
5. abiding
6. non-loss
7. arising again
8. increasing

Paramārthasamudgata contrasts this first-wheel teaching with the second wheel, when Buddha said in the Perfection of Wisdom Sūtras, "All phenomena are natureless; all phenomena are unproduced, unceasing, quiescent from the start, and naturally thoroughly passed beyond sorrow." He concludes by asking Buddha what he meant by the second-wheel teaching.

D̄zong-ka-b̄a summarizes the question as being that the teaching in the middle wheel that all phenomena are natureless, and so forth, and the teaching in the first wheel that the aggregates, and so forth, have an "own-character" would be contradictory if they were left as they are on the surface. Since Buddha's teachings must be non-contradictory, Paramārthasamudgata asks of what Buddha was thinking when he taught the middle wheel of doctrine. D̄zong-ka-b̄a adds that the explicit question about the middle wheel contains an implicit question about what Buddha was thinking when he taught the first wheel of doctrine.

Criticizing Wonch'uk [78] {370}

The Korean scholar Wonch'uk, in his *Great Commentary on the "Sūtra Unraveling the Thought,"* takes the term "own-character" in Paramārthasamudgata's description of Buddha's teaching in the first wheel of doctrine as referring to the unique character or definition of a phenomenon as when Buddha speaks of a phenomenon and then of its unique character that distinguishes it from other phenomena. In the case of form, for instance, this is obstructiveness. D̄zong-ka-b̄a, however, holds that "own-character" refers not to the entity—the distinguishing nature—of form but to form's being established by way of its own character. He points out that the sūtra itself, in the course of Buddha's answer to Paramārthasamudgata's question, says not that imputational natures do not have their own unique character but that they do not subsist by way of their own character. He draws the absurd conclusion that if "own-character," as Wonch'uk says, meant an object's unique character, then it could not be held, as the sūtra says, that imputational natures are character-non-natures. D̄zong-ka-b̄a gives no further explanation, but the commentators agree that he is referring to the fact that imputational nature (as a category) does indeed have a unique characterization—namely, that which is imputed by conceptuality and is not established by way of its own character.

D̄zong-ka-b̄a next criticizes unidentified "commentaries" for mistaking the meaning of "the various and manifold constituents" mentioned in Paramārthasamudgata's question. He says that these should be taken as referring to the eighteen constituents and the six constituents based on another occurrence of these terms in the *Sūtra Unraveling the Thought,* at which point they are identified as the eighteen constituents and the six constituents. (See the footnotes in the Translation for the connection to Wonch'uk.)

Glossing The Meaning Of A Word [81] {370}

He finishes discussion of the question by glossing an obscure term, this being the sixth feature of the thirty-seven harmonies with enlightenment. He glosses "non-loss"[a] with "non-forgetfulness."[b]

---

[a] *mi bskyud pa, asaṃpramoṣatā* (Étienne Lamotte, *Saṃdhinirmocanasūtra: L'Explication des mystères* [Louvain: Université de Louvain, 1935], 67 [1], n. 26).

[b] *mi brjed pa.*

2. Buddha's Answer

Overview. This long chapter [82] {371} has eight basic movements:

1. Citing Buddha's brief indication of his thought behind the teaching in the Perfection of Wisdom Sūtras that all phenomena are natureless and also citing Asaṅga and Vasubandhu on the same issue
2. Based on these, denouncing the Jo-nang-b̄as for holding that the ultimate truly exists
3. Presenting Buddha's extensive explanation of his thought behind the teaching in the Perfection of Wisdom Sūtras that all phenomena are natureless, this being that there are three types of phenomena and three types of non-nature. In this and the above two subsections he makes distinctions between the Mind-Only School and the Middle Way School
4. Through focusing on the description of the ultimate in the *Sūtra Unraveling the Thought* as a mere negation, assailing the Jo-nang-b̄as for holding, on the one hand, that the *Sūtra Unraveling the Thought* is definitive and, on the other hand, that the ultimate is a positive entity
5. Citing the examples used in the *Sūtra Unraveling the Thought* to highlight the three non-natures, or three natures
6. Showing how, from the perspective of the Mind-Only School, when the Consequence School takes the Perfection of Wisdom Sūtras literally, they come to deprecate all three natures
7. Citing Buddha's explanation of the thought behind his teaching in the Perfection of Wisdom Sūtras that all phenomena are unproduced, unceasing, quiescent from the start, and naturally thoroughly passed beyond sorrow—this being from two perspectives, imputational natures and thoroughly established natures
8. Based on Wonch'uk's explanation, showing how the just mentioned description of the teaching—that phenomena are unproduced, unceasing, quiescent from the start, and naturally thoroughly passed beyond sorrow—is from the perspective of **two** of the three natures does not conflict, in essence, with the statement in Asaṅga's *Summary of Manifest Knowledge* that this teaching is from the perspective of all **three** natures

Let us turn to these in more detail.

Brief Indication Of The Thought Behind Buddha's Teaching In The Perfection Of Wisdom Sūtras That All Phenomena Are Natureless [82] {371}

Buddha explains that when, in the Perfection of Wisdom Sūtras, he said that all phenomena are natureless, he was not making a blanket statement with respect to all phenomena but was referring to three types of non-nature:

- A character-non-nature
- A production-non-nature
- Two types of ultimate-non-nature

Ḏzong-ka-ḇa quotes Asaṅga's *Compendium of Ascertainments* and Vasubandhu's *The Thirty,* the latter indicating that the three non-natures are posited with respect to the three natures. Thus, to repeat the charts given in the introduction:

Three Natures	*Three Non-Natures*
Imputational natures	Character-non-natures
Other-powered natures	1) Production-non-natures 2) Ultimate-non-natures
Thoroughly established natures	Ultimate-non-natures

To understand Ḏzong-ka-ḇa's immediate criticism of the Jo-nang-ḇas, it is necessary to flesh out the meaning of these correspondences by drawing from the subsequent extensive explanation. Using that, it is seen that:

Three Natures	*Three Non-Natures*
Imputational natures	Character-non-natures, in the sense that they are posited by names and terminology and do not exist by way of their own character
Other-powered natures	1) Production-non-natures, in the sense that they arise through the force of other conditions and are not self-produced 2) Ultimate-non-natures, in the sense that they are not objects of observation of paths of purification, that is, are not objects of the ultimate, purifying consciousness
Thoroughly established natures	Ultimate-non-natures, in the sense that they are the ultimate and the very absence of a difference of entity of subject and object and the very absence of establishment by way of a phenomenon's own character as the referent of terms and conceptual consciousnesses

This is how the three natures are paired with the three non-natures (the last of the three non-natures having two types).

Denouncing The Jo-nang-ḇas For Holding That The Ultimate Truly Exists [83] {372}

Ḏzong-ka-ḇa accuses the Jo-nang-ḇas of self-contradiction since:

- they must admit that the *Sūtra Unraveling the Thought* reports that in the middle wheel of doctrine Buddha taught that **all** phenomena are natureless, and
- they must admit that the Perfection of Wisdom Sūtras themselves individually mention that the 108 classes of phenomena—which include the 18 emptinesses—are natureless, and in particular that all synonyms of the ultimate, such as emptiness, the element of a (Superior's) qualities, thusness, and so forth are natureless;

- however, they hold that the ultimate is not among the phenomena that the Perfection of Wisdom Sūtras say are natureless.

Also, the *Sūtra Unraveling the Thought,* as well as Asaṅga and Vasubandhu, say that all three non-natures, including ultimate-non-natures, are behind Buddha's statements in the middle wheel that all phenomena are natureless. Thus Ḏzong-ka-ḇa shows amazement that the Jo-nang-ḇas could hold that statements in the Perfection of Wisdom Sūtras that all phenomena are natureless are in consideration only of conventional phenomena and not the ultimate. He concludes that the Jo-nang-ḇas are outside of Asaṅga's and Vasubandhu's Mind-Only system and that they also are outside Nāgārjuna's Middle Way system (since they hold that the ultimate is truly established). This means that they are outside of any Great Vehicle system.

Extensive Explanation Of The Thought Behind Buddha's Teaching In The Perfection Of Wisdom Sūtras That All Phenomena Are Natureless [85] {373}

Character-Non-Nature [85] {373}

Apparently following Wonch'uk's[741] structuring of Buddha's description of the character-non-nature in the *Sūtra Unraveling the Thought,* Ḏzong-ka-ḇa divides it into a (rhetorical) question, an answer, a (rhetorical) questioning of the reason, and an answer to that question. He then advises that this format should be used also with respect to the other two non-natures.

In short, Buddha identifies that it is imputational natures that are character-non-natures because, from the negative side, they are not posited by way of their own character and, from the positive side, are posited by names and terminology.

Ḏzong-ka-ḇa stresses that, therefore, the character that imputational natures do not have is establishment by way of their own character and that whether something is or is not established by way of its own character turns on whether it is not or is posited in dependence upon names and terminology ("terminology" here being taken—in order to avoid redundancy with "names"—to mean a conceptual consciousness). He makes the distinction that whatever is posited by names and terminology does not necessarily exist but, typical to his brevity, does not spell out the point—this being that phenomena, such as uncompounded space and an object's being the referent of a term or conceptual consciousness, which are posited in dependence upon names and terminology, do indeed exist but that the horns of a rabbit or an object's being established **by way of its own character** as the referent of a term or conceptual consciousness, which are also posited in dependence upon names and terminology, do not exist.

He cryptically adds that:

- the Mind-Only School and the Consequence School do not agree with respect to the meaning of being posited in dependence upon names and terminology, and hence
- do not agree with respect to what it means to exist by way of its own character, but
- if a person has the conception of an object as being established by way of its own character according to how this is described in the Mind-Only system, that person also has the conception of its being established by way of its own character according to how this is described in the Consequence School, and yet
- even though Proponents of Mind-Only did not conceive imputational natures in accordance with their own description of what it means to be established by way of their own character, they conceive imputational natures to be established by way of their own character in accordance with the description by the Consequence School.

He gives no further explanation, expecting the reader to know the dictum that the Mind-Only School holds that any existent, including existent imputational natures, is findable when the object imputed is sought and that this is the meaning of "establishment of an object by way of its own character" for the Consequence School.

Production-Non-Nature [87] {374}

In short, Buddha identifies that it is other-powered natures that are production-non-natures because, from the negative side, they are not produced by themselves and, from the positive side, they arise through the force of other conditions. D̄zong-ka-b̄a stresses that, therefore, the nature in terms of production that other-powered natures do not have is production by themselves, that is to say, production under their own power. He buttresses this point with a citation from Asaṅga's *Compendium of Ascertainments* and thereby implicitly emphasizes the consonance between the *Sūtra Unraveling the Thought* and Asaṅga's text.

Contrasting the Mind-Only School with the Consequence School, he reiterates that in the Mind-Only School other-powered natures are natureless due to being without the nature of self-powered production, unlike the Consequence School, which holds that other-powered natures are natureless due to not being established by way of their own character. He seeks to underline that in the Mind-Only School other-powered natures are established by way of their own character.

Ultimate-Non-Nature [88] {375}

In short, Buddha identifies that, from between the two types of ultimate-non-nature,[a] other-powered natures are ultimate-non-natures because the ultimate is what is observed and meditated upon in order to purify obstructions, whereas other-powered natures are not objects of such a process of purification.

Dzong-ka-ba raises the hypothetical question that if something were posited as an ultimate-non-nature merely because of not being an object of observation of purification, imputational natures also would have to be posited as ultimate-non-natures. However, he answers that Buddha at this point in the *Sūtra Unraveling the Thought* is responding to a qualm that stems from the fact that the sūtra itself explains that one is to meditate on **other-powered natures'** emptiness of being established by way of their own character as the referents of words and of conceptual consciousnesses, and thus other-powered natures are the substrata and the imputational nature is what is refuted with respect to them. Specifically, there arises the qualm that since, in that case, a wisdom consciousness must also observe the other-powered natures that are the substrata of the quality of emptiness, those other-powered natures also would be objects of observation of purification, due to which they would be ultimates. This is why such a qualm needs to be alleviated with respect to other-powered natures; however, since the sūtra speaks of the imputational nature as what is refuted, such a qualm does not occur with respect to the imputational nature.

The qualm is that the substratum, since it is observed in the sense of being the basis of the quality of emptiness, would also be an object of observation by a path of purification and hence an ultimate. Dzong-ka-ba declares that this is not the case and draws a parallel to the fact that although the conception that sound is permanent is overcome by ascertaining sound as impermanent, the conception of permanence is not overcome through merely observing sound.

As a final point, he cryptically says that although other-powered natures are not established as ultimates in the sense of being objects which, when observed and meditated upon, bring about purification, they are another type of ultimate. He does not explain the point here, but later it is clear that other-powered natures are ultimates in the sense of being ultimately established, that is to say, established by way of their own character.

Actual Ultimate-Non-Nature [90] {376}

Then, with respect to the second (and main) ultimate-non-nature, Buddha identifies that it is thoroughly established natures that are the ultimate-non-nature because in phenomena **just** the selflessness of phenomena

- is their naturelessness, and
- is the ultimate.

Drawing from the previous description of other-powered natures as not the

---

[a] *don dam pa ngo bo nyid med pa nyid, paramārthaniḥsvabhāvatā* (Lamotte, *Saṃdhinirmocana,* 67[3], n. 5). For discussion of the two meanings of this term see p. 35, footnote c.

ultimate because they are not objects of observation of purification, Dzong-ka-ba emphasizes here that the thoroughly established nature is the object of observation of purification.

The Ultimate As A Mere Negation: Assailing The Jo-nang-bas For Holding The Opposite [91] {376}

In order to counter the Jo-nang-ba notion of a positive ultimate, Dzong-ka-ba cites a passage from the third chapter of the *Sūtra Unraveling the Thought* called the "Questions of the Bodhisattva Suvishuddhamati." It offers more evidence that a thoroughly established nature is a "**mere** selflessness" and a "**mere** naturelessness"; that is to say, only an elimination of an object of negation and not something positive, as the Jo-nang-bas claim. He also cites the fact that the *Sūtra Unraveling the Thought* (94) gives space—which is a mere absence of obstructive contact—as an analog to the thoroughly established nature. Thus, for Dzong-ka-ba it is clear that, according to the *Sūtra Unraveling the Thought,* the thoroughly established nature is a non-affirming negative, a mere absence of the self of phenomena—a mere lack of objects' establishment by way of their own character as the referents of their respective conceptual consciousnesses and as the objects expressed by terms. Based on this, it is self-contradictory for the Jo-nang-bas to hold that the *Sūtra Unraveling the Thought* is definitive in its teachings about the ultimate and yet to hold that the ultimate is a positive, self-powered uncontaminated wisdom and that its appearance to the mind does not depend on the elimination of an object of negation.

Dzong-ka-ba finishes the discussion by making the distinction that in the Mind-Only School it is not said that the thoroughly established nature is natureless due to the negation itself not being established by way of its own character. He says no more, but the point is that in the Mind-Only School the thoroughly established nature is established by way of its own character whereas in the Consequence School it is not. Also, in the Autonomy School it, like all phenomena, is **ultimately** not established by way of its own character although it is conventionally established by way of its own character.

Examples For The Three Non-Natures [93] {377}

Buddha compares character-non-natures, that is, imputational natures, to a flower in the sky. Due to an eye disease,[a] the figure of a flower appears in the sky, but in fact there is no flower in the sky; just so, imputational natures are merely imputed by conceptuality. Dzong-ka-ba points out that, nevertheless, this does not mean that **all** imputational natures do not exist, but he does not give any further explanation. His point is that uncompounded space, for instance, is an **existent** imputational nature, as is an object's being the referent of

[a] *rab rib.*

a term and of a conceptual consciousness—with the qualification that they are not established **by way of their own character**.

Buddha compares production-non-natures, these being other-powered natures which are without self-production, to magical creations. Dzong-ka-ba refers the reader to a later explanation but does not identify it. It is found in chapter 8, on Maitreya's *Ornament for the Great Vehicle Sūtras*. The example is of a magician who takes pebbles or sticks, for instance, puts a salve on them, and recites a mantra, whereupon they appear to the entire audience as well as to the magician to be horses, elephants, and so forth. Jik-may-dam-chö-gya-tso,[742] a late-nineteenth- and early-twentieth-century scholar from northeastern Tibet, aligns the relevant factors of the example and of the exemplified this way:

The pebbles and sticks that are the bases of illusion	Unreal ideation[a] (that is, other-powered natures)
The pebbles and sticks being affected by the mantra and substance, that is, salve, that the magician uses	Unreal ideation (other-powered natures) being affected by predispositions for mistaken dualistic appearance
The appearance—to the audience—of the sticks and pebbles as horses, elephants, and so forth due to being affected by the magician's mantra and salve	The appearance of unreal ideation (other-powered natures) as distant and cut off due to being affected by predispositions for mistaken dualistic appearance

Buddha says that from between the two ultimate-non-natures, other-powered natures—which are posited as ultimate-non-natures since they are not the ultimate—are again to be viewed as like a magician's illusions. Then addressing the (actual) ultimate-non-nature, he says that the thoroughly established nature, which is both the ultimate and the absence of the nature of the self of phenomena, is like space. Dzong-ka-ba merely says that the example is clear. As Jik-may-dam-chö-gya-tso[743] puts it, just as space is distinguished, or posited, by way of a mere negation of obstructive contact and pervades all physical phenomena in the sense of existing with them, so the thoroughly established nature is distinguished by way of a mere elimination of a self of phenomena and pervades all phenomena as their mode of subsistence.

When The Consequence School Takes The Perfection Of Wisdom Sūtras Literally, It Comes To Deprecate All Three Natures [95] {378}

According to the Mind-Only School, when the Perfection of Wisdom Sūtras state that all phenomena are natureless, it must be understood that these statements are in consideration of the three non-natures. Otherwise, one would absurdly have to explain, in accordance with the Consequence School, that all three natures are not established by way of their own character, and this would be unsuitable because one would be adhering literally to the Perfection of Wisdom Sūtras' statements of naturelessness, in which case one would incur a view

a For a discussion of this term, see p. 307ff.

of nihilism. Thereby one would come to have the view that character, that is, establishment by way of its own character, does not exist, because one would be deprecating all three natures:

- Other-powered natures would be deprecated due to the fact that the Mind-Only School, following clear statements in the *Sūtra Unraveling the Thought,* holds that if other-powered natures are not established by way of their own character, production and cessation are not feasible
- Thoroughly established natures would be deprecated due to the fact that the Mind-Only School holds that if the thoroughly established nature does not exist by way of its own character, it could not be the basic disposition of phenomena
- Imputational natures would be deprecated due to viewing that the other two natures are not established by way of their own character, because when those two do not exist by way of their own character, they must be nonexistent, in which case the bases of imputing imputational natures, as well as the terms and conceptual consciousnesses that impute them would not exist

D̄zong-ka-b̄a cites a passage in the *Sūtra Unraveling the Thought* which says that (indented material throughout the synopses is paraphrase except where quotation marks appear):

> There are trainees who, even though they have interest in the profound thoroughly established nature, do not understand, just as it is, the profound reality that Buddha set forth in a non-literal manner. These trainees adhere to the terms as only literal: "All these phenomena are only natureless. All these phenomena are only unproduced, only unceasing, only quiescent from the start, only naturally thoroughly passed beyond sorrow." Due to that, they acquire the view that all phenomena do not exist and the view that establishment of objects by way of their own character does not exist. Doing so, they deprecate all three natures. For, if other-powered natures and the thoroughly established character are established by way of their own character, the imputational character is possible, whereas those who perceive other-powered natures and thoroughly established natures as not being established by way of their own character also deprecate the imputational nature. Thereby, those persons deprecate even all three natures.

D̄zong-ka-b̄a concludes by pointing out that even if one holds that production and cessation do not exist by way of their own character, one deprecates other-powered natures, whereby one also comes to deprecate the imputational and thoroughly established natures. For the Mind-Only School holds that if production and cessation are not established by way of their own character, they would be nonexistent. He says no more, but his point must be that, in that case, the bases of imputation of imputational factors and the substrata of the thoroughly established nature would not exist, and thus all three natures would be deprecated.

The Thought Behind Buddha's Teaching In The Perfection Of Wisdom Sūtras That All Phenomena Are Unproduced, Unceasing, Quiescent From The Start, And Naturally Thoroughly Passed Beyond Sorrow [97] {380}

In the Perfection of Wisdom Sūtras, Buddha taught that all phenomena are unproduced, unceasing, quiescent from the start, and naturally thoroughly passed beyond sorrow. He did this from two viewpoints—character-non-natures and ultimate-non-natures, these being imputational natures and thoroughly established natures, respectively. Thinking of character-non-natures, that is, imputational natures, he said that all phenomena are unproduced, unceasing, quiescent from the start, and naturally thoroughly passed beyond sorrow because imputational natures do not exist by way of their own character and hence are not produced, due to which they do not cease, due to which they are from the start quiescent, due to which they are naturally—without depending on an antidote—devoid of the afflictive emotions, due to which they do not have the least thing to pass beyond sorrow.

D̄zong-ka-b̄a stresses that the reason why imputational natures are not produced and do not cease is that they are not established by way of their own character. He does this to highlight the difference between the Mind-Only School and Chandrakīrti's Consequence School, in which no phenomenon is established by way of its own character.

Thinking of the ultimate-non-nature [98] {381}, that is, thoroughly established natures, Buddha taught that all phenomena are unproduced, unceasing, quiescent from the start, and naturally thoroughly passed beyond sorrow because the ultimate-non-nature is distinguished by the selflessness of phenomena and only subsists in permanent, permanent time and everlasting, everlasting time (these being identified by Wonch'uk as former and later time), and thus the ultimate-non-nature is the uncompounded final reality of phenomena, devoid of all afflictive emotions. Due to being uncompounded, it is unproduced and unceasing, and due to being devoid of all afflictive emotions, it is quiescent from the start and naturally thoroughly passed beyond sorrow.

Non-Contradiction Of This Presentation With That In Asaṅga's *Summary of Manifest Knowledge* [100] {381}

In identifying what was behind Buddha's teaching in the Perfection of Wisdom Sūtras that all phenomena are unproduced, unceasing, quiescent from the start, and naturally thoroughly passed beyond sorrow, the *Sūtra Unraveling the Thought* at this point identifies only character-non-natures and the ultimate-non-nature, that is, imputational natures and the thoroughly established nature.

However, Asaṅga, in his *Summary of Manifest Knowledge,* says that Buddha taught such in consideration of **all three** natures. Ḏzong-ka-ḇa first cites Wonch'uk's description and then refines it, explaining that:

- the *Sūtra Unraveling the Thought* is indicating that, since other-powered natures have production and cessation that exist by way of their own character, the statements in the *Sūtra Unraveling the Thought* concerning no production and no cessation are not in consideration of other-powered natures. Also, since most other-powered natures are included within the class of thoroughly afflicted phenomena, they are not treated as what was behind Buddha's teaching that phenomena are quiescent from the start and naturally thoroughly passed beyond sorrow;
- Asaṅga, on the other hand, sought to demonstrate a correspondence between how each of the three natures is natureless and how they also are unproduced, unceasing, and so forth.

Ḏzong-ka-ḇa's followers[744] flesh out Asaṅga's presentation:

- Imputational natures are said to be "unproduced" because they are not produced by way of their own character. They are said to be "unceased" because they do not cease by way of their own character. They are said to be quiescent from the start and naturally passed beyond sorrow because they are not afflicted phenomena, since they are uncompounded
- Other-powered natures are said to be "unproduced, unceasing" because they are not produced by their own power without depending on conditions and do not cease by their own power. They are said to be "quiescent from the start and naturally passed beyond sorrow" because without depending on conditions they do not exist as thoroughly afflicted phenomena
- Thoroughly established natures are said to be "unproduced, unceasing" because they are not produced and do not cease as the nature that is a self of phenomena or because they are the suchness that is not produced and does not cease as either a self of persons or a self of phenomena. They are said to be "quiescent from the start" and "naturally passed beyond sorrow" because they are without afflictions that are the nature of a self of phenomena, that is, without afflictions that are established by way of their own character as referents of conceptual consciousnesses. On this occasion, "sorrow" consists of the afflictive emotions. Or, in another way, thoroughly established natures are said to be "quiescent from the start" and "naturally passed beyond sorrow" because of being naturally passed beyond the afflictions, in the sense of not being either established as a substantially existent person or established by way of their own character as the referents of conceptual consciousnesses and words.

Ḏzong-ka-ḇa's implication is that since the sūtra and Asaṅga had different purposes in mind, they are not contradictory in essence.

3. The Three Natures

The previous chapter was concerned with the three non-natures that are teamed with the three natures; Ḏzong-ka-ḇa now turns his focus on the three natures themselves through identifying each briefly.

Overview. This chapter [104] {383} has five basic movements:

1. Based on Paramārthasamudgata's description in the *Sūtra Unraveling the Thought,* identifying the imputational nature of a form
2. Identifying the other-powered nature of a form
3. Identifying the thoroughly established nature of a form
4. Based on the sūtra's exposition of the thoroughly established nature as a mere elimination of the imputational nature in an other-powered nature, criticizing the Jo-nang-ḇas for holding that the thoroughly established nature is the absence of the other two natures
5. Explaining Paramārthasamudgata's extension of the three natures to other phenomena

The Imputational Nature Of A Form [104] {383}

Using the example of a form, Paramārthasamudgata renders what he understands Buddha to have said about the three natures. First, he indicates that the imputational nature being discussed here is of two types—imputation of an entity, as in "This is a form," and imputation of an attribute, as in "This is the production of form." Ḏzong-ka-ḇa refers to his own later discussion of this topic, where he says that, since forms and so forth are indeed entities of such imputation, it is not that the mere conception that forms and so forth **are** entities of imputation as entity and attribute is refuted; rather, the superimposition being refuted is that forms and so forth are established as entities of imputation as entity and attribute **by way of their own character**. (This is an important point since it allows language to refer to objects without making referentiality an integral nature of objects.)

The Other-Powered Nature Of A Form [106] {383}

As Paramārthasamudgata says, the bases of imputation of the imputational nature are other-powered natures that have three qualities. Other-powered natures are:

- the objects of activity of conceptuality,
- the foundations of imputational characters, and
- those which have the signs of compositional phenomena.

The first means that other-powered natures are objects of observation of conceptual consciousnesses—both main minds and mental factors. The second means that other-powered natures are bases of imputation of the imputational factor. D̄zong-ka-b̄a says merely that the third indicates the entities themselves of other-powered natures; other-powered natures themselves are compositional phenomena. (In a sense, therefore, the passage indicates the substrata—compositional phenomena—and **two** qualities.)

The Thoroughly Established Nature Of A Form [107] {383}

Paramārthasamudgata indicates that an other-powered nature's non-establishment as the imputational nature is the thoroughly established nature. He calls this the absence of self in phenomena and calls it thusness, as well as the object of observation of purification. D̄zong-ka-b̄a stresses that the sūtra says that the thoroughly established nature is just the naturelessness of only that imputational nature; he does this so that he can contrast this with the Jo-nang-b̄a assertion that the thoroughly established nature is other-empty, in the sense of being empty of other-powered natures and imputational natures. For D̄zong-ka-b̄a, the bases of emptiness are not the thoroughly established nature itself but other-powered natures. He stresses that the sūtra **very clearly** indicates that the emptiness of the imputational nature in those other-powered natures is the thoroughly established nature.

Criticizing The Jo-nang-b̄as' Presentation Of The Thoroughly Established Nature [109] {384}

Based on this very clear delineation in the *Sūtra Unraveling the Thought,* D̄zong-ka-b̄a accuses the Jo-nang-b̄as of self-contradiction in that:

- they hold that the presentation of the mode of emptiness in the *Sūtra Unraveling the Thought* is to be taken literally, and yet
- they assert that the mode of emptiness is that the thoroughly established nature is empty of the imputational and other-powered natures.

He adds that emptiness is not the negation of something that exists elsewhere (as would be the case if emptiness here meant the absence of other-powered natures and existent imputational natures) but is the absence of something that never existed, as in the case of the common Buddhist notion of a person's absence of substantial existence, which a person never had but is imagined to have. This is why the sūtra speaks of emptiness—the thoroughly established nature—as the mere non-establishment of other-powered natures as the imputational nature.

D̄zong-ka-b̄a mentions that, with respect to the imputational nature, the sūtra speaks **only** of factors imputed in the manner of entities and attributes. As he says later, there are other imputational natures, such as uncompounded space, but they are not relevant to the discussion of the imputational nature the emptiness of which is the thoroughly established nature.

Extension Of The Three Natures To Phenomena Other Than Forms [111] {384}

Having used forms, the first of the five aggregates, as a paradigm for laying out the three natures, Paramārthasamudgata extends this threefold formulation to all other categories of phenomena in the seven groups:

The remainder of the five mental and physical aggregates
The twelve sense-spheres
The twelve links of dependent-arising
The four foods
The four noble truths
The eighteen and six constituents
The thirty-seven harmonies with enlightenment

(Dzong-ka-ba does not address the issue that, since permanent phenomena are included among the twelve sense-spheres and the eighteen constituents, an other-powered nature must be posited with respect to them; this conundrum is left for his followers to unravel.)

4. The Overall Meaning

Overview. This summary chapter [114] {386} has four basic movements:

1. Describing the three wheels of doctrine in terms of whether they require interpretation or are definitive and then citing the *Sūtra Unraveling the Thought* on this topic
2. Through drawing on and refining Wonch'uk's commentary, explaining terminology in the sūtra
3. Identifying just what scriptures the *Sūtra Unraveling the Thought* is calling interpretable and definitive and why Buddha made this division
4. Based on these distinctions, indicating briefly that the descriptions of the three wheels of doctrine by the Jo-nang-b̄as, Bu-d̄ön, and others are wrong

Three Wheels Of Doctrine And Whether They Require Interpretation Or Are Definitive [114] {386}

D̄zong-ka-b̄a explains that, according to the *Sūtra Unraveling the Thought,* there are three sets of sūtras:

- a first wheel, which teaches that all phenomena exist by way of their own character
- a middle wheel, which teaches that all phenomena do not exist by way of their own character
- a final wheel, which differentiates well whether phenomena do or do not exist by way of their own character.

These three are put into two classes:

- The first two sets of sūtras do not differentiate well whether the three natures exist by way of their own character and thus require interpretation
- The final set of sūtras differentiates well that other-powered natures and thoroughly established natures exist by way of their own character and that imputational natures do not exist by way of their own character, and thus it is definitive

He then quotes from the *Sūtra Unraveling the Thought* Paramārthasamudgata's rendering of the meaning that implicitly rests in the question and answer, as well as in the presentation of the three natures.

Explaining Terminology In The Sūtra [118] {387}

The First Wheel Of Doctrine [118] {387}

Paramārthasamudgata describes the first wheel of doctrine from nine viewpoints:[745]

- The turner of the wheel is the Supramundane Victor
- The time is the first period (which, according to the late-seventeenth- and early-eighteenth-century Tibetan scholar Jam-ȳang-shay-b̄a, begins with Buddha's enlightenment and extends up to his death)[746]
- The place is the Deer Park called "Sage's Propounding," in the area of Varaṇāsi
- The intended trainees are those of low lineage mainly engaged in the Hearers' scriptural collections through hearing, thinking, and meditating
- The topics are the aspects of the four noble truths
- The mode of teaching is to declare that all phenomena without differentiation are equally established by way of their own character
- The entity is that it is a wheel of doctrine
- The praise is to call it fantastic and marvelous, which none—god or human—had previously turned in a similar fashion in the world
- The differentiation as to whether it requires interpretation or is definitive is to describe the first wheel of doctrine as surpassable, affording an occasion, requiring interpretation, and serving as a basis for controversy

Refining Wonch'uk's presentation of the last set of qualities in both word and meaning, D̄zong-ka-b̄a explains that:

- Surpassable means that there are other teachings of definitive meaning higher than this
- Affording an occasion means that it affords an occasion for the assessment of fault by other disputants (D̄zong-ka-b̄a praises Paramārtha's translation of this as "susceptible to dispute.")
- Requiring interpretation means that its meaning must be interpreted otherwise
- Serving as a basis for controversy means that, since Buddha did not clearly differentiate the status of what from among the three natures exists by way of its own character and what does not, there is controversy about the meaning

The Second Wheel Of Doctrine [123] {388}

Paramārthasamudgata's description of the second wheel of doctrine can be structured by way of the same nine viewpoints:[747]

- The turner of the wheel is the Supramundane Victor
- The time is the second period (which, according to Jam-ȳang-shay-b̄a, begins with the first pronouncement of the middle-wheel sūtras and extends up to Buddha's death)[748]
- The places are not mentioned in the *Sūtra Unraveling the Thought* because they are manifold—it was set forth in sixteen assemblies at four places, such as Vulture Peak

- The intended trainees are those of the Great Vehicle lineage mainly engaged in the scriptural collections of the Great Vehicle through hearing, thinking, and meditating
- The topics are the naturelessness of all phenomena, their absence of production, absence of cessation, quiescence from the start, and being naturally passed beyond sorrow
- The mode of teaching is to declare that all phenomena without differentiation are equally not established by way of their own character (or not established from their own side)
- The entity is that it is the **second** wheel of doctrine relative to the first
- The praise is to call it **very** fantastic and marvelous since, by way of its extensive teaching of emptiness, it is the principal of all sūtras (even in the Mind-Only School)
- The differentiation as to whether it requires interpretation or is definitive is to describe the second wheel of doctrine as surpassable, affording an occasion, requiring interpretation, and serving as a basis for controversy

Ḏzong-ka-b̄a criticizes Wonch'uk for merely saying the final set of four qualities are so "in relation to the third wheel." He also passes off Paramārtha's explanation, cited by Wonch'uk, as not good and thus does not even cite it or explain his disdain. He says the four should be interpreted as above for the first wheel:

- Surpassable means that there are other teachings of definitive meaning higher than this
- Affording an occasion means that it affords an occasion for the assessment of fault by other disputants
- Requiring interpretation means that its meaning must be interpreted otherwise
- Serving as a basis for controversy means that, since Buddha did not clearly differentiate the status of what from among the three natures exists by way of its own character and what does not, there is controversy about the meaning.

The Third Wheel Of Doctrine [124] {388}

As before, Paramārthasamudgata's description of the third wheel of doctrine can be structured by way of the same nine viewpoints:[749]

- The turner of the wheel is the Supramundane Victor
- The time is the third period (which, according to Jam-ȳang-shay-b̄a, begins with the first pronouncement of the third-wheel sūtras and extends through Buddha's death)[750]
- The places are not mentioned in the *Sūtra Unraveling the Thought,* but it was spoken to eight assemblies in seven places, the principal of which is

Vaishālī, since that is where the *Sūtra Unraveling the Thought* was spoken

- The intended trainees are those of the Great Vehicle lineage mainly engaged in the scriptural collections of both the Lesser Vehicle and the Great Vehicle through hearing, thinking, and meditating
- The topics are—as with the middle wheel—the naturelessness of all phenomena, their absence of production, absence of cessation, quiescence from the start, and naturally being passed beyond sorrow
- The mode of teaching is to differentiate a presentation of three natures and three non-natures with respect to each phenomenon
- The entity is that it is the third wheel of doctrine relative to the first two wheels of doctrine
- The praise is to call it fantastic and marvelous
- The differentiation as to whether it requires interpretation or is definitive is to describe **this** *Sūtra Unraveling the Thought* that makes such differentiation—and not other sūtras that do not—as unsurpassable, not affording an occasion for refutation, being definitive, and not serving as a basis for controversy

Dzong-ka-ba points out that the set of four qualities of the third wheel mean the opposite of his earlier explanation with respect to the first wheel. Thus, if we reverse the earlier descriptions and add his further comments:

- Unsurpassable means that there are not other teachings of definitive meaning higher than this
- Not affording an occasion means that it does not afford an occasion for the assessment of fault by other disputants since its literal meaning, unlike the previous two wheels, does not need to be interpreted otherwise
- Being definitive means that its meaning need not be interpreted otherwise
- Not serving as a basis for controversy means that since Buddha clearly differentiated the status of what from among the three natures exists by way of its own character and what does not, there is no controversy about the meaning, for there is no room for controversy when scholars analyze whether the meaning of the sūtra is or is not to be delineated that way, even though there can be other controversies (such as objections by the Proponents of Non-Nature)

Dzong-ka-ba quotes Wonch'uk on these four and laconically faults the first part of his twofold interpretation of the second quality—"Because it does not afford an occasion for something more superior later and does not afford an occasion for later destruction, it does not afford an occasion." Jik-may-dam-chö-gya-tso[751] explains the unsuitability of Wonch'uk's explanation as being that if it means that the third wheel does not allow for there being something superior to it, then (1) it is redundant with the earlier mention that "there is no other exceeding it" and (2) the second wheel would also "not afford an occasion." Jik-may-dam-chö-gya-tso's latter point is that sharp Bodhisattvas can, without further explanation, understand the second wheel as teaching the three natures and three non-natures, and thus the second wheel teaches the three natures and three non-natures even if not on the literal level, and hence the second wheel also does not afford an occasion for there being something superior to it, in this sense.

D̄zong-ka-b̄a [126] {389} agrees with Wonch'uk that the first wheel is to be called the wheel of doctrine of the four truths and that the second is to be called the wheel of doctrine of no character, but he does not agree that the third is to be called the wheel of the ultimate, the definitive. Rather, he prefers "the wheel of good differentiation," based on the sūtra's description:

> The Supramundane Victor turned a third wheel of doctrine for those engaged in all vehicles, **possessed of good differentiation**, fantastic and marvelous.

(Perhaps D̄zong-ka-b̄a seeks to preserve the point that the middle wheel teaches the ultimate, even if not on the literal level.)

Identifying Just What Scriptures The *Sūtra Unraveling the Thought* Is Calling Interpretable And Definitive And Why Buddha Made This Division [128] {390}

D̄zong-ka-b̄a emphatically makes the point that the scriptures that the *Sūtra Unraveling the Thought* says require interpretation or are definitive are not **all** teachings during certain periods. What the *Sūtra Unraveling the Thought* says require interpretation in the first period are the teachings that all phenomena are established by way of their own character (or established by way of their own character as the referents of their respective conceptual consciousnesses), and not other teachings, such as when Buddha told the five ascetics, "The lower robe should be worn in a circular fashion," meaning not to let it sag here and there. Similarly, what require interpretation in the second period are the teachings that all phenomena are not established by way of their own character (or are not established from their own side), and others that do not teach such naturelessness are not the concern. The teachings that the *Sūtra Unraveling the Thought* says are definitive in the third period are those that differentiate clearly between what from among the three natures are established by way of their own character and what are not—that give a clear presentation of the three natures and three non-natures—and not all teachings during the third period, as when, for instance, about to pass away, Buddha told his disciples that it would be suitable to use his earlier declarations concerning similar ethical situations as a basis for deciding new issues that he had not addressed; this type of teaching is not of concern to the *Sūtra Unraveling the Thought* in its declaration that certain third-wheel teachings are definitive.

The purpose [129] {390} behind Buddha's differentiation between what require interpretation and what are definitive is that he is intent that trainees of the *Sūtra Unraveling the Thought* overcome taking literally the teachings that phenomena, without differentiation, either are or are not established by way of their own character. He wanted to teach them that:

- imputational natures are not established by way of their own character,
- other-powered natures and thoroughly established natures are established by way of their own character, and
- other-powered natures' emptiness of the imputational factor is the final ultimate that is the object of observation of the path.

Criticizing The Descriptions Of The Three Wheels Of Doctrine By The Jo-nang-b̄as, Bu-d̄ön, And Others [129] {390}

D̄zong-ka-b̄a ends the section on what the *Sūtra Unraveling the Thought* itself says about differentiating the interpretable and the definitive with a very brief refutation of the Jo-nang-b̄as, Bu-d̄ön, and others without mentioning any of them by name. He accuses them of not having analyzed well Paramārthasamudgata's question, Buddha's answer, or how sūtras are posited as requiring interpretation or being definitive. As Jik-may-dam-chö-gya-tso[752] explains, these scholars hold the mistaken notion that the division of sūtras as to whether they require interpretation or are definitive is made only by way of periods in Buddha's teaching rather than by way of whether teachings do or do not differentiate which from among the three natures is established by way of its own character. Thus, the Jo-nang-b̄as take literally all scriptures of the third period, including a certain type of teaching on the matrix of One Gone Thus (Buddha nature) that says that Buddha qualities are already present in sentient beings' continuums and that actually was given for the sake of non-Buddhists addicted to the conception of self. Bu-d̄ön Rin-chen-drup and so forth, on the other hand, seeing the fallacy of taking such teachings literally, hold that the differentiation of what requires interpretation and what is definitive, as found in the *Sūtra Unraveling the Thought,* is itself not to be taken literally (supposedly even in the Mind-Only system).

In addition, rather than holding that, according to the *Sūtra Unraveling the Thought,* other-powered natures and thoroughly established natures exist by way of their own character and that imputational natures do not exist by way of their own character, the Jo-nang-b̄as hold that only the thoroughly established nature exists by way of its own character, whereas the other two natures are only fancied by a mistaken awareness to exist at all. This is what they hold to be the meaning of the good differentiation by the third wheel of doctrine.

MIND-ONLY SCHOOL: EXPLICATIONS OF THE *SŪTRA UNRAVELING THE THOUGHT* ON DIFFERENTIATING THE INTERPRETABLE AND THE DEFINITIVE

Overview of Chapters 5 Through 12

In the second section of his exposition of the Mind-Only School [135] {392}, Ḏzong-ka-ḇa turns to great Indian Mind-Only treatises for their exegesis of the topic of the interpretable and the definitive in the *Sūtra Unraveling the Thought.* Initially, he shows how Asaṅga, who came to be renowned as the founder of the Mind-Only School, relied on the *Sūtra Unraveling the Thought.* Then, in chapters 6 through 12, he discusses central Mind-Only treatises by Asaṅga and Maitreya and briefly treats others. From among the four contexts mentioned above as operative in the first section,

- Presenting Indian Mind-Only scholarship, so that the architecture of the system can be engaged
- Distinguishing the Mind-Only School from the Consequence School
- Refining the Korean scholar Wonch'uk's seventh-century presentation
- Criticizing the eclectic syncretism of his close thirteenth and fourteenth Tibetan predecessor Jo-nang-ḇa Š̄hay-rap-gyel-tsen,

Ḏzong-ka-ḇa no longer addresses Wonch'uk's interpretations, probably because, from his viewpoint, the refinements he has made are sufficient, but not because Indian exegesis of the *Sūtra Unraveling the Thought* is now his focus, since Wonch'uk, as is obvious from even a quick reading of his commentary, was well versed in Indian treatises, which he very frequently cites.

5. The Importance of the *Sūtra Unraveling the Thought*

As commanding evidence [135] {392} that the *Sūtra Unraveling the Thought* is vital to Asaṅga's system, Ḏzong-ka-ḇa points out that, except for its introductory chapter, Asaṅga cites the sūtra almost in its entirety, chapter by chapter, in his *Compendium of Ascertainments.*[753] Also, he stresses that Asaṅga's three works on the view—the "Chapter on Suchness" in the *Grounds of Bodhisattvas,* the *Compendium of Ascertainments,* and the *Summary of the Great Vehicle*—derive their central theme from the statement in the *Sūtra Unraveling the Thought* that other-powered natures' emptiness of factors imputed in the manner of entities and attributes is the thoroughly established nature. Finally, he indicates that the teachings on emptiness in Maitreya's *Ornament for the Great Vehicle Sūtras, Differentiation of the Middle and the Extremes,* and so forth, as well as their commentaries, accord with the *Sūtra Unraveling the Thought.*

These points not only show the connection of these treatises with the *Sūtra Unraveling the Thought* but also account for Ḏzong-ka-ḇa's own exclusive concentration on this sūtra in the previous section. In addition, the importance of this sūtra to Asaṅga and Maitreya justifies his citing its very clear statements about the thoroughly established nature as a mere absence in order to refute the Jo-nang-ḇa presentation of a positive ultimate. (Indeed, the sūtra's statements to this effect are even clearer than are those in Asaṅga's and Maitreya's treatises.)

Overview of Chapters 6 Through 9

Dzong-ka-ba's exposition of major Indian Mind-Only treatises in terms of their exegesis of the sūtra's discussion about the interpretable and the definitive begins with how these treatises refute the two extremes of superimposition and nihilism in general. These comprise chapters 6 through 9; he gives a more specific refutation of the extreme of superimposition in chapters 10 and 11; and finally in chapter 12 he considers how, in dependence on the determination of the middle free from the extremes, scriptures are differentiated into those that require interpretation and those that are definitive.

In chapters 6 through 9 Dzong-ka-ba focuses on four texts:

- Asaṅga's
  Grounds of Bodhisattvas
  Compendium of Ascertainments
- Maitreya's
  Ornament for the Great Vehicle Sūtras
  Differentiation of the Middle and the Extremes

He secondarily touches on nine texts by four authors:

- Vasubandhu's
  The Thirty
  Principles of Explanation
  Commentary on (Maitreya's) "Differentiation of the Middle and the Extremes"
  Explanation of (Maitreya's) "Ornament for the Great Vehicle Sūtras"
  The Twenty
- Sthiramati's
  Explanation of (Vasubandhu's) Commentary on (Maitreya's) "Differentiation of the Middle and the Extremes"
  Commentary on (Vasubandhu's) "The Thirty"
- Dignāga's
  Summary Meanings of the Eight Thousand Stanza Perfection of Wisdom Sūtra
  Examination of Objects of Observation
- Dharmakīrti's
  Commentary on (Dignāga's) "Compilation of Prime Cognition."[a]

Along the way, he occasionally refers to:

[a] Dharmakīrti's *Ascertainment of Prime Cognition* (*tshad ma rnam par nges pa, pramāṇaviniścaya;* Peking 5710, vol. 130) is mentioned in passing.

- Asaṅga's
  Summary of Manifest Knowledge
  Summary of the Great Vehicle

Dzong-ka-ba frames these four chapters around how these texts avoid the extremes of superimposition (or reification) and deprecation, but the emphases within each chapter differ.

- Chapter 6, on Asaṅga's *Grounds of Bodhisattvas,* introduces the issue of the two extremes of reification and deprecation but focuses on the extreme of deprecation—describing the pitfalls of holding that other-powered natures are not ultimately established and not established by way of their own character, as is asserted by the Proponents of Non-Nature.
- Chapter 7, on Asaṅga's *Compendium of Ascertainments,* continues describing how the extreme of deprecation is avoided; it depicts a debate by Proponents of Mind-Only against the assertion by Proponents of Non-Nature that all phenomena just conventionally exist and do not ultimately exist. In order to dispel confusion between the Mind-Only School and the Naturelessness School, it then explores the complex usage of the vocabulary of (1) the two truths, (2) existing ultimately and existing conventionally, and (3) existing substantially and existing imputedly.
- Chapter 8, on Maitreya's *Ornament for the Great Vehicle Sūtras,* lays out the thought behind the six teachings in the Perfection of Wisdom Sūtras that phenomena are natureless, without production, without cessation, quiescent from the start, and naturally passed beyond sorrow, as well as that practitioners should attain forbearance with respect to the doctrine of non-production. It also explores how an object can be untrue like an illusion and yet truly exist.
- Chapter 9, on Maitreya's *Differentiation of the Middle and the Extremes,* focuses on the Mind-Only doctrine that other-powered natures and emptiness truly exist but duality does not exist, thereby delineating emptiness and the middle path free from the two extremes. As an appendage, brief mention is made of Dignāga's *Summary Meanings of the Eight Thousand Stanza Perfection of Wisdom Sūtra* and Dharmakīrti's *Commentary on (Dignāga's) "Compilation of Prime Cognition";* in the latter Dzong-ka-ba focuses on how Dharmakīrti posits the thought behind the literal reading of the Perfection of Wisdom Sūtras.

Let us consider these four chapters in detail.

6. Asaṅga's *Grounds of Bodhisattvas*

Overview. This chapter [140] {393} has three basic movements:

1. Within drawing out the implications of the vocabulary of the *Grounds of Bodhisattvas,* describing the final nature of phenomena through the route of identifying the extremes of superimposition and deprecation
2. After putting off discussion of the extreme of superimposition until chapter 10, showing how the *Grounds of Bodhisattvas* refutes the extreme of deprecation by depicting a controversy on the final nature of phenomena between the Proponents of Mind-Only and unnamed opponents—who by context are understood to be the Proponents of Non-Nature (the dispute centers on whether other-powered natures are established by way of their own character)
3. Ending with a depiction of the suchness of phenomena that avoids the extremes of superimposition and of deprecation according to the Mind-Only system

Final Nature Of Phenomena [140] {393}

To expose how this system differs from that of the Proponents of Non-Nature, D̄zong-ka-b̄a cites Asaṅga's description of the final nature of phenomena:

> The middle—the final nature of phenomena—avoids the extremes of superimposition and deprecation. The extreme of superimposition is to misapprehend imputational natures as established by way of their own character, and the extreme of deprecation is to misapprehend other-powered natures that are "real things ultimately existing with an inexpressible essence" as not ultimately established by way of their own character.

Those who commit the latter fallacy have fallen away from the doctrine of the Great Vehicle through such deprecatory nihilism; they are the Proponents of Non-Nature.

D̄zong-ka-b̄a makes the distinctions that:

- When Asaṅga speaks of the "nature of imputational words" he is referring not to the words that impute a false nature (words themselves being other-powered natures) but to the false nature that is imputed by words. It is not words that are being refuted but a misconceived nature of things imputed by verbalization and conceptual consciousnesses—the establishment of objects by way of their own character as the referents of their respective terms and conceptual consciousnesses
- When Asaṅga speaks of superimposition, he uses the vocabulary of "own-

character," and when he speaks of deprecation he uses the vocabulary of "not existing ultimately," and thus it can be seen that existing by way of its own character and existing ultimately are equivalent. Hence, conceiving imputational natures to exist ultimately or to be established by way of their own character is a superimposition, and conceiving other-powered natures not to be established by way of their own character or not to exist ultimately is a deprecation

- When Asaṅga speaks of deprecation, he casts the topic only in reference to holding that other-powered natures do not ultimately exist and does not mention thoroughly established natures. However, Dzong-ka-ba extends the explanation of deprecation to include thoroughly established natures since if other-powered natures did not ultimately exist, their final nature—that is, their thoroughly established nature—also would not ultimately exist
- The deprecation of other-powered natures that Proponents of Non-Nature commit is not that they claim that other-powered natures do not exist at all but that they claim that these do not **ultimately** exist, or do not exist by way of their own character. This is a deprecation since, according to the Mind-Only School, other-powered natures do indeed ultimately exist. (Still, for the Mind-Only School, the claim that other-powered natures do not ultimately exist amounts to holding that they do not exist at all even if the Proponents of Non-Nature do not say this, as is seen in the next section.)

Having made these distinctions, he proceeds to show how Asaṅga refutes the extreme of deprecation that is asserted by the Proponents of Non-Nature.

Refuting The Extreme Of Deprecation [143] {396}

To the Proponents of Non-Nature who hold that all phenomena—the five aggregates and so forth—exist conventionally and do not exist ultimately, the Proponents of Mind-Only make the objection:

> When the other-powered natures that are the bases of designation of the imputational nature are established by way of their own character, then imputational natures can be imputed, but if they are not established by way of their own character, imputational natures cannot be imputed. This is like the fact that, for example, when the mental and physical aggregates are established by way of their own character, a person is suitable to be imputed in dependence upon them, whereas if they are not established by way of their own character, then, since the bases of imputation do not exist, a person is not suitable to be imputed in dependence upon them.

Dzong-ka-ba makes the side-point that, nevertheless, the principle that the basis of imputation must be established by way of its own character does not apply to all phenomena, since it is not to be extended to existent imputational natures such as uncompounded space. For it is a cardinal rule, expounded in the *Sūtra Unraveling the Thought* itself, that imputational natures "do not subsist by way of their own character," and thus uncompounded space—which is not an other-powered nature (because it is not produced by causes and conditions) and which is not a thoroughly established nature (because it is not the final reality of phenomena) and thus must be an (existent) imputational nature—must not exist by way of its own character.

The Proponents of Non-Nature cannot respond to the above-stated challenge by saying:

> Other-powered natures are causes and effects for a **mistaken** consciousness that conceives causes and effects to be truly established, but other-powered natures themselves actually are not established as causes and effects.

For then they would have no way to posit actual cause and effect, and the doctrine of karma would be lost. For example, a rope is a snake for a consciousness **mis**conceiving it to be a snake, but it simply is not a snake.

In the Mind-Only School, production that is not established by way of its own character or is not ultimately existent is as good as nonexistent, a mere figment of the imagination. When the Proponents of Non-Nature claim that no phenomenon ultimately exists and that the absence of ultimate existence is the very meaning of suchness, they have fallen into the chief of annihilatory views. Asaṅga cites a sūtra passage saying that those who misapprehend emptiness and thereby deprecate all phenomena neglect proper training and ruin others, as a consequence of which they will be reborn in a hell. (This theme resurfaces in the next chapter, when Ḏzong-ka-ḇa criticizes certain Tibetan scholars for holding that, according to the Mind-Only School, all phenomena only conventionally exist; he says that they mistakenly attribute to the Proponents of Mind-Only the very view that, as shown here, this school considers the pit of nihilism.)

Delineation Of The Middle Position [147] {400}

The chapter concludes with a brief recapitulation of what the actual suchness of phenomena is in the Mind-Only School, based on a pithy statement in the *Grounds of Bodhisattvas* that Ḏzong-ka-ḇa cites in similar form in chapter 9 on Maitreya's *Differentiation of the Middle and the Extremes* from Vasubandhu's commentary. In short, the meaning is that:

- The absence of the ultimate existence of the imputational nature in other-powered natures is the thoroughly established nature
- The remainder—identified as other-powered natures or as both other-

powered natures and thoroughly established natures—ultimately exists
- One who perceives this is non-erroneously oriented to emptiness

In this way, both the extreme of superimposition and the extreme of deprecation are avoided, whereby the true middle is delineated.

Through these points, Ḏzong-ka-ḇa emphasizes the differentiation of the tenets of the Mind-Only School from those of the Naturelessness School—this theme continuing in the next three chapters. By showing how these systems differ from each other, he perforce demonstrates that the Jo-nang-ḇa eclecticism is uninformed and unfounded.

7. Asaṅga's *Compendium of Ascertainments*

Overview. This chapter [149] {402} has four basic movements:

1. Showing how the extreme of deprecation is avoided in Asaṅga's *Compendium of Ascertainments* by citing another debate that Asaṅga carries on with the Proponents of Non-Nature, who accept the literal reading of the statement in the Perfection of Wisdom Sūtras that everything exists conventionally, nothing exists ultimately (Thus the chapter begins with again distinguishing the Mind-Only School from the Naturelessness School.)
2. On the basis of this debate, criticizing those Tibetans who hold that, according to the Mind-Only School, other-powered natures exist only conventionally and do not exist ultimately
3. Handling seemingly divergent usages—in the Mind-Only system itself—of the vocabulary of existing conventionally and existing ultimately, in order to dispel possible criticisms of his interpretation of the Mind-Only system (He shows how statements in Mind-Only texts that seem to suggest that other-powered natures do not ultimately exist do not actually mean this—thereby undercutting the possibility that Proponents of Mind-Only could agree with Proponents of Non-Nature that other-powered natures exist only conventionally.)
4. Ending with a reminder that, through understanding the many meanings of vocabulary for levels of existence in Indian treatises, one can appreciate the need on the part of the Proponents of Non-Nature to refute other schools' assertions, even if their respective positions have superficial similarities

The concern throughout the chapter is with establishing differences between the Mind-Only School and the Naturelessness School.

The Debate [149] {402}

To expose inconsistencies in the position of the Proponents of Non-Nature, Asaṅga asks them:

> What is the ultimate (*don dam, paramārtha*)? What is the concealer (*kun rdzob, saṃvṛti*)?

Ḏzong-ka-ḇa cogently takes the first part of the question as asking what the ultimate truth (*don dam bden pa, paramārthasatya*) is, but he does not take the second part as asking what conventional truths (*kun rdzob bden pa, saṃvṛtisatya*) are. Indeed, the run of the debate bears out his reading that the second part concerns the ignorance, or concealing consciousness, in the face of which phenomena other than emptiness are wrongly considered to be truths, that is to say, to exist the way they appear.[a]

The Proponents of Non-Nature answer:

> The naturelessness, or absence of ultimate existence, of all phenomena is the ultimate. That which conceives those phenomena—which are without ultimate existence—to have ultimate existence is the concealer of the true nature of phenomena.

Asaṅga [151] {404} now grills the Proponents of Non-Nature about the status of the concealing ignorant consciousness itself:

> Does the concealing consciousness arise from causes which are of its own similar type, or is it mere verbalization and convention, that is, imputedly existent? If it arises from causes that are of its own similar type, then since it arises from causes, it is not suitable to say that it does not (ultimately) exist.

Ḏzong-ka-ḇa takes "exist" to mean not mere existence but ultimate existence, since the Proponents of Non-Nature do assert that phenomena conventionally exist. Thus, the debate is about whether an ignorant consciousness misconceiving phenomena to ultimately exist itself ultimately exists; by extension, it also is about whether other-powered natures ultimately exist. (Indeed, although neither Asaṅga nor Ḏzong-ka-ḇa cites it **at this point**, the *Sūtra Unraveling the Thought* itself says,[754] "That which does not exist by way of its own character is not produced," and hence in the Mind-Only system whatever is produced must be established by way of its own character.)

Asaṅga continues:

> If an ignorant, concealing consciousness misconceiving ultimate existence is merely verbal and conventional, then all other-powered natures likewise would be only imputed by conceptuality. In that case, they would be nonexistent, and thus it is not suitable to assert that a consciousness conceiving ultimate existence is imputedly existent.

Next Asaṅga [152] {405} grills the Proponents of Non-Nature about the ultimate:

> Given that other-powered natures are observed to be ultimately existent, how can you claim that their absence of ultimate existence is the ultimate? Why do you claim that things are not existent, that is, are not ultimately existent or are not established by way of their own character?

---

[a] At first blush, his reading seems to be a suspicious maneuver to maintain a facet of his own interpretation of the Mind-Only School; however, further analysis does not support that suspicion.

The Proponents of Non-Nature answer:

> That there is a consciousness that observes, or conceives, phenomena to ultimately exist does not damage our assertion that objects are not ultimately existent, because such a consciousness is erroneous.

Asaṅga responds:

> Do you assert that this erroneous consciousness exists (ultimately) or that it does not exist (ultimately)? If it does, then it is not suitable for you to say that the naturelessness, that is, the absence of ultimate existence, of **all** phenomena, is the ultimate since this erroneous consciousness would exist ultimately. If it does not exist (ultimately), then since it would not exist at all, it is not suitable to say that **because this consciousness erroneously conceives ultimate existence**, what is observed by it is actually natureless, that is, without ultimate existence.

Having described the conflict between the Proponents of Mind-Only and Proponents of Non-Nature on the mode of being of phenomena, D̄zong-ka-b̄a [154] {405} cites Asaṅga's *Compendium of Ascertainments* to show that:

- it describes the two extremes in a way similar to that in the same author's *Grounds of Bodhisattvas,* especially on the issue of what constitutes deprecation—this being to hold that other-powered natures and thoroughly established natures are not established by way of their own character; and
- it indicates that among imputational natures some exist and some do not and that existent imputational natures are imputedly existent and conventionally existent.

On the basis of the latter point, D̄zong-ka-b̄a [156] {406} criticizes a commentary (not the one by Wonch'uk) on the *Sūtra Unraveling the Thought* that holds that imputational natures (and thus **all** imputational natures including existent ones) are not included anywhere in the two truths. That commentary also mistakenly says that subject and object as different entities are other-powered natures and dependent-arisings, whereas in fact subject and object as different entities do not exist at all, as is indicated in Asaṅga's *Summary of the Great Vehicle, Grounds of Bodhisattvas,* and *Compendium of Ascertainments.* These facts make it impossible that Asaṅga, as one scholar claims, wrote the above-mentioned commentary on the *Sūtra Unraveling the Thought,* as does the fact that the commentary cites Dharmakīrti's *Ascertainment of Prime Cognition,* which postdates Asaṅga. D̄zong-ka-b̄a adds that Asaṅga had no need to write a separate commentary on the *Sūtra Unraveling the Thought,* since in the *Compendium of Ascertainments* he cites almost all of the sūtra and delineates the difficult points. (I take the "difficult points" to refer, for instance, to the arguments that are presented in this chapter.)

Criticizing A Recent Interpretation [157] {406}

Having established that in Asaṅga's system other-powered natures ultimately exist, Ḏzong-ka-ḇa criticizes a scholar who claims that Asaṅga holds that other-powered natures do not ultimately exist and only conventionally exist. The criticism is that this scholar thereby attributes to Asaṅga just the position that Asaṅga himself considers the very pit of deprecation. That scholar is variously identified by later exegetes as either of Ḏzong-ka-ḇa's immediate predecessors in the fourteenth century, Bu-ḏön Rin-chen-drup or Jo-nang-ḇa S̄hay-rap-gyel-tsen. Relative to Ḏzong-ka-ḇa's more indirect rebuttals, this strong refutation stands as a theme-repeating crescendo. Still, their opinion is based on statements in Indian Mind-Only texts that other-powered natures exist conventionally, and thus Ḏzong-ka-ḇa begins a detailed analysis of terminology in order to reveal the different contexts in which it is said in some places that other-powered natures conventionally exist and in others that other-powered natures ultimately exist. S̄hay-rap-gyel-tsen, for instance, would stress the former, interpreting conventional existence to mean that other-powered natures exist only for ignorance, whereas Ḏzong-ka-ḇa stresses the latter, interpreting the ultimate existence of other-powered natures as not implying that they are ultimate truths. Since the same Indian texts do say both, Ḏzong-ka-ḇa must show how these two attributions are not contradictory. Thereby any assumed harmony between statements in the Mind-Only School and in the Middle Way School that phenomena only conventionally exist will be undermined.

Handling Complex Vocabulary In The Mind-Only System [158] {407}

He devotes the rest of the chapter to Mind-Only authors' complicated usage of the vocabulary of (1) the two truths, (2) existing ultimately and existing conventionally (including existing as an ultimate and existing as a conventionality), and (3) existing substantially and existing imputedly. The section is framed around a hypothetical objection to his delineation that in the Mind-Only School other-powered natures ultimately exist but are not ultimates.

The objection is that other-powered natures could not ultimately exist if they are not ultimates, that is, ultimate truths. The objector points to the undisputed facts that:

- the *Sūtra Unraveling the Thought* says that whatever is a compounded phenomenon is not ultimate,
- Maitreya's *Differentiation of the Middle and the Extremes* says that the ultimate truth is just the thoroughly established nature,
- Maitreya's *Ornament for the Great Vehicle Sūtras* says (and Vasubandhu's commentary affirms) that other-powered natures are not ultimates, and
- Asaṅga's *Compendium of Ascertainments* says that other-powered natures exist conventionally.

The objector cites the first three on the assumption that whatever is not an ultimate could not possibly ultimately exist, and thus Ḏzong-ka-ḇa answers by distinguishing between ultimate truth and existing ultimately. He points out that other-powered natures can ultimately exist without being ultimate truths. The objector cites the last passage on the assumption that if other-powered natures exist conventionally, they could not also exist ultimately. Thus, Ḏzong-ka-ḇa answers this part by explicating two meanings of "ultimately existing" and "conventionally existing": in the first version other-powered natures ultimately exist and do not conventionally exist, but in the second version the opposite is the case. Let us consider these points.

The First Mode Of Positing Existing Conventionally And Existing Ultimately [160] {409}

In the first way, an existent that is posited through the force of conventions is said to exist conventionally, and an existent that is not posited through the force of conventions but exists by way of its own character is said to exist ultimately. Hence existent imputational natures such as uncompounded space exist conventionally and do not exist ultimately, but other-powered natures and thoroughly established natures exist ultimately and do not exist conventionally.

In an important aside, Ḏzong-ka-ḇa explains the difference between imputed existence and substantial existence. Imputed existence means that the object (such as a person) is not apprehendable without relying on apprehension of other phenomena (such as the mental and physical aggregates) and thus the object must be apprehended in reliance upon apprehending other phenomena. Therefore, it is not contradictory that a phenomenon such as a person (1) ultimately exists—in the sense explained above of not being posited through the force of conventions but existing by way of its own character—and yet (2) imputedly exists.

The Second Mode Of Positing Existing Conventionally And Existing Ultimately [162] {410}

The second mode of existing conventionally and existing ultimately means to exist **as** a conventionality and to exist **as** an ultimate, that is to say, to exist as a conventional truth and to exist as an ultimate truth. Based on Maitreya's *Differentiation of the Middle and the Extremes* and Vasubandhu's commentary, Ḏzong-ka-ḇa analyzes the term for ultimate, *paramārtha,*[a] which is translated into English literally as "highest-object." "Highest" (*dam pa, parama*) is taken as the exalted wisdom of uncontaminated meditative equipoise, and "object" (*don, artha*) is taken as the thusness, or emptiness, that is the object of that exalted wisdom, whereby thusness is called the truth that is the object of the

a *don dam.*

highest (wisdom) (*dam pa'i don, paramasya artha-satya*). In another interpretation, that wisdom itself is called the highest object (*don dam pa, parama-artha*), since it is both highest and object; emptiness is called the truth of the highest object (*don dam pa'i bden pa, parama-arthasya satya*). Given these interpretations of the ultimate, only thoroughly established natures and not other-powered natures are ultimates.

Therefore, according to this second interpretation of "ultimately exist" (that is, exist as an ultimate truth), other-powered natures are not ultimates, but according to the first interpretation of "ultimately exist" (that is, exist by way of their own character), they ultimately exist. Thus, other-powered natures are conventional truths and ultimately exist, whereas existent imputational natures such as uncompounded space are conventional truths but do not ultimately exist—they conventionally exist.

Could A Wisdom Consciousness Be An Ultimate? [163] {411}

D̄zong-ka-b̄a briefly addresses the qualm that, since ultimate truths are objects of the highest wisdom and since the Mind-Only School asserts self-consciousness, the exalted wisdom would be aware of itself, and thus it itself would be its own object, whereby it would be an ultimate truth. (If a wisdom consciousness were the ultimate, this would challenge the point he made with great emphasis in chapter 1 against the Jo-nang-b̄as that, according to the system of the *Sūtra Unraveling the Thought,* the thoroughly established nature is a mere elimination, a simple negative, in which case it could not be a consciousness.) His response is that Maitreya's explanation that the final object observed by the purifying wisdom is the ultimate is in consideration of that object in relation to which suchness is realized; and therefore, the fault that the wisdom consciousness itself would be an ultimate is not incurred. The answer means that even though, roughly speaking, an exalted wisdom is an object of itself, only that object in relation to which a consciousness is said to be an exalted wisdom realizing emptiness is a thoroughly established nature. Thus, since an object is not posited as a thoroughly established nature merely because of being an object of an exalted wisdom, there is no fault that the exalted wisdom itself would be an ultimate truth even though, roughly speaking, it knows itself. (This debate establishes the theme of separating wisdom and emptiness even if, in direct realization of emptiness, wisdom does not distinguish itself from emptiness.) He concludes from this that the ultimate has to be uncompounded and could not be a wisdom consciousness itself but adds that other-powered natures, although not ultimate in the sense of being ultimate truths, are ultimately established in the sense of subsisting by way of their own character without being posited through the force of conventions.

Explaining Away Seeming Contradiction With Āryadeva's Statement [164] {411}

In another brief aside, Ḏzong-ka-ḇa handles evidence by an authoritative Indian master that seems to declare to the contrary that in the Mind-Only School the exalted wisdom itself is an ultimate. Āryadeva's *Compilation of the Essence of Wisdom* seems to say:

> That a consciousness which is released
> From apprehended-object and apprehending-subject exists **as the ultimate**[a] [that is, as the ultimate truth]
> Is renowned in the texts of the Yogic Practitioners
> Who have passed to the other shore of the ocean of awareness.

However, Ḏzong-ka-ḇa holds that the passage actually means:

> That a consciousness which is released
> From apprehended-object and apprehending-subject exists **ultimately** [that is, exists by way of its own character]
> Is renowned in the texts of the Yogic Practitioners
> Who have passed to the other shore of the ocean of awareness.

(Perhaps he must claim that Āryadeva means this in order to forge consistency between his own interpretation of the *Sūtra Unraveling the Thought* on this issue and the highly respected Āryadeva's opinion; the only other, but unacceptable, option would be to hold that he is correcting an errant opinion by Āryadeva.)

Why Does Asaṅga Say That Other-Powered Natures Exist Conventionally? [165] {412}

The remaining question is: Since other-powered natures ultimately exist in the sense that they are established by way of their own character, in what sense does Asaṅga's *Compendium of Ascertainments* say that other-powered natures conventionally exist? Ḏzong-ka-ḇa's answer is that one must understand the two ways in which that text itself speaks of other-powered natures as conventionally existing, that is to say, as existing as conventionalities. The first way that other-powered natures conventionally exist is relative to the statement in the *Sūtra Unraveling the Thought* that ultimates are objects of observation of paths of purification; opposite to this, most other-powered natures give rise to afflictive emotions when they are observed, and thus they are said to exist conventionally, or in an obscuring manner.

The second sense in which Asaṅga's *Compendium of Ascertainments* says that other-powered natures exist conventionally, or as conventionalities, is that they are entities imputed through the conventions of names and terminology and are bases of imputing designations. Ḏzong-ka-ḇa points to Vasubandhu's *Principles of Explanation,* which says that truths, that is, existents, that are ob-

---

a *dam pa'i don du.*

jects understood **by means of conventions** are convention-truths—the objects to which verbalizations refer.

Through these distinctions, Ḏzong-ka-ḇa establishes that, when Asaṅga, in his *Compendium of Ascertainments,* says that other-powered natures exist conventionally, this means that they exist as conventionalities in either or both of these two ways—they give rise to afflictive emotions, or they exist as bases of imputing designations. It is thereby confirmed that statements that other-powered natures conventionally exist do not contradict that other-powered natures exist ultimately, in the sense of existing by way of their own character.

Then, in two asides [166] {413}, Ḏzong-ka-ḇa explains away divergent usages of these terms in Asaṅga's *Compendium of Ascertainments* that might challenge his interpretation:

- Asaṅga speaks of a Superior's exalted wisdom of meditative equipoise directly realizing emptiness as existing ultimately, that is, as an ultimate, contrary to the above explanation that other-powered natures are conventional truths and only emptinesses are ultimate truths. Ḏzong-ka-ḇa explains merely that this is in consideration that such a wisdom consciousness does not have the latter two grounds for being posited as existing conventionally, that is, as a conventionality—namely, it does not give rise to afflictive emotions and is not posited by conventions. His nineteenth-century follower, A-ku L̄o-drö-gya-tso, explains further that a Superior's exalted wisdom of meditative equipoise is **called** an ultimate because the ultimate truth exists as its object of comprehension; in other words, since the ultimate is its object, the wisdom consciousness gets the name of its object but it itself is not an actual ultimate. (These explanations repeat the theme of separating wisdom and emptiness.)
- Asaṅga's *Compendium of Ascertainments* speaks of a Superior's exalted wisdom subsequent to meditative equipoise as existing both conventionally and ultimately, that is, as a conventionality and as an ultimate, but in Ḏzong-ka-ḇa's system the two truths are mutually exclusive—nothing could be both. A-ku L̄o-drö-gya-tso explains away Asaṅga's statement by asserting that it is another case of naming the subject from the viewpoint of the object; he indicates that from the viewpoint of its observing conventional phenomena, a Superior's exalted wisdom subsequent to meditative equipoise is said to exist conventionally, that is, as a conventionality, and from the viewpoint of its understanding emptiness, it is **said** to exist ultimately, that is, as an ultimate, even though it is not an actual ultimate. (Again, wisdom and emptiness are separated through explaining away a statement that seems to suggest the opposite.)

Since Ḏzong-ka-ḇa's presentation requires many distinctions and thus may look like his own creation, he caps his case by citing a passage from Vasubandhu's

Principles of Explanation [168] {413}. This Indian text provides supporting evidence for the non-contradiction of other-powered natures' existing conventionally, that is, as conventionalities, and yet existing ultimately, in the sense of being established by way of their own character. Vasubandhu explains that:

- actions and fruitions **both** exist ultimately, in the sense of existing by way of their own character, and exist conventionally in the sense of existing as bases of the imputation of conventions, that is to say, as conventionalities, and
- persons also exist in these two ways, but, unlike actions and fruitions, they do not substantially exist; they imputedly exist.

In a final step [170] {414}, D̄zong-ka-b̄a handles another seemingly divergent usage of these terms. He explains a passage in Maitreya's *Differentiation of the Middle and the Extremes* saying that thoroughly established natures are verbal **conventionalities**, whereas in his own interpretation thoroughly established natures are only ultimates. His rationalization is that Maitreya is indicating that verbalizations are conventionalities and that even thoroughly established natures are referents of verbalizations—the import being that Maitreya is not indicating that thoroughly established natures are **actual** conventionalities.

Conventional and Ultimate Existence

EXISTING CONVENTIONALLY: *kun rdzob tu yod pa, saṃvṛti(tas)-sat*

Meaning	*What from Three Natures*	*Illustrations*
1. Existing within being posited through the force of conventions (usually translated here as "existing conventionally")	Existent imputations	Uncompounded space, being the referent of terms and conceptual consciousnesses
2. Giving rise to afflictive emotions when they are observed (usually translated here as "existing as a conventionality" or "existing as a conventional truth")	Most other-powered natures (but not a superior's exalted wisdom of meditative equipoise and not a superior's exalted wisdom subsequent to meditative equipoise, for instance)	A beautiful body
3. Existing as entities imputed through the conventions of names and terminology and as bases of imputing designations	Existent imputational natures, most other-powered natures (but not a superior's exalted wisdom of meditative equipoise, for instance, and not a superior's exalted wisdom subsequent to meditative equipoise [?])	Uncompounded space, house
Exceptional usage: referent of a verbalization	Thoroughly established natures	An emptiness (even though it is not an actual conventionality)

EXISTING ULTIMATELY: *don dam par yod pa, paramārtha(tas)-sat*

Meaning	*What from Three Natures*	*Illustrations*
1. Existing within not being posited through the force of conventions but by way of its own character (usually translated here as "existing ultimately")	Other-powered natures and thoroughly established natures	A conceptual consciousness, a chair, a term, a person, a superior's exalted wisdom subsequent to meditative equipoise, an emptiness
2. Existing as a final object of observation by a path of purification (usually translated here as "existing as an ultimate" or "existing as an ultimate truth"	Thoroughly established natures	An emptiness
Exceptional usage: not giving rise to afflictive emotions and not posited by conventions	Pure other-powered natures (?)	A Superior's exalted wisdom of meditative equipoise, for instance.*

* Since the ultimate is its object, the wisdom consciousness gets the name of its object, but it itself is not an actual ultimate.

Hence, if exceptional usages are not considered,

- **all other-powered natures** exist ultimately in only the first sense of existing ultimately,
- **most other-powered natures** exist conventionally in the second and third senses of existing conventionally,
- **all existent imputational natures** exist conventionally in the first and third senses of existing conventionally, and none exist ultimately in any of the senses of existing ultimately, and
- **all thoroughly established natures** exist ultimately in both the first and second senses of existing ultimately, but none exist conventionally in any of the senses of existing conventionally.

Also, since imputed existence (*btags yod, prajñapti-sat*) means that the object (such as a person) is not apprehendable without relying on apprehension of other phenomena (such as the mental and physical aggregates) and thus the object must be apprehended in reliance upon apprehending other phenomena, it is not contradictory that a phenomenon such as a person:

- ultimately exists in the first sense of existing ultimately—that is, not being posited through the force of conventions but existing by way of its own character—and yet
- imputedly exists.

Importance Of Understanding This Vocabulary [171] {415}

D̄zong-ka-b̄a has subjected the multivalent usage of terminology in India, esthetically delightful in its juxtapositions of unlikely combinations of terms, to a rigorous, philosophical analysis in order to expose an internally consistent system. (Of course, whether that consistency is endemic to the Indian text or is superimposed needs to be examined; in any case, it is clear that literary multivalency in India gives way to philosophical rigor in Dzong-ka-ba's system.) In this light, he concludes the chapter on Asaṅga's *Compendium of Ascertainments* by stressing the importance of delineating the actual import of terminology on the status of objects:

- the different meanings of substantial existence and imputed existence, and
- the meanings of existing conventionally and existing ultimately, as well as existing as a conventionality and existing as an ultimate.

He states that, by knowing how these terms are used in different systems, as well as the multiple meanings they have within a single system, one can understand why the Proponents of Non-Nature have to prove to the other Buddhist schools that many phenomena, such as persons, do not exist ultimately even though those phenomena are asserted by those very schools to be imputedly existent and to exist conventionally. He thereby justifies their refutations of other Buddhist systems despite those schools' sometimes using vocabulary superficially similar to that used in the Naturelessness School. Dzong-ka-ba reinvokes an overall purpose for his *The Essence of Eloquence*—delineating the context of the view of emptiness in the Naturelessness School. As was mentioned earlier (p. 12), he wrote this text after beginning a commentary on Nāgārjuna's *Treatise on the Middle;* it may be that he felt that to continue that commentary, he needed to set the historical philosophical context of the critiques of the Mind-Only School, and so forth, by Proponents of Non-Nature.

In sum, the chapter begins with distinguishing the Proponents of Mind-Only from the Proponents of Non-Nature and ends with a reference to understanding criticisms of other systems by Proponents of Non-Nature. The theme of distinction of systems is stressed both to undermine the syncretic doctrine of the Jo-nang-bas and to appreciate the subtleties of the criticisms by the Proponents of Non-Nature.

8. Maitreya's *Ornament for the Great Vehicle Sūtras*

Overview. This chapter [172] {416} has two basic movements:

1. Considering explanations—in Maitreya's *Ornament for the Great Vehicle Sūtras*—of the thoughts behind three groups of teachings in the Perfection of Wisdom Sūtras, whereby it is shown that in this text Maitreya, unlike the Proponents of Non-Nature, does not take the Perfection of Wisdom Sūtras literally
2. Considering an objection that the *Sūtra Unraveling the Thought* and Maitreya's *Ornament for the Great Vehicle Sūtras* use the example of a magician's illusion for other-powered natures and thus would seem to hold the position of the Proponents of Non-Nature—that all phenomena lack true existence—and responding that the Mind-Only School can use this and other examples of illusion without holding that all phenomena lack true existence

Thoughts Behind Teachings In The Perfection Of Wisdom Sūtras [172] {416}

Exploring the esthetic delight that Indian scholars take in creatively positing what is behind certain teachings in the Perfection of Wisdom Sūtras, and so forth, Ḏzong-ka-b̄a finds in Maitreya's text a plethora of types of naturelessness, non-production, and so forth. Indians' creative positing of a multiplicity of specific negations that Buddha had in mind when his words seemed only to be setting forth a general negative teaching draws from a wide variety of Buddhist perspectives on phenomena. As in Indian and Tibetan art, multiplicity—and not simplicity—is what is predominantly considered elegant.

1. That phenomena are natureless was taught in the Perfection of Wisdom Sūtras and so forth in consideration of five facts in two groups:[755]

   Compounded phenomena of the three times are natureless, in the sense that:

   1. a future compounded phenomenon is not produced through its own power,
   2. a past compounded phenomenon is not produced again as itself,
   3. a present compounded phenomenon does not abide for a second moment after its own time.

   Compounded phenomena are natureless, in the sense that five natures of phenomena as conceived by childish beings do not exist:

   4. what is conceived to be clean is actually unclean; what is conceived to be happiness is actually suffering; what is conceived to be

permanent is actually impermanent; what is conceived to be self is actually not self; and

5. whereas object and subject are not different substantial entities, they are conceived to be.

2. That phenomena have no production, no cessation, are quiescent from the start, and are naturally passed beyond sorrow was taught in the Perfection of Wisdom Sūtras and so forth [173] {417} in consideration of the facts that:
   - in just the many ways that phenomena are natureless, so they are not produced;
   - in just the ways that they are not produced, so they do not cease;
   - in just the ways that they are not produced and do not cease, so they are quiescent from the start; and
   - and in those same ways they are naturally thoroughly passed beyond sorrow.

3. In the Perfection of Wisdom Sūtras and so forth [173] {418}, Buddha speaks of attaining forbearance, that is, facility and non-fear, with respect to the doctrine of non-production in consideration that there are eight types of non-production:
   1. No production of a beginning to cyclic existence
   2. No production again of a compounded phenomenon that was produced before
   3. No new production of sentient beings who did not earlier exist in cyclic existence and no production of phenomena that did not exist earlier since something of similar type to what ceased earlier is produced
   4. No production of imputational natures by way of their own character
   5. No production of other-powered natures under their own power without relying on their respective conditions
   6. No production and no change in thoroughly established natures
   7. No production of afflictive emotions in Foe Destroyers
   8. No production of enhancements in a Buddha's Truth Body

The positing of thoughts behind Buddha's teaching—that all phenomena are natureless, have no production, have no cessation, are quiescent from the start, and are naturally passed beyond sorrow, as well as that one is to attain forbearance with respect to the doctrine of non-production—means that these seemingly blanket, negative declarations with respect to all phenomena are not to be taken literally, as the Proponents of Non-Nature do. Rather, there were specific types of naturelessness and non-productions that Buddha had in mind.

(Since there appears to be no evidence internal to the Perfection of Wisdom Sūtras that Buddha had all these limited negations in mind when he made such blanket statements, we can see the strong intention on the part of these commentators to counteract a perceived, excessive sense of negativity found in interpretations by the Proponents of Non-Nature. A tendency toward less negative and more positive interpretations can be seen in many Great Vehicle systems from India to Japan.)

How The Example Of A Magician's Illusion Is Used [176] {419}

Having established that for Maitreya's *Ornament for the Great Vehicle Sūtras* the Perfection of Wisdom Sūtras are not to be taken in accordance with its verbal rendering, D̄zong-ka-b̄a addresses the qualm that it is contradictory for the Mind-Only School to assert that other-powered natures truly exist and yet for both the *Sūtra Unraveling the Thought* and Maitreya's *Ornament* (XI.30) to compare other-powered natures with magician's illusions. This is because comparison with magical illusions is commonly accepted as showing that phenomena are not true.

D̄zong-ka-b̄a implicitly accepts that the example does indicate a lack of trueness, in the sense of showing that phenomena do not exist in accordance with how they appear, but he responds that, nevertheless, comparison with a magician's illusions is not always used to communicate that phenomena do not truly exist, that is to say, do not exist by way of their own character. For the example is also used in the Mind-Only School to indicate the non-duality of subject and object, the selflessness of persons, and how, if there are no external objects, a consciousness could observe an object. Specifically:

- Maitreya's *Ornament* (XI.15-16) itself explains that the example of a magician's illusion is used to demonstrate the false appearance of subject and object in a dualistic mode, and Vasubandhu's commentary substantiates this
- In what may be D̄zong-ka-b̄a's unique interpretation of *Ornament* stanza XI.30, he explains that the example of a magician's illusion is also used in the context of the selflessness of persons
- He caps the argument that comparison with illusions does not always mean that phenomena are not truly existent by referring to the explanation—in Asaṅga's *Summary of the Great Vehicle*—of the import of eight types of illusions, none of which is to show that objects are not truly existent or established by way of their own character

(Implicitly, D̄zong-ka-b̄a thereby shows that the teaching in the *Sūtra Unraveling the Thought* that other-powered natures are established by way of their own character is not contradicted by Maitreya's *Ornament,* even though an explicit statement in the *Ornament* that other-powered natures are established by way of their own character is not forthcoming.)

9. Maitreya's *Differentiation of the Middle and the Extremes* and Other Scholars

Overview. This chapter [182] {422} has four basic movements:

1. Explaining the first two stanzas in Maitreya's *Differentiation of the Middle and the Extremes* that delineate emptiness and the middle path free from the two extremes
2. Refuting, through these distinctions, two Jo-nang-b̄a positions
3. Contrasting how the Proponents of Mind-Only and the Proponents of Non-Nature take a statement in the *Kāshyapa Chapter Sūtra* about the middle path
4. Mentioning Vasubandhu, Sthiramati, and Dignāga and explaining briefly five stanzas from Dharmakīrti

Two Stanzas [182] {422}

D̄zong-ka-b̄a uses the commentaries by Vasubandhu and Sthiramati to unravel Maitreya's elegantly abstruse stanzas, which I will cite here first in their bare form in order to convey a sense of the esthetic enterprise required to penetrate the meaning:[a]

Unreal ideation exists.
Duality does not exist there.
Emptiness exists here.
Also that exists in that.

Not empty and not non-empty,
Thereby all is explained.
Due to existence and due to non-existence, existence.
Therefore that is the middle path.

The unraveling of the three demonstrative pronouns ("that") is done through coordinating their gender with the gender of the nouns in the stanzas, something that cannot be conveyed in a bare English translation without using "he"

---

[a] I.1-1.2; Peking 5522, vol. 108, 19.4.5. The Sanskrit, from Gadjin M. Nagao, *Madhyāntavibhāga-bhāṣya* (Tokyo: Suzuki Research Foundation, 1964), 17, is:

abhūta-parikalpo 'sti dvayan tatra na vidyate/
śūnyatā vidyate tv atra tasyām api sa vidyate//

na śūnyaṃ nāpi cāśūnyaṃ tasmāt sarvvam [Pandeya: *sarvaṃ*] *vidhīyate/*
satvād asatvāt satvāc [Pandeya: *sattvādasattvāt sattvāc*] *ca madhyamā pratipac ca sā//*

See also Ramchandra Pandeya, *Madhyānta-vibhāga-śāstra* (Delhi: Motilal Banarsidass, 1971), 9, 13.

and "she."[a] Let us give the gender identifications in note form: m = male; f = female; n = neuter:

> Unreal ideation^{m} exists.
> Duality^{n} does not exist there.
> Emptiness^{f} exists here.
> Also that^{m} exists in that^{f}.
>
> Not empty and not non-empty.
> Thereby all is explained.
> Due to existence and due to non-existence, existence.
> Therefore that^{f} is the middle path^{f}.

Identifying the antecedents of the demonstrative pronouns and identifying the two adverbs ("there" and "here"), the stanzas read:

> Unreal ideation^{m} exists.
> Duality^{n} does not exist there [in that conceptuality].
> Emptiness^{f} exists here [in this conceptuality]
> Also that^{m} [conceptuality] exists in that^{f} [emptiness].
>
> Not empty and not non-empty.
> Thereby all is explained.
> Due to existence and due to non-existence, existence.
> Therefore that^{f} is the middle path^{f}.

In the first stanza, the identifications provide minimal clarification, but both stanzas remain cryptic, waiting for exposition.

Utilizing Vasubandhu's commentary and Sthiramati's expansive explana-

---

[a] Among those who use this convention are:

- F. Th. Stcherbatsky, *Madhyāntavibhāga, Discourse on Discrimination between Middle and Extremes ascribed to Bodhisattva Maitreya and Commented by Vasubandhu and Sthiramati,* Bibliotheca Buddhica, 30 (1936) (Osnabrück, Germany: Biblio Verlag, 1970; reprint, Calcutta: Indian Studies Past and Present, 1971), 16
- Stefan Anacker, *Seven Works of Vasubandhu* (Delhi: Motilal Banarsidass, 1984), 211.

Among those who do not use this convention are:

- David Lasar Friedmann, *Sthiramati, Madhyāntavibhāgaṭīkā: Analysis of the Middle Path and the Extremes* (Utrechtt, Netherlands: Rijksuniversiteit te Leiden, 1937), 10
- Thomas A. Kochumuttom, *A Buddhist Doctrine of Experience* (Delhi: Motilal Banarsidass, 1982), 29
- Thomas E. Wood, *Mind-Only: A Philosophical and Doctrinal Analysis of the Vijñānavāda,* Monographs of the Society for Asian and Comparative Philosophy, 9 (Honolulu: University of Hawaii Press, 1991), 10
- Ake Boquist, *Trisvabhāva: A Study of the Development of the Three-nature-theory in Yogācāra Buddhism,* ed. Tord Olsson, Lund Studies in African and Asian Religions, 8 (Lund, Sweden: University of Lund, 1993), 71.

tion of his teacher Vasubandhu's commentary, Ḏzong-ka-b̄a interprets the stanzas as meaning:

> Unreal ideation[—ideation being the main other-powered nature—] exists [by way of its own character in that it is produced from causes and conditions].
> Duality [of subject and object in accordance with their appearance as if distant and cut off] does not exist in that [ideation].
> [The thoroughly established nature which is the] emptiness [of being distant and cut off] exists [by way of its own character as the mode of subsistence] in this [ideation].
> Also that [ideation] exists [as an obstructor] to [realization of] that [emptiness].
>
> [Thus, other-powered natures and thoroughly established natures] are not empty [of establishment by way of the object's own character] and are not non-empty [of subject and object being distant and cut off].
> Thereby all [of the mode of thought in the teachings in the Perfection of Wisdom Sūtras, and so forth, of not being empty and of not being non-empty] is explained [thoroughly].
> Due to the existence [of the other-powered nature that is the erroneous ideation apprehending object and subject as distant and cut off, the extreme of non-existence is avoided] and due to the non-existence [of distant and cut off object and subject—in accordance with how they are apprehended by that ideation—as their mode of subsistence, the extreme of existence is avoided, and ideation and emptiness] exist.
> Therefore that [thoroughly established nature which is the emptiness of distant and cut off object and subject and which is the voidness of the two extremes in other-powered natures] is the middle path [that is to say, is established as the meaning of the middle].

Since the passage indicates what exists and what does not exist, it indicates the middle between the two extremes of reified existence and utter non-existence.

The first line of the first stanza. [183] {422} Ḏzong-ka-b̄a cites Sthiramati, who holds that the identification of what exists is in response to those who hold the deprecatory position that all phenomena lack inherent existence. Thereby he again stresses the controversy between the Proponents of Mind-Only and the Proponents of Non-Nature.

Maitreya says that what exists is "unreal ideation."[a] Ḏzong-ka-b̄a does not

---

[a] *yang dag pa ma yin pa'i kun tu rtog pa / yang dag ma yin kun rtog, abhūtaparikalpa.*

explain this term, but Maitreya's *Differentiation of the Middle and the Extremes* itself says:[a]

> Unreal ideation is the minds
> And mental factors of the three realms.

Based on this, the early-twentieth-century commentator Šer-šhül Ḹo-sang-pün-tsok[756] identifies unreal ideation as all consciousnesses of the Desire, Form, and Formless Realms that have dualistic appearance of apprehended-object and apprehending-subject. Thus the term is not limited to conceptual consciousnesses in the division of consciousness into the conceptual and the non-conceptual but includes non-conceptual consciousnesses, such as sense consciousnesses, that have the dualistic appearance of subject and object as different entities. He explains that such ideation is called unreal[b] because:

- apprehended-object and apprehending-subject do not exist in accordance with their dualistic appearance, and
- forms and so forth do not exist in accordance with their appearance as being established by way of their own character as the referents of their respective conceptual consciousnesses.

Thus the mode of appearance to these consciousnesses is unreal. Also, because these consciousnesses observe objects that are merely imputed by conceptuality as referents of terms and conceptual consciousnesses, they are called "ideation," or "conceptuality." For these latter points, Šer-šhül Ḹo-sang-pün-tsok cites Maitreya's *Differentiation of Phenomena and the Final Nature:*[c]

---

[a] I.8. The Tibetan, Peking 5522, vol. 108, 19.5.1:

> *yang dag ma yin kun rtog ni//*
> *sems dang sems byung khams gsum pa//*

The Sanskrit from Nagao (*Madhyāntavibhāga-bhāṣya,* 20) is:

> *abhūtaparikalpaś ca* [Pandeya: *parikalpastu*] *citta-caittās tridhātukāḥ/*

See also Pandeya, *Madhyānta-vibhāga,* 24.

[b] *yang dag ma yin, abhūta.*

[c] *chos dang chos nyid rnam 'byed, dharmadharmatāvibhaṅga:* Peking 5524, vol. 108, 23.1.2:

> *snang ba yang dag ma yin pa//*
> *des na yang dag ma yin pa'o//*
> *de yang thams cad don med cing//*
> *rtog tsam yin pas kun rtog pa'o//*

Other possible translation equivalents for *kun rtog* are "comprehensive imagination" or "comprehensive construction." For an excellent article on this topic, see Hugh B. Urban and Paul J. Griffiths, "What Else Remains In Śūnyatā?: An Investigation of Terms for Mental Imagery in the Madhyāntavibhāga-Corpus," *Journal of the International Association of Buddhist Studies,* 17, no. 1 (1994) 1-25; they favor "unreal comprehensive construction."

> The appearance is **unreal**,
> Therefore it is **unreal**.
> Also **all** are nonexistent as [external] objects and are
> Mere **conceptualizations**; hence **ideation**.

Based on such explanations, Ge-luk-b̄a scholars take "unreal ideation" as a code-word for other-powered natures since, as the late D̄a-drin-rap-d̄en says,[a] they are imbued with the mess of ideation. Other-powered natures are, for common beings, inevitably involved with the pollution of false appearance and misconception of them as different entities in terms of subject and object and as being established by way of their own character as the referents of their respective conceptual consciousnesses and terms. (Still, there are pure other-powered natures, such as a wisdom of meditative equipoise directly realizing emptiness.)

The second line of the first stanza. Maitreya says that what does not exist is duality—the appearance of subject and object as distant and cut off—and that what remain are unreal ideation and emptiness, also called other-powered natures and thoroughly established natures, respectively. The reason why untutored beings do not realize the emptiness of duality is that they have a mistaken conception of duality that serves to obstruct such realization.

The specification of emptiness as the absence of such duality explains the thought behind the statements in the Perfection of Wisdom Sūtras, and so forth, that all phenomena are empty. Therefore, even though it might seem contradictory for the Mind-Only system to hold that other-powered natures exist inherently when some of their own sources, the Perfection of Wisdom Sūtras, say that phenomena are empty of inherent existence, it is not contradictory. For, this system holds that what Buddha had in mind when he said on the literal level that all phenomena are empty is that the duality of subject and object as different entities does not exist—he was not denying their inherent existence. From this point of view, D̄zong-ka-b̄a, without mentioning the Jo-nang-b̄as by name, criticizes them for holding that Maitreya puts forth the system of the Great Middle Way in which it is held that other-powered natures are empty of themselves.

The third line of the first stanza. Sthiramati contextualizes the next line, and D̄zong-ka-b̄a and his followers[757] elaborate on the background:

> Since Maitreya says in the **first** line that ideation, that is, other-powered natures, exist and then says in the **second** line that duality, that is, the imputational nature that is the object of negation, does not exist, it might seem that emptiness might not truly exist. For, if emptiness does truly exist, it should have been mentioned before the second line, along with or after other-powered natures. Also, imputational factors, which do not truly exist, and the thoroughly established nature are similarly uncompounded phenomena, and thus it might

---

[a] *Annotations*, 99.6: *gzhan dbang la kun rtog gi rnyog pa de yod pas na.*

seem that, since imputational natures do not truly exist, thoroughly established natures also do not truly exist.

This is the qualm cleared away by the third line, which says that "The thoroughly established nature which is the emptiness of being distant and cut off exists in this ideation."

Furthermore, Dzong-ka-ba points out that:

- when Sthiramati frames the hypothetical challenge, the objector describes the position of the Proponents of Mind-Only as being that "unreal ideation **ultimately exists inherently**"; and
- since such is not challenged in Sthiramati's answer, the description accurately depicts the stance of the Mind-Only School.

Dzong-ka-ba also cites a similar statement in Sthiramati's *Commentary on (Vasubandhu's) "The Thirty"* and reminds his readers that earlier he provided a similar statement in Asaṅga's *Grounds of Bodhisattvas.*

We can see that he is intent on providing whatever evidence he can from the texts of the Proponents of Mind-Only themselves that they assert that other-powered natures ultimately exist and that existence by way of its own character and ultimate existence are equivalent. His triple purpose is to show that:

- It is not just Chandrakīrti's creation in his critique of the Mind-Only School that the latter assert that other-powered natures ultimately exist and are established by way of their own character
- The Proponents of Mind-Only recognize that the Proponents of Non-Nature assert that phenomena exist, albeit conventionally, and thus that they do not assert that phenomena do not exist at all. (Still, the Mind-Only School assesses their assertion that other-powered natures do not truly exist as ending up in asserting that they do not exist.)
- Because of the great variance between the two schools on these crucial issues, the Jo-nang-ba synthesis of the Mind-Only School and Naturelessness School in a Great Middle Way School is impossible

The second stanza. [188] {426} From the above points, it is clear that in the Mind-Only system:

- unreal ideation—other-powered natures—are **not empty** of themselves, in the sense of being empty of establishment by way of their own character;
- emptiness—the thoroughly established nature—also is **not empty** of itself, in the sense of being empty of establishment by way of its own character; still
- everything is **empty** of a difference of entity between subject and object.

Consequently, it is said that phenomena are neither **uniformly** empty nor

uniformly non-empty. Also, since other-powered natures and thoroughly established natures ultimately exist and imputational natures do not ultimately exist, phenomena also neither **uniformly** ultimately exist nor **uniformly** do not ultimately exist.

Refuting The Jo-nang-b̄as [188] {426}

Since the above is described as the meaning of statements in the Perfection of Wisdom Sūtras, D̄zong-ka-b̄a criticizes the Jo-nang-b̄as for holding that the thoroughly established nature is non-empty, that is, is truly established, and that other-powered natures and imputational natures are empty of true establishment. For he has shown that in the Mind-Only School both thoroughly established natures and other-powered natures are truly established and imputational natures are not. Also, since emptiness here is the absence of a difference of entity between subject and object, he criticizes the Jo-nang-b̄as for holding that the point here is to distinguish that the thoroughly established nature is empty of the other two natures, which, in turn, are empty of the thoroughly established nature.

Contrasting The Mind-Only School And The Naturelessness School [189] {426}

D̄zong-ka-b̄a refers to Sthiramati's association of this description of the middle with that found in the *Kāshyapa Chapter Sūtra:*[758]

> Existence is one extreme; non-existence is the second extreme. That which is the center between these two is unanalyzable [because it cannot be analyzed just as it is by thinking about it], is undemonstrable [because it cannot be explained to another just as it is], is not a support [because it is not an object of the senses], is unperceivable [because from the viewpoint of the mind directly realizing it duality has disappeared], is unknowable [because it cannot be ascertained just as it is by a dualistic mind], and is placeless [because it is a place or source of the afflictive emotions]. Kāshyapa, this is called the middle path, individual analysis of phenomena.

He points out that from Sthiramati's citation it can seen that he (and by extension the Mind-Only School) holds that there is harmony between Maitreya's description in these stanzas and the *Kāshyapa Chapter Sūtra.* D̄zong-ka-b̄a makes the distinction that the Proponents of Non-Nature take the middle path as explained in the *Kāshyapa Chapter Sūtra* to accord with their own description of the middle and thus they consider it to be superior to that described in Maitreya's *Differentiation of the Middle and the Extremes.* Again, he is stressing that the Naturelessness School and the Mind-Only School must be distinguished, and hence the Jo-nang-b̄a synthesis is unfounded.

Indeed, S̄hay-rap-gyel-tsen[759] cites this passage as an instance of one that teaches the Great Middle Way, that is to say, that there is a profound meaning of the middle devoid of the extremes between existence and non-existence that "is not just an elimination, a non-affirming negative that is merely devoid of the extremes, but is established as an inclusionary center or middle that has abandoned the two extremes and is a third category."[760] In his cryptic and implicit rebuttal, D̄zong-ka-b̄a refers to separate interpretations of the passage by separate schools rather than an over-arching meaning beyond the Mind-Only and the Middle Way Schools.

He has reached the end of his exposition on how, in a general way, the two extremes are avoided in Asaṅga's *Grounds of Bodhisattvas* and *Compendium of Ascertainments* and in Maitreya's *Ornament for the Great Vehicle Sūtras* and *Differentiation of the Middle and the Extremes.* The emphasis has been on the extreme of deprecation, since a detailed exposition of the extreme of superimposition is yet to come in chapters 10 and 11.

Other Indian Scholars [190] {426}

Vasubandhu, Sthiramati, And Dignāga [190] {426}

D̄zong-ka-b̄a crisply mentions that he has made occasional citations of Vasubandhu's and Sthiramati's exegesis on these points, the implication being that he has shown their concordance with Asaṅga and Maitreya and that thus these scholars do not require separate treatment. Then, about Dignāga's condensation of the meanings of the *Eight Thousand Stanza Perfection of Wisdom Sūtra* into thirty-two topics, he merely states that Dignāga's exposition agrees with that of Asaṅga's *Summary of the Great Vehicle.*

Jik-may-dam-chö-gya-tso cites the lines of Dignāga's text:[a]

---

[a] *Port of Entry,* 536.4; stanzas 27-29ab; Golden Reprint, vol. 103, 824.6:

shes rab pha rol phyin par ni//
bstan pa gsum la yang dag brten//
btags pa dang ni gzhan dbang dang //
yongs su grub pa kho na'o//

med ces bya la sogs tshig gis//
btags pa thams cad 'gog pa ste//
sgyu ma la sogs dpe rnams kyis//
gzhan gyi dbang ni yang dag bstan//

rnam par byang ba bzhi yis ni//
yongs su grub pa rab tu bsgrags//

The Sanskrit from Giuseppe Tucci, "Minor Texts on the Prajñā-Pāramitā," in *Opera Minora: Parte II* (Rome: Giovanni Bardi Editore, 1971), 433:

The teaching in the Perfection of Wisdom
Thoroughly relies on the three—
Just the imputational, the other-powered,
And the thoroughly established.

Expressions of non-existence and so forth
Refute all imputations.
Examples of magical illusions and so forth
Thoroughly teach the other-powered.

The four purifications
Proclaim the thoroughly established.

According to A-ku Lo-drö-gya-tso,[761] Dignāga holds that in the Perfection of Wisdom Sūtras:

- the statements that phenomena are natureless, unproduced, and so forth are in consideration that imputational natures are natureless in terms of character, that is to say, are not established by way of their own character;
- the teachings by way of the examples of illusions and so forth are in consideration that other-powered natures are natureless in terms of production, that is to say, are without self-powered production; and
- the teachings based on the four purifications—the natural purification which is emptiness, the stainless purification which is true cessations, the path purification which is true paths, and the observational purification which is the Great Vehicle scriptural collections—are in consideration of the thoroughly established nature, that is to say, that thoroughly established natures are the ultimate-non-nature.[a]

Dzong-ka-ba declares that this exposition accords with Asaṅga's *Summary of the Great Vehicle,* and Jik-may-dam-chö-gya-tso identifies the stanza as being from chapter 2:[b]

---

prajñāparitāyāṃ hi trīn samāśritya deśanā/
kalpitaṃ paratantraṃ ca pariniṣpannaṃ eva ca//

nāstītyāpadaiḥ sarvaṃ kalpitaṃ vinivāryate/
māyaopamādidṛṣṭāntaiḥ paratantrasya deśanā//

caturdhā vyavadānena pariniṣpannakīrttanam//

See also Tucci's translation following the text, and Bhikkhu Pāsādika, "On the Meaning of the Perfection of Wisdom: A Summary Composed by Ācārya Dignāga," in *Wisdom Gone Beyond: An Anthology of Buddhist Texts* (Bangkok: Social Science Association Press of Thailand, 1966), 94-102.

[a] Shay-rap-gyel-tsen (*Ocean of Definitive Meaning,* 207.5) cites the same stanzas from Dignāga's commentary as a presentation of the three natures from the viewpoint of the Great Middle Way.

[b] *Port of Entry,* 537.3:

Magical illusions and so forth are taught in relation to the dependent.
Non-existence is taught in relation to the imputational.
The four purifications are taught
In relation to the thoroughly established.

The similarity between this and Dignāga's text is obvious.

Dharmakīrti [190] {426}

About Dharmakīrti's *Commentary on (Dignāga's) "Compilation of Prime Cognition"* Ḍzong-ka-ḃa makes three basic points:

1. He establishes that Dharmakīrti asserts a non-difference of entity between subject and object
2. He describes three ways that Dharmakīrti posits the thought behind the literal reading of the Perfection of Wisdom Sūtras
3. In closing, he briefly refers to a controversy between Dharmakīrti and Proponents of Non-Nature

Dharmakīrti's *Commentary on (Dignāga's) "Compilation of Prime Cognition"* is not a commentary per se on Dignāga's text but an independent text related to that of his predecessor. The seventh-century Dharmakīrti was a student of Īshvarasena, who himself was a direct student of Dignāga. In Tibet, Dharmakīrti's work is said to contain a hundred texts,[a] in the sense that it is open to many interpretations. According to Bu-ṫön's *History,*[762] Dharmakīrti himself asked his student Devendrabuddhi[b] to write a commentary, which, when presented, he found so dissatisfying that he threw it in the river, and then, when presented with the second try, burned it in fire; the third go-around was somewhat successful, so he let it be. As will be exemplified in the last section below (p. 316), Indian and Tibetan scholars have indeed taken Dharmakīrti's work in startlingly different ways.

'byung rten sgyu ma la sogs bstan//
btags la brten nas med pa bstan//
rnam par byang ba bzhi brten nas//
yongs su grub pa bstan pa yin//

Étienne Lamotte, *La somme du grand véhicule d'Asaṅga,* reprint, 2 vols. Publications de l'Institute Orientaliste de Louvain, 8 (Louvain: Université de Louvain, 1973), vol. 1, 38 (II.26); vol. 2, 122; and John P. Keenan, *The Summary of the Great Vehicle by Bodhisattva Asaṅga: Translated from the Chinese of Paramārtha* (Berkeley, Calif.: Numata Center for Buddhist Translation and Research, 1992), 52. Lamotte (vol. 2, 122) refers to the "Abhidarmasūtra, dans Madhyāntavibhaṅga, p. 112" and gives the Sanskrit:

māyādideśanā bhūte kalpitān nāstideśanā/
caturvidhaviśuddhes tu pariniṣpannadeśanā//

a *gzhung brgya ldan.*

b *lha dbang blo.*

Non-Difference Of Entity Between Subject And Object [190] {426}

First Ḏzong-ka-ḇa cites four contiguous stanzas from chapter 3, primarily to make the case that Dharmakīrti also does not take the Perfection of Wisdom Sūtras literally and thus is to be distinguished from Proponents of Non-Nature. An implicit message is that an amalgamation of Great Vehicle masters' works (or parts of those) into a single, unified doctrine is groundless.

Citing chapter 3, stanza 213, of the *Commentary on (Dignāga's) "Compilation of Prime Cognition,"* Ḏzong-ka-ḇa shows that for Dharmakīrti, the final nature of other-powered natures is an emptiness of apprehended-object and apprehending-subject as other substantial entities. Dharmakīrti says:

> Concerning subject and object, due to the absence of a difference of substantial entity of one of them, the other also lacks a difference of substantial entity, and thus the emptiness of duality of one of them is also the suchness of the other one.

Two Ways To Posit The Thought Behind The Perfection Of Wisdom Sūtras [190] {427}

Citing the next two stanzas (III.214-215), he shows how, from this perspective, Dharmakīrti posits in two ways the thought behind the literal reading of the Perfection of Wisdom Sūtras that phenomena are devoid of inherent existence. In the first,[763] Dharmakīrti indicates that the production, abiding, and disintegration—which characterize things—appear to a mistaken mind infected with the appearance of subject and object as if they were different entities, and thus this factor of difference is false, in that it appears to truly exist but does not. Consequently, when in the Perfection of Wisdom Sūtras Buddha says that all phenomena lack inherent existence, what he has in mind is the absence of a truly established factor of difference between these characteristics of things.

In the next stanza[764] Dharmakīrti indicates that when a defining character (or definition) appears to a conceptual mental consciousness, it appears as if cut off on the side of the subject, and its definiendum appears to be cut off on the side of the object. In this way, a definition appears to define, or characterize, something over there, and thus this mode of definition, aside from just being a factor appearing to a conceptual consciousness, does not exist as it appears, since the defining character of an object is the same entity as the object itself. Hence, when in the Perfection of Wisdom Sūtras Buddha says that all phenomena lack inherent existence, what he has in mind is such a lack of difference of entity between definition and definiendum.

A Third Way To Posit The Thought Behind The Perfection Of Wisdom Sūtras [191] {428}

Although, as A-ku Ḻo-drö-gya-tso says,[765] the above explanation of the non-difference of entity between definition and definiendum is that found in the Mind-Only system, Dharmakīrti in the next stanza (III.216) indicates another rendition that is in common with the Hearer schools. Not using the vocabulary of apprehended-object and apprehending-subject, Dharmakīrti speaks of the definition as the agent of the activity of characterization (or that which causes understanding) and the definiendum as the object of the activity. The defining character of fire, for instance, is that which is hot and burning, but it is not an entity other than fire itself, since fire is that which is hot and burning, and that which is hot and burning is fire. A conceptual consciousness, however, sees the two—the definition and the defined—as different entities. Thus when, in the Perfection of Wisdom Sūtras, Buddha says that all phenomena lack inherent existence, what he has in mind is such a lack of difference of entity between definition and definiendum.

Controversy With Proponents Of Non-Nature [192] {428}

In these ways, Dzong-ka-ba shows that Dharmakīrti does not take the Perfection of Wisdom Sūtras literally but posits other meanings as to what Buddha has in mind. To make it even clearer that Dharmakīrti is at odds with the Proponents of Non-Nature, Dzong-ka-ba cites a stanza (III.4) in which Proponents of Non-Nature challenge Dharmakīrti and he answers. As was mentioned above, Dharmakīrti's text is open to many interpretations; thus, let us start with the bare stanza:

> If all are without capacity,
> The capacity of sprouts and so forth is seen in seeds and so forth.
> That is asserted conventionally.
> How? Let it be so!

Dzong-ka-ba mentions only that the stanza makes the same point as what was said earlier in Asaṅga's *Compendium of Ascertainments*—he does not give any commentary.

An interesting exegesis of the stanza is given by the early-nineteenth-century Kalkha Mongolian scholar Nga-wang-bel-den,[766] who treats it in accordance with two different interpretations found in India. The first supports Dzong-ka-ba's point; the second does not. He identifies the first explanation as that of the seventh-century Indian scholar Devendrabuddhi and unnamed others, who interpret the system of Dharmakīrti's text as Mind-Only. In paraphrase:

> Dharmakīrti's position on the two truths is illustrated when he says (III.3):
>
> > That which has the capacity ultimately to perform a function
> > Here ultimately exists.
> > Others exist conventionally.[a]

[a] The fourth line of the stanza ("These describe the specifically and generally characterized,") is not germane to our discussion.

Thus in this interpretation, the first line of III.4 ("If all are without capacity") is a challenge by a Proponent of Non-Nature to that position:

> It follows that the explanation, "That which has the capacity to perform a function ultimately, here ultimately exists," is incorrect, because there is nothing that is ultimately capable of performing a function.

The second line ("The capacity of sprouts and so forth is seen in seeds and so forth,") is a response by a Proponent of Truly Existing Things, including Dharmakīrti himself:

> It is not the case that there is nothing that has the capacity to perform a function ultimately, because the capacity of a cause, such as a seed, to assist in producing an effect, such as a sprout is seen with direct perception.

The third line ("That is asserted conventionally") is a rejoinder by the Proponent of Non-Nature:

> Since the capacity of a cause to assist in producing effects is asserted by us to be so conventionally, there is no fallacy.

The last line ("How? Let it be so!") is a concluding retort by Dharmakīrti, a Proponent of Truly Existing Things:

> Since conventionalities are superimposed factors, how could they be appearing objects of non-mistaken direct perception! Though you Proponents of Non-Nature use the name "conventionality," you have come to assert ultimate establishment.

Thus the stanza according to the first interpretation is:

> [A Proponent of Non-Nature] says: All are [ultimately] without the capacity [to perform functions].
> [*Answer* by a Proponent of True Existence:] The capacity [to produce] sprouts and so forth is seen in seeds and so forth.
> [The Proponent of Non-Nature responds:] That is asserted conventionally.
> [*Answer* by the Proponent of True Existence:] How? Let it be so!

In the second interpretation, Dharmakīrti is taken to be not a Proponent of Mind-Only but a Proponent of Non-Nature. An impressive lineup of Indian scholars—the eighth-century Ravigupta,[a] the eighth-century Shāntarakṣhita and his spiritual son Kamalashīla, the ninth or tenth-century Prajñākaragupta,[b] as

[a] *nyi ma sbas pa.*

[b] Referred to as "the author of the *Ornament*" (*rgyan mkhan po*); the text is

well as Jetāri and so forth—identify Dharmakīrti's stanza in this fashion. They attribute the first line to Dharmakīrti himself as a Proponent of Non-Nature; the second line to the opponent; the third line to Dharmakīrti; and the final to the opponent.

According to the second interpretation, the stanza is:

> [A Proponent of Non-Nature such as Dharmakīrti] says: All are [ultimately] without the capacity [to perform functions].
> [*Response* by a Proponent of True Existence:] The capacity [to produce] sprouts and so forth is seen in seeds and so forth.
> [The Proponent of Non-Nature, for example, Dharmakīrti, responds:] This is asserted conventionally.
> [*Response* by a Proponent of True Existence:] How? Let it be so!

The last line is explained as meaning:

> Since conventionalities are superimpositions, how could they be appearing objects of direct perception! Thus although you Proponents of Non-Nature use the name "conventionality," you have come to accept the meaning of ultimate existence.

It is clear that the second interpretation is not Ḏzong-ka-ḇa's intent. Rather, he seeks to end the brief excursus into Dharmakīrti's *Commentary on (Dignāga's) "Compilation of Prime Cognition"* as well as discussion of the other texts covered in chapters 5 through 9—that focus on the extreme of deprecation—with another reminder of the conflict between the Proponents of Mind-Only and the Proponents of Non-Nature, with Dharmakīrti on the side of the Proponents of Mind-Only.

---

pramāṇavārttikālaṃkāra (*tshad ma rnam 'grel kyi rgyan;* Peking 5719, vol. 132, entire volume). Gnoli (*The Pramāṇavārtikkam of Dharmakīrti,* xxiv) places him in the ninth or tenth century.

10. Superimposition

Ḏzong-ka-ḇa now turns to a detailed exposition of the extreme of superimposition—the exaggeration that constitutes the conception of a self of phenomena. The negation of this superimposed status is emptiness—the thoroughly established nature—and thus the superimposed status itself is what is to be negated.

Overview. This long chapter [194] {430} has seven basic movements:

1. Identifying the superimposition in its artificial (or acquired) and innate forms
2. Raising four hypothetical objections by others to this identification
3. Answering the four objections in an intentionally convoluted way, so that many points can be presented—some detailed and others briefly
4. Laying out the reasonings establishing the selflessness of phenomena that is other-powered natures' emptiness of being established in accordance with the superimposed status of being established by way of their own character as the referents of their respective conceptual consciousnesses
5. In response to a challenge that the two types of selflessness—the emptiness of factors imputed in the manner of entity and attribute and the emptiness of subject and object as different entities—are not related, showing how the reasonings proving that objects are not established by way of their own character as the objects verbalized by their respective terms and as the referents of their respective conceptual consciousnesses bring about entry into cognition-only, that is to say, realization of an absence of external objects
6. Briefly mentioning the reasonings explicitly refuting external objects
7. Emphasizing the importance of understanding the two types of selflessness of phenomena in the Mind-Only School and the reasonings used to establish them

Identifying The Superimposition [194] {430}

Ḏzong-ka-ḇa briefly mentions that in the Mind-Only School two types of positions are refuted by reasoning: deprecation and superimposition. After describing the deprecational as only acquired (and thus not innate) and identifying it as the position of the Proponents of Non-Nature depicted in earlier chapters, he quickly passes on to the superimpositional, of which there are a conception of a self of persons and a conception of a self of phenomena. He postpones discussion of the self of persons to the section on the Consequence School and concentrates on the **innate** superimposition of a self of phenomena, as identified in the Mind-Only School. This is because the artificial version of conceiving a self of phenomena is for the sake of underpinning the innate version and because reasoning is mainly used to counteract belief in the innately conceived self of phenomena. The latter point appears frequently in his works, since he seeks to counter the notion that reasoning is used only to refute philosophical opinions, which are thus artificially acquired conceptions dependent on scripture or reasoning.

With respect to the superimposition of a self of phenomena, Ḏzong-ka-ḇa is sensitive to the fact that although many texts of the Mind-Only School speak only of misapprehending subject and object as different substantial entities, the *Sūtra Unraveling the Thought* itself speaks in a different manner when it repeatedly announces that other-powered natures are not established in accordance with the imputational nature, whereby implicitly it communicates the notion that a consciousness conceiving the opposite of this—that other-powered natures are established in accordance with the imputational nature—is a superimpositional consciousness conceiving a self of phenomena.

Moreover, Asaṅga's *Grounds of Bodhisattvas, Compendium of Ascertainments,* and *Summary of the Great Vehicle* present the middle as the emptiness of such a status and as the thoroughly established nature. Thus Ḏzong-ka-ḇa warns that if one does not know this type of superimposed factor, one will not decisively understand what, in the Mind-Only School, it means to conceive a self of phenomena and hence what the selflessness of phenomena is.

The topic is intriguing since the two types of emptiness are so intimately related that some Ge-luk-ḇa scholars say that through explicitly realizing one of them a practitioner implicitly realizes the other. Does Ḏzong-ka-ḇa mean merely that in these texts Asaṅga is explaining another but equivalent emptiness? Or does he mean that the two types of emptiness are realized serially and are not equivalent? We will return to this subject at the end of the synopsis of this chapter, when he hints at what he means.[a]

First, he succinctly explains that the superimposed factor is the establishment of the aggregates and so forth by way of their own character:

- as the referents of conceptual consciousnesses **thinking about entities** and as the referents of terms **verbalizing entities**, such as "This is a form," and so forth, and
- as the referents of conceptual consciousnesses **thinking about attributes** and as the referents of terms **verbalizing attributes**, such as "This is the production of form."

He emphasizes that since forms and so forth indeed are the referents of thoughts and indeed are objects verbalized by terms, to conceive merely that phenomena are referents of thoughts and objects verbalized by terms is not a superimposition. Rather, the superimposition is to conceive that forms and so forth are **established by way of their own character** as the referents of thoughts and the objects verbalized by terms.

---

[a] For a detailed discussion of this topic, see *Reflections on Reality,* chaps. 18-20.

Four Objections To This Identification [196] {431}

According to Jik-may-dam-chö-gya-tso's cogent exposition,[767] Ḏzong-ka-ḇa considers objections to his presentation that:

- the establishment of forms and so forth by way of their own character as the foundations of name and conception is the self (that is, the exaggerated status) of phenomena that is being negated, and
- the negative of this is the subtle selflessness of phenomena

due to the fact that many Tibetan scholars of his time were uncomfortable with any mode of emptiness in the Mind-Only School except for the emptiness of object and subject as different entities.

The first three of the four objections revolve around the seeming unsuitability that, if the self of phenomena is identified this way, a Lesser Vehicle school could realize the selflessness of phenomena. This is unsuitable because the four schools of Buddhist tenets—Great Exposition, Sūtra, Mind-Only, and Naturelessness Schools—are posited by way of their view of selflessness. The view of selflessness in a higher school must be both different and more subtle.

I would add that since the *Sūtra Unraveling the Thought* itself explicitly presents an ultimate that is beyond the ken of Lesser Vehicle practitioners, the concern with showing how the view that it presents exceeds that of the Lesser Vehicle schools is not brought **to** the sūtra by Tibetan scholars but is already there. The factor that is not in the sūtra and that makes this endeavor so intriguing is that Ḏzong-ka-ḇa recognizes a Lesser Vehicle school following Dharmakīrti—a school that did not pick up on Dharmakīrti's exposition of the subtle selflessness of phenomena of the Mind-Only School but affirmed the existence of external objects. In Ge-luk-ḇa scholarship, Dharmakīrti's *Commentary on (Dignāga's) "Compilation of Prime Cognition"* is seen as having three layers—one unique to the Mind-Only School, in which the position of no external objects is presented, one unique to the Sūtra School, in which external objects are presented, and one shared with those two schools, which does not address this issue—and thus various commentators picked up on different strands. Here the result is that Ge-luk-ḇa scholars must show that Lesser Vehicle followers of Dharmakīrti could not realize the emptiness that is specific to the Mind-Only School.

The First Three Objections [196] {431}

The Proponents of Sūtra following Dharmakīrti realize that objects such as forms—since they have their own unique characteristics that serve as appearing objects of direct perception—cannot be actual objects verbalized by terms; this is because terms cannot evoke an experience of them as they are known in direct perception. The explicit object verbalized by a term is, roughly speaking, a mental image, technically a meaning-generality. Since (oddly enough) internal images such as meaning-generalities are considered to be non-functioning phenomena, they cannot be established by way of their own character, and thus Proponents of Sūtra understand that the explicit objects of terms are not established by way of their own character. Consequently, if understanding such constituted realization of the thoroughly established nature in the Mind-Only School, that school would not delineate an emptiness any more profound than a tenet found in the Sūtra School.

The objector imagines that Dzong-ka-ba has delineated emptiness, the thoroughly established nature, in the Mind-Only School in just this way and thus draws the absurd consequences that a selflessness of phenomena would not be put forth and that meditation on it would not remove the obstructions to omniscience. These supposed positions, in turn, would contradict both the *Sūtra Unraveling the Thought* and Asaṅga's *Grounds of Bodhisattvas,* since the former clearly says that imputational factors' emptiness of establishment by way of their own character is the thoroughly established nature that is the selflessness of phenomena and the latter says that such an emptiness is the object to be meditated upon for purifying the obstructions to omniscience.

In the objector's mind, the only other possibility is that Dzong-ka-ba is saying that in the Mind-Only School other-powered natures themselves are refuted as established by way of their own character. However, this is impossible since the *Sūtra Unraveling the Thought* clearly indicates that other-powered natures are indeed established by way of their own character.

In addition to these points, since Asaṅga in his *Grounds of Bodhisattvas* cites—as a scriptural proof for his delineation of the selflessness of phenomena—passages from **Lesser** Vehicle sūtras, it absurdly seems that Proponents of Sūtra would indeed realize the selflessness of phenomena as presented in the Mind-Only School. Thus the objector draws the conclusion that Dzong-ka-ba's presentation of the thoroughly established nature in the Mind-Only School is unfounded.

Dzong-ka-ba answers these objections first [200] {432} through an appeal to authority. He declares that the emptiness described in the *Sūtra Unraveling the Thought* could not be realized by proponents of Lesser Vehicle schools because Asaṅga, in his *Grounds of Bodhisattvas,* describes it as what is realized by the wisdom purifying the obstructions to omniscience and, in his *Summary of the Great Vehicle,* says that realization of this type of emptiness brings about entry into cognition-only. Since it is axiomatic that Lesser Vehicle schools do not present a path for overcoming obstructions to omniscience—such that all objects of knowledge are realized directly and simultaneously—and since Lesser Vehicle schools, being proponents of external objects, do not propound a path for realizing cognition-only, it is clear that Asaṅga does not hold that proponents of Lesser Vehicle schools could realize this type of emptiness.

Conversely, that Asaṅga [201] {432} holds that the Lesser Vehicle schools **assert** such a self of phenomena is clear from the very way he cites their scriptures to buttress his presentation of emptiness. Since he cites **Buddhist** scriptures, it is clear that he is not refuting non-Buddhists, and since it is obvious that he is refuting neither Proponents of Non-Nature, whose problem is with the extreme of deprecation, nor another type of Proponent of Mind-Only, he must be refuting proponents of Lesser Vehicle tenets. This is why, to present this form of emptiness, he cites three passages from Lesser Vehicle Buddhist scriptures—the *Transmigration Sūtra,* the *Collection of Meanings Sūtra,* and the *Story of Saṃthakatyāyana.* Though the passages are known to proponents of Lesser Vehicle tenets, they are not fully understood by them. Later, he cites the analogy that a Lesser Vehicle school called the Majority School identifies the mention of a "fundamental consciousness" in a Lesser Vehicle scripture as the mental consciousness, whereas Asaṅga takes it to be the mind-basis-of-all.

Ḏzong-ka-ḇa next [203] {432} presents the heart of his response by identifying in more detail the innate superimposition of a self of phenomena. Based on Asaṅga's *Compendium of Ascertainments,* he points out that when we are asked what the meaning of the verbalization "house"[a] is, we say, "That over there is a house," and do not say, "That which is merely nominally imputed with the name 'house' is the meaning of the verbalization 'house.'" From this, it can be concluded that when a house's being a basis of imputation of the convention "house" appears, it does not appear to us to be posited as such by names and conceptual consciousnesses, but its being a foundation of name and thought appears as if established through the force of the house's own mode of subsistence. A consciousness assenting to this appearance is an innate superimpositional consciousness conceiving that a house is established by way of its own character as the object verbalized by the term "house" and as the referent of the thought "house."

This is a conception that imputation in the manner of an **entity** is established by way of its own character. A similar assent to the house's appearing to be established by way of its own character as the referent of the term "beautiful" and of the thought "beautiful" is a conception that imputation in the manner of an **attribute** is established by way of its own character.

Ḏzong-ka-ḇa declares that even though the Lesser Vehicle schools and the Mind-Only School agree that the meaning-generalities that are the explicit objects verbalized by terms are not established by way of their own character, the Lesser Vehicle schools propound tenets supporting that objects themselves are established by way of their own character as the referents of their respective terms and conceptual consciousnesses. (It is noteworthy that, aside from the previously cited appeals to the authority of scripture—the *Sūtra Unraveling the Thought*—and of a special commentator—Asaṅga—no other evidence that Proponents of Sūtra hold this position is cited.)

---

[a] He uses "form" as the example; "house" is my adaptation.

Reasonings Establishing The Selflessness Of Phenomena [206] {434}

Ḏzong-ka-ḇa turns to the reasonings refuting such a superimposed status in order both to gain a better sense of this false notion and to prepare the way for a discussion of how the reasonings provide a door of entry to cognition-only. He points out that the *Sūtra Unraveling the Thought* itself does not offer reasonings (it gives only pronouncements on the nature of reality), and thus he relies on Asaṅga's presentation of reasonings in his *Grounds of Bodhisattvas, Compendium of Ascertainments,* and *Summary of the Great Vehicle.* These three texts give a similar threefold reasoning built around the relationship between an object and its names.

It may be that Ḏzong-ka-ḇa primarily uses the presentation in Asaṅga's *Summary of the Great Vehicle* because it includes a concise, if initially abstruse, verse form. Let us first cite Asaṅga's text without bracketed commentary:[768]

> What makes it evident that other-powered entities which appear to be imputational natures are not of such a nature?...
>
> Because awareness does not exist prior to name,
> Because many, and because not restricted,
> There are the contradictions of its essence, many entities,
> And mixture of entities. Therefore, it is proven.

With commentary, the stanza is understood to mean:

> There are the contradictions that if a bulbous flat bottomed thing able to hold fluid, for instance, were established through the force of its own mode of subsistence as the referent of the verbal convention "pot":
>
> 1. the imputational nature would exist in the essence of that bulbous thing because an awareness of the name of an object would have to exist prior to learning its name;
> 2. one object that has many names would have to be many entities because many names are used for one object; and
> 3. the entities of many objects that have the same name would be mixed because a name is not restricted to one object.
>
> Therefore, it is proven (that objects are not established by way of their own character as the referents of terms and conceptual consciousnesses).

The first reasoning. The most common example in philosophical treatises is a pot—which is defined as that which has a bulbous belly, a flat bottom, and is capable of holding fluid. If this bulbous thing's being a foundation of a term such as "pot" were established by way of the bulbous thing's own mode of subsistence, its being such a foundation would not depend upon language, and thus an awareness thinking "pot" with respect to it absurdly would be generated just through seeing it, prior to learning its name.

The second reasoning. If a person's being the referent of names is established right in the mode of being of the person, the usage of many names—such as Shakra, Indra, Grāmaghātaka, and so forth—for one god, the Lord of the Heaven of the Thirty-Three, must be by way of the force of the god himself since this god is established by way of his own character as the referent of those names. In that case, the one god absurdly would be several gods.

The third reasoning. If a person's being the referent of names is established right in the mode of being of the person, the usage of one name for two persons—two different people called Upagupta, for instance—would mean that the two persons absurdly would be just one person.

The conclusion drawn from these three fallacies is that objects are not established by way of their own character as the objects verbalized by their respective terms and as the referents of their respective conceptual consciousnesses.

Even babies, animals, and so forth—who do not know language and thus do not know specific terms for articles such as pots—nevertheless have awarenesses conceiving that pots and so forth are established by way of their own character as foundations of thoughts about them, and thus the same reasoning is applicable.

Dzong-ka-ba [209] {435} makes only passing reference to Asaṅga's *Grounds of Bodhisattvas* and does not cite the *Compendium of Ascertainments* at all with regard to the reasonings because, as Jik-may-dam-chö-gya-tso says:[769]

- The first reasoning in the *Summary of the Great Vehicle* and in the *Compendium of Ascertainments* is similar to the third reasoning in the *Grounds of Bodhisattvas*
- The second reasoning in the *Summary of the Great Vehicle* and in the *Compendium of Ascertainments* is similar to the first reasoning in the *Grounds of Bodhisattvas*
- The third reasoning in the *Summary of the Great Vehicle* and the third reasoning in the *Compendium of Ascertainments* are similar. (It is difficult to claim that these two are similar to the second reasoning in the *Grounds of Bodhisattvas*.)

The Lesser Vehicle schools [209] {435} use the same reasoning to prove that the meaning-generalities that are the explicit objects of verbalization by words are not established by way of their own character, in that if objects were so established, an awareness thinking "pot" would absurdly be generated without making the linguistic connection, and so forth. However, the Lesser Vehicle schools mistakenly feel that the reasonings do not apply to a phenomenon's existing by way of its own character as an object verbalized by a term and as a referent of a conceptual consciousness.

From this discussion of the superimposed status, it is concluded [210] {435} that imputational factors posited by name and terminology are of two types:

- Those that exist and cannot be refuted by reasoning, such as being an object verbalized by a term or being a referent of a conceptual consciousness
- Those that do not exist and are susceptible to refutation by reasoning, such as an object's being established **by way of its own character** as the object verbalized by a term and as the referent of a conceptual consciousness.

Ď̄zong-ka-b̄a points out that there is nothing odd about the fact that although a form or a consciousness, for instance, is **ultimately established,** a form's or a consciousness's **being** an object verbalized by a term or a referent of conceptual consciousness is an existent imputational factor that is **not ultimately established**. He cites the example that a place without a pot is a common locus of a place and an absence of a pot, the first being a functioning thing and the second being a non-affirming negative that is necessarily not a functioning thing.

As is his frequent refrain, he adds a remark that distinguishes the Mind-Only system from the Proponents of Non-Nature and especially the Consequentialists: Even though the Proponents of Mind-Only can posit something as existing despite its only being posited by name and terminology, they cannot posit cause and effect within such a context, whereas the Consequentialists can.

In a similar way, the Great Exposition and Sūtra Schools cannot posit forms and so forth without their being established by way of their own character as objects verbalized by terms and as referents of conceptual consciousnesses. This sort of "own-character" is not limited to those objects that perform functions (a category that excludes permanent phenomena) since—according to the Mind-Only School—in the Great Exposition School and the Sūtra School all phenomena, both permanent and impermanent, come to be **established by way of their own character** as the referents of conceptual consciousnesses and as the foundations of the imputation of terminology.

In these ways the challenges that a lower school could realize the emptiness of such a superimposed status are countered, and the hierarchy of tenet systems is preserved.

Showing How The Two Selflessnesses Are Related [212] {436}

The Fourth Objection [212] {436}

The last objection in this series is that this description of emptiness does not involve the meaning of cognition-only and thus could not be the object of observation that, when meditated upon, purifies the obstructions to omniscience. Since Ď̄zong-ka-b̄a's cryptic answer is discussed at length in *Reflections on Real-*

ity, part 4 , I will give here my condensed rendition of the argument as formulated by his student Ke-drup:

1. Forms and so forth appear to conceptual consciousnesses to be established by way of their own character as the referents of the conventions of entity and attribute
2. A conceptual consciousness adheres to this mistaken appearance as being correct
3. Reasoning refutes the correctness of this appearance and thus also the correctness of the conceptual consciousness's assenting to this appearance
4. Objects also appear to sense consciousnesses to be established by way of their own character as the referents of the conventions of entity and attribute, and thus the correctness of this appearance to **non-conceptual** consciousnesses, such as sense consciousnesses, is also refuted
5. Thereby, sense consciousnesses are shown to be mistaken with respect to their appearing objects, in that their objects seem to be established by way of their own character as the referents of the conventions of entity and attribute, whereas they are not
6. Thereby, it is refuted that the apprehended-object is produced through the power of an external object. (That is to say, it is refuted that the images of objects apprehended in sense perception are produced through external objects impinging on consciousness; rather, they are produced through the activation of seeds of perception contained within the mind-basis-of-all.)
7. Thereby, it is also refuted that a sense object, such as a patch of blue, exists as an entity other than, or outside of, the sense consciousness that perceives it. (The one seed of perception contained within the mind-basis-of-all produces both the apprehended-object and the consciousness apprehending it, which, although they **appear** to be separate entities, are not.)

After the third point, D̄zong-ka-b̄a cites Asaṅga's *Summary of the Great Vehicle* which details the four examinations and the four thorough knowledges:[770]

1. Examination into whether names are merely adventitious, mere imputation, or whether they are designated through the force of the object's own mode of being
2. Examination into whether objects by way of their character or adventitiously exist as referents of names
3. Examination into whether in the designation of entities the relationship between the word and the object exists substantially
4. Examination into whether objects are established by way of their own character as the referents of the designation of attributes, such as their production, destruction, color, impermanence, and use

1. Knowledge that names do not exist by way of their own character in the objects they denote

2. Knowledge that objects do not exist by way of their own character as the referents of the designation of names
3. Knowledge that the designation of entities based on the relationship of names and objects does not exist by way of its own character
4. Knowledge that the designation of attributes does not exist by way of its own character

Asaṅga concludes by saying, "Through these, practitioners enter into cognition-only concerning those mental **conceptual** consciousnesses to which letters and meanings appear." This leaves Ḏzong-ka-ḇa [214] {437} to counter the qualm that the refutation applies only to conceptual consciousnesses and not to sense consciousnesses. This is accomplished by points four through seven (see p. 327).

That non-conceptual sense consciousnesses are mistaken leads to a further qualm [215] {437}:

> A self-cognizing consciousness apprehending a sense consciousness would also be mistaken in that the sense consciousness's being a referent of a conceptual consciousness would appear to it as being established by way of its own character. This is like the undisputed fact that when a patch of blue, for instance, appears to a sense consciousness, its being a referent of a conceptual consciousness appears to that sense consciousness as being established by way of its own character and thus the sense consciousness is mistaken

The problem is that self-cognizing consciousnesses are supposed to be only non-mistaken.

Ḏzong-ka-ḇa's response is that, since a self-cognizing consciousness is devoid of dualistic appearance, being a referent of a conceptual consciousness does not even appear to it. The reason why being a referent of a conceptual consciousness does not appear to it is that when being the referent of a conceptual consciousness appears, it definitely appears as having dualistic appearance, but a self-cognizing consciousness is necessarily devoid of dualistic appearance.

This line of argument leads to another qualm [215] {438} that, although peripherally related to the issue, must be addressed. Specifically, one might be led to think that **whatever** appears to a conceptual consciousness necessarily appears to have dualistic appearance. Ḏzong-ka-ḇa immediately counters this misimpression by pointing out that when consciousness (or, as some take his meaning, self-cognizing consciousness) appears to a conceptual consciousness (such as when thinking about what consciousness is or what self-cognizing consciousness is), that consciousness itself does not appear to have dualistic appearance; rather, it appears to be just an entity of cognitive experience; this is so even though all conceptual consciousnesses themselves are dualistic. His point is that the **object** on which a dualistic consciousness focuses does not have to be dualistic, as when one conceptually considers a vanishing of dualistic appearance in the state of meditative equipoise that realizes emptiness totally non-dualistically. He makes a distinction between a conceptual consciousness's **having** dualistic appearance and an **object's** appearing to it **as having the aspect** of dualistic appearance. He goes on to say that if a vanishing of dualistic appearance could not appear to a conceptual consciousness, it would not exist—the axiom being that whatever exists can appear (however vaguely) to a conceptual consciousness apprehending it.

Dzong-ka-ba [217] {438} quickly switches back to an extension of the basic question, this being whether being the referent of a conceptual consciousness—which is something that is only posited through the force of **conceptuality**—could appear to a **non-conceptual** consciousness such as an eye consciousness. This question stems from a fundamental tenet in the Mind-Only system that the false sense of objects' being established by way of their own character as objects verbalized by terms and as referents of conceptual consciousnesses appears even to non-conceptual consciousnesses such as an eye consciousness. The basic position is that the infection is so deep that raw sensation is polluted with an erroneous sense of the status of the object. Dzong-ka-ba counters the seemingly fatal flaw—that something posited through the force of **conceptuality** could appear to a **non-conceptual** consciousness—by declaring that, in a magical illusion, pebbles and sticks are used as the bases of emanation of magical display of horses and elephants, that is to say, as the things that will appear to be horses and elephants, and their **being** horses and elephants—despite the fact that it is merely imputed by conceptuality—appears to a visual sense consciousness devoid of conceptuality. (We learn from this that being posited by conceptuality or imputed by terms and conceptual consciousnesses does not necessarily mean that conceptuality is presently operating on the object—an important point laying the groundwork for the stance by the Consequentialists that all phenomena are only imputed by conceptuality even if conceptuality is not presently acting on the object.)

He has shown the connection between (1) realizing that objects are not established by way of their own character as the objects verbalized by terms and as the referents of conceptual consciousnesses and (2) realizing that objects and subjects are not different entities. Thus he summarizes this section on the entry into cognition-only by pointing out that a negation of subject and object as different entities is not absent in the statements in the *Sūtra Unraveling the Thought* that the emptiness of imputational factors imputed in the manner of entities and attributes is the thoroughly established nature. He immediately adds, somewhat cryptically until his references are identified, that in the "Questions of Maitreya Chapter" of the *Sūtra Unraveling the Thought* there is a clear refutation of external objects. (For extensive discussion of these issues see *Reflections on Reality*, part 4.)

Before listing explicit refutations of external objects found in Mind-Only treatises, Ḏzong-ka-ḇa [217] {438}, typical to his style of making refinements that do not fit into the superficial flow of the text but reflect a mind seeking even to take care of peripheral issues, points out that the *Sūtra Unraveling the Thought* does not mention other existent imputational natures, such as uncompounded space and so forth. He says the reason for this is that the sūtra is concerned with identifying the imputational factor the emptiness of which is the thoroughly established nature—the object negated in the view of selflessness of phenomena. He cryptically adds, in seeming contradiction with an earlier statement[a] that equates being posited by names and terminology with being only imputed by conceptuality, that many of those existent imputational natures are **not** posited by names and terminology but **are** only imputed by conceptuality. His followers are left with trying to adjust these two positions so that they fit together coherently.[b]

Reasonings Explicitly Refuting External Objects [218] {438}

He now lists how external objects are refuted in Mind-Only treatises. Though he restricts the discussion to a mere naming of four types of reasoning without any exposition, let us identify the four briefly:

1. Asaṅga, in his *Summary of the Great Vehicle,* draws parallels between the lack of external objects and yet generation of consciousness in illusory states, such as dreams, and the lack of external objects in other types of consciousness

2. Vasubandhu, in his *The Twenty,* attacks the possible building blocks of external objects—partless particles—by considering that they are surrounded by other particles and thus have sides, and hence parts, facing those other particles[c]

3. Dharmakīrti, in his *Commentary on (Dignāga's) "Compilation of Prime Cognition,"* refutes external objects by way of demonstrating that an apprehended-object does not produce an apprehending-subject similar to it; he denies that an external object impinges on a consciousness, making it similar to the object

4. Dignāga, in his *Examination of Objects of Observation,* employs a reasoning analyzing what kind of object could possibly impinge upon a conscious-

[a] The statement (p. 86) is:

Here, the measure indicated with respect to existing or not existing by way of [an object's] own character is: not to be posited or to be posited in dependence upon names and terminology.

[b] See *Reflections on Reality,* chap. 13; and *Absorption,* #105-109.

[c] A reasoning refuting partless particles is also found in the third chapter of Dharmakīrti's *Commentary on (Dignāga's) "Compilation of Prime Cognition."*

ness, generating it into its likeness. In technical vocabulary this is called an observed-object-condition, because it is the object observed that serves as a condition, or secondary cause, generating the consciousness. Dignāga refutes that an aggregation of particles or an individual minute particle could be an observed-object-condition

Re-Emphasizing The Importance Of Understanding The Two Types Of Selflessness Of Phenomena [218] {438}

Having mentioned these other reasonings that refute externality, Ḏzong-ka-b̄a concludes the chapter by returning to his point that understanding the thoroughly established nature as set out in the "Questions of Paramārthasamudgata Chapter" of the *Sūtra Unraveling the Thought*—this being the non-establishment of objects by way of their own character as the objects verbalized by terms and as the referents of their respective conceptual consciousnesses—is crucial to understanding the texts of this system. Otherwise, attempts to delineate the meaning of many types of statements will involve great absurdities, since these will all have to be explained as refuting an otherness of substantial entity of subject and object. Also, it would be difficult to explain the teaching that objects should not be held to be anything—permanent, impermanent, and so forth—for these statements would have to be taken as referring to states of meditative equipoise (whereas the meaning is that one should not hold objects as being established by way of their own character as the foundations of imputations as entity and attribute); also, other passages that do make differentiation of "it is this, it is not that" will have to be explained as referring to states subsequent to meditative equipoise.

He harkens back to the statements in Asaṅga's *Grounds of Bodhisattvas, Summary of the Great Vehicle,* and *Summary of Manifest Knowledge* that the four examinations and the four thorough knowledges are the door of entry to cognition-only and the antidotes to the obstructions to omniscience—those obstructions being the foundations of the afflictive emotions that comprise the defilements preventing release from cyclic existence. He recommends that to understand the four examinations and four thorough knowledges, it is necessary to understand from a subtle level:

- The reasonings refuting the falsely superimposed status of things' establishment by way of their own character as the objects verbalized by terms and as the referents of conceptual consciousnesses
- The types of consciousness that make these false superimpositions
- How these reasonings promote realization of the absence of a difference of entity between subject and object

Concluding, he humbly says that, having seen that few have involved themselves in analyzing these issues, he has written the **start** of such analyses for the intelligent, and indeed the six centuries of analysis of his insights have yielded a stream of reflection and discussion as well as a wealth or written commentary.

11. Handling Objections

Given that in the previous section Ḏzong-ka-ḇa presented the superimposed status in the format of objections and answers, it may seem anticlimactic that he follows with a separate section dispelling more objections. However, here he counters two new challenges.

Overview. This chapter [220] {440} has four basic movements:

1. A challenge that Ḏzong-ka-ḇa's presentation that Bodhisattvas realize the selflessness of phenomena, whereas Hearers and Solitary Realizers do not, contradicts the statement in the *Sūtra Unraveling the Thought* that the path and the practice of the three vehicles is one and that the state of release is one
2. Response that the meaning of the sūtra is that practitioners of all three vehicles attain conquest over the **afflictive emotions** through the same path and practice
3. A challenge that taking other-powered natures as the bases of emptiness contradicts a text attributed to Vasubandhu in which the thoroughly established nature is taken as the basis of emptiness
4. Response that Damṣhṭasena, not Vasubandhu, composed this text, which itself does not accord with either the *Sūtra Unraveling the Thought* or presentations in texts known to be by Vasubandhu

First Challenge: What Does The *Sūtra Unraveling the Thought* Mean When It Says That The Path And The Practice Of The Three Vehicles Are One? [220] {440}

The *Sūtra Unraveling the Thought* describes the process of cyclic existence as follows:

- From conceiving the imputational nature in other-powered natures, the afflictive emotions are produced
- This leads to accumulation of karmas
- These, in turn, result in revolving among the levels of cyclic existence

The sūtra describes release from this invidious process as being through perceiving other-powered natures as without the imputational nature, and it declares that Hearers, Solitary Realizers, and Bodhisattvas through just this path and just this practice attain nirvana, due to which their paths of purification of their vehicles and also the states of purification are one.

Since in this context the sūtra speaks only of a selflessness of phenomena and does not speak of a selflessness of persons, it would seem that when it says that Hearers, Solitary Realizers, and Bodhisattvas attain their release through perceiving other-powered natures as without the imputational nature, it implies that Hearers and Solitary Realizers, and not just Bodhisattvas, realize the selflessness of phenomena. However, this would contradict the explanation that it is only Bodhisattvas who realize the thoroughly established nature that is the selflessness of phenomena. On the other hand, if Hearers and Solitary Realizers do not realize the selflessness of phenomena, what is the meaning of the *Sūtra Unraveling the Thought* when it says that the paths of practice of the three vehicles are one and the states of release of the three vehicles are one?

Response: The Meaning Of The Sūtra Is That Practitioners Of All Three Vehicles Attain Nirvana Through The Same Path And Practice [221] {440}

Ḏzong-ka-ḇa first cites a passage from Asaṅga's *Grounds of Bodhisattvas* that affirms that the conception of a self of persons does indeed have as its root the conception of a self of phenomena. It says that:

> The three:
>
> - the conception that factors imputed in the manner of entity are established by way of their own character,
> - the conception that factors imputed in the manner of attributes are established by way of their own character, and
> - the conception that amorphous wholes are established by way of their own character, as in viewing that a collection of many types of trees is a forest
>
> generate a liking for such superimpositions and thereby a proliferation of conceptuality. Based on this, the conception of a self of persons—called the view of the transitory as substantially established I and mine—is generated, whereby other afflictive emotions are produced and beings travel in cyclic existence. The entire process is overcome through the four examinations and the four thorough knowledges.

By citing this passage that clearly places the conception of a self of phenomena prior to the conception of a self of persons, Ḏzong-ka-ḇa highlights the challenger's question about how Hearers and Solitary Realizers could achieve liberation from cyclic existence without extricating its root—the conception of a self of phenomena.

His answer is that the **final** root of cyclic existence need not be overcome in order to overcome cyclic existence. Hearers and Solitary Realizers overcome the conception of a self of persons that is the root of cyclic existence, but they do not overcome the conception of a self of phenomena that is the **final** root of cyclic existence. He calls attention to a parallel assertion by the Middle Way Autonomists, the followers of Bhāvaviveka, who make a similar difference between the root and the final root of cyclic existence, holding that Hearers and

Solitary Realizers overcome cyclic existence without overcoming its final root.

Still, the *Sūtra Unraveling the Thought,* despite mentioning the selflessness of persons four times,[a] never explicitly says that Hearers and Solitary Realizers meditate on it rather than on the selflessness of phenomena, and thus it might seem that the sūtra refers only to the realization of the selflessness of phenomena when it speaks of "just this path" and "just this practice." To avoid this, D̄zong-ka-b̄a refers to but does not cite a passage in Asaṅga's *Summary of Manifest Knowledge* that speaks of other-powered natures' emptiness of the imputational factor **in terms of the selflessness of persons**, and, seemingly based on this, he draws the conclusion that, when the *Sūtra Unraveling the Thought* says that the paths of purification and the state of purification are the same for all three types of practitioners, it means (1) that the afflictive emotions are purified through realizing the selflessness of persons and (2) that the release—the nirvana—that is a mere abandonment of **afflictive emotions** attained through this path is the same. In this way, he can hold that this statement in the *Sūtra Unraveling the Thought* does not contradict that only Bodhisattvas realize the selflessness of phenomena, gradually overcome the obstructions to omniscience, and attain the supreme liberation of Buddhahood.

To bolster this point, D̄zong-ka-b̄a cites the fact that the sūtra says that the wheel of doctrine of good differentiation, which is mainly the passages under consideration in the *Sūtra Unraveling the Thought* itself, is for the sake of those engaged in **all** vehicles. Thus, when it **explicitly** lays out the three natures in terms of the selflessness of phenomena, it **implicitly** indicates that the emptiness of the imputational factor of a self of persons in other-powered natures—the mental and physical aggregates—is posited as the thoroughly established nature that is the selflessness of persons.

Therefore, it is implicit to the exposition in the *Sūtra Unraveling the Thought* that Hearers and Solitary Realizers, for whom the first wheel was taught, are suitable as vessels for realizing the thoroughly established nature in terms of the selflessness of persons but not suitable as vessels for realizing the thoroughly established nature in terms of the selflessness of phenomena. In this sense the *Sūtra Unraveling the Thought* is for the sake of those engaged in all vehicles.

Second Challenge: Only Taking Other-Powered Natures As The Bases Of Emptiness Contradicts Vasubandhu [225] {441}

The next challenge is put forward by followers of Döl-b̄o S̄hay-rap-gyel-tsen; D̄zong-ka-b̄a pays it particular attention. According to his own interpretation, in the Mind-Only School the thoroughly established nature that is the selflessness of phenomena is:

- other-powered natures' non-establishment by way of their own character as

[a] It is mentioned once in chapter 3 and three times in chapter 8.

imputational natures imputed in the manner of entity and attribute, and
- other-powered natures' non-establishment as other substantial entities of apprehended-object and apprehending-subject.

Hence:

- other-powered natures are taken as the bases of emptiness,
- imputational natures are that of which other-powered natures are empty, and
- other-powered natures' emptiness of the imputational nature is the thoroughly established nature.

The challenger, however, says that Vasubandhu himself, in his *Commentary on the One Hundred Thousand, Twenty-Five Thousand, and Eighteen Thousand Perfection of Wisdom Sūtras* called *Conquest Over Objections about the Three Mother Scriptures,* takes as the basis of emptiness not other-powered natures, but the thoroughly established nature and explains that the thoroughly established nature is empty of the other two natures—other-powered natures and imputational natures. In commentary on a passage in the Perfection of Wisdom Sūtras that says, "The eye is empty of the eye," the *Conquest Over Objections* says in a summary that:

> "The eye" = the eye of reality, which means the reality of the eye.
>
> "Of the eye" = of (1) the eye that is the imputational factor and (2) the eye that is the imputed (the eye itself).
>
> "Empty" = "devoid."
>
> Hence, "The eye is empty of the eye," = "The reality of the eye is empty of the imputational factor of the eye and empty of the imputed,"—the word "imputed" here meaning "the eye itself."

The Jo-nang-b̄as, based on this summary statement in the *Conquest Over Objections,* understandably take the passage to mean:

> The reality, or thoroughly established nature, of the eye is empty of the imputational nature of the eye and is empty of the other-powered nature of the eye.

Taken this way, the passage indicates that the thoroughly established nature is the basis of emptiness in that it is empty of the other two natures; this is the position of "other-emptiness."

This exposition conflicts with D̄zong-ka-b̄a's limiting the selflessness of phenomena to other-powered natures' emptiness of the imputational nature. Hence, he is challenged to explain away this disparity with the word of Vasubandhu.

Response: Realization Of Emptiness As Explained In The *Conquest Over Objections* Is Not Sufficient, And Vasubandhu Did Not Write The *Conquest Over Objections* [226] {442}

Ḏzong-ka-ḇa's often cryptic response basically communicates three points:

1. The challenger's interpretation of the *Conquest Over Objections* is mistaken
2. The explanation of the thoroughly established nature in the *Conquest Over Objections* is not how it is delineated in the context of a view for practice in the basal, or ordinary, state and thus does not offer a practice that would harm the innate conception of a self of phenomena
3. Vasubandhu did not write the *Conquest Over Objections;* Damṣhṭasena did

The Challenger's Interpretation Of The Conquest Over Objections *Is Mistaken* [228] {443}

Ḏzong-ka-ḇa faults the Jo-nang-ḇas for their interpretation of the exposition in the *Conquest Over Objections.* He does this from the viewpoint that the *Conquest Over Objections* itself, since in a longer exposition immediately preceding the above summary statement, it gives a different explanation, which puts the exposition in the context of meditative equipoise realizing emptiness. It also says that:

- The imputational eye = appearances to a conceptual consciousness of means of verbalization and objects of verbalization
- The imputed eye = the appearance as an eye that apprehends color and/or shape
- The eye of reality, that is to say, the reality of the eye = the thoroughly established nature known by individual self-cognition in meditative equipoise
- "The eye is empty of the eye" = the reality of the eye is (1) inexpressible due to being devoid of the means of verbalization and the objects of verbalization and (2) devoid of individual appearances as object apprehended by the eye and the eye as an apprehending-subject

Thus Ḏzong-ka-ḇa's implicit point is that the *Conquest Over Objections* here (and elsewhere) does not offer support for the Jo-nang-ḇa view of other-emptiness.

The Explanation Of The Thoroughly Established Nature In The Conquest Over Objections *Is Not How It Is Delineated In The Context Of A View For Practice In The Basal, Or Ordinary, State And Thus Does Not Offer A Practice That Would Harm The Innate Conception Of A Self Of Phenomena* [230] {444}

Ḏzong-ka-ḇa also criticizes the *Conquest Over Objections* for its exposition of this passage from Perfection of Wisdom Sūtras. For he makes the point that this type of teaching is not sufficient for opposing the ingrained tendency to view objects wrongly, and thus those objects, that is, other-powered natures, have to be taken as the bases of the emptiness of the imputational nature. He mentions that the presentation of the thoroughly established nature in the *Conquest Over Objections* is not how the selflessness of phenomena is delineated as a **view of the basal state**. He says no more than this, but his fifteenth-century commentator B̄el-jor-hlün-drup[771] adds:

> This type of teaching is not in terms of delineating the selflessness of phenomena by hearing and thinking in the basal state; rather, it teaches the mode of appearance to meditative equipoise, a path state.

The point is that the *Conquest Over Objections* indicates how emptiness is experienced in meditative equipoise directly realizing the ultimate. It may be that, since it is merely indicating that in meditative equipoise no conventional phenomena appear, D̄zong-ka-b̄a does not quarrel with the accuracy of such a presentation from the viewpoint of such a path state. However, he insists that, in the basal—or ordinary—state, beings need a presentation related to the phenomena that are misconceived to exist with a false status. The presentation in the *Conquest Over Objections* is from the viewpoint of how the thoroughly established nature appears in meditative equipoise, a path state.

Realization Of Such A Thoroughly Established Nature Would Not Harm The Innate Conception Of A Self Of Phenomena [226] {442}

In order to indicate the inadequacy of the explanation in the *Conquest Over Objections,* D̄zong-ka-b̄a explains the process of entrapment in suffering and its converse, how to undo that process. Beings are trapped into a delusory state, not by misapprehending the thoroughly established nature but by misapprehending other-powered natures, such as bodies and houses, to be established in accordance with the imputational nature. Thus, both the Yogic Practice School (that is, Mind-Only School) and the Naturelessness School take other-powered natures as the bases of emptiness and delineate a thoroughly established nature that is other-powered natures' emptiness of the imputational nature. He compares this to how a person's fright, arisen upon misapprehending a rope to be a snake, is removed. It is done by being shown that the rope is empty of a snake—that it is not a snake. It is not done by being shown that the emptiness of a snake is devoid of being a rope and devoid of being a snake due to being factually other than those two.

D̄zong-ka-b̄a's concern is that realization of the thoroughly established nature must counter the innate misconception of the status of objects that has resided in the mental continuum from beginningless time. Thus the conception of a self of phenomena cannot be like non-innate misconceptions that:

- directionally partless minute particles exist,
- objects of apprehension composed of directionally partless minute particles exist,
- partless moments of consciousness exist, and
- a consciousness that is a continuum composed of partless moments exists.

For these are imagined only by those whose minds have been affected by mistaken systems of tenets and do not occur innately among sentient beings. He sees the refutation of such tenets, which is indeed present in Buddhist texts, as a subsidiary branch of the more important project of refuting that the bases—the phenomena that are innately misconceived to exist in accordance with a self of phenomena—exist this way.

Just these things—that ordinary beings misconceive to be objects and subjects that are different entities or to be established by way of their own character as the referents of words and conceptual consciousnesses—must be the bases of delineating emptiness, the thoroughly established nature. They appear in a false way, and this appearance is assented to; such assent is the innate conception that objects exist the way they appear. The antidote is to realize that appearances in fact are not established as other substantial entities and are not established by way of their own character as the referents of their respective conceptual consciousnesses or objects verbalized by words. This is the delineation of the selflessness of phenomena. Selflessness, therefore, is not like a temple's being empty of monastics (who exist somewhere else) but like a rope's emptiness of a snake—the rope never was a snake.

Since the root error does not come from misconceiving that other-powered natures and imputational natures exist in the thoroughly established nature, delineation of selflessness is not constituted by realizing that the thoroughly established nature is empty of the other two natures. D̄zong-ka-b̄a uses the worldly example of attempting to ward off a spirit. The proper way is to make an effigy of the person and place it in the direction from which the spirit comes to the house. The spirit is fooled into thinking that the effigy (crafted to look like the person) is the actual person and makes trouble for it, whereby the person is relieved. However, if the effigy is put in the wrong direction, the ritual cannot have any effect. The point is that this mistaken assertion attempts to overcome the conception of a self of phenomena without taking into account the actual process of the misconception.

From this perspective, D̄zong-ka-b̄a says that the explanation in the *Conquest Over Objections* of the statement in Perfection of Wisdom Sūtras that "The eye is empty of the eye," means that the thoroughly established nature is empty of imputational natures and other-powered natures in the face of meditative equipoise is not good. Rather, the Perfection of Wisdom Sūtras themselves present three natures each for every phenomenon and explain that the emptiness of the imputational nature in an other-powered nature is the thoroughly established nature, reality. Therefore, the reality of the eye is the imputed eye's emptiness of the imputational eye.

The Conquest Over Objections *Does Not Offer Support For The Jo-nang-b̄a Notion That The Thoroughly Established Nature Ultimately Exists* [230] {444}

Without saying why he is bringing up the matter, D̄zong-ka-b̄a adds that:

- the *Conquest Over Objections* does indeed explain that what exists in the face of a Superior's meditative equipoise ultimately exists, and thus the thoroughly established nature ultimately exists in the sense of existing in the perspective of an ultimate consciousness;
- however, this does not establish that in the system of the *Conquest Over Objections* the thoroughly established nature has the status of ultimate existence as that term is understood in the debate between the Middle Way School and the Mind-Only School on whether an object ultimately exists or not, that is to say, is established by way of its own character or not; and
- in fact, the *Conquest Over Objections* utterly does not accept that there are any ultimate existents in this latter sense, and this can be seen through its specific refutations that the ultimate ultimately exists by way of its own character. (These refutations occur in its discussion of the emptiness of emptiness, the emptiness of the ultimate, and the emptiness of the uncompounded.)[a]

D̄zong-ka-b̄a's implicit point is that such a presentation does not fit Vasubandhu's system or that of authoritative Mind-Only scholars; nor does it accord with the Jo-nang-b̄a position that the thoroughly established nature ultimately exists in the sense of being established by way of its own character. He thereby undercuts one of S̄hay-rap-gyel-tsen's important sources for the ultimate existence of the thoroughly established nature.

Encapsulating points made earlier, D̄zong-ka-b̄a says that, since the Mother Sūtras—the Perfection of Wisdom Sūtras—describe the thoroughly established nature as other-powered natures' emptiness of the imputational nature, it must be said that the imputed eye's emptiness of the imputational eye is reality, the thoroughly established nature. Hence, the *Conquest Over Objections* does not give an explanation relevant to the ordinary state when it posits that the meaning of the sūtra statement that "The eye is empty of the eye" is that the thoroughly established nature of the eye is empty of other-powered natures and of imputational natures in the face of a Superior's meditative equi-

[a] From the fact that the *Conquest Over Objections* speaks of even the ultimate truth of being empty of ultimate existence (this being the Middle Way School's presentation of emptiness acceptable to D̄zong-ka-b̄a), Jik-may-dam-chö-gya-tso (*Port of Entry,* 691.4-693.2) draws the conclusion that D̄zong-ka-b̄a, although criticizing the *Conquest Over Objections* for its treatment of the above sūtra passage, does not see that text as presenting other-emptiness and thus does not refute its mode of emptiness.

poise. Given what has gone before, it may be that Ḏzong-ka-ḇa allows that the *Conquest Over Objections* does indeed give a suitable description of a path state of meditative equipoise but does not do so for the crucial basal state, when the pernicious misconception of the status of phenomena has to be opposed. Ḏzong-ka-ḇa's brevity leaves the point in a pregnant hiatus.

Damshṭasena, Not Vasubandhu, Wrote The Conquest Over Objections [231] {445}

Ḏzong-ka-ḇa offers two proofs that Vasubandhu did not author the *Conquest Over Objections:*

1. The *Conquest Over Objections* cites a text written after Vasubandhu—a *Commentary on the "Twenty-Five Thousand Stanza Perfection of Wisdom Sūtra"* by Bhadanta Vimuktasena (not to be confused with Vasubandhu's student Āryavimuktasena)
2. The *Conquest Over Objections* refutes that both other-powered natures and thoroughly established natures are established by way of their own character or are truly established. However, this explanation is at great variance with Vasubandhu's *Principles of Explanation,* where he says that the thought of the Mother Sūtras must be taken in accordance with the *Sūtra Unraveling the Thought.* The sūtra clearly says that other-powered natures are established by way of their own character and takes other-powered natures, not the thoroughly established nature, as the bases of emptiness

Ḏzong-ka-ḇa concludes that for these reasons Vasubandhu did not compose the *Conquest Over Objections.* Rather, it was written by Damṣhṭasena, as is attested in early catalogues.

12. Differentiating Scriptures

In chapters 6 through 11, Ḏzong-ka-ḇa presented how authoritative authors of treatises on Mind-Only delineate the middle through avoiding the two extremes:

- the extreme of reification, in which even imputational natures are established by way of their own character
- the extreme of deprecation, in which all three natures are not established by way of their own character.

Based on those expositions, he now presents how scriptures are differentiated into those that require interpretation and those that are definitive.

Overview. This chapter [234] {446} has seven basic movements:

1. Through citing Vasubandhu, showing how the first wheel of doctrine requires interpretation
2. Through citing Asaṅga, showing how the middle wheel of doctrine requires interpretation
3. Explaining that the types of interpretation required for the first two wheels of doctrine are markedly different
4. After briefly indicating that the final wheel of doctrine is definitive, referring to Vasubandhu's opinion that the Perfection of Wisdom Sūtras, if taken literally, are self-contradictory
5. Chiding Tibetans who claim to be Proponents of Non-Nature but who do not give sufficient status to conventional phenomena and urging them to learn how to uphold the valid status of conventional phenomena, since otherwise they will be subject to Vasubandhu's criticisms that the Perfection of Wisdom Sūtras, if taken literally, are self-contradictory
6. Briefly identifying the three wheels of doctrine.
7. Finishing the section on the Mind-Only School with a refutation of the way the eleventh-century Indian scholar Ratnākarashānti differentiates what requires interpretation and what is definitive.

Showing How The First Wheel Of Doctrine Requires Interpretation [234] {446}

Once it is an extreme of reification for phenomena to be established by way of their own character as the referents of their respective conceptual consciousnesses or for apprehended-object and apprehending-subject to be separate entities from each other, the first wheel of doctrine that teaches just such an extreme requires interpretation. Vasubandhu's *The Twenty* is cited to show that interpretation is required from three viewpoints:

- **The basis in Buddha's thought**: This refers to the actuality that Buddha had in mind when teaching something that in fact does not exist. Thus, for the first-wheel teaching of a difference of entity between subject and object, the basis in Buddha's thought is said to be (1) the seeds from which consciousnesses arise and (2) the appearance of forms, sounds, odors, tastes, and tangible objects as if they were external objects
- **The purpose for the teaching**: This refers to the liberative purpose for Buddha's teaching something that is non-factual. In the case of the first wheel, it is said that when he taught that subject and object are different entities, he wanted his listeners to realize that, aside from consciousness, there is no permanent self or substantially existent self that perceives objects. As an example, Vasubandhu cites Buddha's teaching of spontaneously arisen sentient beings, that is to say, his teaching that there are sentient beings that just spontaneously exist and thus are permanent and substantially exist; this teaching has—as its basis in Buddha's thought—the intermediate state between lives, and it is given for Nihilists and so forth so that they might understand that there is a basis for the connection of actions in one life to their effects in another life
- **The damage to the literal reading:** These are the scriptures and the reasonings refuting external objects that were given earlier

The discussion thus far has been about the teaching of external objects; hence D̄zong-ka-b̄a adds that:

- when it is taught in the first wheel that all phenomena, without differentiation, are established by way of their own character, the imputational nature—a phenomenon's being a referent of a conceptual consciousness and of words—is included as being taught that it is established by way of its own character;
- however, since it exists but actually does not exist by way of its own character, such scriptures also require interpretation.

Showing How The Middle Wheel Requires Interpretation [236] {447}

The extreme of deprecation is that all three natures are not established by way of their own character (or not established from their own side), and thus the second wheel of doctrine, since it teaches this, requires interpretation. D̄zong-ka-b̄a refers to the statement in Asaṅga's *Summary of Manifest Knowledge* that the declarations in the Perfection of Wisdom Sūtras that all phenomena are natureless are in consideration of the three non-natures and thus require interpretation. He also refers to but does not cite Asaṅga's *Summary of the Great Vehicle,* which says:

> Magical illusions and so forth are taught in relation to the dependent.
> Non-existence is taught in relation to the imputational.

The four purifications are taught
In relation to the thoroughly established.

He finishes describing the second wheel of doctrine by citing a similar statement in Vasubandhu's *Principles of Explanation* refuting the literality of the explanations in the Perfection of Wisdom Sūtras that all phenomena are natureless.

The Types Of Interpretation That The First Two Wheels Of Doctrine Require Are Markedly Different [237] {447}

In the first wheel of doctrine, the basis in Buddha's thought—also called the thought of the speaker[a]—is that there are seeds in the mind-basis-of-all, from the ripening of which the various consciousnesses arise, and that there are appearances of their respective objects as if they are external objects. However, the thought of the first-wheel scriptures, or the meaning that is expressed by those sūtras, is different from the thought of the speaker—namely, that object and subject are different entities, a notion that is contradicted by Buddha's own thought.

With respect to the middle wheel of doctrine, on the other hand, the thought of the speaker and the thought of the scriptures are the same, in that both are the three modes of naturelessness—imputational natures are character-non-natures, other-powered natures are [self-]production-non-natures, and thoroughly established natures are ultimate-non-natures. Thus the **literal reading** of the middle wheel—that all phenomena are natureless—is neither the thought of the middle-wheel scriptures nor the thought of their speaker, whereas the literal reading of the first wheel—the existence of external objects and the establishment of all phenomena by way of their own character as the referents of their respective conceptual consciousnesses—is the thought of the first-wheel scriptures, but not the thought of the speaker.

These distinctions make the important point that the Mind-Only School does not hold that the meaning of the Perfection of Wisdom Sūtras is that all phenomena are natureless; rather, this is just the literal reading of those sūtras. Thus the Proponents of Non-Nature, who erroneously take the Perfection of Wisdom Sūtras to be literal, are not the intended trainees for whom those sūtras were spoken; rather, the intended trainees are sharp Proponents of Mind-Only who understand the meaning of the Perfection of Wisdom Sūtras in accordance with the doctrine of the three non-natures as presented in the *Sūtra Unraveling the Thought* but without needing to rely on an explanation of the three non-natures as in the *Sūtra Unraveling the Thought.* (From this viewpoint, Ge-luk-b̄a scholars say that, even according to the Mind-Only School, the Perfection of Wisdom Sūtras are the supreme of all sūtras).[b]

a *gsung ba po'i dgongs pa.*

b *mdo sde kun gyi mchog.*

The mode of commentary on the literal reading of the Perfection of Wisdom Sūtras is that:

- imputational natures are non-natures, in the sense that they lack establishment by way of their own character;
- other-powered natures are non-natures, in the sense that they lack self-production and also in the sense that they lack being the ultimate that is the object meditated to bring about purification; and
- thoroughly established natures are non-natures, in that they are the very lack of a self of phenomena that exists with each phenomenon. (They are also the ultimate that is the object meditated in order to bring about purification.)

In this way, the thought of the middle and final wheels of doctrine are the same, and those who hold the middle-wheel sūtras to be literal are to be refuted. Hence, the perspective from which the *Sūtra Unraveling the Thought* says that the sūtras of the final wheel of doctrine are definitive is that they are literal. It is not that their thought differs from the middle wheel.

Self-Contradictions In The Literal Reading Of The Perfection Of Wisdom Sūtras [239] {448}

After concluding that the final wheel of doctrine is literal and thus definitive, D̄zong-ka-b̄a skips over the expected topic of the **purpose** behind the teaching of the literal reading of the Perfection of Wisdom Sūtras and proceeds to lay out the **damage to their literal reading**. Nevertheless, his followers have speculated on the purpose for the literal reading of the second wheel. Jik-may-dam-chö-gya-tso,[a] for instance, holds that (the literal reading of) the second wheel is for the sake of leading Consequentialists to the view of the Mind-Only School; he bases this on D̄zong-ka-b̄a's earlier citation from Asaṅga's *Compendium of Ascertainments* (p. 83):

---

[a] *Port of Entry*, 702.4. He (*Port of Entry*, 706.2) also lists other scholars' interpretations of the purpose of the middle wheel of doctrine:

- Both Paṇ-chen S̄ö-nam-drak-b̄a and Jay-d̄zün Chö-ḡyi-gyel-tsen explain that the middle wheel is for the sake of taking care of Proponents of Mind-Only who have sharp faculties. (This speaks to the purpose of the explicit teaching of the middle wheel, not to the purpose of its literal reading.)
- Jam-ȳang-shay-b̄a explains that it is for the sake of leading Consequentialists and so forth
- J̄ang-ḡya explains that it is for the sake of stopping the ten types of distracted conceptuality
- "Others" explain that it is for the sake of stopping the view of reification in which the first wheel of doctrine is held to be literal

> *Question:* Thinking of what did the Supramundane Victor say [in the middle wheel] that all phenomena are natureless?
>
> *Answer:* Here and there he said such through the force of taming [trainees], thinking of three types of non-nature.

Still, he does not explain the crucial point of **how** the teaching of what the Mind-Only School calls a deprecation of all phenomena could be of service to Consequentialists. However, it can be surmised that Consequentialists are able to posit the cause and effect of actions and the practice of virtue **only** in the context of the utter absence of inherent existence in all phenomena, and thus, in relation to their mind-set, Buddha communicates to them that all phenomena are natureless.

With respect to the **damage to the literal reading** of the Perfection of Wisdom Sūtras, Dzong-ka-ba refers to the earlier pronouncements in the *Sūtra Unraveling the Thought* that if they were taken to be literal, this would involve the deprecation that all three natures would not be established by way of their own character—the problem being that other-powered natures and thoroughly established natures are indeed established by way of their own character. He cites Vasubandhu's analysis—in his *Principles of Explanation*—of internal contradictions in the Perfection of Wisdom Sūtras:

> On the one hand, the Perfection of Wisdom Sūtras call for the adoption of practices for the sake of certain effects and call for training in the perfection of wisdom in order to attain levels of the path. On the other hand, those same sūtras propound the naturelessness of all phenomena. Therefore, the latter cannot be taken literally but as having another thought behind it.

Dzong-ka-ba points out that even the Proponents of Non-Nature do not assert that the entities of phenomena utterly do not exist or do not exist conventionally. Vasubandhu's criticism is that if such a denial of **ultimate existence** in other-powered natures were literal, cause and effect would not be feasible.

Advice To Tibetan Proponents Of Non-Nature [241] {449}

Having explained how Vasubandhu interprets the Perfection of Wisdom Sūtras such that they become free of self-contradiction, Dzong-ka-ba turns to indicating how Proponents of Non-Nature should take the Perfection of Wisdom Sūtras so that they are not subject to Vasubandhu's criticisms. He upbraids those

- who claim to be Proponents of Non-Nature but think that cause and effect cannot be established by valid cognition since, according to their wrong notions, valid certification would make cause and effect inherently existent; and

- who therefore hold that cause and effect exist only in the perspective of a mistaken consciousness that fancies production to exist.

He chides these pretenders who cannot uphold the valid status of conventional phenomena by saying that it would be splendid if they followed the interpretation by the Proponents of Mind-Only, for otherwise they are subject to the fault of nihilism. Ḏzong-ka-ḇa, being a Consequentialist himself, is warning that denial of the valid establishment of objects is an extreme of nihilism, according to his exposition of the Consequence School; here he is speaking in his own voice, not from the perspective of the Mind-Only School.

Identifying The Three Wheels Of Doctrine [242] {450}

Ḏzong-ka-ḇa draws the conclusion that the three wheels of doctrine are posited not by way of the assemblies of Buddha's students or by way of periods in the Buddha's life, and so forth, but by way of the topics expressed.

1. Initially, at Varaṇāsi within teaching the selflessness of persons, Buddha taught that all phenomena, ranging from the five aggregates through the thirty-seven harmonies with enlightenment, are established by way of their own character as referents of their respective conceptual consciousnesses and as objects expressed by words
2. Then, he taught that all phenomena, ranging from forms through omniscient consciousnesses, are not established from their own side
3. Finally, he made the distinction that other-powered natures and thoroughly established natures are established by way of their own character but that imputational natures are not established by way of their own character

Thus the three wheels of doctrine that the *Sūtra Unraveling the Thought* elucidates as requiring interpretation or being definitive are very specific teachings, and other sūtras that do not teach these topics are not in any way what Buddha, in the *Sūtra Unraveling the Thought,* is dividing into what require interpretation and what are definitive.

Refuting The Way That Ratnākarashānti Differentiates The Interpretable And The Definitive [243] {450}

To complete his exposition of how the Mind-Only School differentiates the interpretable and the definitive, Ḏzong-ka-ḇa refutes the presentation of this topic by the eleventh-century Indian scholar Ratnākarashānti, who speaks of a threefold division of sūtras:

- Those whose meaning is ascertained through themselves—such as the *Descent into Laṅkā,* the *Sūtra Unraveling the Thought,* and so forth. These themselves clearly teach that imputational natures are not established by way of their own character and that other-powered natures and thoroughly established natures are established by way of their own character

- Those whose meaning is ascertained through another sūtra—such as the *Eight Thousand Stanza Perfection of Wisdom Sūtra,* and so forth. On the literal level, these do not differentiate from among the three natures that other-powered natures and thoroughly established natures are established by way of their own character and that imputational natures are not established by way of their own character; rather, they require elucidation with regard to these facts by other sūtras, such as the *Sūtra Unraveling the Thought*
- Those whose meaning is ascertained through themselves and whose meaning is ascertained through another sūtra—such as the *Twenty-Five Thousand Stanza Perfection of Wisdom Sūtra,* and so forth. The meaning of earlier chapters in the *Twenty-Five Thousand Stanza Perfection of Wisdom* is ascertained through the "Questions of Maitreya Chapter" in that sūtra itself and through the *Sūtra Unraveling the Thought*

With respect to the latter, Ratnākarashānti's point is that the "Questions of Maitreya Chapter" in the *Twenty-Five Thousand Stanza Perfection of Wisdom Sūtra* has an explanation that earlier passages in that sūtra require interpretation regarding their blanket presentation of all phenomena as natureless. He holds that this chapter presents the three natures in the same way as the *Sūtra Unraveling the Thought* does.

D̄zong-ka-b̄a [244] {451} disagrees and, in so doing, indirectly undermines S̄hay-rap-gyel-tsen's amalgamation of the final thought of the middle and final wheels of doctrine into a Great Middle Way through the "Questions of Maitreya Chapter." D̄zong-ka-b̄a holds that on the surface the presentation of the three natures in the "Questions of Maitreya Chapter" in the *Twenty-Five Thousand Stanza Perfection of Wisdom Sūtra* might seem to be like that in the *Sūtra Unraveling the Thought,* but it is not. However, he defers explanation of this point until late in the section on the Consequence School. Because of its importance in understanding his criticisms of S̄hay-rap-gyel-tsen's system, let us pursue it briefly here.

The passage from the *Twenty-Five Thousand Stanza Perfection of Wisdom Sūtra,*[772] for instance, at the least seems to give a presentation of the three natures that accords with that in the *Sūtra Unraveling the Thought,* in that it declares that imputational forms and so forth do not substantially exist but that forms themselves do substantially exist, this being similar to the statement in the *Sūtra Unraveling the Thought* that imputational natures do not subsist by way of their own character but that other-powered natures do. It is cited at length in Jam-ȳang-shay-b̄a's *Great Exposition of Tenets* (the bracketed additions in the last paragraph below represent D̄zong-ka-b̄a's way of explaining away the seeming similarity with the exposition of the three natures in the *Sūtra Unraveling the Thought*):[773]

"In dependence on the name, discrimination, and convention of the term 'form' to these and those things which have the character of compositional phenomena, a nature of forms is imagined. These are imputational forms.

"Maitreya, in dependence on the name, discrimination, designation, and convention of the terms 'feelings,' 'discriminations,' 'compositional factors,' 'consciousnesses'—through to—'qualities of a Buddha' to these and those things which have the character of compositional phenomena, there is imputed a nature of feelings, discriminations, compositional factors, consciousnesses—through to—a nature of the qualities of a Buddha. These are imputational feelings, discriminations, compositional factors, consciousnesses—through to—imputational qualities of a Buddha.

"[Then with respect to other-powered natures] there are the nominal, discriminated, imputed, and conventional 'forms,' 'feelings,' 'discriminations,' 'compositional factors,' 'consciousnesses'—through to—'qualities of a Buddha' that are designated to these and those things which have the character of compositional phenomena, in dependence on conceptuality abiding in just the nature of conceptuality. These are imputed forms, imputed feelings, imputed discriminations, imputed compositional factors, imputed consciousnesses—through to—imputed qualities of a Buddha.

"Whether the Ones Gone Thus appear or not, reality and the sphere of the actual status of phenomena just abide. Reality's forms are imputed forms' permanent, permanent, stable, absence of nature and absence of a self of phenomena as imputational forms—suchness, final reality. These are reality's feelings, discriminations, consciousnesses—through to—reality's qualities of a Buddha." Thus Buddha said.

The Bodhisattva Maitreya asked, "From among these three types of forms [imputational forms, imputed forms, and reality's forms], which forms are to be viewed as not substantially existing? Which as substantially existing? Which as neither not substantially existing nor substantially existing but distinguished by being ultimate objects? From among the three types of feelings, the three types of compositional factors, the three types of consciousnesses—through to—the three types of qualities of a Buddha, which are to be viewed as not substantially existing? Which as substantially existing? Which as neither not substantially existing nor substantially existing but distinguished by being ultimate objects?" Thus [Maitreya] asked.

The Supramundane Victor said to the Bodhisattva Maitreya, "O

> Maitreya, these imputational forms [that is to say, the ultimate existence imagined in forms] should be viewed as not substantially existing [because of not existing at all]. These imputed forms [that is, forms themselves] should be viewed as substantially existing [that is, conventionally existing] because conceptuality substantially exists and not because forms exist under their own power. Reality's forms [that is, emptinesses] should be viewed as neither not substantially existing [because of existing as the nature of phenomena] nor as substantially existing [because of not existing by way of their own character] but as distinguished by being ultimate objects."

Despite the seeming similarities (if we disregard the interpolations in the last paragraph) with how the *Sūtra Unraveling the Thought* treats the status of the three natures, D̄zong-ka-b̄a[774] explains that this chapter presents the three natures in a different way from the *Sutra Unraveling the Thought* and that Ratnākarashānti is not to be followed with regard to this topic. This is because the *Twenty-Five Thousand Stanza Perfection of Wisdom Sutra* itself elsewhere speaks of **all** phenomena as not existing ultimately and only existing conventionally whereas the *Sūtra Unraveling the Thought* indicates that other-powered natures (and, by extension, thoroughly established natures) are established by way of their own character and imputational natures are not. Thus, though it might seem that the "Questions of Maitreya Chapter" of the *Twenty-Five Thousand Stanza Perfection of Wisdom Sūtra* makes a differentiation of status here among the three natures like that of the *Sutra Unraveling the Thought* when it says that imputational forms (the imputational nature imputed to forms) do not substantially exist whereas imputed forms (other-powered natures) substantially exist, D̄zong-ka-b̄a holds that "imputational forms" here refers to the ultimate existence imagined of forms which does not exist at all and "imputed forms" refers to forms themselves which exist conventionally; he asserts that it can be understood that "substantial existence" here means not ultimate existence but just existence, that is, conventional existence. Ratnākarashānti is faulted for not having taken the context of the sutra into proper account. (D̄zong-ka-b̄a uses the rest of the *Twenty-Five Thousand Stanza Perfection of Wisdom Sūtra* to explain the "Questions of Maitreya Chapter," whereas Ratnākarashānti uses this chapter to explain the rest of the sūtra.)

The point is that since here "substantial existence" is equivalent to "existence," which is equivalent to conventional existence, even this passage, which **seems** to accord with the *Sūtra Unraveling the Thought*, is not—for the Mind-Only School—definitive and requires interpretation. D̄zong-ka-b̄a's explanation of the three-natures section of the "Questions of Maitreya Chapter" thereby maintains his position that, for the Mind-Only School, the literal reading of the Perfection of Wisdom Sūtras requires interpretation and does not—on the literal level—present a doctrine of the three natures similar to that in the *Sūtra Unraveling the Thought*.[a]

Shay-rap-gyel-tsen,[b] on the other hand, holds that this presentation in the *Twenty-Five Thousand Stanza Perfection of Wisdom Sūtra* is just the same as that given by Maitreya at the beginning of his *Differentiation of the Middle and the Extremes,* and so forth (see p. 182ff.). Thus Dzong-ka-ba's refutation of Ratnākarashānti's similar notion also is aimed implicitly at Shay-rap-gyel-tsen.

Here in the Mind-Only section, Dzong-ka-ba points out that Vasubandhu establishes that the statements in the Perfection of Wisdom Sūtras that all phenomena are natureless require interpretation as per the *Sūtra Unraveling the Thought* and that Vasubandhu indicates contradictions in the literal reading of those sūtras. Indeed, Vasubandhu does not establish this through citing the "Questions of Maitreya Chapter" in the *Twenty-Five Thousand Stanza Perfection of Wisdom Sūtra.* We can see that this is a reason for Dzong-ka-ba's earlier quotation of Vasubandhu's explicit citation of the *Sūtra Unraveling the Thought* (p. 237):

> Vasubandhu's *Principles of Explanation* refutes the assertion that the explanations in the Mother Sūtras of naturelessness and so forth are literal and says:
>
>> **It is set out in the *Sūtra Unraveling the Thought*** that all such statements that "All phenomena are natureless," and so forth are not of definitive meaning.

---

[a] For treatments of these issues see Edward Conze and Shōtarō Iida, "'Maitreya's Questions' in the *Prajñāpāramitā,*" *Mélanges d'indianisme a la mémoire de Louis Renou,* 229-242 (Paris: Éditions E. de Boccard, 1968); Noriaki Hakamaya, "A Consideration on the Byams Shus kyi Le'u," *Indobukkyogaku Kenkyu* 14, no. 1 (1975): 499-489; Shōtarō Iida, *Reason and Emptiness* (Tokyo: Hokuseido, 1980), 259-269; Ian Charles Harris, *The Continuity of Madhyamaka and Yogācāra in Indian Mahāyāna Buddhism* (Leiden, Netherlands: Brill, 1991), 102-131; and Cyrus R. Stearns, *The Buddha from Dol po and His Fourth Council of the Buddhist Doctrine* (Ann Arbor, Mich.: University Microfilms, 1996), 136-143. The complexities of Dzong-ka-ba's presentation are perhaps what have led Harris (*Continuity of Madhyamaka and Yogācāra,* 110) mistakenly to surmise that Dzong-ka-ba would be put in the uncomfortable position of having to accept that the *Sūtra Unraveling the Thought* is **not** a basic scripture for the Yogic Practice School ("His position seems to entail a denial of the fact that the *Sandhinirmocanasūtra* is *āgama* for the *Yogācāra*...") and (*Continuity of Madhyamaka and Yogācāra,* 120) that Dzong-ka-ba himself "was a *Svātantrika-Mādhyamika*"!

The scholars mentioned in the above paragraph do not consider the "Questions of Maitreya Chapter" to be an integral part of that sūtra but take it to be a later insertion into the text, by reason of the fact that it contains this explanation of the three natures so opposed to the run of the rest of the sūtra. Indeed, this is a way to avoid having to make the forced complexities of interpretation that Dzong-ka-ba employs in order to create a unified whole.

[b] Shay-rap-gyel-tsen (*Ocean of Definitive Meaning,* 205.4-207.6) cites and explains the passage from the *Twenty-Five Thousand Stanza Perfection of Wisdom Sūtra* given above.

It also can be seen that he is buttressing this argument when, earlier on the occasion of presenting the damage to the literal reading of the Perfection of Wisdom Sūtras, he cites Vasubandhu's presentation of the internal contradictions of those sūtras. The point, by extension, is that Vasubandhu did not take literally the exposition of the three natures in the "Maitreya Chapter" of the *Twenty-Five Thousand Stanza Perfection of Wisdom Sūtra*, and thus Ratnākarashānti is wrong to hold that this chapter presents the three natures in the same way as the *Sūtra Unraveling the Thought.*

D̄zong-ka-b̄a adds that if the presentation of the three natures in the "Maitreya Chapter" and in the *Sūtra Unraveling the Thought* were equivalent, then it could not be said, as the Proponents of Non-Nature rightly do, that the meaning of the thought of the Mother Sūtras is that all phenomena are natureless ultimately but exist conventionally. This is because, according to Ratnākarashānti's wrong view, the "Questions of Maitreya Chapter" of the *Twenty-Five Thousand Stanza Perfection of Wisdom Sūtra* would be saying (even on the literal level) that such teaching is not definitive and that other-powered natures **are** established by way of their own character. The Middle Way School absurdly would have to accord with the Cognition School, that is to say, the Mind-Only School, on the topic of the three natures, whereas it is obvious that these scholars differed on this issue.

D̄zong-ka-b̄a's refutation of Ratnākarashānti's opinion in terms of its implications for the Naturelessness School serves as a transition to the following sections on the Naturelessness School. It also calls his readers to apply the principles—that he has seen in basic Indian Mind-Only treatises—in critically examining any and all presentations of the Mind-Only School, whether these be Indian or Tibetan. The suggestion that critical analysis is paramount resonates with the statement in his prologue that the differentiation of what requires interpretation and what is definitive derives from reasoning.

PART FOUR:
CRITICAL EDITION IN TIBETAN SCRIPT

D̄zong-ka-b̄a L̄o-sang-drak-b̄a's

Treatise Differentiating Interpretable and Definitive Meanings: The Essence of Eloquence

Prologue and Section on the Mind-Only School

Preface to Critical Edition

Editions Consulted

Ten editions were used; five were checked exhaustively:

1. "Delhi NG dkra shis lhun po": from the Collected Works of Rje Tsoṅ-kha-pa Blo-bzaṅ-grags-pa, vol. 21 *pha,* 478-714 (Delhi: Ngawang Gelek, 1975); photographic reprint, of the old *dkra shis lhun po* edition. At the end, after an identification of the scribe, *bsod nams blo gros,* it finishes with "*maṅgalaṃ*"
2. "Se rva zhol": 1988 printing at *se rva* Monastic University of the *zhol* blocks (for identification of the blocks, see number 6) from volume *pha* of the Collected Works; 114 folios. It is the same as number 6 except that the latter includes both corrections and flawed attempts at correction. At the end, after an identification of the scribe, *bsod nams blo gros,* it finishes with a prayer that begins with "*svasti*" and ends with "*maṅgalaṃ*"; it frequently employs contractions, such as *gsungso* for *gsungs so*
3. "Zi ling sku 'bum": from *rje tsong kha pa chen po'i gsung 'bum, pha,* 337-526 (Zi ling: mtsho sngon mi rigs dpe skrun khang, 1987); codex fixed-type rendering of the "*sku 'bum byams pa gling*" edition, 337-526. At the end, after an identification of the scribe, *bsod nams blo gros,* and finishing with "*maṅgalaṃ,*" there is an additional colophon that begins with "*svasti*" and identifies the place of publication. It has more *shad* than other editions and creatively uses *shad* to alert the reader to meaning breaks. It is likely that most of its many variations are due to the editors of this edition
4. "Sarnath gtsang": on the cover in roman letters is *Dan-ne-leg-shed nying-po* (Sarnath, India: Pleasure of Elegant Sayings Press, 1973); codex fixed-type flawed rendering of a "*gtsang*" edition with corrections, 251 pages. At the end, after an identification of the scribe, *bsod nams blo gros,* and "*maṅgalaṃ,*" there are an additional prayer by H.H. the Fourteenth Dalai Lama, which is different from that in number 9, and a further identification of sponsors of the publication
5. "Grags pa & rnam rgyal": on the title page is *drang nges legs bshad snying po: The Essence of Eloquent Speech on the Definitive and Interpretable* (Mundgod, India: SOKU, 1991); codex fixed-type critical edition by Geshe Palden Drakpa and Damdul Namgyal, 231 pp. The editors compared four editions—using as the basis the *zi ling mtsho sngon mi rigs dpe skrun khang* edition (1987) which is number 3 above, compared with the Peking edition (number 7 below); the *gtsang dkra shis lhun po* edition (perhaps number 1 above or an earlier version); and the *lha sa rtse zhol* edition (number 2 above but perhaps not printed at *se rva*). At the end, after an

identification of the scribe, *bsod nams blo gros,* it finishes with a prayer that begins with "*svasti*" and ends with "*maṅgalaṃ,*" followed by an additional prayer by H.H. the Fourteenth Dalai Lama and an additional colophon. Since it is based on the Zi ling sku 'bum edition, only instances where it differs from it will be cited

Two closely related editions were consulted:

6. "Delhi GD zhol": from The Collected Works (*gsuṅ 'bum*) of the Incomparable Lord Tsoṅ-kha-pa Blo-bzaṅ-grags-pa, vol. 14 *pha,* 443-669 (New Delhi: Guru Deva, 1979); photographic reprint, of the "1897 old zhol[a] (*dga'-ldan-phun-tshogs-gliṅ*) blocks." This is the same as number 2 above, except that this edition includes flawed attempts at correction. At the end, after an identification of the scribe, *bsod nams blo gros,* and giving the word "*maṅgalaṃ,*" the word "*svasti*" follows; there is a further stanza
7. "sku 'bum 1988": (Ch'ing-hai: sku 'bum Monastic University, 1988); printed from *sku 'bum* blocks of the beginning of the nineteenth century;[b] it is the basis of number 3 above; 124 folios. At the end, after an identification of the scribe, *bsod nams blo gros,* and finishing with "*maṅgalaṃ*" there is an additional colophon that begins with "*svasti*" and identifies the place of publication

[a] E. Gene Smith (personal correspondence) identifies the "old zhol":

The old Zhol Par-khang has the formal name Shar Dga'-ldan-phun-tshogs-gling. This was founded by the 5th Dalai Lama and was the chief printing house of Lhasa until the establishment of the new Zhol Par-khang printery, the Bka'-'gyur Par-khang, styled the Gangs-can-phan-bde'i-gter-mdzod-gling. This was founded during the reign of the 13th Dalai Lama for housing the blocks of the Lha-sa edition of the Bka'-'gyur. After the completion of this project, the Lhasa government initiated the carving of the printing blocks for a number of other important gsung 'bum including Bu-ston, A-khu-ching, Thu'u-bkwan, Gung-thang. The blocks from the Old Zhol printery were under the custody of the Potala authorities. Most seem to have been discarded and are being sold around the Bar-'khor as curios. The New Zhol blocks are under the custody of the TAR Archives and are well kept, for the most part. Regarding the name Shar Dga'-ldan-phun-tshogs-gling for the old Zhol printery, I think this is called Shar in contrast to the Nub Dga'-ldan-phun-tshogs-gling or the old Rtag-brtan-phun-tshogs-gling, the seat of Jo-nang Rje-btsun Tāranātha. This monastery boasted a great printing house with a number of works by the 5th Dalai Lama. Ngawang Gelek Demo published a 1957 survey of the printing houses of Central Tibet in his Three Catalogues. For the history of the Dga'-ldan-phun-tshogs-gling of the west (formerly Rtag-brtan-phun-tshogs-gling), see Champa Thupten Zongtse, *History of the Monastic University Dga'-ldan-phun-tshogs-gliṅ = Geschichte der Kloster-Universität dGa'-ldan-phun-tshogs-gliṅ = Dga' ldan phun tshogs gling gi thog mtha' bar gsum gyi byung ba yid la dran byed kun khyab snyan pa'i rnga sgra* (Göttingen: Im Selbstverlag des Verfassers, 1977).

[b] Many thanks to Leonard van der Kuijp for identifying the date of the carving.

Three other editions were consulted:

8. "Peking": Peking 6142, vol. 153, 168.5.8-209.3.4; volume *nga* of the Collected Works. At the end, after an identification of the scribe, *bsod nams blo gros,* there is a long additional colophon on the occasion of this new edition that identifies it as built on the *dga' ldan phun tshogs gling* edition; it ends with "*sarvamangalaṃ*" and identifies the place of publication
9. "Kalimpong": (Kalimpong, India: Kalsum Laksey, 1968?); fixed-type small Tibetan-style book; 142 folios, on green paper. At the end, after an identification of the scribe, *bsod nams blo gros,* there is an additional prayer by H.H. the Fourteenth Dalai Lama that is different from that in 9 and begins with "*oṃ svasti*" and ends with "*mangalaṃ*"
10. "rje'i gsung lta ba'i skor": from *rje tsong kha pa'i gsung dbu ma'i lta ba'i skor* (Sarnath, India: Pleasure of Elegant Sayings Press, 1975); codex fixed type edition, 262-458. It ends like number 3 above

I also compared portions of the text with citations in the follow works, which are fully cited in the bibliography:

B̄el-den-drak-b̄a's *gzhi gsum gyi dus tshigs la dpyod pa'i legs bśad luṅ rigs dga' tshal*
B̄el-jor-hlün-drup's *Lamp for the Teaching*
D̄a-drin-rap-d̄en's *Annotations*
Dön-drup-gyel-tsen's *Four Intertwined Commentaries*
Gung-ru Chö-jung's *Garland of White Lotuses*
Gung-tang Ḡön-chok-d̄en-b̄ay-drön-may's *Annotations* and *Difficult Points*
Jam-ȳang-shay-b̄a Nga-w̄ang-d̄zön-drü's *Great Exposition of the Interpretable and the Definitive*
Jik-may-dam-chö-gya-tso's *Port of Entry*
S̄er-s̄hül L̄o-sang-pün-tsok's *Notes*
Wonch'uk's *Commentary on the "Sūtra Unraveling the Thought"*

For citations from the *Sūtra Unraveling the Thought* I consulted Étienne Lamotte's critical edition and the *stog* Palace edition, which are also fully cited in the bibliography. For D̄zong-ka-ba's citations of Indian texts, comparisons were made with editions of the Sanskrit, as cited in the footnotes.

Page numbers of two major editions and one minor edition have been inserted into the text in small type as follows:

{2} = Delhi NG dkra shis lhun po
(2a) = Se rva zhol
[2] = Sarnath gtsang (included even though seriously flawed because of the availability of the edition among refugee scholars in India).

Process Of Editing

The editing of D̄zong-ka-b̄a's text involved the work of four graduate students in the University of Virginia Tibetan program:

1. In the summer of 1988, Steven Weinberger typed the entire Tibetan text of the Sarnath gtsang edition into my computer in Wylie transcription, using Microsoft Word. I converted it to Tibetan script via the program by Chet Wood.
2. John C. Powers compared both the Wylie transcription and the Tibetan script of the prologue, the Mind-Only section, and the Autonomy section to the Delhi NG dkra shis lhun po edition, since I had determined that this edition should be the basis because the Sarnath gtsang is an error-laden edition. My editorial decisions on these sections were entered by Nathanial Garson.
3. Nathanial Garson and Steven Weinberger each compared the text of the prologue and the Mind-Only section in hard copy to the Se rva zhol edition.
4. I did a computer spell-check on the Wylie transcription and then made editorial decisions by incorporating changes and making footnotes, based on the work done to date, also checking Ḏzong-ka-ḇa's quotations against the Peking and sometimes the *sde dge*.
5. Nathanial Garson checked the text of the prologue and the Mind-Only section against the Zi ling sku 'bum edition, after which I made editorial decisions.
6. Mark Seibold checked the text of the prologue and the Mind-Only section in hard copy against the Grags pa & rnam rgyal edition, after which I made editorial decisions.

This new critical edition incorporates several features:

- All quotations are indented for easy identification.
- The Sanskrit of quotations is provided, often comparing multiple editions.
- All unspecified references to headings of sections are identified and given in brackets.
- Corresponding page numbers of three editions are given, as indicated above.
- Titles of texts are marked by a broken underline.
- A separate table of contents is provided.
- Marginal line numbers are provided.
- Speculations on possible reasons for variations are given in hopes of provoking discussion.

Many thanks to Steven Weinberger, John C. Powers, Nathanial Garson, and Mark Seibold for their essential assistance in this project.

Table of Contents for Critical Edition: Tibetan Style

There are two tables of contents for the Tibetan text, one here and one at the end of the book. The detailed contents at the end of the book give all subsections in the order in which they appear, whereas the table here gives all subsections together with the larger section to which they belong. This one partially mimics the way a traditional Tibetan table of contents reads.

Using this type of table, a student would memorize and recite all of the sections in large type (except for the first two entries, which have been added for convenience). The entries in small type have no subsections and, as mentioned above, are all included in a larger section. The small-type entries would not be given in a strict traditional format but are added here for convenience in locating the page numbers of these subsections.

The Tibetan Text

ཙོང་ཁ་པ་བློ་བཟང་གྲགས་པས་མཛད་པའི་

ལེགས་བཤད་སྙིང་པོ།།

སྤྱི་བཤད་དང་སེམས་ཙམ་པའི་སྐབས།།

དྲང་བ་དང་ངེས་པའི་དོན་རྣམ་པར་ཕྱེ་བའི་བསྟན་བཅོས་ལེགས་བཤད་སྙིང་པོ་བཞུགས་སོ།།[a]

ན་མོ་གུ་རུ་མཉྫུ་གྷོ་ཥ་ཡ། [65] (251)

བདེ་འབྱུང་སྤྲིན་ལ་ཞོན་དང་གསེར་གྱི་མདངས།།
ལུས་མེད་བདག་པོ་ཐ་གུའི་ལྡོ་ལ་སོགས།།
སྲིད་ན་དྲེགས་པའི་ང་རོ་ཆེར་སྒྲོགས[b]་པའི།།
ཀློམ་པས་འགྱིང་རྣམས་ཀྱིས་ཀྱང་གང་གི་སྐུ།།

མཐོང་བའི་མོད་ལ་ཉེ་མས་མི་ཁྱེར་བཞིན།།
མཛད་པར་གྱུར་ཆེ་མཛེས་པའི་ཙོད་པན་གྱིས།།
གང་གི་ཞབས་པད་གུས་པས་སྟེན་བྱེད་པ།།

---

[a] Delhi NG dkra shis lhun po (478.1) and Peking (168.4.8): *bzhugs;* Se rva zhol (title page): *bzhugso* (with *bzhugs* and *so* elided); Zi ling sku 'bum (337.3) and Kalimpong (title page): *bzhugs so.*

[b] Zi ling sku 'bum (339.2): *sgrog.*

ཐུབ་དབང་ལྷ་ཡི་ལྷ་ལ་ཕྱག་འཚལ་ལོ།།

མཁྱེན་བརྩེའི་གཏེར་མཐའ་ཤིན་ཏུ་དཔག་པར་དཀའ།།
བྱང་ཆུབ་སྤྱོད་པའི་རླབས་ཆེན་ཆལ་ཆིལ་གཡོ།།
ལེགས་བཤད་རིན་ཆེན་གཏེར་གྱུར་འཇམ་པའི་དབྱངས།།
རྒྱལ་ཚབ་རྒྱ་མཚོ་ཆེ་ལ་གུས་ཕྱག་འཚལ།།

བདེར་གཤེགས་གསུང་རབ་ཚུལ་གཉིས་ཤིང་རྟའི་སྲོལ།།
ལེགས་པར་ཕྱེ་བས་རྒྱལ་བའི་བསྟན་པ་མཆོག།
ས་གསུམ་འགྲོ་ན་ཉི་ལྟར་གསལ་མཛད་པ།། {480}
ཀླུ་སྒྲུབ་ཐོགས་མེད་ཞབས་ལ་སྤྱི་བོས་འདུད།།

ཤིང་རྟ་ཆེན་པོའི་སྲོལ་གཉིས་ལེགས་བཟུང་ནས།།
འཛམ་གླིང་བློ་གསལ་བྱེ་བའི་མིག་འབྱེད་པ།།
འཕགས་པ་ལྷ་དང་དཔའ་བོ་སངས་རྒྱས་བསྐྱངས།།
ལེགས་ལྡན་འབྱེད་དང་ཟླ་བ་གྲགས་པའི་ཞབས།།

དབྱིག་གཉེན་ཞབས་དང་བློ་བརྟན་ཕྱོགས་གླང་དང་།།
ཆོས་ཀྱི་གྲགས་པའི་ཞབས་སོགས་འཛམ་གླིང་རྒྱན།།
ཐུབ་བསྟན་མི་ནུབ་རྒྱལ་མཚན་འཛིན་པའི་མཆོག།
མཁས་པའི་དབང་པོ་རྣམས་ལ་གུས་པས་འདུད།།

གཞུང་ལུགས་མང་ཐོས་རིགས་ (2a) པའི་ལམ་དུའང་[a]།། [68] (251)
ངལ་བ་མང་[b] [2] བསྟེན་མངོན་པར་རྟོགས་པ་ཡི།།
ཡོན་ཏན་ཚོགས་ཀྱིས་མི་དམན་དུ་མས་ཀྱང་།།

---

a Zi ling sku 'bum (339.15): *du yang.*

b Delhi NG dkra shis lhun po (480.3) and Peking (168.5.6): *ngal ba med;* Se rva zhol (2a.1), Zi ling sku 'bum (339.15), Sarnath gtsang (1.20), and Kalimpong (3.6): *ngal ba mang.* Gung-tang's *Difficult Points* (18.9) reports that "another" edition reads "without weariness" (*ngal ba med*) rather than "with much weariness" (*ngal ba mang*) but that the meaning is similar. His point must be that both indicate that these scholars worked very hard at the task. Indeed, both readings are feasible; I have chosen the one more frequently cited in the commentaries.

འབད་ཀྱང་རྟོགས་པར་མ་གྱུར་གནས་དེ་ནི།།
འཇམ་མགོན་བླ་མའི་དྲིན་གྱིས་ཞིབ་མཐོང་ནས།།
ཤིན་ཏུ་བརྩེ་བའི་བསམ་པས་བདག་གིས་བཤད།།
བསྟན་པའི་དེ་ཉིད་རྟོགས་པའི་རྣམ་དཔྱོད་ཀྱིས།།
སྨྲ་བ་ཟླ་མེད་འདོད་རྣམས་གུས་པས་ཉོན།།

ཇི་སྐད་དུ་འཕགས་པ་ཡུལ་འཁོར་སྐྱོང་གིས་ཞུས་པ་ལས།[a] [68] (251)

སྟོང་པ་ཞི་བ་སྐྱེ་བ་མེད་པའི་ཚུལ།།
མི་ཤེས་པས་ནི་འགྲོ་བ་ཁྱམས་གྱུར་པ།།
དེ་དག་ཐུགས་རྗེ་ {481} མངའ་བས་ཐབས་ཚུལ་དང་།།
རིགས་པ་བརྒྱ་དག་གིས་ནི་འཇུད་པར་མཛད།།

ཅེས་ཆོས་རྣམས་ཀྱི་དེ་བཞིན་ཉིད་ནི་ཤིན་ཏུ་རྟོགས་པར་དཀའ་བ་དང་། མ་རྟོགས་ན་འཁོར་བ་ལས་མི་གྲོལ་བར་གཟིགས་ནས་ཐུགས་རྗེ་ཅན་གྱི་སྟོན་པས་ཐབས་ཀྱི་ཚུལ་དང་རིགས་པའི་སྒོ་དུ་མ་ཞིག་གིས་དེ་ཁོང་དུ་ཆུད་པ་ལ་འཇུད་པར་གསུངས་སོ།། དེའི་ཕྱིར་རྣམ་དཔྱོད་དང་ལྡན་པ་དག་གིས་དེ་ཉིད་ཇི་ལྟར་ཡིན་ཁོང་དུ་ཆུད་པའི་ཐབས་ལ་འབད་

---

[a] Gung-tang (*Difficult Points,* 28.14) reports that this citation is not found in a small sūtra by the same name (Peking 833, vol. 33) but is found in the eighteenth chapter of the *Pile of Jewels Sūtra* (*'phags pa yul 'khor skyong gis zhus pa zhes bya ba theg pa chen po'i mdo, āryarāṣṭrapālaparipṛcchānāmamahāyānasūtra;* Peking 760, vol. 23, chap. 17). Gung-tang (28.15) also cites a different edition of the sūtra, which varies slightly due to a difference in translation:

stong pa zhi ba skye ba med pa'i tshul//
mi shes pas ni 'gro ba 'khyams gyur te//
thugs rje'i thabs tshul rigs pa brgya dag gis//
de dag rnams ni 'dzud par mdzad pa lags//

(In the last line of the Sarnath Guru Deva edition of Gung-tang's text, 28.18, read *mdzad* for *dzad* in accordance with the Hla-s̄a Go-mang edition, 13a.4.)

The Sanskrit is found in P. L. Vaidya, *Mahāyānasūtrasaṃgraha,* Buddhist Sanskrit Texts, 17 (Dharbanga, India: Mithila Institue, 1961), vol. 1, 154 (II. 310):

śūnyāśca śānta anutpādanaya avijānādeva jagadudbhramati/
teṣāmupāyanayayuktiśatairavatārayasyapi kṛpālutayā//

This version accords with that cited by D̄zong-ka-b̄a, which has the instrumental *thugs rje mnga' bas* for *kṛpālutayā.*

དགོས་ལ་དེ་ཡང་རྒྱལ་བའི་གསུང་རབ་ཀྱི་དྲང་བ་དང་ངེས་པའི་དོན་རྣམ་པར་ཕྱེད་པ་ལ་རག་ལས་ཤིང་། དེ་གཉིས་རྣམ་པར་འབྱེད་པ་ཡང་འདི་ནི་དྲང་བའི་དོན་ནོ་འདི་ནི་ངེས་པའི་དོན་ནོ་ཞེས་གསུངས་པའི་ལུང་ཙམ་གྱིས་ནུས་པ་མ་ (2b) ཡིན་ཏེ། གཞན་དུ་ན་ཤིང་རྟ་ཆེན་པོ་དག་གིས་དྲང་ངེས་འབྱེད་པའི་དགོངས་འགྲེལ་བརྩམས་པ་དོན་མེད་པར་འགྱུར་བའི་ཕྱིར་དང་། གསུང་རབ་ལས་དྲང་ངེས་ཀྱི་ [3] འཇོག་ཚུལ་མི་མཐུན་པ་དུ་མ་གསུངས་པའི་ཕྱིར་དང་། འདི་ནི་འདིའོ་ཞེས་གསུངས་པ་ཙམ་གྱི་ལུང་གིས་དེ་ལྟར་གཞག་པར་ནི་མི་ནུས་ལ་དེའི་ཚེ་སྤྱི་ལ་དེ་ལྟར་མ་ཁྱབ་པ་ན་བྱེ་བྲག་དྲང་ངེས་ལ་ཡང་འདི་འདིའོ་ཞེས་གསུངས་པ་ཙམ་གྱིས་ཀྱང་སྒྲུབ་པར་མི་ནུས་པའི་ཕྱིར་རོ།། དེའི་ཕྱིར་གསུང་རབ་ཀྱི་དྲང་ངེས་འབྱེད་པར་ལུང་བསྟན་པའི་ཤིང་རྟ་ཆེན་པོ་དག་གིས་དྲང་ངེས་ཀྱི་དགོངས་པ་བཀྲལ་ཞིང་དེ་ཡང་ངེས་དོན་གྱི་གསུང་རབ་ཀྱི་དོན་གཞན་དུ་འདྲེན་པ་ལ་གནོད་བྱེད་དང་། གཞན་དུ་དྲང་དུ་མི་རུང་བར་དོན་དེར་ངེས་པའི་སྒྲུབ་བྱེད་ཀྱི་རིགས་པས་ལེགས་པར་གཏན་ལ་ཕབ་པ་ཞིག་གི་རྗེས་སུ་འབྲངས་ནས་དགོངས་པ་འཚོལ་དགོས་པས་མཐར་གཏུགས་ན་དྲི་མ་མེད་ {482} པའི་རིགས་པ་ཉིད་ཀྱིས་དབྱེ་དགོས་ཏེ། རིགས་པ་དང་འགལ་བའི་གྲུབ་མཐའ་ཁས་ལེན་ན་སྨྲ་བ་པོ་ཚད་མའི་སྐྱེས་བུར་མི་རུང་བའི་ཕྱིར་དང་། དངོས་པོའི་དེ་ཁོ་ན་ཉིད་ཀྱང་འཐད་པས་སྒྲུབ་པའི་རིགས་པའི་སྒྲུབ་བྱེད་དང་ལྡན་པའི་ཕྱིར་རོ།། དོན་གྱི་དབང་འདི་གཟིགས་ནས།

དགེ་སློང་དག་གམ་མཁས་རྣམས་ཀྱིས།།
བསྲེགས་བཅད་བརྡར་བའི་གསེར་བཞིན་དུ།།
ལེགས་པར་བརྟགས་ལ་ང་ཡི་བཀའ།།
བླང་བར་བྱ་ཡི་གུས་ཕྱིར་མིན།།[a]

---

[a] Gung-tang's *Difficult Points* (29.1/13a.5) identifies this version of the stanza as being like that found in the translation of Kalkī Puṇḍarīka's (*rigs ldan pad ma dkar po*) *Great Commentary on the "Kālachakra Tantra," the Stainless Light* (*bsdus pa'i rgyud kyi rgyal po dus kyi 'khor lo'i 'grel bshad rtsa ba'i rgyud kyi rjes su 'jug pa stong phrag bcu gnyis pa dri ma med pa'i 'od ces bya ba, vimālaprabhānāmamūlatantrānusāriṇīdvādaśasāhasrikālaghukālacakratantrarājaṭīkā*) by the Translator of Ra, Dor-jay-drak-b̄a (*rwa lo tsā ba rdo rje grags pa*). He also gives the version of the same text by the Translator of Dro, S̄hay-rap-drak (*'bro lo tsā ba shes rab grags*):

bsregs bcad brdar ba'i gser bzhin du//
mkhas pa rnams kyis yongs brtags nas//

ཞེས་གསུངས་སོ།།

དེ་ལྟར་ན་དྲང་ངེས་འབྱེད་པ་ལ་གཉིས། མདོ་སྡེ་དགོངས་འགྲེལ་ལ་བརྟེན་པའི་ཕྱོགས་དང་། བློ་གྲོས་མི་ཟད་པས་བསྟན་པ་ལ་བརྟེན་པའི་ཕྱོགས་སོ།། [73] (255)

---

bdag gsung blang bya dge slong dag//
gus pa'i phyir ni ma yin no//
Like gold that is [acquired] upon being scorched, cut, and rubbed,
My speech is to be adopted by scholars
Upon analyzing it thoroughly,
Not, O monastics, out of respect [for me].

Gung-tang also gives another, unidentified version:

bsregs bcad brdar ba'i gser bzhin du//
legs par brtags la nga yi bka'//
mkhas pa dag gis blang bya yi//
dge slong dag gis gus phyir min//

Like gold that is [acquired upon being] scorched, cut, and rubbed,
My word is to be adopted by scholars
Upon analyzing it well,
Not by monastics out of respect [for me].

The stanza is cited in Shāntarakṣhita's *Compendium of Principles* (*de kho na nyid bsdus pa'i tshig le'ur byas pa, tattvasaṃgrahakārikā*), XXVI.3343 and 3587. The Sanskrit is found in Dwarikadas Shastri, *Tattvasaṅgraha of Ācārya Shāntarakšita, with the Commentary "Pañjikā" of Shri Kamalashīla* (Varanasi, India: Bauddha Bharati, 1968), vol. 2, 1115:

tāpācchedācca nikaṣāt suvarṇam iva paṇḍitaiḥ/
parīkṣya bhikṣavo grāhyaṃ mad vaco na tu gauravāt//

This version accords with that by the Translator of Dro, Shay-rap-drak, which has *dge slong dag* (*bhikṣavo*) in the vocative. For a translation into English, see G. Jha, *The Tattvasaṃgraha of Śāntirakṣita, with the Commentary of Kamalaśīla*, Gaekwad's Oriental Series, 80 and 83 (Baroda, India: Oriental Institute, 1937-1039), XXVI.3344 (p. 1485) and XXVI.3588 (p. 1558). The first citation occurs at the point of discussing the word of Buddha and how it is not annulled by direct perception, inference, and scriptural inference; the second citation occurs at the point of discussing identifying Buddha's "lion's roar" that brings about "the lowering of the arrogance of the maddened elephants in the shape of the False Philosophers" (Jha, *Tattvasaṃgraha*, 1558).

དང་ [4] པོ་ [མདོ་སྡེ་དགོངས་འགྲེལ་ལ་བརྟེན་པའི་ཕྱོགས་]ལ་གཉིས། མདོ་སྡེ་ནས་ཇི་ལྟར་གསུངས་པ་དགོད་ (3a) པ་དང་། དེའི་དོན་ཇི་ལྟར་བཀྲལ་བའི་ཚུལ་ལོ།། [73] (255)

དང་པོ་ [མདོ་སྡེ་ནས་ཇི་ལྟར་གསུངས་པ་དགོད་པ་]ལ་བཞི། མདོ་སྡེ་ལ་འགལ་སྤོང་གི་དྲི་བ། འགལ་བ་དེ་སྤོང་བའི་ལན། ངོ་བོ་ཉིད་གསུམ་གྱི་ངོ་བོ་ངོས་གཟུང་བ། དེ་དག་གིས་གྲུབ་པའི་དོན་ཞུས་པའོ།། [73] (255)

དང་པོ་ [མདོ་སྡེ་ལ་འགལ་སྤོང་གི་དྲི་བ་]ནི་ [75] (257)
དགོངས་འགྲེལ་ལས།

> བཅོམ་ལྡན་འདས་ཀྱིས་རྣམ་གྲངས་དུ་མར་ཕུང་པོ་རྣམས་ཀྱི་རང་གི་མཚན་ཉིད་ཀྱང་བཀའ་སྩལ། སྐྱེ་བའི་མཚན་ཉིད་དང་། འཇིག་པའི་མཚན་ཉིད་དང་། སྤང་བ་དང་ཡོངས་སུ་ཤེས་པ་ཡང་བཀའ་སྩལ། ཕུང་པོ་རྣམས་ཀྱི་ཇི་ལྟ་བ་དེ་བཞིན་དུ་[a] སྐྱེ་མཆེད་རྣམས་དང་རྟེན་ཅིང་འབྲེལ་པར་[b] འབྱུང་བ་དང་ཟས་རྣམས་ཀྱི་བར་[c] ཡང་བཀའ་སྩལ། དེ་བཞིན་དུ་སྡུར་ནས་བདེན་པ་རྣམས་ཀྱི་རང་གི་

---

a Zi ling sku 'bum (341.10): *ji lta ba bzhin du.*

b Zi ling sku 'bum (341.11): *bar,* most likely to accommodate the rule that *ba* follows the suffixes *nga, 'a, ra, la,* and suffixless syllables; see, for instance, *The Important Points of the Rules for Affixing Letters: A Luminous Mirror* (*yi ge'i thob thang nyer mkho rab gsal me long*), Collected Works of A-Kya Yongs-'dzin, vol. 2 (New Delhi: Lama Guru Deva, 1971), 444. On the surface this would seem to contradict the rule that *'brel* has a non-manifest extra suffix *da* that calls for *pa;* however, the presence of a non-manifest extra suffix *da* is often disregarded.

c The syllable *bar* (*zas rnams kyi* ***bar***) does not indicate that anything is deleted in Dzong-ka-ba's paraphrase of the sūtra; it indicates only the range of the list, as can be seen in the sūtra itself (for example, Dön-drup-gyel-tsen's *Four Intertwined Commentaries,* 4.5). Dzong-ka-ba uses the term *bar* at the end of this list; the term usually indicates an ellipsis, but here the entire list is given, and thus Jik-may-dam-chö-gya-tso cogently (*Port of Entry,* 140.6) speculates that it might serve as a *tha tshig* (which he likely is taking to be *tha ma'i tshig*), the meaning of which would be "delimiter," that is to say, indicating the end of a list. The term *tha tshig* often means "synonym" or "equivalent," but that would not make any sense here.

Lamotte (*Saṃdhinirmocanasūtra: L'Explication des mystères* [Louvain: Université de Louvain, 1935], 66 [1, line 9]) mistakenly reads *zas rnams* ***kyis yang,*** which is (1) euphonically impossible (since rules of euphony call for *kyang* after *kyis*), (2) inconsistent (since none

མཚན་ཉིད་དང་ཡོངས་སུ་ཤེས་པ་དང་སྤང་བ་དང་མངོན་དུ་བྱ་བ་དང་བསྒོམ་པ་དང་ཁམས་རྣམས་ཀྱི་རང་གི་མཚན་ཉིད་ {483} དང་ཁམས་སྣ་ཚོགས་པ་དང་ཁམས་དུ་མ་དང་སྤང་བ་དང་ཡོངས་སུ་ཤེས་པ་དང་། བྱང་ཕྱོགས་སོ་བདུན་གྱི་རང་གི་མཚན་ཉིད་དང་མི་མཐུན་པ་དང་གཉེན་པོ་[a]དང་མ་སྐྱེས་པ་སྐྱེ་བ་དང་སྐྱེས་པ་གནས་པ་དང་མི་བསྐྱུད་པ་དང་སླར་ཞིང་འབྱུང་བ་དང་འཕེལ་ཞིང་ཡངས་པ་ཉིད་ཀྱང་བཀའ་སྩལ་ལ། བཅོམ་ལྡན་འདས་ཀྱིས་ཆོས་ཐམས་ཅད་ངོ་བོ་ཉིད་མ་མཆིས་པ་ཆོས་ཐམས་ཅད་མ་སྐྱེས་པ་མ་འགགས་པ་གཟོད་མ་ནས་ཞི་བ་རང་བཞིན་གྱིས་ཡོངས་སུ་མྱ་ངན་ལས་འདས་པ་ཞེས་ཀྱང་བཀའ་སྩལ་ལགས་ན། བཅོམ་ [5] ལྡན་འདས་ཀྱིས་ཅི་ལ་[b]དགོངས་ནས་ཆོས་ཐམས་ཅད་ངོ་བོ་ཉིད་མ་མཆིས་པ་ཆོས་ཐམས་ཅད་མ་སྐྱེས་པ་མ་འགགས་པ་གཟོད་མ་ནས་ཞི་བ་རང་བཞིན་གྱིས་ཡོངས་སུ་མྱ་ངན་ལས་འདས་པ་ཞེས་བཀའ་སྩལ་སྙམ་བགྱིད་ལགས་ཏེ། བཅོམ་ལྡན་ (3b) འདས་ཀྱིས་ཅི་ལ་དགོངས་ནས་ཆོས་ཐམས་ཅད་ངོ་བོ་ཉིད་མ་མཆིས་པ་ཆོས་ཐམས་ཅད་མ་སྐྱེས་པ་མ་འགགས་པ་གཟོད་མ་ནས་ཞི་བ་རང་བཞིན་གྱིས་ཡོངས་སུ་མྱ་ངན་ལས་འདས་པ་ཞེས་[c]ཀྱང་བཀའ་སྩལ་བའི་དོན་དེ་ཉིད་བཅོམ་ལྡན་འདས་ལ་བདག་ཡོངས་སུ་ཞུ་ལགས་སོ།

of the other *bka' stsal* in the same section takes the instrumental), and (3) grammatically impossible (since the instrumental is not used for objects of verbs). Delhi NG dkra shis lhun po (482.6) and Sarnath gtsang (4.10) correctly read *zas rnams* ***kyi bar yang;*** the Karmapa *sde dge* edition of the sūtra (*mdo sde, ca,* 31.4) reads *zas rnams* ***kyi yang;*** and the *stog* Palace edition (*mdo sde, na,* 45.2), which represents a different translation, reads *zas rnams* ***dang.***

[a] In Lamotte (*Saṃdhinirmocana,* 66 [1, lines 17 and 26]), the *stog* Palace (45.5 and 46.1), and the Karmapa *sde dge* (31.6 and 32.1) of the sūtra, "meditation" (*bsgom pa dang*) is included in the list of attributes of the thirty-seven harmonies with enlightenment between "antidotes" and "production of that which has not been produced," whereas Dzong-ka-ba's text (for example, Delhi NG dkra shis lhun po, 483.1) and Dön-drup-gyel-tsen's text (5.1) omit this.

[b] Lamotte (*Saṃdhinirmocana,* 66 [1, line 32]) reads ***ji ltar*** *dgongs nas,* whereas the Karmapa *sde dge* (32.4) edition of the sūtra, the Delhi NG dkra shis lhun po (483.3), and Sarnath gtsang (5.1) more properly read ***ci la*** *dgongs nas;* the *stog* Palace sūtra gives a common variant of the latter, ***ci las*** *dgongs nas.*

[c] Lamotte (*Saṃdhinirmocana,* 193 [3], n. 2) gives the Sanskrit:

niḥsvabhāvāḥ sarvadharmā anutpannāḥ sarvadharmā aniruddhā ādiśāntāḥ prakṛtiparinirvṛtāḥ.

ཞེས་གསུངས་སོ།། འདིས་ནི་མདོ་སྡེ་ཁ་ཅིག་ཏུ་ཆོས་ཐམས་ཅད་ངོ་བོ་ཉིད་མེད་པ་སོགས་སུ་གསུངས་པ་དང་། ཁ་ཅིག་ཏུ་ཕུང་པོ་ལ་སོགས་པའི་རང་གི་མཚན་ཉིད་ལ་སོགས་པ་ཡོད་པར་གསུངས་པ་གཉིས་སྒྲ་སོར་བཞག་ན་འགལ་ནའང་འགལ་བ་མེད་དགོས་པས་ཅི་ལ་དགོངས་ནས་ངོ་བོ་ཉིད་མེད་པ་སོགས་སུ་གསུངས་ཞེས་དྲིས་ཏེ། དེས་ནི་རང་གི་མཚན་ཉིད་ཡོད་པ་སོགས་སུ་གསུངས་པ་ཡང་ཅི་ལ་དགོངས་ནས་གསུངས་པ་ {484} དོན་གྱིས་ཞུས་སོ།། [78] (259) འདིར་རང་གི་མཚན་ཉིད་ཅེས་པ་རྒྱ་ནག་གི་འགྲེལ་ཆེན་སོགས་ལས་ཐུན་མོང་མ་ཡིན་པའི་མཚན་ཉིད་ལ་བཤད་པ་ནི་རིགས་པ་མ་ཡིན་ཏེ། མདོ་ཉིད་ལས་ཀུན་བརྟགས་[a]ཀྱི་སྐབས་སུ་རང་གི་མཚན་ཉིད་ཀྱིས་གྲུབ་པ་ལ་གསལ་བར་གསུངས་པའི་ཕྱིར་དང་། ཀུན་བརྟགས་ལའང་ཐུན་མོང་མ་ཡིན་པའི་མཚོན་བྱེད་ཡོད་པས་མཚན་ཉིད་ངོ་བོ་ཉིད་མེད་པ་ཀུན་ [6] བརྟགས་ལ་བཤད་དུ་མི་རུང་བའི་སྐྱོན་དུ་འགྱུར་བའི་ཕྱིར་རོ།། ཁམས་སྣ་ཚོགས་པ་དང་དུ་མ་ལ་འགྲེལ་པ་རྣམས་ཀྱིས་གཞན་དུ་བཤད་ཀྱང་འོག་ནས་འབྱུང་བའི་མདོ་དང་སྦྱར་ན་ཁམས་བཅོ་བརྒྱད་དང་ཁམས་དྲུག་ལ་བྱའོ།། [81] (260) མི་བསྐྱུད་པ་ནི་མི་བརྗེད་པའོ།།

[a] Zi ling sku 'bum (342.13) have the common variant *btags,* here and throughout the text.

གཉིས་པ་ [འགལ་བ་དེ་སྤོང་བའི་ལན་] ལ་གཉིས། ངོ་བོ་ཉིད་མེད་ཚུལ་གང་ལ་དགོངས་ནས་ངོ་བོ་ཉིད་མེད་པར་གསུངས་པ་བཤད་པ་དང་། གང་ལ་དགོངས་ནས་མ་སྐྱེས་པ་སོགས་སུ་གསུངས་པ་བཤད་པའོ།། [82] (261)

དང་པོ་ [ངོ་བོ་ཉིད་མེད་ཚུལ་གང་ལ་དགོངས་ནས་ངོ་བོ་ཉིད་མེད་པར་གསུངས་པ་བཤད་པ་]ལ་གསུམ། མདོར་བསྟན་པ་དང་། རྒྱས་པར་བཤད་པ་དང་། དེ་དག་གི་དཔེ་བསྟན་པའོ།། [82] (261)

དང་པོ་ [མདོར་བསྟན་པ་] ནི། [82] (261)
དགོངས་འགྲེལ་ལས།

> དོན་དམ་ཡང་དག་འཕགས། ངས་ཆོས་རྣམས་ཀྱི་ངོ་བོ་ཉིད་མེད་པ་ཉིད་རྣམ་པ་གསུམ་པོ་འདི་ལྟ་སྟེ། མཚན་ཉིད་ངོ་བོ་ཉིད་མེད་པ་ཉིད་དང་སྐྱེ་བ་ངོ་བོ་ཉིད་མེད་པ་ཉིད་དང་དོན་དམ་པ་ངོ་བོ་ཉིད་མེད་པ་ཉིད་ལ་དགོངས་ནས་ཆོས་ཐམས་ཅད་ངོ་བོ་ཉིད་མེད་པའོ།། ཞེས་བསྟན་ཏོ་

ཞེས་ངོ་བོ་ཉིད་མེད་པ་གསུམ་ག་ལ་དགོངས་ནས་ངོ་བོ་ཉིད་མེད་པར་གསུངས་སོ།། བསྡུ་བ་ལས་ཀྱང་།

> བཅོམ་ལྡན་འདས་ཀྱིས་ཅི་ལ་[a] དགོངས་ནས་ཆོས་ཐམས་ཅད་ངོ་བོ་ཉིད་མེད་པ་ཞེས་གསུངས་ཤེ་ན། {485}སྨྲས་པ་འདུལ་བའི་དབང་གིས་དེ་དང་དེ་ར་ངོ་བོ་ཉིད་མེད་པ་ཉིད་རྣམ་པ་གསུམ་ལ་དགོངས་ནས་གསུངས་ཏེ་

ཞེས་གསུངས་ཤིང་། སུམ་ཅུ་པ་ལས་ཀྱང་།[b]

---

[a] *rnam par gtan la dbab pa bsdu ba, viniścayasaṃgrahaṇī;* Peking 5539, vol. 111, 71.2.8; Tokyo *sde dge, sems tsam,* vol. 9 (*zi*), 8.4.5. In a typical variant reading, both of these editions read *ci* ***las*** *dgongs* for *ci* ***la*** *dgongs.* Lamotte similarly uses both readings: for instance, ***la*** *dgongs* (*Saṃdhinirmocana,* 66 [1, four lines from the end of the section]) but ***las*** *dgongs* (*Saṃdhinirmocana,* 67 [3, line 4]).

[b] *sum cu pa'i tshig le'ur byas pa, triṃśikākārikā;* Peking 5556, vol. 113, 233.3.3; stanza 23. Wonch'uk cites the same passage (*Extensive Commentary,* Peking 5517, vol. 116, 130.4.8). The Sanskrit from Sylvain Lévi, *Vijñaptimātratāsiddhi / Deux traités de Vasubandhu: Viṃśatikā (La Vingtaine) et Triṃsikā (La Trentaine),* Bibliothèque de l'École des Hautes Études, 245 (Paris: Libraire Ancienne Honoré Champion, 1925), 14, is:

ངོ་བོ་ཉིད་ནི་རྣམ་གསུམ་གྱི།།
ངོ་བོ་ཉིད་མེད་རྣམ་གསུམ་ལ།།
དགོངས་ [7] ནས་ཆོས་རྣམས་ཐམས་ཅད་ནི།།
ངོ་བོ་ཉིད་མེད་བསྟན་པ་ཡིན།།

ཞེས་གསུངས་པས་ [83] (262) གང་དག་ཤེར་ཕྱིན་ལ་སོགས་པའི་མདོ་རྣམས་ལས་ཆོས་ཐམས་ཅད་ངོ་བོ་ཉིད་མེད་པར་གསུངས་པ་ཀུན་རྫོབ་ཀྱི་ཆོས་ཐམས་ཅད་ལ་དགོངས་ཀྱི་དོན་དམ་པ་ལ་དགོངས་པ་མིན་ནོ་ཞེས་འཆད་པ་ནི་དགོངས་འགྲེལ་དང་ཐོགས་མེད་སྐུ་མཆེད་ཀྱི་གཞུང་དང་འགལ་ཞིང་འཕགས་པ་ཡབ་སྲས་ལ་སོགས་པའི་ལུགས་ལས་ཀྱང་ཕྱི་རོལ་ཏུ་གྱུར་པའོ།། འདི་ལྟར་ཅི་ལ་དགོངས་ནས་ངོ་བོ་ཉིད་མེད་པར་གསུངས་པ་དྲིས་པ་ནི་ཅི་ལ་བསམས་ནས་ངོ་བོ་ཉིད་མེད་པར་བསྟན་པ་དང་ངོ་བོ་ཉིད་མེད་ཚུལ་དྲིས་པ་ཡིན་ལ་ལན་གྱིས་ཀྱང་དེ་གཉིས་ (4b) རིམ་པ་བཞིན་སྟོན་པ་ལས་དང་པོ་འཆད་པ་ནི། གཟུགས་ནས་རྣམ་མཁྱེན་གྱི་བར་གྱི་ཆོས་རྣམས་ཀྱི་གསལ་བའི་དབྱེ་བ་མཐའ་ཡས་པ་ལ་ངོ་བོ་ཉིད་དམ་རང་བཞིན་མེད་དོ་ཞེས་གསུངས་པ་རྣམས་ངོ་བོ་ཉིད་མེད་པ་གསུམ་དུ་འདུ་ཞིང་དེའི་ངོ་བོ་ཉིད་མེད་ཚུལ་བཤད་ན་གོ་སླ་བར་དགོངས་ནས་ངོ་བོ་ཉིད་མེད་པ[a] གསུམ་དུ་བསྡུས་ཏེ། དོན་དམ་པ་དང་ཀུན་རྫོབ་པའི་ཆོས་ཐམས་ཅད་དེ་གསུམ་གྱིས་བསྡུས་སོ།། དེ་ལྟར་མཛད་དགོས་པ་ཡང་ཡུམ་གྱི་མདོ་ལ་སོགས་པར་ཕུང་པོ་ལྔ་ཁམས་བཅོ་བརྒྱད་སྐྱེ་མཆེད་བཅུ་གཉིས་ཀྱི་ཆོས་ཐམས་ཅད་ལ་རེ་རེ་ནས་དངོས་པོ་མེད་པ་དང་རང་བཞིན་མེད་པ་དང་ངོ་བོ་ཉིད་མེད་ {486} པར་གསུངས་ཤིང་། ཁྱད་པར་དུ་སྟོང་པ་ཉིད་དང་ཆོས་ཀྱི་དབྱིངས་དང་དེ་བཞིན་ཉིད་ལ་ [8] སོགས་པ་དོན་དམ་པའི་རྣམ་གྲངས་ཐམས་ཅད་སྨོས་ནས་

---

trividhasya svabhāvasya trividhāṃ niḥsvabhāvatām /
saṃdhāya sarvadharmāṇāṃ deśitā niḥsvabhāvatā //

See also K. N. Chatterjee, *Vijñapti-Mātratā-Siddhi (with Sthiramati's Commentary)* (Varanasi, India; Kishor Vidya Niketan, 1980), 122; Thomas E. Wood, *Mind-Only: A Philosophical and Doctrinal Analysis of the Vijñānavāda,* Monographs of the Society for Asian and Comparative Philosophy, 9 (Honolulu: University of Hawaii Press, 1991), 54; and Enga Teramoto, *Sthiramati's Triṃçikābhāṣyaṃ (Sum-cu-paḥi ḥGrel-pa): A Tibetan Text* (Kyoto: Association for Linguistic Study of Sacred Scriptures, 1933), 79.14.

[a] Delhi NG dkra shis lhun po (485.5), Se rva zhol (4b.2), Peking (169.5.2), Sarnath gtsang (7.15), and Kalimpong (10.5): *ngo bo med pa.* Zi ling sku 'bum (344.1) and sku 'bum 1988 more cogently read: *ngo bo* ***nyid*** *med pa.*

དེ་དག་ལ་ངོ་བོ་ཉིད་མེད་པར་གསུངས་པས་མདོ་སྡེ་དེ་དག་ལས་ཆོས་རྣམས་ངོ་བོ་ཉིད་མེད་པར་གསུངས་པའི་ཆོས་ཀྱི་ནང་ན་དོན་དམ་མེད་དོ་ཞེས་སེམས་དང་ལྡན་པ་སུ་ཞིག་སྨྲ།

གཉིས་པ་ [རྒྱས་པར་བཤད་པ་] ནི། [85] (263)

གལ་ཏེ་ངོ་བོ་ཉིད་མེད་པར་གསུངས་པའི་ཆོས་རྣམས་ངོ་བོ་ཉིད་མེད་པ་གསུམ་དུ་སྡུད་ན་དེ་གསུམ་གང་ཡིན་ངོ་བོ་ཉིད་མེད་ཚུལ་ཇི་ལྟར་ཡིན་སྙམ་ན་ངོ་བོ་ཉིད་མེད་པ་དང་པོ་བཤད་པ་ནི་དགོངས་འགྲེལ་ལས།

> དེ་ལ་ཆོས་རྣམས་ཀྱི་མཚན་ཉིད་ངོ་བོ་ཉིད་མེད་པ་ཉིད་གང་ཞེ་ན། ཀུན་བརྟགས་པའི་མཚན་ཉིད་གང་ཡིན་པའོ།། དེ་ཅིའི་ཕྱིར་ཞེ་ན། འདི་ལྟར་དེ་ནི་མིང་དང་བརྡས་རྣམ་པར་བཞག་པའི་མཚན་ཉིད་ཡིན་གྱི[a] རང་གི་མཚན་ཉིད་ཀྱིས་རྣམ་པར་གནས་པ་ནི་མ་ཡིན་པས་དེའི་ཕྱིར་དེ་ནི་མཚན་ཉིད་ངོ་བོ་ཉིད་མེད་པ་ཉིད་ཅེས་བྱའོ་

ཞེས་གསུངས་ཏེ། ཚིག་དང་པོ་གཉིས་ཀྱི་དྲིས་ལན་གྱིས་ཀུན་བརྟགས་མཚན་ (5a) ཉིད་ངོ་བོ་ཉིད་མེད་པར་བཤད་ནས། དེ་ཅིའི་ཕྱིར་ཞེ་ན་ཞེས་པས་དེའི་རྒྱུ་མཚན་དྲིས་པའི་ལན་དུ་དགག་ཕྱོགས་ནས་རང་གི་མཚན་ཉིད་ཀྱིས་མ་གྲུབ་པ་དང་སྒྲུབ་ཕྱོགས་ནས་མིང་དང་བརྡས་བཞག་པ་ཡིན་པའི་རྒྱུ་མཚན་གསུངས་སོ།། མདོ་ཡི་དམིགས་འབྱེད་པ་འདིས་འོག་མ་གཉིས་ཀྱང་ཤེས་པར་བྱའོ།། ཀུན་བརྟགས་ལ་མེད་རྒྱུའི་མཚན་ཉིད་ཀྱི་ངོ་བོ་ཉིད་ནི་རང་གི་མཚན་ཉིད་ཀྱིས་གྲུབ་པའམ་གནས་པ་ལ་བྱའོ།། འདིར་རང་གི་མཚན་ཉིད་ཀྱིས་ཡོད་མེད་བསྟན་ཚོད་ [9] {487} ནི་མིང་དང་བརྡ་ལ་ལྟོས་ནས་བཞག་མ་བཞག་ཡིན་ལ། བཞག་པ་ལ་ཡང་ཡོད་པས་མ་ཁྱབ་ཅིང་འཇོག་ལུགས་ཀྱང་ཐལ་འགྱུར་བས[b] ཡོད་པ་རྣམས་མིང་གི་ཐ་

[a] Zi ling sku 'bum (344.13): *kyi;* the usage of *gyi* perhaps reflects an editor's not heeding the presence of a non-manifest extra suffix *da* at the end of the previous syllable, which calls for *kyi.*

[b] Zi ling sku 'bum (345.2): *pas;* the variation perhaps reflects an editor's seeking to hold to the rule that only *pa* is used for a possessor (*bdag sgra*) although later instances of editing *pa* to *ba* either throw such a suspicion into question or suggest two uncoordinated editors. Indeed, Ṡi-d̄u Chö-ḡyi-jung-ñay (*si tu chos kyi 'byung gnas,* 1700-1774) holds that only *pa* should be used to indicate a possessor and says that possessor words using *ba* "are only the vulgar language of villagers" (*grong pa'i skad phal pa tsam*); see *Explanation of (Tön-mi Sambhoṭa's) "The Thirty" and "Usage of Gender," a Treatise on the Thorough Application of the Language of the Snowy Country: Beautiful Pearl Necklace of the Wise* (*yul gangs can pa'i brda yang

སྐད་ཀྱི་དབང་གིས་བཞག་པ་དང་ཆེས་མི་མཐུན་པས་རང་གི་མཚན་ཉིད་ཀྱིས་ཡོད་མེད་ཀྱི་དོན་ཡང་མི་མཐུན་ནོ།། འོན་ཀྱང་འདིའི་རང་མཚན་གྱིས་ཡོད་པར་འཛིན་པ་ཡོད་ན་ཐལ་འགྱུར་བའི་[a] རང་མཚན་གྱིས་གྲུབ་པར་འཛིན་པ་ཡང་ཡོད་ལ་གཞི་འགའ་ཞིག་སྔ་མ་ལྟར་མི་འཛིན་ཀྱང་ཕྱི་མ་ལྟར་འཛིན་པ་ནི་ཡོད་དོ།། ངོ་བོ་ཉིད་མེད་པ་གཉིས་པ་ནི་ [87]

(264) དགོངས་འགྲེལ་ལས།

ཆོས་རྣམས་ཀྱི་སྐྱེ་བ་ངོ་བོ་ཉིད་མེད་པ་ཉིད་གང་ཞེ་ན། ཆོས་རྣམས་ཀྱི་གཞན་གྱི་དབང་གི་མཚན་ཉིད་གང་ཡིན་པའོ།། དེ་ཅིའི་ཕྱིར་ཞེ་ན། འདི་ལྟར་དེ་ནི་རྐྱེན་གཞན་གྱི་སྟོབས་ཀྱིས་བྱུང་བ་ཡིན་གྱི་བདག་ཉིད་ཀྱིས་མ་ཡིན་པས་དེའི་ཕྱིར་དེ་ནི་སྐྱེ་བ་ངོ་བོ་ཉིད་མེད་པ་ཉིད་ཅེས་བྱའོ་

ཞེས་གསུངས་སོ།། གཞན་དབང་ལ་མེད་རྒྱུའི་སྐྱེ་བའི་ངོ་བོའམ་ངོ་བོ་ཉིད་ཀྱིས་སྐྱེ་བ་ནི་བདག་ཉིད་ཀྱིས་མ་ཡིན་པས་ཞེས་གསུངས་པས་བདག་ཉིད་ཀྱིས་སྐྱེ་བའོ།། དེ་ནི་རང་དབང་གིས་སྐྱེ་བ་ཡིན་ཏེ། བསྡུ་བ་ལས།

འདུ་བྱེད་རྣམས་ནི་རྟེན་ཅིང་འབྲེལ་པར[b] (5b) འབྱུང་བ་ཡིན་པའི་ཕྱིར་རྐྱེན་གྱི་སྟོབས་ཀྱིས་སྐྱེ་བ་ཡིན་གྱི་རང་མི[c] སྐྱེ་བ་ནི་སྐྱེ་བ་ངོ་བོ་ཉིད་མེད་པ་ཉིད་ཅེས་བྱའོ།

---

dag par sbyor ba'i bstan bcos kyi bye brag sum cu pa dang rtags kyi 'jug pa'i gzhung gi rnam par bshad pa mkhas pa'i mgul rgyan mu tig phreng mdzes) (Dharmsala, India: Tibetan Cultural Printing Press, n.d.), 42.11).

[a] Zi ling sku 'bum (345.4): *pa'i;* see the previous footnote.

[b] Zi ling sku 'bum (345.12): *bar;* see p. 368, footnote b.

[c] Delhi NG dkra shis lhun po (487.5), Zi ling sku 'bum (345.13), Peking (170.1.8), and Sarnath gtsang (9.17) read *rang mi skye ba,* as do the Peking (5539, vol. 111, 71.3.2) and the Tokyo *sde dge* (*sems tsam,* vol. 9 [*zi*], 8.4.7) of Asaṅga's text. Se rva zhol (5b.1) and Kalimpong (13.2) read *rang gi skye ba.* Among the commentaries, Gung-ru Chö-jung's *Garland of White Lotuses* (30b.2), Jam-ȳang-shay-b̄a's *Great Exposition of the Interpretable and the Definitive* (70.2), Dön-drup-gyel-tsen's *Four Intertwined Commentaries* (53.4), Jik-may-dam-chö-gya-tso's *Port of Entry* (180.2), B̄el-jor-hlün-drup's *Lamp for the Teaching* (16.5), and S̄er-s̄hül's *Notes* (19a.1) read *rang mi skye ba,* whereas D̄a-drin-rap-d̄en's *Annotations* (17.3) reads *rang gi skye ba.* S̄er-s̄hül specifically indicates that *rang gi skye ba* in the "new edition" (*par sar*) is incorrect.

Ge-s̄hay B̄el-den-drak-b̄a (*dge bshes dpal ldan grags pa; gzhi gsum gyi dus tshigs la dpyod pa'i legs bśad luṅ rigs dga' tshal* [New Delhi: Tibet House, 1983], 198.10) prefers (albeit with considerable circumlocution and understatement which I understood only when he explained the point in person) the second reading (*rang gi skye ba*), since he holds that the *gi* was mistakenly amended to *mi* and is nonsensical. However, I would suggest that both are

ཞེས་གསུངས་པ་ལྟར་རོ།། གཞན་དབང་ལ་རང་བཞིན་གྱིས་སྐྱེ་བ་དེ་འདྲ་བའི་ངོ་བོ་ཉིད་མེད་པས་ངོ་བོ་ཉིད་མེད་པར་གསུངས་ཀྱི་རང་གི་མཚན་ཉིད་ཀྱིས་གྲུབ་པ་ [10] མེད་པས་ངོ་བོ་ཉིད་མེད་པར་གསུངས་པ་མིན་པའི་ལུགས་སོ།། [88] (264) ངོ་བོ་ཉིད་མེད་པ་གསུམ་པ་ལ་འཇོག་ཚུལ་ {488} གཉིས་ལས་གཞན་དབང་ལ་དོན་དམ་པ་ངོ་བོ་ཉིད་མེད་པར་བཞག་པ་ནི་དགོངས་འགྲེལ་ལས།

> ཆོས་རྣམས་ཀྱི་དོན་དམ་པ་ངོ་བོ་ཉིད་མེད་པ་གང་ཞེ་ན། རྟེན་ཅིང་འབྲེལ་པར[a] འབྱུང་བ་ཆོས་གང་དག་སྐྱེ་བ་ངོ་བོ་ཉིད་མེད་པ་ཉིད་ཀྱིས་ངོ་བོ་ཉིད་མེད་པ་དེ་དག་ནི་དོན་དམ་པ་ངོ་བོ་ཉིད་མེད་པ་ཉིད་ཀྱིས་ངོ་བོ་ཉིད་མེད་པ་ཡང་ཡིན་ནོ།། དེ་ཅིའི་ཕྱིར་ཞེ་ན། དོན་དམ་ཡང་དག་འཕགས། ཆོས་རྣམས་ལ་རྣམ་པར་དག་པའི་དམིགས་པ་གང་ཡིན་པ་དེ་ནི་དོན་དམ་པ་ཡིན་པར་ཡོངས་སུ་བསྟན་ལ། གཞན་གྱི་དབང་གི་མཚན་ཉིད་དེ་རྣམ་པར་དག་པའི་དམིགས་པ་མ་ཡིན་པས་དེའི་ཕྱིར་

---

readable, depending on what the last nominative governs. In the first reading, the last nominative governs everything before it:

> ***'du byed rnams ni rten cing 'brel par 'byung ba yin pa'i phyir rkyen gyi stobs kyis skye ba yin gyi rang mi skye ba*** *ni skye ba ngo bo nyid med pa nyid ces bya'o//*

In English, literally:

> That because compounded phenomena are dependent-arisings, they are produced through the power of conditions and are not self-produced is called "production-non-nature."

In the second reading the nominative is confined to the last clause:

> *'du byed rnams ni rten cing 'brel par 'byung ba yin pa'i phyir rkyen gyi stobs kyis skye ba yin gyi* ***rang gi skye ba*** *ni skye ba ngo bo nyid med pa nyid ces bya'o//*

In English, literally:

> Because compounded phenomena are dependent-arisings, they are produced through the power of conditions, and self-production is said to be a "production-non-nature."

The first reading strikes me as more readable and requires less strain. Also, the second (*rang gi*) would read better as *rang gis,* thereby paralleling the *bdag nyid* ***kyis*** of the sūtra.

In D̄zong-ka-b̄a's treatment of Maitreya's *Ornament for the Great Vehicle Sūtras* (see p. 419, footnote b), the very same phrase (*rang mi skye ba, rang gi skye ba*) occurs, with the same variant readings in the various editions. In that context, *rang mi skye ba* is clearly preferable, as explained in that footnote.

[a] Delhi NG dkra shis lhun po (488.1), Se rva zhol (5a.6), Peking (170.2.2), Sarnath gtsang (10.5), and Kalimpong (13.4): *par;* Zi ling sku 'bum (345.19): *bar;* see p. 368, footnote b.

དོན་དམ་པ་ངོ་བོ་ཉིད་མེད་པ་ཉིད་ཅེས་བྱའོ།

ཞེས་གསུངས་སོ།། གཞན་དབང་ནི་དོན་དམ་པའི་ངོ་བོ་ཉིད་དུ་མེད་པས་དོན་དམ་པ་ངོ་བོ་ཉིད་མེད་པ་ཞེས་བྱ་སྟེ། དོན་དམ་པ་ནི་གང་ལ་དམིགས་ནས་གོམས་ན་སྒྲིབ་པ་ཟད་པར་འགྱུར་བ་ཡིན་ན་གཞན་དབང་ལ་དམིགས་ནས་གོམས་པས་སྒྲིབ་པ་དག་པར་བྱེད་མི་ནུས་པའི་ཕྱིར་རོ།། འོ་ན་ཀུན་བརྟགས་ཀྱང་དོན་དམ་པ་ངོ་བོ་ཉིད་མེད་པར་ཅིའི་ཕྱིར་མི་གཞག་ཅེ་ན། རྣམ་པར་དག་པའི་དམིགས་པ་མ་ཡིན་པ་ཙམ་གྱིས་འཇོག་ན་བདེན་ཡང་ལོག་རྟོག་དགག་པ་ལ་ལྟོས་ནས་གཞན་དབང་རྣམ་པར་ (6a) དག་པའི་དམིགས་པ་མིན་པས་དོན་དམ་པ[a]ངོ་བོ་ཉིད་མེད་པར་བཞག་གི་ཀུན་བརྟགས་མ་བཞག་གོ།། [11] ཇི་ལྟར་ཞེ་ན། གཞན་དབང་ཀུན་བརྟགས་ཀྱིས་སྟོང་པ་ལ་དམིགས་ནས་བསྒོམས་པས་སྒྲིབ་པ་དག་པར་འགྱུར་བར་ཤེས་པ་ན། དེ་ལྟ་ན་ཆོས་ཅན་གཞན་དབང་ལ་ཡང་དམིགས་ {489} དགོས་པས་དེ་ཡང་རྣམ་པར་དག་པའི་དམིགས་པར་འགྱུར་བས་དོན་དམ་པར་འགྱུར་རོ་སྙམ་དུ་དོགས་པ་སྐྱེ་ལ་ཀུན་བརྟགས་ལ་དེ་འདྲ་བའི་དོགས་པ་མེད་པའི་ཕྱིར་རོ།། དོགས་པ་དེའི་སྐྱོན་ནི་མེད་དེ་སྒྲ་མི་རྟག་པར་ངེས་པས་སྒྲ་རྟག་འཛིན་ལྡོག་ཀྱང་སྒྲ་ལ་དམིགས་པས་རྟག་འཛིན་མི་ལྡོག་པ་མི་འགལ་བ་བཞིན་ནོ།། གཞན་དབང་རྣམ་པར་དག་པའི་དམིགས་པ་ལ་དོན་དམ་དུ་བྱས་པའི་དོན་དམ་དེ་ར་མ་གྲུབ་ཀྱང་དོན་དམ་གཞན་དུ་གྲུབ་མ་གྲུབ་ནི་འཆད་པར་འགྱུར་རོ།། དོན་དམ་པ་ངོ་བོ་ཉིད་མེད་པའི་འཇོག་ཚུལ་གཉིས་པ་ཡང་དགོངས་འགྲེལ་ལས། [90] (265)

གཞན་ཡང་ཆོས་རྣམས་ཀྱི་ཡོངས་སུ་གྲུབ་པའི་མཚན་ཉིད་གང་ཡིན་པ་དེ་ཡང་དོན་དམ་པ་ངོ་བོ་ཉིད་མེད་པ་ཉིད་ཅེས་བྱའོ།། དེ་ཅིའི་ཕྱིར་ཞེ་ན། དོན་དམ་ཡང་དག་འཕགས། ཆོས་རྣམས་ཀྱི་ཆོས་བདག་མེད་པ་གང་ཡིན་པ་དེ་ནི། དེ་དག་གི་ངོ་བོ་ཉིད་མེད་པ་ཉིད་ཅེས་བྱ་སྟེ་དེ་ནི་དོན་དམ་པ་ཡིན་ལ་དོན་དམ་པ་ནི་ཆོས་ཐམས་ཅད་ཀྱི་ངོ་བོ་ཉིད་མེད་པ་ཉིད་ཀྱིས་རབ་ཏུ་ཕྱེ་བ་ཡིན་པས་དེའི་ཕྱིར་དོན་དམ་པ་ངོ་བོ་ཉིད་མེད་པ་ཉིད་ཅེས་བྱའོ།

ཞེས་གསུངས་སོ།། ཆོས་རྣམས་ཀྱི་ཆོས་ཀྱི་བདག་མེད་ཡོངས་གྲུབ་ནི་རྣམ་པར་དག་པའི་

[a] Zi ling sku 'bum (346.10): *don dam pa;* Delhi NG dkra shis lhun po (488.5), Sarnath gtsang (10.19), Kalimpong (14.3), Se rva zhol (6a.1), and Peking (170.2.7) lack *pa.*

དམིགས་པ་ཡིན་པས་དོན་དམ་པ་ཡང་ཡིན་ [12] ལ། ཆོས་རྣམས་ཀྱི་བདག་གི་ངོ་བོ་ཉིད་མེད་པས་རབ་ (6b) ཏུ་ཕྱེ་བ་སྟེ་དེ་ཙམ་གྱིས་བཞག་པ་ཡིན་པའི་ཕྱིར་ཆོས་རྣམས་ཀྱི་ངོ་བོ་ཉིད་མེད་པ་ཞེས་ཀྱང་བྱ་བས་དོན་དམ་པ་ངོ་བོ་ཉིད་མེད་པ་ཞེས་བྱའོ།། ཡང་དགོངས་འགྲེལ་ལས། [91] (266)

གལ་ཏེ་འདུ་བྱེད་ཀྱི་མཚན་ཉིད་དང་དོན་དམ་པའི་མཚན་ཉིད་ཐ་དད་པ་ཡིན་པར་གྱུར་ན་ནི། {490} དེས་ན་འདུ་བྱེད་རྣམས་ཀྱི་བདག་མེད་པ་ཙམ་དང་ངོ་བོ་ཉིད་མེད་པ་ཙམ་ཉིད་དོན་དམ་པའི་མཚན་ཉིད་ཡིན་པར་ཡང་མི་འགྱུར།

ཞེས་གསུངས་ཤིང་། དཔེའི་སྐབས་སུ་ཡང་ནམ་མཁའ་གཟུགས་མེད་པ་ཙམ་ལ་འཇོག་པ་བཞིན་དུ་བདག་མེད་འཇོག་པར་གསུངས་པས། ཆོས་ཅན་འདུས་བྱས་ལ་ཆོས་ཀྱི་བདག་རྣམ་པར་བཅད་ཙམ་གྱི་སྤྲོས་པ་མེད་དགག་ལ་ཆོས་ཀྱི་བདག་མེད་ཀྱི་ཡོངས་གྲུབ་འཇོག་པར་ཤིན་ཏུ་གསལ་བའི་ཕྱིར། མདོ་འདིའི་[a] དེ་ཁོ་ན་ཉིད་ཀྱི་དོན་བསྟན་པ་ངེས་པའི་དོན་དུ་འདོད་བཞིན་དུ་འགྱུར་མེད་ཡོངས་གྲུབ་དགག་བྱ་བཅད་ཙམ་གྱི་བཅད་ལྡོག་ནས་མི་འཇོག་པར་བློའི་ཡུལ་དུ་འཆར་བ་དགག་བྱ་བཅད་པ་ལ་མི་ལྟོས་པར་སྣང་བ་རང་དབང་བ་ལ་འདོད་པ་ནི་འགལ་བའོ།། ཡོངས་གྲུབ་འདི་ནི་ཆོས་རྣམས་ཀྱི་བདག་གི་ངོ་བོ་རྣམ་པར་བཅད་པ་ཙམ་ཡིན་པས་ཆོས་རྣམས་ཀྱི་དོན་དམ་པ་ངོ་བོ་ཉིད་མེད་པ་ཞེས་གསུངས་ཀྱི་དགག་པའི་རང་གི་ངོ་བོ་ལ་རང་གི་མཚན་ཉིད་ཀྱིས་གྲུབ་པ་མེད་པས་ངོ་བོ་ཉིད་མེད་པར་མི་བཞེད་པའི་ལུགས་སོ།།

གསུམ་པ་ [དེ་དག་གི་དཔེ་བསྟན་པ་] ནི། [93] (266)
ངོ་བོ་ཉིད་མེད་པ་ [13] གསུམ་པོ་དེ་དཔེ་ཇི་ལྟར་འདྲ་བ་ནི་དགོངས་འགྲེལ་ལས།

དེ་ལ་འདི་ལྟ་སྟེ་དཔེར་ན་ནམ་མཁའི་མེ་ཏོག་ཇི་ལྟ་བ་དེ་ལྟ་བུར་ནི་མཚན་ཉིད་ངོ་བོ་ཉིད་མེད་པ་ཉིད་བལྟ་བར་བྱའོ།། དོན་དམ་ཡང་དག་འཕགས། དེ་ལ་འདི་ལྟ་སྟེ་དཔེར་ན་སྒྱུ་མ་བྱས་པ་ཇི་ལྟ་ (7a) བ་དེ་ལྟ་བུར་ནི་སྐྱེ་བ་ངོ་བོ་ཉིད་མེད་པ་ཉིད་བལྟ་བར་བྱའོ།། དོན་དམ་པ་ངོ་བོ་ཉིད་མེད་པ་ཉིད་དེ་ལས་ཀྱང་གཅིག་ཀྱང་བལྟ་བར་བྱའོ།། དོན་དམ་ཡང་དག་འཕགས། དེ་ལ་འདི་ {491} ལྟ་སྟེ་དཔེར་ན་ནམ་མཁའ་

a Zi ling sku ’bum (347.14): *’dis.*

> ནི་གཟུགས་ཀྱི་ངོ་བོ་ཉིད་མེད་པ་ཙམ་གྱིས་རབ་ཏུ་ཕྱེ་བ་དང་ཐམས་ཅད་དུ་སོང་བ་ཇི་ལྟ་བ་དེ་ལྟ་བུ་ནི་དོན་དམ་པ་ངོ་བོ་ཉིད་མེད་པ་དེ་ལས[a]་ཆོས་བདག་མེད་པས་རབ་ཏུ་ཕྱེ་བ་དང་ཐམས་ཅད་དུ་སོང་བ་གཅིག་བལྟ་བར་བྱ་སྟེ།

ཞེས་སོ།། ཀུན་བཏགས་ནམ་མཁའི་མེ་ཏོག་དང་འདྲ་བ་ནི་རྟོག་པས་བཏགས་པ་ཙམ་གྱི་དཔེ་ཡིན་གྱི་ཤེས་བྱ་ལ་མི་སྲིད་པའི་དཔེ་མིན་ནོ།། གཞན་དབང་སྒྱུ་མ་དང་འདྲ་ཚུལ་ནི་འཆད་པར་འགྱུར་ལ་ཡོངས་གྲུབ་ཀྱི་དཔེ་དོན་ནི་དཀྲུས་ན་གསལ་ལོ།། [95] (267) ངོ་བོ་ཉིད་མེད་པར་གསུངས་པའི་ངོ་བོ་ཉིད་མེད་ཚུལ་ནི་དེ་ལྟར་དུ་བཤད་ཀྱི་དེ་ལྟ་མིན་པར་ངོ་བོ་ཉིད་གསུམ་ག་རང་གི་མཚན་ཉིད་ཀྱིས་མ་གྲུབ་པ་ལ་ངོ་བོ་ཉིད་མེད་པར་བཤད་ན་ངོ་བོ་ཉིད་མེད་པར་གསུངས་པའི་མདོ་སྡེ་ལ་སྒྲ་ཇི་བཞིན་པར་ཞེན་པ་ཡིན་ལ། དེ་ལྟ་ན་མེད་ལྟའམ་ཆད་པར་ལྟ་བ་ཐོབ་པར་འགྱུར་ཏེ་ངོ་བོ་ཉིད་གསུམ་ག་ལ་སྐུར་པ[b]་འདེབས་པས་མཚན་ཉིད་མེད་པར་ལྟ་བ་ཅན་ [14] དུ་འགྱུར་བའི་ཕྱིར་རོ།། འདི་ལྟར་གཞན་དབང་རང་གི་མཚན་ཉིད་ཀྱིས་གྲུབ་པ་མེད་ན་སྐྱེ་བ་དང་འགག་པ་མི་རུང་བས་དེ་ལ་སྐུར་པ་འདེབས་པ་ཡིན་ལ་ཡོངས་གྲུབ་རང་གི་མཚན་ཉིད་ཀྱིས་མེད་ན་དངོས་པོའི་གཤིས་སུ་མི་འགྱུར་བའི་ལུགས་སོ།། གལ་ཏེ་རང་གི་མཚན་ཉིད་ཀྱིས་མ་གྲུབ་པར་ལྟ་བ་ངོ་བོ་ཉིད་གཞན་གཉིས་ལ་སྐུར་ (7b) འདེབས་ཡིན་དུ་ཆུག་ཀྱང་ཀུན་བཏགས་ལ་སྐུར་འདེབས་སུ་ཇི་ལྟར་འགྱུར་སྙམ་ན། ངོ་བོ་ཉིད་གཞན་གཉིས་རང་གི་མཚན་ཉིད་ཀྱིས་མེད་ན་དེ་གཉིས་མེད་པར་འགྱུར་ལ་དེ་ལྟ་ན་ཀུན་བཏགས་འདོགས་པའི་གཞི་དང་འདོགས་པ་པོའི་ཐ་སྙད་ཀྱང་མེད་པས་ཀུན་ {492} བཏགས་ཡེ་མེད་དུ་འགྱུར་བའི་ཕྱིར་རོ།། དེ་ལྟར་ཡང་དགོངས་འགྲེལ་ལས།

---

[a] The *stog* Palace edition (49.1) offers a different reading:

> *nam mkha' gzugs kyi ngo bo nyid med pa tsam gyis rab tu phye zhing kun tu 'gro ba de bzhin du* ***de dag las gcig*** *don dam pa ngo bo nyid med par blta ba ni gang chos la bdag med pas rab tu phye ba kun tu 'gro ba'o*

Since *de dag* is dual or plural, I take it as referring to the other two natures; hence, in translation the *stog* Palace version would read:

> Paramārthasamudgata, it is thus: just as, for example, space is distinguished by the mere naturelessness of form and pervades everywhere, so the ultimate naturelessness is to be viewed—as other than those—as distinguished by the selflessness of phenomena and as pervading everything.

[b] Zi ling sku 'bum (348.15): *skur ba* here and throughout, again fulfill the rule that *ba* follows *nga, 'a, ra, la;* however, since *skur* is considered to have a non-manifest extra suffix *da, pa* is also correct. Other instances will not be cited.

ངའི་དགོངས་ཏེ་བཤད་པ་ཟབ་མོ་ཡང་དག་པ་ཇི་ལྟ་བ་བཞིན་དུ་རབ་ཏུ་མི་ཤེས་ཏེ་ཆོས་དེ་ལ་མོས་ཀྱང་ཆོས་འདི་དག་ཐམས་ཅད་ནི་ངོ་བོ་ཉིད་མེད་པ་ཁོ་ན་ཡིན་ནོ།། ཆོས་འདི་དག་ཐམས་ཅད་ནི་མ་སྐྱེས་པ་ཁོ་ནའོ།། མ་འགགས་པ་ཁོ་ནའོ།། གཟོད་མ་ནས་ཞི་བ་ཁོ་ནའོ།། རང་བཞིན་གྱིས་ཡོངས་སུ་མྱ་ངན་ལས་འདས་པ་ཁོ་ནའོ་ཞེས་ཆོས་ཀྱི་དོན་ལ་སྒྲ་ཇི་བཞིན་ཁོ་ནར་མངོན་པར་ཞེན་པར་བྱེད་དོ།། དེ་དག་གཞི་དེས་ན་ཆོས་ཐམས་ཅད་ལ་མེད་པར་ལྟ་བ་དང་མཚན་ཉིད་མེད་པར་ལྟ་བ་འཐོབ་པར་འགྱུར་ཏེ། མེད་པར་ལྟ་བ་དང་མཚན་ཉིད་མེད་པར་ལྟ་བ་ཐོབ་ནས་ཀྱང་ཆོས་ཐམས་ཅད་ལ་མཚན་ཉིད་ཐམས་ཅད་ཀྱིས་སྐུར་པ་འདེབས་ཏེ། ཆོས་རྣམས་ཀྱི་ཀུན་བརྟགས་ [15] པའི་མཚན་ཉིད་ལ་ཡང་སྐུར་པ་འདེབས་ཆོས་རྣམས་ཀྱི་གཞན་གྱི་དབང་གི་མཚན་ཉིད་དང་ཡོངས་སུ་གྲུབ་པའི་མཚན་ཉིད་ལ་ཡང་སྐུར་པ་[a]འདེབས་སོ།། དེ་ཅིའི་ཕྱིར་ཞེ་ན། དོན་དམ་ཡང་དག་འཕགས། འདི་ལྟར་གཞན་གྱི་དབང་གི་མཚན་ཉིད་དང་ཡོངས་སུ་གྲུབ་པའི་མཚན་ཉིད་ཡོད་ན་ནི་ཀུན་བརྟགས་པའི་མཚན་ཉིད་ཀྱང་རབ་ཏུ་ཤེས་པར་འགྱུར་ན། དེ་ལ་གང་དག་གཞན་གྱི་དབང་གི་མཚན་ཉིད་དང་ཡོངས་སུ་གྲུབ་པའི་མཚན་ཉིད་ལ་མཚན་ཉིད་མེད་པར་མཐོང་བ་དེ་དག་གིས་ནི་ཀུན་བརྟགས་པའི་མཚན་ཉིད་ལ་ཡང་སྐུར་པ་བཏབ་པ་ཡིན་པའི་ཕྱིར་ཏེ། དེ་ལྟ་བས་ན་དེ་དག་ནི་མཚན་ (8a) ཉིད་རྣམ་པ་གསུམ་ཆར་ལ་ཡང་སྐུར་པ་ {493} འདེབས་པ་ཞེས་བྱའོ།

ཞེས་སོ།། དོན་ལ་སྒྲ་ཇི་བཞིན་དུ་ཞེན་ཞེས་པའི་སྒྲ་ནི་ངོ་བོ་ཉིད་མེད་པར་སྟོན་པའི་མདོ་སྡེ་ལས་ཆོས་ཐམས་ཅད་དོན་དམ་པར་རང་བཞིན་གྱིས་སྟོང་པ་དང་ངོ་བོ་ཉིད་དང་རང་གི་མཚན་ཉིད་ཀྱིས་སྟོང་ཞེས་གསུངས་པ་རྣམས་ཡིན་ལ་དེ་དག་ལ་ཇི་ལྟར་བསྟན་པ་ལྟར་འཛིན་པ་ནི་སྒྲ་ཇི་བཞིན་པར་ཞེན་པར་འདོད་པའི་ལུགས་སོ།། གཞན་དབང་དང་ཡོངས་གྲུབ་ཀྱི་མཚན་ཉིད་ལ་མཚན་ཉིད་མེད་པར་མཐོང་བ་ནི་དེ་གཉིས་རང་གི་མཚན་ཉིད་ཀྱིས་མ་གྲུབ་པར་ལྟ་བ་སྟེ། དེ་ཅིའི་ཕྱིར་ཞེ་ན། ཞེས་པ་མན་ཆད་ཀྱིས་ངོ་བོ་ཉིད་གསུམ་ག་ལ་སྐུར་འདེབས་སུ་འགྲོ་བའི་རྒྱུ་མཚན་སྟོན་ནོ།། རང་གི་མཚན་ཉིད་ཀྱིས་སྐྱེ་བ་དང་འགག་པ་མེད་པར་གསུངས་པ་ལྟར་བཟུང་ན་ཡང་གཞན་དབང་ལ་སྐུར་འདེབས་སུ་འགྱུར་བའི་

[a] Se rva zhol (7b.5): *skur ba,* though the same word earlier in the line is *skur pa.*

ཕྱིར་ [16] གཞན་གཉིས་ལ་ཡང་སྐྱར་འདེབས་སུ་འགྲོ་བ་ཤེས་པར་བྱ་སྟེ། སྐྱེ་འགག་རང་གི་མཚན་ཉིད་ཀྱིས་མ་གྲུབ་ན་སྐྱེ་འགག་མེད་པར་འགྱུར་བའི་ལུགས་སོ།།

གཉིས་པ་ [གང་ལ་དགོངས་ནས་མ་སྐྱེས་པ་སོགས་སུ་གསུངས་པ་བཤད་པ་]ནི། [97]

(269)

ངོ་བོ་ཉིད་མེད་པའི་ཚུལ་དེ་ལྟར་ཡིན་ན་སྐྱེ་བ་མེད་པ་སོགས་གང་ལ་དགོངས་ནས་གསུངས་ཤེ་ན། འདི་ནི་ངོ་བོ་ཉིད་མེད་པ་དང་པོ་དང་ཐ་མ་ལ་དགོངས་ནས་གསུངས[a]ཏེ། དེ་ཡང་དང་པོ་ནི་དགོངས་འགྲེལ་ལས།

> དེ་ལ་མཚན་ཉིད་ངོ་བོ་ཉིད་མེད་པ་ཉིད་ལ་དགོངས་ནས་ངས་ཆོས་ཐམས་ཅད་མ་སྐྱེས་པ་མ་འགགས་པ་གཟོད་མ་ནས་ཞི་བ་རང་བཞིན་གྱིས་ཡོངས་སུ་མྱ་ངན་ལས་འདས་པའོ་ཞེས་བསྟན་ཏོ།། དེ་ཅིའི་ཕྱིར་ཞེ་ན། དོན་དམ་ཡང་དག་འཕགས། འདི་ལྟར་རང་གི་མཚན་ཉིད་ཀྱིས་མེད་པ་གང་ (8b) ཡིན་པ་དེ་ནི་མ་སྐྱེས་པ་ཡིན་མ་སྐྱེས་པ་ {494} གང་ཡིན་པ་དེ་ནི་མ་འགགས་པ་ཡིན། མ་སྐྱེས་པ་དང་མ་འགགས་པ་གང་ཡིན་པ་དེ་དག་ནི་གཟོད་མ་ནས་ཞི་བ་ཡིན་གཟོད་མ་ནས་ཞི་བ་གང་ཡིན་པ་དེ་ནི་རང་བཞིན་གྱིས་ཡོངས་སུ་མྱ་ངན་ལས་འདས་པ་ཡིན། རང་བཞིན་གྱིས་ཡོངས་སུ་མྱ་ངན་ལས་འདས་པ་གང་ཡིན་པ་དེ་ལ་ནི་ཡོངས་སུ་མྱ་ངན་ལས་བཟླ་བར་བྱ་བ་ཅུང་ཟད་ཀྱང་མེད་དེ།

ཞེས་གསུངས་སོ།། ཀུན་བརྟགས་ལ་སྐྱེ་འགག་མེད་པའི་རྒྱུ་མཚན་དུ་རང་གི་མཚན་ཉིད་ཀྱིས་མ་གྲུབ་པ་བཀོད་པའི་ཕྱིར་སྐྱེ་འགག་ཡོད་ན་རང་མཚན་གྱིས་གྲུབ་པ་དང་གཞན་དབང་ལ་རང་གི་མཚན་ཉིད་ཀྱིས་གྲུབ་པའི་སྐྱེ་འགག་ཡོད[b]པར་ཡང་བསྟན་ཏོ[c]།། [17]སྐྱེ་འགག་དང་

---

a Zi ling sku 'bum (350.10) misreads *sungs.*

b Se rva zhol (8b.3) misreads *yed,* which was corrected in the Delhi GD zhol to *yod.*

c Zi ling sku 'bum (351.1): *bstan to* here. The same is the case for Grags pa & rnam rgyal, 17.9, and so forth. The editors of the Zi ling sku 'bum were seeking to take account of the non-manifest extra suffix *da* in the past form of the verb, which thus calls for *to* as a terminator. It seems that they were intent on correction—ignoring non-manifest extra suffixes as in *skur pa* (perhaps from the sometimes-cited rule that if the addition of the syllable creates an even number of syllables, it should be *pa* and if its addition creates an odd number of syllables, it should be *ba* or perhaps from the commonly accepted notion that there is no certainty, presumably because usage in the locality determines what is done) and paying attention to them in *bstan to.* The other editions seem to have done the reverse.

བྲལ་བ་ནི་འདུས་མ་བྱས་ཡིན་པས་ཀུན་ནས་ཉོན་མོངས་ཀྱི་ཆོས་སུ་མི་རུང་བའི་ཕྱིར་གཟོད་མ་ནས་ཞི་བ་དང་རང་བཞིན་གྱིས་མྱ་ངན་ལས་འདས་པར་བསྟན་ཏེ་མྱ་ངན་ནི་འདིར་ཀུན་ཉོན་ཡིན་པའི་ཕྱིར་རོ།། གཉིས་པ་ཡང་དགོངས་འགྲེལ་ལས། [98] (269)

ཡང་དོན་དམ་པ་ངོ་བོ་ཉིད་མེད་པ་ཉིད་ཆོས་བདག་མེད་པས་རབ་ཏུ་ཕྱེ་བ་ལ་དགོངས་ནས་ངས་ཆོས་ཐམས་ཅད་མ་སྐྱེས་པ་མ་འགགས་པ་གཟོད་མ་ནས་ཞི་བ་རང་བཞིན་གྱིས་ཡོངས་སུ་མྱ་ངན་ལས་འདས་པའོ་ཞེས་བསྟན་ཏོ།། དེ་ཅིའི་ཕྱིར་ཞེ་ན། འདི་ལྟར་དོན་དམ་པ་ངོ་བོ་ཉིད་མེད་པ་ཉིད་ཆོས་བདག་མེད་པས་རབ་ཏུ་ཕྱེ་བ་ནི་རྟག་པ་རྟག་པའི་དུས་དང་ཐེར་ཟུག་ཐེར་ཟུག[a]གི་དུས་སུ་རྣམ་པར་གནས་པ་ཁོ་ན་ཡིན་ལ། དེ་ནི་ཆོས་རྣམས་ཀྱི་ཆོས་ཉིད་འདུས་མ་བྱས་པ་ཉོན་མོངས་པ་ཐམས་ཅད་དང་བྲལ་བ[b]ཡིན་ཏེ། རྟག་པ་རྟག་པའི་ {495} དུས་དང་ཐེར་ཟུག་ཐེར་ཟུག་གི་དུས་སུ་ཆོས་ཉིད་དེ་ཉིད་ཀྱི་རྣམ་པར་གནས་པ་འདུས་མ་བྱས་པ་གང་ཡིན་པ་དེ་ནི་འདུས་མ་བྱས་པའི་ཕྱིར་མ་སྐྱེས་པ་ (9a) དང་མ་འགགས་པ་ཡིན་ལ། དེ་ནི་ཉོན་མོངས་པ་ཐམས་ཅད་དང་བྲལ་བའི་ཕྱིར་གཟོད་མ་ནས་ཞི་བ་དང་རང་བཞིན་གྱིས་ཡོངས་སུ་མྱ་ངན་ལས་འདས་པ་ཡིན་ཏེ།

ཞེས་གསུངས་སོ།། རྟག་པ་རྟག་པའི་དུས་ནི་སྔ་མ་སྔ་མའི་དུས་དང་ཐེར་ཟུག་ཐེར་ཟུག་གི་དུས་ནི་ཕྱི་མ་ཕྱི་མའི་དུས་ལ་རྒྱ་ནག་གི་འགྲེལ་ཆེན་ལས་བཤད་དོ།། [100] (269) འོ་ན་འདིར་ངོ་བོ་ཉིད་མེད་པའི་གཞི་གསུམ་ག་ལ་མཛད་ནས་སྐྱེ་བ་སོགས་ [18] མེད་པའི་གཞི་ངོ་བོ་ཉིད་མེད་པ་བར་པ་ལ་མི་མཛད་པ་དང་། ཀུན་ལས་བཏུས་ལས་ཀྱང་།

ཀུན་བརྟགས་པའི་ངོ་བོ་ཉིད་ལ་མཚན་ཉིད་ངོ་བོ་ཉིད་མེད་པ་དང་གཞན་གྱི་དབང་ལ་སྐྱེ་བ་ངོ་བོ་ཉིད་མེད་པ་དང་ཡོངས་སུ་གྲུབ་པ་ལ་དོན་དམ་པ་ངོ་བོ་ཉིད་མེད་པའི་ཕྱིར་རོ།། མ་སྐྱེས་པ་མ་འགགས་པ་གཟོད་མ་ནས་ཞི་བ་རང་བཞིན་གྱིས་མྱ་ངན་ལས་འདས་པ་ཞེས་འབྱུང་བའི་དགོངས་པ་གང་ཡིན་ཞེ་ན། ཇི་ལྟར་ངོ་བོ་ཉིད་མེད་པ་དེ་ལྟར་མ་སྐྱེས་སོ།། ཇི་ལྟར་མ་སྐྱེས་པ་དེ་ལྟར་མ་འགགས་སོ།། ཇི་ལྟར་མ་

[a] Delhi GD zhol (8b.6) omits this syllable, which is written beneath the line in Se rva zhol.

[b] Se rva zhol (8b.6), presumably taking account of a non-manifest extra suffix *da* at the end of the previous syllable, reads *pa*.

> སྐྱེས་པ་དང་མ་འགགས་པ་དེ་ལྟར་གཟོད་མ་ནས་ཞིའོ།། དེ་ལྟར་རང་བཞིན་གྱིས་ཡོངས་སུ་མྱ་ངན་ལས་འདས་སོ།[a]

ཞེས་མཚན་ཉིད་གསུམ་གའི་[b] དབང་དུ་བྱས་ནས་མ་སྐྱེས་པ་སོགས་སུ་བཤད་པའི་དོན་ཅི་ཡིན་ཞེ་ན། འདི་ལ་རྒྱ་ནག་གི་འགྲེལ་ཆེན་ལས། མདོ་ལས་གཞན་དབང་སྐྱེ་བ་མེད་པ་སོགས་ཀྱི་དགོངས་གཞིར་མ་གསུངས་པ་ནི་རྟེན་ཅིང་འབྲེལ་པར་[c] འབྱུང་བའི་དོན་མེད་པ་ {496} མིན་པར་བསྟན་པའི་ཕྱིར་ཡིན་ལ། ཀུན་ལས་བཏུས་ལས་བཤད་པ་ནི་བདག་ཉིད་ཀྱིས་སྐྱེ་བ་དང་རྒྱུ་མེད་ལས་སྐྱེ་བ་མེད་པའི་དབང་དུ་བྱས་པར་བཤད་དོ།། གཞན་དབང་ལ་རང་གི་མཚན་ཉིད་ཀྱིས་སྐྱེ་བ་དང་འགག་པ་ཡོད་ (9b) པས་སྐྱེ་འགག་མེད་པར་གསུངས་པ་གཞན་དབང་ལ་དགོངས་པ་མིན་ལ་གཞན་དབང་ཕལ་ཆེར་ཀུན་ཉོན་གྱིས་བསྡུས་པས་ཚིག་ཕྱི་མ་གཉིས་ཀྱི་གཞིར་མ་མཛད་པ་ནི་མདོ་འདིའི་དགོངས་པའོ།། ངོ་བོ་ཉིད་གསུམ་གྱི་ [19] རང་རང་གི་སྐབས་ཀྱི་ངོ་བོ་མེད་རྒྱུ་དེའི་དབང་དུ་བྱས་ནས་ཇི་ལྟར་ངོ་བོ་ཉིད་མེད་པ་དེ་ལྟར་མ་སྐྱེས་པ་དང་མ་འགགས་ལ་གཟོད་མ་ནས་ཞི་བ་དང་། གདོད་ནས་མྱ་ངན་ལས་འདས་པ་ཡང་ཡིན་པ་ལ་དགོངས་ནས་ཀུན་ལས་བཏུས་ལས་དེ་ལྟར་བཤད་དོ།།

---

[a] The Peking edition of Asaṅga's *Summary of Manifest Knowledge* (5550, vol. 112, 266.1.5) reads ***ji*** *ltar rang bzhin gyis yongs su mya ngan las 'das so.* Wonch'uk (Peking 5517, vol. 106, chap. 5, 134.2.2) cogently reads ***gzod ma nas zhi ba ji lta ba de bzhin tu*** *rang bzhin gyis yongs su mya ngan las 'das so.*

[b] Delhi NG dkra shis lhun po (495.5), Zi ling sku 'bum (352.3), Sarnath gtsang (18.10), and Kalimpong (22.6): *ga'i;* Se rva zhol (9a.5) and Peking (171.3.6): *ka'i.*

[c] Delhi NG dkra shis lhun po (495.6), Sarnath gtsang (18.14), and Kalimpong (23.1): *par;* Se rva zhol (9a.6), Zi ling sku 'bum (352.5), and Peking (171.3.7): *bar.* Delhi GD zhol shows evidence of being emended to *par.*

གསུམ་པ་ [ངོ་བོ་ཉིད་གསུམ་གྱི་ངོ་བོ་ངོས་གཟུང་བ་]ནི། [104] (271) ཀུན་བརྟགས་མཚན་ཉིད་ངོ་བོ་ཉིད་མེད་པ་ཡིན་ན་ཀུན་བརྟགས་ཉིད་གང་ཡིན་སྙམ་ན། དེ་ནི་དགོངས་འགྲེལ་ལས།

> རྣམ་པར་རྟོག་པའི་སྤྱོད་ཡུལ་ཀུན་བརྟགས་པའི་མཚན་ཉིད་ཀྱི་གནས་འདུ་བྱེད་ཀྱི་མཚན་མ་ལ་གཟུགས་ཀྱི་ཕུང་པོ་ཞེས་ངོ་བོ་ཉིད་དམ་བྱེ་བྲག་གི་མཚན་ཉིད་[a]དུ་མིང་དང་བརྡར་རྣམ་པར་བཞག་པ་དང་། གཟུགས་ཀྱི་ཕུང་པོ་སྐྱེའོ་ཞེའམ་འགག་པ་ཞེའམ་གཟུགས་ཀྱི་ཕུང་པོ་སྤང་བ་དང་ཡོངས་སུ་ཤེས་པ་ཞེས་ངོ་བོ་ཉིད་ཀྱི་མཚན་ཉིད་དམ་བྱེ་བྲག་གི་མཚན་ཉིད་དུ་མིང་དང་བརྡས་རྣམ་པར་བཞག་པ་གང་ལགས་པ་དེ་ནི་ཀུན་བརྟགས་པའི་མཚན་ཉིད་ལགས་ཏེ།

ཞེས་གསུངས་སོ།། དེ་ལ་ཚིག་དང་པོ་གསུམ་གྱིས་ནི་ཀུན་བརྟགས་འདོགས་པའི་གཞི་བསྟན་ལ་ {497} དེ་མན་ཆད་ཀྱིས་ཀུན་ཏུ་བརྟགས་ཚུལ་སྟོན་ཏེ། འདི་གཟུགས་ཕུང་ངོ་ཞེས་ངོ་བོ་དང་གཟུགས་ཕུང་སྐྱེའོ་ཞེས་སོགས་སུ་བཏགས་པ་ནི་བྱེ་བྲག་གམ་ཁྱད་པར་དུ་བཏགས་ཚུལ་ཡིན་ཏེ་ཞིབ་ཏུ་འཆད་པར་འགྱུར་རོ།། གཞན་དབང་སྐྱེ་བ་ངོ་བོ་ཉིད་མེད་པ་ཡིན་ན་གཞན་དབང་གང་ཡིན་སྙམ་ན། [106] (271) དེ་ནི་དགོངས་འགྲེལ་ལས།

> རྣམ་པར་རྟོག་པའི་སྤྱོད་ཡུལ་ཀུན་བརྟགས་པའི་མཚན་ཉིད་ཀྱི་གནས་ [20] འདུ་བྱེད་ཀྱི་ (10a) མཚན་མ་གང་ལགས་པ་དེ་ནི་གཞན་གྱི་དབང་གི་མཚན་ཉིད་ལགས་ཏེ

ཞེས་གསུངས་ཏེ། དང་པོས་གང་གི་ཡུལ་ཡིན་པ་དང་གཉིས་པས་ཀུན་བརྟགས་ཀྱི་གདགས་གཞི་དང་གསུམ་པས་རང་གི་ངོ་བོ་བསྟན་ཏོ།། [107] (272) ཡོངས་གྲུབ་དོན་དམ་པ་ངོ་བོ་ཉིད་མེད་པ་ཡིན་ན་དེ་ཉིད་གང་ཡིན་སྙམ་ན། དེ་ནི་དགོངས་འགྲེལ་ལས།

> རྣམ་པར་རྟོག་པའི་སྤྱོད་ཡུལ་ཀུན་བརྟགས་པའི་མཚན་ཉིད་ཀྱི་གནས་འདུ་བྱེད་ཀྱི་མཚན་མ་དེ་ཉིད། ཀུན་བརྟགས་པའི་མཚན་ཉིད་དེར་ཡོངས་སུ་མ་གྲུབ་ཅིང་ངོ་བོ་ཉིད་དེ་ཁོ་ནས་ངོ་བོ་ཉིད་མ་མཆིས་པ་ཉིད་ཆོས་ལ་བདག་མ་མཆིས་པ། དེ་

[a] Both Lamotte (*Saṃdhinirmocana,* 81 [25, line 9]) and Dön-drup-gyel-tsen's *Four Intertwined Commentaries* (21.4) read *ngo bo nyid* ***kyi mtshan nyid*** *dam bye brag gi mtshan nyid.*

བཞིན་ཉིད་རྣམ་པར་དག་པའི་དམིགས་པ་གང་ལགས་པ་དེ་ནི་ཡོངས་སུ་གྲུབ་པའི་མཚན་ཉིད་ལགས་ཏེ་

ཞེས་གསུངས་སོ།། ཆོས་ལ་ཞེས་སོགས་ཀྱིས་ཆོས་ཀྱི་བདག་མེད་དེ་བཞིན་ཉིད་ཅེས་བརྗོད་པ་གང་ལ་དམིགས་ནས་བསྒོམས་པས་སྒྲིབ་པ་དག་པར་འགྱུར་བ་དེ་ཉིད་ཡོངས་གྲུབ་ཏུ་ངོས་བཟུང་ངོ༎ ཆོས་ཀྱི་བདག་མེད་དེ་གང་ཞི་ན་ངོ་བོ་ཉིད་མ་མཆིས་པ་ཉིད་དེ་ཉིད་ནི་དེ་ཁོ་ན་ཞེས་པའི་དོན་ནོ།། གང་གི་ངོ་བོ་ཉིད་མེད་པ་ཡིན་སྙམ་པ་ལ། ངོ་བོ་ཉིད་དེ་ཁོ་ནས་ཞེས་ཀུན་བརྟགས་ཀྱི་ {498} ངོ་བོ་ཉིད་གོང་དུ་སྨོས་པ་ལ་གསུངས་ནས་ཁོ་ནས་ཞེས་པས་ནི་གཞན་གཅོད་པས་ངོ་བོ་ཉིད་གཞན་གཉིས་ཀྱི་ངོ་བོ་ཉིད་མ་མཆིས་པ་ལ་མི་བྱེད་ཀྱི་ཀུན་བརྟགས་ཁོ་ནའི་ངོ་བོ་མེད་པ་ལ་ཡོངས་གྲུབ་ཏུ་བྱེད་ཅེས་པའི་དོན་ནོ།། དེ་ཉིད་གོང་མས་བཤད་པ་ནི་རྣམ་པར་ [21] རྟོག་པ་ཞེས་པ་ནས་དེ་ཉིད་ཅེས་པའི་བར་གྱིས་གཞན་དབང་སྟོང་གཞིར་བསྟན་ནས་ཀུན་བརྟགས་ཀྱི་མཚན་ཉིད་དུ་མ་གྲུབ་ཅེས་པས་དེ་ཉིད་ཀུན་བརྟགས་ཀྱིས་སྟོང་པ་ལ་ཡོངས་གྲུབ་ཏུ་ཤིན་ཏུ་ (10b) གསལ་བས། [109] (272) མདོ་འདིས་སྟོང་ཚུལ་བསྟན་པ་ངེས་དོན་དུ་འདོད་པ་དང་ངོ་བོ་ཉིད་ཐ་མ་ངོ་བོ་ཉིད་དང་པོ་གཉིས་ཀྱིས་སྟོང་པ[a] ཡོངས་གྲུབ་ཏུ་འདོད་པ་ཡང་འགལ་བའོ།། སྟོང་ལུགས་ཀྱང་ས་ཕྱོགས་བུམ་པས་སྟོང་པ་ལྟར་དོན་གཞན་དུ་ཡོད་པ་བཀག་པ་མིན་གྱི་གང་ཟག་རྫས་སུ་མེད་པ་ལྟར་གཞན་དབང་ཀུན་བརྟགས་ཀྱི་ངོ་བོར་གྲུབ་པས་སྟོང་པ་ཡིན[b] ནོ།། དེ་ཉིད་ཀྱི་ཕྱིར་མདོ་ལས། དེ་ཉིད་ཀུན་བརྟགས་པའི་མཚན་ཉིད་དེར་ཡོངས་སུ་མ་གྲུབ་ཅིང་། ཞེས་གསུངས་སོ།། གང་གིས་སྟོང་པའི་ཀུན་བརྟགས་ནི་མདོ་འདིའི་ཀུན་བརྟགས་ངོས་བཟུང་བའི་སྐབས་གཉིས་ཀར་ངོ་བོ་དང་ཁྱད་པར་དུ་བཏགས་པ་ཙམ་མིན་པའི་ཀུན་བརྟགས་གཞན་མ་གསུངས་པའི་རྒྱུ་མཚན་ནི་འཆད་པར་འགྱུར་རོ།། [111] (273) དེ་ལྟར་གཟུགས་ཕུང་ལ་ཇི་ལྟར་སྦྱར་བ་བཞིན་དུ་ཕུང་པོ་ལྷག་མ་བཞི་དང་སྐྱེ་མཆེད་བཅུ་གཉིས་དང་རྟེན་འབྲེལ་བཅུ་གཉིས་དང་ཟས་བཞི་དང་ཁམས་དྲུག་དང་བཅོ་བརྒྱད་པོ་རེ་རེ་ལ་ཡང་མཚན་ཉིད་གསུམ་གསུམ་སྦྱར་བར་

[a] Delhi NG dkra shis lhun po (498.3) and Sarnath gtsang (21.5): *ba;* Se rva zhol (10b.1), Zi ling sku 'bum (354.5), Peking (171.5.7), and Kalimpong (25.6): *pa.* The former probably is a correction in order to follow either the rule that *ba* comes after *nga* or the sometimes-evoked rule that after adding the syllable, it creates an even number of syllables. Another possibility is that *stong* used to be spelled *stongs,* thereby accounting for *pa.* Other instances of this will not be noted separately.

[b] Peking (171.5.8) misreads *min.*

གསུངས་སོ།། སྡུག་བདེན་ལ་ནི་གདགས་གཞི་སྟེར་ {499} བཞིན་ལ་སྡུག་བསྔལ་གྱི་བདེན་པའོ་ཞེས་ངོ་བོ་དང་སྡུག་བདེན་ཡོངས་སུ་ཤེས་པ་ཞེས་བྱེ་བྲག་ཏུ་མིང་དང་བརྡས་བཞག་པ་ཀུན་བརྟགས་དང་། གཞན་དབང་སྟེར་བཞིན་དང་ [22] ཡོངས་གྲུབ་ཀྱང་སྟེར་དང་འདྲ་ལ་ངོ་བོ་ཉིད་དེ་ཁོ་ནས་ངོ་བོ་ཉིད་མ་མཆིས་པ་ཞེས་གསུངས་ཤིང་། དེ་བཞིན་དུ་བདེན་པ་ལྷག་མ་ལ་ཡང་སྦྱར་རོ།། བྱང་ཕྱོགས་སྡེ་ཚན་བདུན་ལ་ཡང་སྦྱར་ཏེ་གདགས་གཞི་སྟེར་བཞིན་ལ་ཡང་དག་པའི་ཏིང་ངེ་འཛིན་ཞེས་ངོ་བོ་དང་དེའི་མི་མཐུན་ཕྱོགས་དང་གཉེན་པོ་སོགས་སྟེར་བཤད་པ་རྣམས་ལ་དེ་དང་དེའི་འོ་ཞེས་ཁྱད་པར་དུ་བཏགས་པའི་ཀུན་བརྟགས་དང་། ངོ་བོ་ཉིད་གཞན་ (11a) གཉིས་སྡུག་བདེན་བཞིན་གསུངས་སོ།། དེ་དག་ནི་སྟེར་འགལ་སྤོང་དྲིས་པའི་སྐབས་སུ་བཤད་པའི་གཟུགས་ཕུང་ནས་ལམ་གྱི་ཡན་ལག་གི་བར་གྱི་རེ་རེ་ལ་ཡང་མཚན་ཉིད་གསུམ་གསུམ་གྱི་འཇོག་ལུགས་བྱས་ནས་དེ་ལ་དགོངས་ནས་སྟོན་པས་ངོ་བོ་ཉིད་མེད་པ་གསུམ་དུ་བཤད་པར་བདག་གིས་གོའོ་ཞེས་དོན་དམ་ཡང་དག་འཕགས་ཀྱིས་སྟོན་པ་ལ་གསོལ་བའོ།།

བཞི་པ་[དེ་དག་གིས་གྲུབ་པའི་དོན་ཞུས་པ་]ལ་གཉིས། མདོ་དགོད་པ་དང་། དེའི་དོན་ཅུང་ཟད་བཤད་པའོ།། [114] (274)

དང་པོ་[མདོ་དགོད་པ་]ནི། [114] (274)

དེ་ལྟར་ན་གསུང་རབ་ལ་ཆོས་རྣམས་རང་གི་མཚན་ཉིད་ཀྱིས་ཡོད་པ་དང་ཆོས་རྣམས་རང་གི་མཚན་ཉིད་ཀྱིས་མ་གྲུབ་པར་སྟོན་པ་དང་། རང་གི་མཚན་ཉིད་ཀྱིས་གྲུབ་མ་གྲུབ་ལེགས་པར་ཕྱེ་བའི་མདོ་སྡེ་གསུམ་བྱུང་ཞིང་དེ་དག་ཀྱང་ངོ་བོ་ཉིད་ཡོད་མེད་ལེགས་པར་ཕྱེ་མ་ཕྱེ་གཉིས་སུ་འགྱུར་ལ་ཕྱེ་བ་ནི་དོན་གཞན་དུ་དྲང་བར་མི་བྱ་བས་ངེས་པའི་དོན་དང་། མ་ཕྱེ་བ་ནི་དོན་གཞན་དུ་དྲང་དགོས་པས་ {500} དྲང་བའི་དོན་ཡིན་ལ། དེ་ལ་ཡང་གཉིས་ཡོད་པས་ [23] མདོ་སྡེ་གཉིས་དྲང་དོན་དང་གཅིག་ངེས་དོན་དུ་ཐར་བཤད་པ་རྣམས་ཀྱི་ཤུགས་ཀྱིས་ཤེས་པར་འགྱུར་རོ།། ཤུགས་ལ་གནས་པའི་དོན་དེ་ཉིད་དུས་ཀྱི་རིམ་པའི་སྒོ་ནས་འཁོར་ལོ་གསུམ་དང་སྦྱར་བའི་དྲང་ངེས་སུ་འགྱུར་ཚུལ་དོན་དམ་ཡང་དག་འཕགས་ཀྱིས་སྟོན་པ་ལ་ཞུས་པ་ནི་དགོངས་འགྲེལ་ལས།

> བཅོམ་ལྡན་འདས་ཀྱིས་དང་པོར་ཡུལ་བ་ར་ཎ་སིར[a]དྲང་སྲོང་སྨྲ་བ་རི་དྭགས་ཀྱི་ནགས་སུ་ཉན་ཐོས་ཀྱི་ཐེག་པ་ལ་ཡང་དག་པར་ཞུགས་པ་རྣམས་ལ་འཕགས་པའི་བདེན་པ་བཞིའི་རྣམ་པ་བསྟན་པས་ཆོས་ཀྱི་འཁོར་ལོ་ངོ་མཚར་རྨད་དུ་བྱུང་བ་སྔོན་ལྷར་གྱུར་པའམ་མིར་གྱུར་པ་སུས་ཀྱང་མཐུན་པར་ (11b) འཇིག་རྟེན་དུ་མ་བསྐོར་བ་གཅིག་རབ་ཏུ་བསྐོར་ཏེ། བཅོམ་ལྡན་འདས་ཀྱིས་ཆོས་ཀྱི་འཁོར་ལོ་རབ་ཏུ་བསྐོར་བ་དེ[b]ཡང་བླ་ན་མཆིས་པ་སྐབས་མཆིས་པ་དྲང་བའི་དོན་རྩོད་པའི་གཞིའི་གནས་སུ་གྱུར་པ་ལགས། བཅོམ་ལྡན་འདས་ཀྱིས་ཆོས་རྣམས་ཀྱི་ངོ་བོ་ཉིད་མ་མཆིས་པ་ཉིད་ལས་བརྩམས། སྐྱེ་བ་མ་མཆིས་པ་དང་འགག་པ་མ་མཆིས་པ་དང་གཟོད་མ་ནས་ཞི་བ་དང་རང་བཞིན་གྱིས་ཡོངས་སུ་མྱ་ངན་ལས་འདས་པ་ཉིད་ལས་བརྩམས་

[a] The name is spelled many different ways, this spelling indicating that the location is at the junction of the Varaṇa and Asi Rivers. Sarnath gtsang (23.5) reads *wā rā ṇa sīr;* given the consistency of the other editions, this probably represents a misguided "correction" by the Sarnath editors. A-ku Lo-drö-gya-tso (*Precious Lamp,* 141.3) lists three etymologies, of which the two-river version is the third.

[b] Zi ling sku 'bum (355.19) lacks *de.*

ནས་ཐེག་པ་ཆེན་པོ་ལ་ཡང་དག་པར་ཞུགས་པ་རྣམས་ལ་སྟོང་པ་ཉིད་སྨོས་པའི་རྣམ་པས་ཆེས་ངོ་མཚར་རྨད་དུ་བྱུང་བའི་ཆོས་ཀྱི་འཁོར་ལོ་གཉིས་པ་བསྐོར་ཏེ། བཅོམ་ལྡན་འདས་ཀྱིས་ཆོས་ཀྱི་འཁོར་ལོ་བསྐོར་བ་དེ་ཡང་བླ་ན་མཆིས་པ་སྐབས་མཆིས་པ་དྲང་བའི་དོན་རྩོད་པའི་གཞིའི་གནས་སུ་གྱུར་པ་ལགས་ཀྱི། བཅོམ་{501} ལྡན་འདས་ [24]ཀྱིས་ཆོས་རྣམས་ཀྱི་ངོ་བོ་ཉིད་མ་མཆིས་པ་ཉིད་ལས་བརྩམས། སྐྱེ་བ་མ་མཆིས་པ་དང་འགག་པ་མ་མཆིས་པ་དང་གཟོད་མ་ནས་ཞི་བ་དང་རང་བཞིན་གྱིས་ཡོངས་སུ་མྱ་ངན་ལས་འདས་པ་ཉིད་ལས་བརྩམས་ནས་ཐེག་པ་ཐམས་ཅད་ལ་ཡང་དག་པར་ཞུགས་པ་རྣམས་ལ་ལེགས་པར་རྣམ་པར་ཕྱེ་བ་དང་ལྡན་པ་ངོ་མཚར་རྨད་དུ་བྱུང་བའི་ཆོས་ཀྱི་འཁོར་ལོ་གསུམ་པ་བསྐོར་ཏེ། བཅོམ་ལྡན་འདས་ཀྱིས་ཆོས་ཀྱི་འཁོར་ལོ་བསྐོར་བ་འདི་ནི་བླ་ན་མ་མཆིས་པ་སྐབས་མ་མཆིས་པ་ངེས་པའི་དོན་ལགས་ཏེ་རྩོད་པའི་གཞིའི་གནས་སུ་གྱུར་པ་མ་ལགས་སོ།

ཞེས་གསུངས་སོ།།

གཉིས་པ་ [དེའི་དོན་ཅུང་ཟད་བཤད་པ་]ལ་གཉིས། མདོའི་ཚིག་དོན་ཅུང་ཟད་བཤད་པ་དང་། དྲང་ངེས་ཀྱི་ཚུལ་ཅུང་ཟད་བཤད་པའོ།། [118] [274]

དང་པོ་ [མདོའི་ཚིག་དོན་ཅུང་ཟད་བཤད་པ་]ནི། [118] [274]

དེ་ལ་འཁོར་ལོ་དང་པོ་བསྐོར་བ་ལ་གནས་ནི་ཚིག་དང་པོས་བསྟན་ལ་ (12a) གདུལ་བྱ་ནི་གཉིས་པས་སོ།། འཕགས་པའི་ཞེས་པ་ནས་བསྐོར་ཏེ་ཞེས་པའི་བར་གྱིས་འཁོར་ལོའི་ངོ་བོ་བསྟན་ནོ།། བདེན་པ་བཞིའི་རྣམ་པ་བསྟན་ཞེས་པ་ནི་བརྗོད་བྱ་གང་ལས་བརྩམས་ནས་བསྟན་པའོ།། ངོ་མཚར་སོགས་ནི་དེའི་བསྔགས་པའོ།། དེ་ཡང་ཞེས་སོགས་ནི་ངེས་དོན་མིན་པར་སྟོན་པའོ།། དེ་ལ་བླ་ན་མཆིས་པ་ནི་འདིའི་གོང་ན་ཁྱད་པར་ཅན་གྱི་བསྟན་པ་ཡོད་པའོ།། སྐབས་མཆིས་པ་ནི་འདི་ལས་སྐབས་ཁྱད་པར་ཅན་གྱི་བསྟན་པ་ཡོད་པའོ།། སྟོང་པ་ཉིད་མི་སྟོན་ཞིང་ཡོད་པར་སྟོན་པས་དྲང་བའི་དོན་ནོ།། རྩོད་པ་དང་བཅས་པ་ནི་གཞན་གྱིས་ [25]གཞིག་པར་བྱ་བ་དང་ཉན་ཐོས་སྡེ་པ་རྣམས་ཀྱི་རྩོད་པ་སྣ་བའི་གནས་སུ་གྱུར་པའོ།། ཞེས་ཞིན་ཚིག་གིས་བཤད་དོ།། མདོའི་དོན་ནི་དང་པོ་ནི་བླ་ན་{502}སྟེ་འདིའི་གོང་ན་ངེས་དོན་གཞན་ཡོད་པའོ།། གཉིས་པ་ནི། འདིའི་དོན་ཇི་ལྟར་བསྟན་པ་ལྟར་ཁས

བླངས་པ་ལ་རྩོལ་བ་གཞན་གྱི་སྐྱོན་གྱི་སྐབས་མཆིས་པའོ།། འདི་ལ་རྒྱ་ནག་གི་འགྲེལ་པ་ལས་རྩོལ་བ་དང་བཅས་པ་ཞེས་ཀྱང་བསྒྱུར་བས་དོན་དེ་ལྟར་རོ།། གསུམ་པ་ནི་འདིའི་དོན་གཞན་དུ་དྲང་དགོས་པའོ།། བཞི་པ་ནི་དོན་འདི་ལྟར་ཡིན་སྟོན་པས་གསལ་པོར[a]་མ་ཕྱེ་བས་དོན་ལ་མི་མཐུན་པར་རྩོད་པའོ།། [123] (275) འཁོར་ལོ་གཉིས་པ་ལ་ཆོས་རྣམས་ཀྱི་ཞེས་པ་ནས་བརྩམས་ནས་ཞེས་པའི་བར་ནི་བརྗོད་བྱ་གང་ལས་བརྩམས་པའོ།། ཐེག་པ་ཞེས་སོགས་ནི་གང་ལ་བསྐོར་བའི་གདུལ་བྱའོ།། སྟོང་པ་ཉིད་སྨོས་པའི་རྣམ་པས་ཞེས་པའི་དོན་ཆོས་ཀྱི་བདག་མེད་བསྟན་པ་ལ་འགྲེལ་པ་ཁ་ཅིག་གིས་བཤད་ལ། རྒྱ་ནག་གི་འགྲེལ་ཆེན་ལས། མི་ (12b) མངོན་པའི་རྣམ་པས་ཞེས་ཀྱང་འབྱུང་ལ་དེའི་དོན་ཡོད་པ་མཁྱུད་པ་ལ་བཤད་དོ།། འགྱུར་ནི་དེ་ལེགས་ལ་དོན་ནི་འཁོར་ལོ་ཕྱི་མ་གཉིས་བརྗོད་བྱ་ངོ་བོ་ཉིད་མེད་པ་ལས་བརྩམས་ནས་སྟོན་པར་འདྲ་བ་ལ་སྟོན་ཚུལ་གྱི་ཁྱད་པར་ནི་བར་པས་ངོ་བོ་ཉིད་ཡོད་མེད་སྔར་ལྟར་མ་ཕྱེ་བས་མི་མངོན་པའི་རྣམ་པས་ཞེས་གསུངས་ལ་ཐ་མས་ཕྱེ་བས་ལེགས་པར་རྣམ་པར་ཕྱེ་བ་ཞེས་གསུངས་སོ།། སྡེ་སྣོད་གསུམ་པ་ཡྀན་ཚིག་གིས་གསུམ་པ་ལ་ལྟོས[b]་ནས་ལྷ་ན་ཡོད་པ་སོགས་ལས་ [26] མ་བཤད་ཅིང་། རྒྱ་གར་གྱི་མཁན་པོ་ཡང་དག་བདེན་པའི་བཤད་པ་བཀོད་མོད་ཀྱང་ལེགས་པར་མི་སྣང་བས་མ་བྲིས་ལ་རང་གི་ལུགས་ནི་སྔ་མ་ལྟར་རོ།། [124] (276) འཁོར་ལོ་གསུམ་ {503} པ་ལ་བརྗོད་བྱ་གང་ལས་བརྩམས་པ་བར་པ་དང་འདྲ་ཞིང་། གདུལ་བྱ་ནི་ཐེག་པ་ཐམས་ཅད་ལ་ཡང་དག་པར་ཞུགས་པ་སྟེ་སྔ་མ་གཉིས་ནི་ཐེག་པ་ཆེ་ཆུང་སོ་སོ་བ་ཡིན་ལ་འདི་ནི་གཉི་གའི[c]་དབང་དུ་བྱས་པའོ།། ལེགས་པར་ཕྱེ་བ་ནི་སྔར་བཤད་པ་ལྟར་གཟུགས་ལ་སོགས་པའི་ཆོས་རེ་རེ་ལ་མཚན་ཉིད་གསུམ་གསུམ་གྱི་རྣམ་གཞག་དང་དེ་ལ་ངོ་བོ་ཉིད་མེད་ཚུལ་གསུམ་གསུམ་དུ་ཕྱེ་བའོ།། ཆོས་ཀྱི་འཁོར་ལོ་བསྐོར་བ་འདི་ནི་ཞེས་ཉེ་བའི་ཚིག་གིས་སྨོས་པ་ནི་དེ་མ་ཐག་ཏུ་སྨོས་པའི་ལེགས་པར་རྣམ་པར་ཕྱེ་བའི་འཁོར་ལོ་དགོངས་འགྲེལ་དང་དེ་བཞིན་དུ་ཕྱེ་བ་རྣམས་ལ་ཟེར་བ་ཡིན་གྱི། དུས་ཐ་མར་གསུངས་ཀྱང་ངོ་བོ་ཉིད་ཡོད་མེད་ཀྱི་ཚུལ་འདི་བཞིན་དུ་མ་ཕྱེ་བའི་མདོ་སྡེ་རྣམས་ལ་ཟེར་བ་མིན་ནོ།། འཁོར་ལོ་དེའི་ཆེ་བ་ནི་ལྷ་ན་

[a] Zi ling sku 'bum (357.7): *gsal bor;* this again is an application of the rule calling for *ba* after the suffix *la,* within not taking into account the fact that *gsal* has a non-manifest extra suffix *da.*

[b] Se rva zhol (12b.2) misreads *ltes.*

[c] Zi ling sku 'bum (357.20): *gnyis ka'i.*

མ་མཆིས་པ་སོགས་ཀྱིས་སྟོན་ཏེ།

> འདི་མཆོག་ཏུ་རྨད་དུ་བྱུང་ཞིང་དེ་ལས་ལྷག་ (13a) པ་གཞན་མེད་པས་བླ་ན་མ་མཆིས་པ་དང་། ཕྱིས་མཆོག་ཏུ་འགྱུར་བའི་སྐབས་དང་གཞིག་པའི་སྐབས་མེད་པས་སྐབས་མ་མཆིས་པ་དང་། ཡོད་མེད་རྫོགས་པར་བསྟན་པས་ངེས་པའི་དོན་དང་། རྩོད་པ་སླ་བའི་གཞིའི་གནས་མིན་པའོ།

ཞེས་ཝེན་ཚེག་གིས་བཤད་པ་ནི་སྐབས་མེད་པའི་སྔ་མ་མ་གཏོགས་པ་སྤྱིར་བདག་ [27] གིས་བླ་ན་ཡོད་པ་སོགས་ཀྱི་དོན་བཤད་པ་ལས་བཟློག་པ་དང་དོན་འདྲའོ།། མདོ་སྡེ་སྔ་མ་གཉིས་ཀྱི་སྒྲ་ཇི་བཞིན་པའི་དོན་ལ་སྐྱོན་གྱི་སྐབས་ཡོད་ལ་འདི་ལ་མེད་པ་ནི་སྒྲ་ཇི་བཞིན་པའི་དོན་དེ་ལས་གཞན་དུ་དྲང་དགོས་མི་དགོས་ཀྱི་རྒྱུ་མཚན་གྱིས་ཡིན་ལ། རྩོད་པ་ཡོད་མེད་ནི་མདོ་སྡེའི་དོན་ངོ་བོ་ཉིད་ཡོད་མེད་སྟོན་པས་ {504} དེ་ལྟར་གཏན་ལ་ཕབ་པ་ཡིན་མིན་ལ་མཁས་པས་བརྟགས་ན་རྩོད་ས་མེད་པ་ལ་བྱའི་[a] རྩོད་པ་གཞན་མེད་པར་སྟོན་པ་མིན་ནོ།།

གཉིས་པ་[དྲང་ངེས་ཀྱི་ཚུལ་ཅུང་ཟད་བཤད་པ་]ནི། [126] (278)
དེ་འདྲ་བའི་འཁོར་ལོ་དང་པོ་ལ་བདེན་བཞིའི་ཆོས་འཁོར་དང་གཉིས་པ་ལ་[b] མཚན་ཉིད་མེད་པ་དང་། གསུམ་པ་ལ་དོན་དམ་རྣམ་པར་ངེས་པའི་འཁོར་ལོ་ཞེས་རྒྱ་ནག་གི་འགྲེལ་ཆེན་ལས་བཏགས་ལ། མདོ་འདི་ཉིད་ཀྱི་ཚིག་དང་བསྟུན་ན་གསུམ་པ་ལ་ལེགས་པར་རྣམ་པར་ཕྱེ་བའི་འཁོར་ལོ་ཞེས་བྱའོ།། དེ་ལ་མདོ་འདིས་དྲང་ངེས་སུ་འཇོག་པའི་ཚུལ་ནི་ལེགས་པར་ཕྱེ་མ་ཕྱེ་གཉིས་ཡིན་ལ། དྲང་ངེས་སུ་འཇོག་པའི་གཞི་ནི་ཆོས་རྣམས་ལ་[c] རང་གི་མཚན་ཉིད་ཀྱིས་གྲུབ་པའི་ངོ་བོ་ཉིད་ཡོད་མཉམ་དུ་གསུངས་པ་དང་མེད་མཉམ་དུ་གསུངས་པ་དང་ཡོད་མེད་ལེགས་པར་ཕྱེ་བ་གསུམ་ཡིན་པ་ནི། མདོ་སྡེ་ལ་འགལ་སྤོང་གི་དྲི་བ་དང་དེའི་ལན་བཏབ་པ་དང་། ཆོས་རེ་རེ་ལ་ངོ་བོ་ཉིད་གསུམ་ (13b) གསུམ་གྱི་རྣམ་གཞག་བྱས་ནས་དེ་ལ་དགོངས་ནས་ངོ་བོ་ཉིད་མེད་པར་བཤད་ཚུལ་ཞུས་པ་དང་། དེ་

---

[a] Zi ling sku 'bum (358.15 and throughout): *bya yi;* other occurrences will not be cited. This seems to be an unnecessary emendation, since the two have the same meaning and since the disyllabic form is, by rule, limited to poetry. The Zi ling sku 'bum editors, or their predecessors, appear to have been intent on leaving their mark on the text; I doubt that many of this edition's variations stem from an older version.

[b] Zi ling sku 'bum (358.17) mistakenly omits *la.*

[c] Se rva zhol (13a.6) misreads *pa.*

དག་ལ་བརྟེན་ནས་དུས་སྔ་ཕྱིར་གསུངས་པའི་འཁོར་ལོ་གསུམ་གྱི་ [28] དྲང་ངེས་ཤེས་པ་ལས་ཤིན་ཏུ་གསལ་བ་ཡིན་ནོ།། [128] (278) དེའི་ཕྱིར་དུས་དང་པོར་བདེན་པ་བཞི་ལ་བརྩམས་ནས་རང་གི་མཚན་ཉིད་ཡོད་པ་སོགས་སུ་གསུངས་པའི་འཁོར་ལོ་དང་པོ་དྲང་དོན་དུ་སྟོན་པ་ཡིན་གྱི་དུས་དང་པོར་གསུངས་ཚད་ཀྱི་གསུང་རབ་ཐམས་ཅད་ལ་མིན་ཏེ། དཔེར་ན་དུས་དང་པོར་ཝཱ་ར་ཎཱ་སཱིར་[a]ལྔ་སྡེ་ལ་ཤམ་ཐབས་ཟླུམ་པོར་བགོ་བར་བྱའོ།། ཞེས་པ་ལ་སོགས་པའི་བསླབ་བྱ་ {505} གསུངས་པ་ལ་འདིར་དོགས་པ་གཅོད་[b]མི་དགོས་པ་བཞིན་ནོ།། དེ་བཞིན་དུ་གཉིས་པ་ཡང་ངོ་བོ་ཉིད་མེད་པ་སོགས་སུ་གསུངས་པ་ལ་བྱའི། དུས་གཉིས་པར་གསུངས་ཀྱང་ངོ་བོ་ཉིད་མེད་པ་སོགས་ལས་མ་བརྩམས་པའི་མདོ་སྡེ་ལ་འགལ་སྤོང་དྲིས་པ་ལྟར་གྱི་དོགས་པ་མེད་པས་དེ་འདིར་དྲང་དོན་དུ་སྟོན་མི་དགོས་སོ།། འཁོར་ལོ་གསུམ་པ་ངེས་དོན་དུ་བཤད་པ་ཡང་སྔར་བཤད་པ་ལྟར་ལེགས་པར་ཕྱེ་བ་རྣམས་ཡིན་གྱི་ཐམས་ཅད་མིན་པ་ནི་མདོ་ཉིད་ལས་ཀྱང་ཤིན་ཏུ་གསལ་ལོ། དཔེར་ན་མྱ་ངན་ལས་འདའ་ཁར་འདུལ་བ་མདོར་བསྡུས་ཞེས་བྱ་བ་ཙུང་མཐུན་དུ་གྲགས་པ་གསུངས་ཀྱང་དེ་མདོ་འདིས་ངེས་དོན་དུ་སྟོན་པ་མིན་པ་བཞིན་ནོ།། [129] (279) མདོ་འདིས་ཅི་ཞིག་འགྲུབ་པར་འདོད་ནས་ཆོས་འཁོར་གྱི་དྲང་ངེས་ཕྱེ་བ་ཡིན་སྙམ་ན། ཆོས་རྣམས་ལ་སོ་སོར་མ་ཕྱེ་བར་རང་གི་མཚན་ཉིད་ཀྱིས་གྲུབ་པ་དང་མ་གྲུབ་པར་བསྟན་པ་སྒྲ་ཇི་བཞིན་དུ་འཛིན་པ་བཟློག་[c]ནས་ཀུན་བརྟགས་རང་གི་མཚན་ཉིད་ཀྱིས་མ་གྲུབ་ཅིང་། ངོ་བོ་ཉིད་གཞན་གཉིས་རང་གི་མཚན་ཉིད་ [29] ཀྱིས་གྲུབ་པ་ (14a) དང་གཞན་དབང་ལ་ཀུན་བརྟགས་ཀྱིས་སྟོང་པའི་སྟོང་ཉིད་ལམ་གྱི་དམིགས་པའི་དོན་དམ་མཐར་ཐུག་ཏུ་དེའི་གདུལ་བྱ་ལ་བསྟན་པར་བཞེད་ནས་ཡིན་ནོ།། དེའི་ཕྱིར་འཁོར་ལོ་དང་པོ་གཉིས་དྲང་དོན་དང་ཐ་མ་ངེས་དོན་དུ་གསུངས་སོ།། [129] (279) དེའི་ཕྱིར་ཁ་ཅིག་གིས་མདོ་འདི་ལ་བརྟེན་ནས་དུས་གསུམ་པར་གསུངས་པའི་མདོ་ཐམས་ཅད་ངེས་དོན་དུ་བསྒྲུབས་ནས་གཞན་སྡེའི་རིགས་ཅན་བདག་ཏུ་སྨྲ་བ་ལ་ཞེན་པ་རྣམས་དྲང་བའི་ཕྱིར་དུ་གསུངས་པ་འགའ་ཞིག་སྒྲ་ཇི་བཞིན་པར་འདོད་

---

[a] Sarnath tsang (23.5) *wā rā ṇa sīr;* given the consistency of the other editions, it is likely that this unusual spelling represents a "correction" by the Sarnath editors.

[b] Se rva zhol (13b.3) misreads *gcad,* corrected in the Delhi GD zhol to *gcod.* All other editions: *gcod*—Delhi NG dkra shis lhun po (505.1), Zi ling sku 'bum (359.11), Peking (173.1.5), Sarnath gtsang (28.7), and Kalimpong (33.6).

[c] Zi ling sku 'bum (359.20) uses the past form: *bzlogs.*

ཅིང་། {506} ཆོས་ཉིད་མ་གཏོགས་པའི་ཆོས་ཅན་ཐམས་ཅད་འཕྲུལ་པའི་སློས་སློམ་པ་མ་གཏོགས་པ་རང་གི་ངོ་བོ[a]་གྲུབ་པ་ཅུང་ཟད་ཀྱང་མེད་ཅིང་ཆོས་ཉིད་བདེན་པར་གྲུབ་པའི་བདེན་མི་བདེན་རྣམ་པར་ཕྱེ་བ་ནི་སྔར་བཤད་པའི་ལེགས་པར་རྣམ་པར་ཕྱེ་བའི་དོན་དུ་འདོད་དོ།། དེ་ལ་གཞན་དག་གིས་ནི་མདོ་འདིས་དྲང་ངེས་ཕྱེ་བ་ལྟར་ཡིན་ན་ཕྱོགས་སྔ་མས་སྨྲ་བ་ལྟར་འགྱུར་རོ་སྙམ་ནས་དྲང་ངེས་ཀྱི་ཚུལ་དེ་སྒྲ་ཇི་བཞིན་པ་མིན་ནོ་ཞེས་འགོག་གོ། དེ་གཉིས་ཀས་ཀྱང་མདོ་འདིར་མདོ་སྡེ་ལ་འགལ་སྤོང་གི་དྲི་བ་བྱུང་ལུགས་དང་དེ་ལ་སྟོན་པས་ལན་བཏབ་ལུགས་དང་དེ་ལ་བརྟེན་ནས་དྲང་ངེས་སུ་བཞག་ལུགས་རྣམས་ལ་ཞིབ་ཏུ་མ་བརྟགས་པར་དྲང་ངེས་ཀྱི་རྣམ་དབྱེ་བྱས་པའི་སྐབས་ཙམ་ཞིག་ལ་རྩོད་པར་སྣང་ངོ་།།

[a] Ḍa-drin-rap-ḍen's *Annotations* (48.4) misreads *rang gi ngo* ***bos*** *grub pa.*

གཉིས་པ་ [དེའི་དོན་ཇི་ལྟར་བཀྲལ་བའི་ཚུལ་]ལ་གཉིས། སློབ་དཔོན་ཐོགས་མེད་ཀྱིས་གཙོ་བོར་དགོངས་འགྲེལ་ལ་བརྟེན་ཚུལ་དང་། དེ་ལ་བརྟེན་ནས་དེ་ཁོ་ན་ཉིད་གཏན་ལ་ཕབ་པའི་ཚུལ་ལོ༎ [135] (284)[30]

དང་པོ་ [སློབ་དཔོན་ཐོགས་མེད་ཀྱིས་གཙོ་བོར་དགོངས་འགྲེལ་ལ་བརྟེན་ཚུལ་]ནི། [135] (284)

བསྡུ་བ་ལས།

དོན་དམ་པ་མཚན་ཉིད་ལྔ་དང་ལྡན་པ་ཡང་དགོངས་འགྲེལ་ལས་འབྱུང་བ་བཞིན་ཤེས་པར་(14b) བྱའོ།

ཞེས་དགོངས་འགྲེལ་གྱི་དོན་དམ་པའི་ལེའུ་རྣམས་དྲངས་ཤིང་།

ཆོས་རྣམས་ཀྱི་མཚན་ཉིད་ནི་དགོངས་འགྲེལ་ལས་འབྱུང་བ་བཞིན་བལྟ་བར་བྱའོ།

ཞེས་མཚན་ཉིད་གསུམ་སྟོན་པའི་མཚན་ཉིད་ཀྱི་ལེའུ་རྣམས་དྲངས་ལ།

ཆོས་རྣམས་ཀྱི་ངོ་བོ་ཉིད་མེད་པའི་མཚན་ཉིད་ནི་དགོངས་འགྲེལ་ལས་འབྱུང་བ་བཞིན་བལྟ་བར་བྱའོ།

ཞེས་མདོ་སྡེ་ལ་འགལ་སྤོང་གི་དྲིས་ལན་དང་དྲང་ངེས་ལ་སོགས་པ་{507}རྣམས་སྟོན་པའི་ངོ་བོ་ཉིད་མེད་པའི་ལེའུ་རྣམས་དྲངས་སོ༎ དེ་བཞིན་དུ་རྣམ་ཤེས་ཚོགས་བརྒྱད་དང་མཐར་ཐུག་རིགས་ངེས་པ་ཡང་དགོངས་འགྲེལ་ནས་གསུངས་པ་རྣམས་དྲངས་སོ༎ བྱང་སའི་དེ་ཁོ་ནའི་ལེའུ་དང་དེའི་རྣམ་པར་གཏན་ལ་དབབ་པ་དང་ཐེག་བསྡུས་ལས་ཀྱང་དགོངས་འགྲེལ་ལས་གཞན་དབང་ངོ་བོ་དང་ཁྱད་པར་དུ་བཏགས་པའི་ཀུན་བརྟགས་ཀྱིས་སྟོང་པ་ཡོངས་གྲུབ་ཏུ་གསུངས་པ་ཉིད་བཤད་པའི་རྣམ[a]གྲངས་མང་པོས་གཏན་ལ་འབེབས་པར་མཛད་དོ༎ མདོ་སྡེ་རྒྱན་དང་དབུས་མཐའ་ལ་སོགས་པར་དེ་ཁོ་ནའི་དོན་བཤད་པ་དང་དེ་དག་གི[b]འགྲེལ་པ་རྣམས་སུ་བསྟན་པའི་གནད་རྣམས་ཀྱང་མདོ་སྡེ་འདིའི་དོན་དང་ཤིན་ཏུ་མཐུན་པས་ལུགས་འདི་ལ་མདོ་སྡེ་འདིའི་དོན་གཏན་ལ་འབེབས་པ་ནི་ཆ་བར་སྣང་ངོ༎

[a] Se rva zhol (14b.4) misreads *rnams.*

[b] Grags pa & rnam rgyal (30.3) misreads ***de dag ga.***

གཉིས་པ་ [དེ་ལ་བརྟེན་ནས་དེ་ཁོ་ན་ཉིད་གཏན་ལ་ཕབ་པའི་ཚུལ་]ལ་གསུམ། མཐའ་གཉིས་སྤོང་ཚུལ་སྤྱིར་བསྟན་པ།[a] {31}སྒྲོ་འདོགས་ཀྱི་མཐའ་བྱེ་བྲག་ཏུ་དགག་པ། དེས་གསུང་རབ་ཀྱི་དྲང་ངེས་འབྱེད་པའི་ཚུལ་ལོ།། [138] (287)

དང་པོ་ [མཐའ་གཉིས་སྤོང་ཚུལ་སྤྱིར་བསྟན་པ་]ལ་གསུམ། བྱང་ས་ནས་བཤད་པའི་ཚུལ་དང་། བསྡུ་བ་ནས་བཤད་པའི་ཚུལ་དང་། དེ་དག་ལས་གཞན་པའི་གཞུང་ནས་བཤད་ཚུལ་ལོ།། [140] (287)

དང་པོ་ [བྱང་ས་ནས་བཤད་པའི་ཚུལ་]ལ་གཉིས། {15a}སྒྲོ་སྐུར་དུ་ལྟ་བའི་ཚུལ་དང་། དེ་གཉིས་འགོག་པའི་ཚུལ་ལོ།། [140] (287)

དང་པོ་ [སྒྲོ་སྐུར་དུ་ལྟ་བའི་ཚུལ་]ནི། [140] (287)

བྱང་ས་ལས།[b]

> ཇི་ལྟར་ཡོད་ཅེ་ན་ཡོད་པ་མ་ཡིན་པ་ལ་སྒྲོ་བཏགས་པའི་ལེགས་པར་མ་ཟིན་པ་སྤངས་པ་དང་ཡང་དག་པ་ལ་སྐུར་པ[c]་བཏབ་པའི་ལེགས་པར་མ་ཟིན་པ་སྤངས་པ་ཡོད་དེ།

ཞེས་སྒྲོ་སྐུར་སྤངས་པའི་ཚུལ་གྱིས་ཡོད་དོ་ཞེས་གསུངས་པའི་སྒྲོ་འདོགས་དང་སྐུར་འདེབས་ནི་ཇི་ལྟ་བུ་ཞིག་ཡིན་ {508}ཞེ་ན། དེ་གཉིས་ནི་བྱང་ས་ལས།[d]

[a] Delhi NG dkra shis lhun po (507.4) misreads *bstan pa la;* Se rva zhol (14b.5), Zi ling sku 'bum (361.12), Peking (173.3.6), Sarnath gtsang (31.1), and Kalimpong (36.6): *bstan pa.*

[b] Chap. 4; Peking 5538, vol. 110, 144.1.3-144.1.4. The Sanskrit from Unrai Wogihara, *Bodhisattvabhūmi: A Statement of the Whole Course of the Bodhisattva (Being the Fifteenth Section of Yogācārabhūmi)* (Tokyo: Seigo Kenkyūkai, 1930-1936), 44.5, is:

> *kathaṃ vidyate. a-sad-bhūta-samāropā-saṃgrāha-vivarjito* [Dutt: *vivarjitaśca*] *bhūtāpavādāsaṃgrāha-vivarjitaś ca vidyate.*

See also Nalinaksha Dutt, *Bodhisattvabhūmi (Being the XVth Section of Asangapada's Yogacarabhumi),* Tibetan Sanskrit Works Series, 7 (Patna, India: K. P. Jayaswal Research Institute, 1966), 30.6.

[c] Delhi NG dkra shis lhun po (507.6), Peking (173.3.8), Sarnath gtsang (31.8): *ba;* Se rva zhol (15a.1), Zi ling sku 'bum (361.18), Grags pa & rnam rgyal (30.13), and Kalimpong (37.2): *pa.*

[d] The Sanskrit in Wogihara (*Bodhisattvabhūmi,* 45.14) is:

གཟུགས་ལ་སོགས་པའི་ཆོས་རྣམས་དང་[a]གཟུགས་ལ་སོགས་པའི་དངོས་པོ་ལ་འདོགས་པའི་ཚིག་གི་ངོ་བོ་ཉིད་ཀྱི་རང་གི་མཚན་ཉིད་ཡོད་པ་མ་ཡིན་པ་ལ་སྒྲོ་བཏགས་ནས་མངོན་པར་ཞེན་པ་གང་ཡིན་པ་དང་།

ཞེས་པ་འདིས་སྒྲོ་འདོགས་ཚུལ་གསུངས་ལ།

བཏགས་པའི་ཚིག[b]གི་མཚན་མའི་གཞི་བཏགས་པའི་ཚིག[c]གི་མཚན་མའི་རྟེན་དུ་གྱུར་པ། བརྗོད་དུ་མེད་པའི་བདག་ཉིད་ཀྱིས་དོན་དམ་པར་ཡོད་པ་ཡང་དག་པའི་དངོས་པོ་ལ་ཐམས་ཅད་ཀྱི[d]ཐམས་ཅད་དུ་མེད་དོ་ཞེས་སྐུར་པ་འདེབས་ཤིང་ཆུད་གཟོན་པར་བྱེད་པ་གང་ཡིན་པ་འདི་གཉིས་ནི་ཆོས་འདུལ་བ་འདི་ལས[e]རབ་ཏུ་ཉམས་པ་ཡིན་པར་རིག་པར་བྱའོ།

ཞེས་པ་ཕྱི་མས་ [32] ནི་སྐུར་པ་འདེབས་ཚུལ་བསྟན་ལ་ཆུད་གཟོན་ཞེས་པ་མན་ཆད་ཀྱིས་ནི་ཐེག་པ་ཆེན་པོའི་ཆོས་ཟབ་མོ་ལས་ཉམས་པར་བསྟན་ཏོ།། གཟུགས་ཞེས་པ་ནས་དངོས་པོ་ལ་ཞེས་པའི་བར་གྱིས་ཀུན་བརྟགས་འདོགས་པའི་གཞི་བསྟན་ཏེ། དེ་ལ་འདོགས་པའི་ཚིག་གི་ངོ་བོ་ཉིད་ཅེས་པ་ནི་ཚིག་གིས་བཏགས་པའི་ངོ་བོ་ཉིད་ལ་བྱའི། འདོགས་བྱེད་ཀྱི

yaś ca rūpādīnāṃ dharmāṇāṃ rūpādikasya vastunaḥ prajñapti-vāda-sva-bhāvaṃ sva-lakṣaṇaṃ a-sad-bhūta-samāropato 'bhiniviśate. yaś cāpi prajñapti-vāda-nimittādhi-ṣṭhānaṃ prajñapti-vāda-nimitta-saṃniśrayaṃ nir-abhilāpy'ātmakatayā paramārtha-sad-bhūtaṃ vastv apavādamāno nāśayati sarveṇa sarvaṃ nāstīti. a-sad-bhūta-samā-rope tāvad ye doṣāḥ. te pūrvaṃ eva nirūpitāḥ [Dutt: *nirūpitā*] *uttānā viśaditāḥ pra-kāśitāḥ. yaiḥ doṣaiḥ* [Dutt: *yair doṣai*] *rūpādike vastuny a-sad-bhūta-samāropāt pra-naṣṭo bhavaty asmād dharma-vinayād iti veditavyaḥ.*

In Dutt, *Bodhisattvabhūmi,* see 30.26. The Tibetan, in both Dzong-ka-ba's citation and the Peking, abbreviates the end.

a The conjunction *dang* is absent in the Peking edition, as is its equivalent in the Sanskrit; see the previous footnote for the references.

b The Peking (5538, vol. 110, 144.3.1) reads *'dogs pa'i tshig;* the Sanskrit is *prajñaptivāda.*

c Ibid.

d *thams cad kyi thams cad du, sarveṇa sarvaṃ.* Gung-ru Chö-jung's *Garland of White Lotuses* (65b.6) takes this phrase to be *thams cad* ***kyis*** *thams cad du* (which mirrors the Sanskrit) and glosses it as "by all Proponents of Non-Nature in all places, times, and tenets" (*ngo bo nyid med par smra ba thams cad kyis yul dus grub pa'i mtha' thams cad du*); A-ku Lo-drö-gya-tso (*Precious Lamp,* 181.2) has the same reading but interprets it as "all phenomena not existing in all places, times, and tenets" (*chos thams cad yul dus grub mtha' thams cad du med pa*).

e Peking reads *la,* but *las* accords more with the Sanskrit ablative *dharmavinayād.*

ཚིག་ལ་མི་བྱ་སྟེ་བསྐུ་བ་ལ་སོགས་པ་ནས་གསལ་ (15b) བར་བཤད་དོ།། བྱང་སའི་སྐབས་གཞན་དུ་བྱུང་བ་རྣམས་ཀྱང་དེ་ལྟར་ཤེས་པར་བྱའོ།། ཚིག་གིས[a] བཏགས་པའི་ངོ་བོ་དེ་ཉིད་རང་གི་མཚན་ཉིད་ཀྱིས་ཡོད་པ་མིན་པ་ལ་དེའི་རང་གི་མཚན་ཉིད་ཡོད་དོ་ཞེས་ཞེན་པ་ནི་སྒྲོ་འདོགས་སོ།། བཏགས་པའི་ཚིག་གི་མཚན་མའི་གཞི་ནི་བཏགས་པའི་ཚིག་གི་མཚན་ {509} མའི་རྟེན་ཞེས་པས་བཤད་དེ་ཀུན་བརྟགས་ཀྱི་གདགས་གཞིའོ།། དེ་ཉིད་བརྗོད་དུ་མེད་པའི་ཚུལ་གྱིས[b] དོན་དམ་པར་ཡོད་པ་ལ་ཐམས་ཅད་ཀྱི་ཐམས་ཅད་དུ་མེད་དོ་ཞེས་འཛིན་པ་ནི་སྐུར་འདེབས་སོ།། དེ་ལྟར་བྱས་ན་ཀུན་བརྟགས་དོན་དམ་པར་ཡོད་དོ། ཞེས་པ་ནི་སྒྲོ་འདོགས་དང་ངོ་བོ་ཉིད་གཞན་གཉིས་དོན་དམ་པར་མེད་དོ་ཞེས་པ་ནི་སྐུར་འདེབས་ཡིན་ཏེ། དང་པོ་ཀུན་རྫོབ་དང་གཞན་གཉིས་དོན་དམ་པར་ཡོད་པའི་ཕྱིར་རོ།། དོན་དམ་པར་ཡོད་པ་ལ་མེད་པར་ལྟ་བ་སྐུར་འདེབས་སུ་བཤད་པའི་ཟླས་དྲངས་ན་དོན་དམ་པར་མེད་པ་ལ་ཡོད་པར་ལྟ་བ་སྒྲོ་འདོགས་སུ་བཤད་དགོས་ལ་སྐབས་འདིར་ཀུན་བརྟགས་རང་གི་མཚན་ཉིད་ཀྱིས་ [33] ཡོད་པར་འཛིན་པ་ལ་སྒྲོ་འདོགས་སུ་གསུངས་ཀྱིས[c] དེ་དོན་དམ་པར་ཡོད་པར་འཛིན་པ་ཚིག་གིས་གསལ་བར་མ་བསྟན་ཀྱང་རང་གི་མཚན་ཉིད་ཀྱིས་ཡོད་ན་དོན་དམ་པར་ཡོད་པ་གཞུང་གི་དོན་ཡིན་པས་ཀུན་བརྟགས་དོན་དམ་པར་ཡོད་པ་སྒྲོ་འདོགས་སུ་འགྲོ་བའི་ཕྱོགས་སོ།། དགོངས་འགྲེལ་ལས། ཀུན་བརྟགས་པའི་མཚན་ཉིད་ཀྱི་གནས་འདུ་བྱེད་ཀྱི་མཚན་མ་ངོ་བོ་དང་ཁྱད་པར་དུ་འདོགས་པའི་གཞི་གཞན་དབང་ལ་གསུངས་པས། གཞུང་འདིས་བཏགས་པའི་ཚིག་གི་མཚན་མའི་གཞི་དོན་དམ་པར་ཡོད་པ་ལ་མེད་ཅེས་གསུངས་པའི་དངོས་བསྟན་ (16a) གཞན་དབང་ཡིན་མོད་ཀྱང་། དེ་དོན་དམ་པར་མེད་ན་ཡོངས་གྲུབ་ཀྱང་དོན་དམ་དུ་མེད་པར་འགྱུར་བས་གཉིས་ཀ་ལ་བཤད་པ་ལ་སྐྱོན་མེད་དེ་བྱང་ས་ལས།[d]

[a] Sarnath gtsang (32.8) misreads *gi.*

[b] Se rva zhol (15b.2) misreads *gyi;* the other editions: *gyis*—Delhi NG dkra shis lhun po (509.1), Zi ling sku 'bum (362.16), Peking (173.4.7), Sarnath gtsang (32.12), and Kalimpong (38.4).

[c] Zi ling sku 'bum (363.2): *kyi.* It is likely that the change was made to accord with the dictum that the five instrumental endings are not to be used for conjunction-disjunction, whereas the five genitive endings are. However, this rule is contravened repeatedly in Tibetan literature.

[d] Peking 5538, vol. 110, 144.3.5-144.3.6. The Sanskrit in Wogihara (*Bodhisattvabhūmi,* 45.25) and Dutt (*Bodhisattvabhūmi,* 31.6) is:

rūpādīnāṃ dharmāṇāṃ vastu-mātram apavādamānasya [Dutt: *apavādato*] *naiva*

> གཟུགས་ལ་སོགས་པའི་ཆོས་རྣམས་ཀྱི་དངོས་པོ་ཙམ་ལ་སྐུར་པ་འདེབས་པ་ལ་ {510} ནི་དེ་ཁོ་ན་ཡང་མེད་ལ་འདོགས་པ་ཡང་མེད་དེ་དེ་[a] གཉིས་ཀ་ཡང་མི་རིགས་སོ།

ཞེས་གསུངས་པའི་ཕྱིར་ཏེ་དངོས་པོ་གཞན་དབང་ལ་སྐུར་པ་འདེབས་ཚུལ་ནི་ཐ་སྙད་དུ་མེད་དོ་ཞེས་པའམ་སྤྱིར་མེད་དོ་ཞེས་པ་མིན་གྱི་སྔར་གོང་དུ་དོན་དམ་པར་ཡོད་པ་ལ་མེད་ཅེས་པ་སྐུར་འདེབས་སུ་གསུངས་པ་ལྟར་རོ།།

གཉིས་པ་ [དེ་གཉིས་འགོག་པའི་ཚུལ་] ནི། [143] (288)

གལ་ཏེ་སྒྲོ་སྐུར་བྱེད་ཚུལ་དེ་ལྟར་ཡིན་ན་དེ་གཉིས་སྤོང་ཚུལ་ཇི་ལྟར་ཡིན་སྙམ་ན། དེ་ལ་སྒྲོ་འདོགས་ཀྱི་མཐའ་ནི་ཆོས་གང་ལ་ཡང་དེའི་ངོ་བོ་དང་ཁྱད་པར་དུ་བཏགས་པ་དེས་དེ་དོན་དམ་པར་སྟོང་པར་ [34] བསྟན་པས་འགོག་སྟེ་ཞིབ་ཏུ་འཆད་པར་འགྱུར་རོ།། སྐུར་འདེབས་ནི་བྱང་ས་ལས། དེ་མ་ཐག་ཏུ་དྲངས་པའི་ལུང་དེ་དང་དེའི་རྗེས་ཐོགས་སུ[b]

> འདི་ལྟ་སྟེ་དཔེར་ན་གཟུགས་ལ་སོགས་པའི་ཕུང་པོ་རྣམས་ཡོད་ན་གང་ཟག་གདགས་སུ་རུང་གི་མེད་དུ་ཟིན་ན་ནི་དངོས་པོ་མེད་པ་ལ་གང་ཟག་གདགས་སུ་མེད་དོ།། དེ་བཞིན་དུ་གཟུགས་ལ་སོགས་པའི་ཆོས་རྣམས་ཀྱི་དངོས་པོ་ཙམ་ཡོད་ན་གཟུགས་ལ་སོགས་པའི་ཆོས་འདོགས་པའི་ཚིག་ཉེ་བར་གདགས་སུ་རུང་གི། མེད་དུ་ཟིན་ན་དངོས་པོ་མེད་པ་ལ་གདགས་པའི་ཚིག་གིས་ཉེ་བར་འདོགས་པ་མེད་དོ།། དེ་ལ་འདོགས་པའི་གཞི་མེད་དུ་ཟིན་ན་ནི་གཞི་མེད་པར་འགྱུར་བས་འདོགས་པ་ཡང་མེད་པར་འགྱུར་རོ་

ཞེས་གསུངས་པས་བཀག་ (16b) གོ།། དེ་ལ་འདིར་སྐུར་འདེབས་འགོག་པའི་ཕྱོགས་སྔ[c]ཁས་

tattvaṃ nāpi prajñaptis tad-ubhayam etan na yujyate.

a This reading of *de kho na yang med la 'dogs pa yang med de de* is preferable to the Peking *de kho na yang med pa la 'dogs pa yang/ de* since the former accords more with the Sanskrit (see the previous footnote).

b Peking 5538, vol. 110, 144.3.6-144.5.1. The Sanskrit in Wogihara (*Bodhisattvabhūmi,* 46.1) and Dutt (*Bodhisattvabhūmi,* 31.7) is:

> *tad-yathā satsu rūpādiṣu skandheṣu pudgala-prajñatir yujyate. nā-satsu. nir-vastukā pudgala-prajñaptiḥ. evaṃ sati rūpāḍīnām dharmāṇāṃ vastu-mātre sa rūpādi-dharma-prajñapti-vādopacāro yujyate. nā-sati. nir-vastukaḥ prajñapti-vādopacāraḥ. tatra prajñapter vastu nāstīti niradhiṣṭhānā prajñaptir api nāsti.*

c Se rva zhol (16b.1) misreads *sde;* in the Delhi GD zhol, this has been corrected to *snga,* as is the reading in the other editions—Delhi NG dkra shis lhun po (510.6), Zi ling sku

ལེན་མཁན་ནི་གཞན་སྡེར་འོང་དོན་མེད་ལ་རང་སྡེ་ཡང་ཉན་ཐོས་སྡེ་པ་ལ་མིང་དང་བརྡས་ཐ་སྙད་འདོགས་པའི་གཞིའི་ {511} གཟུགས་སོགས་ཀྱི་དངོས་པོ་རང་གི་མཚན་ཉིད་ཀྱིས་མེད་ཅེས་ཁས་ལེན་པ་ཡང་མེད་དོ།། དེས་ན་བསྡུ་བ་ལས་བཤད་པ་ལྟར་ཐེག་པ་ཆེན་པོའི་གྲུབ་མཐའ་སྨྲ་བ་ཡིན་ལ་དེ་ཡང་ཆོས་རྣམས་རང་གི་མཚན་ཉིད་ཀྱིས་མ་གྲུབ་ཅེས་སྨྲ་བའི་ངོ་བོ་ཉིད་མེད་པར་སྨྲ་བ་རྣམས་སོ།། དེ་དག་གིས་ནི་གཞན་དབང་ལ་སོགས་པའི་ཆོས་རྣམས་སྤྱིར་མི་སྲིད་པ་དང་ཐ་སྙད་དུ་མེད་ཅེས་འདོད་པ་གཏན་མིན་པས་དོན་དམ་པར་མ་གྲུབ་ཅེས་སྨྲའོ།། དེས་ན་དངོས་པོ་ཙམ་མེད་ [35] ན་ཞེས་འགོག་པ་ནི་སྔར་བཤད་པ་ལྟར་དོན་དམ་པར་ཡོད་པའི་ཡང་དག་གི་དངོས་པོ་མི་སྲིད་ཅེས་འགོག་པ་ཡིན་ཏེ། འདིའི་ལུགས་ཀྱིས་ཀུན་བརྟགས་ལ་རང་གི་མཚན་ཉིད་ཀྱིས་མ་གྲུབ་པ་དང་དོན་དམ་པར་མེད་ན་མེད་མི་དགོས་ཀྱང་། ངོ་བོ་ཉིད་གཞན་གཉིས་དོན་དམ་པར་རམ་རང་གི་མཚན་ཉིད་ཀྱིས་མ་གྲུབ་ན་མེད་པ་ཡིན་ནོ།། གཞན་དབང་སེམས་སེམས་བྱུང་རང་གི་རྒྱུ་རྐྱེན་ལ་བརྟེན་ནས་སྐྱེ་བ་དེ་རང་གི་རང་མཚན་གྱིས་གྲུབ་པའི་སྐྱེ་བ་ཡིན་ན་དོན་དམ་པའི་སྐྱེ་བར[a]་འགྱུར་ལ། དེ་མིན་ན་བློས་སྐྱེ་བར་རློམས[b]་ནས་སྐྱེའོ་ཞེས་བཏགས་པ་ཙམ་དུ་ཟད་ཀྱི་སེམས་སེམས་བྱུང་གི་དངོས་པོ་ལ་སྐྱེ་བ་ཡོད་པར་མི་འགྱུར་རོ[c]་སྙམ་དུ་ལུགས་འདིས་བསམས་སོ།། དེས་ན་གཞན་དབང་གི་སྐྱེ་འགག་བློ་འཁྲུལ་པས[d]་སྐྱེ་འགག་ཏུ་ཞེན་པ་ཙམ་གྱི་ངོར[e]་ཡིན་པས་ཀུན་རྫོབ་ཏུ་སྐྱེ་འགག་ཡོད་པས་སྐུར་འདེབས་སུ་མི་འགྱུར་རོ་ཞེས་ (17a) པས་ལན་མི་ཐེབས་ཏེ། ཐག་པ་ལ་སྦྲུལ[f]་དུ་ཞེན་པའི་འཁྲུལ་ངོར་ཐག་པ་སྦྲུལ་ཡིན་ལ་སྤྱིར་ཐག་པ་སྦྲུལ་དུ་གྲུབ་

'bum (364.5), Peking (174.1.3), Sarnath gtsang (34.12), and Kalimpong (40.5).

a Se rva zhol (16b.5) misreads *par;* in the Delhi GD zhol, this has been emended to *bar.*

b Zi ling sku 'bum (364.17): *rlom.*

c Se rva zhol (16b.6) lacks *ro,* which has been added in Delhi GD zhol and appears in the other editions—Delhi NG dkra shis lhun po (511.5), Zi ling sku 'bum (364.18), Peking (174.2.1), Sarnath gtsang (35.10), and Kalimpong (41.5).

d Delhi NG dkra shis lhun po (511.5), Delhi GD zhol (16b.6), Sarnath gtsang (35.11), and Kalimpong (41.6): *pas;* Se rva zhol (16b.6), Zi ling sku 'bum (364.19), and Peking (174.2.1): *bas.* The variations reflect whether the presence of the non-manifest extra suffix *da* at the end of the previous syllable is taken into account.

e Delhi NG dkra shis lhun po (511.6), Zi ling sku 'bum (364.19), Delhi GD zhol (16b.6), Sarnath gtsang (35.12), and Kalimpong (41.6): *ngor;* Se rva zhol (16b.6) and Peking (174.2.1) misread *dor.*

f Se rva zhol (16b.5) and Delhi NG dkra shis lhun po (511.6) misread *sprul du;* the other editions: *sbrul du*—Zi ling sku 'bum (365.1), Sarnath gtsang (35.13), Kalimpong (42.1), and Peking (174.2.2). Delhi GD zhol (17a.1) has been wrongly emended to *sbrul* ***bu.***

མ་མྱོང་ཞིས་པ་ {512} དང་འདྲ་བར་གཞན་དབང་གི་རྒྱུ་འབྲས་ཀྱང་རྒྱུ་འབྲས་བདེན་འཛིན་གྱི་འཁྲུལ་ངོར་རྒྱུ་འབྲས་ཡིན་གྱི། གཞན་དབང་པོ་རང་རྒྱུ་འབྲས་སུ་མ་གྲུབ་ཅེས་འདོད་ན་ནི་དེ་འདྲ་ཁས་བླངས་ཀྱང་དགེ་སྡིག་ལས་བདེ་སྡུག་སྐྱེ་བའི་ལས་འབྲས་གཞག་ས་མེད་པར་སོང་བས་སྐུར་འདེབས་སྤོང་མི་ནུས་ལ། དེ་འདྲ་མིན་པའི་རྒྱུ་འབྲས་འདོད་ན་ནི་རང་གི་མཚན་ཉིད་ཀྱིས་གྲུབ་པའི་རྒྱུ་འབྲས་ཡིན་པས་དོན་དམ་ [36] པར་ཡོད་པའི་དོན་གྲུབ་པ་ཡིན་ནོ་སྙམ་དུ་བསམས་ནས། གདགས་གཞི་མེད་ན་འདོགས་པ་ཡང་མེད་པས་ཆོས་ཐམས་ཅད་བཏགས་པ་ཙམ་ཡིན་པ་དང་དེ་ཉིད་དེ་ཁོ་ནའི་དོན་དུ་བྱེད་པ་གཉིས་ཀ་མི་སྲིད་པས་ཆད་ལྟའི་གཙོ་བོར་འགྱུར་རོ་ཞེས་བཤད་དེ། བྱང་ས་ལས།[a]

> དེ་བས་ན་གང་ཟག་ཁ་ཅིག་ཤེས་པར་དཀའ་བའི་མདོ་སྡེ་ཐེག་པ་ཆེན་པོ་དང་ལྡན་པ་ཟབ་མོ་སྟོང་པ་ཉིད་དང་ལྡན་པ་དགོངས་པའི་དོན་བསྟན་པ་དག་ཐོས་ནས་བཤད་པའི་དོན་ཡང་དག་པ་ཇི་ལྟ་བ་བཞིན་དུ་མ་ཤེས་ནས་ཚུལ་བཞིན་མ་ཡིན་པར་རྣམ་པར་བརྟགས་ཏེ་རིགས་པ་མ་ཡིན་པས་བསྐྱེད་པའི་རྟོག་པ་ཙམ་གྱིས་འདི་ཐམས་ཅད་ནི་བཏགས་པ་ཙམ་དུ་ཟད་དེ། འདི་ནི་དེ་ཁོ་ན་ཡིན་ནོ་སུ་འདི་ལྟར་ལྟ་བ་དེ་ནི་ཡང་དག་པར་ལྟ་བ་ཡིན་ནོ་ཞེས་དེ་ལྟར་ལྟ་ཞིང་དེ་སྐད་སྨྲའོ།། དེ་དག་གི་ལྟར་ན་འདོགས་པའི་གཞིའི་དངོས་པོ་ཙམ་ཡང་མེད་པས་འདོགས་པ་དེ་ཉིད་ཀྱང་ཐམས་ཅད་ཀྱི་ཐམས་ཅད་དུ་མེད་པར་འགྱུར་ན་བཏགས་པ་ཙམ་གྱི་དེ་ཁོ་ན་ལྟ་ཡོད་པར་ག་ལ་འགྱུར་ཏེ། དེ་ (17b) བས་ན་རྣམ་གྲངས་དེས་ན་དེ་དག {513} གིས་ནི་དེ་ཁོ་ན་དང་བཏགས་པ་དེ་གཉིས་ཀ་ལ་ཡང་སྐུར་པ་བཏབ་པར་འགྱུར་ཏེ། བཏགས་པ་དང་དེ་

[a] Peking 5538, vol. 110, 144.4.1-144.5.5. The passage immediately follows the previous citation; the Sanskrit in Wogihara (*Bodhisattvabhūmi,* 46.7) and Dutt (*Bodhisattvabhūmi,* 31.10) is:

> *ato ya ekatyā dur-vijñeyān sūtrāntān mahāyāna-pratisaṃyuktāṃ gambhīrāṃ cchūnyatā* [Dutt: *pratisaṃyuktān gambhīrān śūnyatā*]*-pratisaṃyuktān abhiprāyikārtha-nirūpitāṃ* [Dutt: *nirūpitān*] *cchrutvā yathābhūtaṃ bhāṣitasyārtham an-abhijñāyā* [Dutt: *avijñāyā*] *'yoniśo vikalpyā-yogavihitena tarkamātrakeṇaivaṃ dṛṣṭayo bhavanty evaṃ vādinaḥ. prajñapti-mātram eva sarvam etat* [Dutt: *etacca*] *tattvaṃ* [Dutt: *tat-tvam*]*. yaś caivaṃ paśyati sa saṃyak paśyatīti. teṣāṃ prajñapty-adhiṣṭhānasya vastu-mātrasyā-abhāvāt saiva prajñaptiḥ sarveṇa sarvaṃ na bhavati. kutaḥ panaḥ prajñapti-mātraṃ tattvaṃ* [Dutt: *bhaviṣyatīti*]*. tad anena paryāyeṇa tais tattvam api prajñaptir api tad-ubhayam apy apavāditaṃ bhavati. prajñapti-tattvāpavādāc ca pradhāno nāstiko veditavyaḥ.*

ཁོ་ན་ལ་སྐུར་པ་བཏབ་པས་ན་མེད་པར་ལྟ་བའི་གཙོ་བོ་ཡིན་པར་རིག་པར་བྱའོ་ཞེས་གསུངས་ཤིང[a]།

དེ་ལ་དགོངས་ནས་གང་ཟག་ཏུ་ལྟ་བ་ནི་བླའི[b]་སྟོང་ཉིད་ལ་ལོག་པར་ཟིན་པ་དེ་ནི་དེ་ལྟ་མིན་ནོ་ཞེས་གསུངས་ཏེ། སྔ་མ་ནི་ཤེས་བྱ་ལ་རྨོངས་ [37] པ་ཙམ་ཡིན་གྱི་ཤེས་བྱ་ཐམས་ཅད་ལ་སྐུར་པ་མི་འདེབས་ཤིང་གཞི་དེས[c]་དམྱལ་བར་མི་སྐྱེ་ལ། གཞན་ཆོས་འདོད་པ་ཡང་ཕུང་བར་མི་བྱེད་བསླབ་པའི་གཞི་ལ་ཡང་གཡེལ་བར་མི་འགྱུར་ལ། ཕྱི་མ་ནི་དེ་དག་ལས་བཟློག་པར་འགྱུར་བས་སོ་

---

[a] Peking 5538, vol. 110, 144.4.7-144.5.3; Ḏzong-ka-ḇa’s paraphrase is considerable but fair. The Peking reads (with parts missing in the paraphrase in bold print):

> ***bcom ldan ’das kyis/*** *de la dgongs nas/* ***’di na la la*** *gang zag tu lta ba ni bla’i/* ***la la*** *stong* ***pa*** *nyid la log par zin pa ni de lta* ***ma yin*** *no zhes* ***bka’ stsal te/ de ci’i phyir zhe na/ gang zag du lta ba can gyi skye ba po*** *ni shes bya la rmongs pa* ***’ba’ zhig tu zad do//*** *shes bya thams cad la skur pa mi ’debs* ***pa ma yin te/*** *gzhi des* ***sems can*** *dmyal ba* ***rnam su*** *skye* ***bar mi ’gyur*** *la/ gzhan chos ’dod pa* ***dang sdug bsngal las rnam par thar par ’dod pa dag kyang*** *phung bar mi byed* ***cing slu bar ni byed la/ chos dang bden pa la yang ’god par byed do/*** *bslab pa’i gzhi* ***dag*** *la yang g.yel bar mi ’gyur* ***ro/ stong pa nyid la log par zin pa ni shes bya’i dngos po la yang rmongs la/ shes bya thams cad la yang skur pa ’debs te/ gzhi des sems can dmyal ba rnam su yang skye bar ’gyur la/ gzhan chos ’dod pa dang/ sdug bsngal las rnam par thar par ’dod pa rnams kyang phung bar byed do/ bslab pa’i gzhi dag la yang g.yel bar ’gyur te/***

His abbreviations suggest that he was trying to make the passage easier to read (or for the scribe to write down) by avoiding repetitions.

The Sanskrit in Wogihara (*Bodhisattvabhūmi,* 46.21) and Dutt (*Bodhisattvabhūmi,* 31.20) is:

> *idaṃ* [Dutt: *idañ*] *ca saṃdhāyoktaṃ bhagavatā. varam ihaikatyasya pudgala-dṛṣṭir na tv evaikatyasya dur-gṛhītā śūnyateti. tat kasya hetoḥ. pudgala-dṛṣṭiko jantur jñeye kevalaṃ muhyan* [Dutt: *muhyen*] *na tu sarvaṃ jñeyam apavadeta. na tato nidānam apāyeṣūpapadyeta. nāpi dharmārthikaṃ duḥkha-vimokṣārthikaṃ* [Dutt: *vi-mokṣārthikañca*] *paraṃ visaṃvādayen na vipralambhayet. dharme satye ca pratiṣṭhāpayet. na ca śaithiliko bhavec chikṣā-padeṣu. dur-gṛhītayā punaḥ śūnyatayā jñeye vastuni muhyet. apy apavadeta jñeyaṃ sarvaṃ* [Dutt: *sarvam*]. *tan-nidānaṃ cāpāyeṣūpapadyate. dhārmikaṃ ca duḥkha-vimokṣārthikaṃ paraṃ vipādayet. śaithilikaś ca syāc chikṣā-padeṣu.*

[b] Zi ling sku ’bum (365.20) misread *sla yi;* as given in the previous footnote, the Peking reads *bla’i,* and the Sanskrit is *varam.* A-ku Ḻo-drö-gya-tso’s *Precious Lamp* (187.6) glosses *bla* as “suitable or superior” (*rung ’am mchog*); in this context where two wrong views are compared, it has a connotation of “better” and thus, more loosely, “not so bad.”

[c] Zi ling sku ’bum (366.2) misread *de;* as given two notes above, the Peking reads *des* and the Sanskrit is *tato nidānam.*

ཞེས་བྱང་ས་ལས་གསུངས་སོ།། དེ་ལྟར་བྱས་ན་གང་ལ་གང་མེད་པ་དེ་ནི་དེས་སྟོང་ཞིང་ལྷག་མ་གང་ཡིན་པ་དེ་ནི་ཡོད་པ་ཡིན་ལ་དེ་ལྟར་མཐོང་བ་ནི་སྟོང་ཉིད་ལ་ཕྱིན་ཅི་མ་ལོག་པར་ཞུགས་པ་ཡིན་ཏེ། གཟུགས་ལ་སོགས་པའི་དངོས་པོ་རྣམས་དེ་དག་ཏུ་ཚིག་གིས་བཏགས་པའི་ངོ་བོས་སྟོང་པ་ནི་ཚིག་སྔ་མའི་དོན་ཡིན་ལ། ལྷག་མ་ཡོད་པ་ནི་གདགས་གཞིའི་དངོས་པོ་ཙམ་དང་འདོགས་པ་ཙམ་ཡོད་པར་བྱང་ས་[a]ལས་གསུངས་ཏེ། གང་གིས་སྟོང་པ་ནི་ཀུན་བཏགས་དང་གང་སྟོང་པའི་གཞི་གཞན་དབང་དང་སྔ་མས་ཕྱི་མ་སྟོང་པའི་སྟོང་པ་ཡོངས་གྲུབ་ཡིན་ལ་དེ་དག་གི་ཡོད་མེད་ཀྱི་དོན་ནི་སྔར་བཤད་པ་ལྟར་རོ།། [147] (289)

དེ་ལྟར་སྒྲོ་འདོགས་ཀྱི་མཐའ་སྤངས་པས་ནི་ཡོད་པའི་མཐའ་དང་སྐུར་འདེབས་སྤངས་པས་མེད་པའི་མཐའ་སྤངས་པས་གཉིས་སུ་མེད་པར་རབ་ཏུ་ཕྱེ་བ་ཡང་ཡིན་ཞིང་། འདི་འདྲ་བའི་སྟོང་ཉིད་ནི་དོན་ {514} དམ་པའི་མཐར་ཐུག་ཏུ་བཤད་དེ། བྱང་ས་ (18a) ལས[b]

> དངོས་པོ་སྔ་མ་གང་ཡིན་པ་དང་དངོས་པོ་མེད་པ་འདི་གཉིས་ཀྱི་ཡོད་པ་དང་མེད་པ་ལས་རྣམ་པར་གྲོལ་བའི་ཆོས་ཀྱི་མཚན་ཉིད་ཀྱིས་བསྡུས་པའི་དངོས་པོ་དེ་ནི་

---

[a] This is a paraphrase; Peking 5538, vol. 110, 144.5.6-144.5.8, reads:

> *ji ltar na stong pa nyid la legs par zin pa yin zhe na/ gang gi* [text misreads *gis*] *phyir gang la gang med pa de ni des stong par yang dag par mthong la/ 'di la lhag ma gang yin pa de ni 'di na yang dag par yod do zhes yang dag pa ji lta ba bzhin du rab tu shes pa de ni stong pa nyid la yang dag pa ji lta ba bzhin du phyin ci ma log par zhugs pa zhes bya ste/*

The Sanskrit in Wogihara (*Bodhisattvabhūmi,* 47.16; see also Dutt, *Bodhisattvabhūmi,* 32.11) is:

> *kathaṃ ca panaḥ su-gṛhītā śūnyatā bhavati. yataś ca yad yatra na bhavati. tat tena śūnyaṃ iti samanupaśyati. yat punar atrāvaśiṣṭaṃ bhavati. tat sad ihāstīti yathābhū-taṃ prajānāti. iyam ucyate śūnyatā'vakāntir yathā-bhūtā aviparītā.*

In translation:

> How is emptiness apprehended well? One thoroughly sees that, because such and such does not exist in something, that thing is empty of it and thoroughly knows just as it is that what remains here exists here. This is called non-erroneous orien-tation to emptiness just as it is.

[b] Peking 5538, vol. 110, 142.5.1-142.5.3. The Sanskrit in Wogihara (*Bodhisattvabhūmi,* 39.23) and Dutt (*Bodhisattvabhūmi,* 27.5):

> *yat punaḥ pūrvakeṇa ca bhāvenānena cā-bhāvena tad-ubhābhyāṃ* [Dutt: *cābhāvena ubhābhyāṃ*] *bhāvā-bhāvābhyāṃ vinirmuktaṃ dharma-lakṣaṇa-saṃgṛhītaṃ vastu. tad a-dvayaṃ. yad a-dvayaṃ sā* [Dutt: *tan*] *madhyamā pratipad aṃtadvaya-vivarji-taṃ* [Dutt: *vivarjitam*] *nir-uttaretyucyate.*

གཉིས་སུ་མེད་པ་ཡིན་ནོ།། གཉིས་སུ་མེད་པ་གང་ཡིན་པ་དེ་ནི་དབུ་མའི་ [38] ལམ་
མཐའ་གཉིས་སྤངས་པ་བླ་ན་མེད་པ་ཞེས་བྱ་སྟེ་

ཞེས་སོ།།

གཉིས་པ་ [བསྡུ་བ་ནས་བཤད་པའི་ཚུལ་] ལ་གཉིས། ཕྱོགས་སྔ་མ་དགོད་ཅིང་དེའི་དོན་ལ་དྲིས་ལན་བྱ་བ་དང་། ལན་བཏབ་པའི་ཕྱོགས་དགག་པའོ།། (291) [149]

དང་པོ་ [ཕྱོགས་སྔ་མ་དགོད་ཅིང་དེའི་དོན་ལ་དྲིས་ལན་བྱ་བ་] ནི། (291) [149]

བསྡུ་བ་ལས།

ཐེག་པ་ཆེན་པོ་པ་ལ་ལ་རང་གིས་ཉེས་པར་བཟུང་བས[a] འདི་སྐད་ཅེས་ཀུན་རྫོབ་ཏུ་ནི་ཐམས་ཅད་ཡོད་ལ་དོན་དམ་པར་ནི་ཐམས་ཅད་མེད་དོ་ཞེས་ཟེར་རོ།

ཞེས་གསུངས་ཏེ། ཆོས་ཀུན་དོན་དམ་པར་ནི་མེད་ལ་ཐ་སྙད་དུ་ཡོད་པའོ་ཞེས་སྨྲ་བའི་དབུ་མ་པ་རྣམས་ཀྱིས་ཆོས་རྣམས་ཀྱི་ཡོད་མེད་ཀྱི་ཁྱད་པར་ཕྱེ་བ་བརྗོད་པའོ།། དེ་ནས་

དེ་ལ་འདི་སྐད་ཅེས་ཚེ་དང་ལྡན་པ་དོན་དམ་པ་ནི་གང་ཡིན་ཀུན་རྫོབ་ནི་གང་ཡིན་ཞེས་བརྗོད་པར་བྱའོ།། དེ་སྐད་དྲིས་པ་ན་གལ་ཏེ་འདི་སྐད་ཅེས་ཆོས་ཐམས་ཅད་ཀྱི་ངོ་བོ་ཉིད་མེད་པ་གང་ཡིན་པ་དེ་ནི་དོན་དམ་པ་ཡིན་ལ། ངོ་བོ་ཉིད་མེད་པའི་ཆོས་དེ་དག་ལ་ངོ་བོ་ཉིད་དུ་དམིགས་པ་གང་ཡིན་པ་དེ་ནི་ཀུན་རྫོབ་ཡིན་ནོ།། དེ་ཅིའི་ཕྱིར་ཞེ་ན། འདི་ལྟར་དེ་ནི་ཡོད་པ་མ་ཡིན་པ་དག་ལ་ཀུན་རྫོབ་ཏུ་བྱེད་པ་དང་འདོགས་པ་དང་མངོན་པར་བརྗོད་པ་དང་ཐ་སྙད་དུ་བྱེད་པའི་ཕྱིར་རོ་ཞེས་ལན་འདེབས་པར་གྱུར་ན།

ཞེས་པ་ནི་བདེན་ {515} གཉིས་གང་ཡིན་དྲིས་ནས་དེའི་ལན་བཏབ་པ་ཕྱོགས་སྔར་མཛད་པའོ།།

(18b) དེ་ལ་འདིར་དོན་དམ་གང་ཡིན་དྲིས་པ་ནི་དོན་དམ་བདེན་པའི་མཚན་གཞི་དྲིས་པ་ཡིན་གྱི་དོན་དམ་པར་མེད་ཅེས་པའི་ཇི་འདྲ་ཞིག་ཏུ་མེད་པས་དོན་དམ་དུ་མེད་པའི་ [39] མེད་ས་དྲིས་པ་མིན་ཏེ། གཞན་དུ་ན་ཆོས་རྣམས་ཀྱི་ངོ་བོ་ཉིད་མེད་པ་དོན་དམ་མོ་ཞེས་སྨྲ་བར་མི་རིགས་ཏེ། དབུ་མ་པས་དོན་དམ་དུ་འདོད་པའི་ཆོས་ཀྱི་བདག་མེད་དུ་ཡོད་པས་དོན་དམ་དུ་ཡོད་པར་མི་འཇོག་པའི་ཕྱིར་རོ།། ཀུན་རྫོབ་གང་ཡིན་དྲིས་པ་ཡང་ཀུན་རྫོབ་བདེན་པ་ཞེས[b] གང་གི་ངོར་བདེན་པ་འཇོག་པའི་ཀུན་རྫོབ་དྲིས་པ་ཡིན་གྱི་ཐ་སྙད་དུ་

[a] The Peking of Asaṅga's text (5539, vol. 111, 82.4.7) reads *rang* ***gi*** *nyes* ***pa*** *bzung* ***nas;*** the Tokyo *sde dge* (*sems tsam,* vol. 9 [*zi*], 42b.5) reads *rang* ***gi nye*** *bar bzung* ***nas***. In the latter *gi nye bar* is clearly mistaken.

[b] Sarnath gtsang (39.5) misreads *zhes;* the other texts: *zhes pa*—Delhi NG dkra shis lhun

ཡོད་པའི་ཡོད[a]་སའི་ཐ་སྙད་དེ་གང་ཡིན་ཞེས་དྲིས་པ་མིན་ཏེ། གཞན་དུ་ན་ངོ་བོ་ཉིད་མེད་པ་ལ་ངོ་བོ་ཉིད་དུ་འཛིན་པ་ཀུན་རྫོབ་པོ་ཞེས་སྨྲ་བར་མི་རིགས་ཏེ། དེ་ནི་བདེན་འཛིན་ཡིན་པས་དེའི་ཞེན་ཡུལ་ཐ་སྙད་དུ་ཡང་མེད་པར་དབུ་མ་པས་འདོད་པའི་ཕྱིར་ཏེ་ངོ་བོ་ཉིད་མེད་ཅེས་པའི་མེད་རྒྱུའི་ངོ་བོ་ནི་བདེན་པའི་ངོ་བོ་ཉིད་ལ་བྱ་དགོས་པའི་ཕྱིར་རོ།།

གཉིས་པ་[ལན་བཏབ་པའི་ཕྱོགས་དགག་པ་]ལ་གཉིས། གཞན་གྱི་གྲུབ་མཐའ་ལ་འགལ་བ་བསྟན་པ་དང་། རང་གི་གྲུབ་མཐའ་ལ་འགལ་བ་སྤོང་བའོ།། [151] (292)

དང་པོ་[གཞན་གྱི་གྲུབ་མཐའ་ལ་འགལ་བ་བསྟན་པ་]ནི། [151] (292)

དེ་ལ་ཐོག་མར་ཀུན་རྫོབ་ཀྱི་ངོས་འཛིན་འགོག་པ་ནི་བསྡུ་བ་ལས།

> དེ་ལ་འདི་སྐད་ཅེས་བརྗོད་པར་བྱ་སྟེ་ངོ་བོ་ཉིད་དུ་དམིགས་པ་དེ་མངོན་པར་བརྗོད་པ་དང་ཀུན་རྫོབ་ཀྱི་རྒྱུ་ལས་བྱུང་བ་ཡིན་པར་འདོད་དམ་འོན་ཏེ་མངོན་པར་བརྗོད་པ་དང་ཀུན་རྫོབ་ཙམ་ཞིག་ཡིན་པར་འདོད། གལ་ཏེ་མངོན་པར་བརྗོད་པ་དང་ཀུན་རྫོབ་ཀྱི་རྒྱུ་ལས་བྱུང་བ་ཡིན་ན་ནི་དེས་ན་ {516} མངོན་པར་བརྗོད་པ་དང་ཀུན་རྫོབ་ཀྱི་རྒྱུ་ལས་བྱུང་བ་ཡིན་ (19a) པས་ཡོད་པ་མ་ཡིན་ནོ་ཞེས་བྱར་མི་རུང་ངོ་།། གལ་ཏེ་མངོན་པར་བརྗོད་པ་ [40] དང་ཀུན་རྫོབ་ཙམ་ཞིག་ཡིན་ན་ནི་དེས་ན་གཞི་མེད་པར་མངོན་པར་བརྗོད་པ་དང་ཀུན་རྫོབ་ཅེས་བྱར་མི་རུང་ངོ་

ཞེས་གསུངས་སོ།། དེའི་དོན་ནི་འདི་ཡིན་ཏེ་དོན་དམ་པར་ངོ་བོ་ཉིད་མེད་པ་ལ་ངོ་བོ་ཉིད་ཡོད་དོ་སྙམ་དུ་འཛིན་པའི་ཀུན་རྫོབ་དེ་ནང་གི་མངོན་པར་བརྗོད་པར་ཡང་འགྱུར་ལ་དེའི་ཚེ་རང་གི་རིགས་འདྲ་སྔ་མའི་རྒྱུས་བསྐྱེད་པ་ཡིན་ནམ། ཀུན་རྫོབ་པ་དང་མངོན་པར་བརྗོད་པའི[b]་རྣམ་རྟོག་གིས་བཏགས་པ་ཙམ་ཞིག་ཡིན། དང་པོ་ལྟར་ན་རྒྱུས་བསྐྱེད་པས་

---

po (515.3), Se rva zhol (18b.2), Zi ling sku 'bum (367.15), Grags pa & rnam rgyal (37.19), Peking (174.4.8), and Kalimpong (45.6).

[a] Se rva zhol (18b.3) and Peking (174.4.8) misread *yong;* the other editions: *yod*—Delhi NG dkra shis lhun po (515.13), Zi ling sku 'bum (367.16), Sarnath gtsang (39.6), and Kalimpong (46.1).

[b] According to Gung-tang (*Annotations, khu* 89.5) and A-ku Lo-drö-gya-tso (*Precious Lamp,* 192.6), this should read *mngon par brjod pa,* without the genitive ending; they take it to be nominative because, just below, Dzong-ka-ba says *mngon par brjod* ***pa*** *rtog pas btags pa tsam yin na.* However, Ser-shül (*Notes,* 28b.1) cogently questions the emendation.

ཡོད་པ་མིན་ཞེས་པ་མི་རུང་ཞེས་པ་ནི་དོན་དམ་པར་ཡོད་པ་མིན་ཞེས་པ་ཡིན་ཏེ་འདིར་དོན་དམ་དུ་ཡོད་མེད་རྩོད་པའི་སྐབས་ཡིན་པའི་ཕྱིར་དང་། ཕ་རོལ་པོས[a] དོན་དམ་དུ་མེད་པར་ཁས་བླངས་ཀྱི་སྤྱིར་མེད་ཅེས་མ་སྨྲས་པའི་ཕྱིར་རོ།། གཉིས་པ་ལྟར་ན་རྟོག་པས་བཏགས་པ་ཙམ་དུ་མི་རུང་སྟེ། འདོགས་པའི་གཞི་མེད་པའི་ཕྱིར་ཏེ་ཀུན་རྫོབ་དང་མངོན་པར་བརྗོད་པ་རྟོག་པས་བཏགས་ཙམ་ཡིན་ན་གཞན་རྣམས་ཀྱང་དེ་ཙམ་དུ་འགྱུར་བའི་ཕྱིར་རོ།། [152] (292) དོན་དམ་པའི་ངོས་འཛིན་འགོག་པ་ནི་དེ་ཉིད་ལས།

> དེ་ལ་འདི་སྐད་ཅེས་ཚེ་དང་ལྡན་པ་ཅིའི་ཕྱིར་ན་གང་དམིགས་པ་དེ་མེད་པ་ཡིན་ཞེས་ཀྱང་བརྗོད་པར་བྱའོ།། དེ་སྐད་ཅེས་དྲིས་པ་ན་གལ་ཏེ་དེ་འདི་སྐད་ཅེས་ཕྱིན་ཅི་ལོག་གི་དངོས་པོ་ཡིན་པའི་ཕྱིར་རོ་ཞེས་ལན་འདེབས་པར་གྱུར་ན། དེ་ལ་འདི་སྐད་ཅེས་བརྗོད་པར་བྱ་སྟེ་ཕྱིན་ཅི་ལོག་དེ་ཡོད་པར་འདོད་དམ་འོན་ཏེ་ {517} མེད་པར་འདོད། གལ་ཏེ་ཡོད་ན་ནི་དེས་ན་ཆོས་ཐམས་ཅད་ཀྱི་ངོ་བོ་ [41] ཉིད་མེད་ (19b) པ་ཉིད་ནི་དོན་དམ་པའོ་ཞེས་བྱར་མི་རུང་ངོ་།། གལ་ཏེ་མེད་ན་ནི་དེས་ན་ཕྱིན་ཅི་ལོག་གི་དངོས་པོ་ཡིན་པའི་ཕྱིར་གང་དམིགས་པ་དེ་ངོ་བོ་ཉིད་མེད་དོ་ཞེས་བྱར་མི་རུང་ངོ་།

ཞེས་གསུངས་སོ།། དེའི་དོན་ནི་ཆོས་འདི་དག་ལ་རང་གི་མཚན་ཉིད་ཀྱིས་གྲུབ་པའི་རང་མཚན་དམིགས་བཞིན་དུ་དེ་མེད་ཅེས་ཇི་ལྟར་རིགས་ཏེ། དེ་ལ་ནི་དེ་ལྟར་དམིགས་པའི་ཚད་མས་གནོད་པའི་ཕྱིར་རོ།། གལ་ཏེ་དེ་ལྟར་དམིགས་པའི་བློས་མི་གནོད་དེ་བློ་དེ་ཉིད་འཁྲུལ་པའི་དངོས་པོ་ཡིན་པའི་ཕྱིར་རོ། ཞེ་ན། འོ་ན་འཁྲུལ་པ་དེ་རང་གི་མཚན་ཉིད་ཀྱིས་ཡོད་ན་ནི་ངོ་བོ་ཉིད་མེད་པ་དོན་དམ་དུ་མི་རུང་ལ། མེད་ན་ནི་འཁྲུལ་པའི[b] ཕྱིར་དམིགས་ཀྱང་མེད་དོ། ཞེས་པ་དེ་མི་འཐད་དོ།། འདིར་ཡང་དོན་དམ་དུ་ཡོད་མེད་ཀྱི་བརྟག་པ་བྱ་དགོས་མོད་ཀྱང་དོན་འདྲ་ཞིང་བརྟག་པ་སྔ་མ་གོ་སླ་བས་དེ་ལྟར་བཤད་དོ།། [153] དེ་ལྟར་ན་འདིར་ཀུན་བརྟགས་དང་ཡོངས་གྲུབ་གཉིས་དོན་དམ་པར་མེད་ཅིང་ཐ་སྙད་དུ་ཡོད་པ་ལ་སྐྱོན་མ་བསྟན་པར་ཀུན་རྫོབ་པའི་ཤེས་པ་དང་འཁྲུལ་པའི[c] ཤེས་པ་དོན་

[a] Zi ling sku 'bum (368.14): *bos,* again correcting for following the suffix *la,* but *rol* has a non-manifest extra suffix *da.*

[b] Zi ling sku 'bum (369.9): *ba'i,* correcting from not taking account of the non-manifest extra suffix *da* at the end of the previous syllable.

[c] Zi ling sku 'bum (369.13): *ba'i.* See previous footnote.

དམ་པར་ཡོད་མེད་ལ་བརྟགས་ནས་སྐྱོན་བསྟན་པ་ནི། གཞན་དབང་དོན་དམ་པར་མེད་ལ་ཀུན་རྫོབ་ཏུ་ཡོད་པ་བཀག་པ་ཡིན་ཏེ། འདི་ཉིད་ཡོངས་གྲུབ་ཀྱི་ཆོས་ཅན་དང་ཀུན་བརྟགས་ཀྱི་འདོགས་པ་པོ་དང་གདགས་གཞི་ཡིན་པས་མཁས་པ་རྣམས་གཙོ་བོར་འདི་ཉིད་དོན་དམ་པར་ཡོད་མེད་ལ་རྩོད་པ་ཡིན་ནོ།། [154] (293) གཞན་ཡང་བསྡུ་བ་ལས།

དེ་ལ་གཞན་གྱི་དབང་གི་ངོ་བོ་ཉིད་དང་ [42] ཡོངས་སུ་གྲུབ་ {518} པ[a]ལ་ཀུན་བརྟགས་པའི་ངོ་བོ་ཉིད་དུ་མངོན་པར་ཞེན་པ་གང་ཡིན་པ་དེ་ནི་སྒྲོ་འདོགས་པའི་མཐའ་ཡིན་པར་རིག་པར་བྱའོ་

ཞེས་དང་།

སྐུར་པ་འདེབས་པའི་མཐའ་ (20a) ནི་གཞན་གྱི་དབང་གི་ངོ་བོ་ཉིད་དང་ཡོངས་སུ་གྲུབ་པའི་ངོ་བོ་ཉིད་ཡོད་པ་ལ་མེད་དོ་ཞེས་རང་གི་མཚན་ཉིད་ལ་སྐུར་པ་འདེབས་པ་གང་ཡིན་པ་སྟེ་དེ་ལྟར་མཐའ་གཉིས་རྣམ་པར་སྤངས་པའི་ཚུལ་གྱིས་དེ་ཁོ་ནའི་དོན་གྱི་ཚུལ་ཁོང་དུ་ཆུད་པར་བྱའོ།

ཞེས་ངོ་བོ་ཉིད་ཐ་མ་གཉིས་རང་གི་མཚན་ཉིད་ཀྱིས་ཡོད་པ་ལ་དེར་མ་གྲུབ་བོ་ཞེས་པ་རང་མཚན་ལ་སྐུར་འདེབས་སུ་གསུངས་ཏེ། བྱང་ས་དང་འདི་གཉིས་སྒྲོ་སྐུར་གྱི་མཐའ་དང་དེ་སྤོང་ཚུལ་གཅིག་གོ །[154] (293) ཀུན་བརྟགས་མེད་པ་ཡང་དོན་དམ་དུ་ཡིན་གྱི་ཐ་སྙད་དུ་མེད་པ་མིན་ཏེ། བསྡུ་བ་ལས།

མངོན་པར་རྟོགས[b]་པ་དེ་དག་མིང་གང་དང་མངོན་པར་བརྗོད་པ་གང་གིས་རྣམ་པར་འཇོག་པ་དེའི་ངོ་བོ་ཉིད་ཡིན་པར་བརྗོད་པར་བྱའམ་འོན་ཏེ་དེའི་ངོ་བོ་ཉིད་མ་ཡིན་པར་བརྗོད་པར་བྱ་ཞེ་ན། སྨྲས་པ། ཐ་སྙད་ལས་ནི་དེའི་ངོ་བོ་ཉིད་ཡིན་པར་བརྗོད་པར་བྱའོ།། དོན་དམ་པར་ནི་དེའི་ངོ་བོ་ཉིད་མ་ཡིན་པར་བརྗོད་པར་བྱའོ།

ཞེས་དང་།

---

a Tokyo *sde dge, sems tsam,* vol. 8 (*zhi*): *yongs su grub pa'i ngo bo nyid.*

b Reading *mngon par* ***rtogs*** *pa* following Tokyo *sde dge, sems tsam,* vol. 8 (*zhi*) 279b.1, as well as Ser-shül's *Notes,* 410.3, and Jik-may-dam-chö-gya-tso's *Port of Entry,* 410.3 and 421.2. Gung-tang's *Annotations* (91.6), A-ku Lo-drö-gya-tso's *Precious Lamp* (194.3), Da-drin-rap-den's *Annotations* (71.3): *mngon par* ***rtog*** *pa.*

དེ་ལ་མཚོན་པར་བརྗོད་པ་ལ་ཡོངས་སུ་གོམས་པའི་མིང་ལ་བརྟེན་པའི་རྣམ་པར་ཤེས་པའི་དམིགས་པ་ཀུན་བརྟགས་པའི་ངོ་བོ་ཉིད་གང་ཡིན་པ་དེ་ནི་

ཞེས་གསུངས་ནས་

འདི་ལྟར་དེ་ནི་བཏགས་པའི་ཡོད་པ་ཡིན་གྱི་དོན་དམ་པར་ཡོད་པ་མ་ཡིན་པའི་ཕྱིར་རོ་

ཞེས་གསུངས་སོ།། [43]དེས་ན་བདག་གཉིས་ཀྱི་ཀུན་བརྟགས་ལྟ་བུ་ཤེས་བྱ་ལ་{519}མི་སྲིད་ཀྱང་དེ་ཙམ་གྱིས་ཀུན་བརྟགས་ཐམས་ཅད་མི་སྲིད་པ་མིན་པས་རྫས་སུ་ཡོད་པ་དང་དོན་དམ་པར་ཡོད་པ་དགག་ལ་བཏགས་ཡོད་དང་ཐ་སྙད་དུ་ཡོད་པར་གཞག་གོ། [156] (293) དེའི་ཕྱིར་དགོངས་འགྲེལ་གྱི་འགྲེལ་ཆེན་ཁ་ཅིག་ལས་

ཀུན་བརྟགས་བདེན་པ་གཉིས་(20b)ཀར་མེད་ལ་གཟུང་འཛིན་གཉིས་ཀྱི་གཞན་དབང་གི་རྟེན་ཅིང་འབྲེལ་པར[a]་འབྱུང་བ་སྒྱུ་མ་བྱས་པ་དང་འདྲ་བར་ཀུན་རྫོབ་ཏུ་ཡོད་པ་དང་། ཡོངས་གྲུབ་དོན་དམ་པ་ཡང་ཡིན་ལ་ངོ་བོ་ཉིད་མེད་པའི་ཚུལ་དུ་ཡོད་པ་དོན་དམ་པར་ཡོད་པ་ཡིན་ནོ།

ཞེས་བཤད་པ་ནི་མདོ་དེའི་དགོངས་པ་མིན་ནོ།། ཐེག་བསྡུས་སུ་དགོངས་འགྲེལ་དྲངས་ཏེ་ཕྱི་རོལ་མེད་པར་བསྒྲུབས་ནས་ཕྱི་ནང་གི་གཟུང་འཛིན་ཀུན་བརྟགས་སུ་བཤད་པ་དང་འགལ་ཞིང་། བྱང་ས་དང་བསྡུ་བ་དང་ཡང་འགལ་ལ་དེར་རྣམ་ངེས་ཀྱི་ལུང་ཡང་དྲངས་པས། ཁ་ཅིག་དེ་ཐོགས་མེད་ཀྱིས་མཛད་ཟེར་བ་ནི་མ་བརྟགས་པ་ཆེན་པོའོ།། བསྡུ་བར་དགོངས་འགྲེལ་གྱི་གླེང་གཞིའི་ལེའུ་མ་གཏོགས་པ་ལེའུ་ལྷག་མ་རྣམས་ཕལ་མོ་ཆེ་དྲངས་ཤིང་དཀའ་གནས་རྣམས་ལེགས་པར་གཏན་ལ་ཕབ་འདུག་པས་སློབ་དཔོན་འདིས་འགྲེལ་བ[b]་ཟུར་དུ་མཛད་དགོས་པར་ཡང་མི་སྣང་ངོ།། [157] (294) ཕྱིས་ཀྱི་ཁ་ཅིག་ཀྱང་ངོ་བོ་ཉིད་དང་པོ་ཐ་སྙད་དུ་ཡང་མེད་བར་པ[c]་ཐ་སྙད་དུ་ཡོད་ཀྱང་དོན་དམ་པར་མེད་ཐ་མ་དོན་

[a] Zi ling sku 'bum (370.16): *bar.* See p. 368, footnote b.

[b] Zi ling sku 'bum (371.4): *pa,* correcting from not taking account of the non-manifest extra suffix *da* at the end of the previous syllable.

[c] Se rva zhol (20b.4) and Kalimpong (51.2) misread *ba;* the other editions: *pa*—Delhi NG dkra shis lhun po (519.5), Zi ling sku 'bum (371.6), Sarnath gtsang (43.16), and Peking (175.3.5)—the last also misreading *par pa* for *bar pa.*

དམ་པར་ཡོད་པ་ཐོགས་མེད་སྐུ་མཆེད་ཀྱི་དགོངས་པར་འཆད་པ་ཡང་ལུགས་འདི་ལས་ [44] ཕྱི་རོལ་ཏུ་གྱུར་པ་ཡིན་ལ། ཁྱད་པར་དུ་གཞན་དབང་ཐ་སྙད་དུ་ཡོད་པའི་དོན་འཁྲུལ་པའི[a] བློས་དེ་ལ་སྐྱེ་འགག་སོགས་ {520} ཡོད་པར་ཞེན་པ་ཙམ་ཡིན་གྱི། དངོས་པོ་ལ་སྐྱེ་འགག་སོགས་མེད་དོ་ཞེས་འདོད་པ་ནི། གཞན་དབང་ལ་སྐུར་འདེབས་ཀྱི་མཐར་ཐུག་དེའི་རྒྱུ་མཚན་གྱིས་ངོ་བོ་ཉིད་གཞན་གཉིས་ལ་ཡང་སྐུར་པ་བཏབ་པས་མཚན་ཉིད་གསུམ་ག་ལ་སྐུར་འདེབས་ཆད་ལྟའི་གཙོ་བོར་སོང་བར་བྱང་ས་ལས་བཤད་པ་དེ་ཡིན་ཞིང་། (21a) མདོ་སྡེ་དགོངས་འགྲེལ་ངེས་དོན་ཡིན་པར་འདོད་པའི་ཕྱོགས་ལ་སྲིད་དུ་མེད་པའི་འགལ་བར་ཤེས་པར་གྱིས་ཤིག།

གཉིས་པ་ [རང་གི་གྲུབ་མཐའ་ལ་འགལ་བ་སྤང་བ་] ནི། [158] (294)

གལ་ཏེ་བྱང་ས་དང་བསྡུ་བ་ལས། གཞན་དབང་དོན་དམ་པར་ཡོད་པར་གསུངས་པ་ལྟར་ཡིན་ན་དགོངས་འགྲེལ་ལས།

> ཇི་ལྟར་འཕགས་པའི་ལམ་ཡན་ལག་བརྒྱད་པ་ཕན་ཚུན་མཚན་ཉིད་ཐ་དད་པ་ཡིན་པ་དེ་བཞིན་དུ། གལ་ཏེ་ཆོས་དེ་དག་གི་དེ་བཞིན་ཉིད་དོན་དམ་པ་ཆོས་བདག་མེད་པ་ཡང་མཚན་ཉིད་ཐ་དད་པ་ཡིན་པར་འགྱུར་ན་ནི་དེས་ན་དེ་བཞིན་ཉིད་དོན་དམ་པ་ཆོས་ལ་བདག[b] མེད་པ་ཡང་རྒྱུ་དང་བཅས་པ་ཡིན་པར་འགྱུར་རོ[c]།། རྒྱུ་ལས་བྱུང་བ་ཉིད་ཡིན་ན་ནི་འདུས་བྱས་ཡིན་པར་འགྱུར་རོ།། འདུས་བྱས་ཡིན་ན་ནི་དོན་དམ་པ་ཡིན་པར་མི་འགྱུར་རོ།

ཞེས་འདུས་བྱས་ཡིན་ན་དོན་དམ་མིན་པར་གསུངས་པ་དང་། དབུས་མཐའ་ལས[d]།

> དམ་པའི་དོན་ནི་གཅིག་པུའོ།

[a] Zi ling sku 'bum (371.8): *ba'i,* correcting from not taking account of the non-manifest extra suffix *da* at the end of the previous syllable.

[b] Lamotte (*Saṃdhinirmocana,* 52.2): *chos bdag.*

[c] For *dang bcas pa yin par 'gyur ro,* Lamotte (*Saṃdhinirmocana,* 52.3) reads *dang bcas pa yin zhing rgyu las byung ba yin par 'gyur ro.*

[d] III.10c; Peking 5522, vol. 108, 20.3.5. The Sanskrit in Gadjin M. Nagao, *Madhyāntavibhāga-bhāṣya* (Tokyo: Suzuki Research Foundation, 1964), 41, is:

paramārthan tu ekataḥ//

See also Ramchandra Pandeya, *Madhyānta-vibhāga-śāstra* (Delhi: Motilal Banarsidass, 1971), 95.

ཞེས་གསུངས་ཤིང་དེའི་འགྲེལ་པ་ལས་ཀྱང་[a]།

དོན་དམ་པའི་བདེན་ [45] པ་ནི་ཡོངས་སུ་གྲུབ་པའི་ངོ་བོ་ཉིད་གཅིག་པུར་རིག་པར་བྱའོ།

ཞེས་གསུངས་པ་དང་། མདོ་སྡེའི་རྒྱན་ལས་ཀྱང་[b]།

ཡོད་མིན་མེད་མིན་དེ་བཞིན་མིན་གཞན་མིན།།
སྐྱེ[c]་དང་ {521} འཇིག་མེད་འབྲི[d]་བར་མི་འགྱུར་ཏེ།།
འཕེལ་བ་མེད་ཅིང་རྣམ་པར་དག་པའང་མེད།།
རྣམ་པར་དག་འགྱུར་དེ་ནི་དོན་དམ་མཚན།

ཞེས་དོན་དམ་བདེན་པ་མཚན་ཉིད་ལྔ་ལྡན་དུ་གསུངས་པའི་སྐབས་སུ་སྐྱེ་འཇིག་མེད་པར་བཤད་ཅིང་འགྲེལ་པར[e]་ཡང་ཀུན་བརྟགས་དང་གཞན་དབང་གི་མཚན་ཉིད་ཀྱིས་ཡོད་པ་མིན་ལ་ཡོངས་གྲུབ་ཀྱི་མཚན་ཉིད་ཀྱིས་མེད་པ་མིན་པར་གསུངས་པ་དང་། བསྡུ་བ་ལས་ཀྱང་།

རྒྱུ་ (21b) མཚན་ཀུན་རྫོབ་ཏུ་ཡོད་པ་བརྗོད་པར་བྱའམ་དོན་དམ་པར་ཡོད་པར་བརྗོད་

---

[a] Peking 5528, vol. 108, 126.2.2. The Sanskrit in Nagao (*Madhyāntavibhāga,* 41) is:
…paramārtha-satyaṃ/
ekasmāt parinispannād eva svabhāvād veditavyaṃ [Pandeya: *veditavyam*]/
See also Pandeya, *Madhyānta-vibhāga,* 95.

[b] *theg pa chen po'i mdo sde rgyan, mahāyānasūtrālaṃkāra;* VI.1; Peking 5521, vol. 108, 5.1.1. The Sanskrit in S. Bagchi *Mahāyāna-Sūtrālaṃkāra of Asaṅga* [with Vasubandhu's commentary], Buddhist Sanskrit Texts, 13 (Darbhanga, India: Mithila Institute, 1970), 24, is:

na sanna cāsanna tathā na cānyathā na jāyate vyeti na cā[* *nā*] *vahīyate/*
na vardhate nāpi viśudhyate punarviśudhyate tat paramārthalakṣaṇaṃ//

*Added by Bagchi. For the Sanskrit text on which Bagchi's edition was based see Sylvain Lévi, *Mahāyānasūtrālaṃkāra, exposé de la doctrine du grand véhicule selon le système Yogācāra* (Paris: Bibliothèque de l'École des Hautes Études, 1907), vol. 1, 22.

[c] The Peking of Maitreya's text (5521, vol. 108, 5.1.2) reads *skyed;* however, the Peking of Vasubandhu's commentary (5527, vol. 108, 63.5.4) reads *skye.*

[d] Zi ling sku 'bum (372.5): *bri.*

[e] Paraphrasing Vasubandhu's *Explanation of (Maitreya's) "Ornament for the Great Vehicle Sūtras"* (*mdo sde'i rgyan gyi bshad pa, sūtrālaṃkārābhāṣya;* Peking 5527, vol. 108, 63.5.5). The Sanskrit in Bagchi (*Mahāyāna-Sūtrālaṃkāra,* 24) is:
nasatparikalpitaparatantralakṣaṇābhyāṃ, na cāsatparinispannalakṣaṇena/

པར་བྱ་ཞེ་ན། སྒྲས་པ་ཀུན་རྫོབ་ཏུ་ཡོད་པར་བརྗོད་པར་བྱའོ།

ཞེས་དང་།

> རྣམ་པར་རྟོག་པ་ཀུན་རྫོབ་ཏུ་ཡོད་པར་བརྗོད་པར་བྱའམ། དོན་དམ་པར་ཡོད་པར་བརྗོད་པར་བྱ་ཞེ་ན། སྒྲས་པ་ཀུན་རྫོབ་ཏུ་ཡོད་པར་བརྗོད་པར་བྱའོ།

ཞེས་གསུངས་པ་རྣམས་དང་དེ་ལྟར་མི་འགལ་ཞེ་ན། དེ་ལྟར་མི་འགལ་བ་བཤད་པར་བྱ་སྟེ། འདི་ལྟར་ཀུན་རྫོབ་དང་དོན་དམ་པར་ཡོད་པ་ལ་འཇོག་ཚུལ་གཉིས་ཡོད་དེ། [160] (295) དང་པོ་ནི། ཐ་སྙད་ཀྱི་དབང་གིས་བཞག་པའི་ཡོད་པ་ལ་ཐ་སྙད་དུ་ཡོད་པ་དང་། དེའི་དབང་གིས་བཞག་པ་མིན་གྱི་རང་གི་མཚན་ཉིད་ཀྱིས་ཡོད་པ་ལ་དོན་དམ་པར་ཡོད་པར་བཞག་པ་སྟེ། མདོ་ལས་དེ་ཡང་འཇིག་རྟེན་གྱི་ཐ་སྙད་ཀྱི་དབང་གིས་ཡིན་གྱི་དོན་ [46] དམ་པར་ནི་མ་ཡིན་ནོ། ཞེས་མང་དུ་གསུངས་པ་ལྟ་བུའོ།། འདི་ནི་དབུ་མ་པ་དང་རང་གཞན་གྱི་སྡེ་པ་དངོས་པོར་སྨྲ་བ་རྣམས་དོན་དམ་པ་དང་ཐ་སྙད་དུ་ཡོད་མེད་རྩོད་པའི་གཞིར་གྱུར་པའོ།། དེའི་དབང་དུ་བྱས་ན་སྔར་བཤད་པའི་ངོ་བོ་ཉིད་དང་པོ་ཐ་སྙད་དུ་ཡོད་ལ་དོན་དམ་པར་མེད་པ་དང་། ངོ་བོ་ {522} ཉིད་ཐ་མ་གཉིས་དོན་དམ་པར་ཡོད་ལ་ཐ་སྙད་དུ་མེད་པས་བྱང་ས་དང་བསྡུ་བ་ལས་སྔར་ལྟར་གསུངས་ཤིང་། ཡང་བསྡུ་བ་ལས།

> མངོན་པར་བརྗོད་པ་ལ་ཡོངས་སུ་གོམས་པའི་མིང་ལ་གནས་པའི་རྣམ་པར་ཤེས་པའི་དམིགས་པ་གཟུགས་ལ་སོགས་པའི་མིང་ཅན་གྱི་དངོས་པོ་གཟུགས་ལ་སོགས་པའི་བདག་ཉིད་གང་གིས་ཡོད་པ་དེ་ནི་བདག་ཉིད་དེས་རྫས་དང་དོན་དམ་པ་གཉིས་ཀར་ཡང་མེད་དོ།། དེ་ལྟ་བས་ན་གཟུགས་ལ་སོགས་པའི་མིང་ཅན་གྱི་ཆོས་དེ་དག་གི་ངོ་བོ་ཉིད་ཡོད་པ་མ་ (22a) ཡིན་པ་ལས་དེས་ཀུན་བརྟགས་པ་གང་ཡིན་པ་དེ་ནི་བརྟགས་པ་ལས་ཡོད་པ་ཡིན་པར་རིག་པར་བྱའོ།། མངོན་པར་བརྗོད་པ་ལ་ཡོངས་སུ་གོམས་པ་རྣམ་པར་བསལ་[a]བའི་མིང་ཅན་གྱི་རྣམ་པར་ཤེས་པའི་དམིགས་པ་གཟུགས་ལ་སོགས་པའི་མིང་ཅན་གྱི་དངོས་པོ་བརྗོད་དུ་མེད་པའི་བདག་ཉིད་གང་གིས་ཡོད་པ་དེ་ནི། རྫས་དང་དོན་དམ་པ་གཉི་གར་[b]ཡང་དེ་བཞིན་དུ

[a] The Peking (78.1.7) and the Tokyo *sde dge* (*sems tsam,* vol. 9 [*zi*], 32a.4) of Asaṅga similarly read *rnam par bsal ba;* Dön-drup-gyel-tsen's *Four Intertwined Commentaries* (136.50) and Šer-šhül's *Notes* (32a.5) mistakenly read *rnam par gsal ba.*

[b] Zi ling sku 'bum (373.10): *gnyis kar.*

ཡོད་པར་རིག་པར་བྱའོ།

ཞེས་ཀྱང་གསུངས་སོ།། རྫས་བཏགས་ཀྱང་བསྡུ་བ་ལས།

གང་ཅི་ཡང་རུང་སྟེ། དེ་ལས་གཞན་པ་དག་ལ་མི་ལྟོས་ཤིང་། དེ་ལས་གཞན་ [47] པ་དག་ལ་མི་བརྟེན་[a]པར་རང་གི་མཚན་ཉིད་འདོགས་པར་བྱེད་པ་དེ་ནི་མདོར་ན་རྫས་སུ་ཡོད་པ་ཡིན་པར་རིག་པར་བྱའོ།། གང་ཅི་ཡང་རུང་སྟེ་དེ་ལས་གཞན་པ་དག་ལ་ལྟོས་ཤིང་། དེ་ལས་གཞན་པ་དག་ལ་བརྟེན་ནས་རང་གི་མཚན་ཉིད་འདོགས་པར་བྱེད་པ་དེ་ནི་མདོར་ན་བཏགས་པའི་ཡོད་པ་ཡིན་པར་རིག་པར་བྱའི་རྫས་སུ་ཡོད་པ་ནི་མ་ {523} ཡིན་ཏེ།

ཞེས་ཕུང་པོ་ལ་བརྟེན་ནས་བདག་གམ་སེམས་ཅན་དུ་བཏགས་པ་དེའི་དཔེར་མཛད་དོ།། ཆོས་གཞན་བཟུང་བ་ལ་མ་ལྟོས་པར་གཟུང་དུ་མེད་ཅིང་ལྟོས་ནས་གཟུང་དགོས་པའི་བཏགས་ཡོད་དང་ཐ་སྙད་ཀྱི་དབང་གིས་མ་བཞག་པར་རང་གི་མཚན་ཉིད་ཀྱིས་གྲུབ་པ་གཉིས་ཀྱང་ལུགས་འདི་ལ་མི་འགལ་བས་ཀུན་གཞིའི་བག་ཆགས་ལྟ་བུ་བཏགས་ཡོད་དུ་གསུངས་ཀྱང་སྔར་བཤད་པའི་དོན་དམ་པར་ཡོད་པ་མི་འགལ་གྱི། མིང་དང་རྟོག་པས་བཏགས་པའི་བཏགས་ཡོད་དང་ནི་འགལ་ལོ།། [162] (295) འཇོག་ཚུལ་གཉིས་པ་ལྟར་ན་དབུས་མཐའ་ལས[b]།

དོན་དང་ཐོབ་དང་སྒྲུབ་པ་ནི།།
དོན་དམ་རྣམ་པ་གསུམ་ (22b) དུ་འདོད།

ཅེས་གསུངས་པའི་འགྲེལ་པ་[c]ལས་དོན་དོན་དམ་པ་ནི་དེ་བཞིན་ཉིད་དེ་ཡེ་ཤེས་དམ་པའི་

---

a Se rva zhol (20b.4), Delhi NG dkra shis lhun po (522.5), Peking (176.1.2), and Kalimpong (54.5) misread *rten;* Tokyo *sde dge* (*sems tsam,* vol. 8 [*zhi*], 199a.7), Zi ling sku 'bum (373.13), and Sarnath gtsang (47.1) read *brten*—as do all six editions for the same but positive construction in the next sentence, that is, *gzhan pa dag la brten nas.*

b III.11ab; Peking 5522, vol. 108, 20.3.6. The Sanskrit in Nagao (*Madhyāntavibhāga,* 41), is:

artha-prāpti-prapattyā hi paramārthas tridhā mataḥ/

See also Pandeya, *Madhyānta-vibhāga,* 95.

c Peking 5528, vol. 108, 126.2.3. The Sanskrit in Nagao (*Madhyāntavibhāga,* 41) is:

artha-paramārthas tathatā paramasya jñānasyārtha iti kṛtvā/

See also Pandeya *Madhyānta-vibhāga,* 95.

དོན་ཡིན་པའི་ཕྱིར་རོ། ཞེས་དམ་པ་ནི་ཟག་མེད་ཀྱི་མཉམ་གཞག་གི་ཡེ་ཤེས་ལ་བྱས་ནས་དེའི་དོན་ཏེ། ཡུལ་ཡིན་པས་དམ་པའི་དོན་ནམ་དོན་དམ་པ་ཞེས་གསུངས་པ་ནི་བདག་མེད་པའི་དོན་དེ་བཞིན་ཉིད་དེ་དེ་ནི་རྣམ་པར་དག་པའི་དམིགས་པའི་དོན་དམ་ཡང་ཡིན་ནོ།། དེར་ནི་ངོ་བོ་ཉིད་ [48] གཞན་གཉིས་མེད་ཀྱི་ཡོངས་གྲུབ་གཅིག་པུ་ཡིན་པས་དེ་ལྟར་གསུངས་ཏེ། དབུས་མཐའ་ལས།[a]

རྣམ་དག་སྤྱོད་ཡུལ་རྣམ་གཉིས་ཏེ།།
གཅིག་པུ་ཁོ་ནར་བརྗོད་པ་ཡིན།

ཞེས་དང་། དེའི་འགྲེལ་པ་ལས།

ཡོངས་སུ་གྲུབ་པའི་ངོ་བོ་ཉིད་དུ་བརྗོད་དོ་ངོ་བོ་ཉིད་གཞན་ནི་རྣམ་པར་དག་པའི་ཡེ་ཤེས་རྣམ་པ་གཉིས་ཀྱི་ཡུལ་མ་ཡིན་ནོ།

ཞེས་གསལ་བར་གསུངས་སོ།། ཡེ་ཤེས་གཉིས་ནི་སྒྲིབ་པ་གཉིས་དག་པར་བྱེད་པའི་ {524} ཡེ་ཤེས་སོ།། [163] (296) ལུགས་འདིས་ཡེ་ཤེས་དེ་རང་རིག་ཏུ་བཞེད་པས་ཡེ་ཤེས་ཀྱང་ཡུལ་དུ་འགྱུར་རོ་སྙམ་ན། ཡུལ་གང་ལ་ལྟོས་ནས་དེ་ཁོ་ན་ཉིད་ཀྱི་དོན་རྟོགས་པའི་ཡུལ་དེ་ལ་དགོངས་པས་སྐྱོན་མེད་དོ།། དེས་ན་དེ་འདྲ་བའི་དོན་དམ་ནི་འདུས་མ་བྱས་དང་དེ་འདྲ་བའི་དོན་དམ་དུ་མ་གྲུབ་ཀྱང་ཐ་སྙད་ཀྱི་དབང་གིས་བཞག་པ་མིན་པའི་རང་གི་མཚན་ཉིད་ཀྱིས་གནས་པའི་དོན་དམ་དུ་གྲུབ་པ་འདི་པ་ལ་མི་འགལ་ལོ།། ཡེ་ཤེས་སྙིང་པོ་ཀུན་ལས་བཏུས་ལས། [164] (297)

གཟུང་དང་འཛིན་པ་ལས་གྲོལ་བའི།།
རྣམ་ཤེས་དམ་པའི་དོན་དུ་ཡོད།།
བློ་མཚོའི་ཕ་རོལ་ཕྱིན་པ་ཡི།།
རྣལ་འབྱོར་སྤྱོད་པའི་གཞུང་དུ་གྲགས།

ཞེས་གསུངས་པ་ཡང་དོན་དམ་པར་ཡོད་ཚུལ་སྔ་མ་ལ་དགོངས་སོ།། དབུ་མ་པའི་བསྟན་

[a] III.12cd; Peking 5522, vol. 108, 20.3.7. The Sanskrit in Nagao (*Madhyāntavibhāga,* 42) is:

viśuddhi-gocaraṃ dvedhā ekasmād eva kīrttitaṃ [Pandeya: *kīrtitaṃ*]/

See also Pandeya, *Madhyānta-vibhāga,* 99.

བཙོས་དུ་མ་ནས་རྣལ་ (23a) འབྱོར་སྤྱོད་པ་པ་དང་རྩོད་པ་ན་གཞན་དབང་ཡོད་མེད་ལ་རྩོད་པ་ཡང་ཐ་སྙད་ཀྱི་དབང་དུ་བྱས་པ་མིན་གྱི་དོན་དམ་པར་ཡོད་མེད་ལ་རྩོད་པ་ཡིན་པས་དོན་དམ་པ་དེ་གཉིས་ལེགས་པར་ཕྱེད་དགོས་སོ༎ སློབ་ [49] དཔོན་སྐུ་མཆེད་ཀྱི་གཞུང་དུ་ནི་དོན་དམ་པའི་རྣམ་གཞག་ཕྱི་མའི་ཕྱོགས་ལ་བརྟེན་པ་མང་དུ་འབྱུང་ངོ༎ [165] (297) ངོ་བོ་ཉིད་དང་པོ་གཉིས་ཀུན་རྫོབ་ཏུ་ཡོད་ཚུལ་ནི། བསྡུ་བ་ལས། རྒྱུ་མཚན་དང་རྣམ་རྟོག་ཀུན་རྫོབ་ཏུ་ཡོད་པའི་རྒྱུ་མཚན་དུ།

ཀུན་ནས་ཉོན་མོངས་པ་ཀུན་ནས་སློང་བའི་ཕྱིར་དང་གདགས་པའི་གཞི་ཡིན་པའི་ཕྱིར།

ཞེས་གསུངས་པའི་དང་པོ་ནི། དགོངས་འགྲེལ་ལས། རྣམ་པར་དག་པའི་དམིགས་པ་ལ་དོན་དམ་དུ་བཤད་པའི་ཟླས་དྲངས་པ་ན་གང་ལ་དམིགས་པས་ཀུན་ནས་ {525} ཉོན་མོངས་ཀུན་ནས་སློང་བའི་དོན་གྱིས་ཀུན་རྫོབ་ཏུ་ཡོད་པར་བཞག་སྟེ་ཀུན་ལས་བཏུས་དང་མཐུན་ནོ༎ གཉིས་པ་ནི། མིང་དང་བརྡའི་ཐ་སྙད་ཀྱིས་བཏགས་པའི་ངོ་བོ་ཉིད་དང་ཐ་སྙད་འདོགས་པའི་མཚན་མའི་གཞིར་གྱུར་པས་ཐ་སྙད་དུ་ཡོད་པ་ཞེས་བྱའོ༎ རྒྱུ་མཚན་ནི་མངོན་པར་བརྗོད་པའི་ཚིག་གི་གནས་སུ་གྱུར་པའི་དངོས་པོ་ལ་བཤད་དོ༎ རྣམ་བཤད་རིགས་པ་ལས་ཀྱང་།

འཇིག་རྟེན་པའི་ཤེས་པ་མ་འཁྲུལ[a] པའི་ཡུལ་དང་འཇིག་རྟེན་ལས་འདས་པའི་ཤེས་པའི་ཡུལ་ལ་དགོངས་ནས་བདེན་པ་གཉིས་པོ་ཀུན་རྫོབ་ཀྱི་བདེན་པ་དང་དོན་དམ་པའི་བདེན་པ་གསུངས་སོ༎ བརྗོད་པ་ནི་ཀུན་རྫོབ་ཡིན་པས་དེས་ཁོང་དུ་ཆུད་པར་བྱ་བའི་བདེན་པ་ནི་ཀུན་རྫོབ་ཀྱི་བདེན་པ་ཡིན་ཏེ་གང་ལ་བརྗོད་པ་འཇུག་པ་

[a] Delhi NG dkra shis lhun po (525.2), Se rva zhol (23a.5), Peking (176.3.4), Sarnath gtsang (49.14), and Kalimpong (57.5) as well as B̄el-jor-hlün-drup's *Lamp for the Teaching* (49.7) and D̄a-drin-rap-d̄en's *Annotations* (86.2): *shes pa 'khrul pa'i yul.* However, Jik-may-dam-chö-gya-tso (*Port of Entry,* 474.3) and the Peking of Vasubandhu's text (5562, vol. 113, 276.2.5): *shes pa* ***ma*** *'khrul* ***pa'i*** *yul.* Jik-may-dam-chö-gya-tso (*Port of Entry,* 478.6) points out that some editions of D̄zong-ka-b̄a's text, as well as (Guṇamati's) commentary on Vasubandhu's *Principles of Explanation,* read ***ma*** *'khrul.*

Delhi NG dkra shis lhun po appears to have been altered (see the *'a* prefix of *'khrul pa'i*), but this may have no bearing on a possible absent *ma.* Zi ling sku 'bum (375.13): *shes pa* ***la*** *'khrul* ***ba'i*** *yul;* the nonsensical *la* appears to be a replacement for *ma,* which is confirmed by the Peking of Vasubandhu's text. Both readings, with and without the negative, are possible.

> སྟེ། དཔེར་ན་རྐང་པ་གཉིས་ཀྱིས་རྒལ་[a] བར་བྱ་བའི་འབབ་སྟེགས་ལ་རྐང་པའི་འབབ་སྟེགས་ཞེས་བྱ་བ་དང་། ཀོ་གྲུས་ [50] རྒལ་ (23b) བར་བྱ་བའི་འབབ་སྟེགས་ལ་ཀོ་གྲུའི་འབབ་སྟེགས་ཞེས་བྱ་བ་ལྟ་བུའོ།

ཞེས་གསུངས་སོ།། [166] (298) བསྡུ་བ་ལས། དེ་བཞིན་ཉིད་རྟོགས་པའི་མཉམ་གཞག་གི་འཕགས་པའི་ཡེ་ཤེས་ནི་དོན་དམ་པར་ཡོད་པར་གསུངས་ཏེ་ཀུན་རྫོབ་ཏུ་ཡོད་པར་འདོག་པའི་རྒྱུ་མཚན་སྣ་མ་གཉིས་མེད་པ་ལ་དགོངས་སོ།། དེའི་རྗེས་ཐོབ་ཀྱི་ཡེ་ཤེས་ནི་ཀུན་རྫོབ་དང་དོན་དམ་གཉིས་ཀར་ཡོད་[b] པར་གསུངས་ཏེ། ཐ་སྙད་ཀྱི་མཚན་མ་ལ་དམིགས་པའི་སྒོ་ནས་ཐ་སྙད་དུ་ཡོད་པར་གསུངས་སོ།། [168] (298) ཐ་སྙད་འདོགས་པའི་གཞིའི་མཚན་མར་གྱུར་པ་དང་ཀུན་ནས་ཉོན་མོངས་སློང་བའི་དམིགས་པ་བྱེད་པས་ཀུན་རྫོབ་ཏུ་ཡོད་པ་ནི་རང་གི་མཚན་ཉིད་ཀྱིས་གྲུབ་ {526} པའི་དོན་དམ་པར་ཡོད་པ་དང་མི་འགལ་ཏེ། རྣམ་བཤད་རིགས་པ་ལས།[c]

> ཉན་ཐོས་སྡེ་པས་དོན་དམ་པ་སྟོང་པ་ཉིད་ལས། ལས་དང་རྣམ་སྨིན་ཡོད་ལ་བྱེད་པ་པོ་ནི་མི་དམིགས་སོ་ཞེས་གསུངས་པ་དེ་དོན་དམ་པ་ཡིན་ན་ཇི་ལྟར་ན་ཆོས་ཐམས་ཅད་ངོ་བོ་ཉིད་མེད། ཀུན་རྫོབ་ཏུ་ཡིན་ན་ནི་དེར་བྱེད་པ་པོ་ཡོད་པས་དེ་མི་དམིགས་སོ། ཞེས་ཇི་ལྟར་བརྗོད་

---

a Zi ling sku 'bum (375.17, 375.18): *brgal;* this reading is based on the fact that *brgal bar bya ba* is a nominalized future passive participle, which calls for the future form of the verb; however, I have remained with the form used in the other editions.

b Delhi NG dkra shis lhun po (525.6) misreads *yed;* this appears to be a deliberate change made before photo-offsetting.

c This is a paraphrase; according to the Peking edition of Vasubandhu's text (5562, vol. 113, 283.2.7-283.3.3), the passage reads (with material that Dzong-ka-ba condensed in bold):

> *don dam pa stong pa nyid las/ las* ***kyang yod*** *rnam* ***par*** *smin* ***pa yang*** *yod la byed pa po ni mi dmigs so zhes gsungs pa* ***gang yin pa*** *de* ***ci don dam pa nyid du'am*** [text misreads: *lam*] ***'on te kun rdzob nyid yin zhe na/ de las cir "gyur/ gal te*** *don dam pa* ***nyid du*** *yin na/ ji ltar chos thams cad ngo bo nyid med* ***pa yin/ gal te*** *kun rdzob tu yin na byed pa po* ***yang kun rdzob tu*** *yod pas* ***byed pa po ni*** *mi dmigs so zhes brjod* ***par mi bya'o zhe na/ re zhig kun rdzob ces bya ba 'di ci yin/ don dam ni*** [text: *na*] ***gang zhig yin/ de las ci kun rdzob tu yod dam/ ci don dam par yod par shes par bya'o/*** *ming dang brjod pa dang gdags pa dang tha snyad ni kun rdzob yin la/ chos rnams kyi rang gi mtshan nyid ni don dam pa* [text misreads: *ma*] *yin no zhe na/ 'o na de lta na las dang rnam par smin pa gnyis ming du yang yod/ rang gi mtshan nyid du yang yod pas de gnyis ji ltar 'dod par yod du rtog la rag go /*

ཅེས་བརྩད[a]་པའི་ལན་དུ་ཀུན་རྫོབ་དང་དོན་དམ་གང་ཡིན་ཤེས་ན་དེ་ལས་དེ་གཉིས་སུ་ཡོད་པ་ཤེས་པས་དེ་གཉིས་གང་ཡིན་དྲིས་པ་ན།

> མིང་དང་བརྗོད་པ་དང་གདགས་པ་དང་ཐ་སྙད་ནི་ཀུན་རྫོབ་ཡིན་ལ། ཆོས་རྣམས་ཀྱི་རང་གི་མཚན་ཉིད་ནི་དོན་དམ་པ་ཡིན་ནོ་ཞེ་ན། འོ་ན་དེ་ལྟ་ན་ལས་དང་རྣམ་པར་སྨིན་པ་གཉིས་མིང་དུ་ཡང་ཡོད། རང་ [51] གི་མཚན་ཉིད་དུ་ཡང་ཡོད་པས་དེ་གཉིས་ཇི་ལྟར་འདོད་པར་ཡོད་དུ་རྟོག་ལ་རག་གོ།

ཞེས་གསུངས་ཏེ་དོན་དམ་པར་ཡོད་ཚུལ་ནི་སྔ་མ་དང་ཀུན་རྫོབ་ཏུ་ཡོད་ཚུལ་ནི་ཕྱི་མ་ལྟར་ཏེ། དེ་གཉིས་ཀར་ཡོད་ཅེས་པའི་དོན་ནོ།། དོན་དམ་ (24a) དེར་ཡོད་པར་འདོད་ཀྱང་དོན་དམ་པར་ཆོས་ཐམས་ཅད་ངོ་བོ་ཉིད་མེད་པར་གསུངས་པ་ནི་སྒྲ་ཇི་བཞིན་པར་མི་འདོད་པས་འདི་པ[b]་ལ་མི་འགལ་ལོ།། གང་ཟག་ཀུན་རྫོབ་ཏུ་ཡོད་ཀྱང་རྫས་སུ་མེད། ལས་དང་རྣམ་སྨིན་ཀུན་རྫོབ་ཏུ་ཡོད་ཅིང་རྫས་སུ་ཡང་ཡོད་ལ་འཇིག་རྟེན་པའི་ཤེས་པའི་ཡུལ་ཡིན་པས་འཇོག་ཚུལ་གཉིས་པའི་དོན་དམ་དུ་མེད་པ་དང་དེ་གཉིས་འཇིག་རྟེན་ལས་འདས་པའི་ཤེས་པའི་ཡུལ་མིན་ཏེ་དེའི་ཡུལ་ནི་བརྗོད་དུ་མེད་པ་སྤྱིའི་མཚན་ཉིད་ཡིན་པའི་ཕྱིར་རོ་ཞེས་དང་། ཐེག་ཆེན་པ་ཁ་ཅིག་ཆོས་ {527} ཐམས་ཅད་རང་གི་མཚན་ཉིད་དུ་མེད་ལ་ཀུན་རྫོབ་ཏུ་ཡོད་པར་གསུངས་སོ། ཞེས་སྨྲ་བ་ལ་སྔར་གྱི་ཀླན་ཀ་དེ་འཇུག་པར་རྣམ་བཤད་རིགས་པ་ལས་བཤད་པ་འདི་ཡང་ཤིན་ཏུ་གསལ་ལོ།། [170](299) དབུས་མཐའ་ལས[c]།

> བཏགས་པ་དང་ནི་ཤེས་པ་དང་།།
> དེ་བཞིན་བརྗོད་པར་རིགས་པ་ཡིན།

---

a Se rva zhol (23b.4) and Kalimpong (58.6): *brtsod;* Delhi NG dkra shis lhun po (526.2), Zi ling sku 'bum (376.9), Peking (176.4.3), and Sarnath gtsang (50.16): *brtsad.*

b Zi ling sku 'bum (376.17): *ba,* again correcting in order to maintain the rule that *ba* follows *nga, 'a, ra, la,* and suffixless syllables. However, *'di pa* is also correct (or the only correct choice, according to Si-du), since the situation calls for a syllable indicating possession (*bdag sgra*).

c III.10bc; Peking 5522, vol. 108, 20.3.5. The Sanskrit in Nagao (*Madhyāntavibhāga,* 41); and Pandeya (*Madhyānta-vibhāga,* 94) is:

prajñapti-pratipattitas [Pandeya: *pratipattitaḥ*]/
tathodbhāvanayodāraṃ [Pandeya: *audāram*]/

ཞེས་རིགས་པའི་དེ་ཁོ་ན་ཀུན་རྫོབ་ཀྱི་བདེན་པ་ལ་བཏགས་པའི་ཀུན་རྫོབ་དང་ཤེས་པའི་ཀུན་རྫོབ་དང་བརྗོད་པའི་ཀུན་རྫོབ་གསུམ་དུ་མཛད་ནས། ངོ་བོ་ཉིད་གསུམ་དང་སྦྱར་བའི་ཕྱི་མ་ནི་མདོ་གཞན་ལས་དེ་བཞིན་ཉིད་ལ་སོགས་པ་ཀུན་རྫོབ་ཏུ་ཡོད་པར་གསུངས་པའི་དགོངས་པ་འཆད་པ་ལ་ཤེས་ [52] དགོས་སོ།། [171] (300) དེ་ལྟར་གྲུབ་མཐའ་གོང་འོག་གི་རྫས་བཏགས་དང་ཀུན་རྫོབ་དང་དོན་དམ་པར་ཡོད་ཚུལ་དང་གྲུབ་མཐའ་གཅིག་གི་ཡང་དེ་དག་གི་འཇོག་ཚུལ་མི་འདྲ་བའི་ཁྱད་པར་ཞིབ་པར་ཕྱེད་ན་གྲུབ་མཐའ་གལ་[a] ཅན་རྣམས་ལེགས་པར་གཏན་ལ་འབེབས་ནུས་ཤིང་། དངོས་པོར་སྨྲ་བས་བཏགས་ཡོད་དང་ཀུན་རྫོབ་ཏུ་ཡོད་པར་ཁས་བླངས་པ་མང་པོ་དབུ་མ་པས་དེ་དག་ (24b) ལ་དོན་དམ་པར་[b] མེད་པར་སྒྲུབ་དགོས་པ་རྣམས་ཤེས་པར་འགྱུར་ལ། གཞན་དུ་ན་གྲུབ་མཐའ་གོང་འོག་གི་ཁྱད་པར་འབྱེད་པ་ལ་དཀའ་བ་ཙམ་དུ་ཟད་དོ།།

[a] Se rva zhol (24a.6) and Peking (176.5.4) misread *'gal;* the other editions: *gal*—Delhi NG dkra shis lhun po (527.4), Zi ling sku 'bum (377.10), Sarnath gtsang (52.4), and Kalimpong (60.3). The Delhi GD zhol has been corrected to *gal.*

[b] Se rva zhol (24b.1) misreads *yar*. Delhi NG dkra shis lhun po (527.4), Zi ling sku 'bum (377.12), Peking (176.5.5), Sarnath gtsang (52.6), and Kalimpong (60.4): *par*.

གསུམ་པ་ [དེ་དག་ལས་གཞན་པའི་གཞུང་ནས་བཤད་ཚུལ་]ལ་གཉིས། མདོ་སྡེ་རྒྱན་ལས་བཤད་པའི་ཚུལ་དང་། དབུས་མཐའ་ལས་བཤད་པའི་ཚུལ་ལོ།། [172] (302)

དང་པོ་ [མདོ་སྡེ་རྒྱན་ལས་བཤད་པའི་ཚུལ་]ནི། [172] (302)

རྒྱན་ལས།[a]

རང་དང་རང་གི་མཚན་ཉིད་དུ[b]།
མེད་ཕྱིར་རང་གི་ངོ་བོ་ལ།།
མི་གནས་ཕྱིར་དང་འཛིན་བཞིན་དེ།།
མེད་ཕྱིར་ངོ་བོ་ཉིད་མེད་འདོད།

ཅེས་འདུས་བྱས་ཀྱི་མཚན་ཉིད་གསུམ་དང་བྱིས་པས་ཞེན་པ་བཞིན་གྱི་ངོ་བོ་ཉིད་མེད་པ་ལ་དགོངས་ནས་ {528} ངོ་བོ་ཉིད་མེད་པར་གསུངས་པར་བཤད་དོ[c]།། ཀུན་ལས་བཏུས[d]་ལས་ནི། དེ་གཉིས་དང་ངོ་བོ་ཉིད་མེད་པ་གསུམ་ལ་དགོངས་ནས་ཤིན་ཏུ་རྒྱས་པ་ལས་ངོ་བོ་ཉིད་མེད་པར་གསུངས་པར་བཤད་དོ།། ཆོས་རྣམས་རྐྱེན་ལ་རག་ལས་པས་རང[e]་མེད་པའི་

[a] XI.50; Peking 5521, vol. 108, 9.1.3. The Sanskrit in Bagchi (*Mahāyāna-Sūtrālaṃkāra,* 67) is:

svayaṃ svenātmanā 'bhāvātsvabhāve cānavasthiteḥ/
grāhavattadā[*da*] *bhāvācca* [Lévi: *grāhavattadābhāvācca*] *niḥsvabhāvatamiṣyate//*

The Tibetan (*dang 'dzin bzhin* ***de***// *med phyir*) accords more with Bagchi's *grāhavat**tad**abhāvācca.* For the Sanskrit text on which Bagchi's edition was based, see Lévi, *Mahāyānasūtrālaṃkāra,* vol. 1, 67.16; French trans., vol. 2, 121.

[b] For *mtshan nyid du,* the Peking of Maitreya's text (5521, vol. 108, 9.1.3) and of Vasubandhu's commentary (5527, vol. 108, 77.2.1) read *bdag nyid du,* which accords slightly more with the Sanskrit *ātmanā.*

[c] *mdo sde'i rgyan gyi bshad pa, sūtrālaṃkārābhāṣya,* Peking 5527, vol. 108, 77.2.1-77.2.5. Except as noted in the Translation, D̄zong-ka-b̄a is paraphrasing Vasubandhu's commentary. For the Sanskrit, see Bagchi, *Mahāyāna-Sūtrālaṃkāra,* 67.20-67.25; and Lévi, *Mahāyānasūtrālaṃkāra,* vol. 1, 67.18-67.23.

[d] Peking 5550, vol. 112, 266.1.2-266.1.4:

shin tu rgyas pa las chos thams cad ngo bo nyid med do zhes gang gsungs pa de la dgongs pa gang yin zhe na/ bdag nyid kyis mi 'byung ba dang/ rang gi [text reads: *gis*] *bdag nyid du med pa dang/ rang gi ngo bo la mi gnas pa dang/ byis pas bzung ba bzhin du mtshan nyid med pa'i phyir ro// yang kun du brtags pa'i ngo bo nyid la mtshan nyid kyis ngo bo nyid med pa dang/ gzhan gyi dbang la skye ba ngo bo nyid med pa dang/ yongs su grub pa la don dam pa ngo bo nyid med pa'i phyir ro//*

[e] Delhi NG dkra shis lhun po (528.2), Peking (177.1.1), and Sarnath gtsang (52.18):

ཕྱིར་ངོ་བོ་ཉིད་མེད་དོ།། འདིའི་དོན་ནི་རང་གི་བདག་ཉིད་ཀྱིས་སྐྱེ་བ་མེད་པ་ལ་དབུ་མ་སྣང་བར་བཤད་པ་ལྟར་རོ།། ཆོས་གང་འགགས་པ་ནི་སླར་ [53] ཡང་ཆོས་དེའི་བདག་ཉིད་དུ་མི་སྐྱེ་བས་རང་གི་བདག་ཉིད་དུ་མེད་པའི་ཕྱིར་ངོ་བོ་ཉིད་མེད་དོ།། སྐྱེས་ལ་མ་འགགས་པ་ནི་སྐད་ཅིག་མ་ཡིན་པས་རང་གི་ངོ་བོ་ལ་དུས་གཉིས་པར་མི་གནས་པའི་ཕྱིར་ངོ་བོ་ཉིད་མེད་དོ།། མདོར་ན་མྱུ་གུ་མ་འོངས་པ་རང་གི་དབང་གིས་མི་སྐྱེ་ཞིང་མྱུ་གུ་འདས་པ་བསྐྱུར་ནས་མྱུ་གུའི་བདག་ཉིད་དུ་མི་སྐྱེ་ལ་མྱུ་གུ་ད[a]་ལྟར་བ་རང་གྲུབ་པའི་དུས་གཉིས་པར་མི་སྡོད་པས་དུས་གསུམ་གྱི་ཆོས་རྣམས་ལ་ངོ་བོ་ཉིད་མེད་པར་བཤད་ཅེས་པའོ།། བྱིས་པས[b]་གཙང་བདེ་རྟག་བདག་གམ་ཀུན་བརྟགས་ཀྱི་མཚན་ཉིད་གཞན་དུ་ཞེན་པ་ལྟར་གྱི་ངོ་བོ་ཉིད་མེད་པས་ངོ་བོ་ཉིད་མེད་པར་དབྱིག་གཉེན་ (25a) གྱིས་བཤད་དོ།། གཞན་ནི་གཟུང་འཛིན་རྫས་ཐ་དད་དུ་ཞེན་པའོ།། [173] (303) ཇི་ལྟར་ངོ་བོ་ཉིད་མེད་པ་དེ་ལྟར་མ་སྐྱེས་ལ་མ་སྐྱེས་པའི་ཕྱིར་དེ་ལྟར་མ་འགགས་ཞེས་སོགས་སྔ་མ་སྔ་མ་རྒྱུ་མཚན་དུ་བྱས་ནས་ཕྱི་མ་ཕྱི་མ་འགྲུབ་པ་ནི་དེ་ཉིད་ལས[c]།

rang; Se rva zhol (24b.3), Zi ling sku 'bum (378.1), Grags pa & rnam rgyal (51.11), and Kalimpong (61.2): *rang dbang.* This sentence is Ḏzong-ka-ḇa's rerendering of Vasubandhu's commentary:

> That [phenomena] are natureless due to being without ownness is due to the fact that phenomena depend upon conditions *(**rang** med pa'i phyir ngo bo nyid med pa ni chos rnams rkyen la rag las pa'i phyir ro, **svayam**abhāvānniḥsvabhāvatvaṃ dharmāṇāṃ pratyayādhīnatvāt).*

Thus, the *rang* reading would represent a straight reporting of Maitreya's and Vasubandhu's text (*svayam*) with rearranged syntax, whereas *rang dbang* would represent Ḏzong-ka-ḇa's further interpretation of the meaning of *rang.* Both are plausible.

[a] Delhi GD zhol (24b.5) has been mistakenly emended to *de ltar ba;* all other editions: *da ltar ba.*

[b] Ḏzong-ka-ḇa continues his paraphrase of Vasubandhu's *Explanation of (Maitreya's) "Ornament for the Great Vehicle Sūtras"* (Peking 5527, vol. 108, 77.2.4). For the Sanskrit, see Bagchi, *Mahāyāna-Sūtrālaṃkāra,* 67.23; Lévi, *Mahāyānasūtrālaṃkāra,* vol. 1, 67.21.

[c] XI.51; Peking 5521, vol. 108, 9.1.3. The Sanskrit, as restored by Bagchi (*Mahāyāna-Sūtrālaṃkāra,* 67), is:

> *niḥsvabhāvatayā siddhā uttarottaraniśrayāt/*
> *anutpannā niruddhādi-śānta-prakṛti-nirvṛtāḥ//*

Lévi's restoration (*Mahāyānasūtrālaṃkāra,* 67, n. 3) is:

> *niḥsvabhāvatayā siddhā uttarottaraniśrayāḥ/*
> *anutpādo 'nirodhaścādiśāntiḥ parinirvṛtiḥ//*

In his translation Lévi revised this to read:

> *niḥsvabhāvatayā siddhā uttarottaraniśrayāt/*

ཕྱི་མ[a]་ཕྱི་མའི་རྟེན་ཡིན་པས།།
ངོ་བོ་ཉིད་ནི་མེད་པ་ཡིས[b]།།
སྐྱེ་མེད་འགག་མེད་གཟོད་ནས་ཞི།།
རང་བཞིན་མྱ་ངན་འདས་པ་གྲུབ།།

ཅེས་གསུངས་ཏེ་བཤད་ཟིན་ཏོ།། ཡང[c]། [173] (303)

ཐོག་མ་དང་ནི་དེ་{529}ཉིད་གཞན་ཉིད་དང་།།
རང་གི་མཚན་ཉིད་རང་དང་གཞན་དུ་འགྱུར[d]།།
ཀུན་ནས་ཉོན་མོངས་པ་དང་ཁྱད་པར་ལ།།
སྐྱེ་བ་མེད་པའི་ཆོས་ལ་བཟོད་པར་བཤད།

---

anutpannāniruddhādiśāntaprakṛtinirvṛtāḥ//

a Delhi NG dkra shis lhun po (528.6), Se rva zhol (24b.2), Zi ling sku 'bum (378.13), Peking (177.1.6), Sarnath gtsang (53.14), and Kalimpong (62.2) read *phyi ma,* as does the Peking of Vasubandhu's commentary (5527, vol. 108, 77.2.5), but the Peking of Maitreya's text (5521, vol. 108, 9.1.4) reads *snga ma.* This seems to represent merely a difference in translation.

b Delhi NG dkra shis lhun po (528.6), Se rva zhol (24b.2), Zi ling sku 'bum (378.13), Peking (177.1.6), Sarnath gtsang (53.14), and Kalimpong (62.2) read *yin,* but the Peking of Maitreya's text (5521, vol. 108, 9.1.4) and of Vasubandhu's commentary (5527, vol. 108, 77.2.6) read *yis,* which accords with the Sanskrit instrumental *niḥsvabhāvatayā.* Jik-may-dam-chö-gya-tso (*Port of Entry,* 504.1) calls for analysis of D̄zong-ka-b̄a's text, which reads *yin,* since many editions of Maitreya's *Ornament for the Great Vehicle Sūtras* and its commentaries, as well as Asaṅga's *Summary of the Great Vehicle,* read *yis* and since, accordingly, the lines are explained as meaning that "*by reason of* naturelessness non-production and so forth are established."

As S̄er-s̄hul (*Notes,* 38b.1) says:

> The text of the original as well as Asaṅga's *Summary of the Great Vehicle,* and many commentaries read *ngo bo nyid ni med pa yis;* I do not know whether this represents a difference in translation or a corrupt text, but if it is taken as *yis,* it facilitates commentary.

For similar reasons, the text has been emended to *yis.*

c XI.52; Peking 5521, vol. 108, 9.1.4. The Sanskrit in Bagchi (*Mahāyāna-Sūtrālaṃkāra,* 68) is:

> *ādau tattve 'nyatve svalakṣaṇe svayamathānyathābhāve/*
> *saṃkleśe 'tha viśeṣe kśāntiranutpattidharmoktā//*

See also Lévi, *Mahāyānasūtrālaṃkāra,* vol. 1, 68.5.

d All of the editions used read *'gyur,* as does the Peking of Vasubandhu's commentary (5527, vol. 108, 77.2.5), but the Peking of Maitreya's text (5521, vol. 108, 9.1.4) reads *gyur.*

ཅེས་མི་སྐྱེ་བའི་ཆོས་ལ་བཟོད་པ་ཐོབ་ཅེས་གསུངས་པའི་ཆོས་རྣམས་ཀྱི་སྐྱེ་བ་མེད་ཚུལ་བཤད་དོ།། དེ་ལ་ཐོག་མ་ནི་འཁོར་བ་ལ་ཐོག [54] མའི་སྐྱེ་བ་མེད་པ་དང་། དེ་ཉིད་ནི་སྔ་མ་སྟེ་ཆོས་གང་སྔར་སྐྱེས་པ་དེ་དག་སླར་དེའི་ངོ་བོར་སྐྱེ་བ་མེད་པ་དང་གཞན་ནི་ཕྱི་མ་སྟེ་སྔོན་མེད་པའི་རྣམ་པར་མི་སྐྱེ་བ་ལ་འགྲེལ་པས[a] བཤད་དོ།། དེའི་དོན་ནི་འཁོར་བ་ན་སྔོན་མེད་པའི་སེམས་ཅན་མི་སྐྱེ་བ་དང་སྔར་འགགས་པ་དང་རིགས་མཐུན་པ་སྐྱེ་བས་ཆོས་སྔོན་མེད་པ་མི་སྐྱེ་བ་ལ་དབུ་མ་སྣང་བར་བཤད་པ་ལྟར་རོ།། རང་མཚན་ནི་ཀུན་བརྟགས་ལ་སྟེ་དེ་ལ་ནམ་ཡང་སྐྱེ་བ་མེད་དོ།། རང་མི་སྐྱེ་བ[b] ནི་གཞན་དབང་ལའོ།། གཞན་འགྱུར་གྱི་སྐྱེ་བ་མེད་པ་ནི་ཡོངས་གྲུབ་ལའོ།། ཉོན་མོངས་མི་སྐྱེ་བ་ནི་ཟད་པ་ཤེས་པ་ཐོབ་པ་ལའོ།། ཁྱད་པར་དུ་སྐྱེ་བ་མེད་པ་ནི་སངས་རྒྱས་ཀྱི་ཆོས་སྐུ་ལའོ།། ངོ་བོ་ཉིད་མེད་ལུགས་དང་སྐྱེ་བ་མེད་ཚུལ་འདི་བཞིན་འཆད་པ་ནི་ཆོས་ཐམས་ (25b) ཅད་དོན་དམ་པར་ངོ་བོ་ཉིད་ཀྱིས་སྟོང་པ་དང་འདུས་བྱས་རྣམས་ལ་དོན་དམ་པར་སྐྱེ་བ་མེད་པར་བཤད་པ་སྒྲ་ཇི་བཞིན་པར་མི་འདོད་པའི་ལུགས་སོ།། དེ་ལ་དུས་གསུམ་གྱི་ཆོས་ལ་ངོ་བོ་ཉིད་མེད་ཚུལ་གྱི་ད་ལྟར་བ་མ་གཏོགས་པ་དང་། བྱིས་པས་ཞེན་པ་བཞིན་གྱི་ངོ་བོ་ཉིད་མེད་ཚུལ་སྔ་མ་ནི་ཉན་ཐོས་སྡེ་གཉིས་ག[c] དང་ཐུན་མོང་བའོ།། བྱེ་བྲག་ཏུ་སྨྲ་བ་ནི་སྐྱེས་ཟིན་པའི་འོག་ཏུ་གནས་པའི་བྱ་བ་དང་དེའི་འོག་ཏུ་འཇིག་པའི་བྱ་བ་འཇུག[d] པར་འདོད་དོ།། [176] (304)

གལ་ཏེ {530} དགོངས་འགྲེལ་ལས་གཞན་དབང་སྒྱུ་མ་བཞིན་དུ་གསུངས་ཤིང་། རྒྱན་ལས་ཀྱང་འདུས་བྱས་ཐམས་ཅད་སྒྱུ་མ་བཞིན་དུ་གསུངས་པས་བདེན་པར་གྲུབ་ [55] པ་དེ་དག་གི་

---

a Peking 5527, vol. 108, 77.3.2-77.3.5. For the Sanskrit, see Bagchi, *Mahāyāna-Sūtrālaṃkāra,* 68.8-68.14; Lévi, *Mahāyānasūtrālaṃkāra,* vol. 1, 68.7-68.14.

b Delhi NG dkra shis lhun po (529.3), Zi ling sku 'bum (379.3), Peking (177.2.3), and Sarnath gtsang (54.7): *rang mi skye ba;* Se rva zhol (25a.5) and Kalimpong (62.6): *rang gi skye ba.* With the latter reading, the line would be translated as, "'Self-production' is in reference to other-powered natures." Though such a reading also makes sense (since self-production is what is negated with respect to other-powered natures), the former reading is preferable, given that Dzong-ka-ba is paraphrasing Vasubandhu, the Peking edition (5527, vol. 108, 77.3.3) of which reads *rang skye ba* ***med pa****.* Also, the Sanskrit in both Bagchi (*Mahāyāna-Sūtrālaṃkāra,* 68.11) and Lévi (*Mahāyānasūtrālaṃkāra,* 68.10) is *svayam****an****utpattau,* which has the negative *an.*

That these readings parallel those found earlier strongly suggests that Dzong-ka-ba was seeking consistency; see p. 374, footnote c.

c Zi ling sku 'bum (379.10): *gnyis ka.*

d In Dön-drup-gyel-tsen's *Four Intertwined Commentaries* (158.6), read *bya ba 'jug* for *bya ba la 'jug,* in accordance with Delhi NG dkra shis lhun po (529.6), and so forth.

དོན་མིན་ནོ་ཞེ་ན། སྒྱུ་མ་ལ་སོགས་པ་བཞིན་དུ་བཤད་པས་བདེན་པར་མི་སྟོན་པའི་ངེས་པ་མེད་དེ་སྒྱུ་མ་ལ་སོགས་པ་དཔེར་བྱེད་ལུགས་ལ་རག་ལས་སོ།། དེ་ཡང་རྒྱན་ལས[a]

ཇི་ལྟར་སྒྱུ་མ་དེ་བཞིན་དུ།།
ཡང་དག་མ་ཡིན་ཀུན་རྟོག་འདོད[b]།།
སྒྱུ་མའི་རྣམ་པ་ཇི་ལྟ་བར།།
དེ་བཞིན་གཉིས་སུ་འཁྲུལ་པ[c]་བརྗོད།

ཅེས་གསུངས་པ་འདིས་སྒྱུ་མ་དཔེར་བྱེད་ལུགས་བསྟན་ཏེ། འཁྲུལ་པའི[d]་གཞི་བོང་བ་དང་ཤིང་ལ་སོགས་པ་སྒྱུ་མའི་སྔགས་ཀྱིས་བཏབ་པ་ནི་ཀུན་རྟོག་གཞན་དབང་དང་འདྲ་སྟེ་རྐང་པ་དང་པོ་གཉིས་ཀྱི་དོན་ནོ།། སྒྱུ་མའི་རྣམ་པ་རྟ་གླང་ལ་སོགས་པའི་གཟུགས་སུ་སྣང་བ་ནི། གཞན་དབང་གཟུང་འཛིན་རྒྱངས[e]་ཆད་གཉིས་སུ་སྣང་བ་དང་འདྲ་སྟེ་ཕྱི་མ་གཉིས་ཀྱི་དོན་དུ་དབྱིག་གཉེན་གྱིས་བཤད་དོ།། ཡང་རྒྱན་ལས[f]།

ཇི་ལྟར་དེ་ལ་དེ་མེད་པ།།
དེ་བཞིན་དུ་ནི་དོན་དམ་འདོད།།
ཇི་ལྟར་དེ་ནི་དམིགས་གྱུར་ (26a) པ།།
དེ་བཞིན་དུ་ནི་ཀུན་རྫོབ་ཉིད[g]།

[a] XI.15; Peking 5521, vol. 108, 8.3.1. The Sanskrit in Bagchi (*Mahāyāna-Sūtrālaṃkāra,* 59) is:

yathā māyā tathā'bhūtaparikalpo nirucyate/
yathā māyākṛtaṃ tadvat dvayabhrāntirnirucyate//

See also Lévi, *Mahāyānasūtrālaṃkāra,* vol. 1, 59.

[b] For *'dod,* the Peking of Maitreya's text (5521, vol. 108, 8.3.2) and the Peking of Vasubandhu's commentary (5527, vol. 108, 74.4.1) read *brjod.* Also, the next line reads *sgyu ma byas pa ji lta bar.*

[c] Zi ling sku 'bum (379.17): *ba.*

[d] Delhi NG dkra shis lhun po (530.3), Se rva zhol (25b.5), Peking (177.3.1), and Kalimpong (63.6): *pa'i;* Zi ling sku 'bum (379.18) and Sarnath gtsang (55.7): *ba'i.*

[e] Zi ling sku 'bum (380.1 and throughout): *rgyang;* the other instances will not be cited.

[f] XI.16; Peking 5521, vol. 108, 8.3.2. The Sanskrit in Bagchi (*Mahāyāna-Sūtrālaṃkāra,* 59) is:

yathā tasminna tadbhāvaḥ paramārthastatheṣyate/
yathā tasyopalabdhistu tathā saṃvṛtisatyatā//

See also Lévi, *Mahāyānasūtrālaṃkāra,* vol. 1, 59.

[g] The Peking of Maitreya's text (5521, vol. 108, 8.3.3): *kun rdzob 'dod;* the Peking of

ཅེས[a]

སྒྱུ་མ་ལ་གླང་པོ་ཆེ་ལ་སོགས་པ་མེད་པ་བཞིན་དུ་གཞན་དབང་ལ་གཟུང་འཛིན་གཉིས་མེད་པ་དོན་དམ་དང་སྒྱུ་མ་དེ་ཏ་གླང་གི་ངོ་བོར་དམིགས་པ་བཞིན་དུ་ཡང་དག་པ་མིན་པ་ལ་ཀུན་བརྟགས་པ་དེ་ཀུན་རྫོབ་ཀྱི་བདེན་པར་དམིགས་སོ[b]

ཞེས་འགྲེལ་པར་བཤད་དོ།། རྒྱན་ལས། ནང་གི་སྐྱེ་མཆེད་དྲུག་བདག་དང་སྲོག་ལ་སོགས་པར་མེད་བཞིན་དུ་དེར་སྣང་བའི་ཆ་ནས་སྒྱུ་མ་དང་། ཕྱིའི་སྐྱེ་མཆེད་ {531} དྲུག་གང་ཟག་གི་བདག་གི་ཉེ་བར་སྤྱོད་བྱར་མེད་བཞིན་དུ་ [56] དེར་སྣང་བའི་ཆ་ནས་རྨི་ལམ་ལྟ་བུར་མདོ་སྡེ་ལས་གསུངས་པར་བཤད་ཀྱི་ཕྱི་ནང་གི་འདུས་བྱས་རང་བཞིན་གྱིས་སྟོང་བཞིན་དུ་དེར་སྣང་བའི་དཔེར་མ་གསུངས་སོ།། ཐེག་བསྡུས་ལས་ཀྱང་ཡུམ་གྱི་མདོར་གསུངས་པའི་སྒྱུ་མ་ལ་སོགས་པའི་དཔེར་གཞན་དབང་བསྟན་པའི་དཔེ་དོན་སྦྱོར་བ་ན། ཕྱི་རོལ་གྱི་དོན་མེད་ན་ཡུལ་དུ་ཇི་ལྟར་དམིགས་སྙམ་པ་བཟློག་པའི་ཕྱིར་སྒྱུ་མ་དང་། དོན་མེད་ན་སེམས་དང་སེམས་བྱུང་ཇི་ལྟར་སྐྱེ་སྙམ་པ་བཟློག་པའི་ཕྱིར་སྨིག་རྒྱུ་དང་། དོན་མེད་ན་ཡིད་དུ་འོང་མི་འོང་ལ་ཇི་ལྟར་སྤྱོད་སྙམ་པ་བཟློག་པའི་ཕྱིར་རྨི་ལམ་ལ་སོགས་པ་དཔེར་བཤད་དོ།། སྒྱུ་མ་སོགས་མི་བདེན་པའི་དཔེར་བྱེད་པ་ལ་ཡང་དབུ་སེམས་སོ་སོའི་མི་བདེན་ལུགས་ཀྱི་དཔེར་བྱེད་ལུགས་མ་འདྲེས་པར་ཕྱེད་པར་བྱའོ།།

Vasubandhu's commentary (5527, vol. 108, 74.4.4): *kun rdzob nyid.*

[a] Paraphrasing Vasubandhu's *Explanation of (Maitreya's) "Ornament for the Great Vehicle Sūtras."* The Peking (5527, vol. 108, 74.4.4) reads (with the parts that Ḏzong-ka-ḇa has condensed in bold):

> *sgyu ma* ***byas pa de*** *la glang po che la sogs pa med pa* ***de*** *bzhin du gzhan* ***gyi*** *dbang* ***de*** *la* ***kun brtags pa*** *gnyis* ***gyi mtshan nyid*** *med pa don dam* ***par 'dod do// ji ltar*** *sgyu ma* ***byas pa*** *de glang* ***po che la sogs pa'i*** *ngo bor dmigs pa* ***de*** *bzhin du yang dag pa min pa* ***las*** *kun brtag* [sic] *pa de kun rdzob kyi bden par dmigs so//*

For the Sanskrit, see Bagchi, *Mahāyāna-Sūtrālaṃkāra,* 60.7-60.9 and Lévi, *Mahāyānasūtrālaṃkāra,* vol. 1, 59.11-59.13.

[b] This is a paraphrase. The Peking of Vasubandhu's *Explanation of (Maitreya's) "Ornament for the Great Vehicle Sūtras"* (5527, vol. 108, 74.4.4) reads (with the material that Ḏzong-ka-ḇa has condensed in bold):

> *sgyu ma* ***byas pa de*** *la glang po che la sogs pa med pa* ***de*** *bzhin du gzhan* ***gyi*** *dbang* ***de*** *la* ***kun brtags pa*** *gnyis* ***gyi mtshan nyid*** *med pa don dam* ***par 'dod do// ji ltar*** *sgyu ma* ***byas pa*** *de glang* ***po che la sogs pa'i*** *ngo bor dmigs pa* ***de*** *bzhin du yang dag pa min pa* ***las*** *kun brtag* [sic] *pa de kun rdzob kyi bden par dmigs so//*

གཉིས་པ་ [དབུས་མཐའ་ལས་བཤད་པའི་ཚུལ་] ནི། [182] (305)

དབུས་མཐའ་ལས[a]

ཡང་དག་མ་ཡིན་ཀུན་རྟོག་ཡོད།།
དེ་ལ་གཉིས་པོ་ཡོད་མ་ཡིན།།
སྟོང་པ་ཉིད་ནི་འདི་ལ་ཡོད།།
དེ་ལ་ཡང་ནི་དེ་ཡོད་དོ།།

སྟོང་པ་མ་ཡིན་མི་སྟོང་མིན།།
དེ་ལྟ་བས་ན་ཐམས་ཅད་བཤད།།
ཡོད་པས་ (26b) མེད་པས་ཡོད་པས་ན།།
དེ་ནི་དབུ་མའི་ལམ་ཡིན་ནོ།

ཞེས་གསུངས་ཏེ་ [183] (307) ཚོགས་བཅད་དང་པོས་སྟོང་ཉིད་ཀྱི་མཚན་ཉིད་དང་གཉིས་པས་དེ་ཉིད་དབུ་མའི་ལམ་དུ་བསྟན[b]་ནོ།། དེ་ལ་གང་ན་གང་མེད་པ་དེ་ནི་དེས་སྟོང་པ་དང་འདི་ལ་ལྷག་མ་ཡོད་པ་ནི་འདིར་ཡོད་པའོ་ཞེས་ཡོད་མེད་ཡང་དག་པ་ཇི་ལྟ་བ་བཞིན་ཤེས་པ་ནི་སྟོང་ཉིད་ལ་འཇུག་པ་ཕྱིན་ཅི་མ་ལོག་པར་གསུངས་ [57] ལ། འདིས་ཀྱང་དེ་སྟོན་པའི་ཕྱིར་སྟོང་ཉིད་ཡང་དག་པ་བསྟན་ཏོ[c]།། གང་ན་ཞེས་པ་ནི་སྟོང་གཞི་སྟེ་དེ་ནི་ཡང་དག་པ་མ་ཡིན་པའི་ཀུན་རྟོག་ {532} སྟེ་གཞན་དབང་ངོ་།། གང་མེད་ཅེས་པའི་མེད་རྒྱུ་ནི་གཟུང་འཛིན་རྫས་ཐ་དད་པ་གཉིས་པོ་སྟེ་ཀུན་བརྟགས་སོ།། དེ་ལ་ཡོད་མ་ཡིན་ཞེས་པས་ནི་སྔ་མ་དེ་ཕྱི་

---

[a] I.1-2; Peking 5522, vol. 108, 19.4.5. The Sanskrit in Nagao (*Madhyāntavibhāga,* 17 and 18) is:

abhūta-parikalpo 'sti dvayan tatra na vidyate/
śūnyatā vidyate tv atra tasyām api sa vidyate//

na śūnyaṃ nāpi cāśūnyaṃ tasmāt sarvvam [Pandeya: *sarvaṃ*] *vidhīyate/*
satvād asatvāt satvāc [Pandeya: *sattvādasattvāt sattvāc*] *ca madhyamā pratipac ca sā//*

See also Pandeya, *Madhyānta-vibhāga,* 9 and 13.

[b] Delhi NG dkra shis lhun po (531.5), Se rva zhol (26b.1), Peking (177.4.3), and Kalimpong (65.5): *bstan no;* Zi ling sku 'bum (381.2): *bstan to.* Sarnath gtsang (56.17) misreads *bstan na.*

[c] Delhi NG dkra shis lhun po (531.6), Se rva zhol (26b.2), Zi ling sku 'bum (381.5), Sarnath gtsang (57.1), and Kalimpong (65.6): *bstan to.* The Peking (177.4.4) misreads *stan to.*

མ་འདིས་སྟོང་པར་བསྟན་ནོ[a]།། དེ་མེད་ན་དེའི་ཤུལ་དུ་ལྷག་མ་ལུས་པའི་ཡོད་པ་དེ་གང་ཡིན་སྙམ་ན། ཀུན་རྟོག་ཡོད་ཅེས་པ་དང་། རྐང་པ་གསུམ་པས་གཞན་དབང་དང་ཡོངས་གྲུབ་གཉིས་ཡིན་ནོ་ཞེས་བསྟན་ལ་རྐང་པ་བཞི་པས་ནི་དོགས་པ་གཞན་ཞིག་གཅོད་དོ།། དབྱིག་གཉེན་གྱིས་གང་སྟོང་པ་དང་གང་གིས་སྟོང་པའི་དོན་དུ་དེ་ལྟར་བཤད་པ་དེ་ཉིད་བློ་བརྟན་གྱིས་གསལ་བར་བསྟན་པ་ནི་འགྲེལ་བཤད་ལས[b]།

> ལ་ལ་དག་ཆོས་ཐམས་ཅད་རི་བོང་གི་རྭ་ལྟར་རང་བཞིན་ཡེ་མེད་དོ་སྙམ་དུ་སེམས་པ་དེའི་ཕྱིར་ཐམས་ཅད་ལ་སྐུར་པ་དགག་པའི་དོན་དུ། ཡང་དག་མ་ཡིན་ཀུན་རྟོག་ཡོད། ཅེས་བྱ་བ་གསུངས་ཏེ་རང་བཞིན་གྱིས་ཞེས་བྱ་བ་ཚིག་གི་ལྷག་མའོ།

ཞེས་གསུངས་སོ།། ཀུན་རྟོག་ཡོད་ཅེས་པའི་ཚིག་དེ་དེ་ཙམ་གྱིས་མ་རྫོགས་པས་དེའི་ལྷག་མ་དཔྱད་དགོས་ལ་དེ་ཡང་རང་བཞིན་གྱིས་ཞེས་པ་འདེའོ།། དེ་ལྟར་ན་ཀུན་རྟོག་ཡོད་པ་ (27a) ཙམ་མིན་གྱི་རང་བཞིན་གྱིས་ཡོད་པའམ་རང་གི་མཚན་ཉིད་ཀྱིས་གྲུབ་པའི་ཡོད་པའོ།། ཡོད་ཚུལ་དེ་དག་ནི་ཡོངས་གྲུབ་ལ་ཡང་འདྲའོ།། ཚིག་གཉིས་པས་དོགས་པ་སེལ་ཚུལ་ཡང་དེ་ཉིད་ལས[c]། [58]

> དེ་ལྟ་ན་མདོ་ལས་ཆོས་ཐམས་ཅད་སྟོང་པའོ་ཞེས་བཤད་པས་མདོ་དང་མི་འགལ་ལམ་ཞེ་ན། མི་འགལ་ཏེ་འདི་ལྟར། དེ་ལ་གཉིས་པོ་ཡོད་མ་ཡིན། ཡང་དག་པ་མ་ཡིན་པ་ཀུན་ཏུ་རྟོག་པ་གཟུང་བ་དང་འཛིན་པའི་ངོ་བོ་དང་བྲལ་བས་སྟོང་ {533} པ་ཞེས་བྱའི་རང་བཞིན་ཡེ་མེད་པ་ནི་མ་ཡིན་ཏེ་དེའི་ཕྱིར་མདོ་དང་མི་འགལ་ལོ།

[a] Delhi NG dkra shis lhun po (532.1), Se rva zhol (26b.3), Peking (177.4.177.4.5), Sarnath gtsang (57.5), and Kalimpong (66.2): *bstan no;* Zi ling sku 'bum (381.8): *bstan to.*

[b] Peking 5334, vol. 109, 138.1.5. The Sanskrit in Pandeya (*Madhyānta-vibhāga,* 9.25) is:
kecit virundhanti sarvadharmāḥ sarvathā niḥsvabhāvāḥ śaśaviṣāṇavadityataḥ sarvāpavādapratiṣedhārtham āha—

abhūtaparikalpo 'stīti/

svabhāvata iti vākyaśeṣaḥ/

[c] Peking 5334, vol. 109.1.6. The Sanskrit in Pandeya (*Madhyānta-vibhāga,* 9.28) is:
nanvevaṃ sūtravirodhaḥ—sarvadharmāḥ śūnyā iti śāstre vacanāt/ nāsti virodhaḥ yasmāt—

dvayaṃ tatra na vidyate/

abhūtaparikalpo hi grāhyagrāhakasvarūparahitaḥ śūnya ucyate na tu sarvathā niḥsvabhāvaḥ/ ato na sūtravirodhaḥ//

ཞེས་གཞན་དབང་རང་བཞིན་གྱིས་གྲུབ་ན་ཆོས་ཐམས་ཅད་རང་བཞིན་གྱིས་ཡོད་པས་སྟོང་ངོ་ཞེས་གསུངས་པ་དང་འགལ་ལོ་ཞེས་པའི་ལན་དུ་ཀུན་རྟོག་དེ་ཕྱིའི་གཟུང་བ་དང་ནང་གི་འཛིན་པར་སྣང་བའི་གཟུང་འཛིན་རྒྱངས་ཆད་དུ་སྣང་བ་དེ་ལྟར་དུ་ཡོད་པའི་ངོ་བོས་སྟོང་པ་ལ་དགོངས་ནས་ངོ་བོས་སྟོང་པར་གསུངས་ཀྱི་རང་གི་མཚན་ཉིད་ཀྱིས་གྲུབ་པའི་རང་བཞིན་ཡེ་མེད་མིན་ནོ་ཞེས་གསུངས་ཏེ་སྐུ་མཆེད་ཀྱི་གཞུང་གི་དོན་ནི་འདི་ཁོ་ན་ལྟར་ཡིན་ཞིང་དེ་ཉིད་ལ་དོན་དམ་པར་ཡོད་[a]པར་ཡང་བཤད་པས་ལུགས་འདི་ལ་གཞན་དབང་རང་སྟོང་དུ་འཆད་པ་གཏན་མ་ཡིན་ནོ།། ཚིག་གསུམ་པས་དོགས་པ་སེལ་ཚུལ་ཡང་དེ་ཉིད་ལས[b]།

> གལ་ཏེ་དེ་ལྟར་གཉིས་པོ་ནི་རི་བོང་གི་རྭ་ལྟར་ཡེ་མེད་ལ་ཡང་དག་པ་མ་ཡིན་པ་ཀུན་ཏུ་རྟོག་པ་ནི་དོན་དམ་པར་རང་བཞིན་གྱིས་ཡོད་ན་དེ་ལྟ་ན་སྟོང་པ་ཉིད་མེད་པར་འགྱུར་རོ་ཞེ་ན། དེ་ནི་དེ་ལྟ་མ་ཡིན་ཏེ། འདི་ལྟར་སྟོང་པ་ཉིད་ནི་འདི་ལ་ཡོད། ཡང་དག་པ་མ་ཡིན་པ་ཀུན་ཏུ་རྟོག་པ་ལ་གཟུང་བ་དང་འཛིན་ (27b) པ་མེད་པ་ཉིད་གང་ཡིན་པ་དེ་སྟོང་པ་ཉིད་ཡིན་པས་སྟོང་པ་ཉིད་མེད་པར་མི་འགྱུར་ [59] རོ་

ཞེས་སོ།། ཀུན་རྟོག་ཡོད་[c]པ་དང་གཉིས་པོ་མེད་ཅེས་པས་ཡོད་པ་སྔ་མ་དང་མེད་པ་ཕྱི་མ་ཡིན་པར་བསྟན་པས་སྟོང་ཉིད་མེད་སྙམ་པའི་དོགས་པ་བྱུང་བ་བསལ[d]ལོ།། ཀུན་

---

[a] Delhi NG dkra shis lhun po (533.3) misreads *yad.*

[b] Peking 5334, vol. 109, 138.1.7-138.2.1. The Sanskrit in Pandeya (*Madhyānta-vibhāga,* 9.32) is:

> *yadevaṃ dvayaṃ śaśaviṣāṇavat sarvathā nāsti/ abhūtaparikalpaśca paramārthataḥ svabhāvato 'styevaṃ śūnyatā 'bhāvaprasaṅgaḥ/ naitadevaṃ yasmāt—*
>
> *śūnyatā vidyate tvatra*
>
> *iyameva hi śūnyatā yā grāhyagrāhakarahitatā 'bhūtaparikalpasyeti na śūnyatāyā nāstitvaṃ bhavati//*

[c] Delhi NG dkra shis lhun po (533.5) misreads *yang.*

[d] Ser-s̄hul (*Notes,* 40a.1-40a.6) cogently explains that *bsal lo* is correct and should not read *gsal lo;* indeed, *bsal lo* is found in the Peking edition (178.1.2), as well as in Delhi NG dkra shis lhun po (533.6), Se rva zhol (27b.1), Sarnath gtsang (59.3), Zi ling sku 'bum (382.17), and Kalimpong (68.2). Ser-s̄hul explains away the fact that *gsal lo* appears in Gung-tang's *Annotations* (*khe* 122.4), which is cited the same way in Dön-drup-gyel-tsen's *Four Intertwined Commentaries* (168.3). He points out that:

- D̄zong-ka-b̄a takes the third line of Maitreya's stanza as being concerned with how to **clear away** the qualm that emptiness does not exist—"with respect to how the third line clears away a qualm"—not with how that qualm arises; and
- D̄zong-ka-b̄a's text reads *dogs pa byung* ***ba*** and not *dogs pa byung* ***bar*** as it would if the reading were *gsal lo.*

རྟོག་དོན་དམ་པར་རང་བཞིན་གྱིས་ཡོད་ན་ཞེས་རྩོད་པ་ནི་རང་གི་མཚན་ཉིད་ཀྱིས་གྲུབ་ན་དོན་དམ་པར་ཡོད་པར་འདོད་པའི་བསམ་པ་བླངས་པ་སྟེ། ལན་གྱིས་ཀྱང་དེ་ལྟར་ཁས་མ་བླངས་ཞེས་མི་ཟེར་གྱི་དེ་ལྟར་ཁས་བླངས་པའི་ {534} སྐྱོན་ནས་ལན་མཛད་དོ།། སུམ་ཅུ་པའི་འགྲེལ་པ་ལས་ཀྱང་[a]།

> ཡང་ན་རྣམ་པར་ཤེས་པ་བཞིན་དུ་ཤེས་བྱ་ཡང་རྫས་ཉིད་དུ་ཁ་ཅིག་སེམས་པ་དང་། གཞན་དག་ཤེས་བྱ་བཞིན་དུ་རྣམ་པར་ཤེས་པ་ཡང་ཀུན་རྫོབ་ཉིད་དུ་ཡོད་ཀྱི་དོན་དམ་པར་ཡོད་པ་མིན་ནོ་སྙམ་དུ་སེམས་པ་མཐའ་གཅིག་ཏུ་སྨྲ་བ་འདི་རྣམ་པ་གཉིས་དགག་པའི་ཕྱིར་རབ་ཏུ་བྱེད་པ[b]་བརྩམས་སོ།

ཞེས་སློབ་དཔོན་འདིས་གསུངས་སོ།། དེའི་ཕྱིར་གཞན་དབང་ཡི་མེད་མིན་ཞེས་གསུངས་པ་ནི་སྔར་བྱུང་ས་དྲངས་པ་ལྟར་དོན་དམ་པར་ཡོད་པའི་དངོས་པོ་ཡི་མེད་དམ་ཐམས་ཅད་ཀྱི་ཐམས་ཅད་དུ་མེད་ཅེས་པ[c]་འགོག་པ་ཡིན་གྱི་ཤེས་བྱ་ལ་མི་སྲིད་པར་འདོད་པ་བཀག་པ་མིན་ནོ།། ཁང་པ་བཞི་པས་ནི་གཉིས་སྟོང་ཀུན་རྟོག་ལ་གཏན་དུ་ཡོད་ན་ཅིའི་ཕྱིར་མི་རྟོགས་སྙམ་པའི་དོགས་པ་སེལ་ཏེ། སྟོང་ཉིད་དེ་ལ་གཉིས་སྣང་འཁྲུལ་པའི[d]་ཀུན་རྟོག

Given this evidence of D̄zong-ka-b̄a's intention, S̄er-s̄hul doubts that those scholars (*mkhas pa de dag*), that is, Gung-tang and Dön-drup-gyel-tsen, considered *bsal lo* as a corrupt reading that was to be corrected (*dag rgyu*). His implication is that *gsal lo* in Gung-tang's and Dön-drup-gyel-tsen's texts merely represents a scribal error and not their considered intention.

It is amusing that S̄er-s̄hul's own text (40a.3) reads *gsal lo* just before he so carefully explains that it should be *bsal lo;* he was subject to the same scribal error from which, he suggests, Gung-tang and Dön-drup-gyel-tsen suffered.

[a] The Sanskrit in Lévi, *Vijñaptimātratāsiddhi,* 15.12, is:

> *athavā vijñānavadvijñeyamapi dravata eveti kecinmanyante/ vijñeyavad vijñānamapi saṃvṛtita eva na paramārthata ityasya dviprakārasyāpyekāntavādasya pratiṣedhārthaḥ prakaraṃārmbhaḥ/*

See also K. N. Chatterjee, *Vijñapti-Mātratā-Siddhi (with Sthiramati's Commentary)* (Varanasi, India; Kishor Vidya Niketan, 1980), 27.11.

[b] The Peking and Tokyo *sde dge* of Sthiramati's text as well as Teramoto, *Sthiramati's Triṃçikābhāṣyaṃ,* 2.11, all read *rab tu byed pa* ***'di,*** whereas Delhi NG dkra shis lhun po (534.2), and so forth, read *rab tu byed pa* without *'di.* The Sanskrit merely has *prakaraṃārmbhaḥ;* see the previous footnote.

[c] *med ces 'gog* has been emended to *med ces* **pa** *'gog* in accordance with S̄er-s̄hül (*Notes,* 40a.6), who is following Gung-tang. This is to make it clear that the statement is what is being refuted and is not how something else is being refuted.

[d] Zi ling sku 'bum (383.9), not taking into account the non-manifest extra suffix *da* at

ཡོད་པས་དེས་བསྒྲིབས་པའི་ཕྱིར་རོ།། [188] (310) ཆོས་ཐམས་ཅད་མཐའ་གཅིག་ཏུ་སྟོང་པ[a]་དང་མི་སྟོང་པ་དང་ཡོད་པ་དང་མེད་པ་ནི་མཐའ་ཉིད་དུ་འགྱུར་གྱི་དབུ་[60]མའི་ལམ་མ་ཡིན་(28a)པས་དེ་དག་དགག་པའི་དོན་དུ་ཚིགས་བཅད་གཉིས་པ་གསུངས་ཏེ། ཀུན་རྫོབ་དང་སྟོང་ཉིད་ཀྱིས་སྟོང་པ་མིན་ཞིང་གཟུང་འཛིན་གཉིས་ཀྱིས་མི་སྟོང་པ་མིན་པ་ཐམས་ཅད་ནི་ཀུན་རྫོབ་གི་འདུས་བྱས་དང་སྟོང་ཉིད་ཀྱི་འདུས་མ་བྱས་སོ།། བཤད་པ་ནི་ཡུམ་གྱི་མདོ་ལ་སོགས་པ་ལས་འདི་ཐམས་ཅད་ནི་གཅིག་ཏུ་སྟོང་པ་ཡང་མ་ཡིན་ལ་མི་སྟོང་པ་ཡང་མ་ཡིན་ཞེས་བསྟན་པ་སྟེ་དེ་དང་མཐུན་པར་བྱས་པར་དབྱིག་གཉེན་གྱིས་བཤད་པ་ལྟར་བྱའི་[188] (311) སྟོང་པ་མ་ཡིན་པ་ཡོངས་{535}གྲུབ་དང་མི་སྟོང་པ་མ་ཡིན་པ་ངོ་བོ་ཉིད་གཞན་གཉིས་ལ་འཆད་པ་དོན་མིན་ནོ།། ཡོད་པ་ནི་ཀུན་རྫོབ་དང་མེད་པ་ནི་གཉིས་པོ་དང་ཡོད་པ་ནི་ཀུན་རྫོབ་དང་སྟོང་ཉིད་གཉིས་ཕན་ཚུན་ཡོད་པ་ལ་དབྱིག་གཉེན་དཔོན་སློབ་ཀྱིས་བཤད་པ་ལྟར་བྱའི་དེ་གཉིས་གཅིག་དོན་གཞན་དུ་ཡོད་པས་ཅིག་ཤོས་སྟོང་པའོ་ཞེས་འདི་དག་ལས་བཟློག་སྟེ་འཆད་པ་དེ་དག་གི་བཞེད་པར་འཆད་པ་ལྟར་མི་བྱའོ།། [189] (311) འོད་སྲུངས་ཀྱི་ལེའུ་ལས་ཡོད་མེད་གཉིས་མཐའ་རེ་རེར་བཤད་ནས་དེ་གཉིས་ཀྱི་དབུས་ནི་ཆོས་རྣམས་ལ་སོ་སོར་རྟོག་པའི་དབུ་མའི་ལམ་དུ་བཤད་པ་ཉིད་དེ་ནི་དབུ་མའི་ལམ་ཡིན་ནོ། ཞེས་གསུངས་པ་འདིའི་དོན་དུ་བློ་བརྟན་གྱིས་བཤད་དོ།། དེས་ན་རྣམ་པར་རིག་པ་ཙམ་གྱི་ཚུལ་འདི་ཉིད་དབུ་མའི་དོན་དུ་འགྲེལ་པས་དབུ་མ་པ་གཞན་གྱི་ལྟར་ན་དེ་གཉིས་སྔ་མ་ལས་ཕྱི་མ་མཆོག་ཏུ་བཞེད་ཀྱང་ཚུལ་འདིས་དེ་གཉིས་དོན་གཅིག་ཏུ་མཛད[b]་པ་ཡིན་ནོ།། [190] (312) དེ་ལྟར་ན་[61]དབྱིག་གཉེན་དང་བློ་གྲོས་བརྟན་པས་བཀྲལ་ཚུལ་ནི་སྐབས་སྐབས་སུ་བརྗོད་ཟིན་ལ། (28b)ཕྱོགས་ཀྱི་གླང་པོས་ཀྱང་བརྒྱད་སྟོང་པའི་དོན་རྣམས་ཐེག་བསྡུས་དང་མཐུན་པར་བརྒྱད་སྟོང་དོན་བསྡུས་སུ་བཀྲལ་ལོ[c]།། [190] (314) ཆོས་ཀྱི་

---

the end of the previous syllable, reads *ba'i.*

[a] Delhi NG dkra shis lhun po (534.4) and Sarnath gtsang (59.19): *stong ba;* Se rva zhol (27b.6), Zi ling sku 'bum (383.10), Peking (178.1.7), and Kalimpong (69.2): *stong pa.*

[b] Se rva zhol (28a.6) misreads *mdzed;* Delhi GD zhol has been corrected to *mdzad.* Delhi NG dkra shis lhun po (535.4) misreads *mjad.* Zi ling sku 'bum (384.5), Peking (178.2.6), Sarnath gtsang (60.20), and Kalimpong (70.3) correctly read *mdzad.*

[c] Delhi NG dkra shis lhun po (535.5): *la//;* Sarnath gtsang (61.3): *la/;* Se rva zhol (28b.1), Zi ling sku 'bum (384.8), Peking (178.2.7), and Kalimpong (70.4): *lo//.* The latter is more likely, especially given the double *shad* in the Delhi NG dkra shis lhun po.

གྲགས་པས་རྣམ་འགྲེལ་ལས།[a]

དེ་ལ་གཅིག་ནི་མེད་པས་ཀྱང་།།
གཉིས་ཀའང་ཉམས་པར་འགྱུར་བ་ཡིན།།
དེ་ཕྱིར་གཉིས་སྟོང་གང་ཡིན་པ།།
དེ་ནི་དེ་ཡིའང་དེ་ཉིད་ཡིན།།

ཞེས་གཟུང་འཛིན་རྫས་གཞན་གྱིས་སྟོང་པའི་སྟོང་ཉིད་གཞན་དབང་གི་དེ་ཁོ་ན་ཉིད་དུ་གསུངས་ཤིང་། [190] (315) ཆོས་རྣམས་རང་བཞིན་མེད་པར་མདོ་སྡེ་ལས་གསུངས་པའི་དོན་ཡང་དེ་ཉིད་དུ་འགྲེལ་ཏེ[b]།

དངོས་རྣམས་ཐ་དད་གནས་པ་{536}ནི།།
དེ་ཐ་དད་ལ་བརྟེན་པ་ཡིན།།
དེ་ནི་བསླད་པ་ཉིད་ཡིན་ན།།
དེ་དག་ཐ་དད་ཀྱང་བསླད་འགྱུར།།
གཟུང་དང་འཛིན་པའི་རྣམ་པ་ལས།།
མཚན་ཉིད་གཞན་ནི་ཡོད་མ་ཡིན།།
དེས་ན་མཚན་ཉིད་སྟོང་པའི་ཕྱིར།།
རང་བཞིན་མེད་པར་རབ་ཏུ་བཤད།།

ཅེས་དངོས་པོ་རྣམས་སྐྱེ་བ་ལ་སོགས་པར་ཐ་དད་དུ་འབྱེད་པ་ནི་རང་རིག[c]་པ་ཙམ་གྱིས་

---

a *tshad ma rnam 'grel gyi tshig le'ur byas pa, pramāṇavartikakārikā;* III.213. The Sanskrit in Dwarikadas Shastri, *Pramāṇavārttika of Āchārya Dharmakīrtti* (Varanasi, India: Bauddha Bharati, 1968), 164.5, is:

tatraikasyāpyabhāvena dvayamapyavahīyate/
tasmāt tadeva tasyāpi tattvaṃ yā dvayaśūnyatā//

b III.214-215. The Sanskrit in Shastri (*Pramāṇavarttika,* 164.7) is:

tadbhedāśrayiṇī ceyaṃ bhāvānāṃ bhedasaṃsthitiḥ/
tadupaplavabhāve ca teṣāṃ bhedo 'pyupaplavaḥ//

na grāhyagrāhakākārabāhyamasti ca lakṣaṇaṃ/
ato lakṣaṇaśūnyatvānniḥsvabhāvāḥ prakāśitāḥ//

c Sarnath gtsang misreads *rigs.*

མིན་གྱི་གཉིས་སུ་སྣང་བའི་ཤེས་པ་ཉིད་ཀྱིས་འབྲིད་དོ།། གཉིས་སྣང་ཡང་སླད[a]་པ་སྟེ་བརྫུན[b]་པ་ཡིན་པས་དེས་རྣམ་པར་བཞག་པ་ཡང་བརྫུན[c]་པར་འགྱུར་ལ། གཟུང་འཛིན་གྱི་རྣམ་པ་ལ[d]་དོན་གཞན་པའི་མཚན་ཉིད་ཀྱང་མེད་ཅིང་། གཉིས་སུ་སྣང་བའི་མཚན་ཉིད་ཀྱང་ཇི་ལྟར་སྣང་བ་བཞིན་དུ་མེད་པས་རང་བཞིན་མེད་དོ་ཞེས་བཤད་དོ།། [191] (315) ཡང་རྣམ་འགྲེལ་ལས[e]།

ཕུང་ [62] པོ[f]་ལ་སོགས་བྱེ་བྲག་གིས།།
མཚན་ཉིད་ཐམས་ཅད་བྱེད་པ་ཡི།།
ཁྱད་པར་ཅན་དེའང་དེ་ཉིད་མིན།།
དེས་ཀྱང་དེ་དག་མཚན་ཉིད་བྲལ།

ཞེས་གཟུགས་ཕུང་ལ་སོགས་པ་མཚོན་བྱ་དང་། གཟུགས་སུ་རུང་བ་ལ་སོགས་པ་མཚོན་བྱེད་དུ་གསུངས་པ་ནི་ (29a) ཐམས་ཅད་བྱ་བྱེད་ཀྱིས་ཁྱད་པར་དུ་བྱས་ལ། དེ་དག་གི་གཞི་རྫས་སུ་ཡོད་ཀྱང་བྱ་བྱེད་ཀྱི་ཆ་ནས་དེ་ཁོ་ན་ཉིད་དུ་མ་གྲུབ་པ་ལ་དགོངས་ནས་ཀྱང་མཚན་ཉིད་ཀྱིས་སྟོང་ངོ་ཞེས་གསུངས་པར་བཤད་དེ་འདི་ནི་ཉན་ཐོས་སྡེ་པ་དང་ཡང་ཐུན་མོང་བའོ།། [192] (316) རྣམ་འགྲེལ་ལས[g]།

གལ་ཏེ་ཐམས་ཅད་ནུས་མེད་ན།།
ས་བོན་སོགས་ནི་མྱུག་སོགས་ལ།།

---

a Zi ling sku 'bum (384.18): *bslad.*

b Zi ling sku 'bum (384.18): *rdzun.*

c Zi ling sku 'bum (384.18): *rdzun.*

d All of the editions read *la* although *las* may be more appropriate, since Dharmakīrti's text itself reads *las.* Šer-šhül's commentary (*Notes,* 41b.5) similarly reads *las,* as does A-ku L̄o-drö-gya-tso's loose commentary (*Precious Lamp,* 233.1).

e III.216. The Sanskrit in Shastri (*Pramāṇavarttika,* 165.3) is:

vyāpāropādhikaṃ-sarvaṃ skandhādīnāṃ viśeṣataḥ/
lakṣaṇaṃ sa ca tattvaṃ na tenāpyete vilakṣaṇāḥ//

f Delhi NG dkra shis lhun po (536.3) misreads *po'i.*

g III.4. The Sanskrit in Shastri (*Pramāṇavarttika,* 100.4) is:

aśaktaṃ sarvam iti ced bījāderaṅkurādiṣu/
dṛṣṭā śaktiḥ;
matā sā cet saṃvṛtyāḥ;
'stu yathā tathā//

Shastri uses three lines for the last single line in order to make clear the different speakers.

ནུས་མཐོང་གལ་ཏེ་དེ་ཀུན་ཛོབ།།
འདོད་ན་ཇི་ལྟར་དེ་ལྟར་འགྱུར།།

ཞེས་གསུངས་པ་ནི་སྔར་བསྡུ་བ་ལས་གསུངས་པ་དང་གནད་གཅིག་གོ། {537}འདི་དག་གི་བཀྲལ་ཚུལ་ཞིབ་པ་ནི་མངས་སུ་དོགས་ནས་མ་བྲིས་སོ།།

གཉིས་པ་ [སྒྲོ་འདོགས་ཀྱི་མཐའ་བྱེ་བྲག་ཏུ་དགག་པ་]ལ་གཉིས། དགག་བྱ་སྒྲོ་འདོགས་ངོས་གཟུང་བ་དང་། དེ་ཇི་ལྟར་འགོག་པའི་ཚུལ་ལོ།། [194] (319)

དང་པོ་ [དགག་བྱ་སྒྲོ་འདོགས་ངོས་གཟུང་བ་]ནི། [194] (319)

ལུགས་འདིའི་རིགས་པའི་དགག་བྱ་ལ་གཉིས་ཡོད་པའི་སྐབས་འདིར་ནི་གྲུབ་མཐས་བཞག་པ་ཁོ་ན་དང་། དེ་ཡང་རང་སྡེ་ངོ་བོ་ཉིད་མེད་པར་སྨྲ་བའི་ལུགས་སུ་ཞར་བཤད་པ་བཞིན་ནོ།། སྒྲོ་འདོགས་ལ་ནི་ཀུན་བརྟགས་དང་ལྷན་སྐྱེས་གཉིས་ཡོད་ལ་ཀུན་བརྟགས་ནི་གཞན་སྡེ་དང་རང་སྡེ་དོན་སྨྲ་གཉིས་ཀྱི་ལུགས་སོ།། ལྷན་སྐྱེས་ལ་གང་ཟག་གི་བདག་ཏུ་སྒྲོ་འདོགས་པ་ནི་འོག་ཏུ་སྟོན་པས་ཆོས་ཀྱི་བདག་[63]ཏུ་སྒྲོ་འདོགས་པ་བཤད་པར་བྱ་སྟེ། གྲུབ་མཐས་ཆོས་བདག་བཏགས་པ་ཡང་ལྷན་སྐྱེས་ཀྱིས་བཟུང་བའི་ཆོས་བདག་སྒྲུབ་པའི་དོན་ཡིན་པའི་ཕྱིར་དང་རིགས་པའི་དགག་བྱའི་གཙོ་བོ་ཡང་དེ་ཡིན་པའི་ཕྱིར་རོ།། འདིའི་གཞུང་མང་པོར་གཟུང་འཛིན་རྫས་གཞན་དུ་འཛིན་པ་ཆོས་ཀྱི་བདག་འཛིན་དུ་བཤད་པ་མ་གཏོགས་པ་ཆོས་ཀྱི་བདག་འཛིན་གཞན་མ་བཤད་ཀྱང་། མདོ་སྡེ་དགོངས་འགྲེལ་ལས། (29b)གཞན་དབང་ངོ་བོ་དང་ཁྱད་པར་དུ་ཀུན་བརྟགས་པའི་ངོ་བོར[a] རང་གི་མཚན་ཉིད་ཀྱིས་གྲུབ་པ་མེད་པས་མཚན་ཉིད་ངོ་བོ་ཉིད་མེད་པ་ཆོས་ཀྱི་བདག་མེད་དུ་བཤད་པའི་ཤུགས་ཀྱིས་གཞན་དབང་ལ་ངོ་བོ་དང་ཁྱད་པར་དུ་བཏགས་པ་རང་གི་མཚན་ཉིད་ཀྱིས་གྲུབ་པར[b] འཛིན་པ་ཆོས་ཀྱི་བདག་འཛིན་དུ་བསྟན་ལ། བྱང་ས་དང་བསྡུ་བ་དང་ཐེག་བསྡུས་ལས་ཀྱང་དེས་ཇི་ལྟར་བཟུང་བས་སྟོང་པའི་སྟོང་ཉིད་དབུ་མའི་དོན་མཐར་ཐུག་པ་དང་ཆོས་ཀྱི་བདག་མེད་ཀྱི་ཡོངས་གྲུབ་ཏུ་འབད་པ་དུ་མས་བསྒྲུབས་པས། {538}གཞན་དབང་ལ་ཆོས་བདག་སྒྲོ་བཏགས་པའི་ཀུན་བརྟགས་འདི་ཇི་ལྟར་ཡིན་མི་ཤེས་ན་ལུགས་འདིའི་ཆོས་ཀྱི་བདག་འཛིན་དང་ཆོས་ཀྱི་བདག་མེད་མཐའ་ཆོད་པར་མི་ཤེས་སོ།། ཀུན་བརྟགས་རང་གི་མཚན་ཉིད་ཀྱིས་གྲུབ་པར་འཛིན་པ་ཆོས་ཀྱི་བདག་འཛིན་དུ་འདོད་པའི་ཀུན་བརྟགས་ནི་ཕུང་པོ་ལ་སོགས་པ་ལ་འདི་གཟུགས་སོ་ཞེས་ངོ་བོ་དང་འདི་གཟུགས་ཀྱི་སྐྱེ་བའོ་ཞེས་སོགས་ཁྱད་པར་དུ་མིང་དང་བརྡར་བཏགས་པའི་[64]ངོ་བོའོ།། དེ་ཙམ་ཞིག་ཏུ་ནི་ཕུང་པོ་ལ་སོགས་

a Zi ling sku 'bum (386.2): *bo.*

b Delhi NG dkra shis lhun po (537.6), Zi ling sku 'bum (386.5), Peking (178.4.7), and Sarnath gtsang (63.11): *par;* Se rva zhol (29b.2) and Kalimpong (73.2) misread *pa.*

པ་ཡོད་པས་དེར་ཡོད་པར་འཛིན་པ་སྒྲོ་འདོགས་མིན་གྱི་ཕྱུང་སོགས་ངོ་བོ་དེར་རང་གི་མཚན་ཉིད་ཀྱིས་ཡོད་པར་འཛིན་པ་སྒྲོ་འདོགས་སོ།། [196] (321) གལ་ཏེ་གཟུགས་སོགས་མིང་དང་བརྡའི་ཡུལ་ཡིན་པ་རང་གི་མཚན་ཉིད་ཀྱིས་གྲུབ་པ་འགོག་པ་དེ་རྗོད་བྱེད་ཀྱི་དངོས་ཡུལ་ཡིན་པ་འགོག་ན་དངོས་ཀྱི་བརྗོད་བྱ་དང་རྗོད་བྱེད་དོན་སྤྱི་དང་སྒྲ་སྤྱི་དངོས་མེད་དུ་དོན་སྒྲ་རྣམས་ལ་གྲུབ་ཟིན་པས་གཞན་དབང་དེས་སྟོང་པར་བསྒྲུབ་མི་དགོས་པ་དང་། དེས་སྟོང་པར་གྲུབ་པའི་ཚད་མས་ཆོས་ཀྱི་བདག་མེད་མི་འགྲུབ་ཅིང་དེ་ལ་དམིགས་ནས་བསྒོམས་ (30a) པས་ཤེས་སྒྲིབ་དག་པར་མི་འགྱུར་བས་དགོངས་འགྲེལ་ལས་ཀུན་བརྟགས་རང་མཚན་དུ་གྲུབ་པས་སྟོང་པ་ཆོས་ཀྱི་བདག་མེད་ཡོངས་གྲུབ་ཏུ་བཤད་ཅིང་བྱུང་ས་ལས་སྟོང་པ་དེ་ཤེས་སྒྲིབ་དག་པར་བྱེད་པའི་དམིགས་པར་བཤད་པ་དང་འགལ་ལོ།། [198] (321)གཟུགས་སོགས་རྗོད་བྱེད་ཀྱི་ཞེན་ཡུལ་ཡིན་པ་འགོག་པ་ལ་ཞེན་ཡུལ་གྱི་གཞི་ལྡོག་རང་མཚན་གྱིས་ཡོད་པ་འགོག་ན་གཞན་དབང་རང་མཚན་གྱིས་གྲུབ་པ་བཀག་པར་འགྱུར་ལ། ཞེན་ཡུལ་གྱི་རང་ལྡོག་རང་ {539} མཚན་གྱིས་གྲུབ་པ་འགོག་ནའང་རྗེས་དཔག་ཚད་མའི་གཞལ་བྱ་སྤྱི་མཚན་དངོས་པོར་མེད་པར་མདོ་སྡེ་པས་ཀྱང་གྲུབ་པས་མི་འཐད་དོ།། [199] (321) གཞན་ཡང་སྲིད་པ་འཕོ་བའི་མདོ་ལས།[a]

མིང་ནི་གང་དང་གང་གིས་སུ།།
ཆོས་རྣམས་གང་དང་གང་བརྗོད་པ།།
དེ་ལ་དེ་ནི་ཡོད་མ་ཡིན།།
འདི་ནི་ཆོས་རྣམས་ཆོས་ཉིད་དོ། [65]

ཞེས་གསུངས་པའི་ལུང་ཅན་ཐོས་སྡེ་པ་ལ་ཡང་གྲུབ་པས་དེ་ལས་ལྷག་པར་དགོངས་འགྲེལ་གྱི་ཀུན་བརྟགས་ཀྱིས་སྟོང་པའི[b] ཆོས་ཉིད་ལ་ཡང་མི་སྣང་ངོ།། [200] (326) སྟོང་ཚུལ་འདི་ལ་གཟུང་འཛིན་རྫས་ཐ་དད་བཀག་པའི་རྣམ་པར་རིག་པ་ཙམ་གྱི་དོན་མེད་པས་ཆོས་ཀྱི་

---

a *bhavasaṃkrāntisūtra;* Peking 5538, vol. 110, 145.1.6. The Sanskrit—as cited in Asaṅga's *Grounds of Bodhisattvas*—in Wogihara (*Bodhisattvabhūmi,* 48.12) is:

yena yena hi nāmnā vai yo yo dharmo 'bhilapyate
na sa saṃvidyate tatra dharmāṇāṃ sā hi dharmateti [Dutt: *dharmatā// iti*]//

See also Dutt, *Bodhisattvabhūmi,* 33.1, and N. Ayyaswami, "Bhavasamkrānti Sūtra" *Journal of Oriental Research [Madras]* 5, no. 4 (1931): 252, stanza 9; Ayyaswami (252, n. 3) points out that the stanza is cited twice in the *Tattvasaṃgrahapañjikā.*

b Zi ling sku 'bum (387.9): *ba'i;* see p. 426, footnote a.

བདག་མེད་ཤེས་སྒྲིབ་དག་པར་བྱེད་པའི་དམིགས་པར་བཤད་པ་ཡང་ཇི་ལྟར་འཐད། དེས་ན་ལུགས་འདི་ལ་འགལ་བ་དེ་དག་ཇི་ལྟར་མེད་པའི་རྒྱུ་མཚན་བཤད་པར་གྱིས་ཤིག་ཅེ་ན། [200] (322) བཤད་པར་བྱ་སྟེ་སྟོང་ཚུལ་འདི་བྱང་ས་ལས་ཤེས་སྒྲིབ་དག་པར་བྱེད་པའི་ཡེ་ཤེས་ཀྱི་དམིགས་པ་དང་དབུ་མའི་ལམ་མཐའ་གཉིས་སྤངས་པ་གོང་ན་མེད་པར་བཤད་ཅིང་། ཐེག་བསྡུས་ལས་འདིའི་སྒོ་ནས་འཇུག་པ་དེ་རྣམ་པར་ (30b) རིག་པ་ཙམ་དུ་འཇུག་པར་གསུངས་པའི་ཕྱིར་ཉན་ཐོས་སྡེ་པས[a] གྲུབ་ཟིན་པ་མིན་ནོ།། [201] (322) དེའི་ཕྱིར་འདིའི་བཟློག་ཕྱོགས་ཀྱི་སྒྲོ་འདོགས་ངོ་བོ་དང་ཁྱད་པར་དུ་མིང་གིས་བཏགས་པ་དེར་གཟུགས་སོགས་རང་གི་མཚན་ཉིད་ཀྱིས་གྲུབ་པར་འཛིན་པའི་གྲུབ་མཐའི་ཁས་ལེན་ཀྱང་ཉན་ཐོས་སྡེ་པ[b] ལ་ཡོད་དོ།། [201] (322) འདི་ལྟར་འདི་འགོག་པར[c] བྱང་ས་ལས་ལུང་གིས་ཀྱང་བཀག་ཅིང་གཞན་སྡེ་ལ་རང་གི་སྟོན་པའི་ལུང་གིས་འགོག་ཏུ་མི་རུང་བས་དགག་པའི་ཡུལ་ལ་རང་སྡེ་ཡང་ཡོད་ལ། ངོ་བོ་ཉིད་མེད་པར་སྨྲ་བ་དང་རྣལ་ {540} འབྱོར་སྤྱོད་པའི་ཁྱད་པར་ལ་འགོག་པ་མིན་པས་ཉན་ཐོས་སྡེ་པའོ།། དེའི་ཕྱིར་དགོངས་འགྲེལ་གྱི་ལུང་མ་དྲངས་པར་དེ་དག་ལ་གྲུབ་པའི་ལུང་ [66] གསུམ་གྱིས་བཀག་གོ། [203] (323) དེ་ལ་ཐོག་མར་སྒྲོ་འདོགས་ལྡན་སྐྱེས་ངོས་གཟུང་ན་བསྡུ་བ་ལས།

> དེ་ལ་བྱིས་པ་རྣམས་ནི་བརྗོད་པར་བྱ་བའི་དངོས་པོ་ལ་རྒྱུ་ལྡས་མིང་ཇི་ལྟ་བ་དང་
> བརྗོད་པ་ཇི་ལྟ་བ་བཞིན་དུ་ངོ་བོ་ཉིད་དུ་མངོན་པར་ཞེན་པར་རིག་པར་བྱ་སྟེ།

ཞེས་གསུངས་ཤིང་དངོས་པོ་དེའི་ངོ་བོ་ཉིད་གང་ཡིན་དྲིས་ན་ངོ་བོ་ཉིད་གཟུགས་ཡིན་ནོ་ཞེས་ལན་འདེབས་ཀྱི་མིང་གཟུགས་ཡིན་ནོ་ཞེས་ལན་མི་འདེབས་པ་རྒྱུ་མཚན་དང་པོར་བཤད་དོ།། དེའི་དོན་ནི་གཟུགས་ཞེས་བརྗོད་པའི་དོན་དེའི་ངོ་བོ་ཉིད་གང་ཡིན་དྲིས་པ་ན་དེའི་ངོ་བོ་ཉིད་གཟུགས་ཡིན་ཞེས་སྨྲའི[d] གཟུགས་ཞེས་པའི་མིང་དུ་བཏགས་པ་ཙམ་ཞིག་གཟུགས་ཞེས་བརྗོད་པའི་དོན་དེའི་ངོ་བོ་ཉིད་ཡིན་ནོ་ཞེས་སྨྲ་རྒྱུ་མེད་དོ།། དེའི་ཕྱིར་གཟུགས་ཞེས་

---

[a] Zi ling sku 'bum (387.15): *bas.* Again, this is an overcorrection for the rule that *ba* follows the suffixes *nga, 'a, ra, la,* and suffixless syllables, since that rule is contravened by the dictum that only *pa* should be used for ownership (*bdag sgra*) which is the usage here; see p. 373, footnote b.

[b] Zi ling sku 'bum (387.18): *ba;* see the previous footnote.

[c] Zi ling sku 'bum (387.18): *pa la. 'gog par* and *'gog pa la* have the same meaning.

[d] Zi ling sku 'bum (388.8) unnecessarily emends to *smra yi.*

ཐ་སྙད་བཏགས་པའི་ཚེ་སྔོན་པོ་གཟུགས་ཀྱི་ཐ་སྙད་འདོགས་པའི་གཞི་ཡིན་པ་དེ་ཇི་ལྟར་སྣང་བལྟས་[a]པས་ན་མིང་(31a)དང་བརྡས་བཞག་པ་མིན་པར་རང་གི་གནས་ལུགས་ཀྱི་དབང་གིས་གྲུབ་པ་བཞིན་དུ་སྣང་ངོ་།། སྔོན་པོ་དེ་ཇི་ལྟར་སྣང་བ་བཞིན་དུ་གྲུབ་པར་འཛིན་པ་ནི་སྔོན་པོ་ལ་གཟུགས་སོ་ཞེས་མིང་དུ་བཏགས་པ་ལ་རང་གི་མཚན་ཉིད་ཀྱིས་གྲུབ་པར་འཛིན་པའི་སྒྲོ་འདོགས་ཡིན་ལ། དེ་ཕྱིས་པ་རྣམས་ལ་ཡོད་པར་ཐུར་བཤད་པ་དེས་འགྲུབ་ཅིང་དེ་འདྲ་བའི་འཛིན་སྟངས་དེ་འཐད་ལྡན་དུ་དོན་སྨྲ་སྡེ་གཉིས་ཀྱིས་ཀྱང་འདོད་པས་སྒྲའི་བརྗོད་བྱའི་རང་ལྡོག་རྟོག་བཏགས་ཡིན་ཀྱང་དེའི་གཞི་ལྡོག་ཏུ་རང་མཚན་འོང་བའི་[67]ལུགས་དང་ག་{541}ལ་མཚུངས། ཁྱད་པར་དུ་ཀུན་བརྟགས་པ་ལ་སྒྲོ་འདོགས་ཚུལ་དང་ཆོས་གཞན་ལ་འདོགས་ཚུལ་ཡང་དེས་ཤེས་པར་བྱའོ།། དེ་བཞིན་དུ་ཡུལ་ཡུལ་ཅན་གཉིས་སུ་ཤར་བ་ན་གཉིས་ཀ་རྫས་ཐ་དད་དུ་སྣང་བ་བཞིན་དུ་ཡོད་པར་འཛིན་པ་ཡང་ཆོས་ཀྱི་བདག་ཏུ་འཛིན་པའི་སྒྲོ་འདོགས་སོ།། རྩོད་པ་ལྷག་མའི་ལན་ནི་འཆད་པར་འགྱུར་རོ།།

[a] Delhi NG dkra shis lhun po (540.4), Se rva zhol (30b.6), Zi ling sku 'bum (388.11), and Kalimpong (76.4): *bltas;* Peking (179.2.2) and Sarnath gtsang (66.13) misread *ba ltas.*

གཉིས་པ་ [དེ་ཇི་ལྟར་འགོག་པའི་ཚུལ་] ལ་གཉིས། དགག་པ་དངོས་དང་། དེ་ལ་རྩོད་པ་སྤང་བའོ།། [206] (324)

དང་པོ་ [དགག་པ་དངོས་] ནི། [206] (324)

དགོངས་འགྲེལ་ལས་གཞན་དབང་ཀུན་བརྟགས་ཀྱིས་སྟོང་པར་སྒྲུབ་པའི་རིགས་པ་མ་གསུངས་པ་རྫོགས་པར་བྱ་བའི་ཕྱིར་བྱང་ས་དང་བསྡུ་བ་ལས་རིགས་པ་གསུམ་གསུམ་གསུངས་ཤིང་། ཐེག་བསྡུས་ལས་ཀྱང་།

> གཞན་གྱི་དབང་གི་ངོ་བོ་ཀུན་བརྟགས་པའི་བདག་ཉིད་དུ་ཇི་ལྟར་སྣང་བ་དེ་ཡི[a] བདག་ཉིད་མ་ཡིན་པར་ཅི་མངོན་ཞེ་ན།

ཞེས་དྲི་བ་བཀོད་པའི་ལན་དུ།

> མིང་གི་སྔ་རོལ་བློ་མེད་ཕྱིར།།
> མང་བའི་ཕྱིར་དང་མ་ངེས་ཕྱིར།།
> དེ་ཡི་བདག་ཉིད་བདག་མང་དང་།།
> བདག་འདྲེས་འགལ་བས་ (31b) འགྲུབ་པར་འགྱུར།།

ཞེས་གསུངས་སོ།། དེ་ལ་ཆོས་དེའི་བདག་ཉིད་དུ་འགལ་བས་གཞན་དབང་ཀུན་བརྟགས་ཀྱིས་སྟོང་པ་འགྲུབ་ཚུལ་གོ་སླ་བར་བརྗོད་ན། ལྟོ་ལྡིར་བ་བུམ་པའི་ཐ་སྙད་ཀྱི་གཞིའམ་གནས་ཡིན་པ་དེ་ལྟོ་ལྡིར་བའི་གནས་ལུགས་སམ[b] རང་གི་མཚན་ཉིད་ཀྱིས་གྲུབ་ན། བརྡའི་དབང་གིས་མ་བཞག་པར་འགྱུར་ལ་དེ་ལྟ་ན་བརྡའི་ཡུལ་ཅན་གྱི་བློ་ཡང་ [68] བརྡ་ལ་མི་ལྟོས་པས། བུམ་པའི་མིང་བཏགས་པའི་སྔ་རོལ་ནས་ལྟོ་ལྡིར་བ་ལ་བུམ་པའོ་སྙམ་པའི་བློ་སྐྱེ་བར་འགྱུར་རོ།། དོན་གཅིག་ཉིད་དོན་གྱི་བདག་ཉིད་མང་པོར་འགལ་བས་འགྲུབ་པ་ནི་ཕྱོགས་སྔ་ལྟར་ན་དོན་གཅིག་ལ་བརྒྱ་བྱིན་དང་དབང་ {542} པོ་དང་གྲོང་འཇོམས་ལ་སོགས་པའི་མིང་དུ་མ་འཇུག་པ་དེ། དངོས་པོའི་དབང་གིས་འཇུག་དགོས་ལ་རྟོག་པ་ལ་ཇི་ལྟར་སྣང་བ་དེ་བཞིན་དུ་དངོས་པོ་ལ་གནས་པའི་ཕྱིར་དོན་དེ་དུ་མར་འགྱུར་རོ།། དོན་མ་འདྲེས་པའི་ངོ་བོ་འདྲེས་པར་འགལ་བས་འགྲུབ་པ་ནི་ཕྱོགས་སྔ་ལྟར་ན། སྐྱེས་བུ་གཉིས་ལ་ཉེར་སྦྱས་

a Zi ling sku 'bum (389.6) unnecessarily emends to *de'i*.

b Delhi NG dkra shis lhun po (541.5) misreads *sem*.

ཞེས་པའི་མིང་གཅིག་འཇུག་པའི་ཚེ་འདི་ཉེར་སྦྲས་སོ་སྙམ་པའི་བློ་སྐྱེ་བ་ལ་ཁྱད་པར་མེད་པའི་ཕྱིར་དང་། དེའི་མིང་དང་རྟོག་པ་ཡང་དངོས་པོའི་དབང་གིས་དེ་གཉིས་ལ་འཇུག་པའི་ཕྱིར་དོན་གཉིས་དོན་གཅིག་ཏུ་འགྱུར་རོ།། གཟུགས་སོགས་རྟོག་པའི་ཞེན་གཞི་ཡིན་པ་དེ་དོན་དམ་པའམ་རང་གི་མཚན་ཉིད་ཀྱིས་གྲུབ་པར་འཛིན་ནའང་མིང་དུ་བཏགས་པའི་གནས་རང་མཚན་གྱིས་གྲུབ་པར་འཛིན་པ་དང་འདྲ་བས། འདིའི་མིང་འདིའོ་ཞེས་བརྡ་མི་ཤེས་པ་ལ་ཡང་དགག་བྱ་སྒྲོ་འདོགས་ཡོད་ལ་དེ་འགོག་པའི་རིགས་པ་ཡང་འདྲའོ།།

[209] (325) བྱང་སར་

> དོན་སྔར་ཡོད་ལ་འདི་ (32a) འདིའོ་ཞེས་མིང་ཕྱིས་འདོགས་ན་དེ་ལྟར་མ་བཏགས་པའི་ཚེ་དོན་དེའི་ངོ་བོ་མེད་པར་འགྱུར་ལ། མ་བཏགས་པའི་ཚེ་ཡང་ངོ་བོ་ཡོད་པ་ལ་ཕྱིས་འདོགས་ན་མིང་མ་བཏགས་པའི་དུས་ [69] སུ་འདི་གཟུགས་སོ་སྙམ་པའི་བློ་སྐྱེ་བར་འགྱུར་

ཞེས་བཀག་གོ། [209] (325) གང་ལ་བརྡ་འདོགས་པའི་དངོས་ཀྱི་ཡུལ་དེ་དོན་དེའི་ངོ་བོར་རང་མཚན་གྱིས་གྲུབ་ན་བརྡ་འབྲེལ་བྱས་པར[a] མི་ལྟོས་པར་མིང་གི་བློ་སྐྱེ་བ་སོགས་ཀྱི་སྐྱོན་ཡོད་མོད་ཀྱང་། གཟུགས་སོགས་བརྡ་འདོགས་པའི་གནས་དང་རྟོག་པའི་ཞེན་གཞི་ཡིན་པ་དེ་རང་གི་མཚན་ཉིད་ཀྱིས་གྲུབ་པ་ལ་སྐྱོན་དེར་མི་འགྱུར་རོ། ཞེས་ཉན་ཐོས་སྡེ་པ་དག་སྨྲ་མོད་ཀྱང་འདྲའོ།། [210] (326) དེ་ {543} ལྟར་ན་གཟུགས་སོགས་རྟོག་པའི་ཞེན་གཞི་ཡིན་པ་དེ་མིང་དང་བརྡས་བཞག་པའི་ཀུན་བརྟགས་ཡིན་མོད་ཀྱང་ཚད་མས་གྲུབ་པས་དགག་མི་ནུས་ལ། དེ་ཉིད་དངོས་པོ་དེ་དག་གི་རང་གི་མཚན་ཉིད་ཀྱིས་གྲུབ་པ་ནི་མིང་ཙམ་གྱིས་བཞག་པའི་ཀུན་བརྟགས་ཤེས་བྱ་ལ་མི་སྲིད་པ་ཡིན་པས་མིང་དང་བརྡས་བཞག་པ་ལ་ཚད་མས་གྲུབ་མ་གྲུབ་གཉིས་ཡོད་དོ།། འོན་ཀྱང་མིང་དང་བརྡས་བཞག་པ་ཙམ་ཡིན[b] ཕྱིན་ཆད་དེ་ལ་རྒྱུ་འབྲས་མི་རུང་བར་འདི་པ་འདོད་དོ།། དོན་སྨྲ་གཉིས་ཀྱིས་གཟུགས་སོགས་རྟོག་པའི་ཞེན་གཞི་དང་བརྡ་འདོགས་པའི་གནས་སུ་རང་མཚན་གྱིས་གྲུབ་པ་ཁེགས་ན་དེ་དག་ཡོད་པར་འཇོག་མི་ཤེས་ཏེ་ཚད་མ་པ་ལ་གྲགས་པའི་རང་མཚན་ནི་

---

a Zi ling sku 'bum (390.9) unnecessarily emends to *pa la.*

b Delhi NG dkra shis lhun po (543.2), Peking (179.4.5), and Sarnath tsang (69.13) read *yin/ phyin chad,* an obviously faulty scribal error, since the term is *yin phyin chad;* Se rva zhol (32a.5), Zi ling sku 'bum (390.16), and Kalimpong (79.6) correctly lack the *shad.* Delhi GD zhol is mistakenly edited to *yin/ phyin chad.*

མིན་ནོ།། དཔེར་ན་བུམ་མེད་མེད་དགག་ཡིན་ཞིང་དེ་དང་ས་ཕྱོགས་གཞི་མཐུན་དུ་འདུ་ཡང་མེད་དགག་དང་དངོས་པོ་གཉིས་འགལ་བ་མི་འགོག་པ་ལྟར། (32b)རྣམ་ཤེས་རྟོག་པའི་ཞེན་གཞི་ཡིན་པ་དེ་དོན་དམ་པར་མ་གྲུབ་པའི་ཀུན་བརྟགས་ཡིན་པ་དང་ [70]རྣམ་ཤེས་དོན་དམ་པར་གྲུབ་པ་གཉིས་ཀྱང་མི་འགལ་ལོ།། [211] (322) དེའི་ཕྱིར་

མིང་ནི་གང་དང་གང་གིས་སུ།

ཞེས་སོགས་ཉན་ཐོས་སྡེ་པ་ལ་གྲུབ་པའི་མདོ་ཡིན་ཡང་དེ་དག་གིས་བཤད་པ་དང་དོན་ཁྱད་པར་མེད་པ་མིན་ཏེ། དཔེར་ན་ཕལ་ཆེན་སྡེ་པའི[a]ལུང་ལས་རྩ་བའི་རྣམ་པར་ཤེས་པ་ཞེས་འབྱུང་བ་འདི་པས་ཀུན་གཞི་ལ་བཤད་པ་བཞིན་ནོ།། སྔར་བཤད་པའི་ངོ་བོ་དང་ཁྱད་པར་དུ་བཏགས་པ་རང་མཚན་གྱིས་སམ་དོན་དམ་པར་ཡོད་པར་འཛིན་པ་ནི་ཤེས་སྒྲིབ་ཀྱི་གཙོ་བོ་ཡིན་པས་དེས་བཟུང་བ་ལྟར་མེད་པ་གཏན་ལ་ཕབ་པའི་དོན་ནི་ཤེས་སྒྲིབ་དག་བྱེད་ཀྱི་དམིགས་པར་ཡང་འཐད་དོ།། [212] (326) རིགས་པ་འདི་དག་གིས་རྣམ་པར་རིག་པ་ཙམ་ལ་ {544}ཇི་ལྟར་འཇུག་སྙམ་ན། གཟུགས་ནས་རྣམ་མཁྱེན་གྱི་བར་གྱི[b]ཆོས་རྣམས་མིང་གི་ཐ་སྙད་འདོགས་པའི་གནས་དང་རྣམ་རྟོག་གི་ཞེན་པའི་གཞི་ཡིན་པ་དེ་དོན་དམ་པར་གྲུབ་པ་ཁེགས་པ་ན། རྗོད་བྱེད་ཀྱི་མིང་དང་བརྗོད་བྱའི་དོན་དང་མིང་དོན་འབྲེལ[c]བ་ལ་བརྟེན་ནས་བརྗོད་བྱའི་དོན་གྱི་ངོ་བོ་དང་ཁྱད་པར་དུ་སྣང་བའི་ཡིད་ཀྱི་རྟོག་པ་ནི། ཇི་ལྟར་སྣང་བ་ལྟར་གྱི་ཞེན་སའི་དོན་མེད་པས་དེ་ལྟར་འཛིན་པ་མ་འཁྲུལ་བ་ཡང་མེད་དོ་སྙམ་ནས་གཟུང་འཛིན་གཉིས་མེད་པའི་རྣམ་རིག་ཙམ་ལ་འཇུག་སྟེ། ཐེག་བསྡུས་ལས།

འདི་ལྟར་བྱང་ཆུབ་སེམས་དཔའ་རྣམ་པར་རིག་པ་ཙམ་ལ་འཇུག་པར་བརྩོན་པ་དེ་ལྟ་བུ་དེ་ཡི་གེ་དང་དོན་སྣང་བའི་ཡིད་ཀྱི་བརྗོད་པ་དེ་ལ་ཡི་གེའི་མིང་དེ་ཡང་ཡིད་ཀྱི་རྟོག་པ་ཙམ་དུ་ཟད་པར་ [71]ཡང་དག་པར་རྟོག་གོ། ཡི་གེ་ལ་བརྟེན་ (33a)པའི་དོན་དེ་ཡང་ཡིད་ཀྱི་བརྗོད་པ་ཙམ་དུ་ཟད་པ་ཉིད་དུ་ཡང་དག་པར་རྟོག་གོ། མིང་དེ་ཡང་ངོ་བོ་ཉིད་དང་ཁྱད་པར་དུ་བཏགས་པར་ཟད་པ་ཙམ་དུ་ཡང་དག་པར་རྟོག་གོ། དེའི་

a Zi ling sku 'bum (391.4): *ba'i;* see p. 373, footnote b.

b Grags pa & rnam rgyal (69.4) misread *gye.*

c Se rva zhol (32b.4) misreads *'grel pa;* Delhi GD zhol has been corrected to *'brel ba,* which is the reading in Delhi NG dkra shis lhun po (544.2), Zi ling sku 'bum (391.11), Peking (179.5.3), Sarnath gtsang (70.14), and Kalimpong (81.1).

> ཕྱིར་ཡིད་ཀྱི་བརྗོད་པ་ཙམ་དུ་ཟད་པ་ཉིད་དུ་དམིགས་ཤིང་། མིང་དང་བཅས་པའི་དོན་ངོ་བོ་ཉིད་དང་ཁྱད་པར་དུ་བཏགས་པ་དང་བཅས་ཤིང་། ངོ་བོ་ཉིད་དང་ཁྱད་པར་དུ་བཅས་པ་དོན་གྱི་མཚན་ཉིད་དུ་མི་དམིགས་པ་ན་ཡོངས་སུ་ཚོལ[a]་བ་བཞི་དང་། ཡང་དག་པ་ཇི་ལྟ་བ་བཞིན་དུ་ཡོངས་སུ་ཤེས་པ་བཞི་པོ[b]་དག་གིས་ཡི་གེ་དང་དོན་སྣང་བའི་ཡིད་ཀྱི་རྣམ་པར་རྟོག[c]་པ་དེ་དག་ལ་རྣམ་པར་རིག་པ་ཙམ་ཉིད་དུ་འཇུག་གོ།

ཞེས་གསུངས་སོ།། [214] (328) གལ་ཏེ་འདི་ཡིད་ཤེས་རྟོག་པ་ལ་ལྟོས་པའི་གཟུང་འཛིན་ཁེགས་པ་ཡིན་ལ། བག་ཆགས་བརྟན་པ་ལས་བྱུང་བའི་རྟོག་མེད་ཀྱི་ཤེས་པ་ལ་ལྟོས་པའི་གཟུང་ {545} འཛིན་རིགས་པས་ཁེགས་པ་མིན་པས་རྣམ་རིག་ཙམ་ལ་འཇུག་པར་ཇི་ལྟར་འཐད་ཅེ་ན། སྐྱོན་མེད་དེ་འདི་ལྟར་སྔོན་པོ་གཟུང་བ་དོན་གཞན་དུ་འཛིན་པའི་རྟོག་པའི་ཞེན་གཞི་ཡིན་པ་རང་མཚན་གྱིས་ཡོད་པ་རིགས་པས་ཁེགས་ན་སྔོན་པོ་ཞེན་གཞི་ཡིན་པ་སྣང་བའི་སྔོ་འཛིན་དེ་སྣང་ཡུལ་ལ་འཁྲུལ་བར[d]་འགྲུབ་སྟེ། དེ་སྣང་བ་ན་རང་གི་མཚན་ཉིད་ཀྱིས་གྲུབ་པར་སྣང་བའི་ཕྱིར་རོ།། དེ་གྲུབ་ན་སྔོན་པོ་དེ་རང་སྣང་བའི་ཤེས་པ་ལས་རྫས་གཞན་དུ་མེད་པ་གྲུབ་བོ།། [215] (328) འོ་ན་རྣམ་ཤེས་རྟོག་པའི་ཞེན་གཞི་ཡིན་པ་དེ་དོན་ [72] དམ་པར་གྲུབ་པ་རིགས་པས་ཁེགས་ན་དེ་སྣང་བའི་རང་རིག་དེ་སྣང་ཡུལ་ལ་འཁྲུལ་བར་འགྲུབ་སྟེ། དེ་སྣང་བ་ན་རང་མཚན་གྱིས་གྲུབ་པར་སྣང་བའི་ཕྱིར་རོ།། དེ་གྲུབ་ན་རྣམ་ (33b) ཤེས་དེ་མྱོང་བའི་ངོ་བོར་རང་མཚན་གྱིས་གྲུབ་པ་མེད་པས་རྣལ་འབྱོར་སྤྱོད་པའི་གྲུབ་པའི་མཐའ་དོར་བར་འགྱུར་རོ་ཞེ་ན། དེའི་སྐྱོན་མེད་དེ་རང་རིག་ལ་རྣམ་ཤེས་རྟོག་པའི་ཞེན་གཞི་ཡིན་པ་མི་སྣང་ལ་སྔོ་འཛིན་ལ་སྔོན་པོ་ཕྱི་རོལ་ཏུ་ཞེན་པའི་ཞེན་གཞི་ཡིན་པ་སྣང་བའི་ཕྱིར་ཏེ། ཞེན་གཞི་ཡིན་པ་དེ་གཉིས་སྣང་ནུབ་པའི་རང་རིག་ལ་སོགས་པ་ལ་འཆར་དུ་མི་རུང་ཞིང་གཉིས་སྣང་ཅན་གྱི་སྔོ་འཛིན་ལ་སྣང་བ་མི་འགལ་བའི་ཕྱིར་རོ།།

---

a Zi ling sku 'bum (392.2): *'tshol.*

b Zi ling sku 'bum (392.2): *bo*—another overcorrection.

c Following the Chinese translations, Lamotte (*La somme du grand véhicule d'Asaṅga,* reprint, 2 vols. Publications de l'Institute Orientaliste de Louvain, 8 (Louvain: Université de Louvain, 1973), vol. 1, 52.2) reads *snang ba'i yid kyi brjod pa.*

d Se rva zhol (33a.5) and Peking (180.1.3): *'khrul **par;*** Delhi GD zhol has been emended to ***bar,*** as is the reading in Delhi NG dkra shis lhun po (545.2), Zi ling sku 'bum (392.9), Sarnath gtsang (71.17), and Kalimpong (82.3).

[215] (328) རྟོག་པའི་ཞེན་གཞི་དེ་སྣང་བ་ན་གཉིས་སྣང་ཡོད་དགོས་པའི་རྒྱུ་མཚན་ནི་དེའི་ཕྱིར་རྟོག་པ་ལ་འཆར་བ་ན་ངེས་པར་གཉིས་སྣང་གི་རྣམ་པ་ཅན་དུ་འཆར་བའི་ཕྱིར་རོ།།

འདི་ཤེས་པ་ལ་མཚུངས་པ་མ་ཡིན་ཏེ་རྟོག་པ་ལ་ཕྱི་འཆར་བ་ནའང་སྔོན་ཙམ་གྱི་རྣམ་པ་ཅན་དུ་འཆར་བའི་ཕྱིར་རོ།། རྟོག་པ་ལ་གཉིས་སྣང་ངེས་པར་ཡོད་པས་མཚུངས་སོ་ཞེས་སླ་མི་ནུས་ཏེ། རྟོག་པ་ལ་གཉིས་སྣང་ཡོད་པ་དང་ཡུལ་དེ་གཉིས་སྣང་གི་རྣམ་པར་འཆར་བ་གཉིས་དོན་མི་{546}གཅིག་པའི་ཕྱིར་རོ།། དེ་ལྟ་མ་ཡིན་ན་གཉིས་སྣང་ནུབ་པ་རྣམ་རྟོག་ལ་འཆར་མི་སྲིད་པར་ཁས་བླང་དགོས་ན་དེ་ཡང་མི་རིགས་ཏེ་གཉིས་སྣང་ནུབ་པ་མི་སྲིད་པར་འགྱུར་བའི་ཕྱིར་རོ།། [217] (329) གལ་ཏེ་སྔོན་པོ་རྟོག་པའི་ཞེན་གཞི་ཡིན་པ་དེ་རྟོག་པའི་དབང་གིས་བཞག་པ་[73]ཙམ་ཡིན་པའི་ཕྱིར་རྟོག་བྲལ་ལ་མི་སྣང་ངོ་སྙམ་ན། སྒྱུ་མ་རྟ་གླང་ཡིན་པ་ཡང་རྟོག་བྲལ་ལ་མི་སྣང་བར་འགྱུར་ཏེ་རྟོག་པས་བཞག་པ་ཙམ་ཡིན་པའི་ཕྱིར་རོ།། རིགས་ན་ངོ་བོ་དང་ཁྱད་པར་དུ་བཏགས་པའི་ཀུན་བརྟགས་ཀྱིས་སྟོང་པ་ཡོངས་གྲུབ་ཏུ་དགོངས་འགྲེལ་ལས་གསུངས་པ་དེ་ལ་གཟུང་འཛིན་རྫས་གཞན་བཀག་པ་མེད་པ་ཡང་མིན་ནོ།། མདོ་དེ་ལས་ཞི་གནས་ཀྱི་(34a)སྐབས་སུ་ནི་ཕྱི་རོལ་དགག་པ་གསལ་བར་གསུངས་སོ།།

[217] (329) ཕྱིར་ཀུན་བརྟགས་ལ་ཕྱི་མཚན་ཐམས་ཅད་དང་ནམ་མཁའ[a]ལ་སོགས་པ་དུ་མ་ཞིག་ཡོད་ཀྱང་དགོངས་འགྲེལ་ལས་མ་གསུངས་པ་ནི། ཀུན་བརྟགས་གང་གིས་སྟོང་པ་ཡོངས་གྲུབ་ཏུ་འཇོག་པའི་སྐབས་སུ་དེ་དག་མི་མཁོ་བས་སོ།། དེ་དག་གི་མང་པོ་ཞིག་མིང་དང་བརྡས་འཇོག་མི་ནུས་པའི་ཡོད་པ་ཡིན་ཡང་རང་གི་མཚན་ཉིད་ཀྱིས་གྲུབ་པ་མིན་ཏེ་རྟོག་པས་བཏགས་པ་ཙམ་ཡིན་པའི་ཕྱིར། [218] (330) ཕྱི་རོལ་ལ་ལྟོས་པའི་གཟུང་འཛིན་འགོག་པ་ནི་ཐེག་བསྡུས་སུ་རྨི་ལམ་དང་གཟུགས་བརྙན་ལ་སོགས་པའི་རིགས་པ་དང་ཉི་ཤུ་པར་རྡུལ་ཆ་མེད་འགོག་པའི་རིགས་པ་དང་། ཆོས་ཀྱི་གྲགས་པས་གཟུང་འཛིན་གྱི་མཚན་ཉིད་སྐྱེས་ལ་འདྲ་བ་འགོག་པའི་རིགས་པ་དང་། ཕྱོགས་གླང་གིས་རྡུལ་འདུས་པ་དང་ཕྲ་རབ་གཟུང་དོན་ཡིན་པ་འགོག་པའི་རིགས་པ་རྣམས་ཡིན་ནོ།། [218] (331) ཡུམ་གྱི་མདོ་ནས་མེད་ཅེས་གསུངས་པ་ཐམས་ཅད་ཀྱིས་ཀུན་བརྟགས་འགོག[b]{547}པ་ཐེག་བསྡུས་ལས་གསུངས་པ་རྣམས་ལ་དགོངས་འགྲེལ་[74]གྱི་ཀུན་བརྟགས་འགོག་ཚུལ་འདི་མི་ཤེས་ན།

[a] Se rva zhol (34a.1) misreads *na mkha'*, which was most likely intended to be the contraction *namkha'* which is an elision of *nam* and *mkha'*.

[b] Se rva zhol (34a.4) misreads *dgog*.

གཟུང་འཛིན་རྫས་གཞན་[a]གྱི་ཀུན་བརྟགས་ཁོ་ན་ལ་བཤད་པས་རྣལ་འབྱོར་སྤྱོད་པ་བ་དག་[b]གི་ལུགས་ལ་ཡང་ཆེས་མི་རིགས་པ་དུ་མ་ཞིག་སྨྲ་དགོས་ལ། རྟག་མི་རྟག་ལ་སོགས་པ་གང་དུ་ཡང་གཟུང་ས་[c]མེད་པར་གསུངས་པ་རྣམས་ཀྱང་ལུགས་འདིས་བཤད་པར་ཤིན་ཏུ་དཀའ་འོ་[d]།། དེའི་ཕྱིར་གང་དུ་ཡང་གཟུང་ས་[e]མེད་པར་གསུངས་པ་རྣམས་ལ་མཉམ་གཞག་དང་། འདི་ཡིན་འདི་མིན་ཕྱི་ནས་གཟུང་ས་ཡོད་པར་གསུངས་པ་རྗེས་ཐོབ་ཤན་འབྱེད་པའི་དུས་ལ་དགོངས་ (34b) སོ་ཞེས་སྨྲ་དགོས་པ་ཡང་བྱང་སྡེ་ཟེར་རྒྱུས་ཕོངས་པ་ཡིན་ནོ།། བྱང་ས་དང་ཐེག་བསྡུས་དང་ཀུན་ལས་བཏུས་ལ་སོགས་པར་ཚོལ་[f]བ་བཞི་དང་ཡོངས་སུ་ཤེས་པ་བཞི་གསུངས་པ་ནི་རྣམ་རིག་པའི་ལྟ་བ་གཏན་ལ་འབེབས་བྱེད་རྣམ་པར་རིག་པ་ཙམ་ལ་འཇུག་པའི་སྒོ་དམ་པ་ཉོན་མོངས་པ་རྣམས་ཀྱིའང་གཞི་བྱེད་པའི་རྣམ་རྟོག་ཤེས་སྒྲིབ་ཀྱི་གཉེན་པོར་གསུངས་ལ། དེ་དག་གི་དོན་ཤེས་པ་ལ་དགོངས་འགྲེལ་ལས་གསུངས་པའི་ཀུན་བརྟགས་འགོག་པའི་རིགས་པ་དང་དགག་བྱའི་སྒྲོ་འདོགས་ཕྲ་མོ་ནས་ཤེས་དགོས་པར་སྣང་། ཁྱད་པར་དུ་རིགས་པ་དེ་དག་གིས་གཟུང་འཛིན་རྫས་གཞན་ཁེགས་ནས་རྣམ་པར་རིག་པ་ཙམ་ལ་འཇུག་པའི་ཚུལ་ཤེས་དགོས་པར་སྣང་ཡང་དཔྱོད་པ་ཙམ་ཡང་མ་ཞུགས་པར་མཐོང་ནས་བློ་གྲོས་ཅན་རྣམས་ལ་དཔྱོད་པའི་སྒོ་ཙམ་ཞིག་བསྟན་ནོ།།

---

a Sarnath gtsang (74.2) misreads *zhan.*

b Delhi NG dkra shis lhun po (547.1), Se rva zhol (34a.5), Sarnath gtsang (74.2), and Kalimpong (84.6) misread *bdag;* Zi ling sku 'bum (394.3) and Peking (180.3.3) correctly read *ba dag.*

c Delhi GD zhol (34a.5) has been mistakenly emended to *gzugs.* Peking (180.3.1) misreads *gzungs.*

d Zi ling sku 'bum (394.5): *dka'o.*

e Peking (180.3.2) misreads *gzungs.*

f Zi ling sku 'bum (394.8): *'tshol.*

གཉིས་པ་ [དེ་ལ་རྩོད་པ་སྤང་བ་]ནི། [220] (333)

དགོངས་ [75] འགྲེལ་ལས། གཞན་དབང་ལ་ཀུན་བརྟགས་ཀྱི་ངོ་བོ་ཉིད་དུ་མངོན་པར་ཞེན་པས་ཉོན་མོངས་པ་སྐྱེད་ཅིང་དེས་ལས་བསགས་ནས་འཁོར་བར་འཁོར་ལ། གཞན་ {548} དབང་ལ་ཀུན་བརྟགས་ཀྱི་མཚན་ཉིད་ངོ་བོ་ཉིད་མེད་པར་མཐོང་ན་དེ་དག་རིམ་པ་བཞིན་ལྡོག་པར་གསུངས་ནས་ཉན་རང་དང་བྱང་སེམས་གསུམ་གས[a] ལམ་འདི་ཉིད་དང་སྒྲུབ་པ་འདི་ཉིད་ཀྱིས་མྱ་ངན་ལས་འདས་པ་འཐོབ་པས་དེ་དག་གི་རྣམ་པར་དག་པའི་ལམ་དང་རྣམ་པར་དག་པ་ཡང་གཅིག་སྟེ་གཉིས་པ་མེད་པར་གསུངས་ཤིང་། གཞན་དབང་ཀུན་བརྟགས་ཀྱིས་སྟོང་ཚུལ་སྔར་བཤད་པ་ལས་གཞན་པ་ཡང་མ་གསུངས་སོ།། དེའི་ཕྱིར་ཉན་རང་གིས་ཀྱང་ཆོས་ཀྱི་བདག་མེད་རྟོགས་པ་མདོ་འདིའི་དོན་དུ་བྱེད་དམ་མི་བྱེད་བྱེད་ན་སྔར་ཐུན་མོང་མ་ (35a) ཡིན་པར་བཤད་པ་རྣམས་དང་འགལ་ལོ།། མི་བྱེད་ན་མདོའི་དོན་ཇི་ལྟར་བཤད་ཅེ་ན། [221] (334) འདི་ལ་བྱང་སར[b] ཡང་ངོ་བོ་དང་ཁྱད་པར་དུ་རྟོག་པ་དང་རིལ་པོར[c] འཛིན་པའི་རྣམ་རྟོག་གིས་རྣམ་རྟོག་གི་དམིགས་པའི་དངོས་པོ་སྤྲོས་པའི་གནས་སྐྱེད་ལ་དེ་ལ་བརྟེན་ནས་འཇིག་ལྟ་སྐྱེ་ཞིང་དེས་ཉོན་མོངས་གཞན་རྣམས་བསྐྱེད་ནས་འཁོར་བར་འཁོར་ལ། ཚོལ[d] བ་བཞི་དང་ཡོངས་སུ་ཤེས་པ་བཞིས་རྣམ་རྟོག་གིས་བཟུང་བའི་དོན་མེད་པར་ཤེས་ན་དེ་དག་ལྡོག་པར་གསུངས་སོ།། དེ་ལྟར་ན་ཆོས་རྣམས་ལ་ངོ་བོ་དང་ཁྱད་པར་དུ་བཏགས་པར་རང་གི་མཚན་ཉིད་ཀྱིས་གྲུབ་པར་འཛིན་པའི་ཆོས་ཀྱི་བདག་འཛིན་གྱིས་འཇིག་ལྟའི་རྩ་བ་བྱེད་པར་བཞེད་ལ། ཆོས་ [76] ཀྱི་བདག་འཛིན་གྱིས་གང་ཟག་གི་བདག་འཛིན་གྱི་གཞི་བྱེད་པ་ནི་ཉན་རང་ལ་ཆོས་ཀྱི་བདག་མེད་རྟོགས་པ་མེད་པར་བཞེད་པའི་དབུ་མ་པ[e] རྣམས་ཀྱིས་ཀྱང་བཞེད་དོ།། དེ་ལ་ནི་ཆོས་ཀྱི་བདག་འཛིན་ཟད་ན་གང་ཟག་གི་བདག་འཛིན་ལྡོག་ཀྱང་ཆོས་ཀྱི་བདག་འཛིན་མ་ཟད་ན་གང་ཟག་གི་བདག་འཛིན་མི་ {549} ལྡོག་པ་མིན་པས་འཁོར་བའི་གཞི་མཐར་གཏུགས་པ་མ་ལོག་ཀྱང་འཁོར་བ

[a] Sarnath gtsang (75.5) misreads *gis;* Delhi NG dkra shis lhun po (548.1), Se rva zhol (34b.5), Zi ling sku 'bum (394.19), and Kalimpong (86.2): *gas;* Peking (180.3.8): *kas.*

[b] This is a paraphrase; the Peking is 5538, vol. 110, 145.4.5-146.5.8 (Wogihara, *Bodhisattvabhūmi,* 50.22-55.17; Dutt, *Bodhisattvabhūmi,* 34.22-38.3).

[c] Zi ling sku 'bum (395.6): *bor,* not taking into account the non-manifest extra suffix *da* at the end of the previous syllable.

[d] Zi ling sku 'bum (395.8): *'tshol.*

[e] Zi ling sku 'bum (395.13): *ba;* see p. 373, footnote b.

ལས་གྲོལ་བ་མི་འགལ་ལོ།། དེའི་ཕྱིར་ལམ་འདི་ཉིད་ཅེས་གསུངས་པ་ནི་གཞན་དབང་ཀུན་བརྟགས་ཀྱི་མཚན་ཉིད་ཀྱིས་སྟོང་པར་རྟོགས་པའི་ལམ་ལ་བྱེད་ཀྱང་ཆོས་ཀྱི་བདག་མེད་ཀྱི་ལམ་ལ་བྱ་མི་དགོས་ཏེ། གཞན་དབང་ཀུན་བརྟགས་ཀྱིས་སྟོང་པ་ལ་གང་ཟག་གི་བདག་མེད་ཀྱི་དབང་དུ་བྱས་པ་ཡང་ཀུན་ལས་བཏུས་ལས་གསུངས་པའི་ཕྱིར་རོ།། གང་ཟག་གི་བདག་མེད་རྟོགས་པས་ཉོན་མོངས་དག་པར་བྱེད་པ་དང་ཉོན་མོངས་སྤངས་པ་ཙམ་གྱི་ (35b) རྣམ་གྲོལ་ལ་ཐེག་པ་ཆེ་ཆུང་ཁྱད་མེད་པས་རྣམ་དག་གི་ལམ་དང་རྣམ་དག་གཅིག་པར་ཡང་གསུངས་སོ།། ཕུང་པོ་ལ་སོགས་པ་གཞན་དབང་དང་དེ་ལ་ཆོས་ཀྱི་བདག་ཏུ་སྒྲོ་བཏགས་པ་ཀུན་བརྟགས་དང་དེ་དེས་སྟོང་པ་ཆོས་ཀྱི་བདག་མེད་ཀྱི་ཡོངས་གྲུབ་ཏུ་འཇོག་པ་ཐེག་ཆེན་གྱི་མདོའི་དོན་དུ་དགོངས་འགྲེལ་གྱིས་བཀྲལ་བའི་ཞབས་ཀྱིས། ཕུང་པོའི་གཞན་དབང་གང་ཟག་གི་བདག་གི་ཀུན་བརྟགས་ཀྱིས་སྟོང་པ་གང་ཟག་གི་བདག་མེད་ཀྱི་ཡོངས་གྲུབ་ཏུ་འཇོག་པའི་ངོ་བོ་ཉིད་གསུམ་གྱི་རྣམ་གཞག་དེ་ཙམ་ཞིག་ཐེག་ [77] དམན་གྱི་མདོའི་དོན་དུ་གོ་ནུས་ལ། དེའི་ཕྱིར་འཁོར་ལོ་དང་པོ་གསུངས་པའི་གདུལ་བྱ་ནི་གང་ཟག་གི་བདག་མེད་ཀྱི་དབང་དུ་བྱས་པའི་མཚན་ཉིད་ངོ་བོ་ཉིད་མེད་པ་རྟོགས་པའི་སྣོད་དུ་རུང་ལ། ཆོས་ཀྱི་བདག་མེད་ཀྱི་དབང་དུ་བྱས་པའི་མཚན་ཉིད་ངོ་བོ་ཉིད་མེད་པ་རྟོགས་པའི་སྣོད་དུ་མི་རུང་བ་ལ་གསུངས་པར་དགོངས་འགྲེལ་གྱིས་ཞབས་ཀྱིས་འགྲེལ་པས[a]། ལེགས་པར་རྣམ་པར་ཕྱེ་བའི་ཆོས་འཁོར་ཐེག་པ་ཐམས་ཅད་ལ་ཞུགས་པའི་ཆེད་དུ་གསུངས་པའི་དོན་ནི་དེའོ།། [225] (335) གལ་ཏེ་ངོ་བོ་ {550} དང་ཁྱད་པར་དུ་བཏགས་པ་དང་གཟུང་འཛིན་རྫས་གཞན་གྱི་ཀུན་བརྟགས་ཀྱིས་སྟོང་པའི་སྐབས་ཐམས་ཅད་དུ་གཞན་དབང་ཉིད་སྟོང་གཞིར་བྱས་ནས། དེ་ལྟ་མ་གཉིས་ཀྱིས་ཡིན་པའི་ཚུལ་གྱིས་སྟོང་པ་ཡོངས་གྲུབ་ཏུ་བྱ་དགོས་ན། དབྱིག་གཉེན་གྱིས་ཡུམ་གསུམ་གནོད་འཇོམས་ལས།

དེ་ལ[b] མིག[c] ཅེས་བྱ་བ་ནི་ཆོས་ཉིད་ཀྱི[d] མིག་གོ། མིག་གིས་ཞེས་བྱ་བ་ནི་ཀུན་

---

[a] Delhi NG dkra shis lhun po (549.6), Peking (180.5.5), Sarnath gtsang (77.6): *bas;* Se rva zhol (35b.4), Zi ling sku 'bum (396.10), and Kalimpong (88.3): *pas,* the latter appearing to have been crudely emended. The difference is due to whether the non-manifest extra suffix *da* in *'grel* is heeded.

[b] For *de la,* the Peking of the source text (5206, vol. 93, 230.4.4) reads *de la mig mig gis stong zhes bya ba la.*

[c] Se rva zhol (35b.6) misreads *meg,* corrected in the Delhi GD zhol to *mig.*

[d] Zi ling sku 'bum (396.15) misreads *kyis.*

> བཏགས་པ་དང་རྣམ་པར་བཏགས་པའི་མིག་གིས་སོ༎ སྟོང་ཞེས་བྱ་བ་ནི་བྲལ་ཞེས་བྱ་བའི་ཐ་ཚིག་གོ༎ དེ་བཞིན་དུ་རྣ་བ་རྣ་བས་སྟོང་ཞེས་བྱ་ (36a) བ་ལ་སོགས་པ་ལ་ཡང་སྦྱར་བར་བྱའོ།

ཞེས་ཡོངས་གྲུབ་སྟོང་གཞིར་བྱས་ནས་ངོ་བོ་ཉིད་གཞན་གཉིས་ཀྱིས་སྟོང་པར་གསུངས་པ་ཇི་ལྟར་དྲང་[a] ཞེ་ན། [226] (337) དེ་ལ་རྣལ་འབྱོར་སྤྱོད་པ་པ་དང་དབུ་མ་པ་སུའི་ལུགས་ལ་ཡང་ཆོས་ཀྱི་བདག་མེད་ཀྱི་ཡོངས་གྲུབ་གཏན་ལ་འབེབས་པ་ན་སྟོང་གཞི་གང་ལ་བྱ་དགོས་པ་ནི་ཆོས་ཀྱི་བདག་འཛིན་གྱིས་གཞི་གང་ལ་ཆོས་ཀྱི་ [78] བདག་ཏུ་བཟུང་བ་དེ་ལ་རག་ལས་ཏེ། དཔེར་ན་ཐག་པ་ལ་སྦྲུལ་དུ་བཟུང་ནས་སྐྲག་པའི་སྡུག་བསྔལ་བསལ་བར་འདོད་པ་ན་ཐག་པ་སྟོང་གཞིར་བཟུང་ནས་དེ་སྦྲུལ་གྱིས་སྟོང་ངོ་ཞེས་བསྟན་དགོས་ཀྱི། ཐག་པ་སྦྲུལ་གྱིས་སྟོང་པ་སྟོང་གཞིར་བཟུང་ནས་དེ་ཐག་པ་དང་སྦྲུལ་དོན་གཞན་དུ་ཡོད་པས་སྟོང་ངོ་ཞེས་བརྗོད་དུ་མི་རུང་བ་བཞིན་ནོ༎ [227] (338) ཆོས་ཀྱི་བདག་འཛིན་ཡང་རྡུལ་ཕྲ་རབ་ཕྱོགས་ཀྱི་ཆ་མེད་དང་དེ་བསགས་པའི་གཟུང་བ་དང་། དུས་ཐ་མའི་ཆ་ཤས་མེད་པའི་ཤེས་པ་སྐད་ཅིག་མ་དང་དེ་འཐུད་པའི་རྒྱུན་གྱི་ཤེས་པ་ཡོད་པར་འཛིན་པ་ལྟ་བུ་གྲུབ་མཐས་བློ་བསྒྱུར་བ[b]་ཁོ་ནས་བཏགས་པ་རྣམས་ནི་གྲུབ་མཐའ་སྨྲ་བ་ {551} དེ་དག་ཁོ་ན་ལ་ཡོད་ཀྱི་སེམས་ཅན་གཞན་ལ་མེད་དོ༎ དེས་ན་དེ་ཙམ་ཞིག་མེད་པའི་སྟོང་པ་བསྟན་ཡང་ཐོག་མ་མེད་པ་ནས་རྗེས་སུ་ཞུགས་པའི་ལྷན་སྐྱེས་ཀྱི་བདག་འཛིན་ལ་ཅི་ཡང་མི་གནོད་པས། ལྷན་སྐྱེས་ཀྱི་བདག་འཛིན་གྱིས་གང་ལ་བདག་ཏུ་བཟུང་བའི་གཞི་དེ་ཇི་ལྟར་བཟུང་བ་ལྟར་གྱི་བདག་གིས་སྟོང་ངོ་ཞེས་བསྟན་དགོས་ཤིང་། གྲུབ་མཐས་བཏགས་པ་འགོག་པ་ཡང་དེ་འགོག་པའི་ཡན་ལག་ཏུ་ཤེས་དགོས་སོ༎ དེ་ལྟར་བྱས་ན་སེམས་ཅན་རང་དགའ་བ་རྣམས་ཀྱིས་ནི་ (36b) མཐོང་བ་དང་ཐོས་པ་ལ་སོགས་པའི་དོན་མིག་དང་གཟུགས་ལ་སོགས་པའི་ཕྱི་ནང་གི་དངོས་པོ་གཞན་དབང་འདི་ཙམ་ལ་བདག་ཏུ་འཛིན་པས་དེ་ཉིད་སྟོང་གཞིར་བཟུང་ནས་སྟོང་པ་གཏན་ལ་དབབ་དགོས་ཀྱི་ཡོངས་ [79] གྲུབ་ལ་ངོ་བོ་ཉིད་གཞན་གཉིས་དོན་གཞན་དུ་ཡོད་དོ་སྙམ་དུ་བཟུང་ནས་འཁྲུལ་བ་མིན་པས་ཡོངས་གྲུབ་ངོ་བོ་ཉིད་གཞན་གཉིས་དོན་གཞན་དུ་ཡོད་པས་སྟོང་ངོ་ཞེས་བདག་མེད་གཏན་ལ་འབེབས་པ་ག་ལ་ཡིན། ཆོས་བདག་ཡོད་པར་

[a] Sarnath gtsang (77.17): *drangs;* Delhi NG dkra shis lhun po (550.3), Se rva zhol (36a.1), Zi ling sku 'bum (396.18), Peking (180.5.8), and Kalimpong (89.1): *drang.*

[b] Zi ling sku 'bum (397.7): *pa.*

འཛིན་པ་ཡང་ལ་ལ་མི་ཡོད་པར་འཛིན་པ་ལྟ་བུ་དོན་གཞན་ཅིག་[a]ཡོད་པར་འཛིན་པ་མིན་ཏེ། རང་གི་སེམས་ཕྱིའི་ཡུལ་དང་ནང་གི་ཡུལ་ཅན་དུ་སོ་སོ་རྒྱངས་ཆད་དུ་སྣང་བ་ན་ཇི་ལྟར་སྣང་བ་དེ་བཞིན་དུ་གྲུབ་པར་འཛིན་པས་དེའི་གཉེན་པོར་ཡུལ་ཡུལ་ཅན་དུ་སྣང་བ་དེ་གཟུང་འཛིན་རྫས་གཞན་དུ་མ་གྲུབ་ཅེས་སྟོན་གྱི་གཟུང་འཛིན་དོན་གཞན་དུ་དེ་ལ་མེད་དོ་ཞེས་སྟོན་པ་མིན་ནོ།། དེས་ན་དབུས་མཐའི་འགྲེལ་བཤད་ལས་ཀུང་གཙུག་ལག་ཁང་དགེ་སློང་ལ་སོགས་པས་སྟོང་པ་ལྟར་མིན་གྱི་ཐག་པ་སྦྲུལ་གྱིས་སྟོང་པ་ལྟར་ཡིན་པར་གསུངས་ཏེ། ཆོས་བདག་གིས་སྟོང་ཚུལ་གཞན་ཡང་དེ་ལྟར་རོ།། དེས་ན་འཇིག་རྟེན་ན་འདྲེ་ཤར་སྒོར་གནོད་པ་ལ་ {552} གླུད་ནུབ་སྒོར་གཏོང་ཞེས་པ་ལྟར་མ་སོང་བར་གང་ལ་བདག་ཏུ་བཟུང་བའི་གཞི་གཞན་དབང་དེ་ཇི་ལྟར་བཟུང་བ་ལྟར་[b]གྱི་ཀུན་བཏགས་ཀྱི་བདག་གིས་སྟོང་པ་ཡོངས་གྲུབ་ཡིན་པའི་སྟོང་ཚུལ་དེ་འདྲའི་སྟོང་ཉིད་བསྒོམས་ན། བདག་འཛིན་གྱི་གཉེན་པོར་འགྲོ་བ་ཡིན་གྱི་ལུགས་དེ་ལས་གཞན་པའི་སྟོང་ཚུལ་གྱི་སྟོང་པ་བསྒོམས་ན་ནི་བདག་འཛིན་ལ་ཅི་ཡང་མི་གནོད་དོ།། [228] (337) གནོད་ (37a) འཇོམས་ཀྱིས་བཤད་པ་ནི་རྟོག་པ་ལ་རྗོད་བྱེད་སྒྲ་སྤྱི་དང་བརྗོད་བྱ་དོན་སྤྱི་སྣང་ [80] བ་ནི་ཀུན་བཏགས་ཀྱི་མིག་དང་། གཟུང་བ་གཟུགས་ཀྱི་སྐྱེ་མཆེད་ལ་དེ་འཛིན་པའི་བདག་ཉིད་ཀྱི་མིག་ཏུ་སྣང་བ་ནི་རྣམ་བཏགས་ཀྱི་མིག་དང་། སྒྲ་དོན་གྱི་སྤྱིར་གྱུར་པའི་བརྗོད་པར་བྱ་བྱེད་དང་བྲལ་བས་བརྗོད་དུ་མེད་ཅིང་། མིག་གི་གཟུང་འཛིན་དུ་སོ་སོར་སྣང་བར་གྱུར་པ་[c]དང་བྲལ་ཏེ་མཉམ་གཞག་སོ་སོ་རང་རིག་གིས་རིག་པའི་ཡོངས་གྲུབ་ནི་ཆོས་ཉིད་ཀྱི་མིག་ཏུ་འདོད་པས། མིག་གི་ཆོས་ཉིད་དེ་འཕགས་པའི་མཉམ་གཞག་གིས་རིག་པའི་ངོ་ན་[d]བརྗོད་བྱ་རྗོད་བྱེད་དང་གཟུང་

a Zi ling sku 'bum (397.17): *zhig,* not taking into account the extra suffix *da.*

b Se rva zhol (36b.5) misreads *bltar.*

c Delhi NG dkra shis lhun po (552.4), Peking (181.2.7), and Kalimpong (91.5): *ba;* Se rva zhol (37a.2), Zi ling sku 'bum (398.14), and Sarnath gtsang (80.4): *pa.* The latter reflects that it follows a non-manifest extra suffix *da* in the previous syllable.

d Peking (181.2.8) and Zi ling sku 'bum (398.16): *ngo na.* Šer-šhül (*Notes,* 53b.5) also prefers *ngo na;* he points out that in new editions (*spar sar*) there are many mistakes and calls for examination. Delhi NG dkra shis lhun po (552.4), Kalimpong (91.6), Se rva zhol (37a.3), rje'i gsung lta ba'i skor (325.3), and Sarnath gtsang (80.7): *don.* Taken as *don,* the passage would mean:

> Therefore, [such a] reality of the eye is the object known by a Superior's meditative equipoise and is devoid of the dualistic appearance that is the appearance as object of verbalization and means of verbalization and as apprehended-object and apprehending-subject.

འཛིན་དུ་སྣང་བའི་གཉིས་སྣང་དང་བྲལ་བ་ལ་ངོ་བོ་ཉིད་གཞན་གཉིས་ཀྱིས་མཉམ་གཞག་གི་ཡུལ་དེ་སྟོང་ཞེས་བྱ་སྟེ་གཉིས་སྣང་སྔ་མ་ནི་ཀུན་བརྟགས་དང་ཕྱི་མ་ནི་རྣམ་བརྟགས་ཡིན་པའི་ཕྱིར་རོ།། དེ་ལྟར་ཡང་དེ་ཉིད་ལས།

> དེ་ལ་བརྗོད་པར་བྱ་བ་དང་བརྗོད་པའི་རྣམ་པར་བཟུང་བའི་མིག་ཅེས་བྱ་བའི་དངོས་པོ་ནི་ཀུན་བརྟགས་པའི་མིག་ཡིན་ནོ།། དེ་ཉིད[a]གཟུང་བ་དང་འཛིན་པའི་བདག་ཉིད་དུ་གནས་པ་མིག་གི་རྣམ་པར་སོ་སོར་སྣང་བ་ནི་རྣམ་པར་བརྟགས[b]པའི་མིག་གོ།། དེ་ཉིད[c]བརྗོད་པར་བྱ་བ་དང་བརྗོད་པའི་རྣམ་པ་དང་བྲལ་ཞིང་ {553} བརྗོད་དུ་མེད་པ་སྣང་བ་དང་བཅས་པར་གྱུར་པ་དང་བྲལ་ཏེ་སོ་སོ་རང་གིས་རིག་པ་ཡོངས་སུ་གྲུབ་པའི་ངོ་བོ་ཉིད་ནི་ཆོས་ཉིད་ཀྱི་མིག་ཅེས་བྱའོ།

ཞེས་དང་།

> འདི་ལྟར་ཁྱོད་དོན་དམ་པ་ཡིད་ལ་བྱེད་པ་སྒོམ་པའི་ཚེ་འདུ་བྱེད་ཀྱི་མཚན་མའི་དངོས་པོ་མི་སྣང་བས་དོན་དམ་པར་ནི་དེ་མེད་ཀྱི་ཀུན་རྫོབ་ཏུ་ཡོད་པར་ [81] ཤེས་པར་གྱིས་ཤིག།

ཅེས་འཕགས་པའི་མཉམ་གཞག་གི་ངོ་ན་གཉིས་སྣང་མེད་ (37b) པ་ལ་བཤད་པའི་ཕྱིར་རོ།། དེས་ན་ [230] (337) དེ་གཞིའི་ལྟ་བ་ཆོས་ཀྱི་བདག་མེད་ཀྱི་ཡོངས་གྲུབ་གཏན་ལ་འབེབས་པའི[d]ཚུལ་མིན་ནོ།། [230] (340) གནོད་འཇོམས་ལས་འཕགས་པའི་མཉམ་གཞག་གི་ངོ་ན་ཡོད་པ་ཙམ་ལ་དོན་དམ་པར་ཡོད་པ་ཞེས་བཤད་ཀྱང་མཉམ་གཞག་གིས་དེ་ཁོ་ན་ཉིད་རྟོགས་པར་འདོད་པ་ཐམས་ཅད་ཀྱང་རང་གི་ཡུལ་ཅན་གྱི་ངོ་ན་ཡུལ་ཡོད་པར་འདོད་པ་ཁོ་ན་ཡིན་པས་དོན་དམ་པར་ཡོད་མེད་རྩོད་པའི་དོན་དམ་པར་ཡོད་པ་དེ་ག་ལ་ཡིན། ཡིན་ལུགས་དཔྱོད[e]པའི་རིགས་པས་དཔྱད་བཟོད་པའི་དོན་དམ་པར་ཡོད་པ་དེས་གཏན་མི་འདོད་པ་ནི་སྟོང་པ་ཉིད་སྟོང་པ་ཉིད་དང་དོན་དམ་པ་སྟོང་པ་ཉིད་དང་འདུས་

[a] The Peking edition of the source text (5206, vol. 93, 230.4.3) does not have *de nyid;* see 229, footnote d.

[b] Zi ling sku 'bum (399.1) misreads *dag.*

[c] The Peking edition of the source text (5206, vol. 93, 230.4.3) does not have *de nyid;* see 229, footnote d.

[d] Zi ling sku 'bum (399.8) misreads *ba'i.*

[e] Delhi NG dkra shis lhun po (553.4) misreads *dpyed.*

མ་བྱས་སྟོང་པ་ཉིད་ཀྱི་སྐབས་སུ་དེ་ལྟར་འདོད་པ་ལ་དམིགས་ཀྱིས་ཕྱེ་བའི་དགག་པ་དུ་མ་བརྗོད་པས་ཞེས་ཏེ་མངས་པས་འཇིགས་ནས་མ་བྲིས་སོ།། ཡུམ་གྱི་མདོ་ཉིད་ལས། གཟུགས་ནས་རྣམ་མཁྱེན་གྱི་བར་རེ་རེ་ལ་གསུམ་གསུམ་གྱི་རྣམ་གཞག་བྱས་ནས་སྟོང་གཞི་རྣམ་བཏགས་དགག་བྱ་ཀུན་བརྟགས་ཀྱིས་སྟོང་པ་ཆོས་ཉིད་ཡོངས་གྲུབ་ཏུ་བཤད་པས་རྣམ་བཏགས་ཀྱི་མིག་ཀུན་བརྟགས་ཀྱི་མིག་གིས་སྟོང་པ་ནི་ཆོས་ཉིད་དུ་བཤད་དགོས་པའི་ཕྱིར། མཉམ་གཞག་གི་ངོ་ན[a]་སྔ་མ་{554}གཉིས་ཀྱིས་ཕྱེ་མ་སྟོང་པ་མདོའི་དོན་དུ་འཆད་པ་ཡང་ལེགས་པར་མི་སྣང་ངོ་།། [231] (341) འདི་ལས་ཉན་ཐོས་ཀྱི་སྐྱེས་བུ་ཆེན་པོའི་རྣམ་རྟོག་བརྒྱད་རྣམ་འགྲེལ་དུ་ཁ་འཕངས་པ་བཞིན་དུ་ཉི་ཁྲི་རྣམ་འགྲེལ་[82]ན་ཡོད་ཅིང་། གཞན་དབང་དང་ཡོངས་གྲུབ་གཉིས་ཀ་ཡིན་ལུགས་དཔྱོད་པའི་རིགས་པས་དཔྱད་བཟོད་བཀག་པའི་ཕྱིར་དང་། དབྱིག་གཉེན་གྱིས་ཡུམ་གྱི་མདོའི་དགོངས་པའི་དོན་དགོངས་འགྲེལ་(38a)གྱིས་བཤད་པ་བཞིན་དུ་བྱེད་དགོས་པར་རྣམ་བཤད་རིགས་པ་ལས་བཤད་པ་དང་བཤད་ཚུལ་ཆེས་ཤིན་ཏུ་མི་མཐུན་པའི་ཕྱིར་དབྱིག་གཉེན་གྱིས་མཛད་པ་མིན་ལ། སྔོན་གྱི་ཡི་གེ་རྙིང་པ་རྣམས་ལས་དཾཥྚྲ་སེ་ནས་མཛད་པར་གྲགས་པ་ལྟར་ཡིན་ནོ།།

[a] In Sarnath tsang (81.18) and Kalimpong (93.4) read *ngo na* for *don,* in accordance with Delhi NG dkra shis lhun po (553.6), Se rva zhol (37b.5), and Zi ling sku 'bum (399.18), as well as Ḍa-drin-rap-ḍen 153.3. In Peking (181.4.1) read *ngo na* for *ngon.*

གསུམ་པ་ [དེས་གསུང་རབ་ཀྱི་དྲང་ངེས་འབྱེད་པའི་ཚུལ་]ནི། [234] (342)
དངོས་པོའི་དེ་ཁོ་ན་ཉིད་སློབ་དཔོན་ཟླ་མཆེད་ཀྱིས་བཀྲལ་བའི་ཚུལ་དེ་ལྟར་བྱས་ན།
འཁོར་ལོ་དང་པོ་ལས་ཕྱི་རོལ་གྱི་དབང་དུ་བྱས་པའི་གཟུང་འཛིན་གཉིས་གསུངས་པ་དྲང་
དོན་དུ་འགྲེལ་བའི[a] དགོངས་གཞི་ནི་ཉི་ཤུ་པ་ལས[b]།

རང་གི་ས་བོན་གང་ལས་སུ།།
རྣམ་རིག་སྣང་བ[c] གང་འབྱུང་བ།།
དེ་དང་དེ་ཡི་སྐྱེ་མཆེད་ནི།།
རྣམ་པ་གཉིས་སུ་ཐུབ་པས་གསུངས།

ཞེས་གསུངས་པ་དང་། དགོས་པ་ཡང་དེ་ཉིད་ལས[d]།

གཟུགས་སོགས་སྐྱེ་མཆེད་ཡོད་པར་ནི།།
དེས་འདུལ་བ་ཡི་སྐྱེ་བོ་ལ།།
དགོངས་པའི་དབང་གིས་གསུངས་པ་སྟེ།།
བརྫུས་ཏེ་འབྱུང་བའི་སེམས་ཅན་བཞིན།

ཞེས་གསུངས་པ་ལྟར་ཡིན་ཏེ། ཕྱི་ནང་གི་སྐྱེ་མཆེད་ལས་གཟུགས་ལྟ་བ་སོགས་ཀྱི་རྣམ་
ཤེས་འབྱུང་བར་བསྟན་པ་ན་དེ་དག་ལས་མ་གཏོགས་པའི་ལྟ་བ་པོ་ལ་སོགས་པ་མེད་པར་
རྟོགས་པའི་དོན་དུའོ།། སྒྲ་ཇི་བཞིན་པ་ལ་གནོད་བྱེད་ནི་ཕྱི་རོལ་འགོག་པའི་རིགས་པ་ {555}
རྣམས་སོ།། ཆོས་ [83] རྣམས་ལ་ངོ་བོ་དང་ཁྱད་པར་དུ་བཏགས་པའི་ཀུན་བརྟགས་ནི་ཆོས་
ཀྱི་ཁམས་དང་སྐྱེ་མཆེད་ཡིན་པས་དེ་གཉིས་ལ་མ་ཕྱི་བར་རང་གི་མཚན་ཉིད་ཀྱིས་གྲུབ་

a Zi ling sku 'bum (400.9): *pa'i.*

b Stanza 9. The Sanskrit in Lévi (*Vijñaptimātratāsiddhi,* 5.25) is:

yataḥ svabījādvijñaptiryadābhāsā pravartate/
dvividhāyatanatvena te tasyā munirabravīt//

See also Chatterjee, *Vijñapti-Mātratā-Siddhi,* 9.1.

c Delhi NG dkra shis lhun po (554.4) , Zi ling sku 'bum (400.10), and Sarnath gtsang (82.12) misread *la;* Se rva zhol (38a.3) and Kalimpong (94.3): *ba.*

d Stanza 8. The Sanskrit in Lévi (*Vijñaptimātratāsiddhi,* 5.25) is:

rūpādyāyatanāstitvaṃ tadvineyajanaṃ prati/
abhiprāyavaśāduktamupapādukasatvavat//

See also Chatterjee, *Vijñapti-Mātratā-Siddhi,* 8.5.

པར་གསུངས་པ་ཡང་དྲང་དོན་ནོ།། [343] (343) ཀུན་ལས་བཏུས་ལས་ཤིན་ཏུ་རྒྱས་པ་ལས་ཆོས་ཐམས་ཅད་ངོ་བོ་ཉིད་མེད་པར་གསུངས་པ་ངོ་བོ་ཉིད་མེད་པ་གསུམ་ལ་དགོངས་ནས་ (38b) གསུངས་པར་བཤད་ཅིང་། ཐེག་བསྡུས་ལས་ཤིན་ཏུ་རྒྱས་པ་ལས་མེད་ཅེས་གསུངས་པ་ཐམས་ཅད་ཀྱིས་ཀུན་བརྟགས་དང་སྒྱུ་མ་ལ་སོགས་པའི་དཔེ་བསྟན་པ་རྣམས་ཀྱིས་གཞན་དབང་དང་རྣམ་པར་བྱང་བ་བཞིས་ཡོངས་གྲུབ་བསྟན་པར་གསུངས་པའི་མདོ་ནི་ཡུམ་གྱི་མདོར་སྣང་བས་འཁོར་ལོ་གཉིས་པ་དྲང་དོན་དུ་བཤད་པ་ཡང་དེ་ཉིད་དང་དེ་དང་མཐུན་པ་རྣམས་ལ་བཞེད་དོ།། རྣམ་བཤད་རིགས་པར་ཡང་ཡུམ་གྱི་མདོ་ལས་ངོ་བོ་ཉིད་མེད་པ་སོགས་སུ་བཤད་པ་སྒྲ་ཇི་བཞིན་པར་འདོད་པ་བཀག་ཅིང་།

> དགོངས་པ་ངེས་པར་འགྲེལ་བའི་མདོ་ལས་ཆོས་ཐམས་ཅད་ངོ་བོ་ཉིད་མེད་པ་ཞེས་
> བྱ་བ་དེ་ལྟ་བུ་ལ་སོགས་པ་དེ་ཐམས་ཅད་ངེས་པའི་དོན་མ་ཡིན་པར་འགྱུར་ལ།

ཞེས་གསུངས་པས་ཡུམ་གྱི་མདོ་འཁོར་ལོ་གཉིས་པར་བཞེད་དོ།། [237] (344) འདི་དྲང་དོན་དུ་འཆད་ཚུལ་ནི་འཁོར་ལོ་དང་པོ་ལས་གཟུང་འཛིན་གསུངས་པ་དྲང་དོན་དུ་འགྲོ་ལུགས་དང་ཆེས་ཤིན་ཏུ་མི་འདྲ་སྟེ། འདི་ལྟར་མིག་གི་རྣམ་ཤེས་རྣམ་སྨིན་གྱི་བག་ཆགས་ཞེས་བྱ་བ་རང་གི་ས་བོན་སྨིན་པ་གང་ལས་བྱུང་བའི་ [84] ས་བོན་དང་སྣང་བ་ལ་དགོངས་ནས་མིག་དང་གཟུགས་ཀྱི་སྐྱེ་མཆེད་ཡོད་པར་གསུངས་པའི་དགོངས་པའི་དོན་ནི་ཐེག་དམན་ {556} གྱི་མདོ་དེ་དག་གི་བརྗོད་བྱའི་དོན་དུ་མི་རུང་ལ། གང་ལ་དགོངས་ནས་ངོ་བོ་ཉིད་མེད་པར་གསུངས་པའི་ངོ་བོ་ཉིད་མེད་ཚུལ་གསུམ་ནི་ཡུམ་གྱི་མདོའི་དོན་དུ་འཆད་པའི་ཕྱིར་དང་། ཕྱི་རོལ་དོན་གྱི་སྐྱེ་མཆེད་ཡོད་པ་ཐེག་དམན་གྱི་མདོའི་དོན་དུ་འཆད་ལ་ངོ་བོ་ཉིད་མེད་ཚུལ་མ་ཕྱེ་བར་དོན་དམ་པར་ངོ་བོ་ཡེ་མེད་དུ་འདོད་པར་ཡུམ་གྱི་མདོའི་དོན་ཡིན་པར་མི་འཆད་པའི་ཕྱིར་རོ།། དེས་ན་འདི་དག་གིས་ (39a) མ་ཕྱེ་བར་ཆོས་ཐམས་ཅད་དོན་དམ་པར་ངོ་བོ་ཉིད་མེད་པར་འཆད་པ་ཡུམ་གྱི་མདོའི་དོན་ཡིན་ཡང་དེ་དྲང་དོན་ཡིན་ཞེས་མི་འགྲེལ་གྱི་དེ་འདྲ་བ་དེ་སྒྲ་ཇི་བཞིན་པར་གཟུང་དུ་མི་རུང་བའི་ཕྱིར་དོན་དེ་[a] ཙམ་ཞིག་ཏུ་མ་ངེས་ཀྱི་ད་དུང་དེའི་དོན་བཤད་དགོས་པའི་སྒོ་ནས་དྲང་དོན་དུ་འཆད་དོ།། འཆད་ལུགས་ནི་ཀུན་བརྟགས་ཀྱི་ཆོས་རྣམས་རང་གི་མཚན་ཉིད་ཀྱིས་མ་གྲུབ་པས་དོན་དམ་པར་ངོ་བོ་མེད་པ་དང་། གཞན་དབང་གི་ཆོས་རྣམས་རྣམ་པར་དག་པའི་དམིགས་པའི་དོན་

[a] Se rva zhol (39a.1) misreads *do,* corrected in the Delhi GD zhol to *de.*

དམ་དེར་མ་གྲུབ་པས་དོན་དམ་པར་ངོ་བོ་ཉིད་མེད་པ་དང་ཡོངས་གྲུབ་ཀྱི་ཆོས་རྣམས་དོན་དམ་པ་ཡང་ཡིན་ལ་ཆོས་རྣམས་ཀྱི་བདག་གི་ངོ་བོར་མེད་པས་དོན་དམ་པར་ངོ་བོ་ཉིད་མེད་དོ་ཞེས་དེ་ལྟར་འགྲེལ་བའོ[a]།། དེའི་ཕྱིར་སྒྲ་ཇི་བཞིན་པའི་དོན་དུ་འཛིན་པ་ནི་ཡུམ་གྱི་མདོ་གང་གི་ཆེད་དུ་གསུངས་པའི་ [85] གདུལ་བྱར་མི་འདོད་པས་དེའི་ཆེད་དུ་བྱ་བའི་གདུལ་བྱ་ནི་མདོ་དེའི་དོན་དགོངས་འགྲེལ་གྱིས་བཀྲལ་བ་བཞིན་དུ་རྟོགས་པ་ལ་བཞེད་པས་འཁོར་ལོ་ཕྱི་མ་གཉིས་ཀྱི་དགོངས་པ་ནི་གཅིག་ཡིན་ནོ།། [239] (345) ཤིན་ཏུ་རྒྱས་པ་ལ་མོས་ཀྱང་སྒྲ་ཇི་བཞིན་པར་བཟུང་ནས་མདོ་དེའི་དོན་སྒྲ་ཇི་བཞིན་པའི་དོན་ཡིན་ནོ་ཞེས་སྨྲ་བ་བཀག་ནས་སྒྲ་ཇི་ {557} བཞིན་པའི་དོན་མིན་པའི་མདོ་ཡི[b]་དོན་ཡོད་པ་དེ་དགོངས་འགྲེལ་གྱིས་གསལ་བར་འཆད་པས་དེ་ལ་ངེས་དོན་དང་། ཡུམ་གྱི་མདོས་དོན་དེ་གསལ་བར་མ་ཕྱེ[c]་ཞིང་སྒྲ་ཇི་བཞིན་པར་གཟུང་དུ་མི་རུང་བས་དྲང་དོན་ཞེས་ཟེར་རོ།། སྒྲ་ཇི་བཞིན་པ་ལ་གནོད་བྱེད་ནི་སྒྲ་ཇི་བཞིན་པར་བཟུང་ན་མཚན་ཉིད་གསུམ་ག་རང་གི་མཚན་ཉིད་ཀྱིས་མ་གྲུབ་པར་འཛིན་ (39b) པའི་སྐུར་འདེབས་སུ་ཕུར་གསུངས་པ་དེ་ཉིད་དོ།། རྣམ་བཤད་རིགས་པ་ལས་ཀྱང་།

> ཤེས་རབ་ཀྱི་ཕ་རོལ་ཏུ་ཕྱིན་པ་ལས། ཆོས་ཐམས་ཅད་ནི་ངོ་བོ་ཉིད་མེད་པ་ཞེས་བྱ་བ་དེ་ལྟ་བུ་ལ་སོགས་པ་འདི་ལན་མང་དུ་བསྟན་ལ། ཡང་དེ་ཉིད་ལས་བཤད་པ་བྱང་ཆུབ་སེམས་དཔའི[d]་སྐྱོན་མེད་པ་ལ་འཇུག་པར་འདོད་པ་དང་། ཞེས་པ་ནས་སྡིག་པ་ཐམས་ཅད་སོ་སོར་བཤགས་པ་ལ་སོགས་པ་ཡང་བསྟན་པའོ།

ཞེས་པའི་བར་དུ་བཤད་ནས།

> གལ་ཏེ་ངོ་བོ་ཉིད་མེད་པ་ལ་སོགས་པའི་ཚིག་རྣམས་སྒྲ་ཇི་བཞིན་པ་ཁོ་ནའི་དོན་ཡིན་ན་འདི་ཐམས་ཅད་དང་འགལ་བར་འགྱུར་ཏེ། བླང་བར་བྱ་བ་རྣམས་ཅི་ཡང་མེད་པའི་ཕྱིར་རྒྱུ་འདི་ལས་འདི་ལྟ་ [86] བུར་འགྱུར་རོ་ཞེས་དེ་ལྟར་བླང་བ་ནི་རུང་བ་མ་ཡིན་ནོ།། ཡང་ན་དེ་ལྟར་བླང་བར་བྱ་བ་ནི་ ཅི་ཞིག་བླང་བར་སེམས[e]། དེ་ལྟ་བས་

a Zi ling sku 'bum (402.5): *pa'o.*

b Zi ling sku 'bum (402.9): *mdo'i.*

c Se rva zhol (39a.6) misreads *phyi,* corrected in the Delhi GD zhol to *phye.*

d Se rva zhol (39b.2): *dpa.'*

e The Peking of Vasubandhu's text (5562, vol. 113, 279.3.1) more sensibly reads *yang na de ltar blang bar bya ba ni ci zhig blang bar bya bar sems,* rather than *yang na de ltar blang bar*

> ན་ཆོག་དེ་རྣམས་ནི[a]སྒྲ་ཇི་བཞིན་གྱི་དོན་དུ་ངེས་པར་གཟུང་བར[b]མི་བྱའོ།། འོ་ན་ཅི་ཞེ་ན་དགོངས་པ་ཅན་ནོ།

ཞེས་ངོ་བོ་ཉིད་མེད་པ་ལ་སོགས་པ་སྒྲ་ཇི་བཞིན་པ་ཡིན་ན་ནང་འགལ་སྟོན་ནོ།། འགལ་ཚུལ་ནི་ངོ་བོ་ཉིད་མེད་ན་འདི་དང་འདི་ཐོབ་པར་འདོད་པས་ཡུམ་ལ་བསླབ་པར་བྱ་ཞེས་པའི་གླང་བྱ་དང་ཐོབ་འདོད་ཀྱི་འདོད་པ་དང་། སྦྱིན[c]པས་ལོངས་སྤྱོད་ཆེན་པོ་སོགས་སུ་འགྱུར་བའི་རྒྱུ་འབྲས་མི་{558}རུང་ཞེས་སྨྲ་སྡེ་གཙོ་ཆེར་གཞན་དབང་མི་རུང་ཞེས་བཞེད་དོ།། ཡུམ་གྱི་མདོ་ངེས་དོན་དུ་བཞེད་པ་རྣམས་ཀྱང་དེ་ཡང་འཇིག་རྟེན་གྱི་ཐ་སྙད་དུ་ཡིན་གྱི་དོན་དམ་པར་ནི་མ་ཡིན་ནོ། ཞེས་གླང་དོར་དང་རྒྱུ་འབྲས་སོགས་ལ་ཡང་ཡང་གསུངས་པ་ལྟར་འདོད་ཀྱི་སྤྱིར་ངོ་བོ་ཡི་མེད་དམ་ཐ་སྙད་དུ་མེད་པར་མི་འདོད་ལ་མདོ་ནས་རེ་རེ་ལ་མ་སྦྱར་ཡང་སྤྱི་ལ་སྦྱར་ཟིན་པས་(40a)དོན་དམ་པར་མེད་པ་སྒྲ་ཇི་བཞིན་པར་འདོད་ན་རྒྱུ་འབྲས་སོགས་མི་རུང་ཞེས་པའི་དོན་ཡིན་ཏེ། བྱང་ས་དང་བསྡུ་བ་ལས་ཀྱང་དོན་དམ་པར་ཐམས་ཅད་མ་གྲུབ་པ་སྐུར་འདེབས་སུ་བཤད་ཅིང་བཀག་པའི་ཕྱིར་རོ།། [241] (346) དོན་དམ་པ་ལ་བརྩམས་ནས་གསུངས་པའི་གསུང་རབ་ཀྱི་དྲང་ངེས་འབྱེད་པ་ནི་སྒྲ་ཇི་བཞིན་པ་ལ་རིགས་པའི་གནོད་པ་ཡོད་མེད་ལ་ཐུག་ལ་འདིར་གནོད་པ་བསྟན་པ་ལ་ནི། དོན་དམ་[87]པར་ཡོད་པ་ལེགས་པོར་འགོག་ཤེས་ཤིང་དེ་ལྟར་ཁེགས་པའི་དངོས་པོ་ལ་རྒྱུ་འབྲས་དང་འཆིང་གྲོལ་སོགས་ཚད་མས་གྲུབ་པར་འཇོག་ལེགས་པོར་ཤེས་ན་ལན་ཐེབས་སོ།། དེ་ལྟ་མིན་པར་མྱུ་གུའི་སྐྱེ་བ་ཚད་མས་གྲུབ་ན་དོན་དམ་པའི་སྐྱེ་བར་སོང་ནས་འཁྲུལ་ཤེས་ཀྱིས་སྐྱེ་བར་རློམས[d]པའི་ངོར་སྐྱེ་བས་ཀུན་རྫོབ་ཏུ་དེ་དག་ཐམས་ཅད་འཐད་དོ། ཞེས་སྨྲ་བས་ནི་གནོད་པ་སྤོང་མི་ནུས་པས་རྣལ་འབྱོར་སྤྱོད་པ་པ[e]རྣམས་ཀྱིས་བཀྲལ་བའི་ཚུལ་འདི་ལ་བརྟེན་ན་མཛེས་སོ།། དྲང་དོན་དུ་འགྲེལ་ལུགས་ལ་སྒོ་མང་པོ་ཡོད་ཀྱང་རྣལ་འབྱོར་སྤྱོད་པ་

bya ba ni **ci zhig blang bar bya ba ni** *ci zhig blang bar sems,* which is found in all editions of Dzong-ka-ba's text—Delhi NG dkra shis lhun po (557.5), Se rva zhol (39b.3), Zi ling sku 'bum (403.1), Peking (182.2.4), Sarnath gtsang (86.2), and Kalimpong (98.1). The extra phrase appears to be a scribal addition.

a The Peking of Vasubandhu's text (5562, vol. 113, 279.3.1): *de rnams* ***kyi*** *ni.*

b The Peking of Vasubandhu's text (5562, vol. 113, 279.3.1): *gzung* ***ba.***

c Se rva zhol (39b.5) misreads *spyin.*

d Zi ling sku 'bum (403.18): *rlom.*

e Zi ling sku 'bum (403.20): *ba;* see p. 373, footnote b.

པས་འཁོར་ལོ་གཉིས་པ་དྲང་དོན་དུ་འགྲེལ་ལུགས་ནི་དེ་ཁོ་ན་ལྟར་ཡིན་པར་བློ་དང་ལྡན་པ་རྣམས་ཀྱིས་ཤེས་པར་བྱོས་ཤིག། [242] (347) དགོངས་འགྲེལ་ལས་འཁོར་ལོ་རིམ་པ་གསུམ་གསུངས་ {559} པ་ནི་འཁོར་གྱི་འདུ་ཐབས་དང་སྟོན་པའི་སྐུ་ཚེའི་ཚིགས་ལ་སོགས་པས་འཇོག་པ་མིན་གྱི་བརྗོད་བྱའི་ངོས་ནས་ཡིན་ནོ།། དེ་ཡང་བདག་མེད་པའི་དོན་གཏན་ལ་འབེབས་པའི་དབང་དུ་བྱས་པ་སྟེ། དང་པོར་ཝཱ་ར་ཎཱ་སིར་གང་ཟག་གི་བདག་མེད་གསུངས་ཤིང་ཕུང་པོ་ལ་སོགས་པའི་ཆོས་ཅན་ཤས་གཅིག[a] མ་གཏོགས་པ་བདེན་པར་གྲུབ་པ་མ་བཀག་ཅིང་ (40b) བདེན་པར་ཡོད་པ་མང་དུ་གསུངས་པའི་སྐོར་གཅིག་གོ། དེ་ནས་རྣམ་དབྱེ་མ་མཛད་པར་ཕུང་སོགས་ཀྱི་ཆོས་ཐམས་ཅད་བདེན་པར་གྲུབ་པ་བཀག་པའི་སྐོར་གཅིག་གོ། དེ་ནས་དེ་ལ་ངོ་བོ་ཉིད་དང་པོ་རང་གི་མཚན་ཉིད་ཀྱིས་མ་གྲུབ་ཅིང་ [88] གཞན་གཉིས་རང་གི་མཚན་ཉིད་ཀྱིས་གྲུབ་པའི་ཚུལ་སོ་སོར་ཕྱེ་བའི་སྐོར་གཅིག་བྱུང་བས་དེའི་དབང་དུ་མཛད་པ་སྟེ། སྟོན་ཚུལ་དེ་དག་ལས་གཞན་དུ་སྟོན་པའི་མདོ་སྡེ་གཞན་རྣམས་འདིའི་དྲང་ངེས་དཔྱོད་པའི་གཞིར་འོང་དོན་མེད་དོ།། [243] (347) ཤེར་ཕྱིན་མན་ངག་ལས།

> མདོ་གང་དག་གི་དོན་སྒྲ་ཇི་བཞིན་པ་ཡིན་པ་དེ་ནི་ངེས་པའི་དོན་ཁོ་ནའོ།། དོན་དེ་ལ་ནི་དོན་གཉིས་པ་ཡོད་པ་མ་ཡིན་ཏེ་འདིའི་དོན་ངེས་པ་ཁོ་ནའོ་ཞེས་བྱ་བས་ན་ངེས་པའི་དོན་ཏོ།། གང་གིས་དོན་ངེས་ཤེ་ན་མདོ་དེ་ཉིད་དང་དེ་ལས་གཞན་པ་དང་གཉིས་ཀས་ཀྱང་ངོ་།

ཞེས་བཤད་དེ། དང་པོ་ནི་ལང་གཤེགས་དང་དགོངས་འགྲེལ་སོགས་ལ་འདོད་དེ་དེ་དག་གིས་ངོ་བོ་ཉིད་ཡོད་མེད་གསལ་བར་ཕྱེའོ་སྙམ་དུ་བསམས་སོ།། གཉིས་པ་ནི་བརྒྱད་སྟོང་པ་སོགས་ལ་འདོད་དེ་འདི་ལས་ངོ་བོ་ཉིད་ཡོད་མེད་དགོངས་འགྲེལ་བཞིན་དུ་ཕྱེ་བ་མེད་པ་ལ་བསམས་སོ།། གསུམ་པ་ནི་ཉི་ཁྲི་ལ་སོགས་ལ་འདོད་དེ་འདིའི་བྱམས་ཞུས་ཀྱི་ལེའུར་སྒྲ་ཇི་བཞིན་གྱི་དོན་དུ་ {560} ཞེན་པའི་ཕྱིན་ཅི་ལོག་སྤོང་བ་དྲང་དོན་གྱི་བཤད་པ་ཡོད་པ་དང་དགོངས་འགྲེལ་གྱིས་ཀྱང་འདིའི་དྲང་དོན་འགྲེལ་བས་སྙམ་དུ་བསམས་སོ།། བར་བ་ལ་བྱམས་ཞུས་ཀྱི་ལེའུ་མེད་པའི་གནད་ཀྱིས་སོ།། དེའི[b] ལྟར་ན་བྱམས་ཞུས་ཀྱི་ལེའུས[c]

---

a Zi ling sku 'bum (404.6): *zhig.*

b Zi ling sku 'bum (405.2): *de yi.*

c Se rva zhol (40b.6) and Kalimpong (101.2): *le'u;* Delhi NG dkra shis lhun po (560.1),

མཚན་ཉིད་གསུམ་རྣམ་པར་བཞག་པ་དང་དགོངས་འགྲེལ་གྱིས་བཤད་པ་གཉིས་དོན་གཅིག་ཏུ་བཞེད་དོ།། [244] (348) དེ་གཉིས་དོན་ (41a) གཅིག་ན་དེ[a]་ལྟར་འཐད་ཀྱང་ [89] དབྱིག་གཉེན་གྱིས་ཡུམ་གྱི་མདོ་ལས་ངོ་བོ་ཉིད་མེད་པ་སོགས་སུ་གསུངས་པ་དགོངས་འགྲེལ་ལ་སོགས་མདོ་སྡེ་གཞན་གྱིས་དྲང་དོན་དུ་བསྒྲུབས་ཤིང་། ཡུམ་གྱི་མདོ་ཉིད་ལ་ནི་སྒྲ་ཇི་བཞིན་པ་ལ་སྣ་ཕྱིའི་འགལ་བ་བསྟན་གྱི་བྱམས་ཞུས་ཀྱི་ལེའུས་མ་བསྒྲུབས་པས་སྐུ་མཆེད་ཀྱི་དགོངས་པ་མིན་ནོ།། འདི་གཉིས་འདྲ་མོ་ཡོད་པས་ཁྱད་པར་དབྱེ་དཀའ་བ་དང་དེ་གཉིས་དོན་གཅིག་ན་ཆོས་ཐམས་ཅད་དོན་དམ་པར་ངོ་བོ་ཉིད་མེད་ལ་ཐ་སྙད་དུ་ཡོད་པ་ཡུམ་གྱི་མདོའི་དགོངས་པའི་དོན་དུ་བཤད་དུ་མི་རུང་བ་རྣམ་རིག་པ་ལྟར་འགྱུར་ཞིང་དཔྱད་གཞི་ཡང་ཤིན་ཏུ་འགངས་ཆེ་སྟེ་དབུ་མ་པའི་སྐབས་སུ་བཤད་པར་བྱའོ།།

Zi ling sku 'bum (405.7), Peking (182.4.5), and Sarnath gtsang (88.18): *le'us;* the latter accords more with the instrumental in the similar construction in the next line *dgongs 'grel gyis.*

[a] Se rva zhol (41a.1) misreads *da,* corrected to *de* in the Delhi GD zhol.

Appendix 1. Commentaries on the *Sūtra Unraveling the Thought*

Jik-may-dam-chö-gya-tso (*Port of Entry,* 413.4) lists eight commentaries on the *Sūtra Unraveling the Thought* as found in earlier catalogues:

1. A small commentary (*'grel chung*) falsely attributed to Asaṅga, 220 stanzas long, translated by Shang Ye-s̄hay-day (*zhang ye shes sde*)

I take this to be the very short commentary entitled *āryasaṃdhinirmocanabhāṣya* (*'phags pa dgongs pa nges par 'grel pa'i rnam par bshad pa;* Peking 5481, vol. 104, 1.1.1-7.5.1; T3981). Bu-d̄ön in his history (E. Obermiller, *History of Buddhism (Chos-ḥbyung) by Bu-ston* [Heidelberg: Heft, 1932; Tokyo: Suzuki Research Foundation, n.d.], 140) attributes it to Asaṅga.[a]

2. A great commentary (*'grel chen*) falsely attributed to Asaṅga, in forty sections (*bam po*)

This is difficult to identify. D̄zong-ka-b̄a (156) cryptically makes reference to a *Great Commentary:*

> the explanation in a certain *Great Commentary* on the *Sūtra Unraveling the Thought* is not the thought of that sūtra when that commentary says:
>
> > Imputational factors do not exist as either of the two truths [ultimate or conventional]. The dependent-arisings of other-powered natures of apprehended-objects and apprehending-subjects [which are different substantial entities] exist conventionally [and do not exist ultimately] like magical creations. The thoroughly established nature is the ultimate, and its existence in the manner of naturelessness also ultimately exists.
>
> [This is not the thought of the *Sūtra Unraveling the Thought,* because] it contradicts the proof of no external objects in Asaṅga's *Summary of the Great Vehicle*—that is made within citing the *Sūtra Unraveling the Thought*—and thereupon the explanation of external and internal objects and subjects [which are different substantial entities] as imputational factors. It also contradicts Asaṅga's *Grounds of Bodhisattvas* and his *Compendium of Ascertainments.* Furthermore, a passage of [Dharmakīrti's] *Ascertainment [of Prime cognition]* is cited in that [above-

---

[a] For an English translation, see John C. Powers, *Two Commentaries on the Samdhinirmocana-sutra by Asanga and Jnanagarbha* (Lewiston, N.Y.: Edward Mellon, 1992).

> mentioned *Great Commentary*]. Hence, one [scholar's][a] saying that it was written by Asaṅga is a case of a great absence of analysis.[b] In his *Compendium of Ascertainments* Asaṅga quotes, except for the introductory chapter of the *Sūtra Unraveling the Thought,* most of the remaining chapters and settles well the difficult points; hence, there also does not appear to be any need for this master's [that is, Asaṅga's] composing a separate commentary.

This *Great Commentary on the "Sūtra Unraveling the Thought"* is not the one by Wonch'uk but, as S̄er-s̄hül (*Notes,* 29b.4) reports, may be one that Bu-d̄ön says is by a Tibetan and speculates is by L̄u-gyel-tsen (*klu'i rgyal mtshan*). S̄er-s̄hül identifies L̄u-gyel-tsen as the Great Translator J̄ok-ro.[c] Jik-may-dam-chö-gya-tso (*Port of Entry,* 414.3) also cites the Catalogue of the *ldan dkar* Palace Collection (*pho brang stod thang ldan dkar gyi chos 'gyur ro cog gi dkar chags:* Peking 5851, vol. 145; Dharma, 4364; compiled early in the ninth century by dpal brtsegs rakṣita, nam mkha'i snying po, and others,[d] which refers to an extensive commentary by L̄u-gyel-tsen that is in 22,000 stanzas, that is, forty sections (*bam po*); so by sheer similarity in length, I consider it somewhat safe to identify item 2 as by L̄u-gyel-tsen, the Great Translator J̄ok-ro. This is the *Explanation of the "Sūtra Unraveling the Thought"* (Peking 5845, vol. 144, 191.1.1-vol. 145, 89.1.1; Tohoku 4358; *'phags pa dgongs 'grel nges par 'grel pa'i mdo'i rnam par bshad pa, ārya-saṃdhinirmocana-sūtrasya-vyākhyāna;* also Delhi: Delhi Karmapae Choedhey, 1985, vol. 205).

I have not found the reference to L̄u-gyel-tsen in Bu-d̄ön's history, but Ernst Steinkellner ("Who Is Byaṅ chub rdzu 'phrul?: Tibetan and non-Tibetan Commentaries on the *Saṃdhinirmocanasūtra*—A Survey of the Literature," *Berliner Indologische Studien* 4, no. 5 [1989]: 238-241), cites and translates such a passage in Bu-d̄ön's *Catalogue of Translated Doctrine* (*chos bsgyur dkar chag*).

A long commentary is attributed to Jang-chup-dzü-trül (*byang chub rdzu 'phrul*) in the *sde dge* edition, and thus it is also sometimes attributed to the

---

[a] D̄zong-ka-b̄a most likely draws this critique of an unnamed scholar from Bu-d̄ön's *Catalogue of the Translated Doctrine* (*chos bsgyur dkar chag*), which makes this very point to show that the text is not by Asaṅga (see Ernst Steinkellner, "Who Is Byaṅ chub rdzu 'phrul?: Tibetan and non-Tibetan Commentaries on the *Saṃdhinirmocanasūtra*—A Survey of the Literature," *Berliner Indologische Studien* 4, no. 5 [1989]: 239). Bu-d̄ön also does not identify who the scholar is; none of D̄zong-ka-b̄a's commentators does either.

[b] Dharmakīrti, being an indirect student of Dignāga, who was a direct disciple of Asaṅga's half-brother Vasubandhu, is clearly post-Asaṅga, and thus Asaṅga could not have cited him.

[c] *cog ro lo chen.* The Treasure Revealer Karma L̄ing-b̄a (*gter ston kar ma gling pa,* 1356-1405) is considered to be a reincarnation of J̄ok-ro L̄u-gyel-tsen; see Dudjom Rinpoche, *The Nyingma School of Tibetan Buddhism* (Boston: Wisdom, 1991), 1, 800-801.

[d] Edited and published with an index in: Marcelle Lalou, "Les Textes Bouddhiques au Temps du Roi Khri-sroṅ-lde-bcan," *Journal Asiatique* 241, no. 3 (1953): 313-353.

eighth-century Tibetan King Tri-s̄ong-de-d̄zen (*khri srong lde brtsan,* 742-797), since Tri-s̄ong-de-d̄zen was also known by that name. However, both attributions are questionable in the light of Jik-may-dam-chö-gya-tso's citation (*Port of Entry,* 414.2) of a passage from the commentary that refers to Jang-chup-dzü-trül:

> The divisions of those characters are to be viewed in accordance with what appears in the *Validity of the True Word* (*bka' yang dag pa'i tshad ma;* Peking 5839) written by the glorious god emperor Jang-chup-dzü-trül, sovereign of true lords (*dbang phyag dam pa'i mnga' bdag dpal lha btsan po byang chub rdzu 'phrul*).

Jik-may-dam-chö-gya-tso's point is that this text could not have been written by Jang-chup-dzü-trül, that is, Tri-s̄ong-de-d̄zen, and indeed though he **might** cite his own text, he most likely would not have done so in such an exalted manner. (Even with the proviso that the author is not Jang-chup-dzü-trül, Jik-may-dam-chö-gya-tso himself [*Port of Entry,* 423.2] backs off equating the commentary to which D̄zong-ka-b̄a refers with that in the *sde dge,* and so forth.) Also, Steinkellner (Who Is Byaṅ chub rdzu 'phrul?, 238-241, and summary in John C. Powers, *Hermeneutics and Tradition in the Saṃdhinirmocana-sūtra* [Leiden, Netherlands: Brill, 1993], 21) points out that the work does not appear "in the two old inventories we have of the king's works....And Bu ston says nothing about Byaṅ chub rdzu 'phrul, the king, as its possible author."

A-ku L̄o-drö-gya-tso reports that (1) even though he found in the two-volume commentary "possible equivalents" (*dod thub*) of D̄zong-ka-b̄a's citation (or paraphrase?), he did not find the exact passage and (2) although the two-volume commentary cites a passage from the *Ascertainment* (presumably Dharmakīrti's *Ascertainment of Prime Cognition*), beginning *rjes su dpag par bya ba la yod pa nyid,* it does not mention that text by name.[a] He draws no conclusion from these points; thus, it may be that he is not challenging the basic point that D̄zong-ka-b̄a is indeed referring to this two-volume commentary. Given that when D̄zong-ka-b̄a refers to the *Ascertainment,* he is using the very argument employed by Bu-d̄ön to prove that this text was not written by Asaṅga, it is likely that D̄zong-ka-b̄a was indeed referring to that two-volume commentary and was merely paraphrasing instead of quoting that text, something he frequently does.

Jik-may-dam-chö-gya-tso (*Port of Entry,* 411.4) cites the possible passages in (L̄u-gyel-tsen's) *Explanation of the "Sūtra Unraveling the Thought"* from which D̄zong-ka-b̄a may have drawn his "citation" but points out that these

[a] A-ku L̄o-drö-gya-tso also points out that Jam-ȳang-shay-b̄a's *Notes on (D̄zong-ka-b̄a's) "The Essence of Eloquence"* identifies the passage in question as from Vasubandhu's *Commentary on the "Twenty-Five Thousand Stanza Perfection of Wisdom Sūtra,"* but he says that Jam-ȳang-shay-b̄a's text is corrupt at this point. I take this to be a polite way of disagreeing with him.

passages do not explain that other-powered natures exist conventionally and that thoroughly established natures exist ultimately. Rather, they say that other-powered natures exist as conventional truths and that thoroughly established natures exist as ultimate truths. Still, it seems likely that item 2 is the commentary by Ḹu-gyel-tsen, falsely attributed to Jang-chup-dzü-trül, who may be the same person as King Tri-s̄ong-de-d̄zen.

For other, lost commentaries on the *Sūtra Unraveling the Thought,* see the article by Steinkellner cited just above.

3. A condensed commentary (*bsdus 'grel*) falsely attributed to Asaṅga, in one section (?)

4. A great commentary (*ṭīk chen*) in sixty sections (?)

5. An explanation of the "Questions of Maitreya Chapter" by Jñānagarbha in two sections and seventy stanzas

This is the *Small Explanation of the Superior Maitreya Chapter of the "Superior Sūtra Unraveling the Thought"* (*'phags pa dgongs pa nges par 'grel pa'i mdo las 'phags pa byams pa'i le'u nyi tshe'i bshad pa, ārya-saṃdhinirmocana-sūtre-ārya-maitreyakevala-parivarta-bhāṣya;* Peking 5535, vol. 109, 196-211; T4033.[a]

6. A commentary (*ṭīkka*) translated from Chinese in nine sections

I presume that this is a commentary by Paramārtha, frequently cited by Wonch'uk (see item 7) sometimes approvingly and sometimes not; it may be that the text is known only through Wonch'uk's commentary on the sūtra.

7. A great commentary (*'grel chen*) by Wonch'uk in seventy-four sections

This is the *Extensive Commentary on the "Superior Sūtra Unraveling the Thought"* (*'phags pa dgongs pa zab mo nges par 'grel pa'i mdo'i rgya cher 'grel pa; ārya-gambhīra-saṃdhinirmocana-sūtra-ṭīkā;* Peking 5517, vol. 106, entire; Tohoku 4016; also Delhi: Delhi Karmapae Choedhey, Gyalwae Sungrab Partun Khang, 1985, *mdo 'grel,* vol. *ti* [118]). This erudite commentary was translated into Tibetan from Chinese; see p. 39ff.

8 A great commentary (*'grel chen*) by the Chinese master Dzok-s̄el (*rdzogs gsal*) in seventy-five sections

Jik-may-dam-chö-gya-tso mentions that Bu-d̄ön calls for analysis as to whether this and item 7 are the same; *rdzogs gsal* is the Tibetan translation of the Korean Wonch'uk (Chinese: *Yüan tse*), which is often rendered in Tibetan transliteration as *wen tshigs.*

[a] For a translation, see John C. Powers, *Jñānagarbha's Commentary on Just the Maitreya Chapter from the Saṃdhinirmocana-Sūtra: Study, Translation and Tibetan Text* (New Delhi: Indian Council of Philosophical Research, 1998).

Appendix 2. Chinese Translations of the *Sūtra Unraveling the Thought*

Jik-may-dam-chö-gya-tso (*Port of Entry,* 136.1) identifies the *Sūtra Unraveling the Thought* explained by Wonch'uk as having eight chapters:

1. Introduction
2. The Character of the Ultimate Truth
3. The Character of Mind, Sentience, and Consciousness
4. The Characters of All Phenomena
5. The Character of Naturelessness
6. Revealing Yoga
7. The Grounds and Perfections
8. Achieving the Activities of a One Gone Thus

According to Wonch'uk, the second through fifth are what are to be analyzed; the sixth is the yogic path, and the last is the fruit to be attained. Jik-may-dam-chö-gya-tso reports that the second chapter of Wonch'uk's rendering corresponds to the first four chapters of the Tibetan translation of the sūtra and that the remainder of Wonch'uk's version corresponds to the fifth through tenth chapters of the Tibetan translation of the sūtra. Thus, the Tibetan version of the text has an introduction and ten chapters, whereas Wonch'uk's has eight chapters, with the introduction being counted as a chapter.

According to Jik-may-dam-chö-gya-tso (*Port of Entry,* 134.5, citing the description in Wonch'uk's *Great Commentary*), there are four translations of the *Sūtra Unraveling the Thought* into Chinese resulting in four different Chinese editions:[a]

1. The *rnam par 'grol ba'i mdo* in two fascicles (*bam po;* Chinese: *chüan*), put together by the Indian professor (*mkhan po*) Guṇabhadra (*yon tan bzang po*) during the Liu Sung Dynasty (*rgya rje song*) in 443-445 (*Taishō* 678, vol. 16), which consist of only the last two chapters of the eight-chaptered *Sūtra Unraveling the Thought* as listed above:

    7. The Grounds and Perfections
    8. Achieving the Activities of a One Gone Thus

2. The *zab mo rnam par 'grol ba'i mdo* with eleven chapters translated by the Indian master Bodhiruci (*bo de le'u ci*) during the latter Ling Dynasty (*rgya rje 'gris* [?] *phyi ma*) in 514 (*Taishō* 675, vol. 16). The section on the ultimate truth—which in Wonch'uk's version is one chapter (chap. 2)—is

[a] The specific years are from John C. Powers, *Hermeneutics and Tradition in the Saṃdhinirmocana-sūtra* (Leiden, Netherlands: Brill, 1993), 5-6.

treated in this edition as four chapters, whereby, with the other seven, it has eleven chapters:

1. Introduction
2-5. The Character of the Ultimate Truth
6. The Character of Mind, Sentience, and Consciousness
7. The Characters of All Phenomena
8. The Character of Naturelessness
9. Revealing Yoga
10. The Grounds and Perfections
11. Achieving the Activities of a One Gone Thus

3. The *tshigs nges par 'grel pa zhes bya ba'i mdo* in one fascicle, translated by the Indian master Paramārtha (*yang dag bden pa*) during the Ch'en Dynasty (*rgya rje tshin*) in 557 (*Taishō* 677, 679, vol. 16). It has four chapters, consisting of the section on the ultimate which, as in Bodhiruci's version (chaps. 2-5), is divided into four chapters:

1-4. The Character of the Ultimate Truth

4. The *dgongs pa zab mo nges par 'grel pa zhes bya ba'i mdo* in five fascicles translated by the Tripiṭaka master Hsüan-tsang (*hyan tsang*) during the T'ang dynasty (*thang*) in 647 (*Taishō* 676, vol. 16). It has eight chapters, as listed above for Wonch'uk's commentary:

1. Introduction
2. The Character of the Ultimate Truth
3. The Character of Mind, Sentience, and Consciousness
4. The Characters of All Phenomena
5. The Character of Naturelessness
6. Revealing Yoga
7. The Grounds and Perfections
8. Achieving the Activities of a One Gone Thus

Jik-may-dam-chö-gya-tso mentions (but does not identify) a history of China that speaks of the second and the fourth translations as being in five fascicles and that also possibly refers to the other two when it speaks of two extracts (*khol phyung rnam gnyis*). He says that of the two versions of the *Sūtra Unraveling the Thought*—an extensive one the length of a hundred thousand stanzas (that is no longer extant, if it ever was) and a brief one the length of five thousand stanzas—the one studied in Tibet is the latter.

Backnotes

NOTES TO THE PREFACE

1 *sngags rim chen mo / rgyal ba khyab bdag rdo rje 'chang chen po'i lam gyi rim pa gsang ba kun gyi gnad rnam par phye ba; Great Exposition of the Stages of Mantra / The Stages of the Path to a Conqueror and Pervasive Master, a Great Vajradhara: Revealing All Secret Topics;* Peking 6210, vol. 161.

2 *lam rim 'bring/ lam rim chung ngu; Medium Exposition of the Stages of the Path/ Small Exposition of the Stages of the Path To Enlightenment;* Peking 6002, vol. 152-53.

NOTES TO PART ONE, CHAPTER 1

3 London: Wisdom, 1983.

4 Wilfred Cantwell Smith, "The Modern West in the History of Religion," *Journal of the American Academy of Religion,* 52, no. 1 (March 1984), 3.

5 Ibid., 5.

6 Ibid., 5.

NOTES TO PART ONE, CHAPTER 2

7 Stephen Batchelor, *The Tibet Guide* (London: Wisdom, 1987), 145.

8 *tshad ma rnam 'grel, pramāṇavarttika;* Peking 5709, vol. 130.

9 *chos mngon pa'i mdzod, abhidharmakośa;* Peking 5590, vol. 115.

10 *'dul ba'i mdo, vinayasūtra;* Peking 5619, vol. 123.

11 My brief rehearsal of his works is drawn from Elizabeth Napper, *Dependent-Arising and Emptiness* (London: Wisdom, 1989), 6-7.

12 *lam rim chen mo;* Peking 6001, vol. 152. D̄zong-ka-b̄a makes reference to this text in the section on the Autonomy School, "I have explained this mode of reasoning at length elsewhere."

13 *dbu ma rtsa ba'i tshig le'ur byas pa shes rab ces bya ba, prajñānāmamūlamadhyamakakārikā;* Peking 5224, vol. 95.

14 *rigs pa'i rgya mtsho;* Peking 6153, vol. 156.

15 *skyes bu gsum gyi nyams su blang ba'i byang chub lam gyi rim pa;* Peking 6002, vols. 152-153.

16 This material on the request for the teaching is drawn from W̄el-mang Ḡön-chok-gyel-tsen's *Notes on (Ḡön-chok-jik-may-w̄ang-b̄o's) Lectures,* 381.5-382.3; for a partial listing of the transmission of *The Essence of Eloquence* within Ge-luk-b̄a, see the same text, 382.3-384.4.

17 W̄el-mang Ḡön-chok-gyel-tsen's *Notes on (Ḡön-chok-jik-may-w̄ang-b̄o's) Lectures,* 382.1.

18 In his *Explanation of "Freedom from Extremes through Understanding All Tenets": Ocean of Good Explanations (grub mtha' kun shes nas mtha' bral grub pa zhes bya ba'i bstan bcos rnam part bshad pa legs bshad kyi rgya mtsho)* (Thimphu, Bhutan: Kun-bzang-stobs rgyal, 1976).

19 *zab mo stong pa nyid rab tu gsal bar byed pa'i bstan bcos skal bzang mig 'byed.* The work has been translated in its entirety in José Ignacio Cabezón, *A Dose of Emptiness* (Albany, N.Y.: State University of New York Press, 1992).

20 Cabezón, *Dose of Emptiness,* 52.

21 *legs bshad snying po'i dka' 'grel bstan pa'i sgron me.*

22 *rje btsun thams cad mkhyen pa'i gsung 'bum las drang nges rnam 'byed kyi dka' 'grel dgongs pa'i don rab tu gsal bar byed pa'i sgron me.*

23 *drang nges rnam 'byed kyi spyi don rgol ngan tshar gcod rin po che'i phreng ba.*

24 *drang ba dang nges pa'i rnam par 'byed pa legs bshad snying po zhes bya ba'i mtha' dpyod padma dkar po'i phreng ba.*

25 *General Meaning of (D̄zong-ka-b̄a's) "Differentiating the Interpretable and the Definitive": The Essence of Eloquence, Garland of White Lotuses (drang nges rnam 'byed kyi spyi don legs par bshad pa'i snying po padma dkar po'i 'phreng ba)*; and *Decisive Analysis of (D̄zong-ka-b̄a's) "Differentiating the Interpretable and the Definitive" (drang nges rnam 'byed kyi mtha dpyod).*

26 *drang ba dang nges pa'i don rnam par 'byed pa'i mtha' dpyod 'khrul bral lung rigs bai dūr dkar pa'i gan mdzod skal bzang re ba kun skong.*

27 See the table of contents (most likely by Gene Smith) to the Ngawang Gelek edition.

28 *dge ldan thun mong ma yin pa drang ba dang nges pa'i don rnam par phye ba'i bstan bcos legs bshad snying po'i rgya cher bshad pa dang nges bzhi 'dril.*

29 *drang ba dang nges pa'i don rnam par phye ba gsal bar byed pa legs bshad snying po'i don mtha' dag rnam par 'byed pa'i bstan bcos legs bshad snying po'i 'jug ngogs.*

30 *drang nges rnam 'byed kyi zin bris zab don gsal ba'i sgron me.*

[31] *drang nges legs bshad snying po'i dgongs don gsal bar byed pa'i me long.*

NOTES TO PART ONE, CHAPTER 3

[32] Chap. 7; Étienne Lamotte, *Saṃdhinirmocanasūtra: L'Explication des mystères* (Louvain: Université de Louvain, 1935), 70 [10], and 196; and John C. Powers, *Wisdom of Buddha: Saṁdhinirmocana Sūtra* (Berkeley, Calif.: Dharma, 1995), 105-106.

[33] Chap. 7; Lamotte, *Saṃdhinirmocana,* 72-73 [13-14], and 197-198; and Powers, *Wisdom of Buddha,* 111.

[34] Janice D. Willis's translation of the material that Ḏzong-ka-ḇa is summarizing is found in her *On Knowing Reality: The Tattvārtha Chapter of Asaṅga's Bodhisattvabhūmi* (New York: Columbia University Press, 1979; reprint, Delhi: Motilal Banarsidass, 1982), 167 (middle) through 170 (middle).

[35] *theg bsdus, mahāyānasaṃgraha.* For a French translation and edited Chinese and Tibetan texts, see Étienne Lamotte, *La somme du grand véhicule d'Asaṅga,* reprint, 2 vols. Publications de l'Institute Orientaliste de Louvain, 8 (Louvain: Université de Louvain, 1973).

[36] *Annotations,* 110.3.

[37] Chap. 7; Lamotte, *Saṃdhinirmocana,* 79 [17-18], and 199; and Powers, *Wisdom of Buddha,* 115-117.

[38] *rgyud gzhan grub pa zhes bya ba'i rab tu byed pa, saṃtānāntarasiddhināmaprakaraṇa.*

NOTES TO PART ONE, CHAPTER 4

[39] *'phags pa dgongs pa nges par 'grel pa'i mdo'i rgya cher 'grel pa, āryagambhirasṃdhinirmocanasūtraṭīkā;* Peking 5517, vol. 116.

[40] For a brief discussion of the three phases, see Oh Hyung-keun, "The Yogācāra-Vijñaptimātratā Studies of Silla Monks," in *Assimilation of Buddhism in Korea: Religious Maturity and Innovation in the Silla Dynasty,* ed. Lewis R. Lancaster and C. S. Yu (Berkeley, Calif.: Asian Humanities Press, 1991), 106.

[41] The Tibetan translation of his name is *yang dag bden pa.*

[42] See Diana Y. Paul, *Philosophy in Sixth Century China: Paramārtha's "Evolution of Consciousness,"* (Stanford, Calif.: Stanford University Press, 1984).

[43] Robert E. Buswell, trans., Buswell, Robert E., trans. "Wonch'uk (613-696): Memorial Inscription," unpublished manuscript, 2.

[44] Chinese: *Ch'eng wei-shih lun.* There are translations into French and English; see the Bibliography.

[45] The biographical sketch of Hsüan-tsang is drawn from Stanley Weinstein, . "A Biographical Study of Tz'u-en." *Monumenta Nipponica* 15, nos. 1-2 (1959-1960): 119-121; Stanley Weinstein, *Buddhism under the T'ang* (Cambridge, England: Cambridge University Press, 1987), 24-31; and Kenneth K. S. Ch'en, *Buddhism in China: A Historical Survey* (Princeton, N.J.: Princeton University Press, 1964), 235-238, 320-321.

[46] See Samuel Beal, *Buddhist Records of the Western World: Translated from the Chinese of Hiuen Tsiang (A.D. 629)* (London: Kegan Paul; reprint, New York: Paragon, 1968; reprint, Delhi: Motilal Banarsidass, 1981; originally published 1884).

[47] Ch'en, *Buddhism in China,* 237.

[48] See Thomas Waters, *On Yuan Chwang's Travels in India* (Delhi: Munshi Ram Manohar Lal, 1961); and Beal, *Buddhist Records of the Western World.*

[49] Weinstein, *Buddhism under the T'ang,* 31.

[50] Ibid., 121.

[51] Oh Hyung-keun, "Yogācāra-Vijñaptimātratā Studies of Silla Monks," 107.

[52] Ibid., 1.

[53] For references to Nagao and Hatani Ryotai, see Shōtarō Iida, "The Three Stūpas of Ch'ang An," *Papers of the First International Conference on Korean Studies,* Seoul: Academy of Korean Studies, 1980, 489.

[54] Ibid., 146.

[55] Ibid., 486-488. The same opinion is found in Peter H. Lee, ed., *Sourcebook of Korean Civilization* (New York: Columbia University Press, 1993), 166-167.

[56] Lee, *Sourcebook of Korean Civilization,* 167.

[57] For discussion of how the text came to be translated by Fa-ch'eng, see Shōtarō Iida, "A Mukung-hwa in Ch'ang-an—A Study of the Life and Works of Wonch'uk (613-696), with Special Interest in the Korean contributions to the Development of Chinese and Tibetan Buddhism," in *Proceedings, International Symposium, Commemorating the 30th Anniversary of Korean Liberation* (Seoul: National Academy of Sciences, Republic of Korea, 1975), 243-246; and "The

Three Stūpas of Ch'ang An," 490; Inaba Shōju, "On Chos-grub's Translation of the *Chieh-shen-mi-ching-shu,"* in *Buddhist Thought and Asian Civilization*, ed. Leslie S. Kawamura and Keith Scott (Berkeley, Calif.: Dharma, 1977), 105-113; "Daibankoku Daitoku Sanzō hosshi Shamon Hō jō no Kenkyū" (researches on Fa-ch'eng, translator of Wonch'uk's commentary on the *Saṃdhinirmocana-sūtra*), *Tōhō Gukuhō*, 38 (1967): 133-198 and 39 (1968): 119-222; and John C. Powers "Accidental Immortality:: How Wonch'uk Became the Author of the *Great Chinese Commentary*," *Journal of the International Association of Buddhist Studies*, 15, no. 1 (1992): 95-103.

58 For the date, see Gareth Sparham in collaboration with Shōtarō Iida, *Ocean of Eloquence: Tsong kha pa's Commentary on the Yogācāra Doctrine of Mind* (Albany, N.Y.: State University of New York Press, 1993), 17-18.

59 Ernst Steinkellner, "Who Is Byaṅ chub rdzu 'phrul? Tibetan and Non-Tibetan Commentaries on the *Saṃdhinomocanasūtra*—A Survey of the Literature," *Berliner Indologische Studien* 4, no. 5 (1989): 235.

60 The biographical material is drawn from Cyrus R. Stearns, *The Buddha from Dol po and His Fourth Council of the Buddhist Doctrine* (Ann Arbor, Mich.: University Microfilms, 1996), 14-64.

61 *byang chub sems dpa'i spyod pa la 'jug pa, bodhi[sattva]caryāvatāra;* P5272, vol. 99.

62 Stearns, *The Buddha from Dol po*, 20.

63 Ibid., 21.

64 Ibid., 23-24.

65 Ibid., 24.

66 Ibid., 26.

67 Ibid., 34.

68 Ibid., 34.

69 Ibid., 45.

70 Ibid., 51.

71 Ibid., 51; brackets mine.

72 Ibid., 120.

73 Ibid., 52.

74 Ibid., 53.

75 Ibid., 58.

76 Ibid., 63.

77 Ibid., 64.

78 Ibid., 89.

79 Ibid., 148.

80 Shay-rap-gyel-tsen's *Ocean of Definitive Meaning*, 209.4

81 See also Powers, *Wisdom of Buddha*, 255.

82 *Ocean of Definitive Meaning*, 210.1.

83 Ibid., 211.4.

84 Stearns, *The Buddha from Dol po*, 154; brackets are Stearns's.

85 *theg pa mtha' dag gi don gsal bar byed pa grub pa'i mtha' rin po che'i mdzod* (Gangtok, Sikkim: Dodrup Chen Rinpoche, 1969?), 260.

86 Ibid., 267.

87 Ibid., 266.

88 Stearns, *The Buddha from Dol po*, 151.

NOTES TO PART TWO, PROLOGUE

89 Bel-jor-hlün-drup's *Lamp for the Teaching*, 6.3.

90 Jik-may-dam-chö-gya-tso's *Port of Entry*, 56.1.

91 Jay-dzün Chö-gyi-gyel-tsen's *General-Meaning Commentary*, 4b.2.

92 Ibid., 4b.2.

93 Da-drin-rap-den's *Annotations*, 5.3.

94 Ibid., 5.3.

95 Gung-tang's *Difficult Points*, 24.2.

96 Ibid., 24.2.

97 Ibid., 24.4.

98 Ibid., 24.10.

99 Ibid., 24.10, and Ser-shul, 12b.

100 Jay-dzün Chö-gyi-gyel-tsen's *General-Meaning Commentary*, 5b.1.

NOTES TO PART TWO, CHAPTER 1

101 Da-drin-rap-den's *Annotations*, 8.5: *'khor ba 'khor sa.*

102 Ibid., 8.6.

103 Ibid., 8.6; and Gung-tang's *Annotations*, 13.5.

104 Gung-tang's *Annotations*, 13.5.

105 Gung-tang's *Difficult Points*, 76.10.

106 Da-drin-rap-den's *Annotations*, 9.2.

107 Ibid., 9.2.

108 Ibid., 9.3.

109 Ibid., 9.3.

110 Ibid., 9.3.

111 Ibid., 9.4.

112 Ibid., 9.4.

113 Ibid., 9.4.

114 Ibid., 9.4.

115 Da-drin-rap-den's *Annotations*, 9.5.

116 A-ku Lo-drö-gya-tso's *Precious Lamp*, 55.4.

[117] Gung-tang's *Annotations,* 13.7.

[118] D̄a-drin-rap-d̄en's *Annotations,* 9.5; and Gung-tang's *Annotations,* 14.1.

[119] Gung-tang's *Annotations,* 14.1.

[120] Ibid., 14.1.

[121] D̄a-drin-rap-d̄en's *Annotations,* 9.6.

[122] Ibid., 10.4.

[123] Dön-drup-gyel-tsen's *Four Intertwined Commentaries,* 41.5.

[124] Ibid.

[125] D̄a-drin-rap-d̄en's *Annotations,* 10.6.

[126] Ibid., 10.6.

[127] Ibid., 10.6.

NOTES TO PART TWO, CHAPTER 2

[128] D̄a-drin-rap-d̄en's *Annotations,* 11.6.

[129] Ibid., 11.6.

[130] Chap. 7; Étienne Lamotte, *Saṃdhinirmocanasūtra: L'Explication des mystères* (Louvain: Université de Louvain, 1935), 67 [3], and 193; Dön-drup-gyel-tsen's *Four Intertwined Commentaries,* 6.6-7.1.

[131] *rnam par gtan la dbab pa bsdu ba, viniścayasaṃgrahaṇī;* Peking 5539, vol. 111, 71.2.8; Tokyo *sde dge, sems tsam,* vol. 9 (*zi*), 8.4.5.

[132] D̄a-drin-rap-d̄en's *Annotations,* 12.4.

[133] Ibid., 12.3.

[134] This is cited also by Wonch'uk (Peking 5517, vol. 106, chap. 5, 130.4.8). For the Sanskrit, see p. 371, footnote b. For other translations, see Stefan Anacker, *Seven Works of Vasubandhu* (Delhi: Motilal Banarsidass, 1984), 188; and Thomas A. Kochumuttom, *A Buddhist Doctrine of Experience* (Delhi: Motilal Banarsidass, 1982), 258.

[135] S̄er-s̄hül's *Notes,* 14b.5; and D̄a-drin-rap-d̄en's *Annotations,* 12.4.

[136] Jam-ȳang-shay-b̄a's *Great Exposition of the Interpretable and the Definitive,* 45.4; and S̄er-s̄hül's *Notes,* 14b.5.

[137] D̄a-drin-rap-d̄en's *Annotations,* 12.5.

[138] Gung-ru Chö-jung's *Garland of White Lotuses,* 18b.2; and A-ku L̄o-drö-gya-tso's *Precious Lamp,* 70.4.

[139] D̄a-drin-rap-d̄en's *Annotations,* 13.1.

[140] Ibid., 13.2.

[141] A-ku L̄o-drö-gya-tso's *Precious Lamp,* 91.1.

[142] Chap. 7; Lamotte, *Saṃdhinirmocana,* 67-68 [44], and 194; Dön-drup-gyel-tsen's *Four Intertwined Commentaries,* 7.1-7.2; and John C. Powers, *Wisdom of Buddha: Saṁdhinirmocana Sūtra* (Berkeley, Calif.: Dharma, 1995), 99.

[143] S̄er-s̄hül's *Notes,* 15b.1. He glosses *dmigs 'byed pa* with *gsal kha phye ba.*

[144] D̄a-drin-rap-d̄en's *Annotations,* 15.6.

[145] Jam-ȳang-shay-b̄a's *Great Exposition of the Interpretable and the Definitive,* 67.3; and S̄er-s̄hül's *Notes,* 18b.6.

[146] Jam-ȳang-shay-b̄a's *Great Exposition of the Interpretable and the Definitive,* 67.3; and S̄er-s̄hül's *Notes,* 18b.6.

[147] D̄a-drin-rap-d̄en's *Annotations,* 16.1.

[148] Jik-may-dam-chö-gya-tso's *Port of Entry,* 178.4; and D̄a-drin-rap-d̄en's *Annotations,* 16.4.

[149] Chap. 7; Lamotte, *Saṃdhinirmocana,* 68 [5], and 194; Dön-drup-gyel-tsen's *Four Intertwined Commentaries,* 7.2-7.3; and Powers, *Wisdom of Buddha,* 99.

[150] Peking 5539, vol. 111, 71.3.2. Tokyo *sde dge, sems tsam,* vol. 9 (*zi*), 8.4.7.

[151] Jik-may-dam-chö-gya-tso's *Port of Entry,* 182.4; and D̄a-drin-rap-d̄en's *Annotations,* 17.4.

[152] Chap. 7; Lamotte, *Saṃdhinirmocana,* 68 [6], and 194; Dön-drup-gyel-tsen's *Four Intertwined Commentaries,* 7.3-7.5; and Powers, *Wisdom of Buddha,* 99.

[153] D̄a-drin-rap-d̄en's *Annotations,* 18.4.

[154] Gung-ru Chö-jung's *Garland of White Lotuses,* 33b.1.

[155] Jik-may-dam-chö-gya-tso's *Port of Entry,* 184.3.

[156] D̄a-drin-rap-d̄en's *Annotations,* 19.1.

[157] Ibid., 19.2.

[158] Jik-may-dam-chö-gya-tso's *Port of Entry,* 191.2.

[159] Chap. 7; Lamotte, *Saṃdhinirmocana,* 68 [6], and 194; Dön-drup-gyel-tsen's *Four Intertwined Commentaries,* 7.5-7.6; and Powers, *Wisdom of Buddha,* 101.

[160] Chap. 3, "Questions of the Bodhisattva Suvishuddhamati." Lamotte, *Saṃdhinirmocana,* 45 [5], and 177; and Powers, *Wisdom of Buddha,* 43.

[161] D̄a-drin-rap-d̄en's *Annotations,* 22.4.

[162] Ibid., 22.6.

[163] Chap. 7; Lamotte, *Saṃdhinirmocana,* 69 [7], and 194-195; Dön-drup-gyel-tsen's *Four Intertwined Commentaries,* 8.1-8.4; and Powers, *Wisdom of Buddha,* 101.

[164] Jik-may-dam-chö-gya-tso's *Port of Entry,*

199.3.

165 Ibid., 199.6.

166 Ibid., 200.3.

167 Jik-may-dam-chö-gya-tso (*Port of Entry,* 200.5.

168 Ibid., 200.6.

169 Ibid., 201.6.

170 Chap. 7; Lamotte, *Saṃdhinirmocana,* 77 [20], and 200-201; Dön-drup-gyel-tsen's *Four Intertwined Commentaries,* 17.1-17.6; and Powers, *Wisdom of Buddha,* 119.

171 Ḏa-drin-rap-ḏen's *Annotations,* 27.3.

172 Ibid., 27.6.

173 Ibid., 28.3.

174 Ibid., 28.6.

175 Ibid., 29.1

176 Jik-may-dam-chö-gya-tso's *Port of Entry,* 207.5.

177 Chap. 7; Lamotte, *Saṃdhinirmocana,* 69-70 [8], and 195; Dön-drup-gyel-tsen's *Four Intertwined Commentaries,* 8.4-9.1; and Powers, *Wisdom of Buddha,* 103.

178 Ḏa-drin-rap-ḏen's *Annotations,* 30.1.

179 Ibid., 30.3.

180 Jik-may-dam-chö-gya-tso's *Port of Entry,* 209.2.

181 Chap. 7; Lamotte, *Saṃdhinirmocana,* 70 [9], and 195; Dön-drup-gyel-tsen's *Four Intertwined Commentaries,* 9.2-9.6; and Powers, *Wisdom of Buddha,* 103.

182 Jik-may-dam-chö-gya-tso's *Port of Entry,* 211.1.

183 Ḏa-drin-rap-ḏen's *Annotations,* 31.6.

184 Ibid., 32.1.

185 Ibid., 32.1.

186 Ibid., 32.1.

187 Peking 5550, vol. 112, 266.1.3-266.1.6, near the end of the second section, entitled *dharmaviniścayasamuccaya* (*chos rnam par nges pa kun las btus pa*). For fragments and reconstructed Sanskrit text, see Pralhad Pradhan, *Abhidharma Samuccaya* (Santiniketan, India: Visva-Bharati, 1950); for Yashomitra's commentary see N. Tatia, *Abhidharmasamuccayabhāṣyam,* Tibetan-Sanskrit Works Series, No. 17 (Patna, India: K.B. Jayaswal Research Institute, 1976). For a translation into French, see Walpola Rahula, *Le Compendium de la super-doctrine (philosophie) (Abhidharmasamuccaya) d'Asaṅga* (Paris: École Française d'Extrême-Orient, 1980), 142. For Wonch'uk's citation of this passage, see Peking 5517, vol. 106, chap. 5, 134.1.2 and 134.1.8.

188 Jik-may-dam-chö-gya-tso's *Port of Entry,* 212.4.

189 Ḏa-drin-rap-ḏen's *Annotations,* 33.3.

190 Jik-may-dam-chö-gya-tso's *Port of Entry,* 213.1.

Notes to Part Two, Chapter 3

191 Jik-may-dam-chö-gya-tso's *Port of Entry,* 224.6.

192 Chap. 7; Étienne Lamotte, *Saṃdhinirmocanasūtra: L'Explication des mystères* (Louvain: Université de Louvain, 1935), 81 [25], and 203; Dön-drup-gyel-tsen's *Four Intertwined Commentaries,* 21.3-21.21.5; and John C. Powers, *Wisdom of Buddha: Saṁdhinirmocana Sūtra* (Berkeley, Calif.: Dharma, 1995), 131.

193 Ḏa-drin-rap-ḏen's *Annotations,* 34.2.

194 Ibid., 35.1.

195 Jik-may-dam-chö-gya-tso's *Port of Entry,* 229.5.

196 Chap. 7; Lamotte, *Saṃdhinirmocana,* 81 [25], and 203-204; Dön-drup-gyel-tsen's *Four Intertwined Commentaries,* 21.6; and Powers, *Wisdom of Buddha,* 131.

197 Jik-may-dam-chö-gya-tso's *Port of Entry,* 230.3.

198 Ḏa-drin-rap-ḏen's *Annotations,* 36.1.

199 Ibid., 36.4.

200 Ibid., 37.2.

201 Jik-may-dam-chö-gya-tso's *Port of Entry,* 232.2.

202 Ibid., 232.2; Ḏa-drin-rap-ḏen's *Annotations,* 37.3.

203 Ḏa-drin-rap-ḏen's *Annotations,* 37.5.

204 Ibid., 37.6.

205 Jik-may-dam-chö-gya-tso's *Port of Entry,* 233.3.

206 Gung-tang's *Difficult Points,* 207.11.

207 Ḏa-drin-rap-ḏen's *Annotations,* 38.2.

208 Ibid., 38.4.

Notes to Part Two, Chapter 4

209 This and the next two bracketed additions are from Ḏa-drin-rap-ḏen's *Annotations,* 39.4-39.5.

210 Ibid., 39.5.

211 Gung-tang's *Difficult Points,* 232.14; and Ḏa-drin-rap-ḏen's *Annotations,* 40.1.

212 Ibid., 40.1.

213 Jik-may-dam-chö-gya-tso's *Port of Entry,* 279.6.

214 Chap. 7; Étienne Lamotte, *Saṃdhinirmocanasūtra: L'Explication des mystères* (Louvain: Université de Louvain, 1935), 85 [30], and 206; Dön-drup-gyel-tsen's *Four Intertwined Commentaries,* 27.1-28.2; and John C. Powers, *Wisdom of Buddha: Saṁdhinirmocana Sūtra* (Berkeley, Calif.: Dharma, 1995), 139-141.

215 Ḏa-drin-rap-den's *Annotations,* 42.3.

216 Ibid., 42.5.

217 S̄er-s̄hül's *Notes,* 21b.4.

218 Jik-may-dam-chö-gya-tso's *Port of Entry,* 291.1.

219 Ibid., 292.3; and Ḏa-drin-rap-ḏen's *Annotations,* 43.4.

220 Ḏa-drin-rap-ḏen's *Annotations,* 43.5.

221 Peking 5517, vol. 106, chap. 5, 170.2.2.

222 Gung-tang's *Difficult Points,* 240.11.

223 Ibid., 228.-4.

224 A-ku L̄o-drö-gya-tso's *Precious Lamp,* 156.4.

225 Jik-may-dam-chö-gya-tso's *Port of Entry,* 314.5.

226 Ibid., 314.5; 317.2.

227 Ibid., 314.6; 346.3.

228 Ḏa-drin-rap-ḏen's *Annotations,* 47.5.

229 Ibid., 47.6.

230 Jik-may-dam-chö-gya-tso's *Port of Entry,* 314.6; 346.6.

231 Gung-tang's *Difficult Points,* 293.1; A-ku L̄o-drö-gya-tso's *Precious Lamp,* 169.1; Jik-may-dam-chö-gya-tso's *Port of Entry,* 346.6; and Ḏa-drin-rap-ḏen's *Annotations,* 48.3. The first two specify Döl-ḇo S̄hay-rap-gyel-tsen; see his *Ocean of Definitive Meaning,* 173.4ff.

232 Ḏa-drin-rap-ḏen's *Annotations,* 48.3.

233 Ibid., 48.5.

234 Jik-may-dam-chö-gya-tso's *Port of Entry,* 352.1; and Ḏa-drin-rap-ḏen's *Annotations,* 48.6.

235 Jik-may-dam-chö-gya-tso's *Port of Entry,* 352.1.

236 Ibid., 353.3.

237 Ibid., 353.4.

238 Ibid., 353.5.

239 Ibid., 353.3.

240 Ibid., 353.3.

241 Ibid., 353.6.

NOTES TO PART TWO, CHAPTER 5

242 Peking 5539, vol. 111, 83.2.6-87.2.3.

243 Peking 5539, vol. 111, 88.2.2.

244 Peking 5539, vol. 111, 89.2.2.

245 A-ku L̄o-drö-gya-tso's *Precious Lamp,* 176.3; and Ḏa-drin-rap-ḏen's *Annotations,* 51.4.

NOTES TO PART TWO, CHAPTER 6

246 Chap. 4; Peking 5538, vol. 110, 144.1.3-144.1.4; and Janice D. Willis, *On Knowing Reality: The Tattvārtha Chapter of Asaṅga's Bodhisattvabhūmi* (New York: Columbia University Press, 1979; reprint, Delhi: Motilal Banarsidass, 1982), 158; for the Sanskrit, see p. 393, footnote b.

247 For the entire citation, see Peking 5538, vol. 110, 144.2.8-144.3.3; and Willis, *On Knowing Reality,* 160; for the Sanskrit, see p. 393, footnote d. Ḏa-drin-rap-ḏen's *Annotations,* 52.5ff, has extensive explanations of these citations.

248 A-ku L̄o-drö-gya-tso, *Precious Lamp,* 181.1.

249 Dra-ḏi Ge-s̄hay Rin-chen-dön-drup's *Ornament for the Thought,* 51.11.

250 Ḏa-drin-rap-ḏen's *Annotations,* 54.4.

251 Ibid., 55.5.

252 A-ku L̄o-drö-gya-tso's *Precious Lamp,* 182.1.

253 Ḏa-drin-rap-ḏen's *Annotations,* 56.1.

254 Ibid., 56.1.

255 Ibid., 56.2.

256 Ibid., 56.2.

257 Dra-ḏi Ge-s̄hay Rin-chen-dön-drup's *Ornament for the Thought,* 52.15.

258 A-ku L̄o-drö-gya-tso's *Precious Lamp,* 182.6.

259 Peking 5538, vol. 110, 144.3.5-144.3.6; and Willis, *On Knowing Reality,* 161; for the Sanskrit, see p. 395, footnote d.

260 Ḏa-drin-rap-ḏen's *Annotations,* 56.4.

261 Ibid., 56.5.

262 A-ku L̄o-drö-gya-tso's *Precious Lamp,* 183.1.

263 Ḏa-drin-rap-ḏen's *Annotations,* 56.6.

264 Peking 5538, vol. 110, 144.3.6-144.5.1; and Willis, *On Knowing Reality,* 161; for the Sanskrit, see p. 396, footnote b.

265 A-ku L̄o-drö-gya-tso's *Precious Lamp,* 185.6.

266 Ḏa-drin-rap-ḏen's *Annotations,* 57.5.

267 Ibid., 57.6.

268 Ibid., 57.6.

269 Ibid., 57.6.

270 A-ku L̄o-drö-gya-tso's *Precious Lamp,* 186.1.

271 Ibid., 186.1.

272 Ḏa-drin-rap-ḏen's *Annotations,* 58.1.

273 Ibid., 58.1.

[274] Ibid., 58.2.

[275] Ibid., 57.6.

[276] A-ku Lo-drö-gya-tso's *Precious Lamp,* 186.2.

[277] Jam-ȳang-shay-b̄a's *Great Exposition of the Interpretable and the Definitive,* 145.2; and A-ku L̄o-drö-gya-tso's *Precious Lamp,* 186.2.

[278] D̄a-drin-rap-d̄en's *Annotations,* 59.6.

[279] Ibid., 60.4.

[280] Ibid., 60.6.

[281] Ibid., 60.6.

[282] Peking 5538, vol. 110, 144.4.1-144.5.5; and Willis, *On Knowing Reality,* 161; for the Sanskrit, see p. 398, footnote a.

[283] A-ku L̄o-drö-gya-tso's *Precious Lamp,* 187.5.

[284] Jik-may-dam-chö-gya-tso's *Port of Entry,* 392.6.

[285] D̄a-drin-rap-d̄en's *Annotations,* 61.3.

[286] Ibid., 61.3.

[287] Ibid., 61.4.

[288] Peking 5538, vol. 110, 144.4.7-144.5.3; and Willis, *On Knowing Reality,* 162; for the Sanskrit, see p. 399, footnote a.

[289] Jik-may-dam-chö-gya-tso's *Port of Entry,* 394.1.

[290] D̄a-drin-rap-d̄en's *Annotations,* 62.4.

[291] A-ku L̄o-drö-gya-tso's *Precious Lamp,* 188.6.

[292] Ibid., 188.6.

[293] Peking 5538, vol. 110, 142.5.1-142.5.3; and Willis, *On Knowing Reality,* 18, 44, and 163; for the Sanskrit, see p. 400, footnote b.

[294] S̄er-s̄hül's *Notes,* 28a.2; and D̄a-drin-rap-d̄en's *Annotations,* 63.6.

[295] S̄er-s̄hül's *Notes,* 28a.2; and D̄a-drin-rap-d̄en's *Annotations,* 64.1.

Notes to Part Two, Chapter 7

[296] Peking 5539, vol. 111, 82.4.7; and Tokyo *sde dge, sems tsam,* vol. 9 (*zi*), 42b.5.

[297] Peking 5539, vol. 111, 82.4.8; and Tokyo *sde dge, sems tsam,* vol. 9 (*zi*), 42b.6.

[298] D̄a-drin-rap-d̄en's *Annotations,* 64.5.

[299] A-ku L̄o-drö-gya-tso's *Precious Lamp,* 191.4.

[300] Ibid., 191.5; and D̄a-drin-rap-d̄en's *Annotations,* 64.6.

[301] D̄a-drin-rap-d̄en's *Annotations,* 65.1.

[302] A-ku L̄o-drö-gya-tso's *Precious Lamp,* 191.6.

[303] D̄a-drin-rap-d̄en's *Annotations,* 65.2.

[304] A-ku L̄o-drö-gya-tso's *Precious Lamp,* 191.6; and D̄a-drin-rap-d̄en's *Annotations,* 65.2.

[305] A-ku L̄o-drö-gya-tso's *Precious Lamp,* 191.6; and D̄a-drin-rap-d̄en's *Annotations,* 65.2.

[306] Ibid., 65.2.

[307] Jik-may-dam-chö-gya-tso (*Port of Entry,* 417.3-418.3) lists various interpretations of "conceals, imputes, verbalizes, and makes designations"; the one used here for the material in the remainder of the square brackets in the paragraph is from the *Lamp for the Profound and the Manifest* (*zab gsal sgron me*).

[308] Jik-may-dam-chö-gya-tso's *Port of Entry,* 405.2.

[309] Ibid., 405.

[310] Ibid., 406.5.

[311] Peking 5539, vol. 111, 82.5.2; and Tokyo *sde dge, sems tsam,* vol. 9 (*zi*), 42b.7.

[312] D̄a-drin-rap-d̄en's *Annotations,* 66.5.

[313] Ibid., 66.5.

[314] Ibid., 66.5.

[315] Ibid., 66.6.

[316] Ibid., 67.1.

[317] Ibid., 67.1.

[318] Jik-may-dam-chö-gya-tso's *Port of Entry,* 407.2.

[319] D̄a-drin-rap-d̄en's *Annotations,* 67.2.

[320] Ibid., 67.2.

[321] Ibid., 67.3.

[322] Ibid., 67.3.

[323] Ibid., 67.3

[324] Ibid., 67.6.

[325] Ibid., 67.6.

[326] Ibid., 68.1.

[327] Ibid., 68.1.

[328] Ibid., 68.1.

[329] Ibid., 68.2.

[330] Jik-may-dam-chö-gya-tso's *Port of Entry,* 407.4.

[331] Peking 5539, vol. 111, 82.5.4; and Tokyo *sde dge, sems tsam,* vol. 9 (*zi*), 43a.2.

[332] D̄a-drin-rap-d̄en's *Annotations,* 68.3.

[333] Ibid., 68.3-4.

[334] Jik-may-dam-chö-gya-tso's *Port of Entry,* 407.6.

[335] D̄a-drin-rap-d̄en's *Annotations,* 68.5.

[336] Ibid., 68.5.

[337] Ibid., 68.6.

[338] Jik-may-dam-chö-gya-tso's *Port of Entry,* 408.1; and D̄a-drin-rap-d̄en's *Annotations,* 68.6.

[339] D̄a-drin-rap-d̄en's *Annotations,* 68.6.

[340] Ibid., 69.1.

341 Jik-may-dam-chö-gya-tso's *Port of Entry,* 408.1; and D̄a-drin-rap-d̄en's *Annotations,* 69.1.

342 D̄a-drin-rap-d̄en's *Annotations,* 69.2.

343 Jik-may-dam-chö-gya-tso's *Port of Entry,* 408.3; and D̄a-drin-rap-d̄en's *Annotations,* 69.2.

344 Jik-may-dam-chö-gya-tso's *Port of Entry,* 408.2.

345 Ibid., 408.2; and D̄a-drin-rap-d̄en's *Annotations,* 69.2.

346 Ibid., 69.4.

347 Ibid., 69.4.

348 Ibid., 69.4.

349 Ibid., 69.5.

350 Ibid., 69.5.

351 Ibid., 69.5.

352 Ibid., 69.5.

353 Ibid., 69.5.

354 Ibid., 69.6.

355 Jik-may-dam-chö-gya-tso's *Port of Entry,* 408.5.

356 Ibid., 412.1.

357 D̄a-drin-rap-d̄en's *Annotations,* 70.2.

358 Jik-may-dam-chö-gya-tso's *Port of Entry,* 409.3.

359 Tokyo *sde dge, sems tsam,* vol. 8 (*zhi*), 194b.2.

360 Ibid., 194b.4.

361 Jik-may-dam-chö-gya-tso's *Port of Entry,* 409.5; and D̄a-drin-rap-d̄en's *Annotations,* 70.5.

362 D̄a-drin-rap-d̄en's *Annotations,* 71.1.

363 Ibid., 71.2.

364 Ibid., 71.2.

365 Jik-may-dam-chö-gya-tso's *Port of Entry,* 410.2.

366 D̄a-drin-rap-d̄en's *Annotations,* 71.2.

367 Tokyo *sde dge, sems tsam,* vol. 8 (*zhi*), 279b.1.

368 A-ku L̄o-drö-gya-tso's *Precious Lamp,* 194.3; and D̄a-drin-rap-d̄en's *Annotations,* 71.3.

369 Peking 5539, vol. 111, 78.1.8; and Tokyo *sde dge, sems tsam,* vol. 9 (*zi*), 32a.5.

370 D̄a-drin-rap-d̄en's *Annotations,* 72.3.

371 Ibid., 72.3.

372 Peking 5539, vol. 111, 78.2.3; and Tokyo *sde dge, sems tsam,* vol. 9 (*zi*), 32a.6. D̄zong-ka-b̄a has not cited a line that intervenes between this and the last quotation.

373 D̄a-drin-rap-d̄en's *Annotations,* 72.4; I have added the examples.

374 Ibid., 72.5.

375 Ibid, 72.5.

376 Ibid., 72.6.

377 D̄a-drin-rap-d̄en (*Annotations,* 73.1) adds this qualification.

378 B̄el-jor-hlün-drup's *Lamp for the Teaching,* 44.5; and D̄a-drin-rap-d̄en's *Annotations,* 73.2.

379 B̄el-jor-hlün-drup's *Lamp for the Teaching,* 44.5; and D̄a-drin-rap-d̄en's *Annotations,* 73.3.

380 Jik-may-dam-chö-gya-tso's *Port of Entry,* 414.2 and 423.1; the latter lists other attributions, such as to Vasubandhu and Asaṅga.

381 D̄a-drin-rap-d̄en's *Annotations,* 73.4.

382 Jik-may-dam-chö-gya-tso's *Port of Entry,* 414.6.

383 D̄a-drin-rap-d̄en's *Annotations,* 73.6.

384 Ibid., 73.6.

385 Ibid., 74.1.

386 Ibid., 74.1.

387 A-ku L̄o-drö-gya-tso's *Precious Lamp,* 196.3.

388 Ibid., 196.5.

389 D̄a-drin-rap-d̄en's *Annotations,* 77.1.

390 Chap. 4, "The Questions of Subhūti"; Étienne Lamotte, *Saṃdhinirmocanasūtra: L'Explication des mystères* (Louvain: Université de Louvain, 1935), 51.33-52.5, and 181; and John C. Powers, *Wisdom of Buddha: Saṁdhinirmocana Sūtra* (Berkeley, Calif.: Dharma, 1995), 63.

391 III.10c; Peking 5522, vol. 108, 20.3.5; and Stefan Anacker, *Seven Works of Vasubandhu* (Delhi: Motilal Banarsidass, 1984), 236; for the Sanskrit, see p. 407, footnote d.

392 Peking 5528, vol. 108, 126.2.2; and Anacker, *Seven Works of Vasubandhu,* 236; for the Sanskrit, see p. 408, footnote a.

393 Paraphrasing Vasubandhu's *Explanation of (Maitreya's) "Ornament for the Great Vehicle Sūtras"* (*mdo sde'i rgyan gyi bshad pa, sūtrālaṃkārābhāṣya;* Peking 5527, vol. 108, 63.5.5); for the Sanskrit, see p. 408, footnote e.

394 D̄a-drin-rap-d̄en's *Annotations,* 76.2.

395 Peking 5539, vol. 111, 61.4.7.

396 Ibid., 61.5.1; and Tokyo *sde dge, sems tsam,* vol. 9 (*zhi*), 289a.2.

397 A-ku L̄o-drö-gya-tso's *Precious Lamp,* 197.6.

398 For D̄a-drin-rap-d̄en's two explanations of this, see his *Annotations,* 76.5.

399 Jik-may-dam-chö-gya-tso's *Port of Entry,* 423.5; 426.2.

400 Ibid., 426.2.

401 A-ku Lo-drö-gya-tso's *Precious Lamp,* 198.1; Da-drin-rap-den (78.1) misidentifies "this" as referring to other-powered natures (*gzhan dbang 'di ni*).

402 Da-drin-rap-den's *Annotations,* 78.3.

403 Jik-may-dam-chö-gya-tso's *Port of Entry,* 427.2.

404 Peking 5539, vol. 111, 78.1.5; and Tokyo *sde dge, sems tsam,* vol. 9 (*zi*), 32a.2. See Da-drin-rap-den's *Annotations,* 78.4, for commentary.

405 A-ku Lo-drö-gya-tso's *Precious Lamp* 198.4; and Da-drin-rap-den's *Annotations,* 79.2.

406 A-ku Lo-drö-gya-tso's *Precious Lamp,* 198.5; and Da-drin-rap-den's *Annotations,* 79.3.

407 Da-drin-rap-den's *Annotations,* 79.4.

408 Ibid., 79.4.

409 Tokyo *sde dge, sems tsam,* vol. 8 (*zhi*) 199a.7.

410 Da-drin-rap-den's *Annotations,* 80.4.

411 Ibid., 80.3.

412 Jik-may-dam-chö-gya-tso's *Port of Entry,* 441.1; and Da-drin-rap-den's *Annotations,* 80.3.

413 Da-drin-rap-den's *Annotations,* 80.5.

414 Ibid., 80.6.

415 Jik-may-dam-chö-gya-tso's *Port of Entry,* 441.2; and Da-drin-rap-den's *Annotations,* 81.1.

416 Da-drin-rap-den's *Annotations,* 81.5.

417 Ibid., 81.4.

418 Ibid., 81.6.

419 Ibid., 81.6.

420 A-ku Lo-drö-gya-tso's *Precious Lamp,* 215.5.

421 III.11ab; Peking 5522, vol. 108, 20.3.6; and Anacker, *Seven Works of Vasubandhu,* 236-237; for the Sanskrit, see p. 410, footnote b. The three identifications are from Ser-shül's *Notes,* 34b.5, based on Sthiramati's commentary.

422 Peking 5528, vol. 108, 126.2.3; and Anacker, *Seven Works of Vasubandhu,* 237; for the Sanskrit, see p. 410, footnote c.

423 Da-drin-rap-den's *Annotations,* 82.3.

424 Ibid., 82.4.

425 Ibid., 82.5.

426 Ibid., 82.5.

427 Ibid., 82.5.

428 Peking 5528, vol. 108, 126.3.4; and Anacker, *Seven Works of Vasubandhu,* 238.

429 Da-drin-rap-den's *Annotations,* 82.6.

430 Ibid., 82.6.

431 Ibid., 83.4.

432 Ser-shül's *Notes,* 35b.5; and Jik-may-dam-chö-gya-tso's *Port of Entry,* 460.6.

433 Jik-may-dam-chö-gya-tso's *Port of Entry,* 426.2; 471.5.

434 Peking 5539, vol. 111, 61.4.8; and Tokyo *sde dge, sems tsam,* vol. 8 (*zhi*), 288b.7.

435 *rnam par bshad pa'i rigs pa, vyākyhayukti;* Peking 5562, vol. 113, 276.2.5-276.2.7.

436 Da-drin-rap-den's *Annotations,* 86.3.

437 Ibid., 86.4.

438 Ibid., 86.6.

439 A-ku Lo-drö-gya-tso's *Precious Lamp,* 218.2.

440 Da-drin-rap-den's *Annotations,* 88.2.

441 Ibid. I have added "in the literal reading of."

442 Ibid., 88.3.

443 Ibid., 88.5.

444 Jik-may-dam-chö-gya-tso's *Port of Entry,* 483.1.

445 Da-drin-rap-den's *Annotations,* 88.6.

446 Ibid.

447 Ibid.

448 See Ser-shül's *Notes,* 37b.1-37b.5, and Jik-may-dam-chö-gya-tso's *Port of Entry,* 489.2-489.6.

449 Bel-jor-hlün-drup's *Lamp for the Teaching,* 51.6; and Da-drin-rap-den's *Annotations,* 89.1.

450 Ibid., 89.2.

451 Ibid., 89.3.

452 Ibid., 89.3

453 Ibid., 89.4.

454 Ibid., 89.4

455 Ibid., 89.5.

456 Ibid., 89.5.

457 Ibid., 89.6.

458 Ibid., 90.1.

459 Ibid., 90.1.

460 Ibid., 89.6.

461 Ibid., 90.2.

462 Ibid., 90.1.

463 Jik-may-dam-chö-gya-tso's *Port of Entry,* 484.5.

464 A-ku Lo-drö-gya-tso's *Precious Lamp,* 219.2. The cited text is III.10bc; Peking 5522, vol. 108, 20.3.5; for the Sanskrit, see p. 414, footnote c.

465 Ser-shül's *Notes,* 38a.5.

NOTES TO PART TWO, CHAPTER 8

466 A-ku Lo-drö-gya-tso's *Precious Lamp,* 220.1.

467 XI.50; Peking 5521, vol. 108, 9.1.3; for the Sanskrit, see p. 416, footnote a. The material in the square brackets is from A-ku Lo-drö-gya-tso's

Precious Lamp, 220.2. See Sylvain Lévi, *Mahāyānasūtrālaṃkāra, exposé de la doctrine du grand véhicule selon le système Yogācāra* (Paris: Bibliothèque de l'École des Hautes Études, 1907), vol. 1, 67.16; vol. 2, 121.

[468] *Explanation of (Maitreya's) "Ornament for the Great Vehicle Sūtras" (mdo sde'i rgyan gyi bshad pa, sūtrālaṃkārābhāṣya),* Peking 5527, vol. 108, 77.2.1-77.2.5. Except as indicated, Ḏzong-ka-ḇa is paraphrasing Vasubandhu's commentary. For the Sanskrit, see S. Bagchi, ed. *Mahāyāna-Sūtrālaṃkāra of Asaṅga* [with Vasubandhu's commentary], Buddhist Sanskrit Texts, 13 (Darbhanga, India: Mithila Institute, 1970), 67.20-67.25; and Lévi, *Mahāyānasūtrālaṃkāra,* vol. 1, 67.18-67.23; vol. 2, 121.26-122.7.

[469] Ḏa-drin-rap-ḏen's *Annotations,* 93.1.

[470] A-ku Ḻo-drö-gya-tso's *Precious Lamp,* 220.3.

[471] Ibid., 222.2.

[472] Peking 5550, vol. 112, 266.1.2-266.1.4, in the first section, entitled *lakṣaṇasamuccaya;* and Walpola Rahula, *Le Compendium de la super-doctrine (philosophie) (Abhidharmasamuccaya) d'Asaṅga* (Paris: École Française d'Extrême-Orient, 1980), 141-142.

[473] A-ku Ḻo-drö-gya-tso's *Precious Lamp,* 221.4.

[474] XI.51; Peking 5521, vol. 108, 9.1.3; and Lévi, *Mahāyānasūtrālaṃkāra,* vol. 2, 122. For the Sanskrit, see p. 417, footnote c.

[475] A-ku Ḻo-drö-gya-tso's *Precious Lamp,* 221.5.

[476] Dön-drup-gyel-tsen's *Four Intertwined Commentaries,* 157.5, and Ḏa-drin-rap-ḏen's *Annotations,* 94.4.

[477] *Explanation of (Maitreya's) "Ornament for the Great Vehicle Sūtras"* (Peking 5527, vol. 108, 77.3.2-77.3.5). For Lévi's translation, see his *Mahāyānasūtrālaṃkāra,* vol. 2, 123-124.

[478] Ḏa-drin-rap-ḏen's *Annotations,* 95.2.

[479] Ibid., 95.3.

[480] Ibid., 95.5.

[481] Ibid., 96.2.

[482] A-ku Ḻo-drö-gya-tso's *Precious Lamp,* 224.2.

[483] XI.15; Peking 5521, vol. 108, 8.3.1; and Lévi, *Mahāyānasūtrālaṃkāra,* vol. 2, 108. For the Sanskrit, see p. 420, footnote a.

[484] *Explanation of (Maitreya's) "Ornament for the Great Vehicle Sūtras"* (Peking 5527, vol. 108, 74.4.2).

[485] Paraphrasing his *Explanation of (Maitreya's) "Ornament for the Great Vehicle Sūtras"* (Peking 5527, vol. 108, 74.4.4); Lévi's translation, *Mahāyānasūtrālaṃkāra,* vol. 2, 109.11-109.17. For the Sanskrit, see Bagchi, *Mahāyāna-Sūtrālaṃkāra of Asaṅga,* 60.7-60.9; and Lévi, *Mahāyānasūtrālaṃkāra,* vol. 1, 59.11-59.13.

[486] Ḏa-drin-rap-ḏen's *Annotations,* 98.2.

[487] A-ku Ḻo-drö-gya-tso's *Precious Lamp,* 224.4.

Notes to Part Two, Chapter 9

[488] I.1-2; Peking 5522, vol. 108, 19.4.5; for the Sanskrit, see p. 422, footnote a. The bracketed material in these two stanzas is from Ḏzong-ka-ḇa's own commentary, which follows the citation, and from Dra-ḏi Ge-s̄hay Rin-chen-dön-drup's *Ornament for the Thought* (77.12ff) which also is cited in Dön-drup-gyel-tsen's *Four Intertwined Commentaries,* 166.1-166.5; in the latter (166.2 and 166.4), read *kun rtog* for *kun btags,* in accordance with Dra-ḏi Ge-s̄hay Rin-chen-dön-drup's *Ornament for the Thought* (77.17 and 78.7). For translations with Vasubandhu's commentary, see Stefan Anacker, *Seven Works of Vasubandhu* (Delhi: Motilal Banarsidass, 1984), 211-212; Thomas A. Kochumuttom, *A Buddhist Doctrine of Experience* (Delhi: Motilal Banarsidass, 1982), 235-236. For translations with Sthiramati's sub-commentary, see David Lasar Friedmann, *Sthiramati, Madhyāntavibhāgaṭīkā: Analysis of the Middle Path and the Extremes* (Utrecht, Netherlands: Rijksuniversiteit te Leiden, 1937), 10-17; and F. Th. Stcherbatsky. *Madhyāntavibhāga, Discourse on Discrimination between Middle and Extremes ascribed to Bodhisattva Maitreya and Commented by Vasubandhu and Sthiramati,* Bibliotheca Buddhica, 30 (Osnabrück, Germany: Biblio Verlag, 1970; reprint, Calcutta: Indian Studies Past and Present, 1971), 16-24. See also Ake Boquist, *Trisvabhāva: A Study of the Development of the Three-Nature-Theory in Yogācāra Buddhism,* ed. Tord Olsson, Lund Studies in African and Asian Religions, 8 (Lund, Sweden: University of Lund, 1993), chap. 4; and Thomas E. Wood, *Mind-Only: A Philosophical and Doctrinal Analysis of the Vijñānavāda,* Monographs of the Society for Asian and Comparative Philosophy, 9 (Honolulu: University of Hawaii Press, 1991), chap. 1.

[489] The phrase "ideation and emptiness" is drawn from Ḏzong-ka-ḇa's own commentary which follows; Ḏra-ḏi Ge-s̄hay does not mention the last "exist."

[490] Jik-may-dam-chö-gya-tso's *Port of Entry,* 508.5.

491 S̄er-s̄hül's *Notes,* 40a.1; in that, read *dbus mtha'i lung* for *dbu ma'i lung.*

492 D̄a-drin-rap-d̄en's *Annotations,* 100.2.

493 Ibid., 100.2.

494 Ibid., 100.3.

495 Ibid., 100.4.

496 Dön-drup-gyel-tsen's *Four Intertwined Commentaries,* 163.3.

497 Peking 5334, vol. 109, 138.1.5; for the Sanskrit, see p. 423, footnote b. For English translations, see Friedmann, *Sthiramati, Madhyāntavibhāgaṭīkā,* 10.16; and Stcherbatsky, *Madhyāntavibhāga,* 17.19.

498 Peking 5334, vol. 109.1.6; for the Sanskrit, see p. 423, footnote c.

499 D̄a-drin-rap-d̄en's *Annotations,* 101.5.

500 Ibid., 101.5.

501 Ibid., 101.6.

502 Ibid., 101.5.

503 Peking 5334, vol. 109, 138.1.7-138.2.1; for the Sanskrit, see p. 424, footnote b.

504 D̄a-drin-rap-d̄en's *Annotations,* 102.4.

505 Ibid., 102.6.

506 A-ku L̄o-drö-gya-tso's *Precious Lamp,* 228.1-228.3; and S̄er-s̄hül's *Notes,* 40a.2-40a.4.

507 D̄a-drin-rap-d̄en's *Annotations,* 103.3.

508 The citation is from Sthiramati's introduction to Vasubandhu's text in which he gives three different reasons why Vasubandhu composed *The Thirty,* of which this is the third. For the Tibetan, see Peking 5565, vol. 113, 300.3.6; and Enga Teramoto, *Sthiramati's Triṃçikābhāṣyaṃ (Sum-cu-paḥi ḥGrel-pa): A Tibetan Text* (Kyoto: Association for Linguistic Study of Sacred Scriptures, 1933), 2.11; for the Sanskrit, see p. 425, footnote a.

509 Jik-may-dam-chö-gya-tso's *Port of Entry,* 512.5.

510 D̄a-drin-rap-d̄en's *Annotations,* 103.6.

511 Jik-may-dam-chö-gya-tso's *Port of Entry,* 512.5; and D̄a-drin-rap-d̄en's *Annotations,* 103.6.

512 The brackets in this sentence are from Jik-may-dam-chö-gya-tso's *Port of Entry,* 513.5; I have changed his "true existence" to "ultimate existence" to maintain consistency.

513 D̄a-drin-rap-d̄en's *Annotations,* 105.5.

514 A-ku L̄o-drö-gya-tso's *Precious Lamp,* 230.6.

515 Jik-may-dam-chö-gya-tso (*Port of Entry,* 514.5) cites the passages from Vasubandhu and Sthiramati.

516 D̄a-drin-rap-d̄en's *Annotations,* 106.2.

517 Jik-may-dam-chö-gya-tso's *Port of Entry,* 515.2.

518 Ibid., 515.1.

519 Peking 5334, vol. 109, 139.3.2-139.3.4; Friedmann, *Sthiramati, Madhyāntavibhāgaṭīkā,* 17.1-17.8; and Stcherbatsky, *Madhyāntavibhāga,* 26.5-26.13.

520 A-ku L̄o-drö-gya-tso's *Precious Lamp,* 231.1.

521 Ibid., 231.1; S̄er-s̄hül's *Notes,* 40b.3; and D̄a-drin-rap-d̄en's *Annotations,* 106.5.

522 A-ku L̄o-drö-gya-tso's *Precious Lamp,* 231.2; S̄er-s̄hül's *Notes,* 40b.3; and D̄a-drin-rap-d̄en's *Annotations,* 106.6.

523 Jik-may-dam-chö-gya-tso's *Port of Entry,* 536.1.

524 D̄a-drin-rap-d̄en's *Annotations,* 107.3.

525 III.214-215; for the Sanskrit, see p. 427, footnote b. The bracketed material in these two stanzas is drawn from S̄er-s̄hül's *Notes,* 41b.2-42a.1.

526 S̄er-s̄hül's *Notes,* 41b.6.

527 III.216; for the Sanskrit, see p. 428, footnote e. See also Nga-w̄ang-b̄el-den, *Annotations for (Jam-ȳang-shay-b̄a's) "Great Exposition of Tenets," dngos,* 142.6.

528 S̄er-s̄hül's *Notes,* 42a.3.

529 Ibid., 42a.2.

Notes to Part Two, Chapter 10

530 D̄a-drin-rap-d̄en's *Annotations,* 110.1.

531 Ibid., 110.2.

532 Ibid., 110.2.

533 A-ku L̄o-drö-gya-tso's *Precious Lamp,* 235.2.

534 Jik-may-dam-chö-gya-tso's *Port of Entry,* 546.2.

535 D̄a-drin-rap-d̄en (*Annotations,* 110.6) qualifies this as "**explicit** explanation."

536 Ibid., 111.3.

537 Ibid., 111.6.

538 Ibid., 112.2.

539 Ibid., 112.2.

540 Jik-may-dam-chö-gya-tso's *Port of Entry,* 564.1.

541 Jam-ȳang-shay-b̄a's *Great Exposition of the Interpretable and the Definitive,* 186.4.

542 D̄a-drin-rap-d̄en's *Annotations,* 113.2.

543 A-ku L̄o-drö-gya-tso's *Precious Lamp,* 238.2. Jik-may-dam-chö-gya-tso (*Port of Entry,* 565.3) treats this objection as two, beginning the second

with "Also, even if..."

[544] Jam-ȳang-shay-b̄a's *Great Exposition of the Interpretable and the Definitive,* 187.6, and D̄a-drin-rap-d̄en's *Annotations,* 113.4.

[545] Jik-may-dam-chö-gya-tso's *Port of Entry,* 572.5.

[546] D̄a-drin-rap-d̄en's *Annotations,* 113.4.

[547] Ibid., 113.5.

[548] Ibid., 113.6.

[549] Ibid., 114.1.

[550] A-ku L̄o-drö-gya-tso's *Precious Lamp,* 2238.6.

[551] D̄a-drin-rap-d̄en's *Annotations,* 114.2.

[552] Ibid., 114.3.

[553] A-ku L̄o-drö-gya-tso's *Precious Lamp,* 239.2.

[554] D̄a-drin-rap-d̄en's *Annotations,* 114.4.

[555] Jik-may-dam-chö-gya-tso's *Port of Entry,* 567.2.

[556] A-ku L̄o-drö-gya-tso's *Precious Lamp,* 240.1.

[557] D̄a-drin-rap-d̄en's *Annotations,* 115.1.

[558] Ibid., 115.2.

[559] A-ku L̄o-drö-gya-tso's *Precious Lamp,* 240.2-240.4.

[560] Ibid., 240.5.

[561] Ibid., 240.4; and D̄a-drin-rap-d̄en's *Annotations,* 115.6.

[562] A-ku L̄o-drö-gya-tso's *Precious Lamp,* 240.4 and 243.2, the latter being where his commentary begins.

[563] Peking 5539, vol. 111, 73.2.4; and Tokyo *sde dge, sems tsam,* vol. 9 (*zi*), 21a.2.

[564] D̄a-drin-rap-d̄en's *Annotations,* 117.2.

[565] Ibid., 117.2,

[566] Ibid., 117.5.

[567] Ibid., 118.4.

[568] Ibid., 118.5.

[569] Ibid., 118.5

[570] Ibid., 119.1.

[571] Ibid., 118.6.

[572] A-ku L̄o-drö-gya-tso's *Precious Lamp,* 244.1; and D̄a-drin-rap-d̄en's *Annotations,* 119.1.

[573] Ibid., 119.3.

[574] Jik-may-dam-chö-gya-tso's *Port of Entry,* 579.1.

[575] A-ku L̄o-drö-gya-tso's *Precious Lamp,* 256.3.

[576] Peking 5538, vol. 110 144.2.2-144.2.7; and Janice D. Willis, *On Knowing Reality: The Tattvārtha Chapter of Asaṅga's Bodhisattvabhūmi* (New York: Columbia University Press, 1979; reprint, Delhi: Motilal Banarsidass, 1982), 159. D̄zong-ka-b̄a paraphrases it below.

[577] Chap. 2; Peking 5549, vol. 112 224.4.1; Étienne Lamotte, *La somme du grand véhicule d'Asaṅga,* reprint, 2 vols. Publications de l'Institute Orientaliste de Louvain, 8 (Louvain: Université de Louvain, 1973), vol. 1, vol. 1, 36 (24); vol. 2, 118-119; and John P. Keenan, *The Summary of the Great Vehicle by Bodhisattva Asaṅga: Translated from the Chinese of Paramārtha* (Berkeley, Calif.: Numata Center for Buddhist Translation and Research, 1992), 50-51.

[578] D̄a-drin-rap-d̄en's *Annotations,* 120.5.

[579] Ibid., 121.2.

[580] Ibid., 121.4.

[581] Ibid., 121.5.

[582] Ibid., 121.6.

[583] Ibid., 122.1.

[584] Ibid., 122.1.

[585] Ibid., 122.1.

[586] Ibid., 122.1.

[587] Ibid., 122.1.

[588] Ibid., 122.2.

[589] Ibid., 122.4.

[590] Ibid., 122.4.

[591] Ibid., 122.4.

[592] Ibid., 122.4.

[593] Ibid., 122.5.

[594] "Of one continuum" is from ibid., 122.5.

[595] A-ku L̄o-drö-gya-tso's *Precious Lamp,* 254.3; and D̄a-drin-rap-d̄en's *Annotations,* 123.2.

[596] Paraphrasing Peking 5538, vol. 110, 144.2.2-144.2.7; and Janice D. Willis, *On Knowing Reality: The Tattvārtha Chapter of Asaṅga's Bodhisattvabhūmi* (New York: Columbia University Press, 1979; reprint, Delhi: Motilal Banarsidass, 1982), 159.26ff. For the Sanskrit, see Unrai Wogihara, *Bodhisattvabhūmi: A Statement of the Whole Course of the Bodhisattva (Being the Fifteenth Section of Yogācārabhūmi)* (Tokyo: Seigo Kenkyūkai, 1930-1936), 44.22-45.12; and Nalinaksha Dutt, *Bodhisattvabhūmi (Being the XVth Section of Asangapada's Yogacarabhumi)* Tibetan Sanskrit Works Series, 7 (Patna, India: K. P. Jayaswal Research Institute, 1966), 30.17-30.26.

[597] A-ku L̄o-drö-gya-tso's *Precious Lamp,* 258.1.

[598] D̄a-drin-rap-d̄en's *Annotations,* 124.1.

[599] Jik-may-dam-chö-gya-tso's *Port of Entry,* 599.5 (heading at 589.3).

[600] A-ku L̄o-drö-gya-tso's *Precious Lamp,* 259.4.

[601] D̄a-drin-rap-d̄en's *Annotations,* 125.6. The

bracketed additions, except where noted, are drawn from Ser-shül's *Notes,* 43a.1-43a.5.

602 Da-drin-rap-den's *Annotations,* 114.2.

603 Ibid., 126.1.

604 Jam-yang-shay-ba's *Great Exposition of the Interpretable and the Definitive,* 209.4; and A-ku Lo-drö-gya-tso's *Precious Lamp,* 259.4.

605 A-ku Lo-drö-gya-tso's *Precious Lamp,* 260.4.

606 Da-drin-rap-den's *Annotations,* 127.3.

607 Jik-may-dam-chö-gya-tso's *Port of Entry,* 609.2.

608 Ibid., 609.4.

609 Peking 5549, vol. 112, 227.3.1-227.3.5. Lamotte's edition, vol. 1, 51.23ff; vol. 2, 162.1ff; and Keenan, *Summary,* 66.

610 Ser-shül's *Notes,* 47a.2; and Da-drin-rap-den's *Annotations,* 128.4.

611 Ser-shül's *Notes,* 47a.2; and Da-drin-rap-den's *Annotations,* 128.3.

612 Ser-shül's *Notes,* 47a.2; and Da-drin-rap-den's *Annotations,* 128.4.

613 Ser-shül's *Notes,* 47a.3; and Da-drin-rap-den's *Annotations,* 128.5.

614 Ser-shül's *Notes,* 47a.3; and Da-drin-rap-den's *Annotations,* 128.4-5.

615 Ser-shül's *Notes,* 47a.4; and Da-drin-rap-den's *Annotations,* 128.5-6.

616 Ser-shül's *Notes,* 47a.5; and Da-drin-rap-den's *Annotations,* 128.6-129.2.

617 Ibid., 129.3.

618 Ser-shül's *Notes,* 48b.3; and Da-drin-rap-den's *Annotations,* 129.3.

619 Ser-shül's *Notes,* 48b.3; and Da-drin-rap-den's *Annotations,* 129.3.

620 Ibid., 129.5.

621 Jik-may-dam-chö-gya-tso's *Port of Entry,* 616.6.

622 Da-drin-rap-den's *Annotations,* 131.6.

623 Ibid., 132.4.

624 A-ku Lo-drö-gya-tso's *Precious Lamp,* 265.5; Jik-may-dam-chö-gya-tso's *Port of Entry,* 616.6; and Da-drin-rap-den's *Annotations,* 132.4.

625 Da-drin-rap-den's *Annotations,* 132.6.

626 A-ku Lo-drö-gya-tso's *Precious Lamp,* 265.6.

627 Da-drin-rap-den's *Annotations,* 133.3.

628 Bel-jor-hlün-drup's *Lamp for the Teaching,* 86.2.

629 Da-drin-rap-den's *Annotations,* 134.6.

630 Jik-may-dam-chö-gya-tso's *Port of Entry,* 617.1.

631 Da-drin-rap-den's *Annotations,* 135.2.

632 Ibid., 135.3.

633 Ibid., 135.6.

634 Ibid., 135.6.

635 Jik-may-dam-chö-gya-tso's *Port of Entry,* 617.1.

636 Da-drin-rap-den's *Annotations,* 136.3.

637 A-ku Lo-drö-gya-tso's *Precious Lamp,* 273.4; and Da-drin-rap-den's *Annotations,* 136.6.

638 A-ku Lo-drö-gya-tso's *Precious Lamp,* 273.4; *dmigs pa brtag pa, ālambanaparīkṣā* (Peking 5703, vol. 130). He also adds Dignāga's *Compilation of Prime Cognition.*

639 Da-drin-rap-den's *Annotations,* 139.3.

640 Ibid., 139.1.

641 Ibid., 139.2.

642 Ibid., 139.3.

643 See Willis, *On Knowing Reality,* 170-171.

644 Peking 5549, vol. 112, 227.3.1-227.3.5. Lamotte's edition, vol. 1, 51.23ff; vol. 2, 162.1ff; and Keenan, *Summary,* 66.

645 In the first section, entitled *viniścayasamuccaya;* Walpola Rahula, *Le Compendium de la super-doctrine (philosophie) (Abhidharmasamuccaya) d'Asaṅga* (Paris: École Française d'Extrême-Orient, 1980), 136-137.

646 Da-drin-rap-den's *Annotations,* 140.1.

NOTES TO PART TWO, CHAPTER 11

647 A-ku Lo-drö-gya-tso's *Precious Lamp,* 285.5.

648 Ibid., 286.3.

649 Da-drin-rap-den's *Annotations,* 141.1.

650 A-ku Lo-drö-gya-tso's *Precious Lamp,* 286.2; and Da-drin-rap-den's *Annotations,* 141.3.

651 A-ku Lo-drö-gya-tso's *Precious Lamp,* 286.2.

652 Ibid., 286.2

653 Da-drin-rap-den's *Annotations,* 141.5.

654 Ibid., 142.1.

655 A-ku Lo-drö-gya-tso's *Precious Lamp,* 286.5.

656 Ibid., 286.5.

657 This is a paraphrase of Peking 5538, vol. 110, 145.4.5-146.5.8; for the Sanskrit, see Unrai Wogihara, *Bodhisattvabhūmi: A Statement of the Whole Course of the Bodhisattva (Being the Fifteenth Section of Yogācārabhūmi)* (Tokyo: Seigo Kenkyūkai, 1930-1936), 50.22-55.17 and Nalinaksha Dutt, *Bodhisattvabhūmi (Being the XVth Section of Asangapada's Yogacarabhumi)* Tibetan Sanskrit Works Series, 7 (Patna, India: K. P. Jayaswal Research Institute, 1966), 34.22-38.3;

for a translation of the material that Ḏzong-ka-ḇa is summarizing, see Janice D. Willis, *On Knowing Reality: The Tattvārtha Chapter of Asaṅga's Bodhisattvabhūmi* (New York: Columbia University Press, 1979; reprint, Delhi: Motilal Banarsidass, 1982), 167 (middle) through 170 (middle).

658 Ḏa-drin-rap-ḏen's *Annotations,* 142.5.

659 Ibid., 142.5.

660 Ibid., 143.2.

661 Ibid., 144.3.

662 Ibid., 144.4.

663 S̄er-s̄hül's *Notes,* 52a.5.

664 A-ku L̄o-drö-gya-tso's *Precious Lamp,* 288.2.

665 Ḏa-drin-rap-ḏen's *Annotations,* 147.6.

666 Ibid., 148.2.

667 Ibid., 149.1.

668 Ibid., 149.2.

669 This comes at the end of Sthiramati's commentary on I.2. Peking 5334, vol. 109, 139.1.8-139.2.3; Sanskrit: Ramchandra Pandeya, *Madhyānta-vibhāga-śāstra* (Delhi: Motilal Banarsidass, 1971), 12.17-12.22; English translations: David Lasar Friedmann, *Sthiramati, Madhyānta-vibhāgaṭīkā: Analysis of the Middle Path and the Extremes* (Utrecht, Netherlands: Rijksuniversiteit te Leiden, 1937), 15.25-16.4, and F. Th. Stcherbatsky. *Madhyāntavibhāga, Discourse on Discrimination between Middle and Extremes ascribed to Bodhisattva Maitreya and Commented by Vasubandhu and Sthiramati,* Bibliotheca Buddhica, 30 (Osnabrück, Germany: Biblio Verlag, 1970; reprint, Calcutta: Indian Studies Past and Present, 1971), 23.41-24.13.

670 Jik-may-dam-chö-gya-tso's *Port of Entry,* 684.3.

671 S̄er-s̄hül's *Notes,* 53a.5; and Ḏa-drin-rap-ḏen's *Annotations,* 150.6.

672 Peking 5206, vol. 93, 230.4.2-230.4.4. This passage immediately precedes the above citation.

673 Jik-may-dam-chö-gya-tso's *Port of Entry,* 684.6.

674 Ibid., 684.5.

675 Ḏa-drin-rap-ḏen's *Annotations,* 151.4.

676 Ibid., 151.5.

677 Peking 5206, vol. 93.

678 Jik-may-dam-chö-gya-tso's *Port of Entry,* 685.4.

679 Ḏa-drin-rap-ḏen's *Annotations,* 153.2.

680 Ibid., 153.4.

681 Jik-may-dam-chö-gya-tso's *Port of Entry,* 687.6.

682 Ibid., 680.1.

683 Ibid., 680.1.

684 A-ku L̄o-drö-gya-tso's *Precious Lamp,* 289.6; and Ḏa-drin-rap-ḏen's *Annotations,* 153.2.

Notes to Part Two, Chapter 12

685 A-ku L̄o-drö-gya-tso's *Precious Lamp,* 291.2.

686 Jik-may-dam-chö-gya-tso's *Port of Entry,* 698.2.

687 A-ku L̄o-drö-gya-tso's *Precious Lamp,* 291.3.

688 S̄er-s̄hül's *Notes,* 54a.6.

689 Jik-may-dam-chö-gya-tso's *Port of Entry,* 698.2; 700.1.

690 Ḏa-drin-rap-ḏen's *Annotations,* 156.3.

691 Ibid., 156.3.

692 Ibid., 156.5.

693 Peking 5562, vol. 113, 281.4.2.

694 Ḏa-drin-rap-ḏen's *Annotations* (158.1) gives "Vasubandhu's *Principles of Explanation,* Asaṅga's *Grounds of Bodhisattvas,* Asaṅga's *Compendium of Ascertainments,* and so forth"; however, these three are the ones cited just above.

695 Ḏa-drin-rap-ḏen's *Annotations,* 158.2.

696 Ibid., 158.4.

697 Ibid., 158.5.

698 Ibid., 158.6.

699 Ibid., 158.6.

700 Jik-may-dam-chö-gya-tso's *Port of Entry,* 698.2; 703.2.

701 Ibid., 703.2.

702 Ḏa-drin-rap-ḏen's *Annotations,* 159.3.

703 Jik-may-dam-chö-gya-tso's *Port of Entry,* 703.4; Jik-may-dam-chö-gya-tso begins this section one clause earlier.

704 Peking 5562, vol. 113, 278.5.7-279.2.8.

705 Ibid., 279.2.8-279.3.2. This passage immediately follows the previous one.

706 Ḏa-drin-rap-ḏen's *Annotations,* 160.3.

707 Ibid., 160.6.

708 Ibid., 161.2.

709 Jik-may-dam-chö-gya-tso's *Port of Entry,* 704.4.

710 Ḏa-drin-rap-ḏen's *Annotations,* 161.5.

711 Ibid., 161.5.

712 Ibid., 162.2.

713 A-ku L̄o-drö-gya-tso's *Precious Lamp,* 293.4.

714 Ibid., 293.5.

715 Ibid., 293.6.

716 Ḏa-drin-rap-ḏen's *Annotations,* 163.2.

717 Ibid., 163.2.

718 Ibid., 163.4.

719 Ibid., 163.5.

720 Jik-may-dam-chö-gya-tso's *Port of Entry,* 710.4. For an indirectly related refutation of Shay-rap-gyel-tsen, see p. 225ff.

721 *shes rab kyi pha rol tu phyin pa'i man ngag, prajñāpāramitopadeśa;* Peking 5579, vol. 114, 237.5.7. For an outline of the text, see Shoryu Katsura, "A Synopsis of the *Prajñāpāramitopadeśa* of Ratnākaraśānti," *Journal of Indian and Buddhist Studies* [*Indogaku Bukkyōgaku Kenkyū*], 25, no. 1 (1976): 38-41.

722 A-ku Lo-drö-gya-tso's *Precious Lamp,* 296.3.

723 Ser-shül's *Notes,* 55a.5.

724 A-ku Lo-drö-gya-tso's *Precious Lamp,* 296.4.

725 Ibid., 296.4.

726 Ibid., 291.2; 296.2.

727 Ibid., 296.6.

728 Da-drin-rap-den's *Annotations,* 165.4.

729 Ibid., 165.6.

730 Ibid., 165.6.

731 Jik-may-dam-chö-gya-tso's *Port of Entry,* 712.5.

732 Ibid., 712.5.

733 Da-drin-rap-den's *Annotations,* 166.1.

Notes to Part Three, Prologue

734 The presentation here is drawn from Gung-tang's *Difficult Points,* 23.14-24.17.

735 *Garland of Blue Lotuses,* 2a.1.

736 60a.5.

737 72a.6.

738 75b.4.

739 76a.1.

740 76b.6.

Notes to Part Three, Chapter 2

741 Peking 5517, vol. 116, 130.5.4ff.

742 *Port of Entry,* 198.6ff.

743 Ibid., 199.5.

744 See the notes to the Translation for the references.

Notes to Part Three, Chapter 4

745 This synopsis is drawn from Jik-may-dam-chö-gya-tso's *Port of Entry* (287.4-291.3), which makes frequent reference to Wonch'uk's commentary.

746 A-ku Lo-drö-gya-tso's *Precious Lamp,* 142.4.

747 This synopsis is drawn from Jik-may-dam-chö-gya-tso's *Port of Entry* (291.3-294.3), which makes frequent reference to Wonch'uk's commentary.

748 A-ku Lo-drö-gya-tso's *Precious Lamp,* 142.4.

749 This synopsis is drawn from Jik-may-dam-chö-gya-tso's *Port of Entry* (294.3-296.6), which makes frequent reference to Wonch'uk's commentary.

750 A-ku Lo-drö-gya-tso's *Precious Lamp,* 142.4.

751 *Port of Entry,* 296.4.

752 Ibid., 353.5.

Note to Part Three, Chapter 5

753 Peking 5539, vol. 110, 83.2.6-107.4.8.

Note to Part Three, Chapter 7

754 Chap. 7; Étienne Lamotte, *Saṃdhinirmocanasūtra: L'Explication des mystères* (Louvain: Université de Louvain, 1935), 69-70 [8], and 195; and Dön-drup-gyel-tsen's *Four Intertwined Commentaries,* 8.4-9.1.

Note to Part Three, Chapter 8

755 See A-ku Lo-drö-gya-tso's *Precious Lamp,* 220.2.

Notes to Part Three, Chapter 9

756 Ser-shül's *Notes,* 39a.4-39b.2.

757 A-ku Lo-drö-gya-tso's *Precious Lamp,* 228.1-228.3; and Ser-shül's *Notes* (40a.2-40a.4).

758 *'od srung gi le'u'i mdo, kāśyapaparivartasūtra;* Peking 760.43, vol. 24, 194.1.2. Dzong-ka-ba himself does not cite the sūtra. The bracketed material is from Nga-wang-bel-den (*ngag dbang dpal ldan,* born 1797), *Annotations for (Jam-yang-shay-ba's) "Great Exposition of Tenets," Freeing the Knots of the Difficult Points, Precious Jewel of Clear Thought* (*grub mtha' chen mo'i mchan 'grel dka' gnad mdud grol blo gsal gces nor*) (Sarnath, India: Pleasure of Elegant Sayings Press, 1964), *dngos,* 77a.7ff; and *dbu,* 68b.5ff. The passage is also cited in Chandrakīrti's *Clear Words* (Louis de la Vallée Poussin, *Mūlamadhyamakakārikās de Nāgārjuna avec la Prasannapadā, commentaire de Candrakīrti,* Bibliotheca Buddhica, 4 [Osnabrück, Germany: Biblio Verlag, 1970], 358.10). For a citation by Jam-yang-shay-ba in the context of the Consequence School, see Jeffrey Hopkins, *Meditation on Emptiness* (London: Wisdom, 1983; rev. ed., Boston, Ma.: Wisdom, 1996) , 635.

759 *Ocean of Definitive Meaning,* 310.5.

760 Ibid., 309.1-310.1.

[761] A-ku Lo-drö-gya-tso's *Precious Lamp,* 231.5-232.2; and Jik-may-dam-chö-gya-tso's *Port of Entry,* 536.6.

[762] E. Obermiller, *History of Buddhism (Chos-hbyung) by Bu-ston* (Heidelberg: Heft, 1932; Tokyo: Suzuki Research Foundation, n.d.), 152-155.

[763] The explanation is drawn from Ser-shül's *Notes,* 41b.2-41b.5.

[764] The explanation is drawn from A-ku Lo-drö-gya-tso's *Precious Lamp,* 232.6-233.2.

[765] Ibid., 233.1.

[766] *Explanation of the Conventional and the Ultimate in the Four Systems of Tenets* (*grub mtha' bzhi'i lugs kyi kun rdzob dang don dam pa'i don rnam par bshad pa legs bshad dpyid kyi dpal mo'i glu dbyangs*) (New Delhi: Guru Deva, 1972), 39.2-39.6.

Notes to Part Three, Chapter 10

[767] *Port of Entry,* 564.6.

[768] Peking 5549, vol. 112, 224.4.1. Étienne Lamotte, *La somme du grand véhicule d'Asaṅga,* reprint, 2 vols. Publications de l'Institute Orientaliste de Louvain, 8 (Louvain: Université de Louvain, 1973), vol. 1, 36 (24); vol. 2, 118-119; John P. Keenan, *The Summary of the Great Vehicle by Bodhisattva Asaṅga: Translated from the Chinese of Paramārtha* (Berkeley, Calif.: Numata Center for Buddhist Translation and Research, 1992), 50-51.

[769] *Port of Entry,* 593.1, 595.3, and so forth. See A-ku Lo-drö-gya-tso's *Precious Lamp* (257.4) for a different presentation of the correlation; Jik-may-dam-chö-gya-tso (603.1-603.6) calls for analysis of the difference but does not himself settle the issue.

[770] The list is adapted from Jang-gya Röl-bay-dor-jay's *Clear Exposition of the Presentations of Tenets;* see Jeffrey Hopkins, *Meditation on Emptiness* (London: Wisdom, 1983; rev. ed., Boston, Ma.: Wisdom, 1996), 371-372, with translation equivalents updated.).

Note to Part Three, Chapter 11

[771] *Lamp for the Teaching,* 101.5.

Notes to Part Three, Chapter 12

[772] Peking 731, vol. 19 190.1.2ff.

[773] See Jeffrey Hopkins, *Meditation on Emptiness* (London: Wisdom, 1983; rev. ed., Boston, Ma.: Wisdom, 1996), 620-622.

[774] The explanation is drawn from Jam-yang-shay-ba's *Great Exposition of the Middle,* 461b.5-462b.3.

Bibliography

Sūtras and tantras are listed alphabetically by English title in the first section of the bibliography. Indian and Tibetan treatises are listed alphabetically by author in the second section; other works are listed alphabetically by author in the third section.

"P," standing for "Peking edition," refers to the *Tibetan Tripiṭaka* (Tokyo-Kyoto: Tibetan Tripiṭaka Research Foundation, 1956). "Toh" refers to the *Complete Catalogue of the Tibetan Buddhist Canons,* edited by Prof. Hukuji Ui (Sendai, Japan: Tohoku University, 1934), and *A Catalogue of the Tohuku University Collection of Tibetan Works on Buddhism,* edited by Prof. Yensho Kanakura (Sendai, Japan: Tohoku University, 1953). "Dharma" refers to the *sde dge* edition of the Tibetan canon published by Dharma—the *Nying-ma Edition of the sDe-dge bKa'-'gyur and bsTan-'gyur* (Oakland, Calif.: Dharma, 1980). "Tokyo *sde dge*" refers to the *sDe dge Tibetan Tripiṭaka—bsTan hgyur preserved at the Faculty of Letters, University of Tokyo,* edited by Z. Yamaguchi, et. al. (Tokyo: Tokyo University Press, 1977-1984). "Karmapa *sde dge*" refers to the *sde dge mtshal par bka' 'gyur: a facsimile edition of the 18th century redaction of Si tu chos kyi 'byung gnas prepared under the direction of H.H. the 16th rgyal dbang karma pa* (Delhi: Delhi Karmapae Chodhey Gyalwae Sungrab Partun Khang, 1977). "*stog* Palace" refers to the *Tog Palace Manuscript of the Tibetan Kanjur* (Leh, Ladakh: Smanrtsis Shesrig Dpemdzod, 1979). "Golden Reprint" refers to the *gser bris bstan 'gyur* (Sichuan, China: krung go'i mtho rim nang bstan slob gling gi bod brgyud nang bstan zhib 'jug khang, 1989). Works mentioned in the first or second sections are not repeated in the third section.

For an excellent bibliography of Yogācāra texts, see John C. Powers, *The Yogācāra School of Buddhism: A Bibliography,* American Theological Library Association Bibliography Series, 27 (Metuchen, N.J, and London: American Theological Library Association and Scarecrow Press, 1991).

1. Sūtras and Tantras

Collection of Meanings Sūtra

arthavargīyasūtra

don gyi sde tshan dag gi mdo

Sutta Nipāta. Mahāviyuhasutta. Aṭṭhakavagga

Compilations of Indicative Verse

udānavarga

ched du brjod pa'i tshom

P992, vol. 39

English translation: W. Woodville Rockhill. *The Udānavarga: A Collection of Verses from the Buddhist Canon.* London: Trübner, 1883.

Condensed Perfection of Wisdom Sūtra

prajñāpāramitāsañcayagāthā

shes rab kyi pha rol tu phyin pa sdud pa tshigs su bcad pa
P735, vol. 21
Sanskrit: E. E. Obermiller. *Prajñāpāramitā-ratnaguṇa-sañcayagāthā.* Osnabrück, Germany: Biblio Verlag, 1970. Also: P. L. Vaidya. *Mahāyāna-sūtra-saṃgraha.* Part I. Buddhist Sanskrit Texts, 17. Darbhanga, India: Mithila Institute, 1961.
English translation: Edward Conze. *The Perfection of Wisdom in Eight Thousand Lines & Its Verse Summary.* Bolinas, Calif.: Four Seasons Foundation, 1973.

Descent into Laṅkā Sūtra
laṅkāvatārasūtra
lang kar gshegs pa'i mdo
P775, vol. 29
Sanskrit: Bunyiu Nanjio. *Bibl. Otaniensis,* vol. 1. Kyoto: Otani University Press, 1923. Also: P. L. Vaidya. *Saddharmalaṅkāvatārasūtram.* Buddhist Sanskrit Texts, 3. Darbhanga, India: Mithila Institute, 1963.
English translation: D. T. Suzuki. *The Lankavatara Sutra.* London: Routledge and Kegon Paul, 1932.

Eight Thousand Stanza Perfection of Wisdom Sūtra
aṣṭasāhasrikāprajñāpāramitā
shes rab kyi pha rol tu phyin pa brgyad stong pa
P734, vol. 21
Sanskrit: P. L. Vaidya. *Aṣṭasāhasrika Prajñāpāramitā, with Haribhadra's Commentary called Ālokā.* Buddhist Sanskrit Texts, 4. Darbhanga, India: Mithila Institute, 1960.
English translation: E. Conze. *The Perfection of Wisdom in Eight Thousand Lines & Its Verse Summary.* Bolinas, Calif.: Four Seasons Foundation, 1973.

Hevajra Tantra
hevajratantrarāja
kye'i rdo rje zhes bya ba rgyud kyi rgyal po
P10, vol. 1
English translation: D. L. Snellgrove. *Hevajra Tantra,* Parts 1 and 2. London: Oxford University Press, 1959. Also: G. W. Farrow and I. Menon. *The Concealed Essence of the Hevajra Tantra.* Delhi: Motilal Banarsidass, 1992.

Kāshyapa Chapter Sūtra
kāśyapaparivartasūtra
'od srung gi le'u'i mdo
P760.43, vol. 24
Sanskrit: Alexander von Staël-Holstein. *Kāçyapaparivarta: A Mahāyanasūtra of the Ratnakūṭa Class.* Shanghai: Commercial Press, 1926; reprint, Tokyo: Meicho-fukyū-kai, 1977.
English translation: Garma C. C. Chang, ed. *A Treasury of Mahāyāna Sūtras.* University Park: Pennsylvania State University Press, 1983.

King of Meditative Stabilizations Sūtra
samādhirājasūtra / sarvadharmasvabhāvasamatāvipañcatasamādhirājasūtra
ting nge 'dzin rgyal po'i mdo / chos thams cad kyi rang bzhin mnyam pa nyid rnam par spros pa ting nge 'dzin gyi rgyal po'i mdo
P795, vol. 31-2; Toh 127, Dharma, vol. 20
Sanskrit: P. L. Vaidya. *Samādhirājasūtram.* Buddhist Sanskrit Texts, 2. Darbhanga, India: Mithila Institute, 1961.
Partial English translation (of chaps. 8, 19, and 22): K. Regamey. *Three Chapters from the Samādhirājasūtra.* Warsaw: Publications of the Oriental Commission, 1938.

Pile of Jewels Sūtra
ratnakūṭa / mahāratnakūṭadharmaparyāyaśatasāhasrikagrantha
dkon brtsegs / dkon mchog brtsegs pa chen po'i chos kyi rnam grangs le'u stong phrag brgya pa
P760, vols. 22-24
See individual sutra titles.

Questions of Rāṣṭrapāla Sūtra
rāṣṭrapālaparipṛcchā
yul 'khor skyong gis zhus pa
P760.17, vol. 23
Sanskrit: Louis Finot. *Rāṣṭrapālaparipṛcchā. Sūtra de Mahāyāna.* Bibliotheca Buddhica, 2. St. Petersburg, Russia: Académie Impériale des Sciences, 1901; reprint, Osnabrück, Germany: Biblio Verlag, 1970. Also: P. L. Vaidya. *Mahāyāna-sūtra-saṁgraha,* Part I. Buddhist Sanskrit Texts, 17. Darbhanga, India: Mithila Institute, 1961.
English translation: Jacob Ensink. *The Questions of Rāṣṭrapāla.* Zwolle, Netherlands: van de Erven J. J. Tijl, 1952.

Story of Saṃthakatyāyana Sūtra
saṃthakātyāyanasūtra
stums byed ka tya'i bu las brtsams te bka' stsal ba'i mdo
Aṅguttara-Nikāya. Ekādasaka-Nipāta. Nissaya-Vagga X
Pāli: Richard Morris and Edmund Hardy. *The Aṅguttara Nikāya.* Vol. 5: 322-326. Pali Text Society, vol. 46. London: H. Frowde, 1900; reprint, London: Luzac, 1958.
English translation: "Book of the Elevens, Chapter I—Dependence, (10) Sandha." In F. L. Woodward. *The Book of the Gradual Sayings (Anguttara-Nikāya) or More-Numbered Suttas.* Vol. 5: 204-207. Pali Text Society Translation Series, 27. London: Luzac, 1972.
Sanskrit: (Excerpts quoted in) Unrai Wogihara. *Bodhisattvabhūmi: A Statement of the Whole Course of the Bodhisattva (Being the Fifteenth Section of Yogācārabhūmi).* 2 vols. Leipzig: 1908; Tokyo: Seigo Kenkyūkai, 1930-1936. Also: Nalinaksha Dutt. *Bodhisattvabhumi (Being the XVth Section of Asangapada's Yogacarabhumi).* Tibetan Sanskrit Works Series, 7. Patna, India: K. P. Jayaswal Research Institute, 1966.
Tibetan: (Excerpts quoted in) Asaṅga. *Grounds of Bodhisattvas.* P5538, vol. 110.

Sūtra of the Teachings of Akṣhayamati
akṣayamatinirdeśasūtra
blo gros mi zad pas bstan pa
P842, vol. 34.

Sūtra Unraveling the Thought
saṃdhinirmocanasūtra
dgongs pa nges par 'grel pa'i mdo
P774, vol. 29; Toh 106; Dharma, vol. 18
Tibetan text and French translation: Étienne Lamotte. *Saṃdhinirmocanasūtra: L'Explication des mystères.* Louvain: Université de Louvain, 1935.
English translation: John C. Powers. *Wisdom of Buddha: Saṁdhinirmocana Sūtra.* Berkeley, Calif.: Dharma, 1995. Also: Thomas Cleary. *Buddhist Yoga: A Comprehensive Course.* Boston: Shambhala, 1995.

Teachings of Akṣhayamati Sūtra
akṣayamatinirdeśa
blo gros mi zad pas bstan pa
P842, vol. 34.

Transmigration Sūtra
bhavasaṃkrāntisūtra
srid pa 'pho ba'i mdo
P892, vol. 35
Tibetan text, restored Sanskrit and English translation: N. Ayyaswami. "Bhavasamkrānti Sūtra" *Journal of Oriental Research* [Madras], 5, no. 4 (1931): 246-260.

Twenty-Five Thousand Stanza Perfection of Wisdom Sūtra
pañcaviṃśatisāhasrikāprajñāpāramitā
shes rab kyi pha rol tu phyin pa stong phrag nyi shu lnga pa
P731, vol. 19

English translation (abridged): Edward Conze. *The Large Sūtra on the Perfection of Wisdom.* Berkeley, Calif.: University of California Press, 1975.

2. Other Sanskrit and Tibetan Works

A-ku Lo-drö-gya-tso / Gung-tang Lo-drö-gya-tso (*a khu blo gros rgya mtsho / gung thang blo gros rgya mtsho;* 1851-1930)

Precious Lamp / Commentary on the Difficult Points of (Dzong-ka-ba's) "Treatise Differentiating Interpretable and the Definitive Meanings, The Essence of Eloquence": A Precious Lamp

drang ba dang nges pa'i don rnam par 'byed pa'i bstan bcos legs bshad snying po'i dka' 'grel rin chen sgron me

Delhi: Kesang Thabkhes, 1982.

Āryadeva (*'phags pa lha,* second to third century C.E.)

Compilation of the Essence of Wisdom

jñānasārasamuccaya

ye shes snying po kun las btus pa

P5251, vol. 95

Four Hundred / Treatise of Four Hundred Stanzas

catuḥśatakaśāstrakārikā

bstan bcos bzhi brgya pa zhes bya ba'i tshig le'ur byas pa

P5246, vol. 95

Edited Tibetan and Sanskrit fragments along with English translation: Karen Lang. *Āryadeva's Catuḥśataka: On the Bodhisattva's Cultivation of Merit and Knowledge.* Indiste Studier, 7. Copenhagen: Akademisk Forlag, 1986.

English translation: Geshe Sonam Rinchen and Ruth Sonam. *Yogic Deeds of Bodhisattvas: Gyel-tsap on Āryadeva's Four Hundred.* Ithaca, N.Y.: Snow Lion, 1994.

Italian translation of the last half from the Chinese: Giuseppe Tucci. "Study Mahāyānici: La versione cinese del Catuḥśataka di Āryadeva, confronta col testo sanscrito e la traduzione tibetana." *Rivista degli Studi Orientali* 10 (1925): 521-567.

Asaṅga (*thogs med,* fourth century)

Explanation of the Superior Sūtra Unraveling the Thought (perhaps falsely attributed to Asaṅga)

āryasaṃdhinirmocanabhāṣya

'phags pa dgongs pa nges par 'grel pa'i rnam par bshad pa

P5481, vol. 104

English translation: John C. Powers. *Two Commentaries on the Samdhinirmocana-sutra by Asanga and Jnanagarbha.* Lewiston, N.Y.: Edward Mellon, 1992.

Five Treatises on the Grounds

1. *Grounds of Yogic Practice*

yogācārabhūmi

rnal 'byor spyod pa'i sa

P5536-5538, vol. 109-110

Grounds of Bodhisattvas

bodhisattvabhūmi

byang chub sems pa'i sa

P5538, vol. 110

Sanskrit: Unrai Wogihara. *Bodhisattvabhūmi: A Statement of the Whole Course of the Bodhisattva (Being the Fifteenth Section of Yogācārabhūmi).* Leipzig: 1908; Tokyo: Seigo Kenyūkai, 1930-1936. Also: Nalinaksha Dutt. *Bodhisattvabhumi (Being the XVth Section of Asangapada's Yogacarabhumi).* Tibetan Sanskrit Works Series, 7. Patna, India: K. P. Jayaswal Research Institute, 1966.

English translation of the Chapter on Suchness, the fourth chapter of Part I which is the fifteenth volume of the *Grounds of Yogic Practice:* Janice D. Willis. *On Knowing Reality.* New York: Columbia University Press, 1979; reprint, Delhi: Motilal Banarsidass, 1979.

2. *Compendium of Ascertainments*
   nirṇayasaṃgraha / viniścayasaṃgrahaṇī
   rnam par gtan la dbab pa bsdu ba
   P5539, vols. 110-111
3. *Compendium of Bases*
   vastusaṃgraha
   gzhi bsdu ba
   P5540, vol. 111
4. *Compendium of Enumerations*
   paryāyasaṃgraha
   rnam grang bsdu ba
   P5543, vol. 111
5. *Compendium of Explanations*
   vivaraṇasaṃgraha
   rnam par bshad pa bsdu ba
   P5543, vol. 111

Grounds of Hearers
nyan sa
śrāvakabhūmi
P5537, vol. 110
Sanskrit: Karunesha Shukla. *Śrāvakabhūmi.* Tibetan Sanskrit Works Series, 14. Patna, India: K. P. Jayaswal Research Institute, 1973.

Two Summaries

1. *Summary of Manifest Knowledge*
   abhidharmasamuccaya
   chos mngon pa kun btus
   P5550, vol. 112
   Sanskrit: Pralhad Pradhan. *Abhidharma Samuccaya of Asaṅga.* Visva-Bharati Series, 12. Santiniketan, India: Visva-Bharati (Santiniketan Press), 1950.
   French translation: Walpola Rahula. *La compendium de la super-doctrine (philosophie) (Abhidharmasamuccaya) d'Asaṅga.* Paris: École Française d'Extrême-Orient, 1971.
2. *Summary of the Great Vehicle*
   mahāyānasaṃgraha
   theg pa chen po bsdus pa
   P5549, vol. 112
   French translation and Chinese and Tibetan texts: Étienne Lamotte. *La Somme du grand véhicule d'Asaṅga,* 2 vols. Publications de l'Institute Orientaliste de Louvain, 8. Louvain: Université de Louvain, 1938; reprint, 1973.
   English translation: John P. Keenan. *The Summary of the Great Vehicle by Bodhisattva Asaṅga: Translated from the Chinese of Paramārtha.* Berkeley, Calif.: Numata Center for Buddhist Translation and Research, 1992.

Asvabhāva (*ngo bo nyid med pa*)
Connected Explanation of (Asaṅga's) "Summary of the Great Vehicle"
mahāyānasaṃgrahopanibandhana
theg pa chen po bsdus pa'i bshad sbyar
P5552, vol. 113
Extensive Explanation of (Maitreya's) "Ornament for the Great Vehicle Sūtras"
sūtrālaṃkārāṭīkā
theg pa chen po'i mdo sde'i rgyan gyi rgya cher bshad pa
P5530, vol. 108

Atisha (*atiśa / atīśa*, 982-1054)

Lamp for the Path to Enlightenment

bodhipathapradīpa

byang chub lam gyi sgron ma

P5343, vol. 103

English translation with Atisha's autocommentary: Richard Sherbourne, S. J. *A Lamp for the Path and Commentary*. London: George Allen and Unwin, 1983.

B̄el-den-drak-b̄a, L̄o-l̄ing Ge-s̄hay (*dpal ldan grags pa, blo gling dge bshes*)

gzhi gsum gyi dus tshigs la dpyod pa'i legs bshad lung rigs dga' tshal

New Delhi: Tibet House, 1983.

B̄el-jor-hlün-drup, N̄yel-d̄ön (*dpal 'byor lhun grub, gnyal* [or *gnyan*] *ston*, 1427-1514)

Lamp for the Teaching / Commentary on the Difficult Points of (D̄zong-ka-b̄a's) "The Essence of Eloquence": Lamp for the Teaching

legs bshad snying po'i dka' 'grel bstan pa'i sgron me

Delhi: Rong-tha Mchog-sprul-rnam-pa-gnyis, 1969.

Bhāvaviveka (*legs ldan 'byed*, c. 500-570?)

Blaze of Reasoning / Commentary on the "Heart of the Middle Way": Blaze of Reasoning

madhyamakahṛdayavṛttitarkajvālā

dbu ma'i snying po'i 'grel pa rtog ge 'bar ba

P5256, vol. 96

Partial English translation (chap. 3, 1-136): Shōtarō Iida. *Reason and Emptiness*. Tokyo: Hokuseido, 1980.

Heart of the Middle Way

madhyamakahṛdayakārikā

dbu ma'i snying po'i tshig le'ur byas pa

P5255, vol. 96

Partial English translation (chap. 3. 1-136): Shōtarō Iida. *Reason and Emptiness*. Tokyo: Hokuseido, 1980.

Bodhibhadra (*byang chub bzang po*)

Connected Explanation of [Āryadeva's] "Compilation of the Essence of Wisdom"

jñānasārasamuccayanāmanibandhana

ye shes snying po kun las btus pa shes bya ba'i bshad sbyar

P5252, vol. 95

Buddhaguhya (*sangs rgyas gsang ba*)

Commentary on the "Concentration Continuation Tantra"

dhyānottarapaṭalaṭīkā

bsam gtan phyi ma rim par phye ba rgya cher bshad pa

P3495, vol. 78

Bu-d̄ön Rin-chen-drup (*bu ston rin chen grub*, 1290-1364)

Catalogue of the Translated Doctrine

chos bsgyur dkar chag

Collected Works of Bu-ston, vol. 26, 401-644; vol. 28, 343-574. New Delhi: International Academy of Indian Culture, 1966.

Chandrakīrti (*candrakīrti, zla ba grags pa*, seventh century)

[Auto]commentary on the "Supplement to (Nāgārjuna's) 'Treatise on the Middle'"

madhaymakāvatārabhāṣya

dbu ma la 'jug pa'i bshad pa / dbu ma la 'jug pa'i rang 'grel

P5263, vol. 98. Also: Dharmsala, India: Council of Religious and Cultural Affairs, 1968.

Tibetan: Louis de la Vallée Poussin. *Madhyamakāvatāra par Candrakīrti*. Bibliotheca Buddhica, 9. Osnabrück, Germany: Biblio Verlag, 1970.

English translation: C. W. Huntington, Jr. *The Emptiness of Emptiness: An Introduction to Early Indian Mādhyamika*, 147-195. Honolulu, Hawaii: University of Hawaii Press, 1989.

French translation (up to chap. 6, stanza 165): Louis de la Vallée Poussin. *Muséon* 8 (1907): 249-

317; *Muséon* 11 (1910): 271-358; *Muséon* 12 (1911): 235-328.
German translation (chap. 6, 166-226): Helmut Tauscher. *Candrakīrti-Madhyamakāvatāraḥ und Madhyamakāvatārabhāṣyam.* Vienna: Wiener Studien zur Tibetologie und Buddhismuskunde, 1981.

Clear Words, Commentary on (Nāgārjuna's) "Treatise on the Middle"
mūlamadhyamakavṛttiprasannapadā
dbu ma rtsa ba'i 'grel pa tshig gsal ba
P5260, vol. 98. Also: Dharmsala, India: Tibetan Cultural Printing Press, 1968.
Sanskrit: Louis de la Vallée Poussin. *Mūlamadhyamakakārikās de Nāgārjuna avec la Prasannapadā commentaire de Candrakīrti.* Bibliotheca Buddhica, 4. Osnabrück, Germany: Biblio Verlag, 1970.
English translation (chap. 1, 25): T. Stcherbatsky. *Conception of Buddhist Nirvāṇa,* 77-222. Leningrad: Office of the Academy of Sciences of the USSR, 1927; rev. reprint, Delhi: Motilal Banarsidass, 1978.
English translation (chap. 2): Jeffrey Hopkins. "Analysis of Coming and Going." Dharmsala, India: Library of Tibetan Works and Archives, 1974.
Partial English translation: Mervyn Sprung. *Lucid Exposition of the Middle Way: The Essential Chapters from the Prasannapadā of Candrakīrti translated from the Sanskrit.* London: Routledge, 1979; Boulder: Prajñā Press, 1979.
French translation (chaps. 2-4, 6-9, 11, 23, 24, 26, 28): Jacques May. *Prasannapadā Madhyamakavṛtti, douze chapitres traduits du sanscrit et du tibétain.* Paris: Adrien-Maisonneuve, 1959.
French translation (chaps. 18-22): J. W. de Jong. *Cinq chapitres de la Prasannapadā.* Paris: Geuthner, 1949.
French translation (chap. 17): É. Lamotte. "Le Traité de l'acte de Vasubandhu, Karmasiddhiprakaraṇa." *Mélanges Chinois et Bouddhiques* 4 (1936): 265-288.
German translation (chap. 5, 12-26): Stanislaw Schayer. *Ausgewählte Kapitel aus der Prasannapadā.* Krakow: Naktadem Polskiej Akademji Umiejetnosci, 1931.
German translation (chap. 10): Stanislaw Schayer. "Feuer und Brennstoff." *Rocznik Orjentalistyczny* 7 (1931): 26-52.

Supplement to (Nāgārjuna's) "Treatise on the Middle"
madhyamakāvatāra
dbu ma la 'jug pa
P5261, P5262, vol. 98
Tibetan: Louis de la Vallée Poussin. *Madhyamakāvatāra par Candrakīrti.* Bibliotheca Buddhica, 9. Osnabrück, Germany: Biblio Verlag, 1970.
English translation (chap. 1-5): Jeffrey Hopkins. *Compassion in Tibetan Buddhism.* London: Rider, 1980; reprint, Ithaca, N.Y.: Snow Lion, 1980.
English translation (chap. 6): Stephen Batchelor. *Echoes of Voidness* by Geshé Rabten, 47-92. London: Wisdom, 1983.
See also references under Chandrakīrti's *[Auto]commentary on the "Supplement."*

Chim Jam-b̄ay-ȳang (*mchims 'jam pa'i dbyangs* or *mchims nam mkha' grags,* died 1289 / 1290)
Commentary on [Vasubandhu's] "Treasury of Manifest Knowledge": Ornament of Manifest Knowledge
chos mngon mdzod kyi tshig le'ur byas pa'i 'grel pa mngon pa'i rgyan
Buxaduor, India: Nang bstan shes rig 'dzin skyong slob gnyer khang, n.d.

D̄a-drin-rap-d̄en (*rta mgrin rab brtan, tre hor dge bshes;* 1920-1986)
Annotations / Annotations for the Difficult Points of (D̄zong-ka-b̄a's) "The Essence of Eloquence": Festival for the Unbiased Endowed with Clear Intelligence
drang nges rnam 'byed legs bshad snying po dka' gnad rnams mchan bur bkod pa gzur gnas blo gsal dga' ston
Delhi: Lhun-grub-chos-grags, 1978.

D̄ak-tsang S̄hay-rap-rin-chen (*stag tshang lo tsā ba shes rab rin chen,* born 1405)
Explanation of "Freedom from Extremes through Understanding All Tenets": Ocean of Eloquence

grub mtha' kun shes nas mtha' bral grub pa zhes bya ba'i bstan bcos rnam par bshad pa legs bshad kyi rgya mtsho
Thimphu, Bhutan: Kun-bzang-stobs rgyal, 1976
Damṣhṭasena (*damṣṭasena;* attributed so by D̄zong-ka-b̄a; some others identify Vasubandhu as the author)
[Commentary on] the Three Mothers, Conquest Over Harm / Extensive Explanation of the Superior One Hundred Thousand Stanza, Twenty-Five Thousand Stanza, and Eighteen Thousand Stanza Perfection of Wisdom Sūtras
āryaśatasāhasrikāpañcaviṃsatisāhasrikāṣṭadaśasāhasrikāprajñāpāramitābṛhaṭṭīkā
yum gsum gnod 'joms / 'phags pa shes rab kyi pha rol tu phyin pa 'bum pa dang nyi khri lnga stong pa dang khri brgyad stong pa'i rgya cher bshad pa
P5206, vol. 93
D̄en-b̄a-dar-gyay, Ke-drup (*bstan pa dar rgyas, mkhas grub,* 1493-1568)
General Meaning of (D̄zong-ka-b̄a's) "Differentiation the Interpretable and the Definitive": Essence of Eloquence, Garland of White Lotuses
drang nges rnam 'byed kyi spyi don legs par bshad pa'i snying po padma dkar po'i 'phreng ba
Indian ed., n.d. [Photocopy provided by Geshe Lobsang Tharchin]. Also: *Supplementary Texts for the Study of the Perfection of Wisdom at Sera Mey Tibetan Monastic University,* vol. 1, 1-50. Bylakuppe, India: The Computer Center, Sera Mey, 1990.
Decisive Analysis of (D̄zong-ka-b̄a's) "Differentiating the Interpretable and the Definitive"
mkhas grub smra ba'i khyu mchog dge 'dun bstan dar ba chen po'i gsung drang nges rnam 'byed kyi mtha dpyod
Indian ed., n.d. [Photocopy provided by Geshe Lobsang Tharchin]. Also: *Supplementary Texts for the Study of the Perfection of Wisdom at Sera Mey Tibetan Monastic University,* vol. 1, 51-153. Bylakuppe, India: The Computer Center, Sera Mey, 1990.
Dharmakīrti (*chos kyi grags pa,* seventh century)
Seven Treatises on Valid Cognition
1. *Analysis of Relations*
sambandhaparīkṣā
'brel pa brtag pa
P5713, vol. 130
2. *Ascertainment of Prime Cognition*
pramāṇaviniścaya
tshad ma rnam par nges pa
P5710, vol. 130
3. *Commentary on (Dignāga's) "Compilation of Prime Cognition"*
pramāṇavārttikakārikā
tshad ma rnam 'grel gyi tshig le'ur byas pa
P5709, vol. 130. Also: Sarnath, India: Pleasure of Elegant Sayings Press, 1974.
Sanskrit: Dwarikadas Shastri. *Pramāṇavārttika of Āchārya Dharmakīrtti.* Varanasi, India: Bauddha Bharati, 1968.
English translation (chap. 2): Masatoshi Nagatomi, "A Study of Dharmakīrti's Pramāṇavarttika: An English Translation and Annotation of the Pramāṇavarttika, Book I." Ph. D. diss., Harvard University, 1957.
4. *Drop of Reasoning*
nyāyabinduprakaraṇa
rigs pa'i thigs pa zhes bya ba'i rab tu byed pa
P5711, vol. 130
English translation: Th. Stcherbatsky. *Buddhist Logic.* New York: Dover Publications, 1962.
5. *Drop of Reasons*
hetubindunāmaprakaraṇa
gtan tshigs kyi thigs pa zhes bya ba rab tu byed pa
P5712, vol. 130

6. *Principles of Debate*
vādanyāya
rtsod pa'i rigs pa
P5715, vol. 130
7. *Proof of Other Continuums*
saṃtānāntarasiddhināmaprakaraṇa
rgyud gzhan grub pa zhes bya ba'i rab tu byed pa
P5716, vol. 130

Dignāga (*phyogs kyi glangs po,* sixth century)
Compilation of Prime Cognition
pramāṇasamuccaya
tshad ma kun las btus pa
P5700, vol. 130
English translation (partial): M. Hattori. *Dignāga, On Perception.* Cambridge, Mass.: Harvard University Press, 1968.
Examination of Objects of Observation
ālambanaparīkṣa
dmigs pa brtag pa
P5703, vol. 130
Summary Meanings of the Eight Thousand Stanza Perfection of Wisdom Sūtra
prajñāpāramitāpiṇḍārtha / prajñāpāramitāsaṃgrahakārikā
brgyad stong don bsdus / shes rab kyi pha rol tu phyin ma bsdus pa'i tshig le'ur byas pa
P5207, vol. 94

Dön-drup-gyel-tsen (*don grub rgyal mtshan;* fl. late eighteenth and early nineteenth centuries)
Four Intertwined Commentaries / Extensive Explanation of (D̄zong-ka-b̄a's) "Treatise Differentiating the Interpretable and the Definitive, The Essence of Eloquence," Unique to Ge-luk-b̄a: Four Intertwined Commentaries
dge ldan thun mon ma yin pa drang ba dang nges pa'i don rnam par phye ba'i bstan bcos legs bshad snying po'i rgya cher bshad pa dang nges bzhi 'dril
New Delhi: Chophel Legdan, 1975.

D̄ra-d̄i Ge-s̄hay Rin-chen-dön-drup (*rin chen don grub, pra sti dge bshes;* fl. mid-seventeenth century)
Ornament for the Thought / Ornament for the Thought of (D̄zong-ka-b̄a's) "Interpretable and Definitive: The Essence of Eloquence"
drang nges legs bshad snying po'i dgongs rgyan
Bylakuppe, India: Sera Je Printing Press: 1989.

Drak-b̄a-shay-drup, J̄o-nay-wa (*grags pa bshad sgrub, co ne ba,* 1675-1748)
Condensed Essence of All Tenets
grub mtha' thams cad kyi snying po bsdus
in *rje btsun grags pa bshad sgrub kyi mdzad pa'i grub mtha', sa lam dang stong 'khor zhabs drung gi mdzad pa'i don bdun cu bcas bzhugs so.*
Bylakuppe, India: Sermey Printing Press, 1995.

D̄zong-ka-b̄a L̄o-sang-drak-b̄a (*tsong kha pa blo bzang grags pa,* 1357-1419)
Explanation of (Nāgārjuna's) "Treatise on the Middle": Ocean of Reasoning / Great Commentary on (Nāgārjuna's) "Treatise on the Middle"
dbu ma rtsa ba'i tshig le'ur byas pa shes rab ces bya ba'i rnam bshad rigs pa'i rgya mtsho / rtsa shes ṭik chen
P6153, vol. 156. Also: Sarnath, India: Pleasure of Elegant Sayings Printing Press, n.d. Also: *rJe tsong kha pa'i gsung dbu ma'i lta ba'i skor,* vols. 1-2. Sarnath, India: Pleasure of Elegant Sayings Press, 1975. Also: Delhi: Ngawang Gelek, 1975. Also: Delhi: Guru Deva, 1979.
English translation (chap. 2): Jeffrey Hopkins. *Ocean of Reasoning.* Dharmsala, India: Library of Tibetan Works and Archives, 1974.
Extensive Commentary on the Difficult Points of the Mind-Basis-of-All and Afflicted Intellect: Ocean of Eloquence: Ocean of Eloquence

yid dang kun gzhi'i dka' ba'i gnas rgya cher 'grel pa legs par bshad pa'i rgya mtsho

P6149, vol. 154. Also: Delhi: Ngawang Gelek, 1975. Also: Delhi: Guru Deva, 1979.

English translation: Gareth Sparham in collaboration with Shōtarō Iida. *Ocean of Eloquence: Tsong kha pa's Commentary on the Yogācāra Doctrine of Mind.* Albany, N.Y.: State University of New York Press, 1993.

Extensive Explanation of (Chandrakīrti's) "Supplement to (Nāgārjuna's) 'Treatise on the Middle'": Illumination of the Thought

dbu ma la 'jug pa'i rgya cher bshad pa dgongs pa rab gsal

P6143, vol. 154. Also: Sarnath, India: Pleasure of Elegant Sayings Press, 1973. Also: Delhi: Ngawang Gelek, 1975. Also: Delhi: Guru Deva, 1979.

English translation (chaps. 1-5): Jeffrey Hopkins. *Compassion in Tibetan Buddhism,* 93-230. Ithaca, New York: Snow Lion, 1980.

English translation (chap. 6, stanzas 1-7): Jeffrey Hopkins and Anne C. Klein. *Path to the Middle: Madhyamaka Philosophy in Tibet: The Oral Scholarship of Kensur Yeshay Tupden,* by Anne C. Klein, 147-183, 252-271. Albany, N.Y.: State University of New York Press, 1994.

Golden Rosary of Eloquence / Extensive Explanation of (Maitreya's) "Ornament for Clear Realization, Treatise of Quintessential Instructions on the Perfection of Wisdom" as well as its Commentaries: Golden Rosary of Eloquence

legs bshad gser 'phreng / shes rab kyi pha rol tu phyin pa'i man ngag gi bstan bcos mngon par rtogs pa'i rgyan 'grel pa dang bcas pa'i rgya cher bshad pa legs bshad gser gyi phreng ba

P6150, vols. 154-155. Also: Delhi: Ngawang Gelek, 1975. Also: Delhi: Guru Deva, 1979.

Great Exposition of Secret Mantra / The Stages of the Path to a Conqueror and Pervasive Master, a Great Vajradhara: Revealing All Secret Topics

sngags rim chen mo / rgyal ba khyab bdag rdo rje 'chang chen po'i lam gyi rim pa gsang ba kun gyi gnad rnam par phye ba

P6210, vol. 161. Also: Delhi: Ngawang Gelek, 1975. Also: Delhi: Guru Deva, 1979.

English translation (chap. 1): H.H. the Dalai Lama, Tsong-ka-pa, and Jeffrey Hopkins. *Tantra in Tibet.* London: George Allen and Unwin, 1977; reprint, with minor corrections, Ithaca, N.Y.: Snow Lion, 1987.

English translation (chap. 2-3): H.H. the Dalai Lama, Tsong-ka-pa, and Jeffrey Hopkins. *The Yoga of Tibet.* London: George Allen and Unwin, 1981; reprinted as *Deity Yoga.* Ithaca, N.Y.: Snow Lion, 1987.

Great Exposition of the Stages of the Path / Stages of the Path to Enlightenment Thoroughly Teaching All the Stages of Practice of the Three Types of Beings

lam rim chen mo / skyes bu gsum gyi nyams su blang ba'i rim pa thams cad tshang bar ston pa'i byang chub lam gyi rim pa

P6001, vol. 152. Also: Dharmsala, India: Tibetan Cultural Printing Press, 1964. Also: Delhi: Ngawang Gelek, 1975. Also: Delhi: Guru Deva, 1979.

English translation of the part on the excessively broad object of negation: Elizabeth Napper. *Dependent-Arising and Emptiness,* 153-215. London: Wisdom, 1989.

English translation of the parts on calm abiding and special insight: Alex Wayman. *Calming the Mind and Discerning the Real,* 81-431. New York: Columbia University Press, 1978; reprint, New Delhi, Motilal Banarsidass, 1979.

Medium Exposition of the Stages of the Path / Small Exposition of the Stages of the Path to Enlightenment

lam rim 'bring / lam rim chung ngu / skyes bu gsum gyi nyams su blang ba'i byang chub lam gyi rim pa

P6002, vol. 152-153. Also: Dharmsala, India: Tibetan Cultural Printing Press, 1968. Also: Mundgod, India: dga' ldan shar rtse, n.d. (includes outline of topics by Trijang Rinbochay). Also: Delhi: Ngawang Gelek, 1975. Also: Delhi: Guru Deva, 1979.

English translation of the section on special insight: Robert Thurman. "The Middle Transcendent Insight." *Life and Teachings of Tsong Khapa,* 108-185. Dharmsala, India: Library of Tibetan Works and Archives, 1982.

English translation of the section on special insight: Jeffrey Hopkins. "Special Insight: From

Dzong-ka-ba's *Middling Exposition of the Stages of the Path to Enlightenment Practiced by Persons of Three Capacities,* with supplementary headings by Trijang Rinbochay." Unpublished manuscript.

Praise of Dependent-Arising / Praise of the Supramundane Victor Buddha from the Approach of his Teaching the Profound Dependent-Arising: The Essence of Eloquence

rten 'brel bstod pa / sang rgyas bcom ldan 'das la zab mo rten cing 'brel bar 'byung ba gsung ba'i sgo nas bstod pa legs par bshad pa'i snying po

P6016, vol. 153. Also: Delhi: Ngawang Gelek, 1975. Also: Delhi: Guru Deva, 1979.

English translation: Geshe Wangyal. *The Door of Liberation,* 175-86. New York: Maurice Girodias Associates, 1973; reprint, New York: Lotsawa, 1978; rev. ed., Boston: Wisdom, 1995. Also: Robert Thurman. *Life and Teachings of Tsong Khapa,* 99-107. Dharmsala, India: Library of Tibetan Works and Archives, 1982.

Treatise Differentiating the Interpretable and the Definitive: The Essence of Eloquence

drang ba dang nges pa'i don rnam par phye ba'i bstan bcos legs bshad snying po

Editions: see the preface to the critical edition, p. 355

English translation: Prologue and Mind-Only section translated in this book. Also: Robert A. F. Thurman. *Tsong Khapa's Speech of Gold in the Essence of True Eloquence,* 185-385. Princeton, N.J.: Princeton University Press, 1984.

Chinese translation: Venerable Fa Zun. "Bian Liao Yi Bu Liao Yi Shuo Cang Lun." In *Xi Zang Fo Jiao Jiao Yi Lun Ji,* 2, 159-276. Taipei: Da Sheng Wen Hua Chu Ban She, 1979.

Gen-dün-chö-pel, A-mdo (*dge 'dun chos 'phel, a mdo,* 1905-1951)

Eloquent Inquiry into Profound Points concerning the Middle: Ornament for the Thought of Nāgārjuna

dbu ma'i zab gnad snying por dril ba'i legs bshad klu sgrub dgongs rgyan

Gangtok, Sikkim: Palace Monastery, 1983.

Treatise on Desire / Tibetan Arts of Love

'dod pa'i bstan bcos

Delhi: T. G. Dhongthog Rinpoche, 1967; also an edited edition, Delhi: T. G. Dhongthog Rinpoche, 1969; reprinted without preface, Dharmsala: Tibetan Cultural Printing Press, 1983.

English translation: Gedün Chöpel and Jeffrey Hopkins. *Tibetan Arts of Love,* 167-275. Ithaca, N.Y.: Snow Lion Publications, 1992.

Gen-dün-drup, First Dalai Lama (*dge 'dun grub,* 1391-1474)

Commentary on [Guṇaprabha's] "Aphorisms on Discipline" / Essence of the Entire Discipline, Eloquent Holy Doctrine

legs par gsungs pa'i dam chos 'dul ba mtha' dag gi snying po

Collected Works of the First Dalai Lama dge-'dun-grub-pa. Gangtok, Sikkim: Dodrup Lama Sangye, 1978-81.

Explanation of [Vasubandhu's] "Treasury of Manifest Knowledge": Illuminating the Path to Liberation

dam pa'i chos mngon pa'i mdzod kyi rnam par bshad pa thar lam gsal byed

Collected Works of the First Dalai Lama dge-'dun-grub-pa, vol. 3. Gangtok, Sikkim: Dodrup Lama, 1978-81. Also: Buxaduor: n. p., 1967. Also: Sarnath, India: wa na mtho' slob dge ldan spyi las khang, 1973.

English translation (chaps. 1-5): David Patt. *Elucidating the Path to Liberation.* Ann Arbor, Mich.: University Microfilms, 1994.

English translation (chap. 6): Harvey B. Aronson, "The Buddhist Path: A Translation of the Sixth Chapter of the First Dalai Lama's *Path of Liberation.*" *Tibet Journal* 5, no. 3 (1980): 29-51; 5, no. 4 (1980): 28-47; 12, no. 2 (1987): 25-40; 12, no. 3 (1987): 41-61.

Great Treatise on Valid Cognition: Adornment of Reasoning

tshad ma'i bstan bcos chen po rigs pa'i rgyan

Collected Works of the First Dalai Lama dge-'dun-grub-pa. Gangtok, Sikkim: Dodrup Lama, 1978-81.

Gen-dün-gya-tso, Second Dalai Lama (*dge 'dun rgya mtsho,* 1476-1542)

Lamp Illuminating the Meaning / Commentary on the Difficult Points of "Differentiating the Interpretable and the Definitive" from the Collected Works of the Foremost Holy Omniscient [Dzong-ka-ba]:

Lamp Thoroughly Illuminating the Meaning of his Thought
rje btsun thams cad mkhyen pa'i gsung 'bum las drang nges rnam 'byed kyi dka' 'grel dgongs pa'i don rab tu gsal bar byed pa'i sgron me
n.d. [blockprint borrowed from the library of H.H. the Dalai Lama and photocopied] volume *'a*

Ḡön-chok-jik-may-w̄ang-b̄o (*dkon mchog 'jigs med dbang po,* 1728-1791)

Precious Garland of Tenets / Presentation of Tenets, A Precious Garland
grub pa'i mtha'i rnam par bzhag pa rin po che'i phreng ba
Tibetan: K. Mimaki. Le Grub mtha' rnam bzhag rin chen phreṅ ba de dkon mchog 'jigs med dbaṅ po (1728-1791), *Zinbun* [The Research Institute for Humanistic Studies, Kyoto University], 14: 55-112. Also, Collected Works of dkon-mchog-'jigs-med-dbaṅ-po, vol. 6, 485-535. New Delhi: Ngawang Gelek Demo, 1972. Also: Xylograph in thirty-two folios from the Lessing collection of the rare book section of the University of Wisconsin Library, which is item 47 in Leonard Zwilling. *Tibetan Blockprints in the Department of Rare Books and Special Collections.* Madison, Wisconsin; the University of Wisconsin-Madison Libraries, 1984. Also: Mundgod, India: blo gsal gling Press, 1980. Also: Dharmsala, India: Tibetan Cultural Printing Press, 1967. Also: Dharmsala, India: Teaching Training, n.d. Also: A block-print edition in twenty-eight folios obtained in 1987 from Go-mang College in Hla-s̄a, printed on blocks that predate the Cultural Revolution.
English translation: Geshe Lhundup Sopa and Jeffrey Hopkins. *Practice and Theory of Tibetan Buddhism,* 48-145. New York: Grove, 1976; revised edition, *Cutting through Appearances: Practice and Theory of Tibetan Buddhism,* 109-322. Ithaca, New York: Snow Lion, 1989. Also: H. V. Guenther. *Buddhist Philosophy in Theory and Practice.* Baltimore, Md.: Penguin, 1972. Also, the chapters on the Autonomy School and the Consequence School: Shōtarō Iida. *Reason and Emptiness,* 27-51. Tokyo: Hokuseido, 1980.

Presentation of the Grounds and Paths: Beautiful Ornament of the Three Vehicles
sa lam gyi rnam bzhag theg gsum mdzes rgyan
Collected Works of dkon-mchog-'jigs-med-dbaṅ-po, vol. 7. New Delhi: Ngawang Gelek Demo, 1972.

Thorough Expression of the Natures of the One Hundred Seventy-Three Aspects of the Three Exalted Knowers: Vine of Lotuses
mkhyen gsum gyi rnam pa brgya dang don gsum gyi rang bzhin yang dag par brjod pa legs bshad padma dkar po'i khri shing
Collected Works of dkon-mchog-'jigs-med-dbaṅ-po, vol. 6, 625-644. New Delhi: Ngawang Gelek Demo, 1972.

Guṇaprabha (*yon tan 'od*)

Aphorisms on Discipline
vinayasūtra
'dul ba'i mdo
P5619, vol. 123

Commentary on (Asaṅga's) "Grounds of Bodhisattvas"
bodhisatttvabhūmivṛtti
byang chub sems dpa'i sa'i 'grel pa
P5545, vol. 112

Gung-ru Chö-jung / Gung-ru Chö-ḡyi-jung-ñay (*gung ru chos 'byung / gung ru chos kyi 'byung gnas;* fl. most likely in sixteenth century, since he refutes positions like those of Paṇ-chen S̄ö-nam-drak-b̄a and Jay-d̄zün Chö-ḡyi-gyel-tsen)

Garland of White Lotuses / Decisive Analysis of (D̄zong-ka-b̄a's) "Differentiating the Interpretable and the Definitive, The Essence of Eloquence": Garland of White Lotuses
drang ba dang nges pa'i rnam par 'byed pa legs bshad snying po zhes bya ba'i mtha' dpyod padma dkar po'i phreng ba
sku bum, Tibet: sku bum Monastery, n.d. [blockprint obtained by the author in 1988].

Gung-tang Ḡön-chok-d̄en-b̄ay-drön-may (*gung thang dkon mchog bstan pa'i sgron me,* 1762-1823)

Annotations / Beginnings of Annotations on (Ḏzong-ka-b̄a's) "The Essence of Eloquence" on the Topic of Mind-Only: Illumination of a Hundred Mind-Only Texts

bstan bcos legs par bshad pa'i snying po las sems tsam skor gyi mchan 'grel rtsom 'phro rnam rig gzhung brgya'i snang ba

Collected Works of Guṅ-thaṅ Dkon-mchog-bstan-pa'i-sgron-me, vol. 1, 725-876. New Delhi: Ngawang Gelek Demo, 1975. Also: Go-mang, n.d. [ed. printed in India with fixed type].

Difficult Points / Beginnings of a Commentary on the Difficult Points of (Ḏzong-ka-b̄a's) "Differentiating the Interpretable and the Definitive": Quintessence of "The Essence of Eloquence"

drang nges rnam 'byed kyi dka' 'grel rtsom 'phro legs bshad snying po'i yang snying

Collected Works of Guṅ-thaṅ Dkon-mchog-bstan-pa'i-sgron-me, vol. 1, 403-723. New Delhi: Ngawang Gelek Demo, 1975. Also: Sarnath, India: Guru Deva, 1965.

Biography of Ḡön-chok-jik-may-w̄ang-b̄o

dus gsum rgyal ba'i spyi gzugs rje btsun dkon mchog 'jigs med dbang po'i zhal snga nas kyi rnam par thar pa rgyal sras rgya mtsho'i jug ngogs

Collected Works of Dkon-mchog 'Jigs-med-dbaṅ-po, vol. 1, 1-555. New Delhi: Ngawang Gelek Demo, 1971. Also: Collected Works of Guṅ-thaṅ Dkon-mchog-bstan-pa'i-sgron-me, vol. 4, 185-701. New Delhi: Ngawang Gelek Demo, 1972.

Secret Biography of Ḡön-chok-jik-may-w̄ang-b̄o

rje btsun dkon mchog 'jigs med dbang po'i gangs ba'i rnam thar

Collected Works of Dkon-mchog 'Jigs-med-dbaṅ-po, vol. 1, 557-566. New Delhi: Ngawang Gelek Demo, 1971. Also: Collected Works of Guṅ-thaṅ Dkon-mchog-bstan-pa'i-sgron-me, vol. 4, 703-711. New Delhi: Ngawang Gelek Demo, 1972.

Gyel-tsap-dar-ma-rin-chen (*rgyal tshab dar ma rin chen,* 1364-1432)

Commentary on (Maitreya's) "Great Vehicle Treatise on the Sublime Continuum" / Commentary on (Maitreya's) "Treatise on the Later Scriptures of the Great Vehicle"

theg pa chen po rgyud bla ma'i ṭīkka

Collected Works of Rgyal-tshab Dar-ma-rin-chen, vol. 2 (entire). Delhi: Guru Deva, 1982. Also: Collected Works of Rgyal-tshab Dar-ma-rin-chen, vol. 2 (entire). Delhi: Ngawang Gelek Demo, 1981. Also: blockprint in the library of H.H. the Dalai Lama, no other data.

Explanation of (Shāntideva's) "Engaging in the Bodhisattva Deeds": Entrance of Conqueror Children

byang chub sems dpa'i spyod pa la 'jug pa'i rnam bshad rgyal sras 'jug ngogs

Collected Works of Rgyal-tshab Dar-ma-rin-chen, vol. 4, 3-331. Delhi: Guru Deva, 1982. Also: Collected Works of Rgyal-tshab Dar-ma-rin-chen, vol. 4. Delhi: Ngawang Gelek Demo, 1981. Also: Varanasi, India: Pleasure of Elegant Sayings Printing Press, 1973.

How To Practice the Two Stages of the Path of the Glorious Kālachakra: Quick Entry to the Path of Great Bliss

dpal dus kyi 'khor lo'i lam rim pa gnyis ji ltar nyams su len pa'i tshul bde ba chen po'i lam du myur du 'jug pa

Collected Works of Rgyal-tshab Dar-ma-rin-chen, vol. 1, 89-203. Delhi: Guru Deva, 1982. Also: Collected Works of Rgyal-tshab Dar-ma-rin-chen, vol. 1. Delhi: Ngawang Gelek Demo, 1981.

Illumination of the Path to Liberation / Explanation of (Dharmakīrti's) Commentary on (Dignāga's) "Compilation of Prime Cognition": Unerring Illumination of the Path to Liberation

thar lam gsal byed / tshad ma rnam 'grel gyi tshig le'ur byas pa'i rnam bshad thar lam phyin ci ma log par gsal bar byed pa

Collected Works of Rgyal-tshab Dar-ma-rin-chen, vol. 6 (entire). Delhi: Guru Deva, 1982. Also: Collected Works of Rgyal-tshab Dar-ma-rin-chen, vol. 6 (entire). Delhi: Ngawang Gelek Demo, 1981. Also: Varanasi, India: Pleasure of Elegant Sayings Press, 1974.

Haribhadra (*seng ge bzang po,* late eighth century)

Clear Meaning Commentary / Commentary on (Maitreya's) "Ornament for Clear Realization, Treatise of Quintessential Instructions on the Perfection of Wisdom"

spuṭhārtha / abhisamayālaṃkāranāmaprajñāpāramitopadeśaśāstravṛtti 'grel pa don gsal / shes rab kyi pha rol tu phyin pa'i man ngag gi bstan bcos mngon par rtogs pa'i rgyan ces bya ba'i 'grel pa

P5191, vol. 90

Sanskrit: Unrai Wogihara. *Abhisamayālaṃkārālokā Prajñā-pāramitā-vyākhyā, The Work of Haribhadra.* 7 vols. Tokyo: Toyo Bunko, 1932-1935; reprint, Tokyo: Sankibo Buddhist Book Store, 1973.

Jam-b̄el-sam-pel, Ge-s̄hay (*'jam dpal bsam 'phel, dge bshes,* died 1975)

Presentation of Awareness and Knowledge, Composite of All Important Points: Opening the Eye of New Intelligence

blo rig gi rnam bzhag nyer mkho kun 'dus blo gsar mig 'byed

no data [modern blockprint].

Jam-ȳang-shay-b̄a Nga-w̄ang-d̄zön-drü (*'jam dbyangs bzhad pa ngag dbang brtson grus,* 1648-1722)

Brief Decisive Analysis of (D̄zong-ka-b̄a's) "Differentiating the Interpretable and the Definitive"

Collected Works of 'Jam-dbyaṅs-bzad-pa'i-rdo-rdo-rje, vol. 12, 473-456. New Delhi: Ngawang Gelek Demo, 1973.

Decisive Analysis of the Treatise (Maitreya's) "Ornament for Clear Realization": Precious Lamp Illuminating All of the Meaning of the Perfection of Wisdom

bstan gcos mngon par rtogs pa'i rgyan gyi mtha' dpyod shes rab kyi pha rol tu phyin pa'i don kun gsal ba'i rin chen sgron me

Collected Works of 'Jam-dbyaṅs-bzad-pa'i-rdo-rdo-rje, vols. 7-8 (entire). New Delhi: Ngawang Gelek Demo, 1973. Also: Sarnath, India: Guru Deva, 1965.

Great Exposition of the Concentrations and Formlessnesses / Treatise on the Presentations of the Concentrations and Formless Absorptions: Adornment Beautifying the Subduer's Teaching: Ocean of Scripture and Reasoning, Delighting the Fortunate

bsam gzugs chen mo / bsam gzugs kyi snyoms 'jug rnams kyi rnam par bzhag pa'i bstan bcos thub bstan mdzes rgyan lung dang rigs pa'i rgya mtsho skal bzang dga' byed

Collected Works of 'Jam-dbyaṅs-bzad-pa'i-rdo-rdo-rje, vol. 12, 3-379. New Delhi: Ngawang Gelek Demo, 1973.

Great Exposition of the Interpretable and the Definitive / Decisive Analysis of (D̄zong-ka-b̄a's) "Differentiating the Interpretable and the Definitive": Storehouse of White Lapis-Lazuli of Scripture and Reasoning Free from Error: Fulfilling the Hopes of the Fortunate

drang ba dang nges pa'i don rnam par 'byed pa'i mtha' dpyod 'khrul bral lung rigs bai dūr dkar pa'i gan mdzod skal bzang re ba kun skong

Edition cited: Buxaduor: n.d. Also: Collected Works of 'Jam-dbyaṅs-bzad-pa'i-rdo-rdo-rje, vol. 11, 3-288. New Delhi: Ngawang Gelek Demo, 1973. Also: dga' ldan pho phrang [blockprint obtained by author in 1987].

Great Exposition of the Middle / Analysis of (Chandrakīrti's) "Supplement to (Nāgārjuna's) 'Treatise on the Middle'": Treasury of Scripture and Reasoning, Thoroughly Illuminating the Profound Meaning [of Emptiness], Entrance for the Fortunate

dbu ma chen mo / dbu ma 'jug pa'i mtha' dpyod lung rigs gter mdzod zab don kun gsal skal bzang 'jug ngogs

Edition cited: Buxaduor, India: Go-mang, 1967. Also: Collected Works of 'Jam-dbyaṅs-bzad-pa'i-rdo-rdo-rje, vol. 9 (entire). New Delhi: Ngawang Gelek Demo, 1973.

Great Exposition of Tenets / Explanation of "Tenets": Sun of the Land of Samantabhadra Brilliantly Illuminating All of Our Own and Others' Tenets and the Meaning of the Profound [Emptiness], Ocean of Scripture and Reasoning Fulfilling All Hopes of All Beings

grub mtha' chen mo / grub mtha'i rnam bshad rang gzhan grub mtha' kun dang zab don mchog tu gsal ba kun bzang zhing gi nyi ma lung rigs rgya mtsho skye dgu'i re ba kun skong

Edition cited: Musoorie, India: Dalama, 1962. Also: Collected Works of 'Jam-dbyaṅs-bzad-pa'i-rdo-rdo-rje, vol. 14 (entire). New Delhi: Ngawang Gelek Demo, 1973.

English translation (beginning of the chapter on the Consequence School): Jeffrey Hopkins. *Meditation on Emptiness,* 581-697. London: Wisdom, 1983; rev. ed., Boston, Ma.: Wisdom, 1996.

Notes on (Ḏzong-ka-ḇa's) "Differentiating the Interpretable and the Definitive"

'jam dbyangs bzhad pa'i rdo rjes mdzad pa'i drang nges rnam "byed kyi zin bris

Collected Works of 'Jam-dbyaṅs-bzad-pa'i-rdo-rdo-rje, vol. 11, 289-331. New Delhi: Ngawang Gelek Demo, 1973.

J̄ang-ḡya Röl-ḇay-dor-jay (*lcang skya rol pa'i rdo rje,* 1717-1786)

Presentation of Tenets / Clear Exposition of the Presentations of Tenets, Beautiful Ornament for the Meru of the Subduer's Teaching

grub mtha'i rnam bzhag / grub pa'i mtha'i rnam par bzhag pa gsal bar bshad pa thub bstan lhun po'i mdzes rgyan

Varanasi, India: Pleasure of Elegant Sayings Printing Press, 1970. Also: Lokesh Chandra, ed. *Buddhist Philosophical Systems of Lcaṅ-skya Rol-pahi Rdo-rje.* Śata-piṭaka Series (Indo-Asian Literatures), vol. 233. New Delhi: International Academy of Indian Culture, 1977. Also: An edition published by gam car phan bde legs bshad gling grva tshang dang rgyud rnying slar gso tshogs pa, in the royal year 2109.

English translation of Sautrāntika chapter: Anne C. Klein. *Knowing, Naming, and Negation,* 115-196. Ithaca, N.Y.: Snow Lion, 1988. Commentary on this: Anne C. Klein. *Knowledge and Liberation: A Buddhist Epistemological Analysis in Support of Transformative Religious Experience: Tibetan Interpretations of Dignaga and Dharmakirti.* Ithaca, N.Y.: Snow Lion, 1986.

English translation of Svātantrika chapter: Donald S. Lopez Jr. *A Study of Svātantrika,* 243-386. Ithaca, N.Y.: Snow Lion, 1986.

English translation of part of Prāsaṅgika chapter: Jeffrey Hopkins. *Emptiness Yoga: The Middle Way Consequence School,* 355-428. Ithaca, N.Y.: Snow Lion, 1983.

Jay-ḏzün Chö-ḡyi-gyel-tsen (*rje btsun chos kyi rgyal mtshan,* 1469-1546)

General-Meaning Commentary / General Meaning of (Ḏzong-ka-ḇa's) "Differentiating the Interpretable and the Definitive": Eradicating Bad Disputation: A Precious Garland

drang nges rnam 'byed kyi spyi don rgol ngan tshar gcod rin po che'i phreng ba

Edition cited: Bylakuppe, India: Se-ra Byes Monastery, 1977. Also: Sarnath, India: Guru Deva, 1965. Also: Lhasa, Tibet: par pa dpal ldan, 1987.

Presentation of Tenets

grub mtha'i rnam gzhag

Buxaduor, India: n. p., 1960. Also: Bylakuppe, India: Se-ra Byes Monastery, 1977.

Jetāri

Differentiating the Sugata's Texts

sugatamatavibhaṅga

bde bar gzhegs pa'i gzhung rnam par 'byed pa

P5867, vol. 146

Jik-may-dam-chö-gya-tso (*'jigs med dam chos rgya mtsho*); poetic name Mi-pam-ȳang-j̄en-gye-ḇay-dor-jay (*mi pham dbyangs can dgyes* [or *dges*] *pa'i rdo rje;* 1898-1946)

Port of Entry / Treatise Distinguishing All the Meanings of (Ḏzong-ka-ḇa's) "The Essence of Eloquence": Illuminating the Differentiation of the Interpretable and the Definitive: Port of Entry to "The Essence of Eloquence"

drang ba dang nges pa'i don rnam par phye ba gsal bar byed pa legs bshad snying po'i don mtha' dag rnam par 'byed pa'i bstan bcos legs bshad snying po'i 'jug ngogs

bkra shis chos sde, India: 199-?.

Jin-ḇa-dar-gyay, Ga-jang (*sbyin pa dar rgyas, dga' byang*)

Brief Illumination of the Difficult Points of (Ḏzong-ka-ḇa's) "Differentiating the Interpretable and the Definitive": Mirror Illuminating Eloquence

drang nges rnam 'byed kyi dka' gnad gsal bar byed pa bsdus don legs bshad gsal ba'i me long

Buxaduor, India: no other data.

Jñānagarbha (*ye shes snying po*, c. 700)
Commentary on Just the Chapter of the Superior Maitreya
āryasaṃdhinirmocanasūtreāryamaitreyakevalaparivartabhāṣya
'phags pa dgongs pa nges par 'grel pa'i mdo las 'phags pa byams pa'i le'u nyi tshe'i bshad pa
P5535, vol. 109
English translation: John C. Powers. *Two Commentaries on the Samdhinirmocana-sutra by Asanga and Jnanagarbha.* Lewiston, N.Y.: Edward Mellon, 1992; and John C. Powers, *Jñānagarbha's Commentary on Just the Maitreya Chapter from the Saṃdhinirmocana-Sūtra: Study, Translation and Tibetan Text.* New Delhi: Indian Council of Philosophical Research, 1998.
Ke-drup-ge-lek-b̄el-sang (*mkhas grub dge legs dpal bzang*, 1385-1438)
Compilation on Emptiness / Opening the Eyes of the Fortunate: Treatise Brilliantly Clarifying the Profound Emptiness
stong thun chen mo / zab mo stong pa nyid rab tu gsal bar byed pa'i bstan bcos skal bzang mig 'byed
Collected Works of the Lord Mkhas-grub rje dge-legs-dpal-bzaṅ-po, vol. 1, 179-702. New Delhi: Guru Deva, 1980. Also: Collected Works of Mkhas-grub dge-legs dpal, vol. 1, 125-482. New Delhi: Ngawang Gelek Demo, 1983. Also: New Delhi: n. p., 1972.
English translation: José Ignacio Cabezón. *A Dose of Emptiness: An Annotated Translation of the* stong thun chen mo *of mKhas grub dGe legs dpal bzang*, 21-388. Albany, N.Y.: State University of New York Press, 1992.
Extensive Explanation of the General Presentation of the Tantra Sets
rgyud sde bzhi'i rnam par bzhag pa rgyas pa bshad pa
Collected Works of the Lord Mkhas-grub rje dge-legs-dpal-bzaṅ-po, vol. 8, 443-630. New Delhi: Guru Deva, 1980. Also: Collected Works of Mkhas-grub dge-legs dpal, vol. 11, 215-368. New Delhi: Ngawang Gelek Demo, 1983.
L̄o-sang-jam-ȳang-m̄ön-lam, Ḡe-u-tsang (*blo bzang 'jam dbyangs smon lam ke'u tshang*, c. 1800)
Clarification of the Difficult Points in the [Auto-]Commentary on the Root text of [D̄zong-ka-b̄a's treatise on] the Afflicted Consciousness and Mind-Basis-of-All of the Yogic Practice School: Union of the Sun and Moon
rnal 'byor pa pa'i lugs kyi yid dang kun gzhi'i rtsa 'grel gyi dka' gnas gsal byed nyi zla zung 'jug
Collected Works gsuṅ 'bum of Ke'u-tshaṅ Sprul-sku Blo-bzaṅ-'jam-dbyaṅs-smon-lam, vol. 1, 181-254. Dharmsala, India: Library of Tibetan Works and Archives, 1984.
L̄o-sang-w̄ang-chuk (*blo bzang dbang phyug*, 1901-1979)
Notes on (D̄zong-ka-b̄a's) "Interpretable and Definitive, The Essence of Eloquence": Lamp for the Intelligent
dang nges legs par bshad pa'i snying po'i zin bris blo gsal sgron me: *Notes on the Art of Interpretation: A Lamp to Light the Mind,* being a commentary on Je Tsongkapa's *Essence of Good Explanation*
Bylakuppe, India: Sera Jey Tibetan Monastic University, 1993.
L̄ong-chen-rap-jam (*klong chen rab 'byams / klong chen dri med 'od zer*, 1308-1363)
Precious Treasury of Tenets: Illuminating the Meaning of All Vehicles
theg pa mtha' dag gi don gsal bar byed pa grub pa'i mtha' rin po che'i mdzod
Gangtok, Sikkim: Dodrup Chen Rinpoche, 1969[?].
Precious Treasury of the Supreme Vehicle
theg pa'i mchog rin po che'i mdzod
Gangtok, Sikkim: Dodrup Chen Rinpoche, 1969[?].
Maitreya (*byams pa*)
Five Doctrines of Maitreya
1. *Great Vehicle Treatise on the Sublime Continuum / Treatise on the Later Scriptures of the Great Vehicle*
mahāyānottaratantraśāstra
theg pa chen po rgyud bla ma'i bstan bcos
P5525, vol. 108

Sanskrit: E. H. Johnston (and T. Chowdhury). *The Ratnagotravibhāga Mahāyānottaratantraśāstra.* Patna, India: Bihar Research Society, 1950.

English translation: E. Obermiller. "Sublime Science of the Great Vehicle to Salvation." *Acta Orientalia* 9 (1931): 81-306. Also: J. Takasaki. *A Study on the Ratnagotravibhāga.* Rome: Istituto Italiano per il Medior ed Estremo Oriente, 1966.

2. *Differentiation of Phenomena and the Final Nature of Phenomena*
dharmadharmatāvibhaṅga
chos dang chos nyid rnam par 'byed pa
P5523, vol. 108

3. *Differentiation of the Middle and the Extremes*
madhyāntavibhaṅga
dbus dang mtha' rnam par 'byed pa
P5522, vol. 108

Sanskrit: Gadjin M. Nagao. *Madhyāntavibhāga-bhāṣya.* Tokyo: Suzuki Research Foundation, 1964. Also: Ramchandra Pandeya. *Madhyānta-vibhāga-śāstra.* Delhi: Motilal Banarsidass, 1971.

English translation: Stefan Anacker. *Seven Works of Vasubandhu.* Delhi: Motilal Banarsidass, 1984. Also, of chapter 1: Thomas A. Kochumuttom. *A Buddhist Doctrine of Experience.* Delhi: Motilal Banarsidass, 1982. Also, of chapter 1: F. Th. Stcherbatsky. *Madhyāntavibhāga, Discourse on Discrimination between Middle and Extremes ascribed to Bodhisattva Maitreya and Commented by Vasubandhu and Sthiramati.* Bibliotheca Buddhica, 30 (1936). Osnabrück, Germany: Biblio Verlag, 1970; reprint, Calcutta: Indian Studies Past and Present, 1971. Also, of chapter 1: David Lasar Friedmann. *Sthiramati, Madhyāntavibhāgaṭīkā: Analysis of the Middle Path and the Extremes.* Utrecht, Netherlands: Rijksuniversiteit te Leiden, 1937.

4. *Ornament for Clear Realization*
abhisamayālaṃkāra
mngon par rtogs pa'i rgyan
P5184, vol. 88

Sanskrit: Th. Stcherbatsky and E. Obermiller, eds. *Abhisamayālaṃkāra-Prajñāpāramitā-Updeśa-Śāstra.* Bibliotheca Buddhica, 23. Osnabrück, Germany: Biblio Verlag, 1970.

English translation: Edward Conze. *Abhisamayālaṃkāra.* Serie Orientale Rome. Rome: Istituto Italiano per il Medior ed Estremo Oriente, 1954.

5. *Ornament for the Great Vehicle Sūtras*
mahāyānasūtrālaṃkāra
theg pa chen po'i mdo sde rgyan gyi tshig le'ur byas pa
P5521, vol. 108

Sanskrit: Sitansusekhar Bagchi. *Mahāyāna-Sūtrālaṃkāraḥ of Asaṅga* [with Vasubandhu's commentary]. Buddhist Sanskrit Texts, 13. Darbhanga, India: Mithila Institute, 1970.

Sanskrit text and translation into French: Sylvain Lévi. *Mahāyānasūtrālaṃkāra, exposé de la doctrine du grand véhicule selon le système Yogācāra.* 2 vols. Paris: Bibliothèque de l'École des Hautes Études, 1907, 1911.

Sanskrit text and translation into English: Surekha Vijay Limaye. *Mahāyānasūtrālaṃkāra by Asaṅga.* Bibliotheca Indo-Buddhica Series, 94. Delhi: Sri Satguru, 1992.

Nāgārjuna (*klu sgrub,* first to second century, C.E.)

Six Collections of Reasoning

1. *Precious Garland of Advice for the King*
rājaparikathāratnāvalī
rgyal po la gtam bya ba rin po che'i phreng ba
P5658, vol. 129

Sanskrit, Tibetan, and Chinese: Michael Hahn. *Nāgārjuna's Ratnāvalī.* vol. 1. *The Basic Texts (Sanskrit, Tibetan, and Chinese).* Bonn: Indica et Tibetica Verlag, 1982.

English translation: Jeffrey Hopkins. *Buddhist Advice for Living and Liberation: Nāgārjuna's Precious Garland,* 94-164. Ithaca, New York: Snow Lion, 1998. Supercedes that in: Nāgārjuna and the Seventh Dalai Lama. *The Precious Garland and the Song of the Four Mindfulnesses,* translated by Jeffrey Hopkins, 17-93. London: George Allen and Unwin, l975; New York: Harper and Row, 1975; reprint, in H.H. the Dalai Lama, Tenzin Gyatso. *The Buddhism of Tibet*. London: George Allen and Unwin, 1983; reprint, Ithaca, New York: Snow Lion, 1987.

English translation: John Dunne and Sara McClintock. *The Precious Garland: An Epistle to a King*. Boston: Wisdom, 1997.

English translation of 223 stanzas (chap. 1, 1-77; chap. 2, 1-46; chap 4; 1-100): Giuseppe Tucci. "The *Ratnāvalī* of Nāgārjuna." *Journal of the Royal Asiatic Society* (1934): 307-325; (1936): 237-52, 423-35.

Japanese translation: URYŪZU Ryushin. *Butten II, Sekai Koten Bungaku Zenshu*, 7 (July, 1965): 349-72. Edited by NAKAMURA Hajime. Tokyo: Chikuma Shobō. Also: URYŪZU Ryushin. *Daijō Butten*, 14 (1974): 231-316. *Ryūju Ronshū*. Edited by KAJIYAMA Yuichi and URYŪZU Ryushin. Tokyo: Chūōkōronsha.

Danish translation: Christian Lindtner. *Nagarjuna, Juvelkaeden og andre skrifter*. Copenhagen: 1980.

2. *Refutation of Objections*
vigrahavyāvartanīkārikā
rtsod pa bzlog pa'i tshig le'ur byas pa
P5228, vol. 95

Sanskrit: E. H. Johnston. *The Ratnagotravibhāga Mahāyānottaratantraśāstra*. Patna, India: Bihar Research Society, 1950.

Edited Tibetan and Sanskrit: Christian Lindtner. *Nagarjuniana*, 70-86. Indiske Studier 4. Copenhagen: Akademisk Forlag, 1982.

English translation: K. Bhattacharya, E. H. Johnston, and A. Kunst. *The Dialectical Method of Nāgārjuna*. New Delhi: Motilal Banarsidass, 1978.

English translation from the Chinese: G. Tucci. *Pre-Diṅnāga Buddhist Texts on Logic from Chinese Sources*. Gaekwad's Oriental Series, 49. Baroda, India: Oriental Institute, 1929.

French translation: S. Yamaguchi. "Traité de Nāgārjuna pour écarter les vaines discussion (Vigrahavyāvartanī) traduit et annoté." *Journal Asiatique* 215 (1929): 1-86.

3. *Seventy Stanzas on Emptiness*
śūnyatāsaptatikārikā
stong pa nyid bdun cu pa'i tshig le'ur byas pa
P5227, vol. 95

Edited Tibetan and English translation: Christian Lindtner. *Nagarjuniana*, 34-69. Indiske Studier 4. Copenhagen: Akademisk Forlag, 1982.

English translation: David Ross Komito. *Nāgārjuna's "Seventy Stanzas": A Buddhist Psychology of Emptiness*. Ithaca, N.Y.: Snow Lion Publications, 1987.

4. *Sixty Stanzas of Reasoning*
yuktiṣaṣṭikākārikā
rigs pa drug cu pa'i tshig le'ur byas pa
P5225, vol. 95

Edited Tibetan with Sanskrit fragments and English translation: Christian Lindtner. *Nagarjuniana*, 100-119. Indiske Studier 4. Copenhagen: Akademisk Forlag, 1982.

5. *Treatise Called the Finely Woven*
vaidalyasūtranāma
zhib mo rnam par 'thag pa zhes bya ba'i mdo
P5226, vol. 95

Tibetan text and English translation: Fermando Tola and Carmen Dragonetti. *Nāgārjuna's Refutation of Logic (Nyāya) Vaidalyaprakaraṇa*. Delhi: Motilal Banarsidass, 1995.

6. *Treatise on the Middle / Fundamental Treatise on the Middle, Called "Wisdom"*
madhyamakaśāstra / prajñānāmamūlamadhyamakakārikā
dbu ma'i bstan bcos / dbu ma rtsa ba'i tshig le'ur byas pa shes rab ces bya ba
P5224, vol. 95

Edited Sanskrit: J. W. de Jong. *Nāgārjuna, Mūlamadhyamakakārikāḥ*. Madras, India: Adyar Library and Research Centre, 1977; reprint, Wheaton, Ill.: Agents, Theosophical Publishing House, c1977. Also: Christian Lindtner. *Nāgārjuna's Filosofiske Vaerker,* 177-215. Indiske Studier 2. Copenhagen: Akademisk Forlag, 1982.

English translation: Frederick Streng. *Emptiness: A Study in Religious Meaning.* Nashville, Tenn.: Abingdon Press, 1967. Also: Kenneth Inada. *Nāgārjuna: A Translation of His Mūlamadhyamakakārikā.* Tokyo: Hokuseido Press, 1970. Also: David J. Kalupahana. *Nāgārjuna: The Philosophy of the Middle Way.* Albany, N.Y.: State University Press of New York, 1986. Also: Jay L. Garfield. *The Fundamental Wisdom of the Middle Way.* New York: Oxford University Press, 1995.

Italian translation: R. Gnoli. *Nāgārjuna: Madhyamaka Kārikā, Le stanze del cammino di mezzo.* Enciclopedia di autori classici 61. Turin, Italy: P. Boringhieri, 1961.

Danish translation: Christian Lindtner. *Nāgārjuna's Filosofiske Vaerker,* 67-135. Indiske Studier 2. Copenhagen: Akademisk Forlag, 1982.

Nga-w̄ang-b̄el-den (*ngag dbang dpal ldan,* b.1797), also known as B̄el-den-chö-jay (*dpal ldan chos rje*)

Annotations for (Jam-ȳang-shay-b̄a's) "Great Exposition of Tenets": Freeing the Knots of the Difficult Points, Precious Jewel of Clear Thought

grub mtha' chen mo'i mchan 'grel dka' gnad mdud grol blo gsal gces nor

Sarnath, India: Pleasure of Elegant Sayings Press, 1964. Also: Collected Works of Chos-rje ṅag-dbaṅ Dpal-ldan of Urga, vols. 4 (entire)-5, 1-401. Delhi: Guru Deva, 1983.

Explanation of the Conventional and the Ultimate in the Four Systems of Tenets

grub mtha' bzhi'i lugs kyi kun rdzob dang don dam pa'i don rnam par bshad pa legs bshad dpyid kyi dpal mo'i glu dbyangs

New Delhi: Guru Deva, 1972. Also: Collected Works of Chos-rje ṅag-dbaṅ Dpal-ldan of Urga, vol. 1, 3-273. Delhi, 1983.

Nga-w̄ang-ke-drup (*ngag dbang mkhas grub,* 1779-1838)

Presentation of Death, Intermediate State, and Rebirth

skye shi bar do'i rnam bzhag

Collected Works of Ṅag-dbaṅ-mkhas-grub, Kyai-rdor Mkhan-po of Urga, vol. 1, 459-474. Leh, Ladakh: S. Tashigangpa, 1973.

Nga-w̄ang-l̄o-sang-gya-tso (*ngag dbang blo bzang rgya mtsho,* Fifth Dalai Lama, 1617-1682)

Instructions on the Stages of the Path to Enlightenment: Sacred Word of Mañjushrī

byang chub lam gyi rim pa'i 'khrid yig 'jam pa'i dbyangs kyi zhal lung

Thimphu, Bhutan: kun bzang stobs rgyal, 1976.

English translation of the "Perfection of Wisdom Chapter": Jeffrey Hopkins. "Practice of Emptiness." Dharmsala: Library of Tibetan Works and Archives, 1974.

Pa-bong-ka-b̄a Jam-b̄a-d̄en-dzin-trin-lay-gya-tso (*pha bong kha pa byams pa bstan 'dzin 'phrin las rgya mtsho,* 1878-1941)

Presentation of the Interpretable and the Definitive, Brief Notes on the Occasion of Receiving Profound [Instruction from J̄o-ne Paṇḍita L̄o-sang-gya-tso in 1927] on (D̄zong-ka-b̄a's) "The Essence of Eloquence"

drang ba dang nges pa'i don rnam par bzhag pa legs par bshad pa'i snying po'i zab nos skabs kyi zin bris mdo tsam du bkod pa

Collected Works of Pha-boṅ-kha-pa-bstan-'dzin-'phrin-las-rgya-mtsho, vol. 4, 400-476. New Delhi: Chophel Legdan, 1973.

Paṇ-chen S̄ö-nam-drak-b̄a (*paṇ chen bsod nams grags pa,* 1478-1554)

Distinguishing through Objections and Answers (D̄zong-ka-b̄a's) "Differentiating the Interpretable and Definitive Meanings of All the Scriptures, The Essence of Eloquence": Garland of Blue Lotuses

gsung rab kun gyi drang ba dang nges pa'i don rnam par 'byed pa legs par bshad pa'i snying po brgal lan gyis rnam par 'byed pa utpa la'i phreng ba

Collected Works (gsuṅ 'bum) of Paṇ-chen Bsod-nams-grags-pa, vol. 5. Mundgod, India: Drepung Loseling Library Society, 1982.

General-Meaning Commentary on the Perfections / Good Explanation of the Meaning of (Gyel-tsap's) "Explanation of (Maitreya's) 'Treatise of Quintessential Instructions on the Perfection of Wisdom: Or-

nament for Clear Realization' as well as its Commentaries, Ornament for the Essence": Lamp Illuminating the Meaning of the Mother
phar phyin spyi don / shes rab kyi pha rol tu phyin pa'i man ngag gi bstan bcos mngon par rtogs pa'i rgyan 'grel pa dang bcas pa'i rnam bshad snying po rgyan gyi don legs par bshad pa yum don gsal ba'i sgron me
Buxaduor, India: nang bstan shes rig 'dzin skyong slob gnyer khang, 1963.

Prajñākaragupta (*shes rab 'byung gnas sbas pa*)
Ornament for (Dharmakīrti's) "Commentary on (Dignāga's) 'Compilation of Prime Cognition'"
pramāṇavārttikālaṃkāra
tshad ma rnam 'grel gyi rgyan
P5719, vol. 132

Prajñāvarman (*shes rab go cha, pra dznyā wa rmaṃ*)
Commentary on (Udbhaṭasiddhasvāmin's) "Exalted Praise"
viśeṣastavanāmaṭīkā
khyad par du 'phags pa'i bstod pa'i rgya cher bshad pa
2002, vol. 46

Pur-bu-jok Jam-b̄a-gya-tso (*phur bu lcog byams pa rgya mtsho,* 1825-1901)
Explanation of the Presentation of Objects and Object Possessors as well as Awareness and Knowledge from the Presentation of the Collected Topics Revealing the Meaning of the Treatises on Prime Cognition: Magical Key to the Path of Reasoning
tshad ma'i gzhung don 'byed pa'i bsdus grva'i rnam bzhag rigs lam 'phrul gyi sde mig las yul yul can dang blo rig gi rnam par bshad pa
Buxaduor: n.p., 1965.
The Topics of Signs and Reasonings in the "Great Path of Reasoning" from the Presentation of the Collected Topics Revealing the Meaning of the Treatises on Prime Cognition: Magical Key to the Path of Reasoning
tshad ma'i gzhung don 'byed pa'i bsdus grva'i rnam bzhag rigs lam 'phrul gyi sde mig las rigs lam che ba rtags rigs kyi skor
Buxaduor: n.p., 1965.

Ratnākarashānti (*ratnākaraśānti, rin chen 'byung gnas zhi ba*)
Quintessential Instructions on the Perfection of Wisdom
prajñāpāramitopadeśa
shes rab kyi pha rol tu phyin pa'i man ngag
P55798, vol. 114

Sāgaramegha (*rgya mtsho sprin*)
Explanation of (Asaṅga's) "Grounds of Bodhisattvas"
yogācāryabhūmau bodhisatttvabhūmivyākhyā
rnal 'byor spyod pa'i sa las byang chub sems dpa'i sa'i rnam par bshad pa
P5548, vol. 112

S̄er-s̄hul Ge-s̄hay L̄o-sang-pün-tsok (*blo bzang phun tshogs, ser shul dge bshes;* fl. in early twentieth century)
Notes / Notes on (D̄zong-ka-b̄a's) "Differentiating the Interpretable and the Definitive": Lamp Illuminating the Profound Meaning
drang nges rnam 'byed kyi zin bris zab don gsal ba'i sgron me
Delhi: n.p., 1974.

Sha-m̄ar Ge-dün-d̄en-dzin-gya-tso (*zhwa dmar dge 'dun bstan 'dzin rgya mtsho;* 1852-1912)
Notes Concerning Difficult Points in (D̄zong-ka-b̄a's) "Differentiating the Interpretable and the Definitive, The Essence of Eloquence": Victorious Clearing Away Mental Darkness
drang nges legs bshad snying po'i dka gnas las brtsams pa'i zin bris bcom ldan yid kyi mun sel
n.p.d. [mentioned in Jik-may-dam-chö-gya-tso's *Port of Entry*]

Shāntarakṣhita (*śāntarakṣita, zhi ba 'tsho,* eighth century)
Compendium of Principles
tattvasaṃgrahakārikā

de kho na nyid bsdud pa'i tshig le'ur byas pa
P5764, vol. 138
Sanskrit: Dwarikadas Shastri. *Tattvasaṅgraha of Ācārya Shāntarakṣita, with the Commentary "Pañjikā" of Shrī Kamalashīla.* Varanasi, India: Bauddha Bharati, 1968.
English translation: G. Jha. *The Tattvasaṃgraha of Śāntirakṣita, with the commentary of Kamalaśīla.* Gaekwad's Oriental Series, 80 and 83. Baroda, India: Oriental Institute, 1937, 1939; reprint, Delhi: Motilal Barnarsidass, 1986.

Shāntideva (*zhi ba lha,* eighth century)
Engaging in the Bodhisattva Deeds
bodhi[sattva]caryāvatāra
byang chub sems dpa'i spyod pa la 'jug pa
P5272, vol. 99
Sanskrit: P. L. Vaidya. *Bodhicaryāvatāra.* Buddhist Sanskrit Texts, 12. Darbhanga, India: Mithila Institute, 1988.
Sanskrit and Tibetan: Vidhushekara Bhattacharya. *Bodhicaryāvatāra.* Bibliotheca Indica, 280. Calcutta: Asiatic Society, 1960.
Sanskrit and Tibetan with Hindi translation: Rāmaśaṁkara Tripāthī, ed. *Bodhicaryāvatāra.* Baudha-Himālaya-Granthamālā, 8. Leh, Ladākh: Central Institute of Buddhist Studies, 1989.
English translation: Stephen Batchelor. *A Guide to the Bodhisattva's Way of Life.* Dharmsala, India: Library of Tibetan Works and Archives, 1979. Also: Marion Matics. *Entering the Path of Enlightenment.* New York: Macmillan, 1970. Also: Kate Crosby and Andrew Skilton. *The Bodhicaryāvatāra.* Oxford: Oxford University Press, 1996. Also: Padmakara Translation Group. *The Way of the Bodhisattva.* Boston: Shambhala, 1997. Also: Vesna A. Wallace and B. Alan Wallace. *A Guide to the Bodhisattva Way of Life.* Ithaca, N.Y.: Snow Lion, 1997.
Contemporary commentary by H.H. the Dalai Lama, Tenzin Gyatso. *Transcendent Wisdom.* Ithaca, N.Y.: Snow Lion, 1988. Also: H.H. the Dalai Lama, Tenzin Gyatso. *A Flash of Lightening in the Dark of the Night.* Boston: Shambhala, 1994.

Shay-rap-gyel-tsen (*shes rab rgyal mtshan, dol po pa;* 1292-1361)
The Mountain Doctrine: Ocean of Definitive Meaning
ri chos nges don rgya mtsho
Gangtok, Sikkim: Dodrup Sangyey Lama, 1976.
Also: Matthew Kapstein. *The 'Dzam-thang Edition of the Collected Works of Kun-mkhyen Dol-po-pa Shes-rab-rgyal-mtshan: Introduction and Catalogue,* vol. 2, 25-707. Delhi: Shedrup Books, 1992.
The Great Calculation of the Doctrine, Which has the Significance of a Fourth Council
bka' bsdu bzhi pa'i don bstan rtsis chen po
Matthew Kapstein. *The 'Dzam-thang Edition of the Collected Works of Kun-mkhyen Dol-po-pa Shes-rab-rgyal-mtshan: Introduction and Catalogue,* vol. 5, 207-252. Delhi: Shedrup Books, 1992.
English translation: Cyrus R. Stearns. *The Buddha from Dol po and His Fourth Council of the Buddhist Doctrine,* 162-244. Ann Arbor, Mich.: University Microfilms, 1996.

Si-du Chö-gyi-jung-nay (*si tu chos kyi 'byung gnas,* 1700-1774)
Explanation of (Tön-mi Sambhoṭa's) "The Thirty" and "Usage of Gender," a Treatise on the Thorough Application of the Language of the Snowy Country: Beautiful Pearl Necklace of the Wise
yul gangs can pa'i brda yang dag par sbyor ba'i bstan bcos kyi bye brag sum cu pa dang rtags kyi 'jug pa'i gzhung gi rnam par bshad pa mkhas pa'i mgul rgyan mu tig phreng mdzes
Dharmsala, India: Tibetan Cultural Printing Press, n.d.

Sthiramati (*blo gros brtan pa;* fl. late fourth century)
Explanation of (Vasubandhu's) "Commentary on (Maitreya's) 'Differentiation of the Middle and the Extremes'"
madhyāntavibhāgaṭīkā
dbus dang mtha' rnam par 'byed pa'i 'grel bshad / dbus mtha'i 'grel bshad
P5334, vol. 109
Sanskrit: Ramchandra Pandeya ed. *Madhyānta-vibhāga-śāstra.* Delhi: Motilal Banarsidass, 1971.
English translation (chap. 1): F. Th. Stcherbatsky. *Madhyāntavibhāga, Discourse on Discrimination*

between Middle and Extremes Ascribed to Bodhisattva Maitreya and Commented by Vasubandhu and Sthiramati, Bibliotheca Buddhica, 30 (1936). Osnabrück, Germany: Biblio Verlag, 1970; reprint, Calcutta: Indian Studies Past and Present, 1971.

English translation (chap. 1): David Lasar Friedmann. *Sthiramati, Madhyānta-vibhāgaṭīkā: Analysis of the Middle Path and the Extremes.* Utrechtt, Netherlands: Rijksuniversiteit te Leiden, 1937.

Explanation of (Vasubandhu's) "The Thirty"

trimśikābhāṣya

sum cu pa'i bshad pa

P5565, vol. 113

Sanskrit: Sylvain Lévi. *Vijñaptimātratāsiddhi / Deux traités de Vasubandhu: Viṃśatikā (La Vingtaine) et Triṃsikā (La Trentaine).* Bibliothèque de l'École des Hautes Études, 245. Paris: Libraire Honoré Champion, 1925.

Tibetan: Enga Teramoto. *Sthiramati's Triṃçikābhāsyaṃ (Sum-cu-paḥi ḥGrel-pa): A Tibetan Text.* Kyoto: Association for Linguistic Study of Sacred Scriptures, 1933.

Explanation of (Vasubandhu's) "Commentary of (Maitreya's) 'Ornament for the Great Vehicle Sūtras'"

sūtrālaṃkārāvṛttibhāṣya

mdo sde'i rgyan gyi 'grel bshad

P5531, vol. 108

Tso-ña-wa Shay-rap-sang-b̄o (*mtsho sna ba shes rab bzang po*)

Explanation of the Root Text of [Guṇaprabha's] "Aphorisms on Discipline": Clear Light of the Moon, Ocean of Scriptural Eloquence

'dul ba mdo rtsa ba'i rnam bshad nyi ma'i 'od zer legs bshad lung gi rgya mtsho; 'dul ṭik nyi ma'i 'od zer

Buxaduor: blo bzang 'gyur med, 1966.

Tu-ḡen L̄o-sang-chö-ḡyi-nyi-ma (*thu'u bkvan blo bzang chos kyi nyi ma;* 1737-1802)

Mirror of Eloquence Showing the Sources and Assertions of All Systems of Tenets

grub mtha' thams cad kyi khungs dang 'dod tshul ston pa legs bshad shel gyi me long

Sarnath, India: Chhos Je Lama, 1963. Also: Gansu, China: kan su'u mi rigs dpe skrun khang, 1984.

Vasubandhu (*dbyig gnyen,* fl.360)

Commentary on (Asaṅga's) "Summary of the Great Vehicle"

mahāyānasaṃgrahabhāṣya

theg pa chen po bsdus pa'i 'grel pa

P5551, vol. 112

Commentary on (Maitreya's) "Differentiation of the Middle and the Extremes"

madhyāntavibhāgaṭīkā

dbus dang mtha' rnam par 'byed pa'i 'grel pa / dbus mtha'i 'grel pa

P5528, vol. 108

Sanskrit: Gadjin M. Nagao. *Madhyāntavibhāga-bhāṣya.* Tokyo: Suzuki Research Foundation, 1964. Also: Ramchandra Pandeya. *Madhyānta-vibhāga-śāstra.* Delhi: Motilal Banarsidass, 1971.

English translation: Stefan Anacker. *Seven Works of Vasubandhu.* Delhi: Motilal Banarsidass, 1984. Also: Thomas A. Kochumuttom. *A Buddhist Doctrine of Experience.* Delhi: Motilal Banarsidass, 1982. Also, of chapter 1: F. Th. Stcherbatsky. *Madhyāntavibhāga: Discourse on Discrimination between Middle and Extremes Ascribed to Bodhisattva Maitreya and Commented by Vasubandhu and Sthiramati.* Bibliotheca Buddhica, 30 (1936). Osnabrück, Germany: Biblio Verlag, 1970; reprint, Calcutta: Indian Studies Past and Present, 1971. Also, of chapter 1: David Lasar Friedmann, *Sthiramati, Madhyāntavibhāgaṭīkā: Analysis of the Middle Path and the Extremes.* Utrechtt, Netherlands: Rijksuniversiteit te Leiden, 1937.

Explanation of (Maitreya's) "Ornament for the Great Vehicle Sūtras"

sūtrālaṃkārābhāṣya

mdo sde'i rgyan gyi bshad pa

P5527, vol. 108

Sanskrit: S. Bagchi. *Mahāyāna-Sūtrālaṃkāra of Asaṅga* [with Vasubandhu's commentary]. Buddhist Sanskrit Texts, 13. Darbhanga, India: Mithila Institute, 1970.

Sanskrit and translation into French: Sylvain Lévi. *Mahāyānasūtrālaṃkāra, exposé de la doctrine du grand véhicule selon le système Yogācāra.* 2 vols. Paris, Libraire Honoré Champion: 1907, 1911.

Principles of Explanation
vyākyhayukti
rnam par bshad pa'i rigs pa
P5562, vol. 113

Treasury of Manifest Knowledge
abhidharmakośakārikā
chos mngon pa'i mdzod kyi tshig le'ur byas pa
P5590, vol. 115

Sanskrit: Swami Dwarikadas Shastri. *Abhidharmakośa & Bhāṣya of Ācārya Vasubandhu with Sphuṭārtha Commentary of Ācārya Yaśomitra.* Bauddha Bharati Series, 5. Banaras: Bauddha Bharati, 1970. Also: P. Pradhan. *Abhidharmakośabhāṣyam of Vasubandhu.* Patna, India: Jayaswal Research Institute, 1975.

French translation: Louis de la Vallée Poussin. *L'Abhidharmakośa de Vasubandhu.* 6 vols. Brussels: Institut Belge des Hautes Études Chinoises, 1971.

English translation of the French: Leo M. Pruden. *Abhidharmakośabhāṣyam.* 4 vols. Berkeley, Calif.: Asian Humanities Press, 1988.

The Thirty / Treatise on Cognition-Only in Thirty Stanzas
triṃśikākārikā / sarvavijñānamātradeśakatriṃśakakārikā
sum cu pa'i tshig le'ur byas pa / thams cad rnam rig tsam du ston pa sum cu pa'i tshig le'ur byas pa
P5556, vol. 113

Sanskrit: Sylvain Lévi. *Vijñaptimātratāsiddhi / Deux traités de Vasubandhu: Viṃśatikā (La Vingtaine) et Triṃsikā (La Trentaine).* Bibliotheque de l'École des Hautes Études. Paris: Libraire Honoré Champion, 1925. Also: K. N. Chatterjee. *Vijñapti-Mātratā-Siddhi (With Sthiramati's Commentary).* Varanasi, India: Kishor Vidya Niketan, 1980.

English translation: Stefan Anacker. *Seven Works of Vasubandhu.* Delhi: Motilal Banarsidass, 1984. Also: Thomas A. Kochumuttom. *A Buddhist Doctrine of Experience.* Delhi: Motilal Banarsidass, 1982.

The Twenty
viṃśatikā / viṃśikākārikā
nyi shu pa'i tshig le'ur byas pa
P5557, vol. 113

Sanskrit: Sylvain Lévi. *Vijñaptimātratāsiddhi / Deux traités de Vasubandhu: Viṃśatikā (La Vigtaine) et Triṃsikā (La Trentaine).* Bibliotheque de l'École des Hautes Études. Paris: Libraire Honoré Champion, 1925.

English translation: Stefan Anacker. *Seven Works of Vasubandhu.* Delhi: Motilal Banarsidass, 1984. Also: Thomas A. Kochumuttom. *A Buddhist Doctrine of Experience.* Delhi: Motilal Banarsidass, 1982.

English translation (stanzas 1-10): Gregory A. Hillis. *An Introduction and Translation of Vinitadeva's Explanation of the First Ten Stanzas of [Vasubandhu's] Commentary on His "Twenty Stanzas," with Appended Glossary of Technical Terms.* Ann Arbor, Mich.: University Microfilms, 1993.

Vimuktasena, Ārya (*'phags pa grol sde*)
Commentary on the "Twenty-Five Thousand Stanza Perfection of Wisdom Sūtra"
āryapañcaviṃśatisāhasrikāprajñāpāramitopadeśaśāstrābhisamayālaṃkārakārikāvṛtti
'phags pa shes rab kyi pha rol tu phyin pa stong phrag nyi shu lnga pa'i man ngag gi bstan bcos mngon par rtogs pa'i rgyan gyi 'grel pa
P5185, vol. 88

Vimuktasena, Bhadanta (*btsun pa grol sde*)
Commentary on the "Twenty-Five Thousand Stanza Perfection of Wisdom Sūtra"

āryapañcaviṃśatisāhasrikāprajñāpāramitopadeśaśāstrābhisamayālaṃkārakārikāvārttika
nyi khrid nam 'grel / 'phags pa shes rab kyi pha rol tu phyin pa stong phrag nyi shu lnga pa'i man ngag gi bstan bcos mngon par rtogs pa'i rgyan gyi tshig le'ur byas pa'i rnam par 'grel pa
P5186, vol. 88

Vinītadeva (*dul ba'i lha*)
Explanation of (Vasubandhu's) [Auto] Commentary on the "Twenty Stanza Treatise"
prakaraṇaviṃśakāṭīkā
rab tu byed pa nyi shu pa'i 'grel bshad
P5566, vol. 113
English translation (commentary on stanzas 1-10): Gregory A. Hillis. *An Introduction and Translation of Vinitadeva's Explanation of the First Ten Stanzas of [Vasubandhu's] Commentary on His "Twenty Stanzas," with Appended Glossary of Technical Terms.* Ann Arbor, Mich.: University Microfilms, 1993.

W̄el-mang Ḡön-chok-gyel-tsen (*dbal mang dkon mchog rgyal mtshan,* 1764-1853)
Notes on (Ḡön-chok-jik-may-w̄ang-b̄o's) Lectures / Notes on (Ḡön-chok-jik-may-w̄ang-b̄o's) Lectures on (D̄zong-ka-b̄a's) "The Essence of Eloquence": Stream of the Speech of the Omniscient: Offering for Purification
legs bshad snying po'i gsung bshad zin bris su bkod pa kun mkhyen gsung gi chu rgyun dag byed mchod yon
Collected Works of Dbal-maṅ Dkon-mchog-rgyal-mtshan, vol. 2, 376-464. New Delhi: Gyeltan Gelek Namgyal, 1974

Wonch'uk (Tib. *rdzogs gsal / wen tshig / wen tshegs / wanydzeg,* Chin. *Yüan-ts'e;* 613-696)
Extensive Commentary on the "Sūtra Unraveling the Thought"
'phags pa dgongs pa nges par 'grel pa'i mdo'i rgya cher 'grel pa
P5517, vol. 116.
Chinese edition: *Dai-nihon Zokuzōkyō, hsü tsang ching,* 134.d-535.a. Hong Kong Reprint, 1922. Also: *Da Zang Jing,* vol. 34, 581-952, vol. 35, 1-100. Taipei: Xin Wen Fong, 1977. Reconstruction of the first portion of the eighth fascicle and all of the tenth fascicle: Inaba Shōju. *Enjiki Gejinmikkyōsho Sanitsububan no kanbunyaku.* Kyoto: Hōzōkan, 1949.

Ȳang-j̄en-ga-way-l̄o-drö, A-kya-yong-dzin (*dbyangs can dga' ba'i blo gros, a khya yongs 'dzin,* c. 1750)
Mirror Illuminating the Important Points of the Rules for Affixing Letters
yi ge'i thob thang nyer mkho rab gsal me long
Collected Works of A-khya Yoṅs-ḥdzin, vol. 2, 444-446. Delhi: Lama Guru Deva, 1971.

Yashomitra (*yaśomitra, grags pa bshes gnyen*)
Explanation of [Asaṅga's] "Summary of Manifest Knowledge"
abhidharmasamuccayabhaṣya
chos mngon pa kun btus pa'i bshad pa
P5554, vol. 113
Sanskrit: N. Tatia. *Abhidharmasamuccayabhāṣyam.* Tibetan-Sanskrit Works Series, 17. Patna, India: K. B. Jayaswal Research Institute, 1976.

3. Other Works

Anacker, Stefan. Seven Works of Vasubandhu. Delhi: Motilal Banarsidass, 1984.

Apte, Vaman Shivaram. Sanskrit-English Dictionary. Poona, India: Prasad Prakashan, 1957.

Batchelor, Stephen. *The Tibet Guide: Central and Western Tibet* (Boston: Wisdom, 1998.

Beal, Samuel. *Buddhist Records of the Western World: Translated from the Chinese of Hiuen Tsiang (A. D. 629).* London: Kegan Paul, Trench, and Trübner, 1884; reprint, New York: Paragon, 1968; reprint, Delhi: Motilal Banarsidass, 1981.

Boquist, Ake. *Trisvabhāva: A Study of the Development of the Three-Nature-Theory in Yogācāra Buddhism,* edited by Tord Olsson. Lund Studies in African and Asian Religions, 8. Lund, Sweden: University of Lund, 1993.

Buswell, Robert E., trans. "Wonch'uk (613-696): Memorial Inscription." Unpublished manuscript.

Chan, Victor. *Tibet Handbook: A Pilgrimage Guide.* Chico, Calif.: Moon, 1994.

Ch'en, Kenneth K. S. *Buddhism in China: A Historical Survey.* Princeton, N.J.: Princeton University Press, 1964.

Chimpa, Lama, and Alaka Chattopadhyaya. *Tāranātha's History of Buddhism in India.* Simla, India: 1970; reprint, Delhi: Motilal Banarsidass, 1990.

Cleary, Thomas. *Buddhist Yoga: A Comprehensive Course.* Boston: Shambhala, 1995.

Conze, E. The Perfection of Wisdom in Eight Thousand Lines & Its Verse Summary. Bolinas, Calif.: Four Seasons Foundation, 1973.

Conze, Edward, and Shōtarō Iida. "'Maitreya's Questions' in the Prajñāpāramitā." In *Mélanges d'indianisme a la mémoire de Louis Renou,* 229-242. Paris: Éditions E. de Boccard, 1968.

Das, Sarat Chandra. *A Tibetan-English Dictionary.* Calcutta: 1902; reprint, Delhi: Motilal Banarsidass, 1969, 1970; compact reprint, Kyoto, Japan: Rinsen Book Company, 1981.

Dondup, K. *The Water-Horse and Other Years: A History of 17th and 18th Century Tibet.* Dharmsala, India: Library of Tibetan Works and Archives, 1984.

Dorje, Gyurme and Matthew Kapstein. *The Nyingma School of Tibetan Buddhism: Its Fundamentals and History.* Boston: Wisdom, 1991.

Dudjom Rinpoche. *The Nyingma School of Tibetan Buddhism.* 2 vols. Boston: Wisdom, 1991.

Edgerton, Franklin. *Buddhist Hybrid Sanskrit Grammar and Dictionary.* New Haven: Yale University Press, 1953; reprint, Delhi: Motilal, 1972.

Grupper, Samuel M. "Manchu Patronage and Tibetan Buddhism during the First Half of the Ch'ing Dynasty." *Journal of the Tibet Society* 4 (1984): 47-75.

Hakamaya, Noriaki. "A Consideration on the Byams Shus kyi Le'u." *Indobukkyogaku Kenkyu* 14, no. 1 (December 1975): 20-30.

Harris, Ian Charles. *The Continuity of Madhyamaka and Yogācāra in Indian Mahāyāna Buddhism.* Leiden, Netherlands: Brill, 1991.

H.H. the Dalai Lama, Tenzin Gyatso. *Buddhism of Tibet and the Key to the Middle Way.* Translated by Jeffrey Hopkins. London: George Allen and Unwin, 1975. Reprinted in a combined volume, *The Buddhism of Tibet.* London: George Allen and Unwin, 1983; reprint, Ithaca, N.Y.: Snow Lion, 1987.

———. *Kindness, Clarity, and Insight.* Translated and edited by Jeffrey Hopkins; coedited by Elizabeth Napper. Ithaca, N.Y.: Snow Lion Publications, 1984.

H.H. the Dalai Lama, Tenzin Gyatso and Jeffrey Hopkins. *The Kālachakra Tantra: Rite of Initiation.* Translated and introduced by Jeffrey Hopkins. London: Wisdom, 1985; 2d rev. ed. 1989.

Hookham, S. K. *The Buddha Within: Tathāgatagarbha Doctrine according to the Shentong Interpretation of the Ratnagotravibhāga.* Albany, N.Y.: State University of New York Press, 1991.

Hopkins, Jeffrey. "A Tibetan Contribution on the Question of Mind-Only in the Early Yogic Practice School." *Journal of Indian Philosophy* 20 (1992): 275-343.

———. "A Tibetan Delineation of Different Views of Emptiness in the Indian Middle Way School: Dzong-ka-ba's Two Interpretations of the *Locus Classicus* in Chandrakīrti's *Clear Words* Showing Bhāvaviveka's Assertion of Commonly Appearing Subjects and Inherent Existence." *Tibet Journal* 14, no. 1 (1989): 10-43.

———. "The Tibetan Genre of Doxography: Structuring a Worldview." In *Tibetan Literature,* 170-186, edited by José Ignacio Cabezón and Roger Jackson. Ithaca, N.Y.: Snow Lion Publications, 1996.

———. "The Wanderer." *Virginia Quarterly* 53, no. 2 (1977): 284-287.

Hyung-keun, Oh. "The Yogācāra-Vijñaptimātratā Studies of Silla Monks." In *Assimilation of Buddhism in Korea: Religious Maturity and Innovation in the Silla Dynasty,* edited by Lewis R. Lancaster and C. S. Yu, 105-120. Berkeley, Calif.: Asian Humanities Press: 1991.

Iida, Shōtarō. "A Mukung-hwa in Ch'ang-an—A Study of the Life and Works of Wonch'uk (613-696), with Special Interest in the Korean contributions to the Development of Chinese and Tibetan Buddhism." In *Proceedings, International Symposium, Commemorating the 30th Anniversary of Korean Liberation,* 225-251. Seoul: National Academy of Sciences, Republic of Korea, 1975.

———. "The Three Stūpas of Ch'ang An." In *Papers of the First International Conference on Korean Studies,* 484-497. Seoul: Academy of Korean Studies, 1980.

Jackson, David. *Enlightenment by a Single Means.* Vienna: Verlag der Österreichischen Akademie der Wissenschaften, 1994.

Joshi, L. M. *Facets of Jaina Religiousness in Comparative Light.* L.D. Series, 85. Ahmedabad, India: L.D. Institute of Indology, 1981.

Kämpfe, Hans-Rainer. *Ñi ma'i 'od zer / Naran-u gerel: Die Biographie des 2. Pekinger Lcaṅ skya-Qutuqtu Rol pa'i rdo rje (1717-1786).* Monumenta Tibetica Historica, 2 (1). Sankt Augustin: Wissenschaftsverlag, 1976.

Katsura, Shoryu. "A Synopsis of the *Prajñāpāramitopadeśa* of Ratnākaraśānti." *Journal of Indian and Buddhist Studies* (*Indogaku Bukkyōgaku Kenkyū*) 25, no. 1 (1976): 38-41.

Klein, Anne C. *Meeting the Great Bliss Queen: Buddhists, Feminists, and the Art of the Self.* Boston: Beacon Press, 1994.

Kye-hyon, Ahn. "Buddhism in the Unified Silla Period." In *Assimilation of Buddhism in Korea: Religious Maturity and Innovation in the Silla Dynasty,* edited by Lewis R. Lancaster and C. S. Yu, 1-46. Berkeley, Calif.: Asian Humanities Press: 1991.

Lalou, Marcelle. "Les Textes Bouddhiques au temps du roi Khri-sroṅ-lde-bcan." *Journal Asiatique* 241, no. 3 (1953): 313-353.

Lati Rinbochay and Jeffrey Hopkins. *Death, Intermediate State and Rebirth.* London: Rider, 1980; Ithaca, N.Y.: Snow Lion, 1980.

Lati Rinbochay and Elizabeth Napper. *Mind in Tibetan Buddhism.* London: Rider, 1980; Ithaca, N.Y.: Snow Lion, 1980.

Lati Rinbochay, Denma Lochö Rinbochay, Leah Zahler, Jeffrey Hopkins. *Meditative States in Tibetan Buddhism.* London: Wisdom, 1983; rev. ed., Boston: Wisdom, 1997.

Lee, Peter H., ed. *Sourcebook of Korean Civilization.* New York: Columbia University Press, 1993.

Lessing, Ferdinand D. *Yung-Ho-Kung; An Iconography of the Lamaist Cathedral in Peking.* Stockholm: Elanders Boktryckeri Aktiebolag, 1942.

Lessing, Ferdinand D., and Alex Wayman. *Mkhas Grub Rje's Fundamentals of the Buddhist Tantras.* The Hague: Mouton, 1968; reprint, Delhi: Motilal Banarsidass, 1978.

Lindtner, Christian. "A Treatise on Buddhist Idealism: Kambala's Ālokamālā." In *Miscellanea Buddhica,* edited by Christian Lindtner, 109-220. Copenhagen: Akademisk Forlag, 1985.

Lodrö, Geshe Gedün. *Walking through Walls: A Presentation of Tibetan Meditation,* translated and edited by Jeffrey Hopkins. Ithaca, New York: Snow Lion Publications, 1992; restructured as *Calm Abiding and Special Insight: Spiritual Transformation through Meditation,* translated and edited by Jeffrey Hopkins. Ithaca, New York: Snow Lion Publications, 1998.

Obermiller, E. *Prajñāpāramitā in Tibetan Buddhism.* Delhi: Classics India Publications, 1988.

Mimaki, Katsumi. "The *blo gsal grub mtha'* and the Mādhyamika Classification in Tibetan *grub mtha'* Literature." In *Contributions on Tibetan and Buddhist Religion and Philosophy,* edited by Ernst Steinkellner and Helmut Tauscher, 161-167. Vienna: Arbeitskreis für tibetische und buddhistische Studien, 1983.

Nagao, Gadjin M. "What Remains in Śūnyatā? A Yogācāra Interpretation of Emptiness." In *Mahāyāna Buddhist Meditation, Theory and Practice,* edited by Minoru Kiyota, 66-82. Honolulu: University of Hawaii Press, 1978; reprinted in *Mādhyamika and Yogācāra: A Study of Mahāyāna Philosophies,* translated by Leslie S. Kawamura, 51-60. Albany: State University of New York Press, 1991.

Napper, Elizabeth. *Dependent-Arising and Emptiness.* London: Wisdom, 1989.

Obermiller, E. *History of Buddhism (Chos-ḥbyung) by Bu-ston.* Heidelberg: Heft, 1932; reprint, Tokyo: Suzuki Research Foundation, n.d.

Palbar, Tenzin. *The Tragedy of My Homeland* (*nga'i pha yul gyi ya nga ba'i lo rgyus*). Dharmsala, India: Narthang, 1994.

Pāsādika, Bhikkhu. "On the Meaning of the Perfection of Wisdom, A Summary Composed by Ācārya Dignāga." In *Wisdom Gone Beyond: An Anthology of Buddhist Texts,* 94-102. Bangkok: Social Science Association Press of Thailand, 1966.

Paul, Diana Y. *Philosophy in Sixth Century China: Paramārtha's "Evolution of Consciousness"* Stanford University Press: Stanford, 1984.

Perdue, Daniel E. *Debate in Tibetan Buddhism.* Ithaca, N.Y.: Snow Lion Publications, 1992.

Powers, John C. "Accidental Immortality: How Wonch'uk Became the Author of the *Great Chinese Commentary.*" *Journal of the International Association of Buddhist Studies* 15, no. 1 (1992): 95-103.

———. *The Concept of the Ultimate (don dam pa, paramārtha) in the Saṃdhinirmocana-sūtra: Analysis, Translation and Notes.* Ann Arbor, Mich.: University Microfilms, 1991.

———. *Hermeneutics and Tradition in the Saṃdhinirmocana-sūtra.* Leiden, Netherlands: Brill, 1993.

———. *The Yogācāra School of Buddhism: A Bibliography.* American Theological Library Association Bibliography Series, 27. Metuchen, N.J., and London: American Theological Library Association and The Scarecrow Press, 1991.

Rogers, Katherine. *A Tibetan Manual of Logic: An Introduction to Reasoning in the Ge-luk-b̄a Monastic Educational System.* Ann Arbor, Mich.: University Microfilms, 1993.

Ruegg, David Seyfort. "The Jo Naṅ Pas: A School of Buddhist Ontologists according to the *Grub mtha' sel gyi me loṅ.*" *Journal of the American Oriental Society* 83, no. 1 (1963): 73-91.

———. *The Literature of the Madhyamaka School of Philosophy in India.* Wiesbaden, Germany: Otto Harrassowitz, 1981.

———. *La Théorie du Tathāgathagarbha et du Gotra: Études sur la sotériologie et la gnoséologie du bouddhisme.* Paris: École Française d'Extrême-Orient, 1969.

———. *Le Traité du Tathāgatagarbha de Bu-ston rin-chen-grub.* Paris: École Française d'Extrême-Orient, 1973.

della Santina, Peter. *Madhyamaka Schools in India.* Delhi: Motilal Banarsidass, 1986.

Schmithausen, Lambert. "On the Problem of the Relation of Spiritual Practice and Philosophical Theory in Buddhism." In *German Scholars on India,* 235-250. Contributions to India Studies, 2. Bombay: Nachiketa, 1976.

Sherbourne, Richard, S. J. *A Lamp for the Path and Commentary.* London: George Allen and Unwin, 1983.

Shōju, Inaba. "Daibankoku Daitoku Sanzō hosshi Shamon Hō jō no Kenkyū" [researches on Fa-ch'eng, translator of Wonch'uk's commentary on the *Saṃdhinirmocana-sūtra*]. *Tōhō Gukuhō* 38 (1967): 133-198; 39 (1968) 119-222.

———. *Enjiki Gejinmikkyōsho Sanitsububan no kanbunyaku.* Kyoto: Hōzōkan, 1949.

———. "On Chos-grub's Translation of the *Chieh-shen-mi-ching-shu.*" In *Buddhist Thought and Asian Civilization,* edited by Leslie S. Kawamura and Keith Scott, 105-113. Berkeley, Calif.: Dharma, 1977.

Smith, E. Gene. "Introduction." In Collected Works of Thu'u-bkwan Blo-bzang-chos-kyi-nyi-ma, 1: 2-12. Delhi: N. Gelek Demo, 1969.

———. *University of Washington Tibetan Catalogue.* 2 vols. Seattle, Washington: University of Washington Press, 1969.

Smith, Wilfred Cantwell. "The Modern West in the History of Religion." *Journal of the American Academy of Religion* 52, no. 1 (March 1984): 3-18.

Snellgrove, D. L., and Richardson, Hugh. *Cultural History of Tibet.* New York: Praeger, 1968.

Sponberg, Alan. *The Vijñaptimātratā Buddhism of the Chinese Monk K'uei-chi (A. D. 632-682).* Ph. D. diss., University of British Columbia, 1979.

Stearns, Cyrus R. *The Buddha from Dol po and His Fourth Council of the Buddhist Doctrine.* Ann Arbor, Mich.: University Microfilms, 1996.

———. "Dol-po-pa Shes-rab-rgyal-mtshan and the Genesis of the *gzhan-stong* Position in Tibet." *Asiatische Studien/ Études Asiatiques* 59, no. 4 (1995): 829-852.

Steinkellner, Ernst. "Who Is Byaṅ chub rdzu 'phrul? Tibetan and Non-Tibetan Commentaries on the *Saṃdhinomocanasūtra*—A Survey of the Literature." *Berliner Indologische Studien* 4, no. 5 (1989): 229-251.

Stoddard, Heather. *Le mendiant de L'Amdo.* Recherches sur la Haute Asie, 9. Paris: Société d'Ethnographie, 1985.

Strong, John S. *The Legend and Cult of Upagupta: Sanskrit Buddhism in North India and Southeast Asia.* Princeton, N.J.: Princeton University Press, 1992.

Thurman, Robert, ed. *The Life & Teachings of Tsong Khapa.* Dharmsala, India: Library of Tibetan Works and Archives, 1982.

Tucci, Giuseppe. "Minor Texts on the Prajñā-Pāramitā." In *Opera Minora: Parte II,* 429-452. Rome: Giovanni Bardi Editore, 1971.

Ueda, Yoshifumi. "Two Main Streams of Thought in Yogācāra Philosophy." *Philosophy East and West* 17 (January-October 1967): 155-165.

Urban, Hugh B., and Paul J. Griffiths. "What Else Remains in Śūnyatā?: An Investigation of Terms for Mental Imagery in the Madhyāntavibhāga-Corpus." *Journal of the International Association of Buddhist Studies* 17, no. 1 (1994): 1-25.

Van der Kuijp, Leonard W. J. "Apropos of a Recent Contribution to the History of Central Way Philosophy in Tibet: *Tsong Khapa's Speech of Gold.*" *Berliner Indologische Studien* 1 (1985): 47-74.

Wallace, B. Alan. *The Life and Teachings of Geshé Rabten.* London: George Allen and Unwin, 1980.

Waters, Thomas. *On Yuan Chwang's Travels in India.* Delhi: Munshi Ram Manohar Lal, 1961.

Wayman, A., and H. Wayman. *The Lion's Roar of Queen Śrīmālā.* New York: Columbia University Press, 1974.

Wayman, Alex. "Yogācāra and the Buddhist Logicians." *Journal of the International Association of Buddhist Studies* 2, no. 1 (1979): 65-78.

Weinstein, Stanley. "A Biographical Study of Tz'u-en." *Monumenta Nipponica* 15, nos. 1-2 (1959-1960): 119-149.

———. *Buddhism under the T'ang.* Cambridge, England: Cambridge University Press, 1987.

Willis, Janice D. *On Knowing Reality: The Tattvārtha Chapter of Asaṅga's Bodhisattvabhūmi.* New York: Columbia University Press, 1979; reprint, Delhi: Motilal Barnasidass, 1982.

Wilson, Joe B. *The Meaning of Mind in the Mahāyāna Buddhist Philosophy of Mind-Only (Cittamātra): A Study of a Presentation by the Tibetan Scholar Gung-tang Jam-ȳay-ȳang (gung-thang-'jam-pa'i-dbyangs) of Asaṅga's Theory of Mind-Basis-Of-All (ālayavijñāna) and Related Topics in Buddhist Theories of Personal Continuity, Epistemology, and Hermeneutics.* Ann Arbor, Mich.: University Microfilms, 1984.

Wood, Thomas E. *Mind-Only: A Philosophical and Doctrinal Analysis of the Vijñānavāda.* Monographs of the Society for Asian and Comparative Philosophy, 9. Honolulu: University of Hawaii Press, 1991.

Wylie, Turrell. "A Standard System of Tibetan Transcription." *Harvard Journal of Asiatic Studies* 22 (1959): 261-267.

Zongtse, Champa Thupten. *History of the Monastic University Dga'-ldan-phun-tshogs-gliṅ = Geschichte der Kloster-Universität dGa'-ldan-phun-tshogs-gliṅ = Dga' ldan phun tshogs gling gi thog mtha' bar gsum gyi byung ba yid la dran byed kun khyab snyan pa'i rnga sgra* (Göttingen: Im Selbstverlag des Verfassers, 1977).

Detailed Contents

Page-number cross-references for the Translation, the Synopsis, and the Text are given immediately after each appropriate entry in square brackets, parentheses, and curly brackets (braces), respectively.

[ ] = Translation; ( ) = Synopsis; { } = Text

[ ] = Translation; ( ) = Synopsis; { } = Text

Index